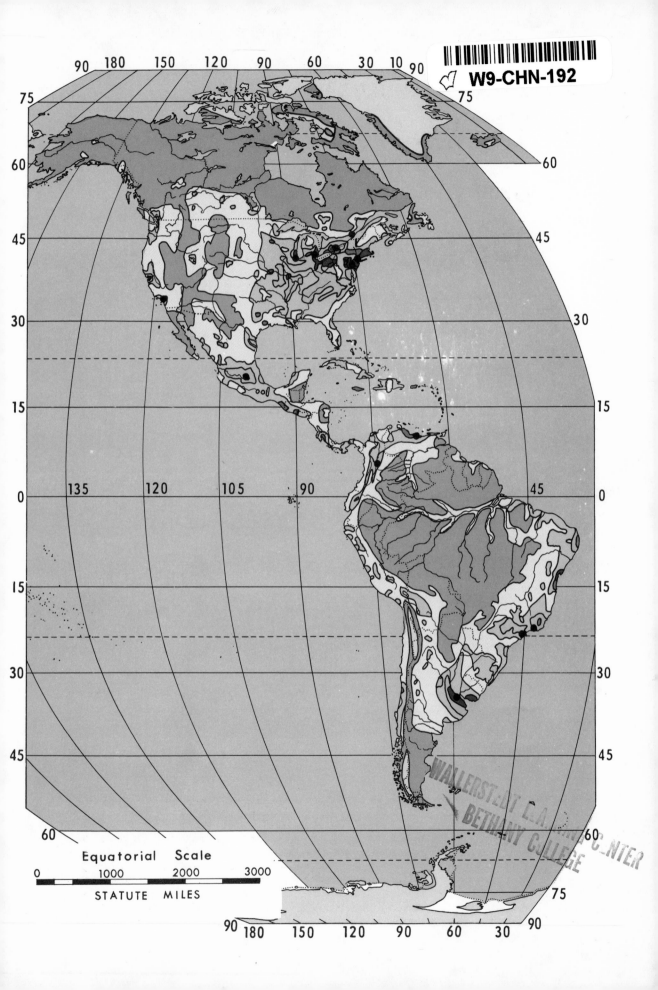

W9-CHN-192

Equatorial Scale

0   1000   2000   3000

STATUTE MILES

301.24
S 845c

62552

CULTURAL GEOGRAPHY

CULTURAL
An Evolutionary Introduction

J. E. SPENCER
*University of California
Los Angeles*

Cartography by ROBERT E. WINTER

GEOGRAPHY

to Our Humanized Earth

WILLIAM L. THOMAS
California State College
Hayward

JOHN WILEY AND SONS, INC. New York · London · Sydney · Toronto

By the same author:
Joseph E. Spencer, *Asia, East by South*, 1954

301.24
S845c

62552
11.10
10/13/71

The pictures on the title page:
On the left, a rural scene in the Phillipines by J. E. Spencer
On the right, New York Harbor, by the Port Authority

Copyright © 1969 by John Wiley & Sons, Inc. Env. 44

All rights reserved. No part of this book may be reproduced by any means, nor transmitted, nor translated into a machine language without the written permission of the publisher.

10 9 8 7 6 5 4 3 2

Library of Congress Catalog Card Number: 67-28950
SBN 471 81550 0
Printed in the United States of America

For Our Children
and Our Children's Children
and All the Other Citizenry of Our Planet Earth
for Whom the Twenty-first Century Is in the Process of Becoming,
So That They May Be Able to Comprehend
the Wonder and Magnificence
of Their Inheritance

Preface

There are many reasons why textbooks are written. This one has been written because no other text has dealt satisfactorily with the subject of cultural geography as we have tried to teach it for years. Teaching without a suitable textbook leads to frustrations. Frustrations lead to discussions of what a suitable text would contain. Such discussions sometimes lead to writing books. This volume is intended as a text in cultural geography. Its value lies in its multilinear evolutionary point of view and synthesis of the material selected for presentation.

The objective of this book is to outline how the surface of the planet Earth has been changing during the time span of human occupance and how, in using that surface, human technology has grown. A basis is thereby provided for the further study of man and society with full realization that man's accomplishments have been based on the limits of the earth's physical and biological conditions.

The organization of this volume is an essential aspect of its point of view. An Introductory chapter provides a brief orientation in the field of cultural geography and in this book's relation to that field. Five principal parts follow. Part One discusses the mosaic of man on the earth in the mid-twentieth century and the comparative position of the United States in this familiar contemporary scene. Part Two examines human beginnings and the eventual spread of mankind over the earth. Part Three treats of the cultural divergences that resulted as earth resources were interpreted differently and portions of the earth's surface were transformed differently by separate human groups, until, in the modern era, a tendency toward convergence set in, involving migrations of people, ideas, and techniques, taking the whole world for its resource base, and tending to override regional differences in the process of transforming the earth. Part Four takes a closer, more systematic look at this modern era with its increasing similarity in man's means for transforming the world's regions for his own purposes. Finally, Part Five discusses the human prospect, the implications of increasing and aging populations, and the demands and limits of technological civilization.

Numerous books have been published with the objective of setting forth a discussion of the cultural geography of the earth. It has been customary to use one of two approaches to accomplish this task in a single volume. One is the systematic or topical approach, without particular regard for the summation or correlation of topics by area or country. The other is the regional approach, which discusses the earth unit by unit or country by country, unconcerned with the principles by which phenomena or processes operate. Neither by itself gets at the full cultural geography of the earth. We have therefore chosen the evolutionary approach as the best means toward a truer understanding of the life circumstances in which man now finds himself. Some topics are treated systematically in order to describe and explain, as distinct from a concern for actual events in specific times and places; regional data are used where necessary to make explicit the environmental relations of things discussed. But, on the whole, this is a volume on cultural geography that considers the transformation of the earth's surface at the hand of man during the whole time span of human existence.

We are indebted to the earliest men who first used tools and fire and so began the human adventure that comprises our subject of study. The annals of time record the efforts of many hundreds of scholars from a host of nations who contributed their hypotheses, observations, and syntheses about the ways of Man on the Earth. We also owe innumerable debts to our mentors and our contemporary colleagues whose insights have led to our comprehension of concepts and clarifications of understanding. From dozens upon dozens of students have come the questions that led to our forming many of the ideas expressed in this book. We appreciate especially the assistance of many graduate students, research assistants, draftsmen, secretaries, and typists who performed the many chores that are involved in preparing a book such as this. Specifically, for his talents as our cartographer, we express our thanks to Robert E. Winter. The shared responsibilities for this textbook, its organization and contents, its errors of commission and omission, are, of course, our own; we would be most appreciative of constructive criticism aiming at improvement.

J. E. S.
W. L. T.

Los Angeles and Hayward, California
October 1968

List of Photograph Clusters

Contents

List of Figures

List of Tables

CULTURAL GEOGRAPHY

Introductory

Study of the evolution of space content on the Earth's surface is geography's research frontier.

Edward A. Ackerman ("Geography and Demography," 1958, p. 724.)

The geographer regards the Earth as more than a globe suspended in space. In general, he is concerned with the planet's lower atmosphere, surface skin, and thin layer of crustal material, or the land-sea-air interface. Here it is that life occurs, localities differ, various conditions appear simultaneously, different processes have been at work since the Earth became relatively stable, and change is continuous.

All this suggests that geography deals with everything that forms the outer section of the earth. In a sense this is so. A "geographer," based on some other planet and possessed of limitless brain and facilities, who is interested in the Geography of the Earth might well accept this holistic approach. On our own planet, however, Man is not yet limitless in brain or facilities. In an effort to focus his attention upon a comprehensible subject he early fell to dividing knowledge into segments, to which he applied diverse terms. The more he understood, the more he divided, until knowledge became so broken into disciplines that, so some feel, no one man can view the whole.

In early Greek times—a formative period of our own culture—geography and history were two great categories of overlapping knowledge which included much that the Greeks knew. Until recent centuries knowledge grew slowly in any one culture, and the divisions of knowledge remained few. Then Occidental culture began to learn rapidly,

and the rates of division increased. Nowadays, for example, geomorphology claims to be the science of landforms and landform processes, and few can say for certain whether this is a branch of geology or geography, or even when geology and geography came to separate. Similarly, anthropology claims to be the science of man. But how to distinguish the sociologist interested in the complexities of Western societies from the anthropologist concerned mostly with cultures other than his own, and either of these from the geographer who also deals with man on a global scale? Though the tolerant geographer may insist upon his holistic view of all Earth phenomena and processes, he must be content to let many nongeographers pursue particular segments of knowledge bearing on the Earth. The Earth remains the focus of our study; how Man divides the separate chores of studying it is of less importance than that such study continue.

Physical, Biological, and Cultural in Geography

The geographer views the earth from three broad orientations. One of these, Physical Geography, stresses the inanimate, purely physical phenomena and processes relating to the air, water, rock, and earth materials that can be described, measured, counted, mapped, and photographed. The second and third deal with living things which

1

exist in a relatively narrow band around the earth's surface extending from slightly above to slightly below the line denoting sea level. Part of the events in this band involve man and his works, and fall under the heading of Human Geography. The rest concern nonhuman forms of life which are considered separately as Biogeography, or are sometimes relegated to the Physical Geography category. This threefold division into inanimate, nonhuman animate, and human is somewhat unwieldy and often causes the nonhuman living elements to be slighted by the scholar who thinks chiefly in terms of the inanimate. It similarly inhibits the thorough study of human phenomena which are inextricably bound to other living elements of the Earth. If a division must be made, it would seem preferable to make it on a twofold basis, distinguishing the inanimate from the animate; and this is the first criterion on which this book rests.

To restrict our interest to living forms is to divide geography into at least two parts; this demands an awareness of the implications of both. Further we label our study Cultural Geography because we wish to focus our attention on man and his works, without including a detailed treatment of man as a biological being. The latter would be essential for development of a full Human Geography. With only given amounts of brain and energy, and because not all living activities have been studied sufficiently to learn the significant things that one should know about them, we cannot hope to achieve an equal assessment of all living phenomena and processes. This volume on cultural geography is only a prologue to the fuller human geography that one day may be written.

Differences in Local Environments

It might be held that a volume concerned with living phenomena and processes becomes a work on "life science" or on anthropology rather than one on cultural geography. Both the life scientist and the anthropologist, however, restrict their coverage and often discuss their findings in the abstract, without concern for the detailed relationships of these data to specific local environments of the physical earth on which we live. Such an anthropology presumes a world uniform in all aspects of its local parts, and somewhat resembles a geology that presumes the Earth to be uninhabited by Man. Recently a good many anthropologists have become interested in ecological and evolutionary relationships, and the approaches of

the ecologically minded anthropologist and the cultural geographer have become similar and more closely intertwined. At the heart of our study is the evolutionary relationship between the life-form and the local environment in which that form thrives. Living forms cannot be or create events unrelated to specific environments. Since the Earth is not uniform, with equivalent physical conditions everywhere, one must take the particular local environment into account when discussing any phenomenon or process involving a living form. This book therefore looks toward the phenomena and processes that operate in a particular place through time, affected by and in turn affecting the immediate environment.

The last statement applies equally to single-celled life forms and processes, to complex forms, and to intricate patterns of group behavior such as a human society. Of the living forms, man is the most significant, in many respects, and has both complex relations with, and reactions to, his local environment. One can perhaps say in fairness that, of all living forms, man is most capable of altering the environment in which he lives, for better or worse. Moreover, his ways of living create situations that are extremely significant to all other life-forms and, perhaps, to the earth itself.

The steady increase in human knowledge has improved Man's ability to free himself from his environment and adapt it to his needs in living on the Earth. But though some men may eventually be able to leave the earth for periods of time and stay elsewhere in the solar system, they cannot disregard the earth, nor upon return disregard the varying sets of local conditions they find in its different parts. It is to Man and his doings in these environments on the Earth that this book addresses itself.

The Evolutionary Approach

The phenomena of the earth's surface, both inanimate and living, are changing phenomena. Their change is so constant and continuous, whether rapid or slow, turbulent or placid, that there is no way to determine a beginning, a norm, a climax, or an end. The whole is a single process— *evolution.* Self-maintaining, self-transforming, and self-transcending, evolution is directional in time and generally irreversible. In its course it always generates novelty, greater variety, more complex organization, higher levels of awareness, and increasingly conscious mental activity among the living forms of life. Thus has life on the Earth evolved.

To understand the organization and complexity of living things one needs to follow the course of many unsynchronized processes. The earth's surface has been changing from one instant to the next. It seems unlikely that by examining physical, biological, and cultural environments in fleeting moments of time we shall be able to recognize the essence of human organization and complexity in relation to the earth and its other living forms. Only by retracing the course of human evolution and exploring each pattern in terms of its predecessor can we expect to comprehend the meaning of our human Earth to Man.

The geographer is therefore advised to approach his subject matter from the evolutionary standpoint. In dealing with inanimate phenomena, this is often termed the "genetic" method, whereas in dealing with phenomena of human civilizations it has customarily been termed the "historical." Not only must the geographer be concerned with what and where, he must also be interested in how and why, for the entire period that the phenomena or processes in question have been in existence. In this book the evolutionary approach is held to be essential; evolution is multilineal but irregularly variate in the broad sense.

A last basic element belongs in this orientation. The story of man also is clearly part of the more general evolutionary process, but the basis and the mechanism are of a different order because man is a unique organism with unique properties. Man is a species of living system that has risen to power and dominance through the development of the special property, intelligence. The appearance of man began the mental period—a new phase of evolution.

The Culture Concept

The word "culture" has long enjoyed wide currency. There is Culture in the sense of tillage or cultivation; there is Culture meaning the possession of standards of value, discrimination, and good taste, and implying good breeding, refinement, and learning. However, as used in this book, Culture has a broader, all-inclusive connotation. Culture is the distillate of total human experience; its possession not only distinguishes Man from other living forms but, indeed, sets him apart as a unique evolutionary product. As a "culture bearer," able to communicate his cumulative ex-

perience, man is the first species capable of consciously and deliberately altering the course of his own evolution.

Through this shareable, transmissible, progressively transformable tradition, human organization achieved a new means of evolution. Man's intelligence has enabled him to penetrate and occupy all parts of the Earth's surface, even though as an animal he is not physiologically equipped to do so. By qualitative increases in social organization and in adapting invented techniques to productive ends, man has made pieces of organized living matter and varieties of inanimate matter serve his own ends and has enabled a quantitative increase in his numbers. His own creation, Culture, has done for him what genetic mechanisms have afforded other animals. His registration and transmittal of human experience has continuously accumulated an unlimited number of complex ideas or techniques and organized them permanently in collective human memory.

A clear distinction must be made between Culture as a collective body and Cultures, the parts of the totality. The splitting and branching of Man over the Earth gave rise to individual cultures. These "cultures"—the technico-mental systems developed as ways of life by the many partially isolated fragments of mankind—gradually came into existence through the unique experiences in space and time of various population groups. But cultures never became completely isolated; they have remained parts of the whole. Through human activity, they have penetrated, metamorphosed, borrowed from, and absorbed one another. Although there is an evolutionary aspect to the growth of individual cultures, like evolution in general, certain traits or trait complexes may fall into disuse, be forgotten, and require relearning. An industrial society obviously knows more than a gathering and collecting society about the physical laws of matter, and certainly uses more complicated techniques of processing materials. Yet the former has forgotten much about the resources, relationships, and processing techniques that the latter knew, and sometimes claims initial discovery for some of the things it has actually relearned or borrowed.

The Framework of Cultural Geography

Physical geographers assert that they are concerned to understand the conditions of the general physical environment of the earth, the processes operative in that environment, and the regional separation of the earth into different specific physical environments. The multiplicity of aspects often leads the physical geographer to delimit his own field of further research, as in geomorphology, physiography, or weather and climate. The human or cultural geographers assert that they are interested in understanding the conditions under which man occupies the earth, the processes operative through that occupance, and the spatial separation of the earth into different kinds of culture regions. The multiplicity of aspects, here too, leads the human geographer to delimit his own field of particular inquiry, as in political geography, urban geography, or agricultural geography. Within the broad zone of nonphysical geography there is also the more specific delimitation into a human geography and a cultural geography separate from political or urban geography. Although the two words "human" and "cultural" sometimes are used, broadly, as synonyms, they are no more synonyms in the specific sense than are geomorphology and physiography.

To speak to the specific, cultural geography is concerned with the systems of human technologies and cultural practices as these are developed in particular regions of the earth through time by human populations conceived as culture groups. To most cultural geographers all geography is developmental, in that physical environments have altered markedly within the time span of the Pleistocene-Recent, in that mankind has occupied most parts of the earth over long periods of time, in that human practices have been altered through time by human inventiveness, and in that human constructs placed on the earth through time have had their forms and functions changed. This leads the cultural geographer to some form of evolutionary and ecological systemization of the human occupance of the earth. The cultural geographer conceives of mankind as an active agent on the surface of the earth, operating in regional units through his differentiated systems of cultures. The cultural geographer is concerned to understand both the reactions of man to the physical environment of the occupied region and the variable impact of man on the occupied environment in terms of the cultural forms that he conceives and places on the landscape as field systems, roads, settlements, crop and decorative plants, and monumental structures. The cultural geographer does not conceive of culture groups operating in isolation, but he is concerned to understand the broad

elements of human interaction, the systems of developmental growth, the systems of cultural transfer between culture groups, and the increasing levels of conceptual growth by which particular culture groups may perceive of their environments during different time periods.

The cultural geographer is seldom primarily interested in the particular functional interpretation of the present landscape of any one region, nor is he primarily interested in the clinical aspects of specific functional systems such as the detailed spatial distribution of population, the spatial particulars of a political system, or the zonal distribution of activities in large settlements; these become the specific concerns for the population geographer, the political geographer, and the urban geographer. The concern of the cultural geographer remains the broad study of spatially oriented and spatially differentiated cultures operating through time on the surface of the earth as a means to the further and deeper understanding of human performance by other geographic specialists. More particular inquiry into the processes and functions of human systems in specific regional environments becomes the concern of some of the more specialized subdisciplines within the broad realm of human geography.

In the pursuit of his studies the cultural geographer is always concerned with origins of human ways; he is interested as to where some human technology began and what were the environmental conditions within which man devised that technology. He is interested in what changes the new technology brought into the human living system and what kinds of change that technology produced in the environmental complex in which it was used. The cultural geographer pursues the questions of whether other societies, using other systems, found the new technology useful and what use each made of it. He is then interested in what changes were brought about by the adoption of the borrowed technology, both in these new living systems and in the environments in which the new technology became utilized. He is interested in how far a newly created technology may spread during a particular millennium and what may be the results in some far environment. The cultural geographer recognizes that such creative accomplishments as developing new technologies require time and effort and that the spread of new ideas requires the passage of time, in one environment, to other living systems in other environments. He recognizes, also, that few technologies are spread intact, but that alterations occur in the process of diffusion. The cultural geographer recognizes clearly that some technologies are strictly material ones, working with stone, iron, fiber, or plastics, and that other technologies are social ones, involving human organization of societal structure systems, systems of perception of the world, systems of beliefs with concern for right and wrong, and systems of administration of both material and social affairs. The cultural geographer observes, broadly, that not all human groups perceive the world in the same ways and that human performances differ widely over the earth, both in regional environments that are quite unequal and in regional environments that may, superficially, be described as possessing somewhat similar physical attributes. He understands that given assemblages of material technologies may be accompanied by many different kinds of social organizational technologies. He recognizes that the conceptual framework within which a people creates its culture and evolves its particular system requires the institutionalizing of that system, and he recognizes, further, that no two institutional systems are identical in all respects. The institutionalized forms of culture systems become the specific elements of study in cultural geography.

Examining the paragraph above for thematic elements, we see that there is a concern for place, site, situation, and ecologic circumstance. There is an interest in human perceptiveness, creativeness, adaptiveness, evolutionary change, and fluctuating levels of life. There is a consideration of time as a factor in human living and a concern for time as a factor in environmental change. There is a concern for origins in space and in time and an interest in change during time in places. Overwhelmingly there is a concern for processes involved in man living on the earth over the long time span; not only processes improving his own levels of living but also processes affecting the environments in which men live. There is little concern for tons, acres, miles, or sheer numbers as the vital statistics of regional occupance (all of which belong to economic geography), for the chief goal is the comprehension of the workings of systems.

In the practice of cultural geography, the practitioner is apt to take the long view, to be less involved in the full elaboration of the operational details of a particular system at a particular time

than with the understanding of the spatial and process interrelations of neighboring systems. The long view is apt to be truly long, concerned for change during millennia rather than during an individual year, and the view is often not focussed upon an explanation of the functional operation of the precisely current year, for the view is that change will take place in succeeding decades through some operational process. The outlook of the cultural geographer, generally, is broadly comparative in the involvement with operational processes, befitting the concern for holistic institutionalized systems. The cultural geographer normally is interested in the specifics of artifacts or systems, such as the type of hoe, the species of crop plant, the kind of loom, the style of buildings, the system of marriage, the manner of social structuring, the kind of economic organization, or the forms of the mutilated landscape, for such specifics are the diagnostic elements by which to measure cultural transfer, evolutionary change, creative skill, or human method. Such interests must be very broad, indeed, for the cultural geographer must use every possible kind of evidence to measure human accomplishment, changes through time, variations in human response to human challenges, and changes in the environmental surroundings. Thus the cultural geographer often uses the procedures, the data, the viewpoints, and the understandings developed by many of our fractionated academic disciplines, particularly within the social sciences, in his long-range endeavor to understand the variable patterns of life upon the whole of the earth. In short, the cultural geographer is a student of institutionalized human systems as these are displayed over the surface of the earth.

Organization of this Book

For the student this book consists of five distinct parts. Part One approaches culture and the contemporary earth from the familiar and immediate so that some basic concepts concerning them may become clear through personally acquired and previous knowledge. Part Two presents the transition from the organic to the human period in the earth's evolution and the beginnings of cultural advance, or improvement of organization. Part Three considers cultural divergence and regional differences in occupance of the Earth by Man. Different cultures have placed different interpretations on what constitute resources and have transformed their wild physical-biological environments into tamed habitats to suit their own cultural goals or values. Part Three then turns to cultural convergence, a trend that is almost absent in animal evolution. Part Four takes a closer look at the technological revolution of the last two centuries. Part Five views the immediate future of the humanized earth on the basis of discernible present trends of cultural evolution.

Within the limits of this one volume we have not tried to deal with all the types of forms of cultural constructs that man places on the landscape. Thus we have not dealt in detail with settlement systems, agricultural systems, patterns of road densities in different regions, the mechanics of mining coal or of making steel, or the specific procedures of turning trees into paper. We are quite conscious that we have, in a sense, told a story of Man's growing ability to adapt the Earth to his own ends, rather than retailing the facts about the occupied earth, rather than setting forth doctrinaire assertions of facts and relationships, rather than asserting laws about human performance documented by assemblages of data ar-

ranged to prove our own interpretations of those laws. We believe that at some point or other in the book we have tried to deal with most of the kinds of human activities (activities that do make marks on the surface of the earth) in ways that depict the growing abilities of our human race. We have intended that this book discuss the systems and principles of human occupation of the earth. For a detailed account of the facts of geography any reader will need recourse to maps, atlases, regional geographies, information almanacs, yearbooks, and statistical compendia, as further contributions to an understanding of the truth about the earth, about man, or about Man on the Earth.

Whatever else we may do or become in our lifetimes, we share one thing with all mankind: the earth is our home, our only sustenance of life. This is our world for as long (or as briefly) as we are upon it. How it has been changed, and continues to change, during its latest phase—the human period—provides the subject of our study. This study we interpret as cultural geography.

PART ONE

Beginning with the
Contemporary Familiar

CHAPTER 1

The Mosaic of Twentieth-Century Man on the Earth

The planet Earth is unique among entities in the infinite series of universes, though other worlds may also possess life. Although the earth has been matchless from the beginning, its individuality has become even more distinctive by virtue of man and the ways in which he has occupied the planet. In no two centuries since man became Man has the Earth been the same, and today's earth is like none before: it has become a mosaic of units of land surface and people. In this setting man has slowly but increasingly developed the body of ways of doing things called culture, which itself has become an element in the total design. The units of Earth, Culture, and Man are now articulated in a manner hitherto unknown.

The relationships among the three involve space and time in an innumerable variety of dimensions. At any given moment some units of earth have been tiny in area, the cultures simple, and the numbers of man have been few, whereas other portions of earth have been vast in size, their cultures complex, and the numbers of Man too great for casual conception. In general, the units of earth have been growing larger through amalgamation of smaller ones, the levels of culture lifting, and the numbers of man increasing. In general, moreover, the relationships among Earth, Culture, and Man have grown increasingly complex and varied. Yet in some parts of the earth the unit of area is still small, the level of culture still simple, and the numbers of man limited. Here man often lives by patterns of the past, whereas elsewhere he brings into practice ways of living that were totally unknown in earlier times. While in some

small units of earth small groups of men still think in units of miniscule size, in others man's outlook has acquired a One World perspective.

This chapter attempts to present elements in these contrasted relationships with a view to setting forth some general concepts that will be developed throughout this book.

Differences in Local Time and Space

The Familiar Local Area

Every human being has been "away from home" at some time and felt the relief and pleasure of getting back. To the small child the home area may be only a few hundred square feet, whereas to the seasoned adult traveler it may encompass a much larger space. Strongly built into human consciousness is the concept of "home"—a sense of territoriality, a feeling of security, and a set of psychological reactions oriented to some sector of the earth (a mental three-dimensional map). Home consists of the truly familiar area (Fig. 1.1A), in which there are no unknowns, no alien patterns, no unfriendly presences, no surprise obstacles to being one's self.

The nature of home varies with Man and with the Earth; no two people react in precisely the same terms to this specific region. It is compounded of varying elements. The configuration of the land surface is one such element, but others lie in the shape and kind of plants that grow on the land, in the form and placement of buildings, in the nature and type of the decorative material applied to land and buildings, in the sounds, sights,

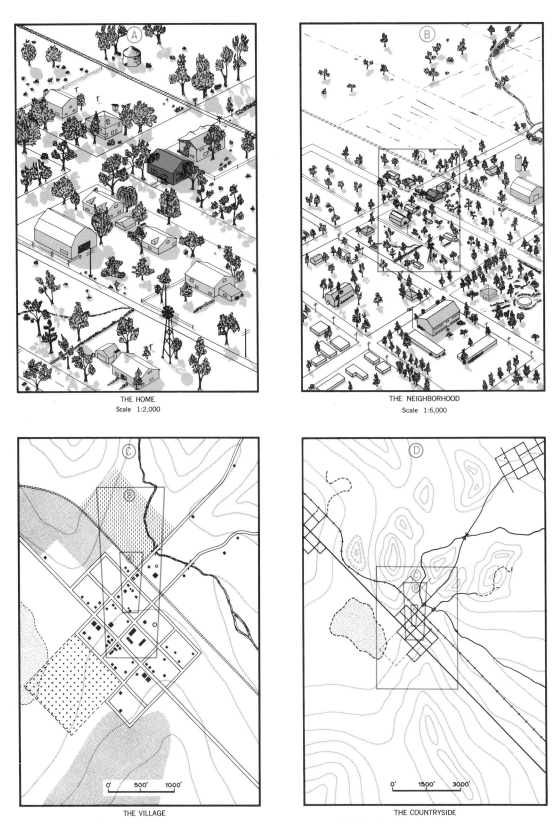

FIG. 1.1 FAMILIAR GROUND. A. The Home (Scale 1:2,000). B. The Neighborhood (Scale 1:6,000). C. The Village (Scale 1:16,667). D. The Countryside (Scale 1:50,000).

and smells that belong to the area, in its language, signs, speech, clothing, and the kinds of animals, big and small, that share its space. Home is a composite of familiar things arranged in familiar manner.

Beyond home lies the "neighborhood," the proximate area within whose range the composition of things on the surface of the earth is also well known (Fig. 1.1B). Here not every detail is precisely memorized. Changes can occur or surprise elements appear in time without upsetting equilibrium. As at home the patterns derive from the shape of the land, the buildings, the plants, the animals, and the people. To the child, the area involved may not be very large, but to the experienced traveler it may be sizable. As the child matures, the home area and the neighborhood tend to expand (Fig. 1.1C), and as the individual travels increasingly, both home area and neighborhood grow, though remaining distinct, strictly local territories. Home and neighborhood have for each of us a special kind of setting on the surface of the earth. To some these must be in or on the hills, to others they must be on the flatlands. There are people oriented to the forests, to the open lands, to the watery surfaces, to the arid lands, to the rainy tropics, or to those parts of the earth having marked seasonal changes and snow in winter. The urban dweller who is ill at ease in the quiet rural scene is matched by the unhappy villager in the great city. Heretofore most people were either rural dwellers or village folk, but the world has increasingly become urban, so that growing numbers of people now orient their homes and neighborhoods to towns and cities, in which Man is less aware of the Earth than formerly.

A short stay in some new environment can easily induce a new sense of "home" and "neighborhood"—remain a few weeks in a different place and new definitions of "home" and "neighborhood" begin to emerge. One set of definitions may fully replace a prior set. Human beings vary greatly in these respects, from the individual who never has more than a single home in his lifetime to the rootless wanderer who seems never to have any home at all. For most men, however, there is the specific identification of each home area, which is a more personal thing than the casual expression of environmental relationships that is often made.

The neighborhood tapers off into a transitional zone in which familiarity with the scene distinctly lessens (see Fig. 1.1C). This may be the village as a whole, within which there are numerous familiar items: homes of friends, particular trees, stores one occasionally visits, a playground, or a movie theater. Within this zone only some of the marks are really well established in the mind, and there are unknown and unfamiliar blanks between these points. One is not lost here, ordinarily, but neither is one as thoroughly at home as within the neighborhood.

Beyond the village lies the countryside (Fig. 1.1D). There will be gross familiarity with the general scene in that one has been here before; true recognition and full familiarity, however, often are restricted to a few particular points one has learned to pick out to maintain a sense of location. One can get lost here at night, and changes through time can deceive one as to one's precise whereabouts. To the stay-at-home the edge of the countryside may be quite close to the home neighborhood, but to the wanderer the inner portion of the countryside may be within the transition zone of fair familiarity.

The Far Country

The transition zone between the home territory and the outer country (see Figs. 1.1C and 1.1D) sometimes is broad and gradual and sometimes it is sharp and sudden, but beyond this zone lies "the far country," a distant, unfamiliar land where things are entirely different (Fig. 1.2). It is another portion of the world, another sector of space inhabited by beings, with conditions of another sort. The transition ends where recognition begins. In early times navigators feared the edge of the sea, landsmen were awed by what lay on the other side of the mountain or beyond the desert. In our time we know these other regions to be part of our same world, yet the uncertainty persists, the curiosity remains. The returned traveler is endlessly pursued with such questions as "What was it like there?" "Did you like the living conditions?" "Did you like the people?"

The human being tends to wonder about the far country, for it must be different from home and neighborhood. How distant the far country lies depends entirely on the human outlook. To the child the far country may begin within a few blocks, to the rural villager it can be the next village a few miles away, whereas to the seasoned traveler it may lie thousands of miles off. What makes the far country different? The very landscape is unfamiliar in that landforms, plant growth,

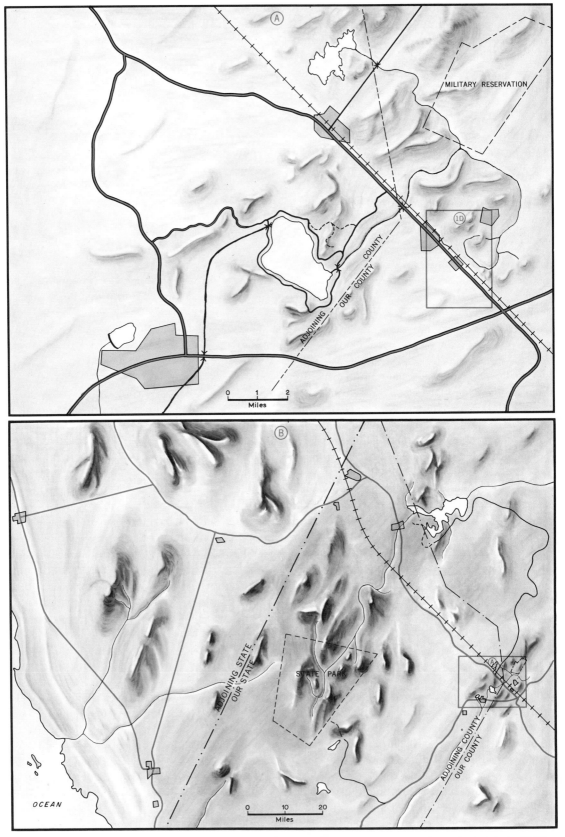

FIG. 1.2   THE FAR COUNTRY.   A. The Next County (Scale 1:200,000).   B. The Next State (Scale 1:1,600,000).

and climate are arranged in combinations unlike those at home, and the fields and crops, the villages and towns, the roads and transport consist of different mixtures. It is also likely that the daily living routine, the diet, the clothing worn, and the songs one hears are dissimilar. The language men speak is apt to differ a little, and the people may themselves seem strange. The habits of living appear to be novel, the social framework is somewhat unfamiliar, and the political structures and organization of regions by which men live also seem different. It *is* the far country in that familiar landmarks are absent, both on the land itself and among the people who inhabit it.

For many portions of the earth, the outermost limits of the transitional zone may lie far from home. In such regions as the United States, the Soviet Union, or Australia, one could proceed a great distance before *everything* became different. These are large areas across which some of the familiar is widespread, mixed with other elements that are new. In other sectors, however, one may find such wholesale changes within so short a distance of one's home base that the scene quickly becomes almost totally foreign.

The Slowly Changing Character of Place with Time

When an adult returns to an old childhood home he is often startled at how near home was to the street corner or tree where he played as a child, though the latter are remembered as spots that had been at the far corner of his neighborhood. Examination discloses that many things remembered are still there, but their relationships seem very different from their remembrance, and totally unfamiliar items have intruded.

This review includes two kinds of changes that occur to areas on the earth's surface. The first is the scale differences that, with the passage of time, humans develop in reaction to areas, and the second is the actual slow changes that come about as areas fill up with human developments, attain growth or suffer depletion in vegetation, and suffer soil erosion as the cultural landscape alters. Both are relatively slow changes in terms of human chronologies, but quite rapid in terms of the full history of Man on the Earth. Were a resident of ancient Athens able today to stand before the Parthenon and survey the city he had known as a child he might well pick out a large number of familiar items, but contemporary Athens would

contain many changes that have emerged slowly during the intervening centuries.

The dimensions of space have altered greatly within the limits of human history, just as space dimensions change during a person's lifetime. People living now are strikingly aware of how effective distance has shrunk within the last generation as modern forms of transport have developed, but the process is as old as human history. The shortening process has not always operated at the same pace, but it has been continuous.

In the time of Man on the Earth the slow processes of landscape change have also been continuous, if uneven. As the numbers of Man have grown greater, all over the world, "vacant lots" have been filling in, forests have gradually been shrinking, planted growth has been growing in bulk and size, and cultivated landscapes have slowly replaced wild ones (Fig. 1.3 and pp. 179–190). Continents and oceans have altered their sizes and shapes, deltas have pushed seaward, and the processes of weathering and transportation of detritus (the loose material that results from the disintegration of rock), aided by accelerated soil erosion in areas where man has been careless, have been altering the detail of the earth's land portion.

Under the hand of man all parts of the world have been slowly changing. Most of the regions of the earth have come to show the accumulating works of man in long-compounded patterns, whereas a few areas show accumulation for a period and subsequent abandonment. For this reason, archaeologists must dig under the present cities to find the traces of earlier human life, whereas such now vacant sites as Troy, Mohenjo-Daro, Jarmo, Machu Picchu, and Chaco Canyon show occupance for certain time periods only.

For any one portion of the earth's surface, a combined pattern of change has been taking place, in which elements of place and time have been interwoven. An early campsite on a natural levee amid the marshy lands near the mouth of the Mississippi River, where New Orleans now stands, formed a useful bit of dry land to early Indian occupants of the lower river country, but the water transport connections with another such site where Pittsburgh stands today were of little consequence. Eventually the marshy delta became a refuge to another people, the Acadian French, who also lived along the levees as subsistence cultivators and hunted in the marsh. Later Andrew Jackson fought the British in the delta country, not for the dry

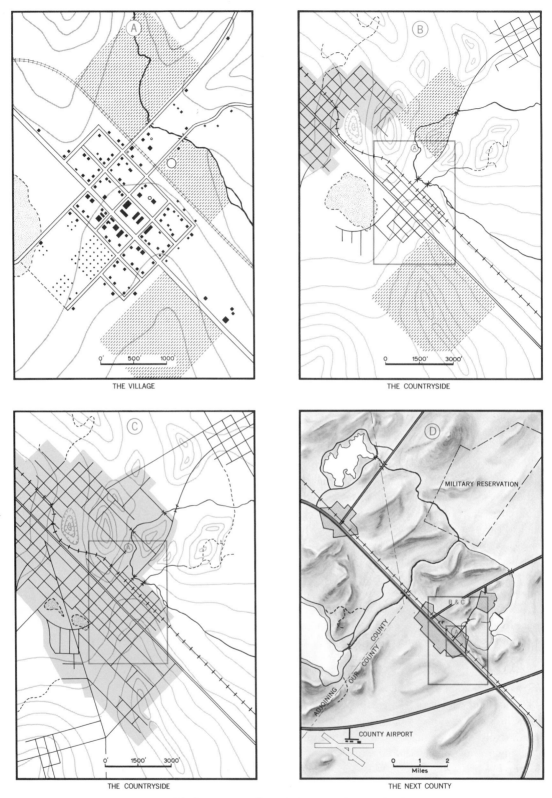

THE VILLAGE

THE COUNTRYSIDE

THE COUNTRYSIDE

THE NEXT COUNTY

FIG. 1.3 CHANGES IN TIME AND PLACE. A. The Village (Scale 1:16,667). B. The Countryside (Scale 1:50,000). C. The Countryside (Scale 1:50,000). D. The Next County (Scale 1:220,000).

14

levees and the marsh hunting, but for the potential connections of the place with other areas of the world.

The great river has changed its course in detail since that first campsite was used. Man has enlarged the dry land strip of the levee, drained some of the marshes, and progressively changed his use of the site. The river continues to alter the mouths of the delta, and man continues to expand his buildings, roads, canals, levees, and fields. Sites for chemical factories, oil fields, and petroleum refineries replace muskrat-hunting grounds. The connections with St. Louis and Pittsburgh have become important, and so have those with Panama, Singapore, Cape Town, and London. New Orleans is today a world port city. Man's concepts of space and time have been altered since the first Indian looked out over the marsh from a levee. The far country is now a larger area at a greater distance than it was in that day.

Abrupt Changes in Time and Space

Not all change on the earth's surface occurs slowly or in great detail. The human record contains numerous examples of abrupt and massive shifts. Its archaeologic phase abounds with puzzles of apparently sudden prehistoric alterations of earlier conditions, many of which the historic record preserves. The physical record also reflects numerous unexpected changes, some of them of quite recent occurrence. These major developments have all taken place in the time that Man has inhabited the Earth, but in the long stream of human occupance they constitute the exceptional and spectacular rather than the normal and average kind of change.

About A.D. 330 the course of the Tarim River, in central Asia, suddenly shifted, altering for centuries the course of the Great Silk Route. In 1883 two thirds of the island of Krakatoa, between Java and Sumatra, disappeared in a volcanic blast that filled world skies with clouds of dust for months and created "tidal" waves (tsunamis) that drowned thousands of people. In 1906 the course of life in San Francisco was suddenly jarred by a major shift of earth along the San Andreas Fault, and another earthquake in central Japan in 1923 took the lives of 143,000 people. Man is restricted in his reactions to such violent expressions of physical force, for there is little that he can do about them other than accept them and adjust his patterns of living accordingly.

The pressure of Man himself upon the occupance of the Earth is sometimes abrupt and has long-lasting results. Although Mohammed taught love, mercy, and social reform during his lifetime, after his death Islam quickly became a violent and militant faith in the hands of fanatics who spread it by force across much of North Africa and Southwest Asia. In the 1860's two great human events produced massive changes in human living conditions, which had severe repercussions on the landscape itself. These were the Civil War in the United States, which caused a half million deaths, and the later portion of the Tai Ping Rebellion in China, which caused over 20 million deaths. More recently, what at first glance seems the abrupt acceptance of Communism by the Chinese will long color the mode of living of a large share of the world's people.

Although sudden changes do affect human living, they are not of primary import in fundamentally modifying the appearance of the earth's surface, though perhaps the power of man may be accumulating to the point where he becomes able to achieve abrupt alterations in certain of that surface's aspects. The earth, as we know it, is the product of a long time sequence of small and specific changes that finally become cumulative. But it is the slowly progressive changes in human culture, the impact of sheer numbers of man, and the accumulation of the detail of man's works that have brought lasting change to the surface of the earth.

Regional and Global Differences in Time and Space

Twentieth-Century Men

People as Vital Statistics. In the time it takes to read this sentence the total population of the world will have increased by about ten persons; by more than ten if one is a slow reader. Thinking of people as vital statistics, the 1967 rate of increase works out at about 125 a minute, 7,500 an hour, 180,000 per day, and roughly 65,000,000 per year. In 1967 the world population stood close to 3400 million, or about 680 million families. Fortunately they are scattered over a large share of the land surface of the earth (see both endpaper maps); at this moment, if they were evenly scattered out over all the land of the earth except Antarctica, there would be about 10 football fields (equal to 11 acres or 4.6 hectares) of area for each person. This seems like a large area, expressed in the arithmetic average of about 58 people per square mile, but, discounting such poor areas as Greenland, Tibet, and the Sahara, the world's people have pushed nearer each other on the better spots. In Japan today there is only about one and a half acres per person, including the top of Mount Fuji and other such difficult places. The Javanese live more tightly packed than the simple area of not quite an acre per person would suggest. In a few parts of southern and eastern Asia the packing reaches two people per acre, which would not be too bad if we were speaking only of housing space, but which is almost impossible when the full sustenance of both persons must also be obtained from this meager area.

About half the world's population consists of young people, and if all couples now marrying intend to have families of three to five children, there will be a lot less space per person in the near future. Owing to the benefits of modern preventive medicine and public health programs, infant mortality has declined. People live longer, so that the rate of population increase has been going up in recent decades. Currently this rate is at its highest level in human history for the world as a whole.

People as Settlers. Our 680 million families are located in many different dwelling sites (Fig. 1.4). Perhaps not more than 85 million families (425 million people) live in dispersed homes scat-

tered in the rural landscape. There are about 3 million villages, in which about 250 million families live (1250 million people), and perhaps 65,000 small towns, housing some 90 million families (450 million people). About 255 million families (1275 million people) live in roughly 1200 large towns and cities, and a great share of the rural annual increase is piling up in cities and their suburbs. The rural settlers change the surface of the earth only slightly with their dwellings, the villages are often inconspicuous, the towns form compact visible sites, but urban environments are increasingly becoming artificial environments as power-using techniques are employed to build cities.

Although more numerous than ever, man still does not live everywhere on the earth's surface (Fig. 1.5). The chief unsettled spots are the really cold polar margins and the higher mountain lands, totaling roughly one fifth of the land surface. Second are the truly dry areas of the world, scattered in fragments among the continents, empty except where some special circumstance has made occupance worthwhile; these account for perhaps another sixth of the world. Third are the very hot and humid sections of the earth, principally in South America, Africa, and southeastern Asia, in which present-day occupance is more notable than in the other empty sectors. The tropical one eighth of the world's land area once thought unlivable is increasingly sustaining large populations and perhaps will be the first "empty zone" to disappear. Today, however, most of the human race (about 80 per cent) occupies the areas of relatively mild conditions—not too cold, not too dry, and not too hot-and-wet—and is thus concentrated on half the world's land area.

People as Ethnic Groups. In the strict sense man is but a single species. Among all forms of man 46 chromosomes are normal, and all forms can interbreed. However, man has always distinguished different groupings of the human family on some specific basis. Skin color has been one common criterion, and something can be done with other criteria such as shape of head, color of eye, nasal index, color and texture of hair, and so on. Different groups perceive these factors differently and attach varying social significance to them. In some parts of the world such recognizable biologic attributes of Man have formed the bases for group organization, whereas in other parts some aspect of culture has been the source

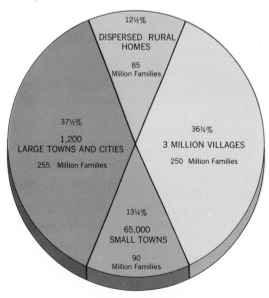

FIG. 1.4 WORLD RESIDENCE PATTERNS.

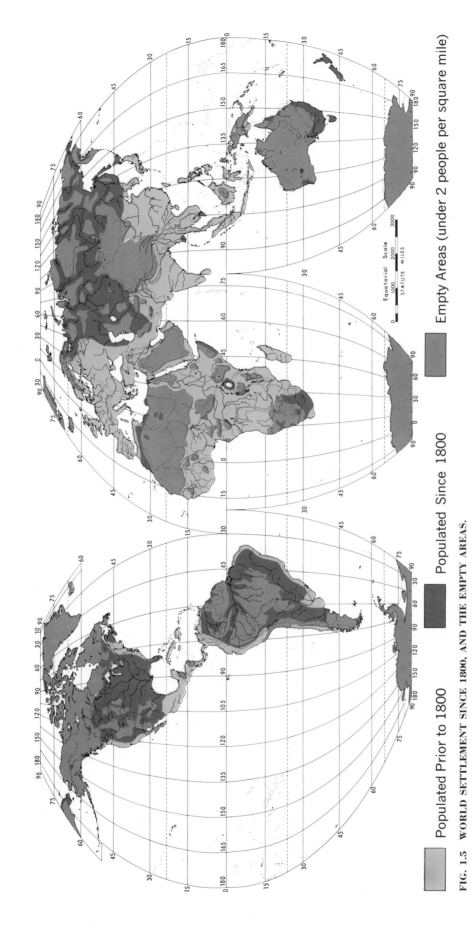

Populated Prior to 1800   Populated Since 1800   Empty Areas (under 2 people per square mile)

FIG. 1.5   WORLD SETTLEMENT SINCE 1800, AND THE EMPTY AREAS.

17

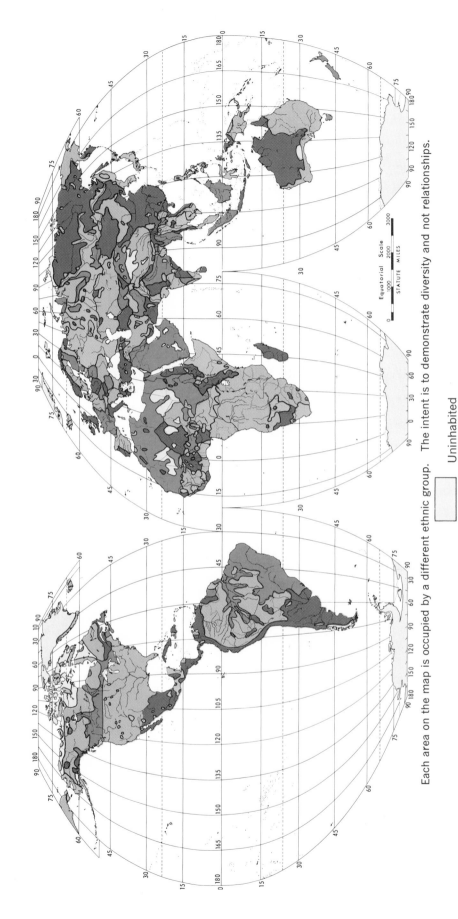

Each area on the map is occupied by a different ethnic group. The intent is to demonstrate diversity and not relationships.

Uninhabited

FIG. 1.6 PEOPLE AS ETHNIC GROUPS. A. World Ethnic Groups.

18

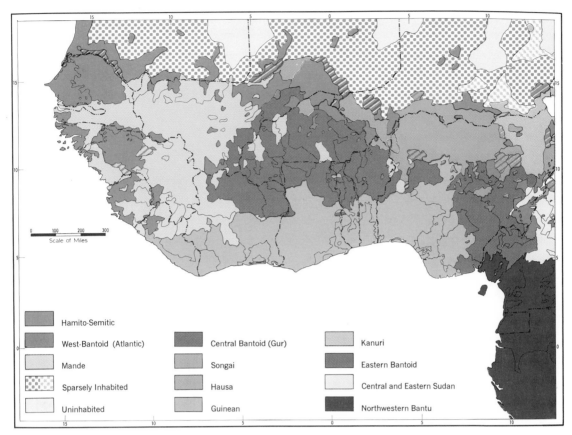

Hamito-Semitic

West-Bantoid (Atlantic)   **Central Bantoid (Gur)**   **Kanuri**

Mande   **Songai**   **Eastern Bantoid**

Sparsely Inhabited   **Hausa**   **Central and Eastern Sudan**

Uninhabited   **Guinean**   **Northwestern Bantu**

FIG. 1.6 (*Continued*)   B. Regional Ethnic Composition—Example of West Africa.

of group cohesion. Frequently, human grouping is predicated on mixed series of biologic and cultural items with the term "ethnic group" often used to express the result (see Fig. 1.6 and pp. 47–58). Nationality is commonly used when political organizational elements play a leading role. "Minority" is still another term for grouping people, usually referring to a proportionately less numerous group politically, socially, or economically which is at the mercy of a dominant group or coalition of groups. According to purpose, the world's people can be ranked into any number of groups from roughly 3 to 400.

People as Linguists. The term language normally presumes an ability restricted to man. Man can be guttural, tonal, or musical in his sounds. He can roll certain of them across his tongue or click his tongue. He can speak in his throat, with his tongue, and with his lips. As a group of people adopts specific techniques for uttering sounds, spoken language emerges.

Languages developed when people were scattered widely over the world in small groups and hence evolved differently. At one time or another some 6000 to 7000 spoken languages have been used. There are still nearly 3000 different systems of composing sounds in use in the modern world, plus almost twice as many dialects (Fig. 1.7). Probably the most widely used language today is Mandarin Chinese. It is spoken, with dialectic differences in particular areas, by perhaps 600 million people. Next most likely is English which, with its dialectic differences, is spoken by about 350 million in regular usage. Spanish, Hindi, Russian, Arabic, Japanese, Indonesian, Portuguese, German, Bengali, French, Italian, and Urdu are other single languages, each spoken by more than 50 million people. These 14 languages encompass more than 60 per cent of the world's people. At the other extreme are a few dozen languages, each spoken by only a few dozens of people; some 500 languages perhaps account for no more than a million persons. Altogether less than half the world's population thus uses about 1500 languages,

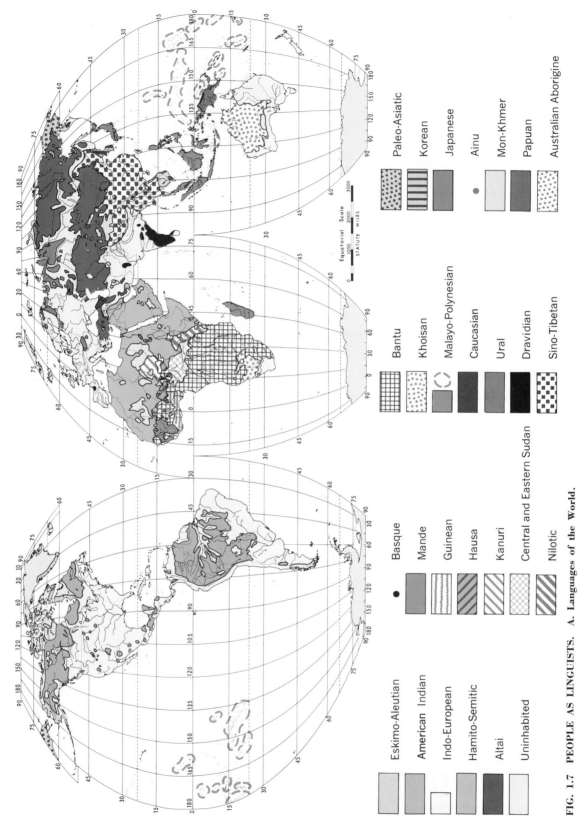

FIG. 1.7 PEOPLE AS LINGUISTS. A. Languages of the World.

Eskimo-Aleutian
American Indian
Indo-European
Hamito-Semitic
Altai
Uninhabited

Basque
Mande
Guinean
Hausa
Kanuri
Central and Eastern Sudan
Nilotic

Bantu
Khoisan
Malayo-Polynesian
Caucasian
Ural
Dravidian
Sino-Tibetan

Paleo-Asiatic
Korean
Japanese
Ainu
Mon-Khmer
Papuan
Australian Aborigine

Equatorial Scale
0   1000   2000   3000
STATUTE MILES

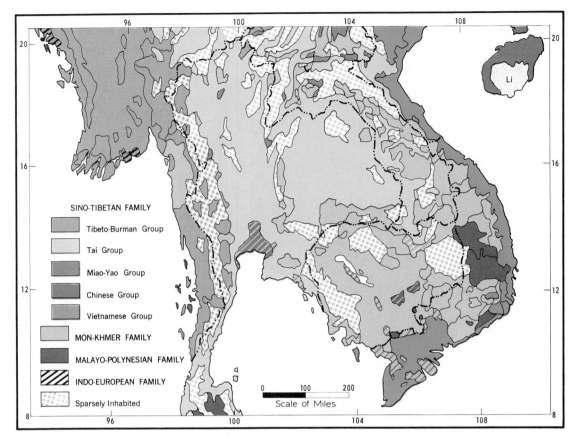

FIG. 1.7 (*Continued*)   B. Regional Language Pattern—Example of Mainland Southeast Asia.

a most inefficient state of affairs for the most rational form of life on our planet. India, southwestern China, the island world of Southeast Asia and Oceania, central Africa, and Soviet Asia are regional areas of greatest contemporary multiplicity in human speech.

Indo-European is the largest family of languages, in which the speech system is technically similar. Speakers of these languages are distributed worldwide today, though their distribution in earlier times extended only from central India to Iceland. Sino-Tibetan comprises another great family of languages, concentrated in China and southeastern Asia. The Ural-Altaic family apparently originated in Siberia but is now scattered from eastern Europe to Central Asia. Hamito-Semitic languages which are chiefly north African, the Bantu language group which is numerous in central Africa, and the American-Indian family—now partly preserved by linguistic anthropologists—constitute the other large families of speech. Perhaps when the New Guinea languages are fully studied they will form

another large family grouping. Some languages cannot be assigned to family groupings. Basque is the standard example of a language whose origin is indeterminate, but Korean, Japanese, Viet-Namese, and even Greek are also hard to place in the complex systems of human speech.

The writing of language, a late development making possible what we call history, is also complex and incompletely understood. Early man tried and discarded many systems before the alphabetic system became dominant over all of the world except China and those areas that have adopted the Chinese system. Written language has been difficult to adapt to the facile human tongue, and no single international language, either spoken or written, can effectively express all the nuances and permutations of human speech and thought. Language is one of the strong cements of culture, whether it be of nationality or of common culture. It becomes the tool of group cohesion in the hands of willful leaders. The United States, in particular, is most fortunate in possessing the basic elements

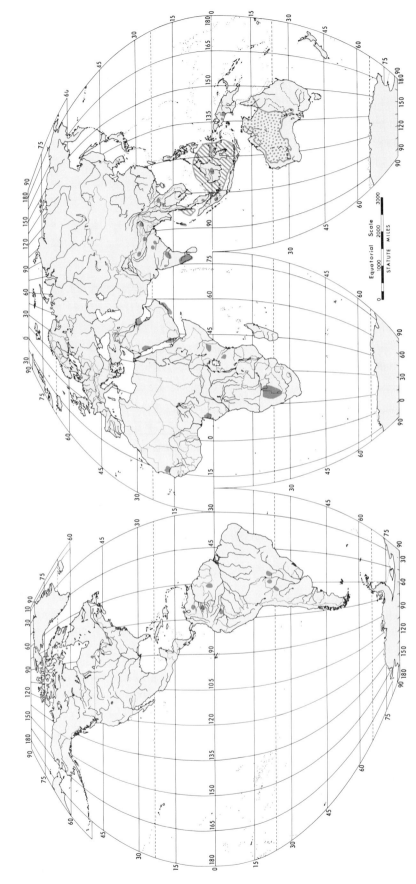

22

FIG. 1.8 SYSTEMS OF GROUP LIVING. A. Subsistence Bands and Groups.

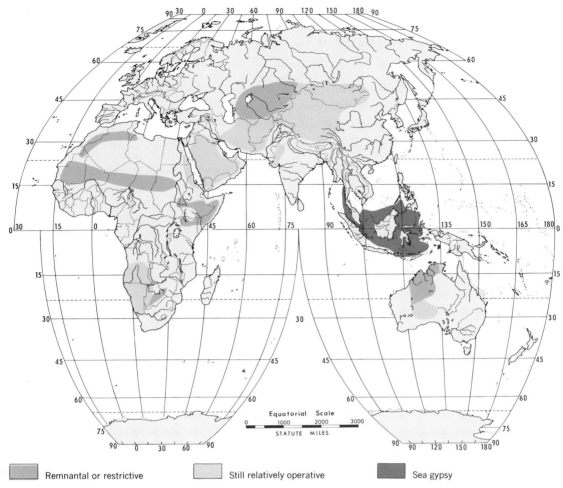

Remnantal or restrictive	Still relatively operative	Sea gypsy

FIG. 1.8 (*Continued*) B. Nomadism.

of a single language, for it is one of the things that has helped to blend members of the country's diverse ethnic subcultures into Americans.

Twentieth-Century Human Organization

Group Living. Scattered around the world are remnant populations that still preserve some of early man's organizational structures. In many early human groups a simple sharing of living problems, techniques, and rewards was characteristic. Organization took various forms, depending on how the food supply was derived, how the group lived together, and what social bounds kept it unified. There were many separate and interlocking motivations to such groupings. The issues of food and shelter and of selection of proper mates in marriage may have been basic, but social arrangement of groups for the practice of magic,

for recreation, for control of territory, for the expression of intergroup friendship or enmity, and for those primordial urges toward individuality was involved in the motivations that led early man to organize his forms of living. We shall purposely place the accent on the elements of economy and residence, but recognition of other factors is implicit.

The simplest, and possibly the earliest, of these groupings was the band of unspecialized gatherers or collectors, then a small mobile unit without permanent housing. This pattern still characterizes a few of the simplest migratory economies pursued by remnant populations in odd spots throughout the tropics (Fig. 1.8). The specialized collector group, concentrating on a localized resource, and sedentarily resident, used a living system developed at a later date. What may be termed a working party, living in a hamlet or small village, linked by lineage to similar entities that practice a self-subsistent economy, is another remnant social structure. The almost total self-subsistence of such groups, either fully sedentary or periodically transferred, is seldom found in the world today, but approximations still appear. In the drier portions of the world seminomadic and nomadic groups still preserve some of the organizational patterns of an early pastoral sort, but these groups also have become fragmented and largely absorbed into more specialized economies.

Among slightly larger units, to be measured in terms of a few hundred people, were amorphous groupings frequently and simply referred to as communal. Organization among such peoples was often a temporary matter, subject to change and realignment as specific needs arose. Economies were frequently combinations of simple crop growing, gathering, and hunting of game, fowl, or fish. Housing also took various forms: associations of hamlets, loose villages, settlements of separate family houses, or the articulated "long house" that sheltered a whole village. Once population totals rose above a few hundred, a variety of suborganizational units appeared, Such sociopolitical structures were widely distributed over the world in early historic time, and a great variety of groupings continued to be employed by the "simpler" cultures (as we today term them) long after the evolution and invention of more formal and complicated sociopolitical forms. The expansion of the European peoples over the earth, after A.D. 1500, encountered large numbers of groups employing all manner of living patterns. All of the simplest groupings can be termed elementary and exist today in remnant distribution only, representing the preservation of the early efforts of man to bring order into the simple problems of group living on the earth.

Multigroup Living. Eventually man conceived an organizational form both more specific and effective than the aforementioned types. Tribal structures and confederacies are more advanced forms, but the most effective one so far has been the political state, which is thought to have been a social invention of the classical Ancient East of southwestern Asia. It was an all-embracing organizational concept combining magic, religion, military power, and power over land, water, wood, crops, animals, minerals, manufactured goods, rights of exchange, and, above all, power over

people as persons. It was clearly an accompanying development of the rather sudden appearance of "civilization" in a few places in the ancient world, and it has been termed the State of the God-King. Its core was a settlement we now term the city; it comprised a controlled area of land around the city which provided economic support; it involved agriculture and manufacturing, taxation, wealth, and organized religious worship of specific gods; it stratified human beings into slaves and other menial classes, into warriors, urban artisans, priests, and nobles; it turned intergroup relations into foreign policy and intragroup relations into a definitive class structure that provided personnel for the operations of an advanced society.

The State of the God-King long antedated the Greek state and was the ancient form of state developed in Dynastic Egypt, Babylonia, the Indus Valley, and North China. Historically, every small "country," kingdom, principality, and state and every colony, empire, commonwealth, and union has employed some modification of this early concept of the state. Greece, at its heyday, abolished the God-King but kept the core city and slavery; early Indian states elevated the role of religion and social structure; the late European national states made one last play upon the Divine Right of Kings; our American democratic state divorced religion from temporal power, made the God-King an elective administrator, and elevated the rights of the individual, but kept the power of taxation and the right of conscription in time of war; the Communist state has returned to an earlier day in respect to control by the holder of power over people as persons and over resources, wealth, and production.

Today most of the world's population lives within the framework of an increasingly complex pattern of organizational forms not to be found in the simpler societies of the past (Fig. 1.9). Many peoples, formerly content with the older forms of organization, now demand all the rights and forms that go with the modern political state. The United Nations, at its origin in 1945, numbered 50 states and governments among the then 71 independent states; since 1943, some 60 newly independent "states" have emerged, and the United Nations in 1967 comprised 122 member nations with numerous units still to gain admission. Within the broad framework of today's varied expressions of the state lie many variants. A few states are ruled by kings, the equivalent of the ancient God-King;

slavery still is a formal legal matter in some; a few have no formal system of taxation of the citizenry; some states, such as the United States, comprise literally thousands of elected and appointed governments within governments.

Special-Purpose Organization. Almost every person in the United States "belongs" to some special-purpose group, organized to further some specific cause or to satisfy some special social urge. But Americans, possessing more leisure and being more "organized" than most societies, merely exhibit a human tendency; people everywhere, and apparently almost from the beginning, have "belonged" to special-purpose organizations, some that have been purely social, serving as an outlet for human gregariousness or providing status, and others that have carved a quasi-official position in the society of which they have been a part. In the United States these range from such groups as the Antique Automobile Club of America, the Improved Order of Red Men, the Society of the Friendly Sons of St. Patrick, the American War Dads, the Daughters of the American Revolution, and Rotary to the American Heart Association, the Association of American Geographers, the Institute of Radio Engineers, the American Rocket Society, and the American Red Cross.

The anthropologist, examining a simple society in a far-off land, notes the presence of the Men's House, the several age groupings, the grouping of the skilled warriors, and that of the skilled Old Men. In other, more advanced societies other kinds of organizational groupings appear. In many instances these special-purpose groupings are status symbols for the membership; in others they represent the effort to serve special needs of a segment, or the whole, of the society. Such special-purpose organizations have become more numerous and often have taken on an international character. There are a great many such groupings today, reaching into almost every country in the world (Fig. 1.10). Increasingly, special-purpose organizational patterns are becoming more numerous and significant in the living relationships of the world.

Twentieth-Century Space Patterns

The Political Earth. Major wars cause geographers much trouble. The political map of the earth undergoes great change at the end of every war. This is a significant truism—in the twentieth century the political map has been constantly changing in almost every part of the world, and it is likely that during the balance of the century there will be more such major changes. Not that this necessarily involves further major wars, for the evolution of the political organization of space on the earth is today in active flux. Colonies become independent, peoples formerly organized as tribes organize political states on modern lines and seek admittance to the United Nations.

What is true of the major outlines of the map of the political earth is also true with regard to the details. Regions of government are multiplying at an astounding rate. Within the continental United States, though the primary boundaries of the contiguous 48 states have not changed for decades, school districts are in constant flux, water-supply and flood-control districts are delimited, and urban governments are absorbing surrounding rural territory. What is true in these matters in the United States also applies, in varying degrees, around the world.

Freedom of the seas, control of territorial waters, and freedom of the air above states are experiencing change. Though the demarcation of political boundaries is going on actively, conflicting claims to earth space are perhaps more numerous than ever. Despite preserving every boundary stone of the separate national entities, the political map of western Europe is overlaid with a series of such new political lines as those formed by NATO, the Iron Curtain domain, and the European Coal and Steel Community (Fig. 1.11). Not all political organization tends toward great combines. Although the U.S.S.R. has outlined the world's largest state, Andorra, Monaco, Liechtenstein, San Marino, Bahrain, and Brunei continue to exist.

What is true in our lifetime has been true over the long term in the past, although there is no certainty that it will always continue. An historical atlas illustrates a bewildering series of political states. From the time of widespread tribalism, through the era of city states, to the first empire, and on toward our present political map, thousands of unit patterns of political organization have been in force. Many present ones seek historic precedent in the formality and outline of some previous state, but many strike out anew.

The Economic Earth. Most comprehensive atlases include one or more maps depicting man's occupations on a global scale. These maps suggest a presently repetitive distribution of economic activities, representing a particular period-condition of world economic development only. People

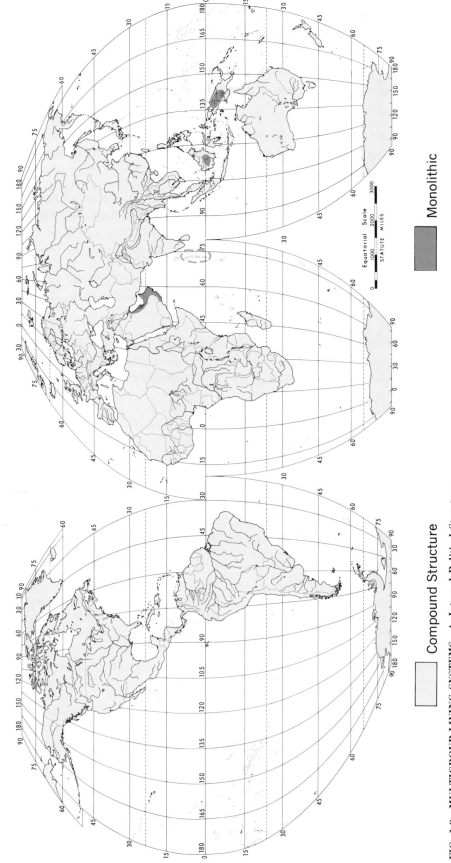

Compound Structure

Monolithic

FIG. 1.9 MULTIGROUP LIVING SYSTEMS. A. Internal Political Structure.

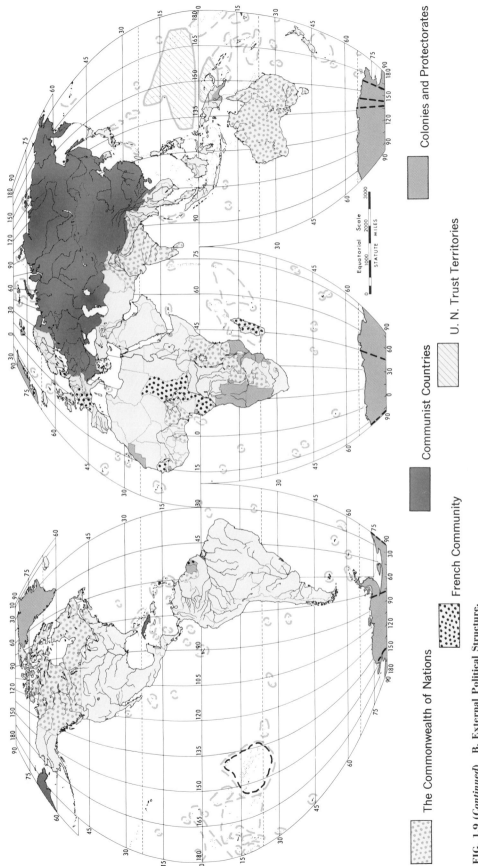

The Commonwealth of Nations

French Community

Communist Countries

U. N. Trust Territories

Colonies and Protectorates

Equatorial Scale

STATUTE MILES

0   1000   2000   3000

FIG. 1.9 (*Continued*) B. External Political Structure.

27

28

ROTARY INTERNATIONAL

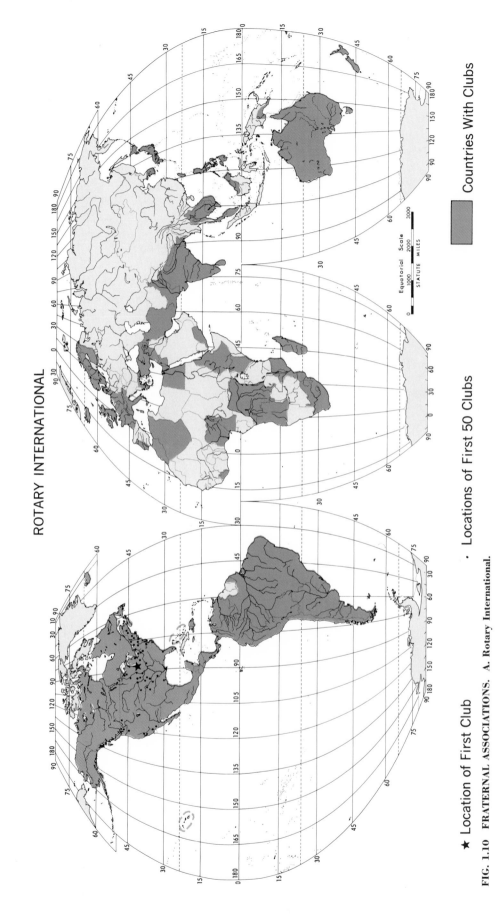

★ Location of First Club   • Locations of First 50 Clubs

Countries With Clubs

FIG. 1.10   FRATERNAL ASSOCIATIONS.   A.   Rotary International.

INTERNATIONAL BOY SCOUTS

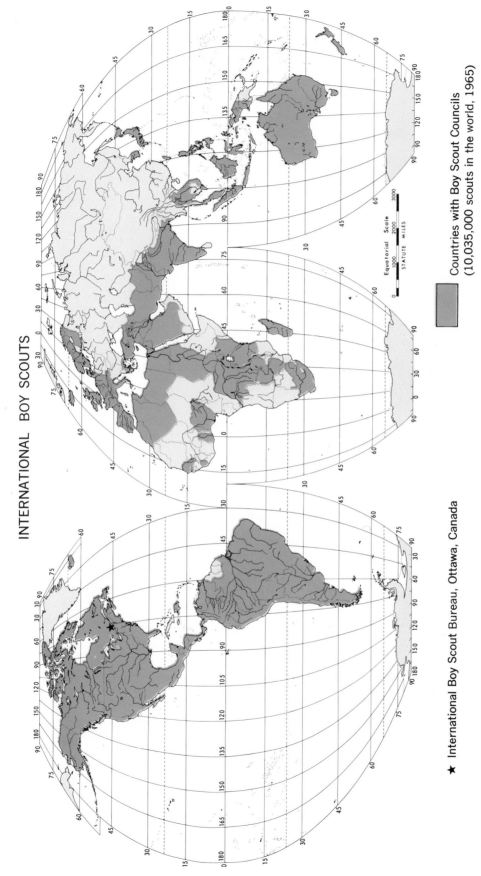

Equatorial Scale
STATUTE MILES

★ International Boy Scout Bureau, Ottawa, Canada

Countries with Boy Scout Councils
(10,035,000 scouts in the world, 1965)

FIG. 1.10 (*Continued*) **B. Boy Scouts.**

THE UNITED NATIONS IN 1967

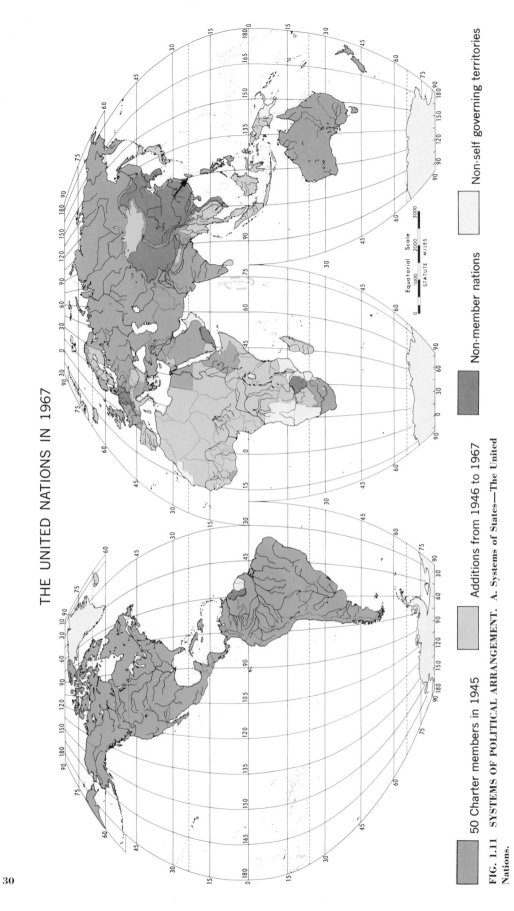

50 Charter members in 1945   Additions from 1946 to 1967   Non-member nations   Non-self governing territories

FIG. 1.11 SYSTEMS OF POLITICAL ARRANGEMENT. A. Systems of States—The United Nations.

30

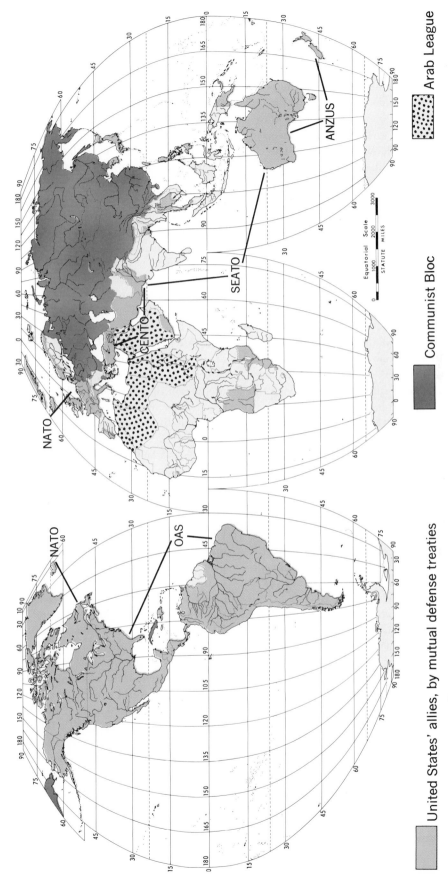

United States' allies, by mutual defense treaties

Communist Bloc

Arab League

FIG. 1.11 *(Continued)* **B. International Participation by the United States.**

31

in tropical regions engage predominantly in certain occupations, produce certain kinds of commodities, and enjoy low or high value patterns by selected criteria. Polar, arid, and midlatitude regions are depicted in other terms. On the composite economic map zones of production of many products, and the flow lines of commodity movement, suggest that the earth has been organized for the better economic support of a relatively small portion of its population.

The composite map makes clear that production and commodity movement is a rather highly elaborated pattern that embraces the whole earth in what might be termed an economic one-world. Contrasting such a map with theoretical constructs for earlier times would clearly indicate that, in the economic sense, the earth now has been rather well integrated. The earlier the composite economic map, the greater would be the separation of its parts into fractionated "little economic worlds." The Pleistocene map would approach true local subsistence patterns. Every other map would indicate the steps being taken by man to increase production and enlarge the regions involving the movement of commodities.

Despite the one-world impression that emerges from scanning contemporary flow charts, there are numerous regionalisms either recently operative or coming into being (Fig. 1.12). Local self-subsistence has almost disappeared from the world, but trade blocs, currency regions, tariff zones, and politically formed trade zones are more numerous than ever. Such terms as "sterling bloc," "dollar bloc," and "ruble bloc" suggest humanly instituted barriers to commodity flow, as do "commonwealth preference," "most-favored nation agreement," and "strategic embargo." Whereas, in 3068 B.C., the barriers to economic exchange were physical problems of transport, distance, and the nature of landscapes separating peoples (leaving aside the problems of technology of production), in A.D. 1968 they were chiefly those set up by man himself. In 3068 B.C. true world trade was not technologically possible; in A.D. 1968 it was technologically possible but practiced only in terms restricted by human barriers.

Twentieth-Century Resource Organization

Local Bases of Food and Raw Materials Supply. The ways in which man secures his food supply vary tremendously in the present world. Australian Aborigines, Indian hillmen, Kalahari

Bushmen, and Amazon Valley Indians still live from day to day by simple gathering or collecting of edible resources during a day's trek within their resource range. Shifting cultivators around the tropics plant tubers, vegetables, and grains in primitive patch units, depend on gathering, hunting, and fishing until the crops ripen, and then undergo "starvation periods" when the crops have been eaten before the next planting period, during which they gather, hunt, and fish again. In the so-called "backward areas," partial subsistence cultivation provides the bulk of local food supplies. Broad zones of the earth do carry on general food-producing cultivation, bartering, exchanging, storing, buying, and selling to balance out the year's needs. Local regions in such areas sell off their annual surpluses, and other regions buy enough to augment their deficits. Other broad zones of the earth engage in production of narrow ranges, but greater surpluses; necessarily these zones are tied to other large regions both for sale of surpluses and purchase of needs. Tropical and subtropical regions contain areas where specialty production of a few commodities occurs concurrently with production of the local food supply. The midlatitudes contain similar large producing units.

Whereas a large share of the world's people was once closely connected with food production, a lesser share is so linked today. This has resulted from the appearance of more advanced production techniques in terms of tools and management of land. Increasingly some element of corporate operation has become prevalent, as in the tropical plantation or the midlatitude farm. The evolution of trade has vastly altered the regionalism of food production and, today, certain commodities such as grains, meats, fish, fruits, and condiments move from producing sites to consuming sites every day of every year. As urbanism grows the nonproductive consuming sites increase, both in number and size. Without trade in food supplies, a large segment of the world's population would starve. However, the primary basis of world food supply is a regional matter (Fig. 1.13A). The share in nutrition of commodities from "the ends of the earth" is not truly great. These items add flavor, variety, zest, and spice, but not the bulk of calories. The foods Americans, Japanese, or Filipinos forwent during World War II, did not, for the most part, seriously impair regional health.

The supply of raw materials is not essentially

different from that of food. Old Stone Age man chiefly picked up his tool stone from the surface of his local area, though long distance trade in rarities did occur. He built his housing from local materials, and adapted other local materials for clothing. Modern man picks up much of industrial minerals off the local surface, and other raw materials normally come from regions relatively close at hand (Fig. 1.13B). Housing materials are chiefly local materials and, as synthetic fibers come more to the fore, so are clothing materials. Coal-mining regions are scattered all over the earth, as are producing forests. Cotton, wool, flax, industrial clay, salt, and petroleum are widely produced in our modern world and flow chiefly to local or regional markets.

Regional and World Bases of Food and Materials Supply. The shift from local to distant sources did not come about simply, even among commodities that eventually moved out of their indigenous production regions. For example, cane sugar remained a commodity produced, bartered, and consumed within the local regions of southeastern and southern Asia for a long time before knowledge of its value gradually filtered westward beyond India into the Mediterranean, to become gradually known in northwestern Europe. This knowledge promoted the growth of the tropical plantation system, and after A.D. 1500 sugar became a commodity of international trade. India still is a leading sugar producer, though little involved in international trade in sugar. Silk also illustrates this situation. Production began in China, spread slowly within the Orient, and not much of it got out of China until the modern period when silk became an important trade commodity. Natural silk production has now decreased owing to the competition of synthetic fibers; there is little world trade in silk, but its production and use are still common within the Orient, China remaining the biggest producer and consumer.

Much of the regional trade in many commodities, both food and raw materials, occurs between or among peoples of like cultural habits (Fig. 1.14). World trade in wheat, for example, has developed among wheat-eating people, that in rice among rice-eating people. Although this analogy can be carried too far, it points up the distinct regionalisms in the production, trade, and consumption of food supplies and raw materials. These regionalisms comprise many different elements of culture, many of which are very old. The regionalisms'

existence, the rise of modern political states, the impact of economic systems and trade blocs, and the question of value versus bulk have all meant that there are broad regional bases to the production and disposal of much of the food and raw materials supply of the world. The phrase "there is no market for it" indicates that cultural preferences restrict truly worldwide movement, trade, and use of a large number of commodities.

When this view is extended to include processed and manufactured goods, and when we look at the world as a whole, other kinds of regionalisms are to be seen beyond the basic environmental characteristics of the earth's areas (Fig. 1.15). Certain zones stand out clearly as great food producers, whereas others are almost insignificant. Although North America is producing significant surpluses of food commodities, China produces the largest volume of the world's food. The Sahara is a very small producer, as is Tibet. Currently Southwest Asia stands out as a producer of petroleum, but this is a regionalism of a single raw material only. The higher latitudes of the northern hemisphere stand out as producers of wood and mineral products. The ocean margins of the continents in the northern hemisphere supply most of the world's aquatic consumption—fish, shellfish, seaweeds.

On the consumption side there are also regionalisms, for every production pattern is a result of a consumer-demand pattern. North America, in per capita terms, is currently the chief consuming region of the world, though in terms of volume the whole of the Orient, with almost half the world population, can be considered the chief consuming region. Regionalisms of particular sorts exist. North America is a meat-consuming region contrasted to Japan, a fish-consuming region, and a coffee-consuming region contrasted to China, a tea consumer. Mexico and southern Asia are regional consumers of the hot spices, just as the Mediterranean Basin is a leading consumer of olive oil. Yet none of these is unique, for other portions of the world have somewhat similar tastes in each case.

Many causal factors may be isolated in the production and consumption regionalisms of the current world. The tastes, preferences, and changing habits of culture groups are basic to the development of world patterns of commodity production. The growth and availability of transport, aided by the application of capital resources, facilitates the satisfaction of these preferences.

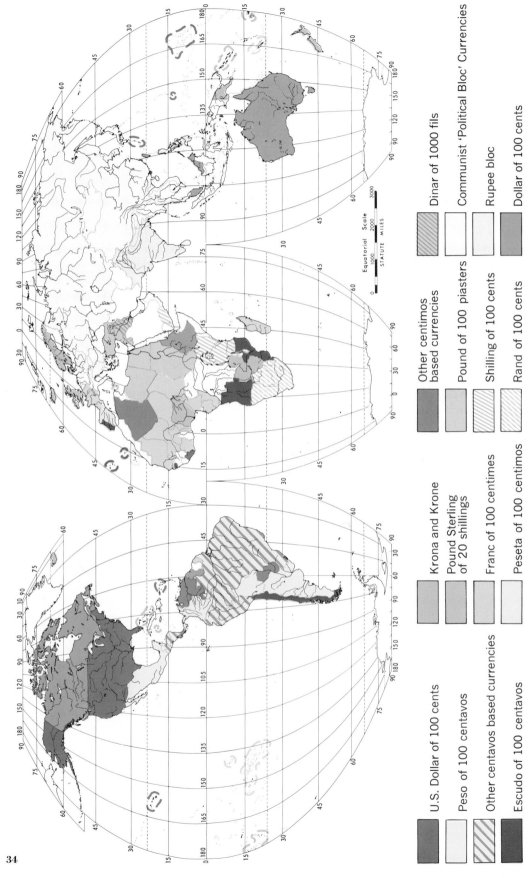

34

FIG. 1.12 SYSTEMS OF ECONOMIC ARRANGEMENT. A. Currency Blocs.

U.S. Dollar of 100 cents

Peso of 100 centavos

Other centavos based currencies

Escudo of 100 centavos

Krona and Krone

Pound Sterling of 20 shillings

Franc of 100 centimes

Peseta of 100 centimos

Other centimos based currencies

Pound of 100 piasters

Shilling of 100 cents

Rand of 100 cents

Dinar of 1000 fils

Communist 'Political Bloc' Currencies

Rupee bloc

Dollar of 100 cents

Equatorial Scale

0   1000   2000   3000
STATUTE MILES

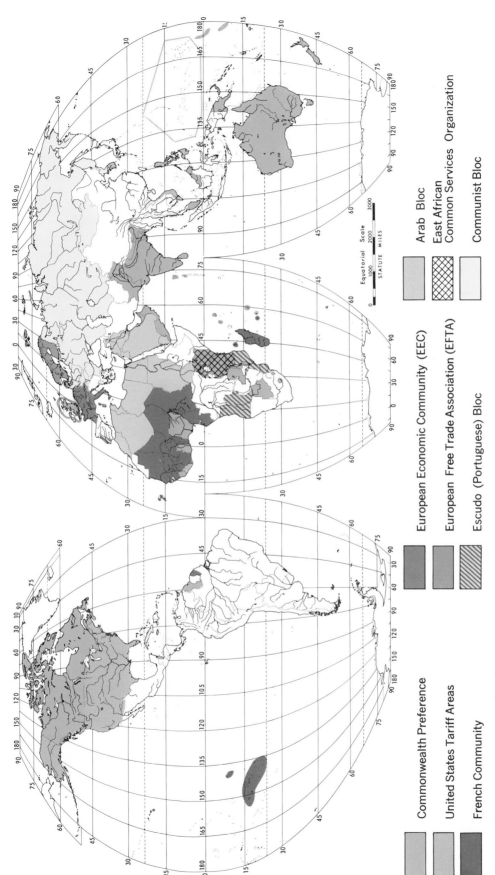

Commonwealth Preference

United States Tariff Areas

French Community

European Economic Community (EEC)

European Free Trade Association (EFTA)

Escudo (Portuguese) Bloc

Arab Bloc

East African Common Services Organization

Communist Bloc

Equatorial Scale
0   1000   2000   3000
STATUTE MILES

FIG. 1.12 (*Continued*) B. Tariff and Trade Blocs.

35

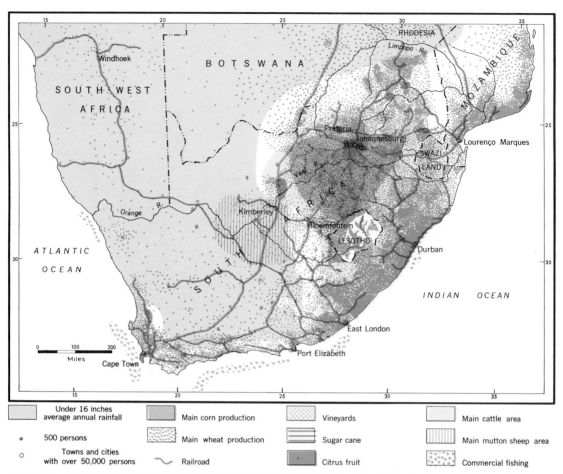

FIG. 1.13   REGIONAL PROVISION OF FOODS AND RAW MATERIALS.   A. Food Patterns—Example of South Africa.

Despite the effectiveness of modern transport the issue of value versus bulk continues to loom large in the world picture of regionalism in both supply and consumption. Highly valuable items of small bulk move widely over the earth, whereas items of large bulk but low value are restricted to localized distribution. The willingness of regional populations to cater to, or develop, productivity in certain lines is critical. Either as a simple bulk exchange point or as a processor, the assembly center has facilitated the whole modern evolution.

Style and fashion, and changes in them, are important in the changing character of production, distribution, and supply. The rise of production in homologous regions, creating secondary regionalisms, has sometimes led to changing the rank of these regions. This is followed by roughly analogous rises of consumption and by the changing rank of consuming regions. In no two portions of the earth do production and consumption operate equally, so that no two regions in the world are complete likenesses as to production and supply of foods, raw materials, or manufactured goods.

The Time Element in Regional and Global Differences

The Persistence of Local Customs in Space. The travel ad reads: "Go back three thousand years to fairytale towns and folklore provinces—go by jet plane to live in luxury in modern hotels." How is this possible on the earth—our one world? The very lure of the ad, of course, is the far country where things are different. To the American, having a short history, who lives in "today," with the expectancy of living in "tomorrow," this means ways of doing things that belong to the "day before yesterday." Were the ad written for the occupant

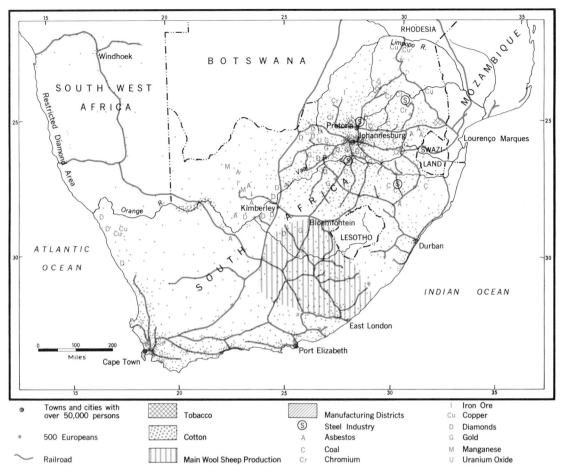

●	Towns and cities with over 50,000 persons	▨	Tobacco	▨	Manufacturing Districts	I	Iron Ore
				Ⓢ	Steel Industry	Cu	Copper
∗	500 Europeans	▦	Cotton	A	Asbestos	D	Diamonds
				C	Coal	G	Gold
∼	Railroad	▥	Main Wool Sheep Production	Cr	Chromium	M	Manganese
						U	Uranium Oxide

FIG. 1.13 (*Continued*) B. Raw Materials—Example of South Africa.

of the fairytale town, to lure him to North America, it would be couched in other terms.

American travel literature exploits the "differentness" arising out of persisting regional customs. These customs are the habits of people, expressed in their houses, clothes, foods, arts, and manufactures—in short, in their landscapes and cultures. Although inventiveness, the desire to do it better, and the hope for new ways of living are common human attributes, the love of the familiar ways, the maintenance of familiar techniques, and the preservation of familiar patterns of living are equally common. The American way puts much stress on inventiveness, novelty, and change. Another way may stress preservation of the tried and true, the familiar and the old. Still another way may combine the two extremes.

The world is currently made up of peoples who follow many combinations of the old and the new

(Fig. 1.16). In terms of human technology a few local regions have just emerged from the stone age, and a few are on the verge of the space age. The element of time shows its clear imprint in the thousands of local regions, ethnic groups, and cultures now active in the world. Human custom, technology, the attitude toward the world and toward the environment, and the composite will of the group vary from region to region and from time to time.

Revolution as a Regional Phenomenon. As applied to human life on the earth, "revolution" denotes widespread change in both areal and population organization. The term is used here in the broad sense, and not just in a political context. Revolution proceeds from dissatisfaction with the way things were; it seldom begins with total dissatisfaction but normally derives from extreme unhappiness about a few matters. Dissatisfaction may

38

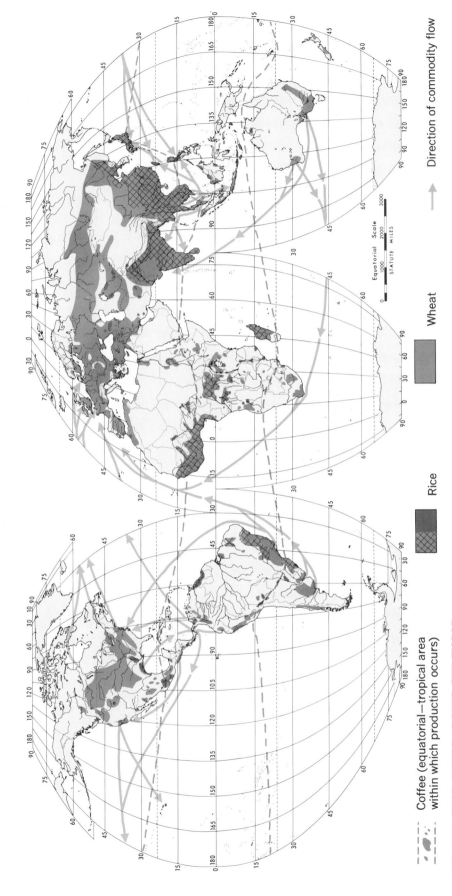

Coffee (equatorial−tropical area within which production occurs)

Direction of commodity flow

Wheat

Rice

FIG. 1.14 FOOD SUPPLY AROUND THE WORLD.

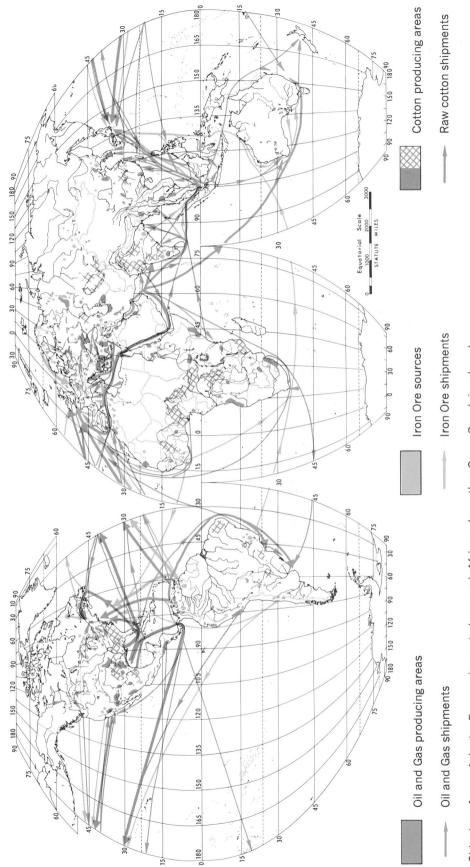

Oil and Gas producing areas

Oil and Gas shipments

Iron Ore sources

Iron Ore shipments

Cotton producing areas

Raw cotton shipments

Shipping from Asia to Europe is routed around Africa when the Suez Canal is closed.

FIG. 1.15 RAW MATERIALS SUPPLY AROUND THE WORLD.

39

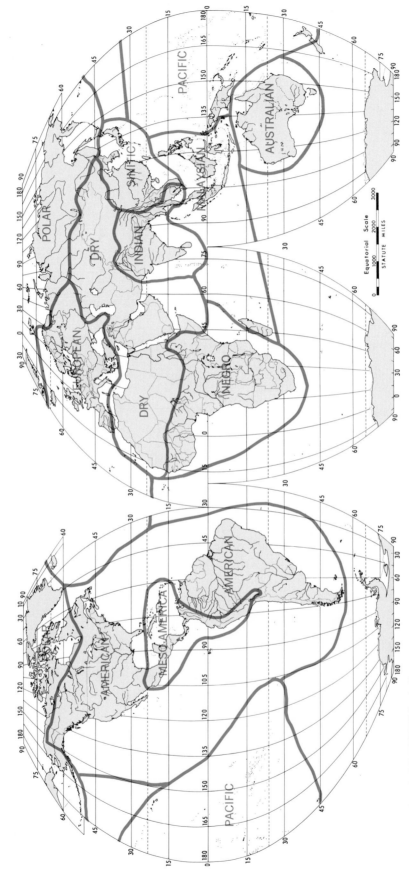

FIG. 1.16 CULTURE WORLDS. A. In A.D. 1450.

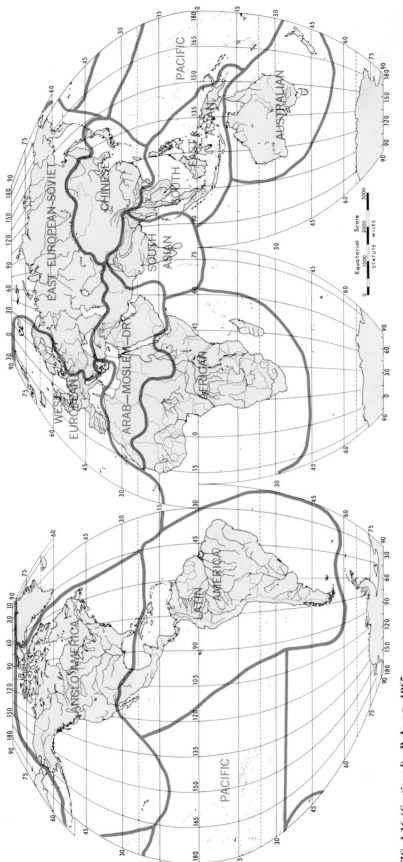

FIG. 1.16 (*Continued*). B. In A.D. 1965.

41

spread from one group of causes to others and end by producing large changes over a wide range of items. Revolution is precipitous, occurring at a faster rate than normal change. Revolution does not occur often in a given region, but when it does appear it may create a notable break with the past. Since few revolutions in human living are ever even reasonably total, there is normally a voluminous retention of prerevolutionary elements. The retention of customs, techniques, material works, commodities, and human preferences, therefore, preserves a considerable share of past patterns in a landscape and in a manner of living.

As applied to human culture, to living systems, and to the landscape in which man lives, most change is nonrevolutionary. Most regional landscapes are slow accretions of elements of different age. But change is almost continuous in some aspect of the living pattern or the landscape itself, despite man or by his hand. Trees grow large and die, houses grow old and crumble, new crop plants enter the field, whether as conscious selections or as weeds that evolve into useful plants, and populations never remain totally static, for emigrants leave and immigrants arrive. New human concepts emerge, resulting in new cultural materials; they may gain only minor acceptance until their value is unquestioned.

By slow accretion the landscape, and human living in it, alter (Fig. 1.17). If by chance a long interval of gradual change does not bring maladjustment, a given region may slowly acquire a patina of stability, and a culture group a tradition of continuity. But more often maladjustment within the region itself, or in a nearby region, brings human dissatisfaction to a boiling point which promotes revolution. Then occurs the drastic change that introduces a disconformity into the stratification of human living in a portion of the earth, and often carries with it major changes in the landscape.

The Spread of Change, and Its Nature in Regions. Changes in human living patterns result occasionally from the invention of new developments within a region, but more customarily from the introduction of new features from outside, a process known as diffusion. The region may be a large area of the earth's surface or a very small one. If a large zone, it may possess sufficient ecologic variety, in the sense of total environment, to contain subregions in which new developments may take place. New features may be passed along through trade or barter, they may be introduced by human migration from one region to another, they may be seen and acquired by the itinerant wanderer for his homeland, or they may be diffused as ideas or techniques, later to be reproduced in a new place. Particular aspects of an item may not gain acceptance, yet the item is used in a way compatible with the new area's old patterns.

As applied to regions, cultural change of the sort suggested produces new manifestations in the landscape itself. New items displace old, take their places beside them, or form a veneer over the old while never totally eradicating them. In the travel ad at the beginning of this section the process is evident. Three-thousand-year-old fairytale towns cannot be too far from jet-age airports, and new hotels with American fittings have intruded on the landscape. The American tourist would not be expected to enjoy living in a type of inn that properly belonged in the fairytale town and the folklore province.

The Twentieth-Century Mosaic—Man on the Earth

Composite Regionalism

For purposes of mapping, the earth may be divided, according to any of various criteria, into major and minor component areas, with lines drawn between them, regionalisms discerned, and patterns of rank established. By geographic region the geographer normally means a cohesive unit, with a certain number of criterion boundaries falling into place around it. Areas that have no such cohesive unity, since they are frequently bisected by the boundaries of particular criteria, are sometimes called shatter belts. Both regions and shatter belts are essentially abstract concepts, but are employed as tools of convenience.

Like the geographer, the anthropologist deals with issues of the regionalism of Man on the Earth. Normally he starts with a broad concept of culture as his most significant criterion. This corresponds to the geographer's use of climate or landforms. Subcultures, particular aspects of culture, and regional biological anthropology next concern him, and ordinarily he adds a time series of criteria for the extinct cultures that can be studied only archaeologically. This volume attempts to combine the concepts and conclusions of both geography and anthropology; hence the factors of regional-

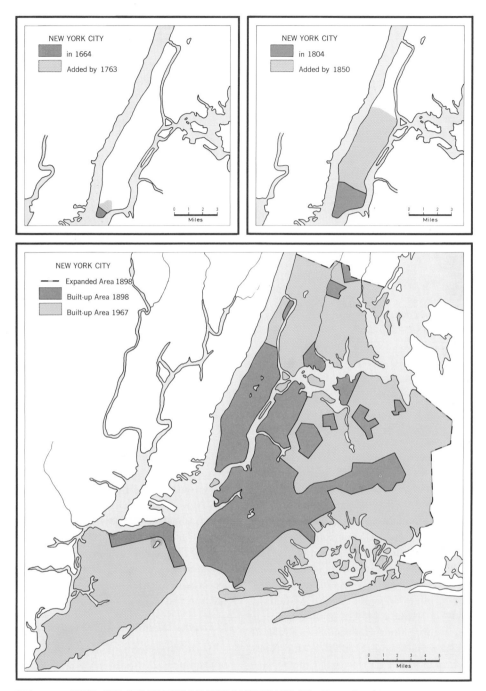

FIG. 1.17 TIME AND ITS MARKS ON THE LANDSCAPE. The Example of New York City, 1664 to 1967.

ism that we consider here are more numerous than those commonly employed by the geographer.

In this view, the earth is a large complex of regionalisms, a complicated, three-layered, translucent mosaic-mural. The fragments forming the mosaic are of three kinds: Earth space, People,

and Culture. The units of Earth space exhibit such aspects of nature as physical size and shape, landform, climate, drainage, vegetation, animal life, and soil. The units of Culture exhibit the customs and ways of human living, settlements, field systems, buildings, roads, mine and erosion scars, politically

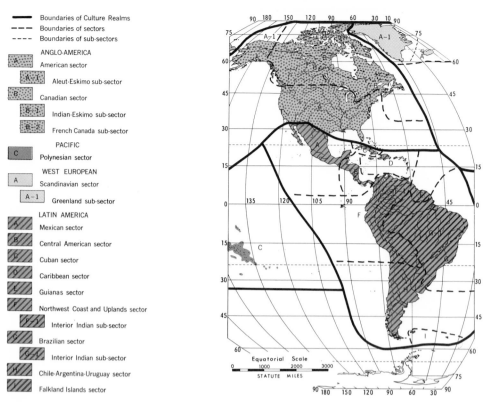

Legend:

Boundaries of Culture Realms
Boundaries of sectors
Boundaries of sub-sectors

ANGLO-AMERICA
[A] American sector
[A-1] Aleut-Eskimo sub-sector
[B] Canadian sector
[B-1] Indian-Eskimo sub-sector
[B-2] French Canada sub-sector

PACIFIC
[C] Polynesian sector

WEST EUROPEAN
[A] Scandinavian sector
[A-1] Greenland sub-sector

LATIN AMERICA
[A] Mexican sector
[B] Central American sector
[C] Cuban sector
[D] Caribbean sector
[E] Guianas sector
[F] Northwest Coast and Uplands sector
[F-1] Interior Indian sub-sector
[G] Brazilian sector
[G-1] Interior Indian sub-sector
[H] Chile-Argentina-Uruguay sector
[I] Falkland Islands sector

Equatorial Scale
0   1000   2000   3000
STATUTE MILES

FIG. 1.18   CULTURE WORLDS, 1965, FIRST AND SECOND ORDER.   A. The New World.

organized territories, languages, religions, clothing patterns, social organisms, manufacturing, music, art, food and game patterns, agricultural and trade systems, and others. The units of People exhibit such aspects of population distribution as ethnic groups, migrations, density variations, birth and death rates, age structures, and regional totals. The separate pieces of the mosaic can be "seen" in their three layers, pieces of each being different in size, shape, density, intensity, value, gravity, and color. Viewed quickly, certain bold motifs stand out, comprising all three kinds of pieces. Seen in detail other motifs become highlighted. Here and there motifs show up in which Earth space, Culture, and People seem in rather full unity; these are the units most geographers would call geographic regions. But parts of the mural have no unity and the separate designs of the three layers do not at all agree—these are the shatter belts.

Certain great groups of pieces show up in master designs on the composite (Fig. 1.18). They form the great realms such as North America, Latin America, or western Eurasia. Each possesses a series of smaller designs, motifs, and patterns that are individual, yet particular elements transgress

the smaller units and the larger masses alike. For example, the Indo-European languages spread from southern Asia through western Eurasia into two New World forms, and the food habit of the bread wheat consumers reaches far through the mural. In some parts of the mosaic the motifs are simple, the pieces are few, and there is neat order in the arrangement. In other sectors the patterns are complex, there seem innumerable fragments, and the order seems intricate, if not confused.

Changing Regionalism through Time

In the long term of Man living on the Earth, environmental values have actually changed in downright practical terms. A Canada covered with glacial ice was worth less to early man than a deglaciated Canada is worth today, and a more-watered Sahara, in immediate terms, was worth more to early man (when northern Europe was covered with ice) than the Sahara is worth now. But a small number of early men possessed too little culture to have made really great use of a deglaciated Canada or a more-watered Sahara. Man in larger numbers is today applying his advanced culture to Canada, and to the Sahara, finding that

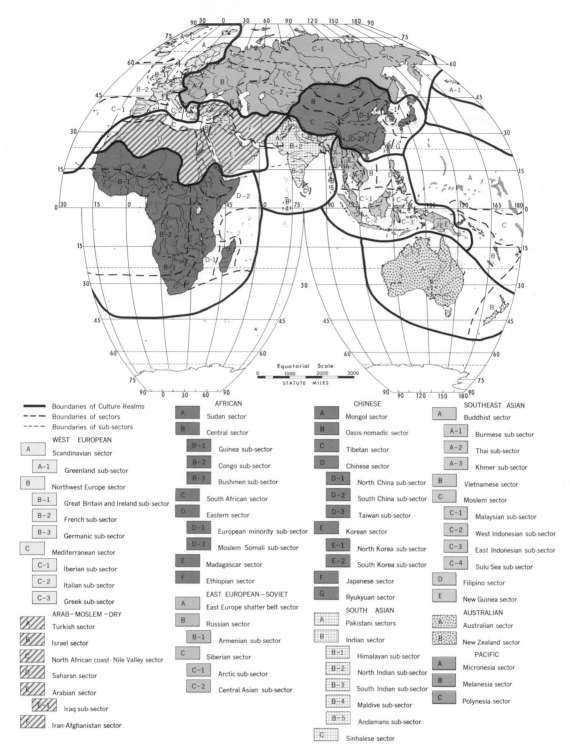

FIG. 1.18 (*Continued*) B. The Old World.

there are real values in each never before suspected.

The history of the occupation of the Earth by Man, therefore, possesses a triple time variable—physical-biotic-environmental time, culture time, and human time. Each aspect of our mosaic—Earth, Culture, and Man—has waxed and waned, increased and decreased in value, been new and old, rejuvenated and declined. The state of affairs in any recognizable region of the earth, today, is a composite of these three variables. To omit the time factor for any one of them is to portray less than the whole.

The Significance of Regionalism

Although innumerable single factors operate in the physical-biotic environment, and man functions culturally according to his ability, the pattern of life in an area or a unit of the earth is determined by group living. But since man is a thinking animal, with a power of initiation beyond that of other animals, he can alter, convert, or rearrange many of the conditions of his occupance of the earth. Traditionally he has done so by units, areas, and regions. Although one can argue the pros and cons of a "geography of Antarctica" before man ever set foot thereon, our concern is with natural regional environment containing man and culture.

It is this interplay of Man and Culture in Regions that writes our story and fashions the tiles in the rich mosaic of Man upon the Earth. Although human cultures operate through human groups, group culture is almost infinitely variable, since it

may alter with time and space. Man himself is variable in numbers, both in time and in space. Physical-biotic environments also vary, but their rates of change, both horizontally and through time, usually are less sharp and less rapid than those of culture or those of man. Whereas man may not as yet greatly alter the size and shape of the physical-biotic environmental tiles of the mosaic, he certainly may muddy the intensity of their value, as with smog or war, by the superstructure he erects, maintains, or allows to deteriorate.

Said more conventionally, there are endless differences in Man-Land relationships. We prefer to think, however, in terms of Man, Culture, and Earth. In the twentieth century this three-dimensional mosaic has been constructed, or has accumulated, in the most complicated set of regional designs that has ever existed on earth. Although we should recognize that, in the future, we shall further complicate the great world mural by continuing to redesign it, it is the patterns now existing, and how they arrived at their present state, that concern us throughout this book.

PEOPLES AND COSTUMES

GEORGE HOLTON, PHOTO RESEARCHERS

Choco Indians, Panama

Australian Aborigine

AUSTRALIAN NEWS & INFORMATION BUREAU

Chimbu Tribesman, New Guinea

Zulu, South Africa

DIANE RAWSON, PHOTO RESEARCHERS

GRETE MANNHEIM, PHOTO RESEARCHERS

Navajo, Arizona, U.S.

HARVEY CAPLIN

Japanese, tattooed

49

SHELDON A. BRODY

Mexican

AMERICAN AIRLINES

50

Bedouin, Algeria

HECTOR ACEBES, PHOTO RESEARCHERS

CARL FRANK, PHOTO RESEARCHERS

Peruvian Highland Indians

51

Gurkha, Nepal

DIANE RAWSON, PHOTO RESEARCHERS

EASTFOTO

Chinese

Japanese

J. E. SPENCER

Malay

JAPAN NATIONAL TOURIST ORGANIZATION

Indian

LONDON DAILY EXPRESS, PICTORIAL PARADE

53

Uganda, East Africa

HAROLD S. JACOBS, D.P.I.

SOVFOTO

54

Koryak, Eastern Siberia

Turk

Dolgan, Yenisei Valley, Siberia

NOVOSTI FROM SOVFOTO

FRITZ HENLE, PHOTO RESEARCHERS

55

J. ALLEN CASH, RAPHO GUILLUMETTE

Portuguese

PORTERFIELD-CHICKERING, PHOTO RESEARCHERS

Romanian

EASTFOTO

Danish

J. ALLEN CASH, RAPHO GUILLUMETTE

British Australian

AUSTRALIAN NEWS & INFORMATION BUREAU

CANADIAN CONSULATE GENERAL

Canadian Logger

PART *TWO*

The Humanization of the Earth

The development and elaboration of any one culture in its particular place and time has been possible only because a particular, ever-changing combination of cultural traits has been assembled from all parts of the world. As one example, very few of the elements of American culture are truly independent inventions of American origin. Rather, almost all resulted from the diffusion of objects or ideas from other places and their introduction, acceptance, and further diffusion in North America. Most of the content of each of the world's cultures has been similarly acquired, either diffused by migrating peoples who carried with them their values, ideas, and material goods, or diffused by the borrowing of ideas that one people learned from another. The latter implies the transmission of knowledge or goods without any migration or mass movement of peoples, as in the exchange of inventions, techniques, or ideas through the trading and discussions that go on between the representatives of one group and those of another.

Our concern is not merely with directly visible features, but also with the changes and processes of development that have produced them. Every object that owes its place in a landscape to human action was either invented, imported, or borrowed. The pyramid and sphinx in the contemporary Egyptian scene were invented and built during the dynastic periods of several millennia B.C. Both the camel toiling slowly around the water-lifting device on the riverbank and the date palms thus irrigated were brought into Egypt when prehistoric peoples from Southwest Asia migrated, bringing such domesticated animals and plants with them. Each element in a landscape has its own origin, its own cultural history of acceptance and modification within a particular culture, its diffusion outward to other cultural regions, and hence its spread through time and over space on the earth's surface. The distribution of all cultural features in various landscapes can be explained historically; each is a part of the evolution of its particular culture.

The spread of American culture from the Atlantic seaboard westward across the midlatitudes of an entire continent, now to include both tropical Hawaii and subarctic Alaska, is but the latest intensification of a process as old as man himself and his invasions of the earth to inhabit a whole planet. Man began with a pristine earth, a surface that had evolved with a near-infinite variety of living forms. From these, he emerged and rose to biological dominance, in a way that no other plant or animal ever has. Men created culture, as a new means of evolution. Knowledge transmitted from person to person and generation to generation can be improved upon, and these additions can become cumulative. Slowly man acquired the ability (through fire, tools, clothing, shelter) to survive and flourish far beyond the range of his biological limitations. And, in the process of securing his sustenance, he has transformed the pristine earth into a human habitat.

The purpose of this part of the book is threefold:

1. To examine the changing nature of the earth's surface during the unique period in which man appeared on the scene.
2. To discuss what we now know about the conditions of man's emergence and where the first halting, tentative steps were taken that led onward to accumulation of culture.
3. To describe how man, as culture bearer, has been able to spread over the earth to become its dominant form of life.

Truly, this has been astounding achievement, and always we shall be asking: Where did these events of cultural invention take place? Whence did they diffuse, through migration and cultural borrowing? And, owing to varying acceptances, modifications, and amalgams of the diffused cultural traits, what cultural complexes were thus developed in particular regions, so that each regional culture formed a distinctive pattern of ideas regarding behavior?

In this part of the book we turn back in time to concern ourselves with fundamentals, the evolutionary base from which man began. The explanation of why many things are present in a landscape can be found only by digging among the roots of culture below the surface of the present time level. Our object is clearly twofold: to understand (1) the present-day complexities in the distributions of man-made features and (2) the results of man's actions and agencies in transforming the face of the earth. Toward these ends, a first consideration dictates a knowledge of what the earth surface was like before the beginning of that process which we have here termed "the humanization of the earth."

CHAPTER 2

The Pleistocene Inheritance

The Earth as a planet has had its unique and long history, now computed at some $4\frac{1}{2}$ billion years (see the Time Chart, Table 2.1). Comparatively, the Age of Man, the period during which Man rose to become the dominant species on the face of the earth, has been brief, being measured in terms of the last two million years. To this latest epoch in the history of the earth, the English geologist Sir Charles Lyell in 1839 gave the name Pleistocene—"most recent."

Since the middle of the nineteenth century a truly fantastic amount of evidence has been gathered about this "most recent" epoch. The vision emerging from the meticulous piecing together of bits of information is that the Age of Man has occurred simultaneously with profound changes in the physical aspects of the earth and in the distributions of plants and animals. Man has witnessed extensive and repeated glacial action, with huge ice sheets occupying as much as three times the area occupied by glaciers today. The climates of great zones over the earth have changed markedly in temperatures and precipitation, snow lines have lowered and raised, sea levels all over the world have fallen and risen vertically through more than 500 feet, ground in the northern latitudes has frozen and thawed, great lakes have grown and dwindled, rivers have altered courses, and whole populations of plants and animals have shifted locations. The Pleistocene was a time of great changes in the character and distribution of physical-biotic environments over the earth's surface. And man's own story, the long era of human emergence from other biological forms and the great time span of human prehistory, is inextricably linked with the whole of the Pleistocene record. An appreciation of the earth's changing character during the Pleistocene epoch is vitally necessary for an understanding of the humanization of the earth.

The Present in the Past

The late twentieth century is terribly important for those of us fortunate enough to be experiencing it. Contemporary events literally shout at us, commanding our attention. In the time of our lives, we devote most of our efforts to understanding and solving many pressing and perplexing problems. But the present moment of our individual short time spans on the earth is scarcely more than a random point in the long continuous history of life. A meaningful and satisfying conception of how man's present circumstances of earthly existence have come about can only be achieved through an awareness of the conditions of the immediate past—the "most recent"—from which man and his present companions on the earth emerged.

Our present landscapes are mostly not the products of solely the physical and biotic processes or forces now acting upon them. Rather, most phenomena whose distribution we seek to understand have their own histories of having been molded or shaped or influenced by the changing forces active during the Pleistocene. The earth that man inherited was a Pleistocene earth. This chapter proposes to examine the wealth of that inheritance—those characteristics of the Pleistocene epoch that were of fundamental significance for the successful emergence of our human ancestors.

TABLE 2.1 TIME CHART OF EARTH HISTORY[a]

Era	Period	Epoch	Year before present (in Millions)	Chief Developments
CENOZOIC 73 million years' duration	QUATERNARY	HOLOCENE (Recent)		Man dominant on earth; birds in air; fishes in ocean competing with insects on land and in air
			0.011	
		PLEISTOCENE	2	Latest Ice Age; evolution of *Homo sapiens*; extinction of some mammals ———
	TERTIARY	PLIOCENE	13 ± 1	
		MIOCENE	25 ± 1	Apes
		OLIGOCENE	36 ± 2	
		EOCENE	58 ± 2	All main groups of mammals exist
		PALEOCENE	73 ± 2	Widespread expansion of flowering plants; mass extinction of reptiles; first birds; vast sea incursions; mammals small and inconspicuous
MESOZOIC 157 million years' duration	CRETACEOUS		135 ± 5	Rich land flora: conifers, cycads, ferns ———
	JURASSIC		180 ± 5	Reptiles more important as amphibians decrease / Dinosaurs; first lizards; first true mammals
	TRIASSIC		230 ± 10	Mammal-like forms from reptiles
PALEOZOIC 370 million years' duration	PERMIAN		280 ± 10	Reptiles start evolutionary line toward mammals —— / Modern insect groups appear / 2nd Ice Age ———
	CARBONIFEROUS	PENNSYLVANIAN	310 ± 10	First reptiles / Rich swamp flora; first conifers ———
		MISSISSIPPIAN	345 ± 10	Earliest land vertebrates ———
	DEVONIAN		405 ± 10	Conquest of land by plants and animals / Enormous mountain-building ———
	SILURIAN		425 ± 10	Age of reef-corals; first land plants
	ORDOVICIAN		500 ± 10	First vertebrates
	CAMBRIAN		600 ± 50	Free oxygen in atmosphere; higher proportion CO_2 / Atmosphere clears; sunshine reaches earth
PROTEROZOIC (ARCHEOZOIC)	——— PRECAMBRIAN ———		1,500	1st "Ice Age" / Several cycles of mountain building / Dawn of life in water ——— / First oceans, without life / Laurentian revolution
AZOIC (ARCHEAN)			3,500	
			4,500	Anhydrous phase, ammonia added to atmosphere / "Glowing" gas, liquid, and skin phases ———

[a] After Harland and Rudwick, *Scientific American*, August 1964, p. 29.

The Longevity of Evolution

To conceive of the Pleistocene epoch, one needs to think about a time span of two million years. This is not easy for contemporary man to grasp in a meaningful way. One image that might be useful is to think of a football field, which is 100 yards long from goal line to goal line. If this field represented a time span of two million years, the distance between successive chalk stripes, marked across the field at five-yard intervals, would represent 100,000 years. Each yard would represent 20,000 years. The whole duration of the

Christian era (almost 2000 years) would be 3.6 inches wide, no wider than the chalkmark indicating the goal line. This imagery provides a glimpse into the depth of time necessary for truly understanding man's longevity on the earth.

But the Pleistocene is just the "near-recent." The vast expanse of earth history must be conceived in immense units and measured in millions of years. In order to understand the physical world that mankind was to inherit, it is necessary to visualize the succession of events during the whole 73 million years of the Cenozoic (see Table 2.1), the era of recent life. (This would cover 37 football fields stretching end to end for more than two miles at the scale of one yard to 20,000 years). Most of the animal species of the present day, including man himself, evolved in this vast arena of time and space, as did the formation and sculpture of the present landform features of the earth.

And the Cenozoic is only the era of "recent" life. It was preceded by the Mesozoic era, something of a medieval period in earth history, toward the end of which the great reptiles became extinct, but during which the earliest mammals came into existence. Compared to the length of the Cenozoic, the Mesozoic was more than twice as long: about 157 million years in duration—or almost $4\frac{1}{2}$ miles of football fields, a seemingly endless vista.

The time span of evolution is far longer. The greatest development of life-forms occurred during a veritable "Golden Age of classical antiquity" in earth history, the Paleozoic era, which had a duration of some 370 million years—longer than the Cenozoic and Mesozoic combined. For conceptualizing the time span of the Paleozoic, during which the first vertebrates appeared, the earth's land surface became covered with plants and animals, the conifers evolved, and amphibians, reptiles, and insects came into being, the image of a football field as a unit of measure representing two million years is wholly inadequate.

The dawn of life on earth is thought to have begun about $1\frac{1}{2}$ billion years ago, after two thirds of earth time already had elapsed. How can anyone grasp the immensity of $4\frac{1}{2}$ billion years for the age of the earth, or $1\frac{1}{2}$ billion years for the evolution of life-forms, or even the 500 million years for the development of the vertebrates? But it is precisely these great spans of time that have been necessary for the slow rate of change required by the evolutionary process. Recent reviews of all the fossil evidence lead to the conclusion that it may take as long as 500,000 years for the evolutionary development of a new animal species and that some modern species may have a longevity of at least 30 million years.

The Variety Manifested by Life

The process of discovering, describing, and classifying the many kinds of organisms now in existence is still going on. A recent estimate for the number of animal forms is about one million; for animals and plants together there are probably several millions of species. Significantly, the number of extinct species greatly exceeds the total number of those now living. One of the greatest facts of life is, and has been, its diversity.

Populations and Species

That organisms vary and that they change in time is a lesson learned from grasping the concept of evolution. But it is *populations* of organisms, not individuals, that are significant for evolutionary variation. The basic unit, *a population*, is a group of more or less similar organisms that live together and interbreed. All populations contain a range of variation among the individual organisms forming them. The basic unit for classifying plants and animals, *the species*, comprises one or more such interbreeding populations. If composed of only a single population, the species occupies a contiguous area, usually a small one having relatively few individuals. If composed of several or many populations, a species occupies discontinuous areas that isolate the populations from one another, though not completely.

Species Formation

The species is the distinct evolutionary unit. Its variations and changes through time are restricted, since it does not normally interbreed with other species. Differences between species arise by a splitting (isolation, migration) of formerly interbreeding populations of one species. As a result of the cessation of interbreeding plus the beginnings of divergence, two species emerge from a common ancestry. As the two species continue to diverge, continuation of the process over a longer time span brings about further changes in different lines of descent. Fossil records show that succession took place through long periods of time, that various groups normally arose on the basis of variation and continuous change, and hence that evolution did occur.

In our present-day classification schemes, the more or less similar, but related, species of plants and animals are grouped together (as genera, families, and so on) into an ascending hierarchy. The primary steps in the hierarchy, as now used (from larger to smaller units) are the following:

KINGDOM (e.g., Animalia, all animals; or Plantae, all forms employing photosynthesis)
    PHYLUM (e.g., Chordata, animals mostly with backbones; or Teropsida, all vascular plants)
        CLASS (e.g., Mammalia, mammals; or Angiospermae, plants having seeds enclosed in an ovary)
            ORDER (e.g., Primates, composed of monkeys, apes, man; or Rosales, composed of rose-like plants)
                FAMILY (e.g., Hominidae, near humans and humans; or Rosaceae, the roses in general)
                    GENUS (e.g., *Homo*, humans; or *Rosa*, roses)
                        SPECIES (e.g., *Homo sapiens*, the one living species of mankind; or *Rosa multiflora*, a specific species of rose)

The Dominance of Angiosperm Plant Life

Among the roughly 350,000 living species of plants that have been studied sufficiently for classification, about 700 species belong to the *Gymnospermae* and over 250,000 species to the *Angiospermae*. The gymnosperms include the coniferous forest trees of the earth which provide much of the commercial timbers, firewoods, and woodpulps. Of rather ancient lineage, numerous members of their group are now extinct since they proved not highly adaptable to changing conditions of environments. The angiosperms, on the other hand, appeared relatively late in earth history and today dominate the earth's plant life. Subdivided into the *Dicotyledoneae* (250 families and over 200,000 species) and the *Monocotyledoneae* (45 families and about 50,000 species), each subclass having quite different characteristics and values the angiosperms are frequently called "dicots" and "monocots." They represent the climax of plant evolution to date and, by their particular characteristics, produced a new kind of vegetation that spread widely over the earth to become the dominant form in Cenozoic time. Very able to adapt quite readily to all aspects of environmental change, the angiosperms also developed superior abilities in both reproduction and wide-ranging distribution.

Whereas the gymnosperms still living are all woody perennials and evergreens, the angiosperms differentiated into plants of many kinds of widely varying characteristics. Although many angiosperms are woody perennials, large numbers of them developed into biennials and annuals with herbaceous characteristics, and others also differentiated into the group of plants known as herbs. The angiosperms differentiated both aboveground in stem, leaf, and seed features and belowground in root characteristics. Important aboveground features are the deciduous leaf shedding that occurs with seasonal change and the fruiting-seeding that makes for rapid reproduction. An important belowground feature has been the root modifications by which food becomes stored in fleshy "roots" permitting, in turn, reproduction by vegetative propagation.

The botanist is interested in many other aspects of the evolution of the angiosperms, but for speciation the foregoing items are the chief ones. In the development of animal life the seasonality of herbaceous plants, the fruiting-seeding, and the "root" storage items are of primary importance, for the wide variety of leafy grasses and herbs, and the many kinds of seeds, fruits, nuts, tubers, and edible flowers, facilitated the evolution of new kinds and varieties of land bird and animal life. In the development of the mammals, the herbaceous plants of seasonal growth habit, producing crops of nutritious seeds and soft leaves, greatly aided the evolution of many of the "herd animals" familiar to us today. The seeding characteristics of large numbers of the angiosperms made possible the appearance of much of the bird and small-animal life of the earth's land areas in the Holocene epoch. It is these same characteristics that provided evolving hominids, the family of mammals to which mankind belongs, with a useful and widely distributed food supply and made it possible for early forms of man to become gatherers of seeds, fruits, nuts, roots, and tubers.

During Permian-Triassic time the evolution of the angiosperms probably began in tropical uplands, inland and away from the relatively uniform lowland sea-margin environments, capitalizing on the variable environmental conditions of those uplands. Increasingly, specialization and further evolutionary change took place among the new angiosperms, to the end that in particular regions they began to assume dominance over the older kinds of plant forms.

During the more recent periods, the marked adaptability of the angiosperms allowed evolutionary processes to keep pace with the increasing differentiation of the crust of the earth into highly varied environments, particularly in the northern hemisphere. Pleistocene conditions of both cold and aridity in several parts of the earth several times put increasing stress upon the survival abilities of the now dominant angiosperms. One of the chief developments in angiosperm history during the Quaternary has been the appearance of plant combinations that evolved toward the vegetative associations that characterize the Holocene.

The alternation of glacial periods with interglacial periods, coupled with the continuance of mountain building and the distribution of climatic zones, caused rapid migrational movements among the angiosperm combinations and associations, and also rapid differentiation among the older angiosperm plant stocks. This gave rise to some new families and large numbers of new species. The maturing of the land birds, the mammalian animals, and man himself has added organic agencies to the complex of inorganic agencies which has affected the formation, distribution, and migration of angiosperm plants during the Holocene. It is clear that the last glacial era strongly upset many of the patterns of distribution of plant life on the earth. It is equally clear that the interval since the peak of the last glacial era must be regarded as one during which the angiosperms in particular have been trying to realign themselves to an altered world containing a new set of ecological environments. Plant migration, in response to these new conditions, has been going on actively during this period, more speciation has been occurring, and so has the development of some new balance in plant associations. This period, however, has also been a period during which the organic agencies, most notably man, have also been active in causing changes in the balancing operation. In many areas man has furthered the whole program, whereas in others he has both interrupted and interfered with that development.

The Dominance and Distribution of Mammals

About 6000 species of mammals, including man, exist on the earth. Mammals originated in the Triassic period, but remained few and insignificant throughout the Mesozoic era, having been overshadowed by the dominant reptiles until the end of the Cretaceous period. Marsupials and placentals (an ancient subclass of mammals) existed together well before the end of the Cretaceous, but the rise to dominance and the main dispersal of mammals began only about the beginning of the Tertiary period. The evolution of such characteristics as hair, warm-bloodedness, lungs, the four-chambered heart, and improved reproduction led to emergence from a reptilian ancestry, and in turn to great variety in tooth formations, adaptations of the foot, and eventually to increased intelligence.

During the Tertiary period, mammals achieved a widespread dispersal over the world. Now, the northern limits of land mammals are the limits of land at the higher latitudes; sea mammals (whales, seals, etc.) live even farther north. Southward, mammals inhabit the farthest reaches of Africa, Tasmania, New Zealand, and South America. Recent, habitable, continental-type islands always have mammals, but usually they are fewer in kind than on adjacent mainlands, the water barrier having had a screening effect upon migration.

But most families of mammals are less than worldwide in their distribution. Man shares his most unusual cosmopolitan distribution with only three families of bats and some mice and rats. Families of rabbits, squirrels, dogs, weasels, and cats are native and widely distributed on all continents except Australia. All other existing families of land mammals are even more limited in distribution, being profoundly influenced by the arrangement of climatic zones. The tropics are the richest (containing more species) and most diverse (having more widely distributed families) in composition of mammal faunas, the temperate zones less diverse, and the arctic still less, only about eight species of land mammals reaching any given northernmost point of land. This diversity is primarily a matter of subtraction: temperate faunas are essentially tropical faunas from which much has been subtracted; arctic faunas are the result of much more subtraction. The overall pattern shows a primarily placental fauna of terrestrial animals over most of the world, a mixed placental-marsupial fauna in South America, and a primarily marsupial fauna in the Australia–New Guinea region.

Direction in the dispersal of mammals (result of adding and subtracting two-way interchanges) has been from the main part of the Old World toward Australia and toward North America, and from North to South America. Excluding human intervention, only one group (*Phalanger*) has moved from the Australian region as far as the island of Sulawesi (Celebes), whereas no South American groups have reached the Old World. Since the greatest mammal faunas are tropical, the greatest single center of radiation of mammals would seem to have been the main tropical regions (Africa and South Asia) of the Old World.

The Uniqueness of the Pleistocene

The Pleistocene or "near-recent" epoch has, in many respects, been the most unusual period in the history of the earth. During the last two million years the long, gradual evolution and dispersal of plants and animals was abruptly disrupted by a host of causally related factors: *isolation*, by upheaval of mountain barriers and by creation of relict life zones through climatic change or separation of islands from continents by rising sea levels; *extinction*, by failure to adapt to changing climatic conditions or to migrate with shifting life zones; *succession*, the replacement of old groups by the spread of new dominant forms. The Pleistocene superimposed an overlay of intricately detailed minor changes upon the underlying distribution of plants and animals that had slowly evolved during the preceding geologically "normal" periods of earth history.

Mountain Building and Climatic Change

One of the "abnormal" features of the present earth is the widespread existence of high mountains (Fig. 2.1 and Plate 5). For most of earth history, the landforms of the surface consisted of plains or low rolling hills, which are thought of as seldom exceeding 1000 feet in altitude. The mountain-building deformations and deep subsurface intrusions of granite substances that began in the late Cretaceous marked the first significant shapings of the continents with which we are familiar and also began the alteration of the monotony of the ancient earth's land surface. The first outlines of the mountain systems we recognize today perhaps began to take shape during the Miocene, and the formal outlines of our familiar continental structures perhaps date from about the end of this epoch. The unusual character of the last two million years was ushered in by a series of mighty upheavals that elevated the previous lowland landscapes, with their somewhat regular skylines, by 10,000 feet or more. Whether in New Zealand, Switzerland, the Andes, or the Himalayas, the resulting mountains are everywhere youthful,

having been carved into deep, narrow valleys only shortly before the Pleistocene; too little time has elapsed for these young mountains to have been reduced to lower forms.

Maximum upheaval, into great fault blocks or great arches, generally occurred during the Pliocene and early Pleistocene over the past 14 million years, but in many regions uplift and displacements continue, as man is made well aware by the abrupt, though small, displacements that destroy his works and sometimes lives. Modern mountain ranges not only follow the trend lines of earlier epochs of mountain making, but also affected many of the great stable blocks or shields (see also Fig. 2.1). The latter, relatively quiescent sectors of the earth throughout its long history, have been uplifted into plateaus that have often been deeply dissected by streams and rivers.

Continental Structures

Huge areas of the continents appear to have been relatively stable for long periods of time, exempt from strong mountain formation. These are called shield areas and upon them very ancient rock series lie essentially horizontally over wide areas. All the shield areas of the earth were in existence well back into Precambrian times more than a billion years ago and their intensely metamorphosed rock types (gneisses and schists) underlie all younger rock systems of the continents as a "basement," out to the very edges of the continental shelves beneath the oceans.

The relative stability of shield areas does not mean that they have been motionless. Some of them have subsided (e.g., Congo Basin, Gulf of Mexico, Yellow Sea, and Gulf of Po Hai), so that hundreds to thousands of feet of sediment have been deposited in broad basins. But the chief movement has been broad intermittent uplift, a few feet at a time. Flexing during this movement has created local arches with intervening basins on the earth's surface, or has formed rift valleys through the relative downward displacement of blocks of the earth's crust (e.g., East Africa and the São Francisco valley of eastern Brazil).

The major shield areas (see Fig. 2.1) are: (1) Africa (all but the north) with an extension into western Arabia; (2) the Brazil-Guiana area of eastern South America bisected by the Amazon lowlands; (3) a smaller mass of Patagonia in southern Argentina; (4) all of east Antarctica; (5) western and central Australia; (6) the whole peninsula of

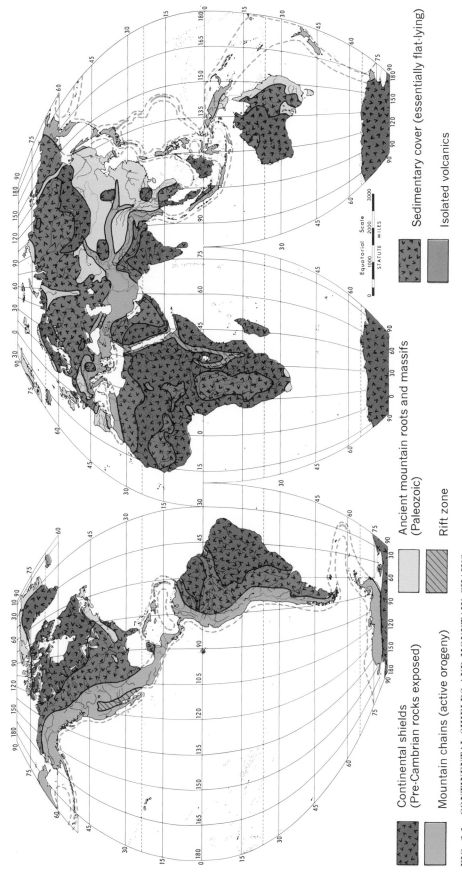

Continental shields
(Pre-Cambrian rocks exposed)

Mountain chains (active orogeny)

Ancient mountain roots and massifs
(Paleozoic)

Rift zone

Sedimentary cover (essentially flat-lying)

Isolated volcanics

Equatorial Scale

1000   2000   3000

STATUTE MILES

FIG. 2.1 CONTINENTAL SHIELDS AND MOUNTAIN CHAINS.

67

southern India; (7) four different nuclei in south-eastern and eastern Asia: Borneo-Cambodia–north-east Thailand, southeast Yunnan–northern Viet-Nam, Ordos platform, and Tarim Basin; (8) the Angara shield of Siberia, from Lake Baikal to the Arctic Ocean and from the Ural Mountains eastward to the Lena River; (9) the Scandinavian shield, with its Baltic Basin drowned by the sea, and its extension stretching eastward and southeastward beneath European Russia to the Caspian Sea; and (10) the Canadian shield of northeastern North America.

In contrast with the smooth, broad deformations of the old shields (which show earlier distortions), the greatest altitudes on the earth are restricted to narrow linear zones, the mountain chains, whereas the greatest depressions are also long and narrow, forming the ocean deeps. The mountain chains are composed chiefly of great thicknesses of sedimentary rock, sometimes with igneous cores or with volcanic caps. The crest of Mt. Everest, now perched at more than 29,000 feet altitude, consists of rock originally laid down beneath the sea. These mountain chains record violent deformations and movements of the earth's crust, which are always in relation to adjacent continental areas. As Fig. 2.1 indicates, the mountain chains do not extend into deep ocean basins. None is known without "basement rocks" of shield or continental type. Their sedimentary rock types (predominantly sandstones, shales, and limestones) are drawn from their neighboring continents, and they join one or more of the shield areas, which also have participated in earth movement, though in modified form. The mountain chains, whether of the Pacific Rim or of the Eurasia-African belt, are those continental areas that have been subjected to more violent vertical movement than the rest of the continents, the shield areas.

Recent Mountain Ranges

The Pacific Basin is completely rimmed by huge mountain ranges, along the western edges of the Americas, and in island arcs in the western Pacific from the Aleutians to New Zealand. In western North America, movements of earth occurred in the Pliocene and in the mid-Pleistocene, creating domes, anticlines, fault blocks, and basins. The Sierra Nevadas were elevated to their full height by uplift and tilting to the west. The modern Andes of South America were created by violent arching, accompanied by extensive block faulting and over-thrusting. In Bolivia and Peru, the Altiplano is a broad meadowed upland, composed of former lake plains at 11,000 to 14,000 feet altitude and surrounded by volcanic uplands of moderate relief. On the east and west rise higher ridges; the great volcanic peaks (18,000 to over 21,000 feet) are scattered atop the western rim of the Andes.

New Zealand, with its steep hillslopes, is a youthful terrain. On New Guinea, late Pliocene and early Pleistocene uplift ranged from 5000 to 7000 feet. The island arcs, such as Japan, owe their present form to great expansion during late Pliocene and strong elevation caused by active faulting in the Pleistocene. In southeast Asia, areas of moderate folding cover Burma, Sumatra, north Java, and other islands eastward to New Guinea.

The Himalayas display much evidence of very late vertical movements. For example, in the Kashmir valley a series of Pleistocene lake and river deposits has been tilted and elevated to between 5000 and 6000 feet. Also, three great rivers, the Indus, Sutlej, and Brahmaputra, begin on the northern flanks of the Himalaya system and cross the mountains to the south side through deep gorges, indicating that river entrenchment kept pace with uplift. South of the Himalayas, within the trough drained by the Indus and Ganges rivers, Pleistocene alluvium is now from 6000 to 15,000 feet thick. The mighty plateau of Tibet exceeds an altitude of 12,000 feet with much of it at 15,000 feet and mountain peaks and ranges rising above 20,000 feet. It is unique on the earth for its great area at such high altitudes.

From Tibet to the Aegean Sea, the festoons of mountain chains, Hindu Kush, Elburz, and Caucasus, are everywhere the result of uplift during Pliocene to Holocene time, with high passes and deep valleys. Volcanic and earthquake activity continue to the present. The modern Alps of Europe are the result of a former Pliocene lowland mightily uplifted and overthrust as an arched surface into which most of the present peaks and valleys have been carved. And, throughout their extent, the existing Atlas Mountains of northwest Africa have been created by a main Plio-Pleistocene uplift followed by profound cutting through of streams.

Relations of Recent Mountain Systems to Climate

The elevation of the young mountain chains around the world has altered many specific aspects of the climates of the earth. In many locations, the young mountain systems are sufficiently tall to alter the general sweep of terrestrial air masses in the lower section of the atmosphere. The specific locations of modern rain shadows, the effective occurrence of orographic precipitation, the precise paths taken by air masses in their broad systemic movements around or through mountain country, the sheltering of basins from polar air masses, and the precise distributions of highland and polar-condition climates in the equatorial zones all are specific and detailed effects of the present arrangement of the earth's young mountain systems. On an earth possessing fewer irregularities both weather and climate would more closely approximate the system of latitudinal belts often presented in the theoretical diagram. In more detailed terms, such local wind systems as mountain and valley breezes, sea and shore breezes, seasonal foehn systems, localized storm systems, and local air drainage systems all are expressions of the specific build and arrangement of the present irregularities on the surface of the earth.

The Impact of Glaciation

The changes that took place among Pleistocene terrestrial floras and marine invertebrate faunas reveal that mean annual temperatures had been diminishing since Miocene time. Rainfall decreased on the lowlands and became greater on the windward slopes of the rising uplands. A slight reduction of temperature converted rainfall concentrations into snowfall and thence into glaciers. The record of long-term climatic change is clear.

The idea that glaciers were formerly far more extensive than at present began with observations in the Alps less than two centuries ago. By the 1850s, evidence from Britain and the Alps indicated that the spread of glacial ice over extensive lowland areas was not a single event but had occurred several times. What we now know is that within the Pleistocene there were several brief but distinct cooler stages when glaciers expanded to cover about a third of the world's land area; these stages were separated by longer periods of warmer time (called interglacials) when temperatures were at least as high as at present.

Nearly 85 percent of the area now covered by glacial ice is in Antarctica (4,862,200 square miles) and more than 11 percent (666,200 square miles) in Greenland. The rest of the world's present glaciers (Fig. 2.2) together constitute less than 4 percent, by area, of the total. Most of the present

glacial ice occupies polar regions where ice persists because of cold climates (minimum solar radiation received), despite small snowfalls.

In middle and low latitudes, glaciers were and are more unstable. A small variation in one or more factors of climate (temperature, precipitation, evaporation) is capable of large and rapid changes in glacier volume. A very slight change, such as tipping the scales from excess melting to excess accumulation of snow, will push a glacier over a critical threshold and touch off a rapid expansion; the reverse change will cause contraction. During the Pleistocene expansion took place and glaciers accumulated to cover three times their present surface. This expansion was brought about chiefly through the creation and growth of glaciers in high middle latitudes. The largest areas, at maximum extent, were (see Fig. 2.2):

1. North America (6,033,400 sq mi), where the Laurentide ice sheet merged with the coalescent Cordilleran ice to cover an area larger than present Antarctica and Greenland combined.
2. Antarctica (5.093,700 sq mi).
3. Scandinavian ice sheet (2,300,000 sq mi) combined with glaciers of British origin.
4. Siberian ice sheet (1,627,000 sq mi).
5. Greenland ice sheet (833,500 sq mi).

It is clear that the continental glaciers of the Pleistocene were unequally distributed over the world's continents. Nearly 35 percent of them by area lay on North America, very little in the tropical or equatorial regions or in the southern continents, except for Antarctica.

In addition to the large ice sheets there were a great many local areas at high elevations in which small glaciers accumulated. The mountain (valley) glaciers, some piedmont glaciers, and other local forms of accumulated ice expanded and retracted repeatedly during the Pleistocene, affecting only local landscapes.

At times an ice sheet filled part of a valley, blocked the normal drainage outlets, and forced the melted waters to spill over and cut a new course around the sheet. One such temporary diversion of the Columbia River in the state of Washington formed the Grand Coulee. Another example is the formation of the course of the middle and upper Missouri River across the Dakotas, where former eastward-flowing streams were diverted and permanently connected southeastward to become tributary to the Mississippi.

The rivers leading away from the melting fronts

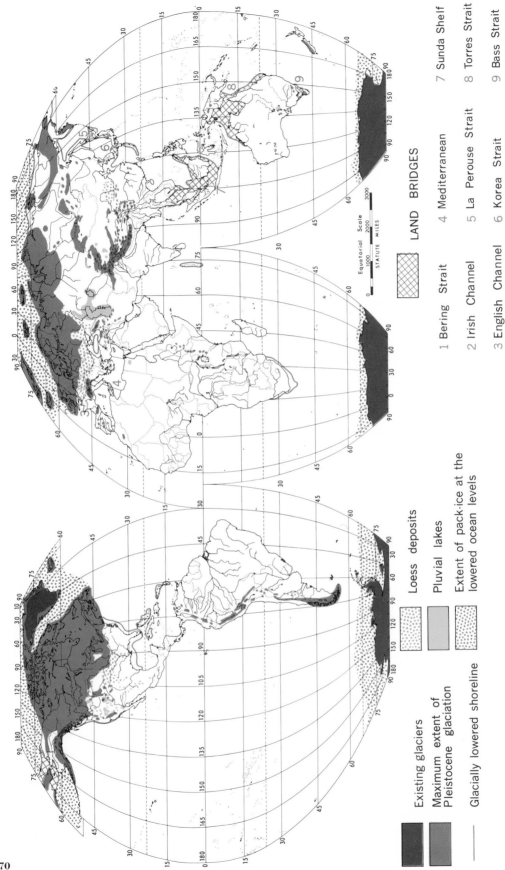

Existing glaciers

Maximum extent of
Pleistocene glaciation

Glacially lowered shoreline

Loess deposits

Pluvial lakes

Extent of pack-ice at the
lowered ocean levels

LAND BRIDGES

1 Bering Strait   4 Mediterranean   7 Sunda Shelf

2 Irish Channel   5 La Perouse Strait   8 Torres Strait

3 English Channel   6 Korea Strait   9 Bass Strait

Equatorial Scale
0   1000   2000   3000
STATUTE MILES

FIG. 2.2 EXISTING GLACIERS AND THE EXTENT OF PLEISTOCENE GLACIATION.

of the ice sheet (such as the Hudson, Ohio, and upper Mississippi in North America and the Rhone, Danube, and Volga in Europe) discharged larger volumes of water and sediment loads than today. These streams, with their pattern of alternate trenching and filling of river valleys, greatly extended the indirect influence of the ice sheets over a vast territory not itself subjected to glacial activity.

As the Pleistocene great ice sheets gradually wasted away, by melting, there became exposed two new kinds of landscapes, both of which are very significant to the contemporary world. These are the icescoured plains, hills, and lower mountains reduced to pitted (now lake-strewn) hard rock surfaces and the glacial drift plains on which the eroded sediments were deposited in a wide variety of minor landforms. Such surfaces make up significant portions of North America and northwestern Europe. Smaller areas of glacial ice locally reproduced both the scoured and drift surfaces in many areas of the earth.

The Pleistocene ice sheets were marked by unusually strong and continuous winds blowing outward from the ice margins. Sand dunes were created in close proximity to glacial outwash. Finer particles were carried farther by the wind to be laid down as loess deposits (see Fig. 2.2). Huge volumes of loess were deposited in great thicknesses (50 to over 500 feet) during the Pleistocene glacial stages. Such deposits tend to be thicker near the rivers (sources of silt), and often were reworked and redeposited by streams.

Loess deposits (some reworked by streams) are widespread in central North America and are scattered over central and eastern Europe. A wide but discontinuous band of sand and loess stretching from the Caspian Sea to northwest China seems related both to glacial outwash and to the action of wind deposits on the sometimes bare and arid expanses of Central Asia. Much of the North China loess has been reworked by streams. There are smaller patches of loess scattered at numerous spots around the drier margins of the earth which may have had only incidental relationships to glacial activity (see Fig. 2.2). In general, loessal soils have been among the more easily cultivated and productive soils of the earth, a fact significant to the whole history of crop growing.

In some regions peripheral to the ice sheets, the process of seasonal freezing and thawing of moisture in the ground was of overriding significance.

In other areas, at particular times, the ground was perennially frozen. The present limit of frozen subsoil or bedrock represents a lingering distribution of a former more widely spread distribution. Permafrost still accounts, however, for 25 percent of the world's land surface in continental areas with long, severely cold winters, vitally affecting many human activities in such areas.

Rise of the Baltic coasts of Scandinavia and of the Great Lakes of North America has resulted from broad doming upward because of the removal of the weight of the last Pleistocene ice sheet. A time lag of several thousands of years exists between ice removal and warping of the earth's crust, hence uplift is still in progress, at the rate of a fraction of an inch per year. Uplift of another 35 feet would convert the Baltic Sea into a chain of lakes; in North America, the projected uplift of about 250 feet eventually will result in the total disappearance of Hudson Bay, which is bordered at present by a 150-mile wide belt of postglacial raised beaches as much as 500 feet above the bay.

Arid and semiarid regions in the interior of all the continents, except Antarctica, contain many saline lakes and basins of numerous extinct lakes, now dry. During the growth of the glacial ice sheets, the belts of eastward-moving storms shifted progressively toward the equator. Increased storminess produced increased rainfall; greater cloudiness combined with lowered temperatures reduced the evaporation rate. As a result, surface runoff created lakes in previously dry basins. Such temporary cooler and wetter or pluvial conditions are most evident in the subtropical deserts, as in western North America (Fig. 2.3), north and east Africa, Turkey, and central Asia. Alternations of pluvial and dry stages occurred all over the earth. Pluvial stages are considered to coincide with glacial advances, whereas dry interpluvials occurred during interglacial stages.

Within the margins of glacial drainage many of the minor landforms, the depositional surfaces, the old lake conditions, and the old stream drainage systems contribute to the present specific arrangements of the contemporary landscapes of many portions of the earth. Beyond the zones directly affected by glaciation or by glacial drainage, the climatic sequences operative during the Pleistocene have also produced impacts on the regional landscapes in the forms of drainage systems, old lake plains covered by particular soils, and particular combinations of local landforms.

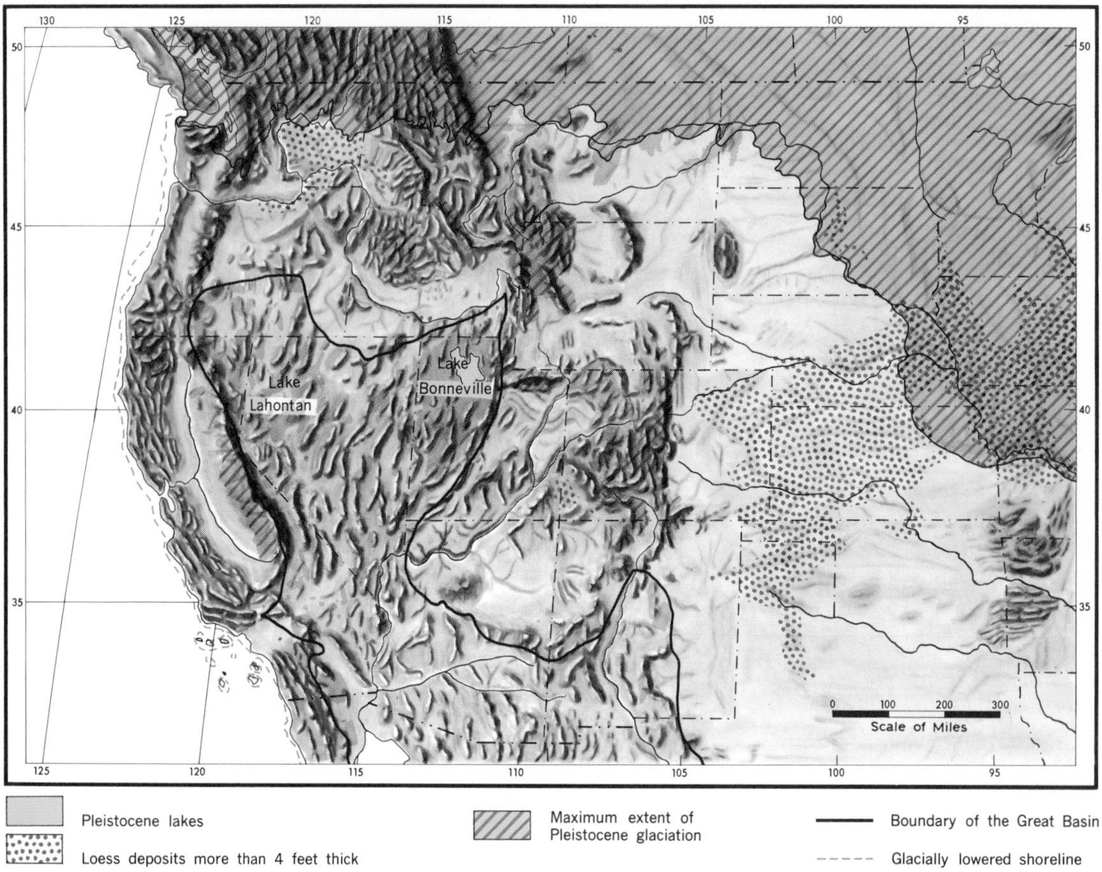

Lake
Lahontan
Lake
Bonneville
Scale of Miles
Pleistocene lakes
Loess deposits more than 4 feet thick
Maximum extent of Pleistocene glaciation
Boundary of the Great Basin
Glacially lowered shoreline

FIG. 2.3 THE PLEISTOCENE LANDSCAPE OF WESTERN NORTH AMERICA.

The Patterns of Land and Sea

All evidence indicates that there was no single, simultaneous advance and retreat of ice sheets in North America, Europe, and Siberia. Following an early and prolonged cold phase, the Pleistocene culminated in a sequence of three ice advances or glacial stages, of different extents and durations, separated by three interglacial stages of different but longer durations (Table 2.2).

Sea-Level Changes

The glacial (pluvial) stages consisted of periods that included both expansions of vast ice sheets and widespread growth of lakes on the continents. When so much water was "locked up" on land in a frozen state or trapped in closed basins, normal runoff of surface waters back to the sea was reduced. Consequently, the level of the sea was conspicuously lowered, resulting in worldwide emergence of shallow continental shelves. These changes in sea level (falling as ice and lakes expanded, rising again as glaciers melted and lakes evaporated) were worldwide, or *eustatic*, since the whole ocean was affected uniformly.

The tentative conclusions that can be made about sea-level changes during the Pleistocene are the following:

1. Last glacial stage (Würm–Wisconsin) lowering of sea level, relative to present sea level, was at least 300 feet and probably near to 350 feet.
2. Previous interglacial stage rise of sea level, relative to land, was about 100 feet above present sea level.
3. Total sea-level drop, from last warm interglacial stage to the subsequent glacial stage minimum position was at least 400 feet.
4. Repeated interim Pleistocene sea stands approximated present sea level, and also contributed work toward creation of various present coastal features.

Changing Land Areas, Coasts, and Rivers

The changes in land areas caused by "glacial control" of sea level varied with seaward slopes and depths. On steep, rugged coasts the sea rose and fell nearly vertically, but on gentle, shallow shelves it receded and returned across a broad area. These exposed shelves were trenched and channeled by rivers whose courses were extended to reach the lowered sea level. In turn, as glacial gave way to interglacial conditions, the rising sea drowned the mouths of all the streams entering it. The general effect upon river valleys of the slowly swinging sea level was twofold: as sea level lowered, the acceleration of rivers eroded valleys; then, as it rose, slackened streams dropped the loads of sediments into embayed river mouths. During glacial stages, large land areas were added, coastlines changed location, and former islands were connected to the mainland by exposure of narrow straits or land bridges (see Fig. 2.2).

An additional element in the changing outlines of the continental littorals has been the mountain-building activities of the late Pliocene and Pleistocene. When true mountain formation occurred as the result of a disturbance in the earth's crust, this orogenic activity was responsible for the particular shaping of coastal fringes, since the intensity of movement exceeded that of any eustatic shift of sea level. However, when gentler movements took place along or near coastal fringes, it often is uncertain whether eustasy or orogeny was responsible. In some cases it would appear that eustatic and orogenic activities may have canceled each other out, whereas in other cases orogenic activity,

either upward or downward, may have been greater or less than eustatic change.

Land Bridges

The similarity of animal life, especially of mammals, on nearby land areas separated by shallow water provides evidence of the recent existence of land bridges, supporting the idea of lowered sea levels during the Pleistocene ice stages. The major Pleistocene land bridges over the world (see Fig. 2.2) are listed in Table 2.3.

Two examples, Bering Strait and the Sunda Shelf, will suffice to indicate the significance of the existence of land bridges. The glacial-stage exposure of Bering Strait created a broad plain 600 miles wide, north to south, connecting Siberia and Alaska. Warmed by the Japan current, at least the southern margin of this plain probably became covered with long thick grass, ideal fodder for herbivores. Animal traffic was two-directional: North American camels and possibly the wolf and rodents moved westward to Asia, but there always seems to have been more movement eastbound from Asia to North America, including musk-oxen, antelope, reindeer, elephants, bears, cats, moose, cattle (*Bison*), sheep, and man.

The Sunda Shelf is a broad projection southeastward from mainland Southeast Asia, mostly covered by shallow water less than 150 feet deep. The Malay Peninsula and the large islands of

TABLE 2.2   TIME CHART OF GLACIAL (PLUVIAL) AND INTERGLACIAL (INTERPLUVIAL) STAGES OF THE PLEISTOCENE

Time Units	Stage		Years (before Present)
HOLOCENE (Recent)	Postglacial or interglacial		11,000
UPPER PLEISTOCENE	Würm (Wisconsin) glaciation		70,000
	Eem (Sangamon) interglacial		110,000
MIDDLE PLEISTOCENE	Riss (Illinoian) glacial complex		200,000
	Holstein (Yarmouth) interglacial		275,000
	Elster (Kansan) glacial complex		
LOWER PLEISTOCENE	Cromerian interglacial		500,000
	Kedischem (Nebraskan) complex	Menapian (Gunz) glacial	
		Waalian interglacial	1,000,000
	A great complex of cold and warm phases prior to the first major continental glaciation	Eburonian glacial	
BASAL PLEISTOCENE			
	Tiglian (first interglacial)		
	Villafranchian (in restricted sense)		
PLIOCENE			2,000,000

TABLE 2.3 MAJOR PLEISTOCENE LAND BRIDGES

Land Bridge	Connecting	Now Covered by the Sea to a Depth Below Present Sea Level of (in feet)
1. Bering Strait	Siberia (Asia)—Alaska (North America)	180
2. Irish Channel	Ireland—Britain	150
3. English Channel	England—France (continent)	150
4. Mediterranean Straits (several)	Europe—Africa	Various
5. La Perouse Strait	Siberia—Sakhalin—Hokkaido (Japan)	200
6. Korea Strait	Korea—Honshu (Japan)	250
7. Sunda Shelf	Malaya (Asia)—Sumatra—Java—Borneo	130
8. Torres Strait	Australia—New Guinea	250
9. Bass Strait	Tasmania—Australia	250

Sumatra, Java, and Borneo are at present the exposed higher portions of land atop the Sunda Shelf, but during the Pleistocene glacial stages they were all connected together and to the mainland. Animal life in these islands is almost completely continental, but not equally distributed. For example, Sumatra has more, including some different, land mammals than Java or Borneo, as shown in Table 2.4.

The differences among the islands in animals are not solely owing to differences in diffusion (animal migration) as affected by fluctuations of Pleistocene sea levels. Fossil evidence from Java also clearly indicates a reduction of fauna caused by extinction.

Shifting Life Zones of the Pleistocene

The ice ages and interglacial periods of the Pleistocene dramatically disrupted the distribution of all previously evolved life-forms. Though the overall effects were worldwide, Eurasia and North America were particularly affected. Additional disruption was provided by early Pleistocene orogenic developments in those areas in which there was significant mountain formation. In some cases one factor complemented the other by increasing the disruptive impact, whereas in other areas the orogenic effect was to maintain relative continuity on a less changeable level of conditions as the shift from glacial to interglacial to glacial occurred.

TABLE 2.4 COMPARISON OF LAND MAMMAL FAUNAS OF THE GREATER SUNDA ISLANDS

Mammal	Occurs on		
	Sumatra (about 164,000 sq mi)	Borneo (about 287,000 sq mi)	Java (about 51,000 sq mi)
Leopard	—	—	x
Proboscis monkey	—	x	—
Banting (wild ox)	—	x	x
Orangutan	x	x	—
Bear	x	x	—
Two-horned rhinoceros	x	x	—
Wild dog	x	—	x
Tiger	x	—	x
One-horned rhinoceros	x	—	x
Elephant	x	—	—
Tapir	x	—	—
Total units	55	47	33

The three successive episodes of continental glacial activity were the most spectacular manifestations of Pleistocene cold, for average temperatures were 8 to 14°F below present ones. Rainfall increased over much of the earth so that wet parts tended to be wetter and dry parts less dry than they now are. Midlatitude storm tracks and rain belts shifted toward the equator closer to what are now the dry subtropical zones; lakes increased in size; and the now arid regions were evidently better watered and better vegetated. And sea level fell, exposing considerable expanses of coastal plains along some continental margins and connecting continents and islands formerly separated by shallow seas.

Between glacial movements, during the longer interglacial stages, climates over much of the world apparently were sometimes warmer and also drier than now. At times during the interglacial periods there was little or no ice on the continents (Greenland and Antarctic ice sheets were gone also), and sea level was 65 to 100 feet higher than at present, so that low edges of continents and low islands were submerged.

Northern faunas and floras were dislocated at least four times by the advances and retreats of the ice sheets. They receded toward the equator during glacial stages and then returned toward the pole during interglacial stages. Successive patterns of distribution did not fully duplicate previous ones. Sometimes arctic-type populations moved upward on mountains during interglacial stages, rather than respreading northward, and survived at high altitudes as isolated relicts.

The post-Pleistocene period of the last 11,000 years, the Holocene epoch, may be considered a partial interglacial period, at less than its highest point since ice sheets still lie on Greenland and Antarctica. The complex northward spreading of readvancing forms of life, following the withdrawal of the last ice sheet, is still going on. But the readjustment of northern life-forms to recent climatic changes is a short-term modification on the periphery of the world's land masses; the major continental areas were not so drastically disturbed.

In the northern midlatitudes south of the ice sheets, there were southward, then northward movements of plants and animals in accordance with the fall and rise of temperatures. These were overlain by a secondary pattern of westward and eastward movements that correlated with increased rainfall followed by return to more arid conditions.

During the rainy glacial stages, forests expanded, then receded as the steppes and deserts were enlarged during the drier interglacial periods. Different animals fled and returned with their shifting habitats, with some becoming isolated in detached relict areas.

The environments of Europe during the main Würm glacial stage are shown in Fig. 2.4. A frost or ice-cap climate (Köppen EF) correlated with the three areas covered by the Scandinavian-British ice sheet and alpine glaciers. A tundra belt with permafrost (Köppen ET) was characteristic for most of France, central Europe, and northern Russia. A forest-tundra-loess belt with permafrost (Köppen Dwc) occupied Hungary, Romania, and southern European Russia. A cold-temperate forest (Köppen Dfd/Dfc) without permafrost was found along the southern shores of the Caspian and the Mediterranean borderlands. Clearly, the Würm glacial period was a rugged environment for early man.

Around the Mediterranean, during the main Würm glacial stage, local mountain-valley glaciers occupied highlands above 5000 feet in the Pyrenees and above 10,000 feet in southwest Asia. Snow lines were thus from 3000 to 2500 feet below their present levels. Alpine meadows or parklands frequented by cold-tolerant animals existed above 3000 feet in the highlands of southern Europe and at 5000 to 7000 feet in North Africa and southwest Asia. The upland tree line was thus at about 3000 to 3500 feet below present altitudes in Spain, Italy, and Crete, about 2500 feet lower in Morocco, and 2000 feet lower in southwest Asia. Temperate species of woodlands, together with temperate fauna, occupied southern Europe and the coastal zones of northern Africa and the eastern Mediterranean. There was greater, torrential, seasonal precipitation at the onset of the Würm glacial stage, but thereafter the region's rainfall was about the same as now.

Closer to the equator, across the Sahara, an increase in rainfall occurred during the last glacial stage. Mediterranean tree species and varieties of grasses grew in what are now desert uplands, suggesting a warm, subhumid climate, and sand dunes were deposited 250 to 350 miles south of the present southern margins of the Sahara.

In the tropics and on the southern continents, the effects of the Pleistocene were much less, slight modifications rather than drastic disruption. During the pluvial (equivalent to the glacial) stages, the expansion of forest and spread of forest animals

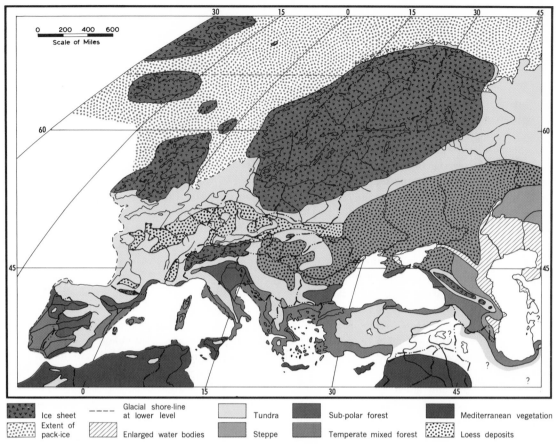

| | Ice sheet | - - - - - | Glacial shore-line at lower level | | Tundra | | Sub-polar forest | | Mediterranean vegetation |
| | Extent of pack-ice | | Enlarged water bodies | | Steppe | | Temperate mixed forest | | Loess deposits |

FIG. 2.4 PLEISTOCENE ENVIRONMENTS OF EUROPE DURING THE MAIN WÜRM
GLACIAL STAGE.

were favored. Periods of lowered sea level allowed many islands to be populated by plants and animals from the continents. During the longer, drier interpluvial periods, analogous to the interglacial, the drier regions, hence the range of steppe and desert animals, expanded. For example, southwestern North America and southern South America were connected by drier regions (seasonally dry tropics, semiarid subtropics) across Central America, which permitted an exchange of plants and animals, including man, from North to South America.

The overall evolutionary trend during the Pleistocene was a gradual withdrawal and extinction of large mammals, which is still going on. There were many more mammals in existence during the early Pleistocene than survive today. For example, among those that have become extinct and become part of the Pleistocene fossil record are: (in Europe) straight-tusked elephants, cave bears, cave lions, woolly mammoth, woolly rhinoceros, and

saber-tooth cat; (in North America) all the camels, all the horses, all the ground sloths, giant bison, giant beaver, stag-moose, several cats including saber-tooth, several mammoths, and mastodon. Mammals, then, as the predominant form of life in this world, are definitely declining.

Human Ancestors

The Primates, as one order of mammals, possess the common characteristics of all mammals, but they also have special characteristics of their own, not held by other mammals. These distinguishing general features of primates are the following:

Prehensile hands and feet
Nails instead of claws on digits (fingers and toes)
Opposability of thumb or big toe to the other digits
Completely enclosed bony orbit (eye socket), directed forward rather than to the side
Relatively enlarged brain
Only one pair of mammary glands, located on the chest

The primates arose at the beginning of the Tertiary period (Cenozoic era), about 73 million years ago, and in time diverged into the suborder Anthropoidea (the anthropoids) (Fig. 2.5). It is likely that all primate development took place in a humid sector of the subtropics or the margins of the tropics.

Anthropoids, as distinguished from the suborder of prosimians, which include tree shrews, lemurs, and tarsiers, are characterized by such a combination of features as stereoscopic vision and the ability to distinguish colors, well-developed ma-

nipulative ability, facial muscles that permit a variety of expression, tongues unsuitable for lapping, brain enlargement to the rear, and a high degree of dependence upon social learning. Anthropoids include the Old World monkeys (Cercopithecoidea), the New World monkeys (Ceboidea), and the Hominoidea. These forms diverged from early primate (tarsioid) stock in, or before, the Oligocene epoch, at least 36 million years ago. The Old World monkeys developed into today's monkeys of Europe, Africa, and Asia, such as macaques, baboons, mandrills, langurs, and Barbary apes. The

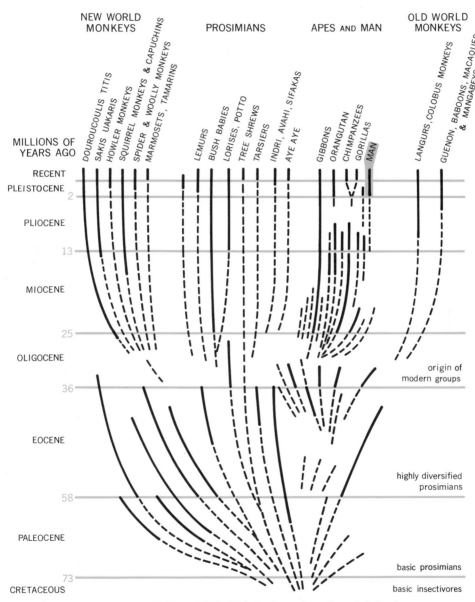

FIG. 2.5   TIME CHART OF PRIMATE RELATIONSHIPS. Redrawn from Time Life Books, *The Primates*, 1965.

present New World monkeys, of North, Central, and South America, include howler monkeys, capuchins, spider monkeys, marmosets, squirrel monkeys, and woolly monkeys. The Hominoidea, which diverged from an early Old World monkey ancestral stock and then evolved separately, include the two families Pongidae (apes) and Hominidae (man).

The Hominoidea (apes and man) differ from Old World monkeys in the following respects:

Larger head and brain relative to body size
Longer neck
Absence of tail
Fewer vertebrae
Wider shoulders, chest, and pelvis
Longer hands and thumbs relative to body size
Longer arms
Longer periods of pregnancy and of growth to adult size

There are four clearly distinct varieties of Pongidae living today. Two are in Africa: the chimpanzee and the gorilla; the other two, the orangutan and the gibbon, are found in Southeast Asia. The gibbon is small (about 12 pounds), whereas the other three are large (chimpanzee and orangutan about human size, with gorilla very large—400 to 800 pounds and often standing six-feet high). But in the past, as evidenced from fossil remains, there were many other varieties of apes, some dating back to the Oligocene epoch. There was thus an adequate time span throughout each stage of the primate evolution for the adaptations required for the ensuing stage to take place, until finally the hominid pattern of existence emerged. Man differs from apes and monkeys in the following ways:

Canine teeth same length as other teeth
No difference between sexes in size of canine teeth
Largest relative brain size
Prominent chin
Least prominent browridges
Lips (everted mucous membrane)
Least prognathism (snout)
Complete erect posture and bipedal gait
Longer legs relative to shorter arms
Greater relative length of thumb and its complete opposability to other fingers
Loss of opposability of big toe

In sum, man has certain morphological and anatomical similarities with each of the various groups of primates, but in certain ways he is clearly unique among the primates. The most significant of man's peculiarly human characteristics are:

Habitual bipedal gait
Completely erect posture
Articulate speech
Capacity for abstract and symbolic thought
Elaborately convoluted and relatively large brain, which makes possible the two previous traits as well as the great potential for learning (memory and problem posing)

Thus far, the oldest among the many hominid fossils has been found to date from just after the beginning of the Pleistocene epoch. The affirmation of man's antiquity began with the discovery of the Olduvai child, found by Mary and Louis B. Leakey in East Africa in 1960, with an age determined at about 1,750,000 years. Most hominid fossils consist of but few teeth or limb bones or skull fragments that have revealed all too little additional information to our meager stock of knowledge about human evolution. What seems to be clear is that three kinds of hominid fossils can be distinguished: the earliest, called *Homo habilis*; an intermediate form called *Homo erectus* who was quite different from modern man and who evolved about 500,000 years ago; and the other, *Homo sapiens*, who emerged, in a form practically identical to modern man, in the late Pleistocene and has persisted to the present day as the single existing human species.

Although the broad outlines of man's ancestry are known and a clear line of man's relationships to other primates has been determined, much more needs to be known about the ancestral forms of the great apes, about the very earliest Pleistocene hominid fossils, and the connections between the two forms.

Summary Notations on Pleistocene Environmental Change

Many of the features sketched so briefly in this chapter possess intrinsic interest in their own right, as attributes of a changing world, but they have been sketched primarily because many of them are of profound significance in the development of animal and bird forms of life in the Holocene epoch on the matured land areas of the earth. Moreover, several of them are critical to the cultures of, and the growth in numbers by, man as an occupant of the earth. Several of these environmental changes have been intricately bound up with the coming to dominance of man as one particular life-form in all parts of the earth.

It is very clear that the surface of the earth in

recent time displays a great variety of surface form. In the sheer range of altitudes, the variety of surface features, and the wealth of variation within comparatively small areas, the world of recent time may well be the most complex assemblage of earth forms that has ever existed. It is probably true that the sheer variety of conditions now existing just above the solid crust of the earth, in the lower atmosphere, presents the widest range of weather and climate that has ever obtained for our earth. Certainly the mineral and rock materials assembled within the earth's crust are now richer in variety than those existing during Ordovician or Triassic times. Although the animal life-forms, aside from man, currently living on the earth often seem somewhat less interesting than some of the forms dominant during the Cretaceous (in the sense that such dinosaurs as the formidable *Tyrannosaurus* and the huge *Triceratops* are much more intriguing than a Holstein dairy cow or a Poland-China pig, and can only be equaled by Hollywood movie creations), the wealth of animal forms in the early Pleistocene was greater than ever. Similarly, in the realm of plant life none of the grasses or stone-fruit trees is as spectacular as some of the *Calamites* of the Mississippian or the cycads of the Cretaceous, but the wealth, range, and sheer variety of plants during late Pleistocene time became far greater than it had ever been. All in all, the physical world of recent times is the most varied, the most richly assembled, and the most fully endowed physical world that has ever existed on our planet.

The very rapidity with which Pleistocene developments took place has been a factor in the wide range of variation existing in the world today. There has not yet been time for the elimination of many different features and life-forms. But the very adaptability of many of these forms has made possible not only the initial populating of physical environments of very great range of ecological conditions, but also the rapid readjustments to the exceedingly large-scale changes in gross environmental conditions that did take place during the Pleistocene-to-Holocene. No such rapid readjustments could have been made by the life-forms prevalent during the Mississippian interval.

Three simple examples illustrate this point. The loess deposits scattered about the earth, regional accumulations of soft windblown silt often reworked somewhat by the action of water, surely are not permanent depositions in terms of the geologic time scale, for they are deposits that will

certainly be removed by subaerial processes during the time interval of a geologic period. Almost immediately upon the deposition of the first thicknesses of loess, different kinds of plants and animals were able to colonize these new landscape surfaces, the forms varying somewhat on the different continents under varied local climatic conditions. Man early found several of the loess areas to possess utilitarian variety of plant forms and rich populations of herd and browsing animals, both of which were available for the gathering and the hunting. Later he found the loess areas to be easily cultivable, rich soil surfaces that could be turned into "breadbaskets" to produce food supplies for considerable numbers of people. The loess areas have proven of great value to man at different stages of his cultural development, yet they are a time-period product only, and man has been fortunate in having them present.

Such a peculiar local environment as the Inland Sea of Japan, with its islands and littoral fringes of lowland shores, presents a time-interval environment with very distinctive conditions probably never equaled by any bay of the great Tethys Sea that stretched from the modern Mediterranean Sea to the modern South China Sea during the late Paleozoic. The sheer wealth of marine life, the sheer variety of land plant life, and the variety of potential living habitat for any form of life, including man, along the Inland Sea represent an environmental complex never before assembled in one geographic locality. The Inland Sea is but the time-interval product of sea level at a particular stage of an interglacial period. During the height of glacial times it may have been an inland valley, whereas the coming of the full extent of an interglacial interval would flood the locality so deeply as to cover the small islands and the lowland shores. The whole major physical construct is in no small degree the product of Pleistocene orogeny. The significant thing as that the Inland Sea exists today as a regional entity in the environmental complex that is Japan.

The sheer volume of Pleistocene orogenic activity which created the Sierra Nevada and the Coast Ranges of California has produced a wider variety of local, regional physical environments than ever existed previously in this zone. The ability of plant and animal forms to populate these environments so that they approach a semblance of short-term ecological balance has in recent times greatly enriched the physical landscape. Man still is seeking a variety of ecological balance in his occupance of geographic environments, and one of his problems is the very richness and regional variation in the assemblage with which he must deal; certainly this is a more fortuitous set of problems than would have been the case in any earlier geological era.

By the workings of evolutionary processes, man came into a world of tremendously varied environmental conditions and has evolved during a period of some of the most spectacular changes of all geologic time. Perhaps better equipped by surrounding plant and animal assemblages than at any other time, modern man finds himself an important occupant of what may be the best world the earth has ever known.

The Meaning of Evolution

All living things are related. There is unity to life, since all forms have evolved from one source by means of one process, admittedly intricate. As in all relationships, some life-forms are more closely related than others. Man, for example, is more closely related, in material origin as well as in functional and structural similarities, to all animals than to any plant. The degree of relationship can be further narrowed: man is a vertebrate, not an invertebrate; he is a mammal, not a fish or an amphibian, or a bird, or a reptile; and, among mammals, man is a primate.

A preceding section of this chapter concerned our human ancestors. The purpose was to demonstrate the close relationship of man to other primates, living and fossil. The conclusion may be drawn that all living primates have evolved each in its own way from a common ancestor, and that the question of how close a relationship exists between man and tarsier, monkey, ape, or other living primate, is irrelevant to our understanding of the human story on the earth. Once the early divergence among the primates had taken place, the evolution of modern lemurs was a separate development. Similarly, later divergence produced the stock ancestral to modern monkeys. A somewhat later divergence led to the apes, and a fourth divergence within the primate order made man's emergence possible. All contemporary primate forms are continuing to evolve, each in its own way. All share a common ancestry, but none has evolved, nor could evolve, from any other form of living primate.

Thus we conclude that man was not planned; that is, he was not an intended goal of evolution. Life has displayed innumerable inconstant trends. Man was not inevitable, and yet he *did* originate after a long continuous sequence of occurrences. Enough changes did come to pass that man did result. For our study, that result is of prime significance. The Pleistocene earth is man's inheritance, and man, the most highly endowed organization of matter that has yet appeared on the earth, is the Pleistocene's principal product. As that principal product, man reaps the value of the balance of the evolutionary process at a time during which the earth is at the most varied and richest stage in its history.

SELECTED REFERENCES

About Plant and Animal Evolution and Distribution
Axelrod, Daniel I.
  1952 "A Theory of Angiosperm Evolution," *Evolution*, Vol. 6, pp. 29–60.
  1960 "The Evolution of Flowering Plants," pp. 227–305 in Tax, Sol (ed.), *Evolution After Darwin*, Vol. 1, *The Evolution of Life.* Chicago: University of Chicago Press. 629 pp.
Bastian, H.
  1963 *And Then Came Man* (translated from the German by D. I. Vesey; D. H. Dalby, ed.). London: Museum Press Ltd. 354 pp.
Colbert, Edwin H.
  1961 *Evolution of the Vertebrates* (Science Editions). New York: Wiley. 479 pp.
Darlington, Philip J., Jr.
  1957 *Zoogeography: The Geographical Distribution of Animals.* New York: Wiley, 675 pp.

Simpson, George Gaylord
  1951 *The Meaning of Evolution* (Mentor MD 66). New York: The New American Library. 192 pp.
  1953 *Life of the Past: An Introduction to Paleontology*. New Haven, Conn.: Yale University Press. 198 pp.

About the Pleistocene Epoch
Butzer, Karl W.
  1964 *Environment and Archeology: An Introduction to Pleistocene Geography*. Chicago: Aldine. 524 pp.
Charlesworth, John K.
  1957 *The Quaternary Era: With Special Reference to Its Glaciation*. London: E. Arnold, 2 vols. 1700 pp.
Cornwall, I. W.
  1964 *The World of Ancient Man*. New York: John Day. 271 pp.
Flint, Richard Foster
  1957 *Glacial and Pleistocene Geology*. New York: Wiley. 553 pp.
King, Lester C.
  1962 *The Morphology of the Earth: A Study and Synthesis of World Scenery*. New York: Hafner. 699 pp.
Schwarzback, Martin
  1963 *Climates of the Past: An Introduction to Paleoclimatology* (translated from the German and edited by Richard O. Muir). London: Van Nostrand. 328 pp.
Wright, M. E., Jr. and David C. Frey (eds.)
  1965 *The Quaternary of the United States*. Princeton: Princeton University Press. 922 pp.
Zeuner, Frederick E.
  1959 *The Pleistocene Period: Its Climate, Chronology, and Faunal Successions*. London: Hutchinson. 447 pp.

About Primates
Eimerl, Sarel, Irvin De Vore, and the Editors of *Life*
  1965 *The Primates* (Life Nature Library). New York: Time, Inc. 199 pp.
Howells, William
  1959 *Mankind in the Making, The Story of Human Evolution*. Garden City, N.Y.: Doubleday. 382 pp.
Hulse, Frederick S.
  1963 *The Human Species, An Introduction to Physical Anthropology*. New York: Random House. 504 pp.
Kraus, Bertram S.
  1964 *The Basis of Human Evolution*. New York: Harper and Row. 384 pp.
Lasker, Gabriel Ward
  1961 *The Evolution of Man, A Brief Introduction to Physical Anthropology*. New York: Holt, Rinehart, and Winston. 239 pp.
LeGros Clark, W. E.
  1960 *The Antecedents of Man, An Introduction to the Evolution of the Primates*. Chicago: Quadrangle Books. 374 pp.
  1961 *History of the Primates, An Introduction to the Study of Fossil Man* (Phoenix Books P21). Chicago: University of Chicago Press. 188 pp.

CHAPTER 3

Man's Invasion of the Earth: The Whole Planet Inhabited

All living men are of one species, *Homo sapiens*. And man is the most generalized of all mammals, since he has never depended upon any one skill at the expense of many others. The first way in which man's primate ancestors separated themselves from other mammals was in standing erect, legs extended and with the head directly over the feet. Subsequent to this development other distinctions became possible, as the human body was rearranged to accommodate to habitual upright posture and bipedal locomotion. For example, the human foot changed from a grasping to a more specialized, stable, weight-sustaining organ, with the result that our hands and feet have come to have quite different shapes. Perhaps the most satisfactory way of describing man's status is to say that he is unique in having a singular combination of abilities, rather than in the possession of any single exclusive ability.

The large primates of the late Miocene and early Pliocene were distributed across subtropical Eurasia and throughout much of Africa. Most of their food had to be found on or near the ground. A primate with a previously existing habit of erect posture in climbing and not fully adapted for brachiation (swinging by the arms) would have been most likely to move upright on two legs at least some of the time. Even if not habitual, erect posture made it easier to see things at a distance and to carry food and tools in the hands and arms freed from the necessity of supporting the body. However, a primate group living mostly on the ground is much more vulnerable to attack from predators, and would tend to remain close to some

trees for safety and nighttime sleeping. The more restricted the territory, the better would be the group's knowledge of routes and havens for escape and of sources for food and water supply, and the more adequately could the territory be defended against other groups.

The larger primates long ago added meat to their diet. Vegetative diets contain much roughage and lots of vitamins but have little protein and add only a few calories per unit of volume. As a result, animals that depend almost entirely upon vegetation for their food must spend much of their time eating, even though that food be readily accessible and easy to collect. Since flesh contains little roughage and is highly nutritious and full of calories, meat eaters spend less of their time attending to activities no farther than the ends of their snouts. A large primate which had taken to running over the ground on its hindlegs and was able to include meat in its diet had time for play, exploration, and inquisitiveness. Our ancestors did just this, using their upright posture, manipulative hands, evolving (expanding) brains, and free time for all sorts of activities not previously attempted by other forms of life. Out of such events as social cooperation in food-gathering, communication through gesture and sounds, and the sharing of food, human culture emerged.

In many respects, human evolution is unique in the living world. Modern man, of course, is a biological species (*Homo sapiens sapiens*) and, as such, is a product of organic evolution. But the singularity of human evolution lies in the fact that the human species evolved culture. Man's key

TABLE 3.1 FOSSIL MAN IN THE TIME PERSPECTIVE OF THE LAST TWO MILLION YEARS

Time Units	Stage	Years (before Present)	Climatic Oscillation	Evolution of Life-Forms	Years (before Present)	Emergence of Hominid Forms	Cultural Phase (Tool Types)
HOLOCENE (Recent)	Postglacial or interglacial		Warm	Fully modern fauna	9,000 — 11,000		NEOLITHIC — "MESOLITHIC"
		— 11,000					
UPPER PLEISTOCENE	Würm (Wisconsin) glaciation (last major cold climatic phase)		Cold		— 35,000		UPPER PALEOLITHIC (blades)
		— 70,000		Division of fauna into alternating glacial and interglacial assemblages		Homo sapiens sapiens	MIDDLE PALEOLITHIC (varieties of tools; regional specializations)
	Eem (Sangamon) interglacial		Warm			Homo sapiens neanderthalensis	
		— 110,000			— 110,000		
MIDDLE PLEISTOCENE	Riss (Illinoian) glacial complex { Warthe glacial / Ohe interstadial / Saale glacial }		Cold / Warm / Cold				
		— 200,000					
	Holstein (Yarmouth) interglacial		Warm				LOWER PALEOLITHIC
		— 275,000					
	Elster (Kansan) glacial complex (first major continental glaciation) { Elster II / Cortonian / Elster I }		Cold / Warm / Cold				(bifacial tools; hand axes) Use of fire (Choukoutien)
	Cromerian interglacial		Warm	Largely modern genera		Homo erectus	Dispersal through Old World
		— 500,000			— 500,000		
LOWER PLEISTOCENE	Menapian (Gunz) glacial / Waalian interglacial / Eburonian glacial		Cold / Warm / Cold	Great floral and faunal changes as most Pliocene elements disappear			
	Kedischem (Nebraskan) complex (great complex of cold and warm phases prior to the first glaciation)	— 1,000,000					BASAL PALEOLITHIC
BASAL PLEISTOCENE (or Villafranchian in the broad sense)	Tiglian (first interglacial)		Warm		— 1,750,000	Homo habilis	Crude chopping tools in use
	Villafranchian (in restricted sense)		Mainly Cold	Pliocene fauna		Australopithecus	Crude chopping tools in use
		— 2,000,000			— 2,000,000		
PLIOCENE			Warm				

peculiarity is his educability, his plasticity, his ability to learn in order to change his behavior in light of experience and circumstance. By means of culture that he himself invented, man profoundly modified his own biological evolution to become so much unlike any other life-form that his evolution cannot adequately be understood in terms only of those causative factors that operate in the biological world outside. Man's evolution, a uniquely human phenomenon, can be understood only as the result of an intricate continuous interplay between organic change and cultural development.

The Earliest Hominids: *Australopithecus* and *Homo habilis*

Table 3.1 places what we know about fossil man into a time perspective. Its purpose is to emphasize correctly the immensity of that stretch of time—some two million years—during which the gradual evolution of human forms and the accompanying cultural development took place. The first three quarters of the Pleistocene were spent in coping with the cultural transition from tool using to toolmaking and its biological consequences. Table 3.1 also outlines the present consensus that human evolution progressed by orderly discrete states: (1) *Australopithecus*, (2) *Homo habilis*, (3) *Homo erectus*, and (4) *Homo sapiens*. But we must guard against presenting too simple a picture. In his evolution, early man behaved exactly as did the other mammals. He branched out, with some branches existing for a while side by side before disappearing and becoming extinct. The surviving branch, evolving at an increasingly rapid rate, gave rise to ourselves.

That there was only one kind of man after the Middle Pleistocene is the result of the cultural development of *Homo sapiens*. He was an efficient enough hunter to be too tough to have any long-existing competition from other members of the genus *Homo*. The more our ancestors became like us, in toolmaking, fighting, hunting, and making fires, the less likely that there could be two species of man existing in the same region at the same time. It is not especially surprising that *Australopithecus*, the early emergent, coexisted with *Homo habilis*. The remarkable thing, however, is that both became extinct after the appearance of *Homo erectus*, and the latter after *Homo sapiens*. This diminution of speciation is a measure of the effectiveness of human culture.

Australopithecus provides fossil evidence of the

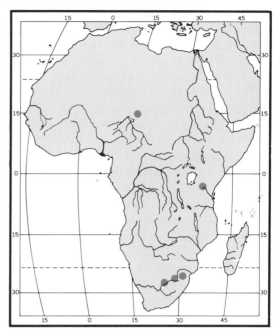

FIG. 3.1 *AUSTRALOPITHECUS* SITES IN AFRICA.

earliest branch to become extinct (Fig. 3.1). Remains of several dozen individuals, the first discovered in 1924 in South Africa, offer evidence of upright posture. *Australopithecus*, which evolved toward *Homo*, was of considerably smaller stature (about four feet tall and weighing about 50 to 60 pounds) than most modern humans. Jaws were short and light; front teeth small. Cranial capacities of adults average between 450 and 600 cubic centimeters, as large as a typical modern gorilla but less than half of modern human. *Australopithecus* represents an early member of the family Hominidae, although the least like *Homo sapiens*, and was a stage through which our ancestors passed from being exceptionally clever animals to becoming human.

The oldest, nearly complete *Australopithecus* skull, from Olduvai Gorge in northern Tanzania of East Africa and dated at 1,900,000 years, was found in association (at the same level) with the broken bones of various small animals and with stone choppers and flakes of a type considered to be the earliest African chopping tools. These tools are made from pebbles by removing two or three flakes from two faces in order to obtain a jagged cutting edge on one side. The tools suggest temporary camps for scavenging or killing, or both, some forms of the more than 160 species of mammals found in the Olduvai deposits.

Between 1958 and 1964, it was thought that *Australopithecus* was the maker of the stone tools (Olduvai choppers) found at the same level as their remains. Now, with further discoveries since 1960 combined with reanalyses of earlier finds, a new species of *Homo* has been identified as the tool-maker. The total evidence from a dozen living sites of early hominids with or without early tools is remarkably consistent: stone tools are absent from purely *Australopithecus* sites, but found with *Australopithecus* only where remains of more advanced hominids also occur. The earliest species of *Homo* was given the name, in 1964, of *Homo habilis*.

Australopithecus clearly was a tool user and tool modifier. He was able to employ his hands effectively, not only in using tusks, femur ends, and teeth as *bone* tools, but also in deliberately modifying the bones, by breaking, splitting, and sharpening them to make them more serviceable for a specific purpose. What is lacking is evidence that *Australopithecus* deliberately fashioned *stone* tools to a set, regular, and evolving pattern; that is, he is not known to have been a cultural toolmaker. It seems highly unlikely that *Australopithecus* possessed the conceptual skills to take the crucial step of learning how to use a tool to make another tool.

The discoveries, since 1960, of *Homo habilis* remains from Bed I at Olduvai Gorge have provided evidence of a species intermediate between the smaller *Australopithecus* and the later *Homo erectus*. The estimated cranial capacity for the type specimen of *Homo habilis* is 675 to 680 cubic centimeters. This falls beyond the upper end (600 cc) of the sample range for *Australopithecus* but short of the lower end (775 cc) of the sample range for *Homo erectus*. *Homo habilis* represents the advancement of *Australopithecus* to a small kind of man, probably weighing not more than 80 or 90 pounds. Other characteristics of *Homo habilis* are also intermediate: large incisor teeth but smaller molars than *Australopithecus*. Such humanizing processes as reduction of tooth and jaw size and expansion of brain size had not progressed very far, yet were sufficient to provide a distinctive quality to *Homo habilis* and open the way toward further development.

There is no question that both *Australopithecus* and *Homo habilis* used tools of bone, stone, and presumably wood. The intentional manufacture by *Homo habilis* of a tool for future use, however, indicated a new mental capacity. Conscious preparation of stabbing or cutting tools with which to attack an animal, then skin and cut it up, implies imagination and foresight. The first halting steps of *Homo habilis* toward a technology opened a wholly new way for reevaluating the external environment. *Homo habilis* embarked upon a long-term program for cultural advance, which altered his ability to cope with his surroundings and better equipped him for survival.

Australopithecus lived in Africa for nearly a million years. South Africa, which has produced so many of his remains, presumably was not the place of origin but rather a cul-de-sac, an area in which he could survive later than elsewhere. The evolution of *Australopithecus* into *Homo habilis* went hand in hand with the habitation of eastern Africa. Since no similar evidence is available from any other part of the world, Africa must be considered, at least temporarily, as the place where man emerged. But it would not be surprising if further research turned up an advanced type of *Homo habilis* in Java, where the remains of his successors have been discovered.

Before the end of the Pliocene our primate ancestors had adapted to habitual tool using and erect posture, which resulted in the freeing of the hands; and during the Pleistocene that followed our hominid ancestors, as their brains increased, adapted to the manufacture of tools to set patterns. As cultural toolmaking became the mark of man, it also became the method by which man was to refashion the earth's surface into a human habitat.

Food-Gathering and Man's Tropical Origins

Man is omnivorous, but with rare exceptions in special times or places, the great bulk of human foodstuffs has been of plant origin. The exceptions to this generalization have attracted much more attention, and provide better archaeological evidence, through bones of animals, birds, and fish, than the more perishable organic remains of plant materials. For most of human time on the earth, man's technological abilities limited him to unspecialized food-gathering. A great variety of locally available edible roots and plants, as well as many smaller mammals, insects, and birds were used. Flesh of larger animals probably was eaten on a scavenging basis. In this sense, *Australopithecus* and *Homo habilis* were probably more the hunted than the hunter. They were no match for the larger carnivores, but quite capable of finishing off the remains of the carcasses of larger animals that the carnivores left behind, including the breaking open of skulls and marrow bones to obtain maximum food value from them.

Wild vegetable foods are obviously more abundant and more varied in lower (equatorial and tropical) latitudes where moisture is available, at least seasonally, and year-round warmth permits continual plant growth. Seasons of cold and drought in any region reduce the volume and variety of plant materials potentially useful to man. Several hundreds of species of plants in a localized area would provide roots and tubers, seeds and nuts, bark and fruits in quantity for consumption. Unspecialized food-gatherers also consumed such readily available edibles as insects, grubs, lizards, snakes, tortoises, birds, small rodents, bats, eggs, and the helpless young of larger animals. Shrimp, bivalves, snails, crabs, and fish were obtainable from inland waters, and the varied shellfish of the seashore supplied a valuable source of protein and iodine for people of limited technological skill. In sum, the humid and subhumid tropical and subtropical climatic regions, particularly in association with lake, river, or coastline, were optimal areas for early man.

Food-gathering was not a process of free wandering. Continuous and assured access to potable water was a first essential, followed by the need for adequate food. The logic of supply indicates the need to keep the expenditure of human effort within the limits of the energy value derived from the food secured. Least effort and continuous food supply were fundamental early principles to be followed for success in perpetuating life. Progress was possible not by diffuse and uncertain dispersal but by success in locating and occupying areas where resources suitable for human food were superior, thus giving an initial advantage to those groups who occupied such regions.

The suggestion has been made that early man's richest habitat lay along the shores of water bodies: lakes, rivers, or the sea. Man requires water to drink as replenishment for the profuse water loss caused by exertion, and he needs to drink often. A shore is also an ecological transition zone: in the water, along the strand, on the land can be found a great diversity of plant and animal life. One type of locale that could provide living sites richer than inland locations was the tropical seashore. A considerable assemblage of life-forms can be had for the taking: turtle eggs, fish, crustaceans, clams and other shellfish, and marine mammals. The strand and sea cliff provide a variable fauna and flora: nestlings of seabirds, eggs, fruits, roots, and edible shoots. There was good opportunity along the shore to eat, settle, learn, and increase.

Wood, Shell, Stone, and Bone

The concentration of attention lavished by archaeologists upon the tools of man is something of an enforced expedient. In the course of even his brief life span, a Pleistocene tool user and toolmaker fashioned and discarded a greater number and volume of implements and weapons than there were bones in his body. Many of his tools—for example, those made of wood—presumably decayed, under conditions of warmth, moisture, soil acidity, and bacterial action, at rates even faster than that which destroys human bone. Shells and some bones have similar and greater degrees of resistance to organic decay. The most durable of early man's tools were those that he made of stone. Since so many of these have been recovered, in comparison to human fossil remains, our knowledge of the spatial distribution and the cultural development of man the toolmaker can be inferred with considerably more confidence than if it were based solely upon the often fortuitous, rare, and scattered finds of fossilized human bone.

It is now recognized that *Homo habilis* was the earliest maker of tools. The only kind of tools that have survived, from the Basal Pleistocene (Basal Paleolithic) of tropical Africa, are not those of wood, shell, or bone, but of stone. The word Paleolithic means "Old Stone Age." These tools are crudely flaked chopping tools (Fig. 3.2), haphazardly manufactured, but intended for future use. The rounded pebbles of quartzite taken from stream beds and sedimentary deposits were broken into rough edges and blunt points flaked from two or more faces for use as cutting and smashing tools. They were crude because they represent the very beginning of the development of a technique. Small game were driven into swamps or water or were cornered in caves or on rocky ground, then killed by clubbing and stoning, dismembered, and eaten. Rats, mice, lizards, frogs, crabs, snakes, tortoises, and the young of pigs, antelopes, ostriches, and baboons were the principal prey; larger animals were acquired mostly by scavenging carcasses and the clubbing of the old, the sick, and the lame.

The *Homo habilis* phase of hominid evolution merged imperceptibly with that of the *Homo erectus* phase during the Lower Pleistocene. The

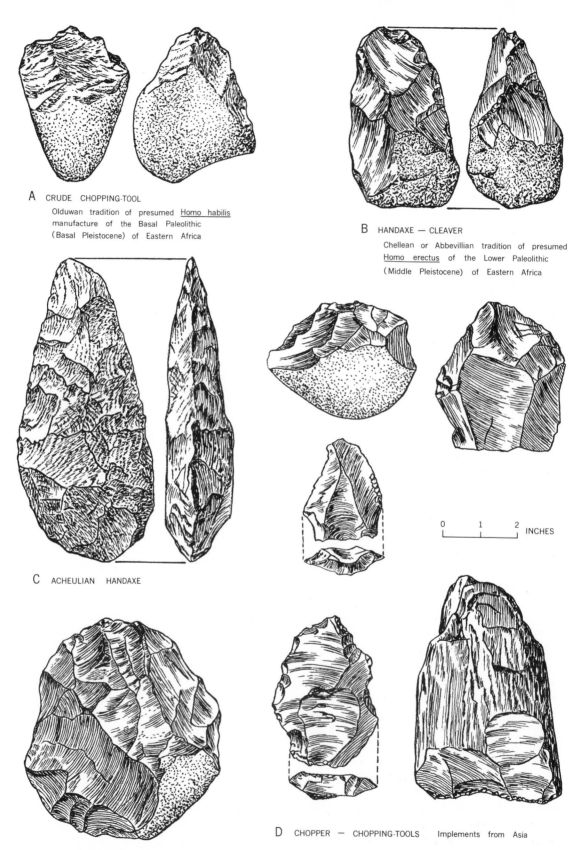

A CRUDE CHOPPING-TOOL

Olduwan tradition of presumed <u>Homo habilis</u> manufacture of the Basal Paleolithic (Basal Pleistocene) of Eastern Africa

B HANDAXE — CLEAVER

Chellean or Abbevillian tradition of presumed <u>Homo erectus</u> of the Lower Paleolithic (Middle Pleistocene) of Eastern Africa

0 1 2 INCHES

C ACHEULIAN HANDAXE

D CHOPPER — CHOPPING-TOOLS   Implements from Asia

FIG. 3.2 STONE TOOLS OF THE BASAL AND LOWER PALEOLITHIC. From *Prehistory and the Beginnings of Civilization* by Jacquetta Hawkes and Sir Leonard Woolley (1963): Harper & Row. (After K. P. Oakley, *Man The Tool-Maker*, 4th edition, London: British Museum (Natural History) 1958.)

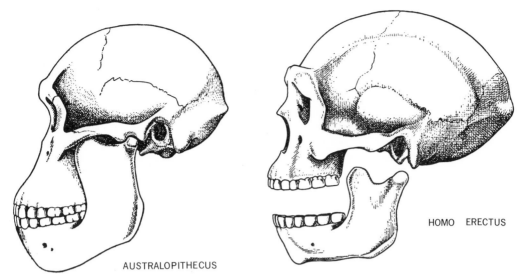

FIG. 3.3 THE SKULLS OF *AUSTRALOPITHECUS* AND *HOMO ERECTUS*. Reprinted from
The Fossil Evidence for Human Evolution by W. E. Legros Clark (1964) by permission of The
University of Chicago Press.

doubling of cranial capacity during the *Homo habilis* stage created a *Homo erectus* with twice the brain size as that of *Australopithecus* (Fig. 3.3). The logical inference is that *Homo erectus* was more effectively organized than were *Australopithecus* and *Homo habilis*; he was better able to survive and he had the capacity for further elaboration of his tools. The excavations at Olduvai Gorge in eastern Africa have produced evidence to show how pebbles gradually came to be shaped with increased care and, presumably, improved techniques. Out of the earliest Olduvai chopping tools slowly matured the finely made hand axes of the Chellean (Abbevillian) tradition of toolmaking and its successor, the Acheulian (see Fig. 3.2B and C).

The Acheulian living sites in Africa were close to water. Those from which the most stone tools have been recovered were butchery sites adjacent to a good source of raw materials for making stone tools. More relics remain at sites deliberately occupied for several days or weeks during which a number of animals were killed, cut up, and eaten, perhaps in conjunction with a seasonal harvest of vegetable foods. The site distribution of stone implements clearly demonstrates that different activities (toolmaking, butchering, scraping) were carried on in different parts of the camp. One of the main uses for the hand axes and cleavers was as meat mattock for dismembering thick-skinned larger game animals, making possible the consumption of all their edible parts.

Homo erectus had to be fully mobile. Tools made for a particular purpose were discarded when the group moved on. It was easier to manufacture new tools as needed than to transport large quantities of stone tools. One or more hand tools, a throwing stick or club, and a wooden spear were the likely tools (weapons) carried by men of the Lower Paleolithic cultural tradition until the control of fire permitted the occupation of caves, as at Choukoutien, China, for shelter, protection, and a semipermanent home. The working of wood must have been greatly eased by the use of fire, including the felling of trees by lighting a fire at the base of the trunk. Easy woodworking, in turn, provided new methods of hunting, as in the construction of traps and pitfalls. The greatly increased number of sites known from the Middle Pleistocene (end of the Lower Paleolithic phase) indicates an increase in overall population.

Early man used stone not only directly as a tool, but also as a way to make other equipment more efficient—in other words, he had invented toolmaking tools. For example, the making of a sharp point on a digging stick increased the range of foods available to the toolmakers. The stone tools of the Lower and Middle Pleistocene indicate that they were used for special activities that could be performed in a variety of physical-biotic environments. One of the difficulties in using stone tools and bones as evidence of ways of life of early man is that emphasis is placed upon the obvious and the positive, that which was the most durable. The connections of stone tools with meat eating has probably been overstressed. The most important tools must have been of wood, as clubs, throwing sticks, knocking sticks, and pointed sticks as spears or for digging, and carrying receptacles of bark or rind, or of animal origin, as bladders, stomachs, and skins to contain liquid. The evidence for the consumption of vegetative foods in a people's diet is not likely to survive in the archaeological record. Such foods, even if overwhelmingly predominant in the diet, as vegetables, grasses, roots, fruits, fish, and lizards are perishable. A campsite may be preserved in the form of a hearth, remains of a windscreen, a grinding stone, and little else save for bone debris and occasional stone tools.

No tools made before the Elster glacial complex (end of the Lower Pleistocene) have as yet been found in any part of Asia, although *Homo erectus*, as found in Java, undoubtedly crossed southern Asia as a toolmaker and eventually, with further search, some of his tools will be found. The earliest tools, as recovered in the Punjab of West Pakistan, in Burma, and in the caves at Choukoutien, are roughly defined types of choppers and chopping tools (see Fig. 3.2D) made on large round, oval, and flat pebbles. The development of working from pebbles advanced in southern and eastern Asia only to the level of chopper-chopping tools and crude scrapers, and this basic tradition persisted throughout the Pleistocene. Eastern and southeastern Asia during the Upper Pleistocene was thus a peripheral region to those areas of Africa and western Eurasia where the dramatic cultural developments of the Middle and Upper Paleolithic occurred.

Fossil Man: *Homo Erectus* of the Lower and Middle Pleistocene

The idea of the existence of fossil man—of man as part of the extinct life-forms of the world—has gained universal acceptance only within the last century, a surprisingly recent conquest of the modern mind. Finds of the remains of early man are widely scattered in place and time (Fig. 3.4). Most research has been done in Europe, where the concept of fossil man first took hold; the spectacular finds there, however, have revealed that man in Europe was a relatively latecomer and could not have originated there.

In 1890, a Dutch army surgeon, Dr. Eugene Dubois, searching in central Java for remains of fossil man, excavated at Trinil an unusual skullcap.

He named this creature *Pithecanthropus erectus*, or the erect ape-man. During the 1930s, other fossils were found, representing five other individuals of the same type. *Homo erectus*, as *Pithecanthropus* is now termed, inhabited Java during the Lower Pleistocene.

As the name *Homo erectus* indicates, these creatures stood erect. They had an average adult stature of about five feet two inches, with normal brain sizes of 800 to 950 cubic centimeters (later finds elsewhere increased the upper range to 1300 cc). Adults had large browridges that lacked recognizable foreheads (see Fig. 3.3), because the frontal lobes of their brains, not yet having evolved and expanded, were distinctly smaller than ours. Short faces, broad noses, and thick skulls are typical of many early types of men.

A great deal more knowledge of early man in eastern Asia has come from the discoveries made in north China, near Peking. Peking man is another variety of the species *Homo erectus*, resembling Java man in such features as thick skull bone, massive browridges, short face with a low and sloping forehead, broad nose, and chinless jaw. But the skull vaults of the Peking specimens are a bit longer and higher or more rounded as if more fully evolved. Consequently the cranial capacity is greater: the average is 1000 cubic centimeters and the largest is 1300 cubic centimeters, the latter being only slightly below the average for *Homo sapiens*.

In the same deep cave deposits with Peking man were found the broken bones of some 60 species of animals, including bears, horses, camels, rhinoceroses, and elephants. Evidently venison was the preferred or most abundant food, since deer bones outnumber those of any other animal by over three to one. Many animal bones appear to have been cut and, along with the greater number of bones of Peking man, exposed to fire. The stone tools present were chipped from quartz and chert and shaped in the chopper-chopping tool tradition (see Fig. 3.2D) which persisted in eastern Asia for hundreds of thousands of years. Their workmanship is distinctly superior to the crude chopping tools of *Homo habilis*. Peking man, who lived during the later part (Elster II) of the first major (Elster) glacial stage, was an able hunter who used fire. The manner in which the skulls were broken open suggest extraction of the brains and the practice of cannibalism. Forty percent of the nearly 40 individuals whose bones have been recovered

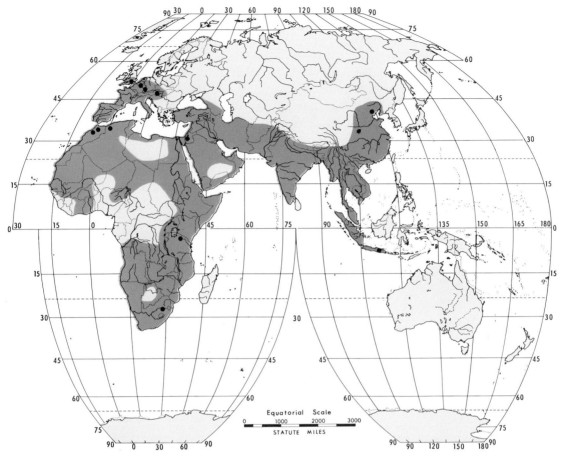

● Fossil Sites

FIG. 3.4   MID-PLEISTOCENE DISTRIBUTION OF *HOMO ERECTUS*.

from the caves at Choukoutien had died before reaching maturity.

Discoveries of fossil remains from several other parts of the Old World permit us to infer that *Homo erectus* was widely distributed. Figure 3.4 illustrates the location of the more than 60 *Homo erectus* finds made through 1964, including:

1. Swartkrans, South Africa (Telanthropus), Cromer interglacial
2. Sangiran, Java (Pithecanthropus robustus), Cromer or very early Elster glacial complex
3. Heidelberg, Germany (Paleoanthropus), Cortonian
4. Choukoutien, near Peking, China (Sinanthropus), Elster II
5. Ternifine, Algeria (Atlanthropus), Elster II
6. Olduvai Bed II, Tanzania (Chellean Man), Elster glacial complex
7. Sidi Abderrahman, Morocco, late Lower Pleistocene
8. Sangiran, Java (Pithecanthropus erectus), late Lower Pleistocene

9. Vertesszöllos, Hungary, *in situ* remains with stone implements and remains of slaughtered animals, Elster I/II
10. Ubeidya, Israel
11. Lantian, China

Homo erectus, making rather efficient use of available animal resources, ranged over a wide variety of physical-biotic environments, from the African savannas and open woodlands to the temperate woodlands of Germany and the forest-tundra of Spain. But there is no evidence that *Homo erectus* inhabited either the equatorial rain forests or the cold Eurasian steppes, the boreal forests, or the tundra.

In Europe the transitional development of *Homo erectus* led to the enlargement of the skull, which became more rounded at the back, although still retaining the heavy browridges and low forehead at the front. The evidence consists of two skulls, one from Steinheim, Germany, and the other from

Swanscombe, England, both discovered in the 1930s, and dated at between 200,000 and 300,000 years ago. The evolutionary development of *Homo erectus* thus led to greater and earlier changes on the back of the head, hence increasing the brain size, before significantly altering the *Homo erectus* form of face.

Fire: The Greatest Discovery

The greatest—certainly the bravest—of man's early triumphs, leading to subsequent successes, was his discovery, utilization, and control of fire. The knowledge of how to make a fire, keep it burning, and use it for other purposes was a masterful achievement. No other animal can do it! No other animal has even begun to understand combustion in any form. As a technological accomplishment, the conquest of fire ranks with, or perhaps exceeds, toolmaking in importance. Exploiting fire long ago became one of the few universal traits of human culture; evidence of its use dates back to Peking man (*Homo erectus*) during the Elster II glacial stage of the Pleistocene.

Today, we take our knowledge of fire making and fire using for granted. Matches are cheap and plentiful, furnaces are automatic and thermostat-regulated. Asking a stranger for "a light" is done as easily as asking "can you tell me the time?" But what would life today be like without fire—our knowledge to produce heat or flame? Almost every object we use in our daily life would be gone, since at some stage in their making each required the use of fire. And without fire we would promptly starve, since there is not enough food now being produced that the world's people could consume in an uncooked form.

Fire for early man was both tool and weapon. Its presence in the form of heat and light at night deterred or drove away other animals; it provided warmth that enabled man to extend his range and to survive in hitherto unexploited territories with cooler climates. It provided a focus of activity for a group of families, a sense of belonging to a common "hearth," for which provision of fuel and keeping the fire or sparks alive were of over-whelming concern.

The natural sources from which fire can be taken are lava flows, craters, and steam vents of volcanic areas, lightning strikes, friction of dry branches moved by wind, or forest or grass fires ignited by these agencies. All of these sources were available to early man in the eastern African uplands as well as along the subtropical zone of southern and southeastern Asia.

Man first made fire according to one of four basic principles, the two most widespread being by friction (fire-plow, fire saw, or fire drill using rotation) and by striking sparks from minerals (flint, pyrites). Each involved the kindling of a bit of fine dust, then "catching" this spark in prepared tinder (dried grass, bark, or pith), which was then ignited by fanning or blowing so that the increased oxygen supply caused the spark first to glow, then to burst into flame. Less common, because more intricate, and restricted to peoples of Southeast Asia, is the fire piston or cylinder, struck percussively, in which tinder is heated by the rapid compression of air. A fourth principle used steam under pressure in volcanic areas: a stick thrust into one of the fissures from which superheated steam emerges will smoke and blacken, then burst into flame when brought out into open air.

The mastery of the animals' fear of fire was a bold step of early humanity. The small band gathered round its hearth derived a tremendous benefit from the discovery that cooking makes meat more edible and digestible and that the plant starches and tough vegetable fibers are broken down by heat into forms digestible by man. Possessing fire, man could and did move outward from his "home territory" with greater confidence. No matter what newfound wild plant materials were gathered, they could be rendered palatable and provide for his sustenance, and no matter what new wild animals would be encountered, they could be driven by fire into bogs or traps or pits or over cliffs, thence killed and eaten as a source of meat. Fire made possible not only an extension of man's range over the earth, from the subtropics into the higher latitudes, but also was one of the cultural achievements that improved man's chances for slowly increasing his numbers, maintaining kin-group solidarity, and further differentiating himself from other animal forms.

Another Cultural Achievement: Shelter

The shelters that man learned to create also greatly aided his adaptation to living in a variety of physical environments more extreme than those of the tropics, hence enabled him to extend vastly his range over the earth. Man's dwellings are exceedingly varied, in the raw materials used, in the climatic conditions (winds, temperatures, precipitation, seasonalities) being countered, in their sites, and in their forms and functions (see pp. 231–248). Men today erect shelters of bamboo and tropical leaves, build with boughs, twigs, and mud, with bones and stone, grass sod and tamped earth, adobe and brick, timber and metal, snow and ice. Men situate their shelters in swamps, over the edge of lakes, streams, and canals, by the shore, on hillslopes and mountain ridges, in open grasslands, and in tropical clearings. The shelter may house a single family or a dozen side by side under one roof; it may be set apart in isolation or built as one of a cluster.

Homo habilis and *Homo erectus* of Paleolithic Africa, living as unspecialized food gatherers and collectors under conditions of natural warmth, had little need for shelter; most likely they lived in the open with only occasional need for protection from tropical downpours. Ready-made shelters were formed by overhanging rocks or cliffs, cracks or fissures, and natural caves. The latter, however, were more likely the lairs of carnivores, until man acquired fire to light their darkness and defend his occupance. Caves, in the midlatitudes where winter cold had to be countered, have been occupied since the end of the Lower Pleistocene. The caves of *Homo erectus* at Choukoutien are the earliest known human habitations. The occupation of caves and rock shelters (formed by overhanging cliffs) by early man is perhaps overemphasized, simply because the archaeologic record is so much better preserved in their littered and buried floors and debris mounds than in the open-air living sites along streams and lake shores where materials were both greatly scattered and exposed, and later more easily removed by running water, waves, and wind.

The Emergence of *Homo sapiens neanderthalensis*

The evolutionary position of *Homo sapiens neanderthalensis* and the significance of his cultural development have taken nearly a century to decipher. Thus far there have been 87 sites where his remains have been found (Table 3.2). Of these, 12 were discovered during the nineteenth century, another 45 by 1947, and 30 since 1949. In other words, one half of all the finds of Neanderthal man have been made since 1930. The discoveries of the nineteenth century all were in Europe; more than half of the discovery sites since 1920 have been

outside of Europe, in Africa and Asia. The considerable recent increase in knowledge has forced continuous revision of our thinking about the relationship of Neanderthaloids to modern man.

Neanderthal man provides ample proof that human fossils have been interpreted according to the theories of human evolution that were current at the time of their discoveries. For example, the first publicized discovery of skeletal remains of fossil man occurred in western Germany in 1856, three years prior to publication of Charles Darwin's *Origin of Species*. The name Neanderthal derives from the cave-site locality near Dusseldorf, in the valley (*thal*) of the Neander River, a tributary of the Rhine. At the time no other similar skeletal material existed (the 1830 and 1848 finds in Belgium and Gibraltar became publicly known only sometime later) as a basis for comparison and no proof could be given for its age. For many years the Neanderthal specimen was regarded simply as pathologically peculiar, neither normal nor really ancient, when actually not enough was known to make an accurate judgment.

The numerous spectacular finds in France between 1907 and 1909, as described in subsequent voluminous scientific publications (1911–1913), established a "climate of opinion" about the "classic" European Neanderthals that was not much altered until the further finds in Palestine (present Israel) in 1929 to 1934. The early twentieth-century view was that Neanderthal cavemen were not ancestral to modern forms of men (not a form of *Homo sapiens*), that they became extinct without issue, being exterminated by a culturally superior *Homo sapiens* who succeeded them so suddenly that too little time existed for biological evolution to have produced modern man from Neanderthal forms. From this view derives our caricature of a Pleistocene caveman as a scantily clad, squat, clumsy, brutish, stupid oaf with a slouching, shuffling, bent-knee, semierect posture. The finds in Palestine during the early 1930s should have altered this view, but did not. The Palestinian discoveries (the Skhul population at Mount Carmel) revealed a form morphologically intermediate between European Neanderthal and modern man, but its age was then determined as interglacial (Lower Pleistocene) and prior to the primitive Neanderthalers. The interpretation of the time was thus reinforced; Neanderthal was not the ancestor to modern man.

TABLE 3.2 DISTRIBUTION OF NEANDERTHALOID SITES BY PLACE AND TIME OF DISCOVERY[a]

Country or Region	Number of Neanderthaloid Sites Discovered in Each Decade														Total
	1830s	1840s	1850s	1860s	1870s	1880s	1890s	1900s	1910s	1920s	1930s	1940s	1950s	1960s	
EUROPE															
Jersey									1						1
Belgium	1			1		1	1								4
Germany			1			1		1			1				4
France						1	1	7		1	1	3	4		18
Spain						1					1		1		3
Gibraltar		1								1					2
Italy										1	2		5		8
Yugoslavia							1								1
Switzerland													1		1
Czechoslovakia						1		1		1			1	1	5
Hungary											1				1
Romania										1					1
Greece											1				1
AFRICA															
Morocco											2		3	1	6
Libya													1		1
Ethiopia								1							1
Kenya									1						1
Tanzania										2				1	3
Rhodesia										1					1
South Africa											1	1	1		3
ASIA															
U.S.S.R.										1	1		1		3
Lebanon											1	1			2
Israel										5	2			1	8
Iraq												2			2
Iran												2			2
Java											1				1
China											1		2		3
Totals	1	1	1	1	0	5	3	10	2	14	16	7	22	4	87

[a] Data tabulated from Oakley, 1964, pp. 296–310.

The more numerous Neanderthaloid discoveries after 1930, when combined with the present accurate techniques for absolute dating, have brought about a reassessment of Neanderthal's place in human evolution: he has been restored to ancestral respectability and is now labeled *Homo sapiens neanderthalensis*. Neanderthal man was the creator of Mousterian culture (multifunctional tools) *prior* to the reduction in the form and dimensions of the Middle Pleistocene face (Fig. 3.5). Neanderthal man was *not* an "Alley Oop" character, but was fully *Homo*. He stood as erect as we do today, with only slightly more robust joints and muscle attachments.

The fundamental morphological distinction between Neanderthaloids and modern man is in the facial dimensions: the Neanderthal face was larger because its larger jaw contained bigger teeth with longer roots. The front teeth (incisors) of Neanderthal were about the largest ever developed in man by biological evolution, and they were a heavily used part of Neanderthal man's tool kit. Large strong incisors were needed not only for biting food but also for many other functions: scraping, cutting, prying, peeling bark, cracking nuts, and to hold objects being manipulated or shaped by the hands. As a result of such use, Neanderthal man's front teeth were remarkably

LATERAL VIEWS

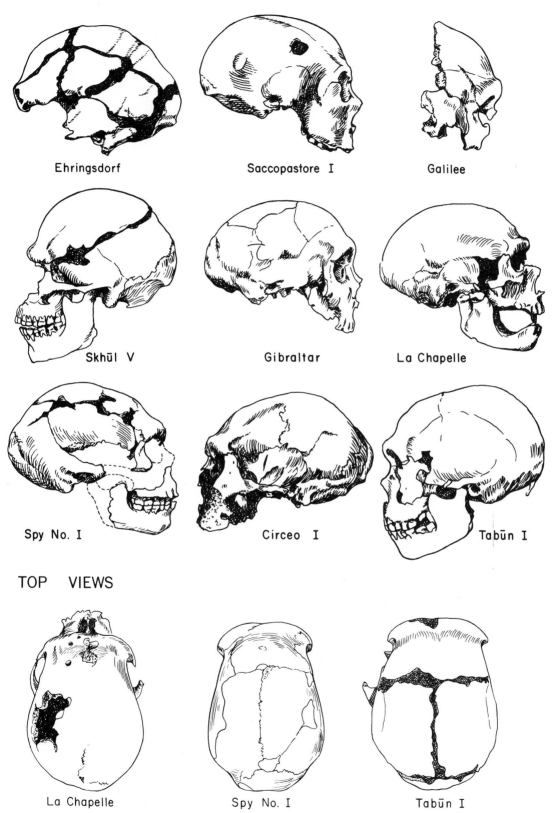

Ehringsdorf

Saccopastore I

Galilee

Skhūl V

Gibraltar

La Chapelle

Spy No. I

Circeo I

Tabūn I

TOP VIEWS

La Chapelle

Spy No. I

Tabūn I

FIG. 3.5 NEANDERTHALOID SKULLS. From *The Basis of Human Evolution* by Bertram S. Kraus, (1964) Harper & Row.

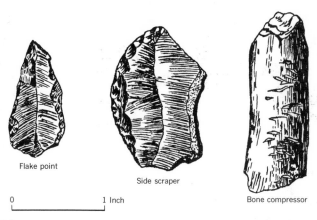

Flake point

Side scraper

0   1 Inch

Bone compressor

FIG. 3.6 MID-PALEOLITHIC STONE TOOLS (MOUSTERIAN CULTURE). From *Prehistory and the Beginnings of Civilization* by Jacquetta Hawkes and Sir Leonard Woolley (1963): Harper & Row. (After K. P. Oakley, *Man The Tool-Maker*, 4th edition, London: British Museum (Natural History) 1958.)

rounded and, for individuals reaching full maturity, were usually worn down to the gums.

The Neanderthal stage of human evolution began at the onset of the last (Eem) interglacial stage, about 110,000 years ago, and continued for some 85,000 years, to the maximum of the main Würm glacial stage, about 35,000 years ago. The culture of *Homo sapiens neanderthalensis* is identified as the Middle Paleolithic. In Europe and Africa the cultural development from the artifacts of *Homo erectus* (see Fig. 3.2) to the stone tools of *Homo sapiens neanderthalensis* (Fig. 3.6) proceeded without a break. Skeletal evidence, consisting of retention of large browridges and large jaws while the brain size was being enlarged, confirms the transition between the two stages.

Neanderthaloids, over a span of 85,000 years, developed a greater sophistication than *Homo erectus* in toolmaking, as the cruder hand axes were replaced by flake blades (compare Figs. 3.2 and 3.6) and superbly worked smaller hand axes of triangular or heart-shaped form. The emphasis was upon more precise shaping of flints and cherts into multipurpose tools, such as scrapers and points with finer cutting edges, by the secondary trimming of flakes on one or both edges. The first beginnings of regional differentiation in toolmaking occur in Europe, where sites with hand axes are mainly

confined to the maritime lowlands of western Europe, which were forest-covered, whereas hand axes were mostly lacking in the climatically more severe tundra conditions of the hilly and mountain interior, where forests were absent. The Neanderthal tool kit was expanded to include dozens of different styles of scrapers, knives, borers, choppers, axes, chisels, planes, and saw-toothed blades, with antlers and animal bone increasingly used as tool materials.

Neanderthal man began with the Old World distribution of *Homo erectus* (see Fig. 3.4) from which he evolved. As a result of improved cultural adaptation, the Neanderthal populations extended their range toward the poles into central Europe and central Asia, and are the first we know to have lived in a truly cold climate. That is, before the time of glacial intensity Neanderthaloids were able to penetrate north of the frost-free zone into the midlatitudes that experienced winter cold. Toward the end of the interglacial period, about 75,000 years ago, Neanderthaloids effectively occupied Europe. In considerable number and over a wide expanse of territory, caves were occupied wherever available, and all year round where food resources permitted, as in southwestern France; these sites, in turn, improved the probabilities for preservation of tools and human bones. The trend toward specialized tools, such as flint scrapers, implies that animal skins, hides, and furs were prepared for use as covering and warmth and that there was an increase in the hunting of the larger game animals. Cave interiors were made more comfortable by the use of coverings of branches and hides over the cave openings and by the use of hearth fires. The main animal food was the reindeer, but the wooly mammoths and rhinos also were hunted, as well as various fish and birds. A direct measure of the cultural success of Neanderthals was their survival, at the edge of Europe's ice sheet and through the winters of the Eurasian midlatitudes, made possibly by their use of clothing, shelter, and their sure control of fire.

Another measure of cultural advance by Neanderthaloids is indicated by their development of the custom of human burials. Graves were cut or dug and bodies placed into them in crouched or flexed positions, as if asleep, accompanied by animal bones and sometimes red ochre. The careful disposal of the dead and the inclusion with them of objects for use after death are actions indicative of funeral rituals that served to reassure the living. This behavior clearly suggests a more sophisticated culture, an increasing awareness of man's social bonds, and a considerable degree of abstract and symbolic thought pointing toward religion and metaphysics. Neanderthaloids reached a crucial stage in personal awareness and a mark of humanization, the recognition of death as the fate of the individual.

The accompanying chart (Table 3.3) presents the contemporary view of the place of *Homo sapiens neanderthalensis* in Pleistocene time and Paleolithic cultural development. Neanderthal was fully *Homo sapiens;* his brain had a capacity equal to our own. Perhaps 75,000 to 80,000 years ago man's brain reached its present state of development and since then has scarcely changed. The explanation for lack of further increase in brain size is twofold:

1. There was an upper limit to brain size in the newborn. Brain sizes larger than could be passed through the birth canal of the female pelvis were at a reproductive disadvantage for survival of both child and mother.
2. Cultural development, as reached by early Neanderthals, made a larger, more complex brain unnecessary. As experiences were shared through language, individuals learned from one another, and knowledge was passed from one generation to the next. Beyond

a critical point of brain complexity sufficient for the individual to be able to speak and to learn, further increases in intelligence conferred no advantages for a person to survive and attain sexual maturity.

During the Middle Paleolithic stage, the most obvious cultural change made by Neanderthaloids was their invention and use of many new kinds of stone tools for cutting and manipulation. As the number of tools increased and they became more specialized for particular uses, a very gradual reduction was possible in the heavy use made, as by early Neanderthaloids, of the front teeth. In other words, cultural adaptations (the invention and use of new tools) replaced the adaptive significance of a biologic feature (the incisor teeth). As the very large teeth of Neanderthals lost their significance for survival (once he was in possession of the new-type stone tools, it did not matter how large or sturdy were the teeth of a Neanderthal), the sizes of teeth and jaw were free to vary. The result of the accumulation of genetic mutations, made at random, was the natural selection of teeth and jaws of reduced size. Instead of teeth that met together, there developed overbite (upper teeth extending forward beyond lower teeth as in modern man). Thus the interplay of cultural development and natural selection led to the creation of the smaller modern face of *Homo sapiens sapiens* (Fig. 3.7).

Food-Gathering and Food Collecting: The Trend Toward Specialization

The basic connection that early men established with their physical-biotic environment in order to sustain themselves hinged upon their methods of obtaining food and securing shelter (settlement) within the territory occupied. Throughout the long duration of the Pleistocene, man's survival depended upon his skills in locating and securing food, which grew as a result of natural biotic processes. Not until the beginning of the postglacial stage, about 11,000 years ago, did man achieve that cultural breakthrough toward incipient food production, based in part upon crop growing and limited keeping of domesticated animals, that enabled him to gain some control over the amounts, kinds, and places of origin of foodstuffs. The duration of the Pleistocene, culturally known as the Paleolithic (Old Stone Age), was 200 times as long as the Holocene period, which culturally began with the stages known as the Mesolithic (Middle Stone Age) and Neolithic (New Stone Age).

TABLE 3.3 UPPER PLEISTOCENE MAN IN THE TIME PERSPECTIVE OF THE LAST
110,000 YEARS

Years (B.C.)	Glacial Stages in Midlatitude Europe	Climate
5,000	RECENT	
10,000	8,000 . . . . . . Last glacial relapse; minor readvance of ice 9,000 . . . . . . Temperate insterstadial (Alleröd interval); ice margin in central Sweden 11,000 ————— Temperate oscillation (Bölling interval) —————	Cold Temperate Cold, but warming
15,000	14,000 . . . . . . Protracted glacial retreat . . . . Halt at Pommeranian moraine 16,000 . . . . . . Halt at Frankfurt moraine	
20,000	18,000 . . . . . . Brandenburg stage (greatest cold) LATE WÜRM (III) **(Full glacial stage)** Readvance of ice front to its maximum position	Very cold
25,000	—26,000——————————————————————————————— Interstadial (Paudorf) retreat of ice front into Scandinavia (?) —28,000———————————————————————————————	Cool Temperate
30,000		
35,000	MAIN WÜRM (II) Ice front south of the Baltic Sea (?)	Very cold
40,000		
	—42,000———————————————————————————————	
45,000	Temperate phase (Gottweig interstadial) —46,000———————————————————————————————	
50,000	EARLY WÜRM (I)	
60,000	57,000 . . . . . . Temperate phase (Brorup interstadial) 62,000 . . . . . . Temperate phase (Amersfoort interval)	
70,000	Formation of Scandinavian glacier Beginning of Würm glacial End of Eem interglacial	Cold
80,000		
90,000	EEM INTERGLACIAL	
110,000	Beginning of Eem interglacial UPPER PLEISTOCENE	
	End of Riss glacial complex MIDDLE PLEISTOCENE	

Hominid Form	Cultural Phases (in Europe)		Tool Types (in Europe)
	NEOLITHIC		
		5,500	
	MESOLITHIC		TARDENOISIAN-MAGLEMOSIAN SAUVETERRIAN
			Bow and arrow
		11,000 — AZILIAN	
		12,500	
HOMO SAPIENS SAPIENS			CRESSWELL-HAMBURG MAGDALENIAN — Specially equipped for reindeer hunting / Eyed needles, cave art, reindeer-antler artifacts
		17,000	
	UPPER PALEOLITHIC		SOLUTREAN — Extraordinary pressure-flaking; willow-leaf and laurel-leaf lance points
		21,000	
			GRAVETTIAN — Smaller knife blades / Ivory wedges for splitting wood and bone
		25,000	
CRO-MAGNON			AURIGNACIAN — Most skillful flintworking / First true boneworking (pins, awls, light spearheads)
		31,000	
			CHÂTELPERRONIAN — Earliest blade cultures / Slender, straight, keen-edged flakes
		35,000	
		40,000	
			MAIN MOUSTERIAN
	MIDDLE PALEOLITHIC		UPPER LEVALLOISIAN — Wooden hafts added to stone tools
			EARLY MOUSTERIAN and MIDDLE LEVALLOISIAN — Multifunctional tools, thick, heavy flakes / Improved techniques of manufacture rather than functional specialization / Two standard types of tools / 1. D-shaped sidescrapers / 2. Triangular point or knife
HOMO SAPIENS NEANDERTHALENSIS			
			LEVALLOISIAN — Small, bifacial, hand axes
		100,000	
HOMO ERECTUS	LOWER PALEOLITHIC		LATER ACHEULIAN (Tayacian and Micoquian) — Sidescrapers

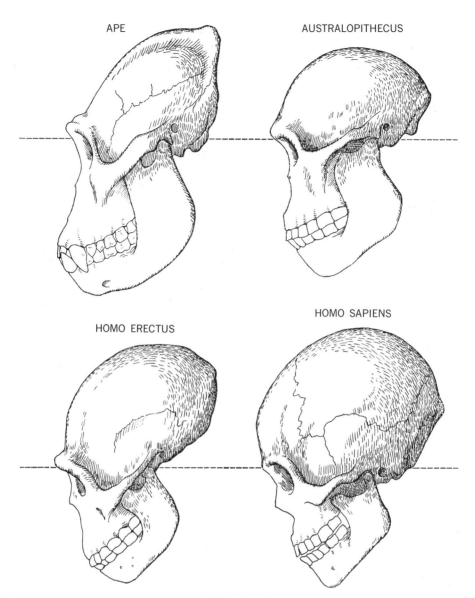

APE AUSTRALOPITHECUS

HOMO ERECTUS HOMO SAPIENS

FIG. 3.7 EVOLUTION OF THE SKULL FROM APE TO MODERN MAN. From "Tools and Human Evolution" by Sherwood L. Washburn in *Scientific American* **(September, 1960).**

Only in these latter cultural stages did man cross the threshold from food-gathering and food collecting to food production. The present chapter focuses upon the effect of man's slow and gradual acquisition of skills (Paleolithic culture) during the long period of the Pleistocene. These are precisely the skills that modern sedentary urbanized men have all but discarded as no longer necessary, except for purposes of sports, guerrilla warfare, or survival from accidents of shipwreck or air crashes in remote regions.

It is useful to distinguish among several types of existence for Pleistocene man:

1. *Unspecialized food-gathering* (example: the *Homo habilis* group).

    Naturally determined mammalian subsistence.

    Wandering within limited territories.

    Temporary shifting settlements of one or only a few days' duration.

    Tools fashioned but not yet standardized (e.g., the very crude and variable chopping tools).

    Materials consumed where gathered; no spatial distinction in activities.

2. *Unspecialized food collecting* (example: *Homo erectus*).

    Selective hunting, strand gathering, and fishing, in particular brief seasons.

    Increased skill in harvesting temporary surpluses of food beyond what could be consumed immediately.

Restricted wandering, within fixed (known) limits, including identification with, and defense of, a "home territory."

Mostly temporary settlements, but occasionally seasonal settlements perhaps of several weeks' or even several months' duration.

Variety in standardized tool forms (mixed tool assemblages) within regions, including "tools to make tools."

Distinction in space between where food collected and where consumed; beginning of techniques for preservation of surplus food collected.

3. *Specialized food-gathering* (example: *Homo sapiens neanderthalensis*, in Europe).

Increased skill in hunting of larger animals (herbivores).

A greater proportion of meat (high protein content) in the diet.

Wandering within somewhat delimited territories with increased knowledge of the better locations for food-gathering.

Temporary shifting settlements of one to several days' duration; less mobility whenever an increased supply of food permitted.

Earliest standardized toolmaking traditions: core bifaces, flakes, and choppers with broad distributions for each tool type.

Materials consumed where gathered, no spatial distinction in activities, but more feasts than famines though seasonal "starvation periods" were possibly annual affairs.

4. *Specialized food collecting* (example: some groups of *Homo sapiens sapiens*).

Intensified hunting, fishing, and plant-product (seeds, berries, nuts) collecting, with emphasis upon maximizing food surpluses.

Seasonal differentiation in activities between plant collecting and hunting for game, fishing, or both.

Trend from restricted wandering toward center-based wandering; that is, toward seasonal settlements of some months' duration to which human groups returned each year. In regions of especially great food surpluses, as along coastlines with continuous supplies of shellfish or huge seasonal salmon runs, the beginning of semipermanent settlements of some years' duration became possible. Lessened frequency of "starvation periods" became normal.

Beginning of plant manipulation (fibers, poisons, drugs) and greater concentration on the taking of fish, fowl, mollusks, and the fleeter mammals (ungulates).

Marked regional distributions of tool types; great skill in food preservation (drying, salting, fermenting) and storage (baskets, bamboo tubes, pit caches)

Spatial separation of food collecting and food consumption, the latter including preservation and storage activities at campsites.

5. *Incipient food production* (example: Mesolithic cultural stage at end of the Pleistocene).

Experimental manipulation by specialized food collectors of favored plants and animals within their natural habitats (e.g., watering or weeding of plants, protection of particular animals from other carnivores, burning of grazing areas to improve the food supply, hence increase the number of those animals favored in hunting).

Semipermanent to near-permanent settlements; less wandering necessary as greater volume and variety of food-stuffs obtained as a result of increased skills (knowledge of all the useful things to be found in a local region; techniques for acquiring, preserving, and storing food surpluses); famines become fewer, but "starvation periods" recur among less successful cultures or in seasonally poor environments.

These five types of existence were developed, in different times and places, by varieties of early man. The differences among them were very real for those who lived by their means. What seem to us, with our advantage of hindsight, to be only miniscule differences in conditions for human existence were precisely those that made "all the difference" in those cultural developments that enabled some groups of Paleolithic men to surpass others. It seems difficult to imagine that it required all but the last 11,000 years of human time on earth for man to attain the cultural stage of incipient food production, but it did. The Holocene period, by comparison, is an "explosive" age of civilizations of increasing cultural complexity.

The Significance of Mental Activity

Among all the animal forms, only birds, carnivores, and primates possess an extrasensitive spot on the retina of the eye that makes possible great acuteness of sight. When the sharpening of sight was combined with stereoscopic vision and a dexterous hand, the way was open for further primate development. Improvement of skills in finger and hand manipulations was all of a piece with intense scrutiny of new objects, whether branches, fruits, insects, or stones. The hand with its fully opposable thumb, remaining unspecialized in man in contrast to the hands of apes or monkeys, was very significant for human evolution. So was the beginning of conscious apprehension made possible by a developing brain.

Man's increased mental capacity coincided with the great expansion of the cerebral cortex, with its deep folds and convolutions, in the brain (see Fig. 3.7). Particularly characteristic of modern man, *Homo sapiens sapiens,* is the vast size of the frontal and temporal lobes, with their nerve cells used for the association and storing of memories. *Within man's brain lies the evolutionary bridge from the biological to the cultural.* Infinite varieties of experience are accumulated as memories stored in the brain, there reshaped into a limited number of generalized ideas or concepts. The development of recognizable and meaningful symbols, both graphic and acoustic, enable men to share experiences and transfer ideas from one individual to another. The seeming small step of the sharing of memory and experience among men made all the difference in human evolution. What started as random, fleeting reactions to external stimuli by an animal were very slowly indeed changed over into a new form of cultural tradition made possible by the evolution of a brain more efficient than that of any other mammal in storing memories, associating ideas, and exercising foresight or planning.

Man's cerebellum, which is concerned more with skill functions, is just as large as his cortex. With its large areas devoted to manipulation of thumb and hand, the cerebellum of man is about three times the size of that of a great ape. From this difference in size and distribution comes the conclusion that the parts of the brain involved with skills had to evolve before tool-use could be effective. This conclusion makes it easier to understand why millions of years of human evolution were necessary before *Homo sapiens* rose to dominance. It is easy for modern man to learn manual skills because the way his brain evolved makes possible such skills. For an ape, however, the things that man does with little effort, such as the precise manipulation of the fingers, are impossible and even inconceivable.

Man's self-awareness which developed along with his cerebral cortex made possible a number of cultural achievements. One very early activity was in toolmaking, which had the extremely practical goal of achieving greater control over the external environment. Another activity was synthesis of thought—an improved capacity to visualize, to conceptualize, to reach conclusions, and to act upon them. Early man did not live to make stone tools. He made his tools, whether of wood, shell, bone, or stone, following definite patterns regularized by conceptual thought, and transmitted them to others not only as material objects whose methods of preparation were observable, but also as idealized forms engraved in human memory later to be duplicated. The development of conceptual thought, expressed as art, mysticism, and ritual, was progressing all the while men were battering away at cobbles to produce chopping tools and hand axes. The evidence is clearly visible in the many fine tools whose design and workmanship are far more elaborate than need be for their purely practical functions of cutting, scraping, or pounding. Aesthetics, as a sense of style or of correct form, also was an early human achievement, fulfilling inner satisfactions.

Organization of Experience

Any delineation of the qualities of humanness must include man's considerable ability to communicate with others in elaborate symbolic ways: speech, writing, printing, whistling, drumming, and gestures. Spoken language, a purely mental achievement, leaves no material embodiment. Nevertheless, its development by man was every bit as significant for human evolution as the capability for toolmaking and tool using. The idea of language, the patterned association of certain sounds with certain meanings, was an invention of the first magnitude.

The origin of language will always remain hidden; the steps were taken across the threshold from hominoid to hominid in the far distant past before it was possible to record events that left no tangible evidence. One hunch is that language began as the association of meaningful sounds with gestures of the hands, face, or both. From pantomime and mouth babbling to precise gestures associated with precise sound symbols is suggested as the way in which language and speech emerged. The point, of course, is that language *was* begun; no human group ever known has been without a fully developed richly symbolic means of verbal communication.

Language, the systematization of signs and words, requires directed thought. No longer was animal life a continuous procession of total events; experiences or objects could be isolated—everything could have a name. Once analytical thought was possible, language expanded rapidly with increasingly complex vocabulary and word order. The growth of language both made possible and was the record of the general elaboration of total human culture.

Consider, for a moment, the basic features of a language as a communication system. It is vocal-auditory (mouth to ear), which has the advantage of leaving the rest of the body free for carrying on other activities at the same time. A vocal signal fades rapidly (does not last long) but its source (distance and direction) can be localized by the two ears (dual receiver system) of a listener. Language signals are interchangeable and are fed back; that is, one can both produce the sounds heard from others like himself and hear the sounds that he himself produces. All land mammals possess these capabilities.

Speech is specialized; its sounds serve no functions except as signals. The signals have meanings (semanticity) which are arbitrary. The great advantage of arbitrariness is that no limit is imposed upon what subjects can be communicated. All primates possess these three characteristics.

Language sounds are discrete; within the huge variety of sounds that can be produced by human vocal organs, any one language uses only a relatively small set of them. Language is transmitted by tradition—by learning and teaching. All hominoids are capable of discreteness and of traditional transmission of speech.

Only man has further capabilities, such as the ability to range freely in his thinking about time or space, or both, and in the remoteness of things talked about—the quality of displacement. Man also can exercise creativity—that is, say things that have never before been said or heard, coining new phrases by assembling pieces familiar from old utterances. The whole enormous stock of words (morphemes) of a language can all be said by rearrangements of a relatively small stock of distinguishable, but in themselves meaningless, sounds (phonemes). Examples: "bad," "bag," "ban," and "bat," as distinct from "dab," "gab," "nab," and "tab." The latter three capabilities—displacement, creativity, and rearrangement of sounds to achieve different meanings—have made human languages very useful for man's evolutionary development and cultural growth. These developments, which characterize human languages and make them at once so complex, so various, so flexible, and so useful, could have come about only by the evolution of large and convoluted brains. Better brains were necessary for the storage and manipulation of the elements of more complex communication systems than exist among any other animal species.

Since all primates are social animals with strong gregarious instincts, man too can be assumed to have always acted in groups, beginning with the family and the associations of families. As the human body and the human mind slowly but continuously evolved from an animal ancestry, so did human society. Without companions of like kind, man could never have developed his mental powers through communication or conceptual thought. The individual is born into a group; the whole process of growing up through a long period of helplessness and immaturity is as important for the society as it is for the survival of the individual. Over a protracted period of childhood the individual acquires the language of his community, learns the socially approved ways of behavior, and gains the necessary skills to manipulate the artifacts of the society—he becomes enculturated. Society thus insures its survival by constant replenishment and education of its individual members.

In the time span of the late Pliocene and Basal Pleistocene (see Table 3.1), primate animal behavior evolved into human social conduct; the herd of kin groups became the tribe with its bands and clans; instincts and habits became socially regulated. There were many steps along the way from animal life, with its patterns set mainly by biological inheritance, to a social organization which was traditionally acquired and consciously enforced. But the steps *were* taken, although so gradually that a better image than one of a series of steps is that of a continuum of slow change over nearly two million years from *Homo habilis* through *Homo erectus* to *Homo sapiens*. There was no point in time that can be identified as *the* moment (or indeed millennium) when hominoid became hominid. There was no threshold across which *Australopithecus* stepped to become a man. Rather, the changes took place down a long corridor of time. What emerged was forever after different from what entered, but no one can say when animal mating became marriage or the animal horde became human society.

The Rise to Dominance of *Homo sapiens sapiens*

Homo sapiens sapiens is a product of the last glacial stage, coming into his own as the successor to Neanderthal man during the Main to Late Würm (see Table 3.3). In Europe, the replacement of Neanderthal man may have taken as long as 10,000 years (from 40,000 to 30,000 years ago), a slow process by our present time dimension, but rather abrupt in the light of the two million years of human evolution. In ecological terms, specialized food-gatherers with flake tools were replaced by specialized food collectors whose advantage lay in their ability to make and use a more complex tool kit, essentially a wide range of blades and burins. The process of replacement was slow, involving both extinction and interbreeding in a complex of small regions, as different small groups confronted one another, defending and shifting and expanding or losing their territories. The end result was the rise to dominance of *Homo sapiens sapiens*, in a variety of forms virtually indistinguishable from those of the present day.

The essence of the newer stone technology was the making of specialized blade tools (Fig. 3.8), a technique that maximized the lengths of cutting edges by three to ten times over that of the previous technology of pebble tools and core tools. The Upper Paleolithic tool kit included the following types of worked flint or obsidian:

Blade: long, parallel-sided flake with sharp cutting edges; a useful knife.

Burin or *graver:* chisel-shaped blade; used for making grooves in wood and engravings in bone or antler.

Backed blade: one sharp edge, the other length a blunt edge for holding.

Notched blade: scraper or shaver for preparing shafts of arrows or spears.

Borer: blade with thin sharp point for drilling or punching holes.

End scraper: blunt-ended, to hollow out wood or bone or to scrape hide or bark.

Tanged point: projectile point, as tips of arrow or light spears, fixed in a wooden shaft.

The specific designations for type styles (variously termed industries or cultural levels) for the Upper Paleolithic of western Europe (see Table 3.3) are, from oldest to youngest, the following:

Châtelperronian: a local development in southwestern France from flint tools of Mousterian type.

Aurignacian: caves and shelters; projectile heads of bone, flint scrapers with a keel, flint burins of beaked form; first evidence of fishing.

Gravettian: artificial shelters in open loessland; mammoth hunting; flint knives, projectile tips, and barbs; female figurines carved in ivory; first cycle of cave art; ceremonial burials, with jewelry, headdresses, and red ochre.

Solutrean: noted for "laurel-leaf" points—thin, sharp-edged knives or daggers—and smaller "willow-leaf" points—for spear or arrow tips; persistence of naturalistic art.

Magdalenian: marked development in the use of bone, especially antler: spear-throwers, harpoons, fishhooks, eyed needles; reindeer hunting; use of sewed skin clothing; cave art carried to the highest peak of development.

Stone implements of the Paleolithic have largely been interpreted as the tools of hunters: as weapons for killing, blades for skinning and cutting, scrapers for preparing hides. As a result of dependence upon that which is best preserved, hence recovered by archaeology, we perhaps have a distorted picture of the significance of hunting in the life of early man. But there is no doubt that Upper Paleolithic man in Europe during the late Würm glacial stage was a skilled hunter of big game. This particular specialization in Europe was the result of a unique time-and-culture coincidence, in which man's evolving cultural abilities allowed him to achieve big-game kills just before and during the period when the large mammals of the Late Pleistocene were becoming extinct. Over most of the rest of the Old World, Upper Paleolithic man went on using his stone tools for cutting and splitting wood, for cutting bark, and in digging. The various types of blades and knives served for shaping wood, bark, and bast, preparing roots and fruits, and dressing meat and skin.

Further astounding evidence from the Upper Paleolithic reveals the heights of human achievement then attained: the fantastic paintings in reds, yellows, browns, and black on the walls and ceilings of great caves. The most elaborate, imaginative, and expressive cave art comes from three areas of southern France and northern Spain, where limestone regions contained a great number of natural caverns created by underground solution channels. In the dark uninhabited depths of caverns, far removed from the inhabited portions of the cave entrances where light could enter and smoke escape, the artists worked by the light of torches or of tiny lamps filled with animal fat or blubber. Paleolithic art was specialized in that it was the work of men who practiced and perfected a variety of techniques: drawing, engraving, outlining, painting, sculpturing in relief. By the thousands these engraved and painted murals were created, almost exclusively of animal subjects: mammoth, bear, lion, horse, bison, reindeer—the great animals of the Pleistocene upon whose successful conquest Paleolithic man depended. The artists were preoccupied with portraying mostly game animals and some beasts of prey, rather than with man. This evidence of a spiritual-ritual life was clearly expressed in the hunter's quest for assurance of a continued supply of abundant game (the repetition of seasonal cycles of migration) and of his success as a hunter of certain preferred kinds of animals.

As we refer, according to widespread custom, to the divisions of the prehistoric and historic periods as "Ages" (e.g., Upper Paleolithic, Mesolithic, Neolithic, Bronze, and Iron), it should be remembered that these designations signify cultural (technological) stages rather than precise chronological periods. An "Age" was not everywhere contemporaneous, but varied in different parts of the world both in the time of its appearance and its duration. Furthermore, in some areas, certain "Ages" were completely skipped. The cultural evolution from one stage to another was never

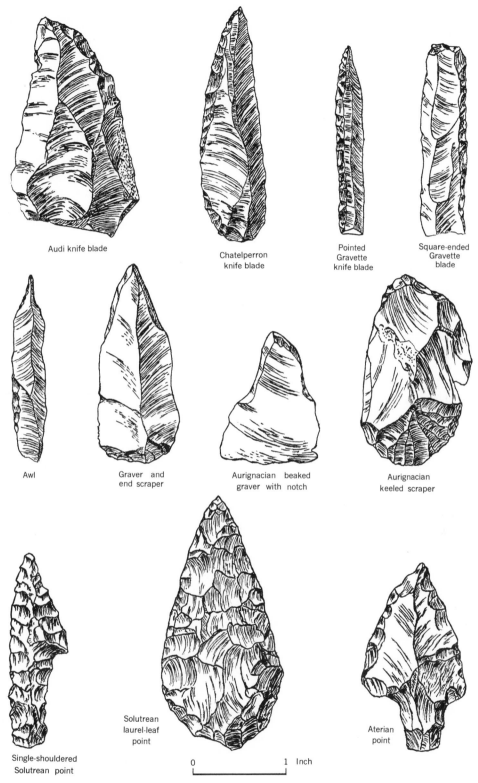

Audi knife blade

Chatelperron
knife blade

Pointed
Gravette
knife blade

Square-ended
Gravette
blade

Awl

Graver and
end scraper

Aurignacian beaked
graver with notch

Aurignacian
keeled scraper

Single-shouldered
Solutrean point

Solutrean
laurel-leaf
point

0   1 Inch

Aterian
point

FIG. 3.8 SPECIALIZED TOOLS OF THE UPPER PALEOLITHIC. From *Prehistory and the Beginnings of Civilization* **by Jacquetta Hawkes and Sir Leonard Woolley (1963): Harper & Row. (After K. P. Oakley,** *Man The Tool-Maker,* **4th edition, London: British Museum (Natural History) 1958.)**

worldwide; each stage represented the acceptance and diffusion of a newly invented technology of tool manufacturing, which occurred at a particular place and diffused outward across the face of the earth. Just as the several stages could not begin simultaneously all over the world, so their endings (the beginning of new stages) were also not simultaneous. It took nearly 3000 years for the Iron Age to spread from the highlands of southwest Asia to North America; the Nuclear Age began here less than 350 years later (less than a century after the introduction of the Steel Age), and spread back to Israel within two decades.

The End of the Ice Age and Its Witnesses

In human prehistory, the customary divide between glacial and postglacial conditions would seem to differ greatly from place to place depending upon the presence and then the absence of ice. Deglaciation, the melting back and wasting away of the great ice sheets, was a process not an event.

The beginning of the last great deglaciation occurred at the instant just after the continental ice sheets reached maximum size, that is, from the very peak of the last major ice advance, about 35,000 years ago. The full postglacial stage was not reached until the end of the deglaciation process, which occurred at different times at different places; the continued rise of sea level made possible marine transgression of continental shelves to a position of near stability resembling the present shoreline about 7000 years ago. Lower courses of streams were flooded to form estuaries and bays, and former smooth coastlines became more irregular. At this time, also, began the formation of present coastal landforms: the erosion of sea cliffs; the building of bars, spits, and beaches; and the filling of lagoons to become salt marshes.

Into this period of the last major deglaciation falls the cultural revolution known as the Mesolithic, a coincidence of great environmental and cultural change. The duration of the Mesolithic, from 35,000 to 11,000 years ago, was not equal to the whole of the deglacial period, but it did encompass a long period of human trial and error in adapting to a new set of conditions for living, hence a great change in culture.

For man's living on the earth, the period of waning ice sheets created considerable changes in the physical-biotic environment, hence changes in human opportunities. The hunting folk disappeared from the more arid parts as they followed the migrating big game. Those who stayed on were gatherer-collectors of less specialized habits, but their habitation sites became fewer and their ranges more restricted as water could be found less readily.

Millions of square miles of land in the higher latitudes were opened for human colonization. The newly created lakes, ponds, and marshes were replenished by aquatic life and migrant waterfowl. Northern woodlands, wet prairies, and marshes became feeding ranges for such big game as muskox, moose, elk, bison, deer, and the hunting peoples followed these animals northward.

The coastal peoples were crowded back by the rise of the sea. But as the shorelines became longer and more diversified, more people could live as strand collectors, distinguishing among the fauna of rocky reefs, gravel beds, sand, and mud flats. The newly formed shallow lagoons and embayments offered a favorable setting for experimentation with rafts and boats.

Valleys filled with alluvium, and river floodplains grew to include natural levees, meander scars, oxbow lakes, and backwater swamps. The various grasses, reeds, lilies, and palms all colonized the marshy parts of the floodplains, as a new world took form, developing the physical-biotic geography of the earth we recently have known.

In Europe, the big-game hunters and masters of stone blade making of the Upper Paleolithic were replaced by new cultural forms from North Africa and southwest Asia. During the waning of its glaciers, Europe underwent the natural process of reforestation, the restocking of the former glacial and near-glacial areas by plants and animals adapted to the increasingly milder climatic conditions. Forests replaced tundras as the focal zones of human habitation, and this is clearly reflected in the component skills and artifacts of Mesolithic culture. The kill of big game became incidental; stonework was less in amount; and heavy projectiles, great knives, and daggers became less useful as Mesolithic men worked more with perishable plant materials.

Characteristic features of the Old World Mesolithic were the following. (1) Most stone artifacts were reduced in size; microliths (very small worked-stone tools) became diagnostic. (2) The bow and arrow became widely used, the arrowhead being a form of microlith. (3) Fishing gear became varied, as fishhooks, sinkers, and floats were introduced, and use of the harpoon became most advanced. (4) Boats came into greater use. (5) Woodworking tools were developed. (6) Grinding slabs appeared. (7) Stone was shaped by deliberate grinding. (8) The dog was domesticated and spread widely. (9) In the late Mesolithic, pottery began to be made.

Man's Slow Deployment over the Continents

Upper Paleolithic blade tools have been found across almost all of the Eurasian landmass. During the Würm glacial stage man was able to range far northward, over all parts of ice-free Europe and Asia, as far east as Lake Baikal in Siberia, and in North China. Regional diversity, in animals hunted, in tools made, in types of shelter, in seasonal changes in ways of life, was greater than at any previous time. Whether settlement was seasonally migratory or semipermanent depended upon the habits of the principal herd animals of particular regions: mammoths occupied the forest-and-loess steppe of eastern Europe year round, whereas the reindeer herds of western Europe shifted northeast in summer and southwest in winter across the tundra at the margin of the continental glacier. There appears to have been no significant change in the size of hunting bands or of their respective territories. What is suggested, however, is that the overall number of bands was greater, and the increased efficiency of Upper Paleolithic man as a specialized food collector had made possible a significant rise in the total human population on the earth.

Upper Paleolithic man possessed the cultural combination of fire, shelter, clothing, containers, and weapons that enabled him to compete with carnivores in following the herd animals anywhere, confident that he could feed himself and his family from the hunted game. The growth in stature of man placed him among the elite as a large land mammal. As any well-stocked modern zoo can testify, there are only about 60 species of mammal of our size or larger. It is not surprising that larger animals require disproportionally more territorial space than smaller animals: for feeding and drinking, for concealment, for breeding and reproduction. Any increase in man's numbers would have increased the territorial pressure on the Old World, either through more intensive use of particular ranges or expansion into new territories.

The way was open, through cultural means, for man as a species to occupy all the landmasses he was able to reach from the Old World. The record indicates that Upper Paleolithic man was the first to invade Australia and the Americas.

The ancestors of the Tasmanians emigrated from southern Asia at the low sea level stage during the Main Würm. Isolated in Australia by rise of sea level, they conservatively preserved the Paleolithic traits that they possessed when crossing from the mainland. They changed little in their habits only because they were shut off from contact with ideas from the rest of the world. The principal weapons and tools of the Tasmanians were of wood: clubs, spears, digging sticks; their stone tools were chiefly used for woodworking: cutting, scraping, and notching steps for climbing.

Pleistocene colonists camped in the mountains of interior east-central Australia around 16,000 B.C. During the last glacial stage, Australia, Tasmania, and New Guinea were a single landmass, and the interior possessed permanent rivers and brimming lakes. Giant herbivorous marsupials still inhabited the land during late Pleistocene times. Massive core tools and flaked quartzite pebbles were elements in a tool kit of Middle Paleolithic style that preceded development of microliths. With these tools, human migrants from tropical Asia discovered new pastures. Their exploration of a new land and their cultural adaptation to life in Australia were achievements of the late Pleistocene.

Ancestors of the Australian Aborigines became isolated from the Asian mainland at a later time than did the Tasmanians. Their culture was more advanced in that they had such products as the dart-thrower, the bark canoe, the boomerang, the bull-roarer, and the shield, all unknown to the Tasmanian.

The suggestion has been made that the Asian invasion of the New World also took place via two different routes at two different times during the last (Würm) glacial stage. The earliest, about 40,000 years ago, was along the Pacific coastal zone out of North China; the later, from central Siberia along the Arctic shores. The significance of the dual movements, in both space and time, is that such would explain the differentiation in cultural traditions, abilities, and artifacts of New World men.

Until very recently, the prevailing assumption was that no American cultures were older than those that contain stone projectile points, and therefore man's arrival in the New World could be no older than 15,000 years. Now, however, recognition has been given to an earlier presence of New World man who was not only preceramic,

Pre-Projectile Point (more than 20,000 years ago)
(Low-Level Technology)

Paleo-Indian (to 10,000 years ago)

Proto-Archaic (to 9,000 years ago)
(Food-Grinding)

FIG. 3.9 EARLY MAN IN THE NEW WORLD: DISTRIBUTION OF HIS TOOLS.

but also preprojectile-point in his traditions (Fig. 3.9). The very general stages for early man in the New World are the following:

1. Preprojectile-point stage (Middle Paleolithic?: as early as 40,000 years ago)
2. Paleo-Indian stage (Upper Paleolithic?: beginning 15,000 years ago)
3. Protoarchaic stage (Mesolithic?: beginning 10,000 years ago)
4. Archaic stage (Neolithic?: beginning 7000 years ago in eastern Mexico)

At the lowest level of stoneworking all objects were made by percussion only. Apparently, man was not yet technologically capable of grinding and polishing stone artifacts into thin, flat projectile points and knives. His products were cores, flake tools, pebble tools, often large and heavy. Splinters of leg bones of large mammals were also used. Shallow hearths have been found, but as yet no human burials in dug graves. Associated animal remains include many late Pleistocene mammals,

which became extinct in the New World, such as horse, camel, giant ground sloth, mammoth, mastodon, and large bison. This Preprojectile-point culture has been the most easily overlooked in American archaeology. The products are least readily recognizable; the sites are small, slight, and infrequent. More search and study needs to be done.

In the Paleo-Indian stage, percussion chipping of stone artifacts became more advanced and better controlled, to produce fluted projectile points and knives, usually of leaf shape. These are most often found at kill sites, where Pleistocene mammals were butchered. True campsites are rarer, except in the eastern United States. Simple forms of chipped-stone and bone artifacts and hearths are present. The dominant economic pattern was that of hunting the late Pleistocene big-game animals.

The Protoarchaic stage is distinguished by the presence of food-grinding implements: milling stones (grinding slabs) and manos, mortars and pestles, shaped by a pecking process. The Pleistocene big game was fast disappearing, and the preparation of collected plant foods became most important in providing sustenance to replace the dwindling meat supply. The new grinding process added much to the resources of primitive kitchens. Whereas plant foods were hitherto limited to things eaten raw, or to starchy roots, stalks, leaves, and fleshy fruits roasted on coals and ashes or baked in pits, it was now possible to use the hard seeds and the small ones, and to leach the bitter ones such as acorns or aroids. The ground meal could be baked into cakes, cooked as gruel, or mixed with other foods. With a greater range of local food resources, more permanent locations, such as caves and rock shelters, were able to be inhabited more intensively. Projectile points continued to be made, in a wide range of styles, mostly unfluted. Other traits that appear are drills or perforates, bone awls, eyed bone needles, shaft smoothers of sandstone, and human burials in dug graves (the first known in North America). Most of the late Pleistocene animals had become extinct, though some survived in a lingering way, such as ground sloth, large bisons on the Great Plains, some mastodons in eastern North America, and some horses at the southern tip of South America.

On the basis of archaeological finds, all three of the preceramic stages were widespread in their extent, reaching to the far tip of South America (see Fig. 3.9). Man migrated into the New World during the Würm (Wisconsin) glacial stage, over 40,000 years ago. Once men had reached the western plains, south of the ice sheet, the occupance of the rest of the Western hemisphere was relatively rapid.

What cannot be assumed is that the entry of man into the New World occurred but once. More reasonable is the assumption that it occurred several or numerous times and that each group that entered from northeastern Asia possessed somewhat different ranges of skills and different tool kits. How else can one explain the relict nature of some New World cultures that possessed only very limited technology? The absence of the dog, for example, among many South American tribes suggests that such people migrated before the dog was domesticated. The Timbira of interior Brazil do not cook by boiling, but only by roasting and baking; they make casual or no use of pots and use gourds for carrying water. Could these be examples of ancient arrivals from the Old World who have remained conservative in pockets of isolation, thus insuring their survival?

The Archaic stage opened the way for a wholly new way of life based upon food production rather than solely food collecting. Shelters were more permanent. The inventory of artifacts was rich; it included chipped, pecked, and polished stone as well as shell and bone. Cemetery areas, the burial of groups rather than isolated individuals, have been uncovered. There is evidence of effective water transport. Most striking was the complete disappearance of late Pleistocene mammals, except for the rare anomaly of the ground sloth isolated in Cuba. A new era for the earth was emerging in that man was beginning to make his presence felt as an effective agent in changing the earth's physical-biotic surface into regional habitats.

During the late Upper Pleistocene, man learned to live successfully in all the world's physical-biotic environments except the true deserts, the high plateaus and mountains, and the oceanic islands. By 15,000 years ago, he not only had reached all the world's continents except Antarctica, but also had spread to their far extremities, such as Tierra del Fuego, clearly establishing a range of subsistence groups, from specialized food-gatherers to specialized food collectors, in a host of local territories. Pleistocene man not only survived, but also learned to thrive, to multiply, and to take possession over the earth. No other single animal species has ever accomplished as widespread a dispersal over the earth as has man. The astounding accomplishment was all but completed before the time when civilization (and history) began. It was no mean achievement for small groups with limited skills and without plan or foreknowledge of final destinations. But, significantly for man's later developments, the whole planet was at last inhabited.

Culture as the New Method of Evolution

Man's greatest prehistoric accomplishments, his dispersal across nearly the whole of the earth, his adaptation to nearly the whole enormous variety of the earth's physical-biotic environments, and his growth in numbers to a population of about five million (an average density of about one person per ten square miles) by 10,000 years ago, resulted from the development of culture. The achievement entailed an immense journey, in both space and time, since the cumulative increase in cultural ability was extraordinarily slow, by any modern measure. Man emerged from being wholly an animal to become forever more than an animal.

Man's capacity to acquire, develop or modify, and transmit culture emerged because of the adaptive advantages that this capacity conferred upon its possessors. The biological and cultural components of human evolution serve the same basic function—adaptation to and control of man's environments. But culture is a vastly more efficient instrument of adaptation than the biological processes because it is more rapid, since culture is wholly acquired from other human beings, and not just from one's parents, during the course of one's lifetime.

Cultural development provides yet another means, beyond the biological method, for adaptation. People achieve adaptation to their environments through learned rather than inborn automatic responses, and most do so successfully. Knowledge enables more individuals to survive by choosing or creating suitable environments for themselves. The development of the human faculty for symbolic and cultural transmission was certainly a radical innovation, transforming the whole of human life so that man lives in a new dimension of reality compared to other life-forms.

The possession of culture, as a social means for transmitting the cumulative experience of a group to the new young members of society, made "all the difference" for human development. Culture served as a buffer that provided a range of choice among possible courses of activity, and this ability gave man an adaptive advantage greater than that possessed by any other life-forms. The unique capability of man was that cultural traditions, when learned, opened further possibilities for unlimited growth.

Culture is transmitted not only between generations within a society, but also across societal lines and among adults. Cultural evolution is dependent on transmissible inventions, instead of, as in other biological forms, on changes in the composition of the gene pool of a breeding population. A man may leave no biological offspring and yet be a significant contributor to cultural evolution by changing the ability of all future men to reorganize modes of human life or draw energy from the environment.

How does an individual participate as an active force in cultural evolution? A "genius" with an idea capable of altering the course of history operates through a "cluster," an initially small group of individuals, to whom he has been able to communicate ideas and without whose aid the "genius" may be unfruitful. The "genius" may represent a synthesis in which larger numbers of persons achieve cohesion or in which individuals experience a greater freedom of creative development. Initially at least, the "genius" who symbolizes a different kind of social or cultural integration may be made to suffer for his deviation from established behavior and organizational standards. The badge of suffering, of course, is no proof of the rightness of his cause. But if the faith that he and his cluster offer becomes infectious, then it serves as a turning point in history.

Human evolution, as a natural process, has two components—biological and cultural, which are interrelated and interdependent. Man is the result of the interaction of biological and cultural processes. But, in producing culture, biological evolution transcended itself. The capacity to learn a symbolic language and a variety of cultural forms was added to other characteristics of the species *Homo*, which made possible his educability and his ability to profit by experience and adjust his behavior to the requirements and expectations of his surroundings.

Culture is a new emergent in the biology of man, but is transmitted socially. Cultural evolution has become adaptively the most potent extension of biological evolution, because it permits an increasing adaptation of genes to multiple environments. But the evolution of culture has not suspended and superseded biological evolution. Cultural evolution and biological evolution are not alternatives, but are superimposed upon each other. Culture is part of the evolution of man, and through this new means of evolution man became able to evolve more rapidly than any other species.

A Sense of Interrelationships in Human Living

At the conclusion of Part Two of this book, which has dealt so specifically with Pleistocene man and the close connections he formed with the earth that sustained him and made possible his evolution, it seems appropriate to return to one of the concerns set forth in the Introductory to this book. We wish here to expand the concept of "Cultural" in geography, to examine it in a more sophisticated manner, and to present a more meaningful theoretical base for the discussions that follow.

One aspect of cultural geography is the study of the interrelations between a particular culture and its physical-biotic environment. The word culture, of course, implies that the particular organism for our study not only is man but men in a group, a human population, possessing a self-recognized and distinctive way of life that includes particular forms of social organization and a particular level of technology. Such a study can only be complex, since it must deal with *four* concepts that are points of reference but functionally interdependent, and *six* interrelationships among them (Fig. 3.10). Perhaps other scholars would arrange these items in somewhat different sequences, or would number concepts and rela-

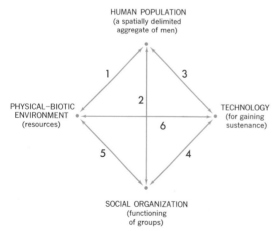

FIG. 3.10 FUNCTIONAL CONCEPTS AND INTERRELATIONS IN CULTURAL GEOGRAPHY.

tionships differently, but we choose to state the concepts and relationships in the following manner. The *four* concepts are:

1. **Population:** a human population group occupying a territory that is spatially defined.
2. **Physical-biotic environment:** the processes and phenomena of a physical and biotic character which, although neutral to population survival, offer resources potentially useful for the maintenance of life.
3. **Social organization:** the way in which the population is integrated and functions; the interdependence of units (families, kin groups, associations) in a more or less elaborated division of labor. This is an aspect of culture, since individuals are unequipped to survive in isolation.
4. **Technology:** the set of techniques (abilities, ideas, tools) employed by the population to gain sustenance from its environment. This also is an aspect of culture, yet a dependent variable.

The *six* interrelationships are:

1. *Population ⟷ Environment.* Not only does a physical-biotic environment (climate, landforms, drainage, and water supplies, earth materials, soils, wild vegetation, wild animal life) provide a range of limits for a population, but a population reacts upon an environment. On the one hand, population size is limited by certain factors of its resource base, that is, the limitations imposed by the content of the space occupied. The size of a population, in turn, affects the quantity of resources to be extracted or converted: the higher the resource-population ratio (R/P) the more complex the culture may become; the lower the ratio the poorer are the cultural opportunities. This interrelationship of population and environment is not static; it changes as the size of the population changes, or whenever a new resource is discovered or a greater or less intensive use is made of the environment.
2. *Population ⟷ Social organization.* The interrelationship between the size and distribution of a population and the organization of the society is fundamental. The larger the population size, the more varied (more complex) will be the ways of social control and means of accomplishing the desired goals. A cluster of 100 people cannot possibly form an urban society, nor require an elaborate formal structure of government. On the other hand, more elaborate social organizations are indispensable to the maintenance of collective life by man. They tend to be functionally persistent (that is, to maintain themselves) and make possible an increase in numbers of their populations, since organizations enhance probabilities of survival for most of their individual members.
3. *Population ⟷ Technology.* A population provides the manpower for creating, maintaining, and operating a technology. The larger the population, the more likely that the technology will be more complex; that is, the application of labor will be increasingly specialized, more widespread, or both. The level of technology (skills, ideas, tools) of the population relates to the number that can be supported, because technology is used by people to find, extract, and convert resource materials and to adjust and intensify their spatial qualities. Of course, there are some very large populations in some large regions (e.g., the Ganges Plain), which have lower technologies than do some smaller populations in particular environments (e.g., Switzerland).
4. *Organization ⟷ Technology.* Social organization adapts to the repertory and techniques at the command of the population. For example, large numbers of people can form remarkably cohesive units with a great number of subsidiary specialized social forms, provided that they are literate, possess sophisticated technologies for nearly instantaneous verbal or pictorial communication and rapid means of transportation, or both. The level of technology, on the other hand, depends upon the degree to which the population, through its social organization, has appreciated and accepted innovation, and absorbed new ideas from others, either by cultural diffusion (borrowing) or by migration. For example, an organization of weavers presupposes a technology that includes looms; an improvement in loom making and usage is most likely to come from an organized need for and acceptance of such an innovation on the part of skilled and experienced weavers.
5. *Environment ⟷ Organization.* It is unavoidable that individuals must cope with the specific environmental conditions in which they find themselves. A sense of tribalism, based upon similarity in language and custom and on social collaboration, cannot develop among local groups, such as bands of specialized food collectors, if each group is environmentally isolated. Tribal social structures without central authority can effectively occupy only a limited space, hence have claim to very limited, almost exclusively local, resources. Organizations of craftsmen and tradesmen and clerks can develop only where the environment affords a food surplus, on the basis of which manufacturing, trade, and regulation (taxation, tribute, marketing) can develop as complex functions. Once developed, such complex organizations through their specialized activities (granaries, distribution facilities) can offset the effects of such environmental local calamities as killing frosts, floods, or destructive insects.
6. *Environment ⟷ Technology.* Early (pre-*sapiens*) man had to depend completely upon what the local environment had to offer by way of water and food

supply, and did not occupy the tropical rain forests, deserts, cool steppes, boreal forests, and tundra. The use of fire and of hides and furs as clothing together made possible man's occupation of subarctic climates. A technology of stone tools specialized for meat cutting and skin scraping was an adaptation to an environment that included a quantity of large game animals. A technology based upon boneworking was developed in a tundra environment that lacked wood. In other words, a technology is not just a random assemblage of artifacts, but a set of techniques invented and diffused, using material available in the environment of a group.

On the other hand, a technology enables a people not only to occupy an environment and exploit its resources, but also to modify that environment in the process. That is, cultural changes are added to the normal processes of geologic and organic change. For food, fuel, fiber, a population (an effective organization employing its technology, whether directly or indirectly through other animal species or inanimate energy) deforms a pristine landscape and tends to create a human habitat. With every change of technology, a new evaluation is possible of what constitutes a resource. The resource-technology interrelationship is not a "static equilibrium" but a continuing dynamic process, based on changing perception of worth, ever since man first used fire for clearing vegetation to improve his hunting grounds.

Some studies of the interrelations between a particular culture and its physical-biotic environment assume a short time span, in order to deal with the four referential concepts as constants and focus upon one or more of the six interrelationships. Such studies are wholly functional in outlook, seeking answers to the question, How does it operate? These studies are called "Cultural Ecology."

Other studies of the interrelations between a particular culture and its physical-biotic environment recognize that some or all of the referential concepts are in the process of evolving and that adding a longer-term time dimension to the system (see Fig. 3.10) is a closer approach to reality, albeit creating more complexities for understanding. These studies, utilizing the genetic approach, have variously been termed "Historical Cultural Geography," or simply "Historical Geography." We suggest that a more appropriate term is Evolutionary Cultural Geography.

SELECTED REFERENCES

Baker, Herbert G.
    1965   *Plants and Civilization.* Belmont, Calif.: Wadsworth Publishing Co. 183 pp.
Baldwin, Gordon C.
    1964   *Stone Age Peoples Today.* New York: Norton. 183 pp.
Bishop, Walter W. and J. Desmond Clark (eds.)
    1967   *Background to Evolution in Africa.* Chicago: University of Chicago Press. 935 pp.
Brace, C. L.
    1967   *The Stages of Human Evolution.* Englewood Cliffs, N.J.: Prentice-Hall. 116 pp.
Brace, C. L., and M. F. Ashley Montagu
    1965   *Man's Evolution, an Introduction to Physical Anthropology.* New York: Macmillan. 352 pp.
Braidwood, Robert J.
    1967   *Prehistoric Men* (7th ed.). Glenview, Ill.: Scott, Foresman and Company. 192 pp.
Braidwood, Robert J., and Gordon R. Willey (eds.)
    1962   *Courses toward Urban Life: Archeological Consideration of Some Cultural Alternates.* (Viking Fund Publications in Anthropology, No. 32). New York: Wenner-Gren Foundation for Anthropological Research. 371 pp.
Buettner-Janusch, John
    1966   *Origins of Man: Physical Anthropology.* New York: Wiley. 674 pp.

Burkitt, Miles Crawford
    1963   *The Old Stone Age; A Study of Paleolithic Times* (4th ed.). New York: Atheneum. 270 pp.

Butzer, Karl W.
    1964   *Environment and Archeology: An Introduction to Pleistocene Geography.* Chicago: Aldine. 524 pp.

Clark, J. Desmond and Eve Kemnitzer
    1967   *Atlas of African Prehistory.* Chicago: University of Chicago Press. 12 maps, 32 overlays, 62 text pp.

Clark, John Grahame Douglas
    1952   *Prehistoric Europe; The Economic Basis.* New York: Philosophical Library. 349 pp.
    1960   *Archeology and Society; Reconstructing the Prehistoric Past* (3rd ed.). London: Methuen; New York: Barnes & Noble. 272 pp.
    1961   *World Prehistory, An Outline.* Cambridge, England: University Press. 284 pp.

Clark, Grahame, and Stuart Piggott
    1965   *Prehistoric Societies.* New York: Knopf. 356 pp.

Clark, W. E. Le Gros
    1964   *The Fossil Evidence for Human Evolution* (2nd ed.). Chicago: University of Chicago Press. 200 pp.

Current Anthropology
    1965   "The Origin of Man" (a symposium of 12 articles with comments by 20 scholars), *Current Anthropology*, Vol. 6, No. 4, October, pp. 342–431.

Daniel, Glyn E.
    1963   *The Idea of Prehistory.* Cleveland, Ohio: World Publishing. 220 pp.

DeVore, Paul L. (ed.)
    1965   *The Origin of Man* (Transcript of a Symposium, University of Chicago, April 2–4, 1965). New York: Wenner-Gren Foundation for Anthropological Research. 152 pp.

Dobzhansky, T. G.
    1962   *Mankind Evolving: The Evolution of the Human Species.* New Haven, Conn.: Yale University Press. 381 pp.

Dubois, René J.
    1965   *Man Adapting.* New Haven, Conn.: Yale University Press. 527 pp.

Ehrich, Robert W. (ed.)
    1965   *Chronologies in Old World Archaeology.* Chicago: University of Chicago Press. 557 pp.

Garn, Stanley M. (ed.)
    1964   *Culture and the Direction of Human Evolution.* Detroit, Mich.: Wayne State University Press. 98 pp.

Hawkes, Jacquetta
    1962   "Part One: Prehistory—Section One: The Paleolithic and Mesolithic," pp. 3–218 in *Prehistory and the Beginnings of Civilization* (UNESCO History of Mankind, Cultural and Scientific Development, Vol. 1). New York: Harper & Row. 873 pp.

Howell, F. Clark, and François Bourliere (eds.)
    1963   *African Ecology and Human Evolution* (Viking Fund Publications in Anthropology, No. 36). New York: Wenner-Gren Foundation for Anthropological Research. 666 pp.

Howell, F. Clark, and The Editors of *Life*
    1965   *Early Man* (Life Nature Library). New York: Time, Inc. 200 pp.

Howells, William
    1963   *Back of History, The Story of Our Own Origins* (rev. ed., The Natural History Library, No. 34). Garden City, N.Y.: Doubleday. 384 pp.

Hulse, Frederick S.
    1963   *The Human Species, An Introduction to Physical Anthropology.* New York: Random House. 504 pp.

Hutchinson, G. Evelyn
    1965   *The Ecological Theater and the Evolutionary Play.* New Haven, Conn.: Yale University Press. 139 pp.

James, Edwin Oliver
1957 *Prehistoric Religion; A Study in Prehistoric Archaeology.* New York: Praeger. 300 pp.

Jennings, Jesse D., and Edward Norbeck (eds.)
1964 *Prehistoric Man in the New World.* Chicago: University of Chicago Press. 633 pp.

Kraus, Bertram S.
1964 *The Basis of Human Evolution.* New York: Harper. 384 pp.

Lasker, Gabriel Ward
1961 *The Evolution of Man, A Brief Introduction to Physical Anthropology.* New York: Holt. 239 pp.

Lorenz, Konrad
1965 *Evolution and Modification of Behavior.* Chicago: University of Chicago Press. 121 pp.

Low, A. M.
1941 *Romance of Fire.* London: The Book Club. 239 pp.

Mather, Kenneth
1964 *Human Diversity; The Nature and Significance of Differences Among Men.* New York: Free Press. 126 pp.

Mayr, Ernst
1963 *Animal Species and Evolution.* Cambridge, Mass.: Belknap Press of Harvard University Press. 797 pp.

Montagu, M. F. Ashley (ed.)
1964 *The Concept of Race.* New York: Free Press of Glencoe. 270 pp.

Munn, Norman Leslie
1965 *The Evolution and Growth of Human Behavior* (2nd ed.). Boston: Houghton Mifflin. 594 pp.

Nougier, Louis René
1959 *Géographie humaine préhistorique.* Paris: Gallimard. 325 pp.

Oakley, Kenneth P.
1964 *Frameworks for Dating Fossil Man.* Chicago: Aldine. 355 pp.

Raphael, Max
1945 *Prehistoric Cave Paintings* (The Bollinger Series, IV). Translated by Norbert Guterman. New York: Pantheon Books. 100 pp.

Sayce, Roderick Urwick
1963 *Primitive Arts and Crafts; An Introduction to the Study of Material Culture.* New York: Biblo and Tanner. 291 pp.

Semenov, S. A.
1964 *Prehistoric Technology; An Experimental Study of the Oldest Tools and Artefacts from Traces of Manufacture and Wear.* New York: Barnes & Noble. 211 pp.

Simpson, George G.
1964 *This View of Life: The World of an Evolutionist.* New York: Harcourt Brace & World. 308 pp.
1965 *The Geography of Evolution; Collected Essays.* Philadelphia: Chilton Books. 249 pp.

Sonneborn, T. M. (ed.)
1965 *The Control of Human Heredity and Evolution.* New York: Macmillan. 127 pp.

Washburn, Sherwood L. (ed.)
1961 *Social Life of Early Man* (Viking Fund Publications in Anthropology, No. 31). New York: Wenner-Gren Foundation for Anthropological Research. 299 pp.
1963 *Classification and Human Evolution* (Viking Fund Publications in Anthropology, No. 37). New York: Wenner-Gren Foundation for Anthropological Research. 384 pp.

SETTLEMENTS

GRANT HEILMAN

Dispersed Settlement, Iowa, U.S.

MARC AND EVELYNE BERNHEIM, RAPHO GUILLUMETTE

116

Dispersed Settlement, Kenya, East Africa

Zulu Hamlet, South Africa

GRETE MANNHEIM, D.P.I.

J. E. SPENCER

Village, China

Town and Dispersed Settlement, Kansas, U.S.

GRANT HEILMAN

Scattered Villages, Madagascar

FREDERICK AYER, PHOTO RESEARCHERS

118

APSA, PERUVIAN AIRLINES

119

Town, Machu Picchu, Peru

Village, Sudan, Africa

MARC AND EVELYN BERNHEIM, RAPHO GUILLUMETTE

ALASKA PICTORIAL, MONKMEYER

SAUDI ARABIAN PUBLIC RELATIONS BUREAU
P.F.I.

(Left top) Logging Camp, Alaska

(Left middle) Date Palm Oasis, Hofuf, Saudi Arabia

(Left bottom) Montmartre, Paris, France

P.F.I.

Grand Canal, Venice, Italy

Rockport, Massachusetts, U.S.

LAWRENCE LOWRY

Phoenix, Arizona, U.S.

AMERICAN AIRLINES

122

Canberra, A.C.T., Australia

AUSTRALIAN NEWS & INFORMATION BUREAU

Levittown, Long Island, New York, U.S.

LITTON INDUSTRIES, AERO SERVICE

Melbourne, Victoria, Australia

AUSTRALIAN NEWS & INFORMATION BUREAU

CANADIAN INFORMATION OFFICE

Vancouver, British Columbia, Canada

New York region, United States

PORT OF NEW YORK AUTHORITY

PART *THREE*

Cultural Divergence
Followed by Cultural Convergence

During the early eras as man spread over the world, groups of people began dropping out of each traveling company to settle down in particular regions which they came to like and consider as their home territories. Curious and restless groups splintered off, creating new settler groups and, in unplanned pulsating movements, kept on until man's occupance of the earth became complete. Inevitably, under primitive conditions, these groups became separated from one another in almost all respects, and among each group there arose a traditional account of how the world began and how its ancestors were the first men on earth. The human outlook of each society was a local one, which viewed the country beyond the horizon as the far country, the country of unknown conditions, of immense dangers, of strange creatures, and of ways unbefitting "our people."

In this early development men often sought the guidance of Nature, learned by trial and error of the environmental boundaries to home territories, and fitted their lives to the living conditions of their particular region. This is the regional differentiation of human culture that characterized early human history. Sometimes, changing physical factors altered living conditions to the extent that a people no longer were able to cope with their environment and felt compelled to migrate into a nearby region. Struggle for control of the new territory often resulted, with a weaker society forced out, required to seek and perhaps fight for another home. Sometimes, with a good environment, a society prospered, its numbers increasing to the point where some members felt the need for more space. Expansion into a nearby region often brought the same result, a fight for new territory. Occasionally, a group migrating into not fully occupied country could settle peacefully with almost no contact with other peoples. Human history is replete with variations on this theme, but they all have one common thread, the attempted or successful identification of a culture group with a regional environment.

Within each regional environment there evolved an individual system of living, built around local conditions of life. Utilizing landforms, plants, animals, waters, minerals, and such other resources as the society perceived or learned to use, each society fashioned its own way of life, and all aspects of its culture bore the imprint of that fashioning, from beliefs and ways of thinking through language to diet, housing, and "land use". Each society also reflected its own particular reactions to and interpretations of its environment, indicating the intrinsic variability within the human species. Most of these regional environments, in a world of primitive culture, were self-contained, almost isolated from each other by factors of time and space. Thus the earth became differentiated into thousands of local regions, each with its own way of life and each with its own local culture. To the degree that physical separation was present, life within short distances could be very unlike, and patterns of culture could be built that differed extremely, one from another.

Territories within and on the margins of large environmental regions, where factors of separation were not prominent, were less conducive to strong human differentiation. Here the patterns of variation in human culture were transitional, most often in small details only. Within such regions interregional and intercultural contacts were greater than elsewhere. Great areas of plains, seacoasts inviting lateral movement, great piedmonts, and great river valleys constitute such transitional regions, as do archipelagos and chains of islands. Intermittently, throughout human history man moved steadily along these major lineaments of the great physical regions, often creating traditional routeways of migration and cultural contact. Such routeways are scattered over the earth, in large or smaller aspect, forming zones of linkage between groups of smaller regions, but they have not been continuously open, since strong groups of peoples could sometimes dominate them and prevent active contacts for long periods. Where too much open ocean formed the zone of separation, human contact was lessened, but man has always been able to go everywhere, and no part of the earth remained untouched by early human occupance, except possibly Antarctica and some very remote oceanic islands.

Early human culture produced no means of tying the whole earth together into a single operating region, despite human ability to go everywhere, so that early human history is a story of the differentiation of peoples, of cultures, and of regions within which people lived. The processes of differentiation remained dominant throughout the early Historic Era, as they had during the Paleolithic, Mesolithic, and Neolithic eras. The creation of the great empires, such as the Persian, the Chinese, the Indian, the Roman, the Aztecan and the Incan, began the process of reducing small regional cultures into gross regional combines, and started linking the earth together. But these very efforts were, for the most part, discontinuous in time and separated in space, so that they could not fundamentally alter the patterns of regionalism and regional cultures for the world as a whole.

The fundamental breakthrough in world linkage came only in modern time and fell to the peoples of Europe to initiate. The Geographical Explorations, which began in a limited way from northwest Europe in the twelfth century, expanded their thrust in succeeding centuries to reach primary completion by the end of the sixteenth century, ultimately linking the whole earth of the twentieth century into a single zone of contact. This breakthrough commenced with land travel and ended with sea travel that bridged the open oceans. Although the breakthrough initiated a revolution in systems of human contact that even now has not been completely consummated, the isolation of the separate regions of the earth has been irrevocably shattered. Never again can the earth operate in total regional seclusion.

Once the basic elements of worldwide contact had been established by the Geographical Explorations, the peoples of the earth very busily altered Nature's recent patterns of botanical and biological distributions and Man's early cultural distributions. Plant monopolies, as regional possessions, were broken by the wholesale transfer of both decorative and utilitarian plants between continents and between hemispheres. Animals were moved around the world for many different reasons. Resource exploitation developed in far areas, both to enrich distant homelands and to facilitate local development, and the redistribution of earth resources became a passion with European traders. Human migration took on totally new proportions after new means of transport became possible, and millions of people (and their descendants) have been trying out new regional environments that appeared to offer better ways of living. The cultural forces unleashed by the linkage of the whole earth, through the means of giving man mobility and moving tonnages of commodities, have made tremendous changes in our earth, both peacefully and through militant procedures, but it seems certain that the process by no means has run its course. The very continuance of the struggle for individuality on the part of small and large cultural groups is evidence of the strength of the process of cultural convergence that may (or may not) turn the earth into one uniform cultural realm in which life is almost alike everywhere around the globe.

This portion of the book covers the twofold process of: (1) differentiation of the earth into separate regions followed, by the (2) convergence of the gross patterns of culture toward a system of cultures in which the common denominator elements steadily increase. Differentiation is the primary theme of the first two chapters, and convergence the primary theme of the third and fourth chapters of this section. Each theme will be dealt with systematically. The coverage is intentionally worldwide and generalized, for discussion of the details of regional cultures in particular geographical zones cannot be included in a volume of moderate size.

CHAPTER *4*

Differential Cultural Development: The Growth of Regionally Separated Human Cultures

A primary characteristic of man is his insistence on changing things as they occur in nature. The things that human beings learn to do form the substance of culture. A method for handling a single concept or artifact is termed a culture trait; a complicated activity involves a number of culture traits grouped into a culture complex. Habitual ways of doing things among even a small group possessing a simple culture involve hundreds of culture traits organized into dozens of culture complexes, and the total integral system of traits and complexes forms a culture. Modern American daily living in the course of a year involves thousands of culture traits arranged into hundreds of culture complexes, the whole of which constitutes what we term the American Way of Life. Another primary characteristic of man is his proneness to do things differently from other people when he can. The American Way of Life includes a large number of subcultures in which particular ways of doing some things are adhered to by those who prefer not to follow the course of the majority.

When we view the beginning of man and the initial development of culture, we cannot make many comparisons between different assemblages of subcultures, between culture complexes, and between culture traits. We cannot assume a single small Garden of Eden, in which it all began, nor can we assume that man, everywhere, was totally creative of such culture as he needed in the face of his necessities. That the Paleolithic Age was nearly two million years long, during which time man advanced only partially toward the state of

civilization, is ample proof of the inaccuracy of the old adage "Necessity is the Mother of Invention"; man remained quite needy at the end of the Paleolithic. We cannot settle, once and for all, the issue of who created culture and where did it take place. The examination of the evidence through archaeological research indicates clearly that Paleolithic man lived almost everywhere, had certain broad attributes in common, and possessed certain basic culture traits and complexes. Archaeological evidence does suggest differences in living patterns in separate parts of the world, clearly hinting that culture was not uniform everywhere, although the ranges within which variation occurred were not very broad.

There are two general concepts that we must take into account in the gradual development of regional world cultures during early human occupation of the earth. The first is independent invention, and the second is the process of diffusion. Historically, modern anthropology first held strongly to the concept of unilinear evolutionary development of culture. Such a view necessarily included the concept of independent invention of every needful item as each group evolved through stages from savagery to civilization. The evolutionary concept, in its early limited form, was replaced by the diffusionist concept, which advocated that each culture trait was formulated but once and then copied by all other peoples exhibiting it; the process of borrowing, copying, or taking over from another is the essence of diffusion. Currently, most students of culture believe that some mixture of the two processes, invention and diffusion, is responsible for human culture in any particular regional or group form, although there is considerable spread of opinion on the relative significance of the two processes to any culture. A sector of contemporary geographic theory actively pursues studies in diffusion theory, the propagation of innovation waves, and the development of network geometry as reliably explaining many aspects of the historical spread of human occupance over the earth. Certainly such studies have merit in parts of the earth in which reliable data may be found pertaining to subject issues. There has been less work done on problems of spatial dimensions and time frequencies of inventiveness, and no clear body of theory has yet developed around this side of the discussion. It may well be that when both sides of the whole problem of culture development have been explored, geographers can significantly contribute to a solution of the relative importance of independent invention as against the significance of diffusion. Certainly there are fascinating problems in both aspects of historical growth of culture on the earth. Lacking adequate data for an effective worldwide treatment of the issues, we do not indulge in the luxury of a few illustrative models of particular cases for the very early section of human history, although parts of our discussion in this chapter tend toward the conjectural.

Viewing the length of the Paleolithic Age, however, suggests quite clearly that the development of culture started slowly, that it grew by very small accretions, and that the numbers of new developments were very small in any one region or during any single time interval. Comparatively, the Neolithic was an era of increase in fundamental advances, whereas the rate of change has increased with fantastic rapidity in the millennium ending with the twentieth century. All reconstructions of the life of early Paleolithic man conclude that he made only slight additions to culture in any one place during any one time interval, but that in many different specific ecological environments he was acquiring rudiments of knowledge about earthly conditions and human practices. This meager knowledge promoted only a slow increase in his numbers but gave ability to survive in a primordial series of environments. To a degree at least this basic knowledge was shared by all of earliest man. The regional patterns of knowledge began to vary only as he learned particular things about particular regional environments, began to

make particular discoveries, and completed a few elementary inventions or subinventions suitable to the particular surroundings.

Magic, Religion, and Culture Systems

Earliest man could not have intelligently argued the issues implicit in the modern discussion of Science versus Religion. Neither could he have debated the view that too much religion in a society becomes an opiate. He certainly knew that he did not understand all the happenings of Nature and that some of these occurrences disturbed him terribly. In this lack of comprehension, fear of the unknown, and quest for assurance lie the human origins of all religious beliefs, practices, and activities and all formulations of religious systems as such. The attribution of power in this sense to both physical objects and natural phenomena, and belief in spiritual beings and things of another world, in magic, ritual, mysticism, and formal ceremonialism, form a complex continuum designed to deal with the supernatural. They also develop an account of the relationship between man and his world, provide a concept of, and explanation for, the universe, and establish mechanisms for assuaging forces that lie outside the control of man both as an individual and in groups. The forms, practices, and creeds developed by man in this broad range of situations vary from the simplest animistic beliefs and practices to the most complex theological and philosophical constructs. Animism describes the beliefs (that good spirits and demons inhabit natural objects) normally held by early (and a few contemporary) simple societies; the organized religions are constructs of sophisticated and civilized man during historic time; and the recent development of secularism expresses the thought of the World of Science that everything can be rationally understood and explained without recourse to mystical appeasement of the supernatural.

Regardless of the specific design of the religious system, the gregariousness of man reinforces the felt need for a faith and produces a social grouping of mankind into units larger than the natural family. This social grouping by religious systems is one of the basic structural patterns of human life on earth that continues in force. Religious social grouping becomes a regional phenomenon; the basic attitudes involved become strong elements in the formation of culture systems; thus religious patterns become dominant elements in the differentiation of cultures all over the earth. The very denial of religion by Communist doctrine yields a culture system with territorial bounds as significant as the affirmation of a particular religion within a regional territory. In early eras of mutually separable cultures, there was often little intermixing of peoples and culture systems. Today, of course, with the intricate interlinkage of all parts of the earth, the movement of people about the earth, and the diffusion of conceptual schemes, it is often difficult to visualize the cultural bonding in religious beliefs. However, this is a recent development quite atypical of most of the earth during human occupance. Our concern here is for the formative role of religion in the development of culture in early time.

Among all human groups there have been those persons best able or most interested in interpreting supernatural phenomena for the rest of the group. The shaman, the soothsayer, the fortuneteller, the priest, the minister, the evangelist, the lay preacher, and the religious reformer, all belong to the cult, fraternity, or order that specializes in establishing contact with the supernatural. These agents practice the arts of appeasement and interpretation, developing and maintaining the beliefs and rituals or the ceremonies and creeds by which the group may receive comfort, understanding, and interpretation. In all societies, these individuals normally have been the formulators, the documenters, and the interpreters of the belief proper to the group in question. Initially their function was formulation, whereas later it became preservation and maintenance of the proper beliefs and doctrines. As such, they oversee the social formulation of culture systems and serve as bulwarks of precedent against untoward change.

Although the initial demand for a system of dealing with the supernatural might seem to have specific limits, every such system developed influences extending throughout the culture, for who could be certain as to what human act, or what failure in human action, annoyed the gods? The development of the religious system, therefore, extended not only to interpretation of supernatural phenomena, but also to the regulation of the daily life of all members of a group, toward the end that the group lived in some conceived and orderly behavioral system designed and governed by the most active minds of the group. In these terms religious forces became highly significant in the shaping of early culture systems; the role of reli-

gions in culture systems remains strong today throughout most of the world of man.

Territoriality, Space Relations, and the Regional World

The concepts of home, neighborhood, and far country were discussed in Chapter 1. This feeling of an individual for a home territory is related to the broader concept of biologic territoriality, something now understood to be widely distributed throughout the vertebrate world of animals and birds. It would appear that man inherited a sense of territoriality from his animal background which did not disappear in his biologic evolution from primordial man. Territoriality among birds and animals takes many forms and variations and, in man, its development shows varying degrees of completeness both in space and through time. Territoriality in some form is one of the strongest expressions of human personality, and one to which man has applied all sorts of embellishments in the creation of his patterns of culture.

In earliest man, the sense of territoriality probably took a form somewhat related to that of many animals. A unit area was marked out as a private preserve for purposes of food acquisition, as the home range of the young, and with perimeters within which defense of the territory was carried out. The gregariousness of man, and the tendency to social grouping, probably made the basic territorial unit one occupied by a population of convenient size. As for other animal forms, the area within the territorial unit probably depended rather directly on the ecologic productivity of the general region. The near-animal status of earliest man undoubtedly established a direct ecological relationship between the territory and the population, and thus one can say that earliest man was quite directly dependent on his environment.

The first human increments to culture could have had one of several results, although, at this distance in time, it is impossible to determine their precise nature. These possible results can be suggested:

1. Concentrating an interest in particular parts of the territorial range, recognizing some parts as more valuable than others.
2. Increasing the range of man's mobility as a food acquirer, thus extending the area of the territorial unit.
3. Increasing the efficiency of food acquisition, thus contracting the area of the territorial unit.

4. Increasing the ease of defense of the perimeters, thus solidifying a group's hold on the territorial unit.
5. Increasing the population that could subsist on the territorial unit, thus reinforcing its occupancy of the territory, creating pressure for expanding that territory, or both.

Regardless of which result came first, any increment in culture could well have altered the definition of what constitutes a group's unit of territoriality. All later increments could have had some impact upon the concept of the territorial unit.

We must recognize that environmental change took place, during the Pleistocene, as man was first refining notions of human territoriality. Shifts in glacial activity, in climatic aridity, in vegetative cover, in animal populations, in form of the littorals, and in surface-water supplies would not have allowed him to develop fixed ideas of territoriality, or attitudes toward geographic space or lowlands or uplands such as characterize many of the bird and animal forms. Regardless of the relationships of primordial man to whatever environments may have been his first home region, man developed the ability to adjust his concepts to many kinds of environments in many sizes, areas, shapes, and schemes of conformality. In part this can be ascribed to biologic evolution of the human species, but increasingly it must be ascribed to increments of culture. If man became biologically adaptable to varied physical environments, the development of rudiments of culture began to lessen man's direct ecological dependence upon his environment.

Whatever early man's intrinsic ability to live in different kinds of environments, the habits of territoriality remained with him. Having divided up earth space to begin with, in a sort of biologic instinct for territoriality man has been redefining his concept of territoriality with every significant change in culture. This has meant a continued shift in patterns of human regionalism throughout human history.

The human attitudes toward space in general have both varied and changed. Some groups of humans came to prefer large amounts of geographic space per unit of population, whereas others seemingly have preferred smaller units and a greater degree of social contact. In the same way there has developed a wide range of attitude toward landscape in general; some peoples have sought the littorals, whereas others have sought the high mountains, the open plains, or the deep forests of lowlands.

We cannot be certain, at any time with any people considered a living group, how old is its preference for a particular kind of geographic space; we can only say, for a short span of human time, that certain groups have lived for specific periods in particular environments. Many human groups within historic time have had to occupy space that might be termed second, third, or fourth choice, since they have been deprived of territorial and spatial occupance of a more preferred choice.

It is clear that as man has occupied the earth, he has lived under many different conditions in many different kinds of environments. When human groups could do so, they have often chosen particular types of territoriality, particular kinds of landscapes, and have displayed particular attitudes toward the habitable world. In the long run of human history, human groups separated themselves into an enormous number of distinct living groups on the several bases comprising the criteria for the occupance of the habitable world. That these territories in early time were often discrete units isolated from other territorial units was a factor in developing divergent trends in human patterns of culture. With each different kind of occupied environment there was a different kind of life to be led.

Housing and Settlement

The smallest of functioning human groups is the natural or nuclear family, although quite probably the "loner" and the hermit have always been with us. It is unlikely that human occupance of the earth began through the dispersal of units consisting only of nuclear families; much more likely the band formed the first living group. The band can also be viewed as an economic working unit, in terms of food acquisition, movement, defense, and reproduction, a group of individuals ranging from a dozen to perhaps a hundred. As basic social groups the bands of early human beings developed rules of association, mate choice, sharing of food supplies, patterns of inheritance, and social status. We are concerned here not with the development of kinship or genealogical systems (how members of a band are related), but with the band as a settlement unit. Once man learned the rudiments of building shelters, the band campsite became a settlement unit perhaps most closely corresponding to the unit now termed a hamlet, a small collection of several to a dozen or more shelter units with cooking fires.

There is allusion, in the phrase "caveman era," to the cave as the first human habitation. The thought is poetic but unreal, for man never restricted himself only to territories possessing caves located at convenient intervals; most of the earliest settlement sites were in the open. Man certainly used caves when they were handy, and such caves have provided us with some of the best-preserved archaeologic records and art forms. But, having to spend nights and winters in the open, early man developed shelter building as one of his early cultural skills; even the apes build sleeping shelters for themselves, and man has similar need for protection from the weather and predators.

There is no way of fully knowing what the earliest human shelters were like, for they undoubtedly were built of perishable materials, subject to collapse and rapid decay (see Fig. 4.1 and pp. 231–248). The earliest evidence of housing suggests oval-to-near-rectangular shallow pits dug into the ground, entered by a ramp at one end and, presumably roofed with some kind of perishable organic materials. These pits range in size from 4 by 6 feet to 6 by 12 feet, the latter containing more than one fire-hearth. There seem to be evolutionary forms of the pit dwelling, which grow larger in floor plan and suggest the use of vertical posts for lifting the roof. The pit dwelling was a northern-hemisphere form that may have begun during a cold period in the Paleolithic Age. Scattered versions of the form continue down into the present century among a variety of northern-hemisphere peoples.

By early Neolithic Age, marking the onset of food production as opposed to food collecting, a notable expansion in domestic building had taken place, although its technological and regional origins are quite unclear. Both the circular and rectangular floor plans were in use, and construction involved wattle and daub (reeds, twigs, and small branches interwoven and daubed with mud plaster), sundried bricks, poles, crude log slabs, and stone, as evidenced by archaeologic sites; building in more perishable materials also must have continued but evidence does not remain. Structures ranged from small beehive units to large and complicated units of multiple stories. There is disagreement over the timing and roles of fortification, palace, storehouse, factory, and temple building, but all of the forms are part of the Neolithic record. Neolithic architecture blossomed quite fully, and many regions present a wide variety of architectural types and technological systems. The diffusion of Neolithic technologies in architecture moved rapidly to many parts of the world and post-Neolithic architectural techniques are highly developed.

We should note, in passing, that along with domestic residential forms there also came a variety of auxiliary buildings for purposes of storage, penning, sheltering of animals, and perhaps the development of the workshop. There is considerable evidence that very early in the development of domestic shelter building, religious motifs appear in the siting, directional facing, inclusion of shrines, focusing on sacred objects, and disposal of the dead. Among some peoples the cooking fire was inside the primary structure, but among others it became excluded from the living quarters, requiring thereby an attached auxiliary structure. Numerous aspects of the sanctity of a house developed, requiring the building of structures for such diverse purposes as childbirth, age ceremonies, and burial rituals.

Once the primary technological elements of architecture had diffused widely, there developed regions of specialization in particular forms and with particular traditions. Many of the former may be summarized in broad terms as developed to fit climatic patterns, such as the flat roof and sundried brick of the arid regions and the pitched roofs with overhangs in humid regions. The particular traditions, however, become the expressions of regional cultures, such as the cone-on-cylinder grass hut in the Sudan and eastern Africa, or the wooden construction amplified by elaborate carving in the Sumatran highlands and the Himalayan border of Tibet. Throughout historic time the technologies and styles of architecture increased, as did the materials employed, becoming elaborated into a bewildering variety and wealth of cultural forms in which regional diversity became extremely marked.

There has been a common assumption that earliest man was nomadic or, at least, rather steadily on the move as a gatherer and collector, and that permanent settlements necessarily awaited the beginnings of cultivation. Need this everywhere have been the case? There is no question that early man moved over sizable territories, but did all men have to wander equally widely? The size of some of the kitchen-midden shell mounds suggest rather sedentary occupance of a fine site for fish, oysters, or clams. Highly productive resource ranges, such as the lower courses of some of the rivers of the American northwest coast frequented by salmon,

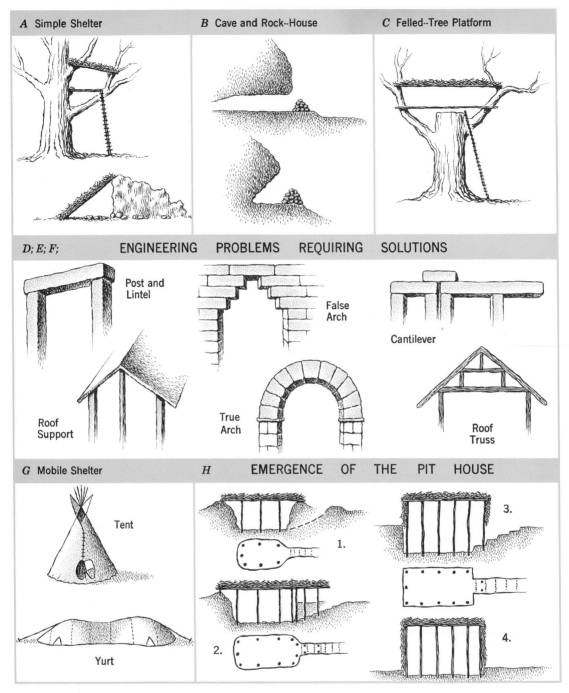

FIG. 4.1 ELEMENTS OF HOUSING SYSTEMS.

suggest possible sedentary situations at a very early point in the occupancy of such regions. In the primordial environments of the Paleolithic Age, when man had not yet highly disturbed the biology of ecological sites that he found, small bands of people could have found many attractive resource ranges in many parts of the world that would have provided ample resources within rather small areas. Throughout the humid tropics and subtropics there were many such sites along the littoral. It is possible, therefore, to suggest that sedentary living patterns began in many parts of the Paleolithic world rather promptly after the elaborating of basic subsistence systems. Earliest man must have tried

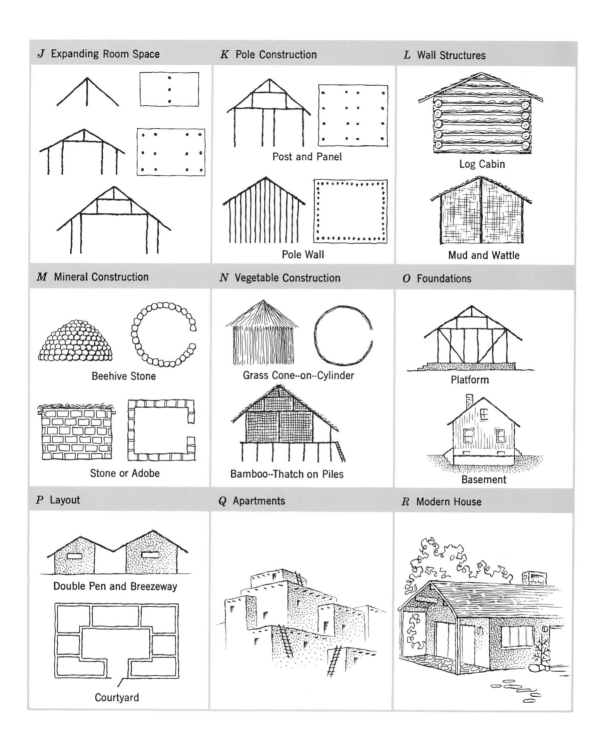

J Expanding Room Space

K Pole Construction

Post and Panel

Pole Wall

L Wall Structures

Log Cabin

Mud and Wattle

M Mineral Construction

Beehive Stone

Stone or Adobe

N Vegetable Construction

Grass Cone--on--Cylinder

Bamboo--Thatch on Piles

O Foundations

Platform

Basement

P Layout

Double Pen and Breezeway

Courtyard

Q Apartments

R Modern House

many kinds of ways of working out these subsistence systems, and the elaboration of the periodic travel route through a given territorial resource range, as a nomadic system, must be reckoned as only one of many alternatives.

Taking the fair assumption that early human economic subsistence systems may have ranged from quite sedentary to quite nomadic, it is possible to suggest that all the basic forms of settlement, short of the town-city, really date from the Paleolithic Age (Fig. 4.2 and pp. 115–124). The evolution of social structure, among large numbers of working bands of human beings subject to different solutions to problems of human organization,

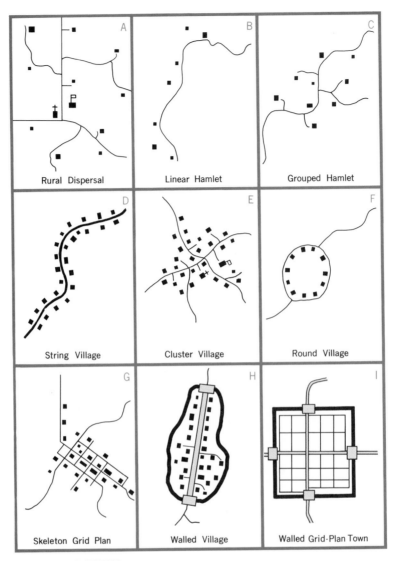

FIG. 4.2 BASIC SETTLEMENT FORMS.

certainly varied greatly in early times, as it continued to do in later times. A given regional population in loose contact only could have varied in
its living patterns from full dispersal of nuclear
families throughout a peaceful zone to relatively
tight concentrations of bands in given favored sites.
Such patterns would have promoted rural dispersion of population, scattered or clustered hamlets,
straggling linear patterns, and compact villages.

Warfare is normally held to be a matter that
causes concentration of settlement and the development of defense systems. This it can do, but for
a people subjected to external stress there is another alternative—retreat, dispersion, and refuge.
A village defense system may be the expression of

a strong group's possessing a good resource that
they choose to protect. A weak population facing
pressure from stronger groups may choose to disperse into very small units of population, which
then live in hidden and widely scattered locations,
maintaining their necessary social contacts in a
near-clandestine manner. The hill country and
lower mountain lands of several parts of the earth
have long marked zones of retreat and dispersion.
Earlier, heavy forests also marked such zones, but
the opportunities for refuge are as broad as the
earth once such a choice is made.

Although we view war today as largely a political
and economic issue, there is ample ground for
suggesting that the earliest warfare among peoples

was chiefly a social institution marked by ritual, ceremonial, sham battling, and large amounts of bluffing. Warfare, in the punitive sense, is a product of civilization and culturally advanced technology, whereas what resulted from the earliest of human disputes was more in the nature of gang fighting. By the Neolithic Age warfare probably had become sufficiently developed that it had implications for settlement. Certainly the construction of formal fortifications derives from the onset of the Neolithic, and the diffusion of fortifying devices to villages probably followed.

Taking the long view, then, it would appear probable that the basic forms of settlement, from rural dispersion through the various forms of hamlets to villages, became established during the Paleolithic Age according to primary social urges and subsistence considerations. The dispersion of man over the earth carried these patterns to all parts of the earth that were populated in Paleolithic time, their selective development becoming a local matter.

Tribes, Confederacies, and the Grouping of Friends and Enemies

The formal sociopolitical organization of early mankind, by groups and units, developed only slowly and as a rather direct result of competitive maneuver for particular territories. We never can know certainly its actual historical development and can only draw inferences from such simple societies as have been studied in modern time. Our presentation here follows anthropological data and theory. The simplest organizational grouping, the band, is not properly a political organization but a loose and changeable working unit. The band had a leader or a headman who was more a peace-maintainer against intragroup bickering than a political officer, more a wise old overseer of the daily routine than a political administrator. Early Paleolithic populations were small, and their patterns of dispersion were such that political organization was unnecessary, since the headman could manage intragroup problems without formal status. Conflicts that could not be resolved ended in withdrawal by a splinter group which functioned thereafter, itself, as a band. The splintering-off of band members into new band units was a normal result of good conditions and growing numbers. Several bands could operate in an adequate region without essential conflict of serious nature.

With significant growth in population to a point where competition for territories came into play, the basis for political organization developed. The affiliation of a group of bands for mutual objectives required the placing of authority in the hands of an individual. The tribe and the chief are one of the first marks of political organization, and a result of tribal organization was the greater formalization of territoriality. In the development of tribal organization around the earth, the functions and powers of the chief varied greatly, as did the pattern of succession. In all cases a degree of authority and something of social status marked the role of the tribal chief. A primary function became the dealing with external relationships through negotiation or warfare. Depending upon whether the tribe thus formed became an aggressive entity aspiring for more or different territory, or a defensive organization concerned with the maintenance of the existing territorial range, the role of the chief varied markedly. The formation of an aggressive entity often resulted in territorial changes and the redistribution of peoples, and sometimes in structuring a larger regional organization through dominance by the stronger tribe and subservience or tributary status of weaker culture groups.

In regions where considerable competition arose among peoples no longer closely related by ethnic or cultural ties, tribal organization sometimes matured into the confederacy. Such a grouping is chiefly political and territorial in objective, bringing together tribes that are culture groups discretely separated by many different attributes. The confederacy normally resulted in a linked relationship, in a formal and negotiated way, for a period of time for a single or several objectives, but confederacies by nature are bound to dissolve, since the component elements are discrete political or cultural units. Each, in its own right, is possessed of autonomies, particularistic concerns, jealousies, and ambitions. It is doubtful if confederacy was significantly achieved until the onset of the Neolithic Age, for earlier situations did not call for such territorial affiliation.

There are other organizational patterns that have had territorial significance as forms of grouping. Above the nuclear family there developed the joint family, linked on either the paternal or maternal side. This is a larger population unit bound together by kinship. The joint family formed both a working and a social grouping of friendly relations who normally lived within the same neighborhood.

Although the joint family may have local territorial expression as to location, such a family is not a unit of formal organization in any administrative sense. The lineage group is similar to the joint family in role and function; essentially the lineage group is an extended unilateral kinship group whose chief functions are the handing-on of rights of various sorts and the maintenance of lines of marriage patterns. In sparsely populated regions without competitive pressures the lineage group may be the only structural social element present. In more heavily populated regions the lineage group may be a structural element of the clan; there normally are several lineage groups combined into the clan.

The clan is an organizational unit with some territorial significance, although clan members may be widely scattered as to residence. The clan is a social organization developed on the basis of unilateral kinship; normally one is born into a clan rather than joining it. A clan whose numbers increase markedly may contain thousands of individuals, and large clans may have subdivisions. As a kinship group hereditarily maintained, a clan does not ordinarily have discrete territorial status, since a given population may possess several clans within the same territorial range. Chiefly the role of the clan has always been what might be termed domestic government, although clan leadership became involved in external relations. Clans normally were the owners of rights to appropriation of resources and, in Neolithic and later time, were the owners of land in common. Clans served as administrators of justice and security, the interpreters of law, and the administrators of intragroup government. The clan also served as the regulator of marriage patterns, which in turn involved patterns of economic security, mutual aid, and control over property and rights to resources. Although the clan obviously exercised political functions, these functions did not perpetuate themselves into formal territorialism in discrete terms, for there has to be two or more interacting clans for the system to exist; the presence of clans, therefore, has been a divisive element rather than an aggregative one in any regional territory so far as political organization is concerned.

There are other organizational elements in social structure among the world's peoples, a few of which go far back into human history, but they are of lesser general significance. It is clear that none of the early forms of organization possessed aggrega-tive powers, but that all tended to work only with local territories and local regions. All the early forms of organization freely permitted the differentiation of the earth's early population into separatist groups in terms of residential location, the evolution of patterns of culture, and the development of local regionalisms. It is only as we approach the middle Neolithic Age that we see organizational forms tending to work toward cohesion, aggregation, and unity. All the early forms of grouping proceed out of motivations in social structure designed first to regulate control of the nuclear family in terms of who might marry whom. Secondary functions were the establishment and maintenance of friendly relations between culture groups or, if friendly relations could not be maintained with all, the alignment of friends and enemies. In the case of unfriendly relations, organizational groupings sought to establish the bases on which belligerency could be regulated and kept to a minimum.

There is a tendency in the modern world to consider peace as normal and to consider militant competition (war) as abnormal. Competition for living space is, however, a normal state of affairs for all life-forms, reckoned in the concept of territoriality. Throughout human history, militant competition for living space has been more normal than has peaceful existence. The bid by human groups for territorial living space leads to the condition described as war. Once human organization developed beyond the level of the band, a share of that organization's people, time, resources, and energy always has been devoted either to the acquisition of new territory or to the defense of the existing territory. The first "war party" sent forth to acquire either space or goods from the territory of another group set in motion the formal competition for territory that remains a segment of the way of life of human beings in their occupance of the earth. However much we, today, may deplore "selfish motives" and the "destructiveness of war," we must reckon with the territorial groupings of friends and enemies; friends may become enemies when they seek to control our earth space, and enemies may seek new friends in order to defend their home territory.

The Evolution and Application of Power Technology

Earliest man was little different from some of the smaller animals in that he could not run very fast or leap very far, he could not carry heavy loads, and his pushing-pulling-pounding strength was relatively slight. It is true that man is differentiated from animals by being both a toolmaker and tool user, but during most of human history the tools that man could create and employ were small ones whose utilization depended heavily on the application of human muscle. In terms of massive accomplishment, none of the early tools was highly productive. Until a very late date a mass-productive task required large numbers of human laborers over long periods of time. The completion of a major task could result only from the accumulated total volume of very small inputs of human energy.

Once the stone axe was well developed, a man could cut down a very large tree in a surprisingly short time, but the task of doing anything with the felled trunk was a very different story. The spear-thrower added considerable leverage to the arm of a skilled and strong man, but the device only made it possible to fell game, or enemies, at a slightly greater distance (Fig. 4.3). The same may be said for the blowgun, the boomerang, the sling, and the bola. Once man learned to use fire as a specific tool, as in burning the heartwood out of a log in shaping a dugout canoe, his skill in manipulating fire could speed up certain kinds of operations. And hunting game by firing the grass cover of grazing ranges could help produce huge volumes of fresh meat at the bottom of the cliff off which the game was driven, but then all that man could do was gorge himself on the yield of meat.

The devising of various agents to extend the power of human muscle has ranged through a wide variety of props and aids. The carrying basket, for shoulder, back, or head load, is one of a series of devices (Fig. 4.4). The shoulder pole is another, as are the pack frames and the travois rigs. Skid boards, rollers, and various systems of "greasing" a surface played their separate roles in various areas at different times. Learning to package loads into sizes suitable to human strength was an early skill. Allied are the skills of chipping, scraping, boring, grinding, and pounding, by which small amounts of human energy could be applied to repeated operations to accomplish work of different types. Using different materials in wood, stone, bone, and plants locally available, diversified skills and traditions of work accumulated around the earth in the application of human energy.

Once animal domestication began, man acquired another work agent of varying ability. Even dogs, goats, and sheep were put to work carrying, pulling, and grinding in parts of the earth in which they were available. As larger animals were domesticated, the process of power application was extended in many different ways in distinct regional patterns. In regions without domesticable animals the delivery of power remained dependent on human muscle. The travois, the sled, the skid road, and finally the wheel were means of utilizing animal power more efficiently (see Fig. 4.4). Invention of the plow, seeding tube, cultivator, leveler, and scraper using animal power provided another range of applications. The pack train of groups of animals, according to their availability, was still another variant. Early man had to learn gradually how to use more than one animal at a time in harnessing animal motive power, and the late-nineteenth-century harvester-combine of the American Middle West utilizing a hundred horses as motive power was a final evolutionary step in a long series involving animal power. In different parts of the earth man still employs most of the traditional methods of utilizing animal power, according to his skills and the availability of animals of particular kinds, thus representing a continuation of late Neolithic systems.

The harnessing of wind in the development of power production was a slow matter that did not appear on land for a very long time. The development of sail systems on watercraft came much earlier for varying portions of the earth, and probably relates to certain wind zones. A fair number of sail systems developed in many parts of the Old World, and possibly in a few parts of the New World. Such systems were integrally linked to the skills of building the craft themselves, possibly being climaxed in the American "Yankee Clipper Ship" of the nineteenth century and contemporary racing yachts. The use of wind in power production reached its productive climax in the windmill. Although the origin of the windmill may lie in a device involving a prayer wheel, its development in ancient Persia as a source of economic power was for grinding grain. The Arabs adapted it to pumping water; in this usage it spread almost around the world in later time.

The use of water in power development was also slow and dependent on other kinds of inventions. The simple waterwheel for grinding grain, and later for lifting water, seems to have originated somewhere in the Middle East (Fig. 4.5). Its spread

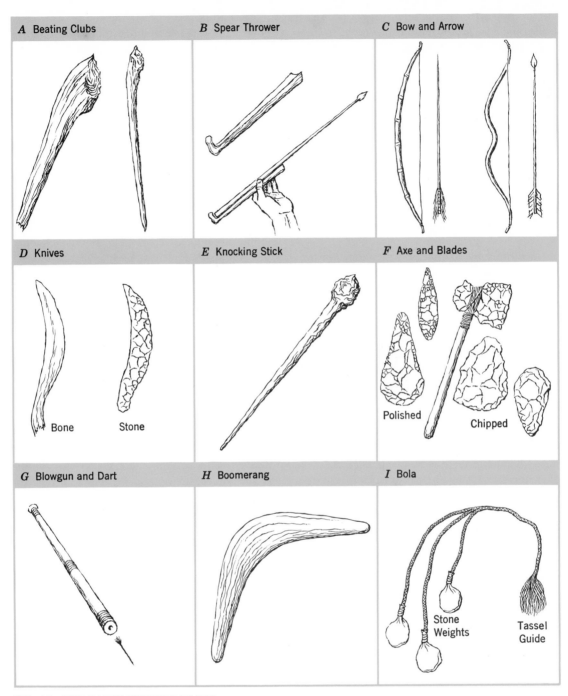

FIG. 4.3   THE EARLY HUNTING TOOLS.

involved variations in both construction and usage in developing power for man. Repeatedly, in the classical periods of ancient history in the Old World, ideas were conceived for using water in power development, but the inadequacy of engineering and construction knowledge prevented their fruitful development. Not until the seventeenth century did real advances in the development of waterpower come about, and the modern evolution of hydroelectric power is the climax in this series. Ideas for harnessing ocean tides to develop power are quite old, but the economic technology for this still has to be perfected.

In a sense, the learning to make and use charcoal

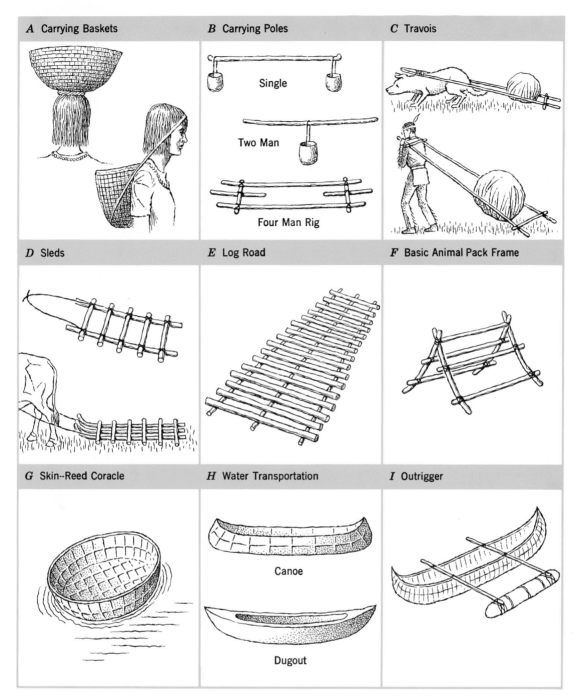

FIG. 4.4 THE TOOLS OF SIMPLE TRANSPORT.

in firing operations is a special development of power. However, the early operations that involved firing different kinds of fuels never matured into the production of power useful in separate applications until the invention of the steam engine and other forms of engines burning some kind of fuel.

Throughout early human history, therefore, man was severely restricted in the kinds of operations that he could conduct. The restrictions to accomplishment meant that only when man devised techniques for dividing work units into small bits or devised ways of using large numbers of human laborers in concerted effort could large tasks be completed. The wonder is, of course, that early

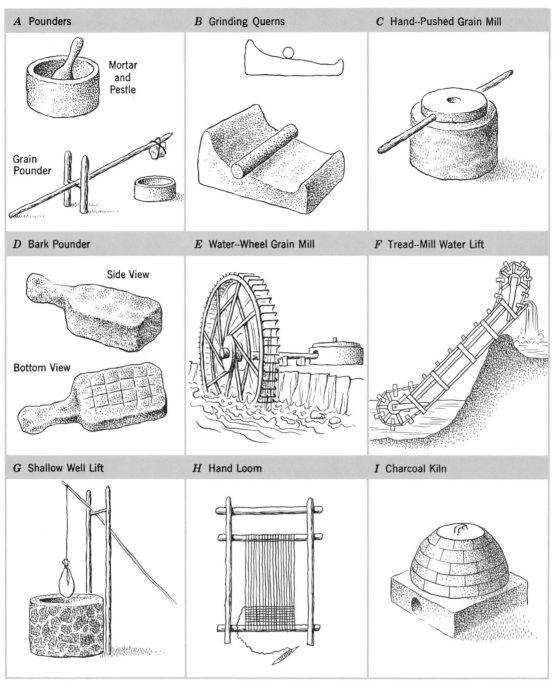

| A Pounders | B Grinding Querns | C Hand--Pushed Grain Mill |

Mortar and Pestle

Grain Pounder

| D Bark Pounder | E Water--Wheel Grain Mill | F Tread--Mill Water Lift |

Side View

Bottom View

| G Shallow Well Lift | H Hand Loom | I Charcoal Kiln |

FIG. 4.5   THE TOOLS FOR PROCESSING.

man occasionally could have accomplished as much as he did in this manner, but these results did not come during the Paleolithic. The huge mounds, the pyramids, the excavations, the long canals, the walls, and the other massive marks of man upon the earth came only during the late Neolithic and protohistoric periods at which time

social and political organization finally permitted the massing of human energies upon a given task.

Food Habits, Dietary Systems, Gathering, and Production

Man, as an animal life-form, is really omnivorous, in contrast to such herbivores as the grazing animals and such carnivores as the cat family. In man's earliest existence the human habit was to try eating almost everything available in the local habitat. Upon ranging into new and strange habitats early man continued this omnivorous tendency. Through watching companions die of varied poisonings, he gradually learned to reject and avoid certain kinds of plants and animal-marine foods. Taboos became attached to certain items through experience, although the true reasons for the nonedibility of certain food sources were slow in coming. A hunting band locally resident in a given resource range gathered knowledge and experience as to what was safely edible. Knowledge of fruiting seasons, spawning periods, migrating periods, and other life-cycle elements of both plant and animal forms accumulated slowly for the different regions in which man lived. In becoming widely distributed over the earth, man took the first steps in the evolution of a whole series of dietary systems based upon local resources.

Through trial and error in human campsites various simple processings evolved, such as aging, drying, soaking in water, leaching in water, pounding, roasting, and grinding. The discoveries and inventions in domestic food-processing technology, such as boiling, baking, parching, broiling, and frying, were important in making possible the better utilization of many food sources and in crystallizing human food habits and dietary systems. Such developments raised human feeding above the animal level and began the processes leading to cultured dietary systems. Regional resources, of course, stimulated the development of multiple systems of dietary support. Migrations of human groups resulted in spreading essential techniques, and also in further experimentation with food sources, sometimes involving considerable shifts in dietary systems that had not yet become stereotyped.

On the production end of the food supply the knowledge of seasonalities, as in the ripening of fruits and tubers, developed annual patterns of harvest patterns for many resources and stimulated varying techniques of acquisition. Hunting and fishing procedures, seed-gathering techniques, and other means of acquisition stimulated the invention of specific tools, utensils, and implements for specific use. Improving design and manufacturing technology perfected many of these into effective instruments by which considerable volumes of food supply could be accumulated.

On the processing side continued experimentation resulted in the devising of a wide range of utensils, implements, tools, and their related procedures. Such processing included means of rendering initially poisonous items palatable, inedible items edible, and momentary surpluses storable. These procedures systematized the acquisition of food in response to sheer biologic need, further differentiating human dietary systems from animal systems.

The steady elaboration of this whole complex of regional developments in regard to food supply became surrounded by numerous habitual ideas, taboos, human insistences, preferences, likes, and dislikes. In the variance of the natural resource range lay the basic origins of multiple systems, but in human extension of taboos and preferences lay the cultural sources of variation that led to a great multiplicity of dietary systems in the occupance of the earth.

Such simple systems based on almost daily acquisition from the resource range characterized earliest human groups. In many regions other cultural developments led to improvements that raised human dietary patterns into complex systems. Yet in many regions very simple patterns of acquiring and processing food supplies long continued. The modern world contains only fragmentary distributions of these Paleolithic systems, but they do remain in a few restricted corners of the earth, characterized under the general term Gathering and Collecting Cultures. Although simple in all aspects, such systems display most of the cultural characteristics of like, dislike, preference, taboo, rules, and standards that may be found in more complex systems.

Fishing, Fishing Systems, and Aquatic Resources

Beachcombing for edible, interesting, curious, and strange things is probably one of man's oldest activities. The tide zone has always yielded a return of something for anyone who searched. As a fishing technique, beachcombing is extremely varied, widely developed, and one of man's ancient procedures. Some human groups, in appropriate resource ranges, came to depend heavily on beachcombing. Along seacoasts, lakeshores, in river estuaries, and in shallow lake waters the trapping of marine products is an old technique using different specific procedures and materials. The simplest of trapping procedures is the building of

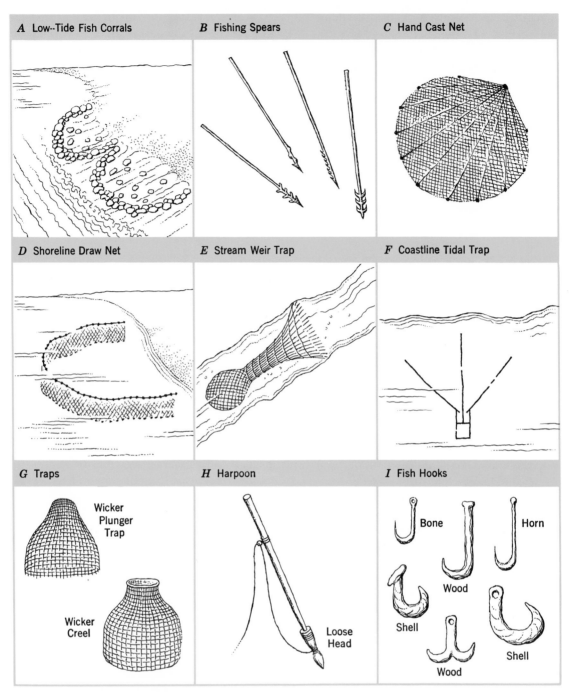

A Low--Tide Fish Corrals	B Fishing Spears	C Hand Cast Net
D Shoreline Draw Net	E Stream Weir Trap	F Coastline Tidal Trap
G Traps	H Harpoon	I Fish Hooks

G: Wicker Plunger Trap; Wicker Creel

H: Loose Head

I: Bone; Horn; Wood; Shell; Wood; Shell

FIG. 4.6 THE TOOLS OF FISHERMEN.

rock-ringed enclosures which, at low water, trap a variable product in a procedure closely related to beachcombing in natural tide pools (Fig. 4.6). At its most advanced level, fish trapping involves some very complex constructions in fairly deep water with ingenious recovery systems.

Fishing, as a technology, displays a bewildering range of procedures which are dependent on the local environment, the cultural circumstances, and the marine biota present. From the mud of a drying pond in a seasonally inundated lowland in Southeast Asia certain forms of fish may be dug from their dry-season estivation sites. Damming a small section of a shallow body of water and emptying out all the remaining water can be an effective fishing technique in southern Asia and parts of Africa. The placing of certain plants containing poisons into pools of relatively still water is an effective technique, in that the poisons temporarily suffocate the fish and cause them to float to the top of the water for easy recovery. Spearing of fish in clear water in pools and rivers can be both interesting and remunerative. Though seemingly a curious practice, restricting the neck of a cormorant, tying a string to its leg, throwing the bird into the water, and letting it catch a fish was once widely employed throughout the Orient. Scooping out ascending fish is an effective procedure in freshwater streams at spawning seasons. Somewhat more dangerous is line-trailing a chunk of pork in the water from an outrigger canoe in the South Pacific and fighting the shark that grabs the bait during a long session in which the boat may be towed some miles. According to the environment and the life-forms involved there are many ways of fishing.

The array of nets and fishhooks employed around the world is vast. The nets range from the simple, circular, weighted-margin cast nets to elaborate affairs requiring large crews for their placement and retrieval. Except for some of the modern powerboat nets used in trawling, most of the forms are ancient and widely distributed, but regional specializations are also numerous. The range of line-suspended hooks is enormous, going from thorns through branched sticks to carved shells, and from bent "pins" through elaborate devices. Along with the variation in the hook itself has been the variation in the bait employed. The traditional lore of "where the fish are," "what the fish will bite," and "how to catch a fish" extends from the mystical to the pseudoscientific, for the fisherman normally lives in a world of his own. Historically the fisherman's lore is both ancient and wide-roaming; in some modern societies science is altering the old processes. The element of sport seems always to have been attached to fishing, along with the staid need for subsistence.

The variation in means of catching fishery products has been accompanied by a wide variation in their processing, storage, and consumption, around which, also, a rich lore has developed. Out-of-the-water prompt consumption, both raw and processed in some manner, lies at one extreme; traditional forms of drying, salting, smoking, fermenting, and pickling processes lie at the other. To the latter

have been added the modern procedures of canning and freezing. With these modern exceptions, the processing of fishery products represents an ancient set of techniques.

Whereas to some peoples, in particular environments, the fishery operation became a primary means of support, for other peoples it became an auxiliary activity, and for still others it represented only a scarcity-season guarantee of support. Fishery activity developed its sporting aspect at a very early date among some culture groups and remained that for many. Large portions of the world, of course, could do little with fishing, yet it is only during the more recent time period, the era of drying out after the last glacial period, in which the arid lands of the earth have failed to provide a resource for those who would fish. In more recent time, with the evolving of complex dietary systems motivated by religious principles, fishery products have become either taboo or periodic alternatives to other food sources. With the evolution of agriculture the fishery resources of the world became an alternative, applicable in many different ways. All in all, the regional variety of fishing and the utilization of fishery products have added greatly to cultural variety in a developing world population.

The Beginning of Plant Domestication and Crop Production

Early man became skilled in his knowledge of the properties of plants long before he began to domesticate them into purposeful producers. The selection of fuel for fires, the processing of string and cord, the making of particular wooden tools, the securing of poisons for several uses, the building of shelters, the processing of plant materials for clothing, and their employment in magic rituals and ceremonials all lie beyond the direct appropriation of plant products for food usage. Simple culture groups living close to their plant world know and differentiate many hundreds of species of herbs, roots, grasses, shrubs, and trees. Some modern shifting cultivators, still living close to the plant world, distinguish nearly two thousand species of useful plants in their local environment. Even modern, remnantal gatherers and collectors distinguish hundreds of species of plants for particular utilities, properties, and consequences.

Prior to purposeful planting and harvesting, early man must have affected the qualities and growth habits of a large number of plants in an aimless and unconscious way by cutting, picking, burning, scattering of seeds and, in the humid tropical and subtropical regions, by the dropping of portions of plants that reproduce by vegetative means. The late Pleistocene was a period of rapid change in the intrinsic and highly plastic characters of the angiosperms by purely natural processes, and it is most likely that Paleolithic man stimulated the patterns of change for a good many species of plants. The accumulated results of change, both natural and by human influence, by the Late Paleolithic, plus man's accumulated knowledge of plants, began to lead to increasing activity by man. This was a forerunner of domestication as a distinctive process.

Discussions normally speak of crop plants, as opposed to what we now term weeds, but in dealing with the early human manipulation of plants it is necessary to remember that any plant deemed useful to early man must be considered. We cannot be certain just why early man seemed interested in certain particular plant products, and it is clear that, as domestication took place, man was gathering the products from some plants that we have long considered to be weeds. A weed, essentially, is any unwanted plant that is growing spontaneously (and usually vigorously) in the midst of a plot of desired plants, so that a cucumber plant may be a weed in a pumpkin patch, or a maize plant may be a weed in a flower garden. The continued association of "weed" species with "crop-plant" species (and "weed" varieties with "crop" varieties) was an important aspect of the development of domestication, as man began the serious manipulation of the plants that were to end up as crop plants. The reason for this is that cross-pollination between varied members of a gene pool, as some of them begin to change, is an important element in the further progress of the selection and mutation processes.

There is good cause to ascribe domestication of useful plants to more than one reason, and not to lay the whole development on the process of working with food plants. The interests were significant in fibers, colors, dyes, poisons, glues, spicy flavorings, strange exotics, "magic" plants useful in religious ritual, and plants yielding items of medicinal value. One of the very old traditions around certain domesticated plants is the "sacredness" theme, owing to rather peculiar growth characteristic. Our modern viewpoints, when most of us no longer live in vitally close relationships with the plant world, may well see the whole matter in too secular and too scientific a manner.

The time period during which domestication occurred used to be set at roughly 5000 years ago, but that period has been moved further and further back with the increases in archaeologic knowledge. In the late 1960s the onset of significant plant domestication often is placed at about 11,000 years ago. It should be recognized, however, that the first domestication processes were somewhat unplanned and slow-moving, so that it is very likely that the date will be set still further back. Domestication has been a continuing kind of process, in one part of the world or other, and some of the domestications have been accomplished within only the last millennium. Even today domestication is in process with such plants as the *Hevea* rubber tree, some of the palms, and some of the forage grasses.

There has been much discussion as to where domestication first yielded crop plants and where crop growing began. One theory places both beginnings in the Middle East, in the humid lower hill country regions, holding that around the wheats and barleys lie the beginnings of all agriculture. We do not question this as one of the locales of origin for domestication and crop growing, but was this the only center? How could all crop growing derive from these beginnings? Recent evidence points to the conclusion that domestication and the beginnings of crop growing were multiple developments, taking place in several equable, regional environments in which early culture groups had thoroughly established themselves for long terms of residence which afforded them a period of working with plants in those regions. The accompanying maps and table depict the distribution and development of the more common crop plants (Figs. 4.7, 4.8; Table 4.1). It also seems likely that there is more than one kind of origin to domestication and crop growing, in that procedures developed around the seeding plants are quite different from those developed around the plants that reproduce by vegetative propagation. As a tentative thesis, we can say that the beginnings of domestication, and the origins of crop growing, have several different specific processes, involving different sets of plants. There is a large range of territory of appropriate climatic and ecologic suitability, within which a number of vegetative concentrations presented early man with useful plant combinations (see Fig. 4.7).

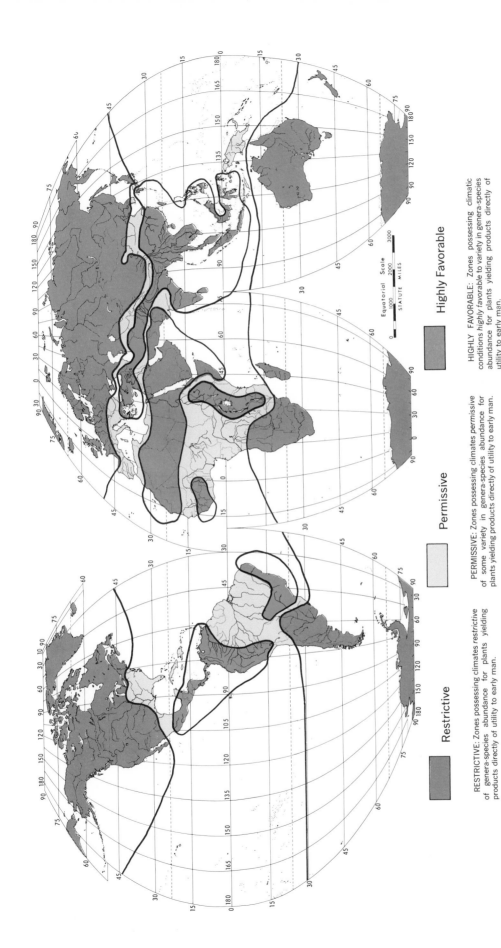

Restrictive

RESTRICTIVE: Zones possessing climates restrictive of genera-species abundance for plants yielding products directly of utility to early man.

Permissive

PERMISSIVE: Zones possessing climates permissive of some variety in genera-species abundance for plants yielding products directly of utility to early man.

Highly Favorable

HIGHLY FAVORABLE: Zones possessing climatic conditions *highly favorable* to variety in genera-species abundance for plants yielding products directly of utility to early man.

FIG. 4.7 GENERALIZED LATE PLEISTOCENE–EARLY RECENT CLIMATIC CONDITIONS AND VEGETATIVE DISTRIBUTIONS.

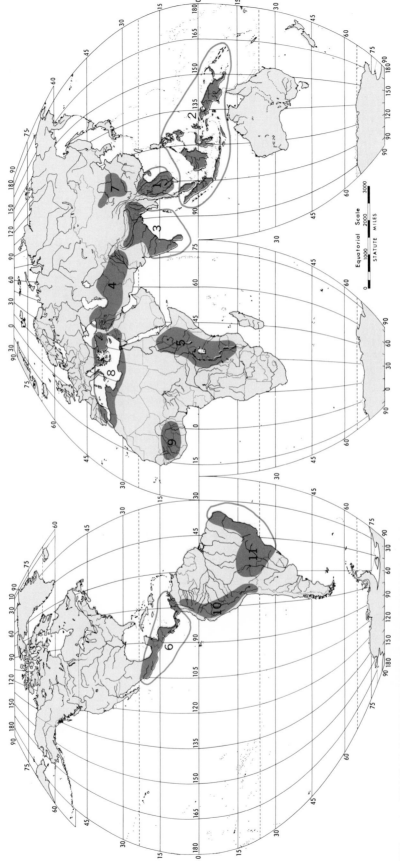

FIG. 4.8A REGIONS OF SIGNIFICANT PLANT DOMESTICATION. (Numbers on map correspond with regions listed on Table 4.1, pages 150–151).

Equatorial Scale

STATUTE MILES

0   1000   2000   3000

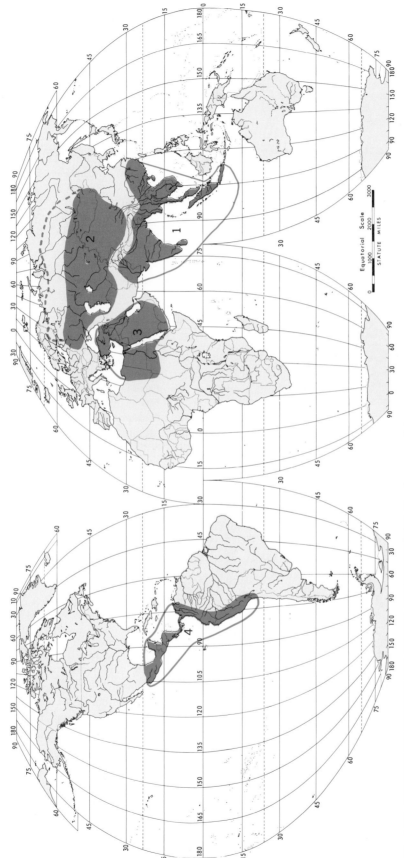

FIG. 4.8B REGIONS OF SIGNIFICANT ANIMAL DOMESTICATION. Numbers correlate
with regional names on Table 4.2, p. 157.

149

TABLE 4.1   CHIEF SOURCE REGIONS OF CROP PLANT DOMESTICATIONS

A. PRIMARY REGIONS OF DOMESTICATIONS

1. THE UPPER SOUTHEAST ASIAN MAINLAND

Citrus fruits*	Yams*	Eugenias*	Teas
Bananas*	Cabbages*	Job's tears	Tung oils
Bamboos*	Rices*	Lichi	Ramie
Taros*	Beans*	Longan	Water chestnut

2. LOWER SOUTHEAST ASIAN MAINLAND AND MALAYSIA (INCLUDING NEW GUINEA)

Citrus fruits*	Yams*	Sugarcanes	Lanzones	Gingers*	Cardamom
Bananas*	Almonds*	Breadfruits	Durian	Brinjals*	Areca
Bamboos*	Pandanuses	Jackfruits	Rambutan	Nutmeg	Abaca
Taros*	Cucumbers*	Coconuts	Vine peppers*	Clove	

3. EASTERN INDIA AND WESTERN BURMA

Bananas*	Rices*	Peas*	Vine peppers*	Kapok*	Sunn Hemp
Yams*	Amaranths*	Grams	Gingers*	Indigo	Lotus
Taros*	Millets*	Eggplants	Palms*	Safflower	Turmeric
Beans*	Sorghums*	Brinjals*	Mangoes	Jute	

4. SOUTHWESTERN ASIA IN GENERAL (NORTHWEST INDIA–CAUCUSUS)

Soft wheats*	Oil seeds*	Carrots*	Flax	Soft Pears*	Grapes*	Tamarind
Barleys*	Poppies*	Turnips	Hemp	Cherries*	Jujubes*	Alfalfa
Lentils*	Oat*	Beets	Apples	Plums*	Pistachio	
Beans*	Rye*	Spinach	Almonds*	Figs	Walnuts	
Peas*	Onions	Sesames	Peaches*	Pomegranates	Melons	

5. ABYSSINIAN AND EAST AFRICAN HIGHLANDS

Hard wheats*	Barleys*	Oil seeds*	Coffees
Millets*	Peas*	Cucumbers*	Castor beans
Sorghums*	Beans*	Melons*	Okras
Rices*	Vetches	Gourds*	Cottons*

6. MESOAMERICAN REGION (SOUTHERN MEXICO TO NORTHERN VENEZUELA)

Maizes	Sweet potatoes	Custard apples	Muskmelons	Cottons*
Amaranths*	Squashes	Avocados	Palms*	
Beans*	Tomatoes*	Sapotes	Agaves	
Taros*	Chili peppers	Plums*	Kapok	

Domestication procedures, with crop plants resulting, were the work of a sedentary people who had lived with those plants for a period of time, to be familiar with them, to have gathered their seeds, fruits, berries, roots, tubers, or leaves, to have subsisted upon their products as wild plants, and to have selected out particular varieties for specific qualities. This did not necessarily mean the largest, the most productive, or the most nutritious, but it did mean the selection for certain preferences. Domestication procedures probably worked with a large number of plant species and plant varieties, all of which grew in situations in which cross-pollination or mutations could occur and were observed by man. In time new varieties took the place of previous ones, as both the plants themselves and the patterns of preference altered. At first harvesting procedures differed little from gathering procedures employed upon purely wild plants; actually it is likely that the gathering procedures continued long after the first crop planting took place, for the first planting activities certainly would not have yielded full subsistence to the planters. In time, as trial-and-error learning pro-

TABLE 4.1 *(Continued)*

B. SECONDARY REGIONS OF DOMESTICATIONS

7. NORTH CENTRAL CHINA (INCLUDING THE CENTRAL ASIAN CORRIDOR)

Millets*	Cabbages*	Rhubarb	Bush cherries*	Jujubes*
Barleys*	Radishes*	Mulberries	Hard pears*	
Buckwheats	Naked oat*	Persimmons	Apricots	
Soybeans	Mustards	Plums*	Peaches*	

8. MEDITERRANEAN BASIN—CLASSICAL NEAR EASTERN FRINGE

Barleys*	Grapes*	Parsnips	Carrots*
Oats*	Olives	Asparagus	Garlic
Lentils*	Dates	Lettuces	Sugar beet
Peas*	Carobs	Celeries	Leek

9. WESTERN SUDAN HILL LANDS AND THEIR MARGINS

Sorghums*	Fonio	Peas*	Gourds*	Kola nut
Millets*	Yams*	Oil seeds*	Oil palms	
Rices*	Beans*	Melons*	Tamarind*	

10. ANDEAN HIGHLANDS AND THEIR MARGINS

White potatoes	Strawberries	Quinoa	Arrocacha
Pumpkins	Beans*	Oca	Ulluco
Tomatoes*	Papayas	Cubio	

11. EASTERN SOUTH AMERICA (CENTERED ON EASTERN BRAZIL)

Taros*	Pineapples	Cacao	Tobaccos
Beans*	Cashew nut	Passion fruits	
Peanuts	Brazil nut	Cottons*	

* The asterisk indicates domestication of related species or hybridized development of new species during domestication in some other region or regions. Some of these secondary domestications were later than in the original region, but clear evidence of chronologic priority seldom is clear-cut.

The plural rendering of the crop name indicates that several different varieties/species either were involved in initial domestications or followed thereafter.

The term "oilseeds" indicates several varieties/species of small-seeded crop plants grown for the production of edible oils, without further breakdown.

In regions 2 and 3 the brinjals refer to the spicy members of the eggplant group used in curries, whereas in region 3 the eggplants refer to the sweet vegetable members.

None of the regional lists attempts a complete listing of all crop plants/species domesticated within the region. Table has been compiled from a wide variety of sources.

ceeded, planting efforts accrued to the point of realization of the culture complex; a people became aware that a production process, which they had developed, could be manipulated toward a culturally determined end.

In regions wherein wild seeding plants formed the bases of a gathering economy, a crop-planting system based upon seed-planted species could have resulted. Where wild seed-bearing plants were less common, but roots, tubers, and fleshy growths formed the bases of a gathering economy, a crop-planting system stemming from vegetative repro-

duction would have resulted. The two sets of procedures are not interchangeable in the beginnings of crop planting. In situations in which domestications were developing, the regional distributions of wild-plant associations were significant to the whole utilization of plant products. The seeding grain plants are not native to the tropics and the warmer, more humid subtropics, whereas originally few of the plants yielding large roots and tubers and propagating themselves by vegetative reproduction were at home far outside these two regions. The distinctive wild-plant associations of the large territory forming the humid tropics and subtropics meant that a great range of wild-plant material lay open to manipulative procedures by early man. Regional concentrations of such efforts could only turn out different crop-plant assemblages; the whole collective effort resulted in a large number of highly varied plants being brought into domestication, each group ecologically at home in a small regional environment. These environmental niches constituted the key areas and the symbiotic nodal points around which cropping systems evolved. Culturally, each of these environments contained human groups that had already developed preference systems, food habits, and manipulative systems based on wild plant products by the time domestication can be considered to have yielded assemblages of crop plants.

Sometimes domestication is inferred to have been accomplished in a short span and spoken of dramatically as an Agricultural Revolution. The truth is that it took a rather long time to bring the earlier domestication processes to effective fruition. Manipulative procedures certainly began in the late Paleolithic. The term Mesolithic denotes the era of transition away from Paleolithic exclusive dependence on gathering and collecting. At first thought to be a relatively brief interval of sudden, almost overnight advances, the Mesolithic more properly should be regarded as a fairly long interval involving a good many millennia during which late Paleolithic man was bringing about a whole group of cultural advances that would enable the Neolithic to be typified by a fundamentally different way of life. By definition, the Neolithic is an era in which the most advanced peoples utilized production systems rather than appropriation systems.

The Evolution of Cropping Complexes and Cropping Systems

The processes involved in plant domestication are but the means to an end, although they began without any clear concept of the goals sought. Trial-and-error efforts at plant domestication resulted in the accumulation of a group of domesticated plants that could support a population for a large part of the year with a varied food supply. In each region in which the domestication processes went on there emerged a group of crop plants more or less ecologically suited to the local environment, and suited to the provision of a reason-

able diet. We cannot look backward at this development to ascribe too much foresight to the whole complicated operation, for regional populations could only slowly work with the wild plants occurring locally in each region. However, it is clear that wherever domestication proceeded, an assemblage of crop plants resulted that served the several purposes in the dietary complex and in the provision of raw materials for nondietary uses.

In each region wherein domestication occurred there developed a crop plant of major importance which provided the bulk of the carbohydrate food supply. This plant became the staple crop, most attention centered on it, and around it developed the key practices in crop growing, the religious rituals, the primary calendar of the crop year, and the basic arrangement of seasonal living and working practices. In each regional domestication center other crop plants eventually appeared, serving a variety of subordinate roles and fitting into the primary scheme. Normally a secondary staple was developed, in case the primary crop failed for some reason. Some vegetable-oil producer usually became a subsidiary but important crop item. A source of sugars resulted in most cases. A variety of "green-vegetable" crop plants usually appeared, although among many peoples this dietary element long continued to be secured through the gathering of some type of wild greens. Also there were usually crop plants providing what may be termed snack foods, for casual or between-meal consumption. Subsidiary crop plants that add variety to the diet, lessening the sheer monotony of staple consumption, formed part of the crop assemblage. Almost every regional center provided some fruit and nut products, some of them serving as snack foods and some fulfilling general purposes ranging even to basic support at certain times of year. Medicinal plants appear to have become minor but important crop species in almost every regional area in which crop domestication was carried on.

Important in the crop-development sequence were crops designed for nonfood purposes. One group formed a series of fiber plants to provide all sorts of products from string and nettings to clothing textiles. Some kind of beverage crop resulted in almost every case of regional domestication, although many of these crops either were not too satisfactory or also served other purposes. Learning to make a beer or an infusion appears to have gone hand in hand with domestication of certain plants. Plants used in making magic and in providing ritual materials, or deemed sacred in some way, usually found a significant position in the crop sequence. The odd and peculiar shapes of tubers, rhizomes, seedpods, and fruits, or the spectacular colors of leaves and fruits, seemed to appeal to early domesticators, and there is a series of crop plants to which it is now difficult to ascribe a specific role to its early growers.

Early man, engaged in trial-and-error plant domestication, knew nothing about the qualities of soils or the means of handling them. He knew almost nothing about cultivation practices and little about issues of productivity and how to implement yields. He had no specific tools or implements to aid his operations when he began, few concepts of weeds and of how to control plant growth he did not want, and little knowledge of crop seasonality, the planting calendar, and the timing of events with crops other than what he had observed in the annual cycle of wild-plant growth. Early man knew that the gods often produced annual sequences of weather that altered the normal patterns of seasonality, resulting in abundances and scarcities, and he remembered the old stories handed down from his ancestors that at times strange things had happened; there had been great floods, periods of drought, and all manner of strange storms. Not understanding these things, early man placated and supplicated the gods in many different ways to make his efforts at growing crops turn out favorably.

Looking at maps of climatic regions and of the richness of vegetative regions (see Fig. 4.7), we can see that plant domestication could not have gone on all over the earth. There were regions in which large numbers of plants yielded useful products, and climatic zones in which the hazards were comparatively slight. The processes of plant domestication were cumulative in a series of areas of mild climate, humid situations, and locally varied ecological circumstances. In these regions assemblages of domesticated plants accrued, no two of which were identical but each of which provided a group of domesticated plants yielding a broad variety of products useful to early man. These assemblages formed crop complexes or crop systems, around which practices of crop growing were to develop, ending in the maturing of agriculture.

Slowly Neolithic man worked out procedures and combinations of procedures for planting, weeding, cultivation, harvesting, and for making representations to the Gods of Nature. In doing so he began several learning processes in which small steps were taken in the developments of systems pertaining to crop growing. There began the development of tool systems, of clearing-planting-weeding systems, of selection systems aimed at better crops, and of harvest and storage systems (Fig. 4.9). In each region in which crop growing was maturing these systems were devised to suit the ecologic environment, taking advantage of environmental circumstances. Neolithic man had no preconceptions of what constituted a good agricultural system, and his earliest "fields" were jungle plots in which all kinds of things, including weeds, grew in profusion, in an approximation of the conditions of nature, modified only little by man. It is likely that shifting cultivation was one of the first cropping systems.

A Neolithic remnant still practiced widely around the earth, shifting cultivation once may have been the only cropping system. It is a natural rotation system in which patches of ground are cleared (chiefly by cutting and burning), planted with a little preparation of the ground, given some weeding, assisted by some magic performance, and then hand-harvested. The ash residue from the burning provided a dressing of soluble nutrients to assist productivity. After a few croppings, and heavy weed growth, a new plot is chosen and the routine repeated. Good yields normally accompany such operations, the vegetative association rapidly regenerates on plots no longer cropped, and little harm results to the landscape when the cultivator can move at his own discretion in a territorial range not heavily overpopulated. As a cropping system, shifting cultivation operates on the principle of usufruct; the cultivator does not own the land but holds rights to the clearing, cropping, and harvest of the yield of land, whereas the social group to which he belongs (lineage, clan, culture group, ethnic group) holds ownership-in-common for the land within the territorial range. Several kinds of site shift are used today, each of which is traditional among its users, as illustrated in Figure 4.10. The first two sketches indicate rural dispersal of settlement, the second pair involves periodic shift of hamlets or villages, and the third pair is accompanied by permanent village settlement. Working systems, tool systems, commodity exchange systems, and the recultivation of particular plots in specific years all form a part of the group's system of cultivation.

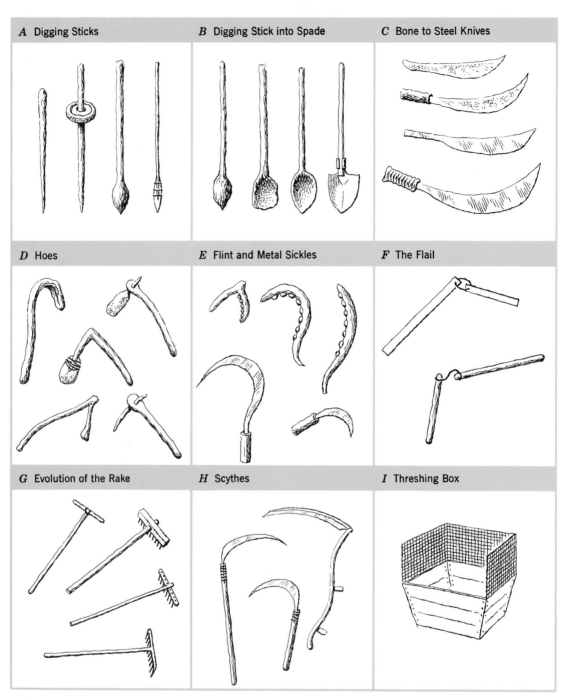

A Digging Sticks
B Digging Stick into Spade
C Bone to Steel Knives
D Hoes
E Flint and Metal Sickles
F The Flail
G Evolution of the Rake
H Scythes
I Threshing Box

FIG. 4.9 THE TOOLS OF GARDENERS.

Shifting cultivation, as perhaps the earliest basic cropping system, spread gradually over the inhabited earth in which Neolithic man learned to grow crops and could cope with environmental conditions. Crop plants were moved from their home regions to different regions, and new trial-and-error procedures were needed to adapt them to new conditions; new crop varieties resulted from selection procedures, and new practices were developed to accommodate to the new sets of conditions. Crop plants were exchanged with other peoples, and assemblages became mixed, for one of the things that has always accompanied crop growing is the interest of the cultivator in new kinds of crops.

We cannot follow this theme in full detail, since it is a complex matter with tremendous variation, not all of which is understood by modern man. It is clear that crop growing diffused among peoples who formerly had been gatherers and collectors, for the procedures could be copied and transferred without the migration of peoples. Within the Old World many crop plants, their usages, and their cropping systems spread steadily, so that crops, tools, systems, and usages covered long distances to far regions. Thus it is that wheat, as a crop plant and a dietary staple, moved from southwest Asia northeastward to North China and northwestward to the British Isles over a period of perhaps two thousand years. Within the New World maize was transferred both northward and southward from its Middle America home region, with a wide range of varieties resulting between what is now New England and the southwestern part of the United States, and between eastern Brazil and the Altiplano of Peru.

We cannot be certain of the regional origins of all domesticated plants, but we can form certain broad generalizations about their beginnings. Most of the tubers, rhizomes, and plants reproducing themselves by vegetative propagation derive from the humid tropics and the mild humid subtropics.

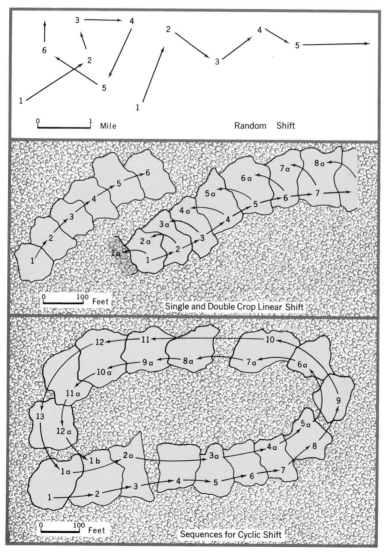

FIG. 4.10 SYSTEMS OF FIELD SHIFT IN SHIFTING CULTIVATION.

Most of the annual seed-producing domesticated plants come from the central humid subtropics wherein a distinctive seasonal range of conditions prevails, with a dry season during the year. Most of the stone fruits and many of the nuts were originally at home in the higher hill country of the cooler subtropical margins where a cool to cold winter prevailed. Many of the leafy vegetables, small root vegetables, grapes, berries, and related items originated in local regional environments in the seasonally wet-and-dry, mild subtropics, but most of these have been drastically altered by man during the domestication process. A few plants derive from midlatitude zones of varied kinds of local ecological environments. All told, man has domesticated about 1850 distinct species and subspecies of crop plants out of the 350,000 species of higher plants. Meanwhile several hundred species now on the threshold of domestication are grown as almost wild plants. Many of the forage grasses fall into this category. These figures do not, of course, include the decorative plants, of which there are several thousands, with many more steadily coming into the status of domesticated plants as growers keep working on improving the "wild flowers."

In the early development of crop complexes and cropping systems man in different regional sectors of the earth concentrated on particular groups of plants. Thus it is that the basic cropping system of Neolithic southeastern Asia can be said to be based chiefly upon taro, yams, bananas, and a series of other plants that reproduce by vegetative association. Similarly the cropping systems of southwest Asia came early to depend chiefly upon wheat, barley, and a series of minor seed crops, whereas in the New World maize, the squashes, and a series of beans became the primary base of the cropping system in Middle America and its northern and southern margins.

Animal Domestication and Its Consequences

It is uncertain just how animal domestication came about, but calculated and consciously purposeful action for economic ends does not seem to describe the development. Such action is not in accord with the other very early kinds of cultural development. More likely domestication began as an unconscious thing involving the symbiotic relationships between man and the small birds and animals who both scavenged his campsites and found in them a refuge from their own predators. It is likely that the initial aspects of animal domestication took place prior to the significant onset of crop growing and that the taming of very young animals and birds secured from litters and nests close to the timing of psychological imprinting of the young is involved along with the symbiotic relationships between small animals and man, and the liking by man for young playmate-pets. Once the process was initiated, additional elements in its continuation may have been such features as totemism, religious sacredness and sacrifice, and economic utility. Paleolithic man, once having acquired some familiarity with animals and birds, relative to keeping, breeding, and managing them, could have extended the process as a purposeful and conscious matter to other animals of more significant economic value. That in their wild, or semiwild, state early man ate all of the small animals as part of his regular dietary could only have been an additonal factor in the whole process.

Most likely the dog, the cat, the pig, the jungle chicken, and perhaps some of the pigeons were among the first animals to enter into the domestic relationship with man (Table 4.2). Of these, all but the dog and the pigeons still maintain a sort of a will of their own, often going back into the wild environment for breeding or for periodic forays on their own. The modern symbiotic relationship between the cat and man often seems to indicate that the advantage lies with the cat, rather than man, but as early man often ate cats, this could have made the relationship mutual.

Archaeologic evidence seems to suggest that the goat and the sheep came early into a similar symbiotic relationship with man, and the gradation in skeletal remains on archaeologic sites for both animals implies a gradual shift from wild to domesticated types of animals.[*] The goat and the sheep were large enough and strong enough, when well-domesticated and trained to the operation, to be of utility to man in carrying pack loads, though we cannot be certain how early such usage really began.

The chronology of other domestications of larger

[*] Domestication, as a status, is not clearly defined biologically, but a general consensus is that when skeletal remains show marked osteological variations from the types considered normal to the wild species, then domestication, and the breeding of specific varieties, is assumed to have taken place. Modern zoo and "farm" breeding of "wild" animals suggests a broadened definition including human control over animal breeding, but the point remains under discussion.

TABLE 4.2 ZONAL PROVENANCE OF ANIMAL DOMESTICATIONS

1. SOUTHERN AND EASTERN ASIA, SOUTH OF THE HIMALAYAS-YANGTZE VALLEY

Pigs*—*Sus* spp   Chicken*—*Gallus* spp   Ducks*—*Anas* spp
Dogs*—*Canis* spp   Pheasant*—*Phasianus* spp   Geese*—*Cygnopsis* spp
Cats*—*Felis* spp   Peacock—*Pavo cristalus*   Silkworm*—*Bombyx mori* & spp

Zebu cattle—*Bos namadicus* & spp into *Bos indicus* breeds[a]
Water buffalo—*Bubalis bubalis*
Mithan—*Bos gaurus* & spp (?)
Banteng—*Bos banteng* & spp (?)

2. INTERIOR EURASIA, NORTH OF THE HIMALAYAS AND WEST OF CHINA PROPER

Goats*—*Capra* spp   Camel*—*Camelus bactrianus*
Sheep*—*Ovis* spp   —*Camelus dromedarius*
Horses*—*Equus* spp   Reindeer—*Rangifer tarandus*
Yak—*Bos grunniens*

Taurus cattle—*Bos primigenius* & spp into *Bos taurus* breeds[a]

3. CLASSICAL NEAR EAST, MEDITERRANEAN BASIN, NORTHEAST AFRICA

Pigs*—*Sus* spp   Donkey*—*Equus asinus* & spp
Cats*—*Felis* spp   Horses*—*Equus* spp
Dogs*—*Canis* spp   Goats*—*Capra* spp
Ducks*—*Anas* spp   Sheep*—*Ovis* spp
Geese*—*Anser* & *Alopochen* spp   Rabbit*—*Oryctolagus cunuculus*
Pigeon*—*Columba* spp   White rat—an albino form of one of the *Rattus* spp
Guinea fowl*—*Numida* spp

4. MESOAMERICA, INCLUDING THE ANDES

Llama—*Lama glama*
Alpaca—*Lama pacos*
Muscovy duck—*Cairina moschata*
Turkey—*Meleagris gallopavo*
Guinea pig—*Cavia porcellus*

5. MISCELLANEOUS AND MARGINAL NOTATIONS

Swan—*Cygnus olor* appears to relate to northwest Europe at a late date.
Elephant—*Elephas maximus*. Often considered domesticated, the Indian elephant seldom has bred in captivity and cannot be considered fully domesticated.
Onager—*Equus hemionus*. Now extinct, the onager sometimes is considered a historic domestication, but extinction makes this doubtful.

Honeybee—*Apis mellifera*
Stingless bee—*Melipona beechii*   Although kept in captivity and productive for mankind, it can be argued that
Cochineal—*Dactylopius coccus*   these forms are only manipulated by man and are not fully domesticated.
Lac insect—*Lacciffer lacca*

Many of the modern laboratory animals, the fur-farm animals, and the zoo-bred animals comprise a large group of animal forms to which the older definition of domestication does not fully apply. Current manipulation of many animal forms may eventually produce new breeds and new conditions of animal maintenance that will require redefinition of the term domestication.

---

[a] The interbreeding of *Bos taurus* and *Bos indicus* cattle in both eastern and western Eurasia, both very early and more recently, has produced many mixed breeds of cattle. Occasional interbreeding between varied members of the Bovini tribe has produced several localized breeds in small numbers.

The use of the plural name indicates domestication in more than one region.

The use of the asterisk suggests that several species and/or sub-species of wild forms probably entered into the evolution of the domesticated breeds.

animals is quite uncertain, for the dates have been moved progressively back into earlier time as archaeological research continues. A suggestive sequence of domestication would put cattle, the donkey, the horse, the reindeer, the camel, and the elephant in that order with the first domestic cattle dating from as early as 6000 B.C., and the elephant from perhaps 2500 B.C.

The locations of domestications of all the animals are still uncertain. Once the processes began, there apparently was diffusion of the concept and numerous secondary domestications presumably occurred from southeastern Asia to the Atlantic Ocean. Arguments for almost every one of the domesticated animals of the Old World favor either North Africa, the Middle East, India, or southeastern Asia. Apparently many attempts were made to domesticate animals that have not matured into populations of domestic races, such as the onager and some of the antelopes. The wide regional distribution of many of the wild stocks which provided the domesticated species is such that repeated domestications could easily have taken place. The accompanying chart (see Table 4.2) presents an attempt to categorize all of the animal domestications, but many problems remain surrounding many species on the list. Notably, animal domestication succeeded far better in the Old World than in the New World, for which the list is both small and not significant. There is reason to suggest that New World domestication possibly took place only after an early pre-Columbian transfer of the idea from the Old World.

Concerning cattle, domestication activity clearly involved several groups in different regions of the earth. The genus *Bos* contains numerous species and subspecies, some of which were native to Eurasia north of the Himalaya Mountains and some of which were native to southern Eurasia. What are commonly called taurus cattle (*Bos taurus* L.) apparently derive from a wild *Bos primigenius* but with several patterns of development across north-central Eurasia, and several domesticated breeds were clearly in existence by 3000 B.C., so that the beginnings of this line of domestication must reach rather far back. The cattle varieties commonly termed zebu or brahman (*Bos indicus* L.) seem derived from a wild *Bos namadicus* of India, and this line seems equally old. The water buffalo (*Bubalis bubalis* L.) derived from India but may not be as old as the zebu form of cattle. The cattle of North China, Central Asia,

southwest Asia, and Europe are those related to *Bos taurus*, whereas most of the Southeast Asian and African cattle are related to *Bos indicus*. Taurus cattle were brought to the New World very soon after the Columbian Discoveries, but in the twentieth century zebu cattle have been interbred with them in the warmer parts of the New World to produce crossbreeds that endure the warmer climates and the poorer forage of the American tropics and subtropics.

Prior to domestication Paleolithic man apparently had learned to drive, round up, or direct the movements of wild herd animals sufficiently to be able to exert some regional control over their seasonal movements. Many of the small animals and some of the birds are not strongly migratory, but alternate seasonally between local regional ecological situations. Evidently Paleolithic man could derive considerable food support from many of the animals in a semicontrolled situation. It is likely that large herd animals often threatened to overrun the patches of crop plantings when these early farming patterns lay near the herd ranges; driving off the animals could be combined with hunting. Certainly this was also true in forested regions in which wild pigs and deer formed a serious threat to early crop-growing efforts. The consequences of domestication, of course, were to render control over a group of animals more complete, so as to provide a steadier source of supply.

The domestication of animals gave Neolithic man an alternative means of production. It made possible the occupation of some of the drier regions in which crop growing could not be carried on effectively in earlier periods. The two patterns of domestication, of plants and animals, broadened the range of economic capabilities, made possible the integration of animal economies with plant economies, and permitted a powerful production system which, for the first time, gave man considerable freedom from dependence on harvests from the natural environment. In some regions animal keeping probably preceded crop growing, but the net effects were to increase the range of variations by which man could live in different parts of the earth and to initiate significant population increase.

The Evolution of Animal Husbandry and Its Systems

A common theme in the older literature of the social sciences refers to the hunter's first learning to become a pastoralist and then evolving into an agriculturist. Among some culture groups this has been the line of development, but there have also been cases in which hunters learned to become crop growers and then improved their lot by becoming pastoralists. There is little truth in the former theory of unilinear development as the standard of cultural evolution. In the equatorial tropics and Pacific islands Neolithic man could grow crops but could not keep many animals. In the seasonally dry grasslands and the increasingly dry territories of North Africa, southwest Asia, and central Asia, early Neolithic man could herd animals but could not grow crops except at oases. It is evident that in certain territorial ranges animal husbandry offered an alternative to early Neolithic man. The pastoral nomadism of history was not born full-blown, but represented a pattern of economy that had to be developed into a successful system of its own. Pastoral nomadism represented a means of support for those Neolithic peoples who either preferred the open and drier country, or the colder northern country, or who could not secure for themselves a sufficiently humid, mild-temperatured, and adaptable territorial range where crop growing could be practiced.

Animal husbandry, in its initial stages, required much experiment and trial-and-error effort. In its pursuit many localized breeds of animals were developed to fit particular ecological situations, and Neolithic man worked with particular animals in different kinds of country. Thus some of the Neolithic inhabitants of rocky and rough country containing only poor browse developed particular varieties of goats, whereas other groups in better country suited for grazing, could succeed by breeding varieties of sheep, and still others in different territorial ranges could center their efforts on cattle or horses. In northern Eurasia lay the range of the people who centered their efforts on reindeer. The elaborate schedules of seasonal pasturage, the patterns of transhumance, and the varieties of combinations of animals that could be employed by different groups all attest to a long series of experiments and developmental efforts by people who became pastoral nomads. As portions of southwest Asia and North Africa became deforested, overcropped, and overgrazed, the domesticated dromedary camel came into its own in the first millennium B.C.

In the more humid and more heavily forested tropical regions only the elephant was at home and here no animal economy early became a primary pattern. In southeastern Asia various small, territorially localized animals and birds could be selectively utilized as an auxiliary means of support but not as a primary source of animal husbandry. The use of water buffalo outside of India appears to be rather late. Various of the peoples of south Asia have kept a small number of a particular breed of cattle, the mithan, but seldom have made more than religious-sacrificial use of them.

It was in the northwestern portions of India, in Turkestan, and throughout southwest Asia, where forests and open lands alternated on local territorial ranges of varying ecological conditions, that animal husbandry evolved its most productive possibilities. Here the two basic systems, crop growing and animal keeping, could be integrated in variable proportions. Somewhere in this geographical range the domesticated animal was first put to draft purposes in the furtherance of crop growing. Animals could be fed on the wastes of cultivation, the leftovers, and the less desired crop products to enrich the economies of the culture groups engaging in the variable practices.

As a source of meat, blood, milk, hair, wool, bone, horn, leather products, and eventually fertilizer and fuel, domestic animals replaced the wild animal sources of these products to a great extent throughout the regions in which animal husbandry became part of the economy. Whatever its local or regional form, it expanded the patterns of living of all peoples employing it. As a variant to crop growing, and an improvement upon hunting economies, animal husbandry was susceptible to a tremendous range of variation and a high degree of development. Animal husbandry was, therefore, one more means by which Neolithic man secured a degree of freedom from the limits of his environment, and one more means by which cultural practices evolved to promote differential cultural development. It is notable that New World man, with the llama and the alpaca, made but few steps in this direction in pre-Columbian time, although it must be pointed out that the variety of New World wild animals as a source of domestics was much less than for the Old World.

The Maturing of Agricultural Systems

Shifting cultivation was the first system to employ different crop plants and specific cropping practices. With these plants and practices went other practices such as those related to control over land and cultivation rights, kin-oriented labor, and strong continuation of appropriation from wild-food resource ranges. There eventually appeared a different complex of practices and customs in which the most significant elements were the cultivation of permanent fields and the development of a land-control system in which land and crops went together in what is termed *agriculture.* It is not at all certain just where these latter practices originated, but it is likely that their development took place in some portion of southwest Asia, for certain other ramifications of a sedentary agricultural system show up there earlier than elsewhere. There were, of course, innumerable variants on these two basic systems; many of the features were dependent on the precise arrangement of social structure of a particular culture group and on the local plant and environment ecology in different regional sectors of the earth.

Growing crops in small field patches by hand labor with extremely simple tools is really a type of gardening operation rather than constituting what we today term agriculture. In gardening operations of the early period a variety of specific technological developments took place to increase productivity in different sites, situations, ecological environments, and regionally dissimilar settings. We know too little of the developmental history of these features to permit elaboration of their chronology and distribution, and here it must be enough to suggest them briefly. The development of terracing of planting patches to provide a smoother and flatter surface on which to work is one such feature that seems to go with the permanent-field practice of crop growing. The initiation of irrigation concepts is another, involving provision of water to seedbeds or patches of growing plants on sites too dry for natural plant growth. The development of such tools as the hoe, the rake, and the spade for soil handling and planting, improved knives, sickles, and the scythe for reaping, and the harvest box, the flail, and the threshing sled for threshing are part of the maturing of sedentary cropping procedures.

The integration of animal husbandry and crop growing made possible some basic advances and altered the basic forms of crop gardening. The presence of the domesticated animals as a source of power spurred the development of new tools such as the plow, the seeding tube, the harrow-cultivator, the land-leveling drag, and the wheeled wagon. Although the first prototypes of these tools

can not have been very efficient, a primary result of their presence was to extend the planting patch into a field of larger size. It is easier to keep a recalcitrant animal going in a straight line than to work it in circles or odd-shaped areas, so that the linear to rectangular field was a normal consequence. The increased potential in plantable area led to greater crop production, but also to a change in labor practices, probably having repercussions on group social structure. Increased yields created local surpluses of crop products, requiring new kinds of transport arrangements and crop storage facilities and permitting the evolution of new kinds of disposition of the crop yields. A surplus yield became a capital resource, and gardening for subsistence evolved into agriculture as a productive enterprise. The control over land, animals, tools, and labor underwent a variety of cultural changes in economic, social, legal, and political terms. We are not here attempting to suggest a linear evolution to civilization stemming singly from the harnessing of a domestic animal to a plow to provide power beyond the range of human muscle. The onset of civilization is a highly multiple complex of many developments. We are, however, suggesting that the provision of animal power turned simple gardening into agriculture, and that accompanying the change in cropping practices were changes in the control over land, labor, crop disposition, and technological practices that altered the whole basic structure of crop growing and animal husbandry to permit the development of several different agricultural systems.

Within the period from about 3000 B.C. to about A.D. 400, agriculture in the Old World matured in a number of respects. The concept of the sedentary field as a cropping surface evolved into the system of private landownership of agricultural lands. This involved such elements as the land tax (on land itself rather than a tribute from the crop yield), the concept of legal title to land, the concept of mortgaging the land itself, the systems of land tenure, and the concept of tenancy as applied to agricultural lands. Not only did these concepts develop, but also the whole growing set of complexes diffused over much of the Old World (Figs. 4.11 and 4.12). The spread of many of these items was much more rapid than the earlier diffusion of ideas about domestication of plants and the growing of crops. Almost the whole complex gradually spread throughout the Mediterranean Basin to form the basic structure of Mediterranean

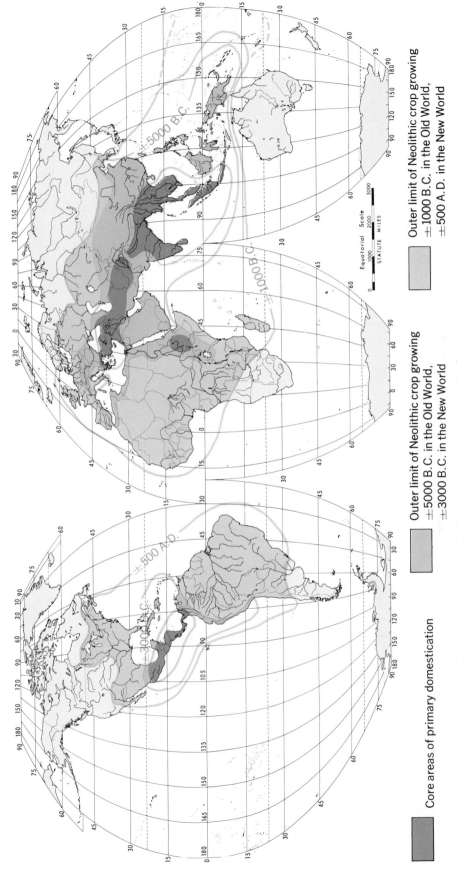

Outer limit of Neolithic crop growing
±1000 B.C. in the Old World,
±500 A.D. in the New World

Outer limit of Neolithic crop growing
±5000 B.C. in the Old World,
±3000 B.C. in the New World

Core areas of primary domestication

Equatorial Scale
0   1000   2000   3000
STATUTE MILES

FIG. 4.11 THE SPREAD OF GARDENING AND OF PLOW AGRICULTURE. A. The Spread of Gardening.

161

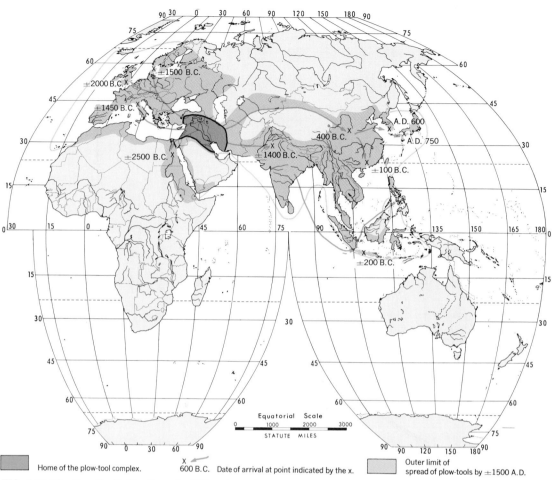

Home of the plow-tool complex.

X ← 600 B.C. Date of arrival at point indicated by the x.

Outer limit of spread of plow-tools by ±1500 A.D.

FIG. 4.11 (*Continued*) B. The Spread of Plow Agriculture in the Old World.

agricultural economy. In the other direction the entire set of ideas was introduced into North China in the first millennium B.C., to constitute a basic structural change in the nature of the Chinese economy.

Within the same interval many regional patterns of crop growing and animal husbandry were maturing within the central sectors of the Old World. What is termed irrigation agriculture, within the drier parts of the Old World, developed specific technologies in which terracing, irrigation, particular crops, seasonal practices, and particular customs developed. Winter wheat, spring vegetable and fruit crops, the olive tree, and other features, all form a distinctive Mediterranean-southwest Asian agricultural system in which animals play a minor but significant role. Farther north in Europe, irrigation was not needed and wheat could still be grown in many areas as a winter crop, but animals became more significant in the whole operation. Also in Europe the fewer kinds of fruits

were of different and hardier types, and summers were more important in minor crop production than spring or winter periods. Agriculture in India, on the other hand, developed a different crop sequence, seasoned to the monsoon cycle, and used dairy products, but slowly developed a taboo on the eating of beef which gradually extended itself to the flesh of other animals. Agriculture in North China early centered itself on the growth of millets as a basic staple but slowly adopted wheat as the food of a larger share of the population, declined to use dairy products, kept some cattle as draft power, developed the pig and the chicken for food supplies, domesticated a series of crop varieties distinctive to eastern Asia, while keeping the whole production complex much nearer to crop gardening than had agriculture in western Europe. Somewhere in South China-Southeast Asia, rice became a crop staple to replace the taros and yams, and involved the wet-field principle in which water control and terracing went together in a humid-

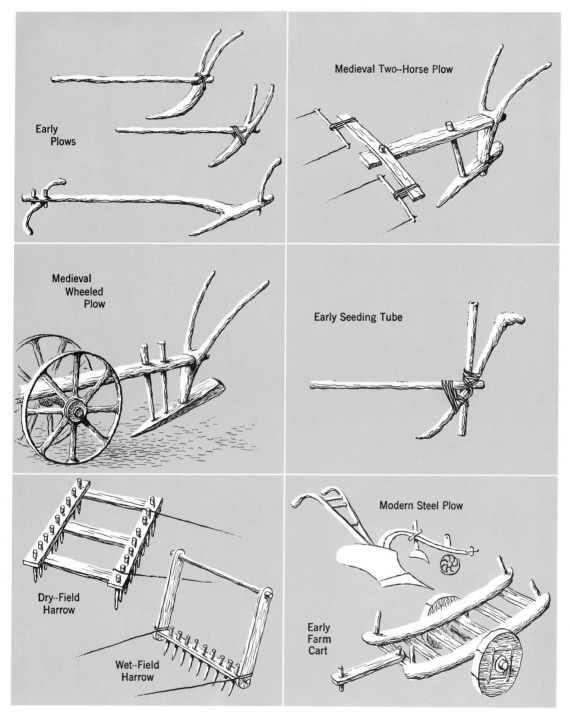

FIG. 4.12   THE BASIC TOOLS OF AGRICULTURE.

land modification of the irrigation concept. Here water buffalo replaced cattle as draft power in the muddy fields, and the basic agricultural tools became modified to suit wet-field cultivation.

There were basic similarities among all Old World agricultural systems in that private land-ownership and the permanent field were present, as opposed to the still prevalent but older gardening system of shifting cultivation with rights of use to the clearing only until cessation of crop harvesting. But in broad regional terms no two agricultural systems were fully alike, for ecological conditions varied in different environments, and cultural patterns of ethnic groups developed different twists in practice. In North China, for example, slavery gradually died out, whereas in the Greek and Roman culture cheap slave labor often performed much of the arduous work. In late Roman times great private landholdings began to build up, operated by slaves and tenants in the evolution of the systems of *latifundia* which the Spanish and Portuguese were later to take to their New World colonies. The serfdom that later characterized northern Europe was a particular regional aspect of an agricultural system which had its origins in ancient Rome.

In the New World during its habitation by American Indians, no such basic changes in crop gardening took place, since no animal husbandry of an equivalent sort evolved. There were no domestications of the big animals suitable to the provision of draft power, meat supplies, dairy products, and related aspects. Sedentary gardening did appear, along with irrigation, terracing, and sundry aspects of improved crop growing, but the origins of these elements are subject to the position taken with regard to whether there were extensive pre-Columbian contacts between the New and Old worlds; the issue is whether these cultural elements were diffused from the Old World or independently invented at a later time in the New World.

The maturing of agricultural systems in various portions of the earth gave strong impetus to the development of differential cultural development. The developments not only had the obvious impact upon the earth's surface itself, in terms of agricultural landscapes, but also upon dietary systems, land-control systems, social-labor systems, and many varieties of cultural practice.

Traditions of Materials Supply, Processing, and Consumption

Paleolithic man began early to express his curiosity about the nature of the physical materials around him on the surface of the earth. He tasted, chewed, cut, dug, roasted, burned, pounded, stripped, washed, rubbed, and otherwise investigated most of the plants, animals, rocks, minerals, and waters in a trial-and-error sort of experimentation. What was it? Could he eat it, drink it, wear it, use it as a body paint, turn it into a decorative trinket, make a tool or a weapon of it, or use it as an agent in doing something else? His earliest knowledge of physical properties, of chemical re-

actions, of mechanics, and of physical laws was very slight, and the technologies available to him were very limited, but he kept trying because he was man and his mind was stimulated and never satisfied. Living close to the physical materials of his world, he learned the rudiments of a great many things in nature that many of us do not know today.

Slowly Paleolithic man accumulated a vast lore of knowledge. Much of what he did not understand became associated with mysticism, awe and superstition, reverence and worship, or dislike and taboo. But his knowledge kept increasing, and folktales and tall stories spread from people to people. And the things he found useful were exchanged, stolen, lost and found by others, seized, or given away, so that much of the knowledge spread widely over the earth, stimulating other people to new kinds of trial-and-error experimentation in production, processing, or utilization.

As technology improved, early man returned to materials and things he remembered but with which he previously could do nothing. A small discovery of a reaction or a property restarted a series of trials. A small invention made possible a new kind of processing which rendered a useful result or a product that, in turn, allowed further experimentation. Small step after small step the process became cumulative, but it must be remembered that by the end of the Paleolithic Age man had lived on the earth for nearly two million years and progress had been extremely slow. By the late Paleolithic, however, the small steps had become numerous and the total accomplishment had reached the point where the integration of knowledge began to produce an increasing rate of progress. The Mesolithic, the time of significant changes in the physical earth during the terminal phases of the last glacial stage, was a period of notable upward spiraling in human activity and inventiveness.

By the end of the Mesolithic period man had learned to find, process, and use most of the plant materials; he had learned a good deal about rock and stone materials; he knew what to do with most bird and animal materials; and he understood a good deal about the various kinds of waters on the surface of the earth. This is to say he had solved the basic technologies employable in processing and supplying raw materials, agents, and end products. He had not yet solved the problems around those minerals that yielded metals, but he understood and worked with many of the water-soluble minerals. Production and processing traditions were established, and many of the consumption patterns were already fairly well fixed among one or another people. The basic developments had taken place in textile making, in pottery manufacture, in tool-stone mining and fabrication, and in processing the several staple food types that formed the heart of the diet in many parts of the world. The key exchange routes were beginning to function in the Old World and, to a lesser extent, in the New World, as forerunners to the great trade routes of later time.

In the Neolithic age technologies in the processing and production of materials for human use flowered, since many of these materials sprang from production rather than remaining dependent on the bounty of nature. Processing technology advanced rapidly, for there were large quantities of materials to be processed. Consumption patterns also increased and became stabilized through cultural preferences. Many of the basic regional cultural preferences of the world thus date from this time. It is in the Neolithic, for example, that wheat products came to be the staple food from southwest Asia northwestward across Europe and northeastward into North China. In this same interval the peoples of eastern India, mainland southeastern Asia, southern China, and southern Japan evolved into rice eaters, whereas the island world of the Southwest Pacific concentrated upon the taros, yams, and bananas, and the central portions of the New World became eaters of maize, squashes, and beans. Similarly, clothing systems, housing systems, tool systems, and other phases of production-consumption crystallized into regional systems. As the regional systems matured, the diversity of patterns over the earth increased.

The Age of the Metals: Mining, Ores, and Smelting

By definition, the end of the Neolithic is established around the timing of the first conscious metallurgy, that is, the mining, smelting, and fabricating of metals from ores rather than the usage of free copper, gold, and silver. The date is an arbitrary one, dependent on accurate historical record, though most date references to the Age of Metals are still prefixed by such words as "perhaps," "probably," or "about." As yet we do not know for certain the location and date of the first purposeful metallurgy. Actually it is uncertain that smelting operations began around metal-yielding minerals, but it is common to relate metallurgy to the copper-oxide ores and their smelting into metallic copper. As archaeologic work continues, the dates move back a bit, and may continue to do so. Here we resort to the usual procedure and place the date at about 3700 B.C., and the location as some portion of the classical Near East or its borders, very possibly near what today is northwestern Iran.

Once the basic technology of smelting was devised involving a crude furnace, an ore mix, the charcoal fuel, and a time sequence, mining became a new kind of operation. It now sought mineral ores rather than rocks and stones. Although the first "prospector" had been an early Paleolithic man who went hunting for a particular kind of a stone, the craft of the prospector now involved new skills. Mining began to change its technology, and there came distinctions among the prospector, the miner, and the smelter. Although it is common to refer to copper smelting as the first variety, it is doubtful if there was a significant Copper Age (Chalcolithic), since the early artifacts are commonly bronze, involving a mixture of tin and copper. Our firm knowledge of early developments of smelting is unclear, but before long the mining and smelting of copper, tin, gold, silver, lead, and iron were involved, possibly in that order. The order of mining and smelting varies regionally by mineral, but the technology appears very similar in respect to the furnace build, charcoal as the fuel, the timing sequences, and the product patterns. Volumes were but a few pounds per furnace per day. The last of the basic minerals, iron, may date as late as 1500 B.C., although recent archaeologic work promises to push the date back in northern Iran.

In contrast to the rather slow diffusion of crop growing over the Old World, the spread of metal smelting moved much less slowly, and bronze products are dated close to 2500 B.C. in regions as far from the Near East as Britain, North China, and northern India (Fig. 4.13). Curiously, early metal smelting was slow in moving into Africa beyond Egypt, but, once begun, iron smelting spread widely. In the New World metal smelting is usually attributed to independent invention sometime after the start of the Christian Era, working first with gold and silver and then with bronze, but the diffusionists hold that its introduction came from the Old World.

The handling of smelted metals is not well

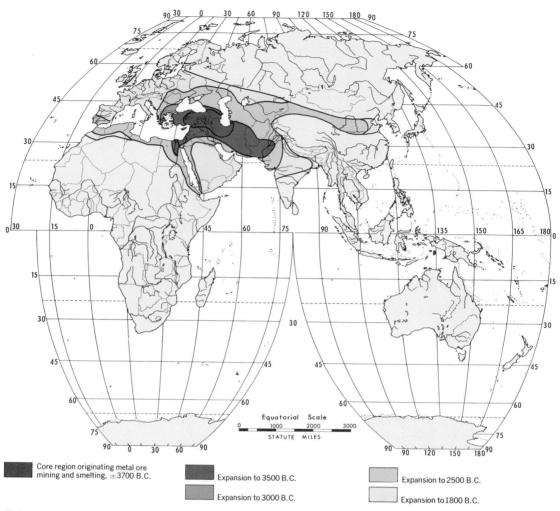

	Core region originating metal ore mining and smelting, ±3700 B.C.		Expansion to 3500 B.C.		Expansion to 2500 B.C.
			Expansion to 3000 B.C.		Expansion to 1800 B.C.

FIG. 4.13 THE DIFFUSION OF MINING AND SMELTING.

known for the earliest periods, but it appears that the melting and reforming of free copper and gold preceded smelting of ores. The handling of bronze and iron after smelting is a more difficult operation. Forging and casting evolved within the home region of smelting, both spread widely, and the crafts of the smith and of the founder became widespread and technically highly skilled. In the diffusion of metalworking there was regional variation in the choice of forging or casting. Forging became almost the only practice employed with iron in northwestern Europe until the modern era, Africa became dominantly a region of forging, India practiced both forging and casting, and North China dominantly employed casting with both bronze and iron. Working out the processing technology was not easy and took some time to develop; the period from perhaps 2600 to 2100 B.C. was one during which the smelting, forging,

casting, and other fabricating techniques made rather rapid advances. After about 2000 B.C. there were few really significant advances in smelting and fabricating procedures until almost the modern era, and the classical empires of the Old World continued to use the standard techniques.

There are two kinds of mining, surface mining and lode mining. The modern strip miner for coal or copper employs exactly the same techniques as the Paleolithic jade miner; both picked up their product from the surface, with the advantage, of course, lying with the modern operator who can pick up a huge volume at a single grasp of his enormous machine. Although Paleolithic man dug some fairly deep holes and pits in mining for flint, jade, and other valuable tool stones, lode mining did not properly begin until well into the Neolithic when miners began driving galleries into lode veins carrying free gold, copper, and precious stones.

The essential techniques of filling exhausted galleries with rubble, leaving pillars of natural stone for support of the roof, and opening ventilating shafts are all Neolithic innovations. Water was another problem; excess water in lode mines was not effectively handled until the invention of pumps in the modern era. By the onset of metal smelting, however, the essential procedures in mining had been developed and perfected to the point that miners could work ore bodies almost to any desired depth provided the mines were not beset with excess water. The essential mining techniques, horn and stone picks, lamps, and carrying devices to remove rubble or product, changed but little from the Neolithic to the modern era, although horn and stone in the tools were replaced by bronze and iron.

In the early world the mineral cycle was a simple boom and bust, with little redevelopment of an old mining site. In particular regions exhausted mining sites were abandoned to the elements, many of them worked out thoroughly, within the limits of early technology. It is only in the modern era that the concept of the mineral cycle has been developed, a subject dealt with in a later chapter.

The coming of metallurgy had a tremendous effect upon economic technology in all parts of the world to which it spread. Metallurgy was a further element that sparked the growth of civilization, and its effects were ramified. Metals went into agricultural tools, into fabricating tools of all sorts for cutting, grinding, filing, and shaping, and metals went into consumer goods of a wide range indeed, from decorative jewelry to cooking pots. Many of our common implements of today date from an inventive application of metallurgy dating as far back as 2500 B.C.; there is little essential difference in heating efficiency between the cast iron cooking pot of 2500 B.C. and the gleaming stainless steel cooking pan of today; the modern stainless steel fingernail file may be lighter and more easily carried than its bronze replica of 2500 B.C., but it serves the purpose with little more efficiency; and the Chinese woman of the Shang Dynasty in the eighteenth century B.C. could apply her makeup as easily with her bronze mirror as can any teen-ager using a stainless steel mirror today. We are not speaking, here, of the wood fire that blackened the old cooking pot or of the neatly packaged lipstick of today, but of the basic application of metals to consumer goods.

Actually, fewer persons possessed metal tools and goods then than now, and the per capita consumption of metal products per year was a low figure in comparison to that in the United States today. An estimate places the total smelter yield of copper, down to 1300 B.C., at about 10,000 tons. However, about 2000 B.C. a single temple at Thebes, Egypt, received an annual tribute of some 120 pounds of gold per year, plus other volumes of other metals; this gold at today's U.S. Treasury value would amount to about $50,000. By 1400 B.C. the Nubians were paying an annual tribute to Egypt approaching 800 pounds of gold, worth $300,000 at today's prices, and gold in Egypt had become more highly valued than copper. In the fourteenth century B.C. in Egypt iron still was valued at five times the value of gold and 40 times the value of silver but, with tribute of both flowing inward, Egypt found it more convenient to import iron from the Near East than to mine and smelt it. The use of iron for making common tools came slowly and, outside portions of the Near East, did not become common in the Mediterranean Basin until after 700 B.C. In Britain it was not common until after the coming of the Romans and in China about the fourth century B.C. A gift of 30 pounds of "steel" to Alexander the Great, in the late fourth century B.C. was considered munificent. Iron was difficult to work at best, and steel could be made only in very small amounts by hand-forging iron and by carburizing it for long periods in a charcoal fire.

By about 2000 B.C. the properties of most common metals had been learned, their ores had been located, the smelting and basic fabricating techniques had been worked out, and most of the basic alloy compositions had been approximated. Until almost the modern era, after about 2000 B.C., the history of metallurgy is chiefly one of diffusion of basic knowledge and techniques, with each regional culture group reacting slightly differently to the whole complex. Although the knowledge of metals had developed soundly, the cultural inventiveness in how to use them had to await the modern era.

Textile Materials, Techniques, and Clothing Systems

Paleolithic man learned fairly early the rudiments of preparing string and rope from various kinds of materials, by devising the essential elements of the spinning process. Later he added basketry in various forms with many different types of materials. The weaving of baskets from plain or processed materials, in late Paleolithic time, became so close to what is termed weaving with textiles that the distinction may often be hard to make. True textiles woven from spun materials, however, are most commonly considered to be Neolithic in timing. Archaeologic research is broadening the range and distribution of textiles and their processing, and it is almost safe to assert that textile spinning and weaving had a worldwide distribution by the end of the Neolithic, although there were specific culture groups that did not employ any of these processes.

By the end of the Neolithic period, man was using bast, flax, hemp, abaca, jute, ramie, sisal-henequen, silk, cotton, wool, and the hair of many different animals in the preparation of textiles of some kind. Spinning of the "thread" could be done in many ways, but the spinning whorl is one of the common archaeologic artifacts. Weaving is the most widespread of the methods of preparing a textile, and the variety of weaving systems is great, but all are merely variations on basic systems, using some variant of the simple handloom. There is regional concentration, of course, in the development of the textile fibers, silk being East Asian, jute being South Asian, abaca being Philippine, sisal-henequen being Middle American, cottons being East African–Northeast Indian and Middle American, and the "wools" and "hair" being regionally distributed per the specific animal. Ramie, flax, and hemp were, however, widely distributed in the Neolithic Old World; bast, of course, refers to the soft inner-bark from some tree species and was obtained from numerous kinds of trees in many parts of the earth.

Various fibers must be processed prior to their use in textiles. Ramie, flax, hemp, sisal-henequen, and abaca must be retted or scraped to free the fiber from the fleshy overcoating, and each specific process was developed very early. Silk has a specific processing of its own to remove the fiber from the cocoon. Wools and hairs of different types must be hackled or combed and washed to make them usable.

In addition to the normal textiles we must, for a discussion of clothing systems, include the animal skins, furs, and leathers, and the sheet bast normally termed bark cloth. Each of these also had its own processing sequences of curing, tanning, and pounding.

Weaving is but one of the methods of preparing

a "textile," although it perhaps was the most common in early times and, as suggested, seems nearly worldwide. Felting, on the other hand, appears rather late as a Central Asian development. The making of a floss from raw silk to serve as a liner for a quilted garment or piece of bedding is Chinese, as the making of a floss of cotton appears to be derived from East Africa–North India. Knitting is little studied as a technique and seldom reported, but it is known from ancient southwest Asia, and became widely distributed in western but not eastern Eurasia. In other local regions there were minor techniques for preparing something approximating a textile, such as the interleaving of palm spathes to form a crude raincoat, or the twisting and knotting done to straw to make sandals.

The wearing of garments is but one aspect of what here is thought of as clothing systems. A better term for the whole complex is adornment, for the complex includes a wide range of elements from tattooing and scarification to the application of body paints and cosmetics, the wearing of jewelry, the styling of the hair, and the wearing of garments. There is far more to the adornment system than protection from the physical elements; it involves the concepts of modesty, the attraction of the opposite sex, the establishment of social, occupational, or political status, the ornamentation of the body, and the sometime protection from insects or rough vegetation. Special status or occupations have at times dictated special garment elements, such as the yellow and red feather cloaks of Hawaiian nobility, the garb of Roman Catholic cardinals, or modern enforcement of the "hard hat" to be worn around high buildings under construction. The concept of modesty varies from culture to culture, and from era to era, chiefly under religious stimulation, and may involve any of the elements of adornment rather than just garments. In effect the concept is a cultural definition which is not based simply on the degree of exposure of the human body.

With these patterns in existence and operative, the utilization of textile materials may be voluminous or lacking in a regional culture. The adornment system may be composed chiefly of nontextiles, for a large share of the earth's lowlands can now be occupied by the human species with a minimum of protection from the physical elements. The changing definition of human comfort may result in a given individual's feeling of discomfort in a rainstorm without a raincoat, but in many regions his biological survival does not depend on the raincoat. The same is true of the definition of comfort as regards exposure to cold or to the sun. In Paleolithic times, during the last glacial stage, man had to retreat from many regions for biological survival, owing to freezing cold, but modern man lives on a milder earth, and has defined the conditions of comfort, which his culture permits him to do.

Intrinsically, there are three possible classifications to garments and the garment-wearing system (see pp. 47–58). The oldest is the draped pattern, by which a skin, a piece of bark cloth, or a piece of textile was wrapped around the body. Such draped clothing patterns involve almost no processing of the materials in the matter of cutting and fitting, often requiring large enough pieces of material that the whole body may be swathed or covered. Such draped elements as the sarong of the South Seas fall within this pattern, as do the poncho, the Roman toga, the Arab burnoose, and the Indian dhoti and sari. A second garment-wearing system stems from the knitted garment. The knitted garment may produce formfitting or loosely draped items, but the lack of knowledge about the history and distribution of knitting precludes extensive comment. Post-Roman northwest Europe apparently made more out of knitted garment wearing that most other portions of the world. The third garment system involves the tailored garment, by which pieces of material are cut, fitted, and sewn together to produce the desired result.

It is evident that draped garments long sufficed throughout the tropics and subtropics, reaching into the milder midlatitude regions. Such garment patterns became stylized into "national dress" for many cultures in protohistoric time and some of them have continued right down to the contemporary era, as almost any news picture out of India or the South Seas will indicate. The knitted garment may have originated in the colder parts of the Middle East or central Asia after the domestication of sheep, for in the early traditions knitting seems always related to wool as a textile. It is thought that many of the close-fitting garments of the early Medes and the Persians were knitted of wool, for they were very different from the draped garments of the Greeks. The employment of knitting in northwestern Europe was related to the prevalence of sheep and the rise of the woolen industries.

Tailoring seems to have developed on the Arctic fringe of Eurasia out of the need for true protection from the cold. Cured furs were cut into pieces to fit the body and then sewn together into a series of upper and lower garments, gloves, and boots. Tailoring came southward into several parts of Eurasia in early time and, in the early Christian Era, seemed about to rearrange the clothing pattern of northern Europe, but the styles changed and the early diffusion did not create a lasting system of tailored clothing. It was in eastern Asia that tailoring first clearly diffused out of the Arctic fringe to affect the clothing styles of Mongolia and China. From China tailoring spread westward during the seventh to twelfth centuries, coming back into northwestern Europe during the early period of the Crusades to take hold permanently. It matured in the modern era into what is now termed "occidental dress" when the import of cottons came about and the modern cotton and wool textile industries began to flourish.

Throughout the earth culture groups have expressed traditional preferences for systems and materials that adorn the body. The cultural definitions in these matters have become so highly specific that the pattern of adornment has often been an obvious declaration of membership in a particular culture group. The widely ranging distribution of materials out of which ornaments and garments can be made has permitted great latitude for any people. Particular groups have strongly expressed their cultural habits in body adornment, ornamentation, and garment wearing. Styles, colors, items, and particular modes all are part of this complex, the whole of which is one of the strong elements that early began to differentiate cultural regionalisms during the Neolithic Age and continued to proliferate to the nineteenth century.

Science, Urbanism, the State, and Its Defense

In the regions in which a system of crop growing developed to the point that it could become sedentary and integrate the new element of animal husbandry into agriculture, the system no longer required the daily labor of every member of the group, since animals now contributed to the energy input for production. A certain share of the population was, therefore, freed from its daily routine and released to the realm of leisure or creative activity. In this newfound freedom, rather than in the sheer necessity of want, lies the seed of creative cultural development. Elements of the population now could begin to investigate the world around them in any number of ways, spending their time in all kinds of trial-and-error efforts that yielded the advances which resulted in the growth of civilization to a level superior to that referred to under the term "simple culture."

We are concerned here with such attributes of culture as the systems of writing, enumeration, and mathematics, some aspects of the rise of science, the development of urbanism, the evolution of organized religions, the maturing of political organization into the concept of the state, and the development of military defense systems. The list could be elaborated to include such features as economic elements of transport, trade, and manufacturing, the growth of metallurgy, and the growth of specific systems of mores, customs, and social patterns. The beginnings of some of these features must certainly antedate the maturing of agriculture, but their productive developments came with and after this occurrence.

Protohistoric man in different parts of the earth developed several different systems for recording speech, records, orders, warnings, and claims. Some of the earliest systems still cannot be read as to meaning or phonetic system employed. Pictorial, ideographic, hieroglyphic, and semialphabetic systems gradually gave way to syllabic alphabetic systems in the classic Near East. Variations of these systems diffused over much of the Old World, in time giving rise to all alphabetic systems of writing, but in doing so greatly increased the number of specific variants. Only in eastern Asia did the Chinese system of ideographic writing withstand the spread of the alphabetic systems to mature into the traditional Chinese system of writing.

Numerous simple systems of enumeration rose above the finger-counting level and, in time, related systems were distributed from the shores of the Indian Ocean to the Mediterranean Basin and to the North China Sea. Out of this common heritage finally came what we now term Arabic (really Indian) numerals, Roman numerals, and Chinese numerals. In the same manner the early elements of mathematics, geometry, gnomonics, and astronomy spread throughout the same broad region. The early glimpses of scientific methodology share the same general distribution throughout the Old World. At present it is hard to place the regions of origin for many of the specific aspects and elements of this whole interrelated subject matter, but their precise utilization and specific regional development characterized one or more of the old cultural centers: Egypt, Mesopotamia, Persia, Transcaspia, North India, and North China. There were variations among the several regional sectors of this large territory concerning the order in which each of the developments took place, but there can now be no question of the broad distribution of most of them or of the cultural significance of the developments within each major region. Then Greece, next the Arabic culture world, and finally, after the Renaissance, Europe carried the torch of the development of science into the twentieth century.

The growth of urbanism may best be viewed as a fairly direct result of the maturing of agriculture and animal husbandry to the level that production surpluses made possible the feeding of populations no longer directly concerned with primary production on their own account. What is often termed the urban revolution involves a number of creative developments and innovations that greatly expanded cultural patterns and ways of living, but these are results rather than causes of urbanism. Urbanism certainly required integration of political and social practice and organization, the redefinition of settlement and housing concepts, and the development of new kinds of architectural structures. Involved in the latter sector were buildings for the storage, processing, and distribution of agricultural surpluses, for the housing and feeding of transients and their animals, for the factory sites for nonagricultural processing, for the housing of political and religious performance and institutions, and possibly for the restrained custody (in a prison) of the wrongdoer. Finally, in architecture, there came the need for defensive construction of various types ranging from walls and battlements to the garrison barracks. The accumulation of large numbers of structures on specific sites also led to the formalizing of the morphology of the urban entity in the grid plan layout of the streets, drains, and lines of access. The institutionalizing of human activity in such varied social circumstances as the inn, the restaurant, the factory, the shop, and the temple went right along with the development of the physical structures.

With the appearance of urbanism, a redefinition of old concepts of territoriality probably went hand in hand with evolving concepts of control over land as a productive facility. Herein we see the evolution of the concept of the state as a formal territorialism carrying with it evolving rules regarding how members of a culture group could obtain and retain rights to land and its cultivation. Herein we also see the evolution from simple systems of giving portions of crop yields as tribute to group leaders and shamans into formal systems of taxation of the productive land of the territorial unit, whether for crop growing, for animal husbandry, for continued hunting of game and the appropriation of wild-plant products, for the securing of building materials, or for the mining of ores used in metallurgy.

The formal appearance of the state as a territorial entity was accompanied by the appearance of the superchief as a political officer in command and control. This was marked in the Near-Middle East, perhaps most clearly related to Egypt, by the figure of the God-King who was all-powerful and was the holder of both temporal and spiritual power. The God-King's residence was both a palace and a temple: as a palace it became both the treasury and the seat of political administration; as a temple it became the sacred ritual place and the center of pilgrimage. Both as a palace and a temple the seat of the God-King required a secular and religious bureaucracy to carry out the manifold functions. This concept spread in one manifestation or another throughout the whole region from the Mediterranean Basin to the Indian Ocean and to the North China Sea; sometimes the King was also God, but in some cases the King was only the earthly and human representative of the gods. The elaboration of both formal political and religious institutions followed, each in its own regional patterns to the end that the record of the title to land, and its taxation, and the observance of religious ritual found its eventual manifestation in each culture. In American culture today we still see these specific items separately in the offices of the County Recorder and the County Tax Assessor, and in the periodic religious service under ministration of a member of the priesthood.

Within specific regions, among particular culture groups, and from time to time, history records the revolt against either the temporal or religious power of the God-King. Among the Greeks political revolt veered toward democracy, the separation of temporal and religious power, and the development of new kinds of political institutions, both administrative and territorial. In Palestine religious reform movements crystallized in the teachings of Jesus and the institutionalizing of the Christian Church by Paul. In India the village council of an earlier day continued to operate at the local level as the God-King took over at the national level, and Buddhism sought a reform to the religious dominance of the God-King. In China the emperor held temporal power through the "mandate of Heaven" only as a representative of the gods, and he could lose his mandate by poor performance. In early modern Europe we know of the decline of the doctrine of the Divine Right of Kings, although the titular role of the King as the head of the Church continued.

Implicit in the formalization of the political state was the development of military defense systems. Three aspects characterize this pattern. One element is the military force itself, the growth of the war party into the army and navy. Second is the development of weapons and tactics, and third is the development of fortification. Among different peoples in different regions the three elements developed variably, with first one and then another taking a lead. The urban settlement could provide increased manpower, it could devise tactics and manufacture equipment, and it turned into a variably fortified settlement that could resist the siege of the attacker. The military defense system was amenable either to defense or to aggressive attack, and it became formalized into an instrument of the political state.

Urbanism settled on the city the wealth, power, culture, and initiative-in-development for the territorial unit that became the state. In that the city drew in the produce of the surrounding regions and became the center of administration, it came to hold sway over rural territory and to have the power of creative orientation. To the degree that a city's population was aggressive and creative it flourished, and with it the territory round about. Whereas the first feeble Paleolithic cultural advances had depended on small groups in relative isolation without the integrative stimulus of interested neighbors, the city became a cultural incubator in which close associations of peoples with different interests had a stimulating effect upon one another. Henceforth, the city became the seat and the source for cultural advancement.

The Formation and Appearance of Civilizations

Our English word "civilization" acquired its current meanings during the eighteenth century, based upon sixteenth- and seventeenth-century elaborations of the concepts citizen and citizenship around the two words "civic" and "civil." The terms derive from a Latin root having reference to a citizen, implying an organized society in a political state of some sophistication. Culture is a continuum, however, and there is no inherent distinction between the culture of a noncivilized group and a civilized people except that there are more numerous culture complexes among the latter. For all that, it is common to speak of civilization as possessing certain attributes which are greater than those characterizing the so-called simple culture. The distinctions connoting civilization are subjective in the minds of the civilized, who then regard certain other peoples and cultures as noncivilized, uncivilized, or barbaric. Europeans perhaps began to make such distinctions in the fourteenth century, but the tendency is a very old one, and the Chinese have always regarded non-Chinese as barbarians. How, then, do we specify the maturing of relatively simple cultures into civilizations, and what are the attributes, culture components, and culture complexes that signify civilization?

Many scholars have concerned themselves with this problem. There are answers that center on political organization and territorial administration; that focus on the creative impact of the formalizing and institutionalizing of religious systems; that see in the drying out of the post-Pleistocene earth the concentration of culture groups and ways of living in restricted territories which possess water resources available to limited technologies; or that find in the particular physical environments of the Mesopotamian lowland or the Nile Valley the requisite sort of cradle for an irrigation agriculture which could have turned Neolithic village communities into civilized political states built around cities. Into every explanation comes the city, the political state, the impact of organized religion, the social kinship system matured into the citizenship system, the effect of agriculture-animal husbandry, the growth of handicraft manufacturing, metallurgy, systems of writing, and the elements of science. There is neither full agreement upon the dating of the maturing of civilization, upon its total construct, nor upon the specific elements that distinguish civilization from noncivilization. We can add no mystical element in explanation, although we see civilization as a further and significant step in the growth of human culture on an earth upon which man could plant his own impress; perhaps civilization implies that the cultural processes had to a degree become conscious rather than undirected gropings. Although life for the slave in an early city was not really civilized, it does appear that in achieving civilization man, collectively, had put together a culture system which gave him a larger measure of self-determined independence from nature than that possible to small culture groups during the Neolithic.

How many regional examples of early civilization were there? Again there is no full agreement, and the number of regional culture centers achieving civilization ranges from two to seven, depending on the criteria and the view taken (Fig. 4.14). Mesopotamia and the Nile Valley show up in every list; Crete is sometimes added by the scholars who see civilization wholly as a creation of the classical Near East. Northwest India and North China are normally added by those partial to the Old World but not blinded to Asian developments. The Middle American and Andean Highland regions are included by those scholars who take a cross-cultural, worldwide view of the growth of human accomplishment. The beginnings are normally spread no wider than these seven regions, other units being considered offshoots of some one of them. The dating employed varies with the number of regions included; few opinions yet credit the New World centers with the antiquity of Mesopotamia and the Nile Valley as the oldest centers. A more detailed consideration of these early centers of civilization is presented in the chapter that follows.

Important points about all seven regions are that, except for the Mayan sector of Middle America, they lie outside the humid tropical lowlands, that none of them lies in truly formidable climatic regions, that they all are regions having relatively good physical situations affording human contact with surrounding regions, that each was relatively close to a plant region affording numerous domesticable plants, and that all possess small to large tracts of land easily cultivable by early crop-growing technologies. Beyond these attributes not all seven regions equally possess characteristics sometimes held important in the growth of civilization. The five Old World centers were all in situations affording contact among the whole number, and the two New World centers were likewise in contact with each other. An important point is that

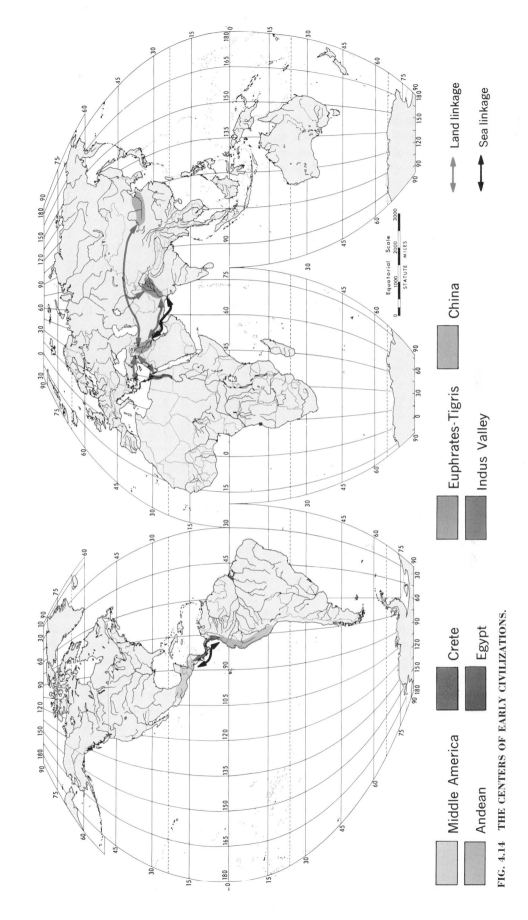

Middle America   Crete   Euphrates-Tigris   China

Andean   Egypt   Indus Valley

← → Land linkage

↑ ↓ Sea linkage

Equatorial Scale
0   1000   2000   3000
STATUTE MILES

FIG. 4.14 THE CENTERS OF EARLY CIVILIZATIONS.

173

these core regions are the places in which the critical assemblages of Neolithic culture complexes were welded together, although many of the regional origins of particular complexes lie well outside these cores.

Whatever may be the elusive key to the spark that produced civilization out of Neolithic culture, it remains true that in a number of separate regions on the earth man did succeed in devising a system of culture that intensified the collective level of living. These regions, within their broad territories, served as the sources of traits, complexes, and cultures that spread to outlying territories and regions of lesser cultural development.

Regional Differentiation, Civilizations, and Barbarians

In scattering widely over the earth, man continuously worked out a great many different living systems in relation to his sources of food and shelter, his tool systems and operational procedures, and the compatible social constructs. Every significant advance contributed to the greater variety of human cultural development. The elaboration of the basic outlines of such development distinguished man from the rest of the animal kingdom, and the further increases in human cultural design differentiated human culture groups, one from another, in different parts of the earth until the range varied from the levels of high civilization to levels describable as the simplest of cultures.

By mid-Paleolithic time, in a few parts of the world, earliest man had worked out only the most basic of the elementary systems of human living. By the end of the Paleolithic, man had about completely inhabited the earth, experimented with such of its resources as he comprehended, and probably derived most of the systematic modes that can be described under the rubric of gathering and collecting. These procedures owed something to the differential development of cultural technology, but in greater degree they reflected variation in the natural ecological conditions of environment.

The Mesolithic Age was a period during which man, in a few regions, was able to begin converting plants and animals, sticks and stones, local ecological niches and small environmental regions into forms, patterns, systems, and entities unlike those nature provided. The human technologies were rendered effective through trial and error, but they expressed the intent and ability of man to interfere with natural evolutionary processes and turn these into directions of growth and change significantly influenced by and useful to him. In carrying on these diverse activities in separate localities, man came to different solutions, with different materials, in the many distinct environments of the earth, again increasing the variety in human culture.

In the Neolithic Age the Mesolithic experiments diffused widely over the earth and matured into systems of production not entirely dependent on what man could harvest from natural processes. Man had finally created his own instruments, which permitted him to determine something of his own systems of living and the places in which he would live. In upsetting the schemes of nature man was undoubtedly destructive on occasion since he did not understand principles and conditions of ecologic balance, but many of his efforts greatly accelerated some of the natural evolutionary trends in plant and animal development. One marked result was the creation of increasing variety in human living, for in the zones of accomplishment human culture came to be something quite different from cultural forms that continued to hold in the zones and regions in which man still depended upon the bounty of nature.

As civilization matured there was marked acceleration in numerous technologies, the creation of new ones, and an increased appreciation of natural resources not previously comprehended. With the greater ability in technologies and greater control over the basic elements of the environment, human cultural modes were created that were far in advance of any that man had been able to organize theretofore. From these new creative efforts in particular locations arose the wide diffusion of new cultural complexes, technologies, social constructs, and forms of living. Although we cannot be positive when such diffusion spread throughout the Old World, and from the Old World to the New, we can see that the key regions of both Old and New Worlds shared many of the developments.* These regions also exhibited numerous

---

*We have equivocated as to the total impact of diffusion over the earth, since there is disagreement on the basic issue of independent invention as opposed to worldwide diffusion. One of the chief points of argument concerns the issue of pre-Columbian contact between the Old World and the New World. Although we lean to the side of repeated pre-Columbian diffusion to the New World, the routes, timings, peoples, and diffusion content are sufficiently uncertain that we take no flat stand in the matter.

differences even when they displayed similarities. Evidently men reacted quite differently in different regional environments in developing the ecological possibilities and utilizing their cultural resources. Such developments both added to the breadth and range of human culture and continuously created ever-widening divergence between the most advanced and least developed systems.

Basic human characteristics are the identification of the individual with a group of other persons and the tendency of the group to distinguish itself from other groups. In earliest Paleolithic time such groupings varied little in ways of living. Increasingly, however, these ways came to differ throughout the earth and, by the time civilization developed in a few key regions, the distinctions had become strong. Qualitative comparisons began to judge the variations and some cultural groups came to look upon themselves as superior to others, regarding themselves as cultured and all others as barbarians. Competivenesses between groups for territories in which different kinds of living systems could be practiced became a regular part of the human cultural spectrum, resulting in the stronger groups' driving out the simpler ones or taking over territories by subjugating the weaker. Further creative developments in regions thus acquired sometimes increased the levels of living still more. In response, weaker groups sometimes sought refuge in rough, dry, or impenetrable regions in order to maintain their existing ways of living, thereby tending to preserve older, less developed systems.

During historic time the civilized peoples have, by virtue of their superior technologies, cultural tools and instruments, transport mobility, and creative and acquisitive outlooks, continued to explore the earth, both in terms of space and materials. In their search and exploration these aggressive groups have continued to find new regions and new materials that they could utilize (what we now term "natural resources") and to devise new technologies for dealing with both space and materials, so that the systems of culture have gone on expanding.

Without dealing in detail with the historical geography of the earth from about 700 B.C. to A.D. 1900, one may summarize the processes of human activity as involving two kinds of patterns. First, there have been the creative developments that expanded human capacities and ways of living in selected, easily used, productive regions of the earth. Second, there has been the persistence of the old ways in other regions to the end that a few examples of Paleolithic and a good many cases of Neolithic living systems are still preserved. The inevitable result has been that an increasing divergence has continued among the kinds and levels of human living on the earth. At the dawn of the twentieth century the face of the earth showed greater variety in human development than at any time before, and there was the greatest known contrast and variation in the outlook of culture groups. Advancing groups were moving more rapidly and the most conservative lagged farther behind than ever. The sheer variety of content man had poured into the earth's regions and the differentiation of cultural development was more striking than it had been at any other time in the history of the universe.

SELECTED REFERENCES

Adams, Robert McC.
  1966 *The Evolution of Urban Society; Early Mesopotamia and Prehistoric Mexico.* Chicago: Aldine. 191 pp.
Ames, Oakes
  1939 *Economic Annuals and Human Culture.* Cambridge, Mass.: Botanical Museum of Harvard University. 153 pp.
Ardrey, Robert
  1966 *The Territorial Imperative.* New York: Atheneum. 390 pp.
Bagby, Philip
  1959 *Culture and History.* Berkeley and Los Angeles: University of California Press. 244 pp.
Beals, Ralph L., and Harry Hoijer
  1965 *An Introduction to Anthropology* (3rd ed.). New York: Macmillan. 788 pp.

Braidwood, Robert J., and Gordon R. Willey (eds.)
  1962 *Courses Toward Urban Life.* Chicago: Aldine. 384 pp.
Burkitt, Miles C.
  1963 *The Old Stone Age* (2nd ed.). New York: Atheneum. 270 pp.
Cottrell, Leonard
  1958 *The Anvil of Civilization.* London: Faber & Faber. 288 pp.
Coulborn, Rushton
  1959 *The Origin of Civilized Societies.* Princeton, N.J.: Princeton University Press.
        200 pp.
Curwen, E. Cecil, and Gudmund Hatt
  1953 *Plough and Pasture, The Early History of Farming.* New York: Schuman.
        329 pp.
Ehrich, Robert W. (ed.)
  1965 *Chronologies in Old World Archaeology.* Chicago: University of Chicago Press.
        557 pp.
Forbes, R. J.
  1950 *Man the Maker.* London: Constable. 355 pp.
Haggett, Peter
  1966 *Locational Analysis in Human Geography.* New York: St. Martin's Press.
        339 pp.
Hutchinson, Joseph (ed.)
  1965 *Essays on Crop Plant Evolution.* Cambridge, England: Cambridge University
        Press. 204 pp.
Kohler, Carl
  1963 *A History of Costume.* New York: Dover Publications, 464 pp.
Krader, Lawrence
  1968 *Formation of the State.* Englewood Cliffs, N.J.: Prentice-Hall, Inc. 118 pp.
Kramer, Fritz L.
  1966 *Breaking Ground: Notes on the Distribution of Some Simple Tillage Tools.*
        Sacramento, Calif: Sacramento Anthropological Society. Paper 5. 141 pp.
Kroeber, Alfred L.
  1962 *A Roster of Civilizations and Culture.* Chicago: Aldine. 96 pp.
  1963 *An Anthropologist Looks at History.* Berkeley and Los Angeles: University
        of California Press. 213 pp.
Linton, Ralph
  1959 *The Tree of Culture.* New York: Knopf. 692 pp.
Needham, Joseph
  1954–
  1965 *Science and Civilization in China.* Cambridge, England: Cambridge University
        Press. Vol. 1, 1954, 318 pp.; Vol. 2, 1956, 692 pp.; Vol. 3, 1959, 874 pp.;
        Vol. 4, Part 1, 1962, 434 pp.; Vol. 4, Part 2, 1965, 759 pp.
Piggott, Stuart
  1965 *Ancient Europe, from the Beginnings of Agriculture to Classical Antiquity.*
        Chicago: Aldine. 343 pp.
Raglan, Lord
  1964 *The Temple and the House.* New York: Norton. 218 pp.
Sahlins, M. D., and E. R. Service
  1960 *Evolution and Culture.* Ann Arbor: University of Michigan Press. 131 pp.
Sauer, Carl O.
  1952 *Agriculture Origins and Dispersals.* New York: American Geographical Society.
        110 pp.
Sayce, R. U.
  1963 *Primitive Arts and Crafts, An Introduction to the Study of Material Culture.*
        London: Hafner Publishing Co. 291 pp. (Reissue of a 1933 publication by
        Cambridge University Press.)
Schwanitz, Franz
  1965 *The Origin of Cultivated Plants.* Cambridge, Mass.: Harvard University Press.
        175 pp.
Schwartz, Marc J., Victor W. Turner, and Arthur Tuden, (eds.)
  1966 *Political Anthropology.* Chicago: Aldine. 390 pp.

Singer, Charles, E. J. Holmyard, and A. R. Hall (eds.)

    1954   *A History of Technology.* London: Oxford University Press. Vol. 1, 827 pp.; Vol. 2, 802 pp.

Spencer, J.E.

    1966   *Shifting Cultivation in Southeastern Asia.* Berkeley and Los Angeles: University of California, Publications in Geography, Vol. 19, 256 pp.

Steward, Julian H.

    1955   *Theory of Culture Change: The Methodology of Multilinear Evolution.* Urbana, Ill.: University of Illinois Press. 244 pp.

Taton, Rene (ed.)

    1957   *Ancient and Medieval Science from the Beginnings to 1450.* New York: Basic Books. 551 pp.

Tax, Sol. (ed.)

    1964   *Horizons of Anthropology.* Chicago: Aldine. 288 pp.

Thomas, William L. Jr. (ed.)

    1956   *Man's Role in Changing the Face of the Earth.* Chicago: University of Chicago Press. 1193 pp.

Turner, Ralph

    1941   *The Great Cultural Traditions.* New York: McGraw-Hill. 2 vols., 1333 pp.

Washburn, Sherwood L. (ed.)

    1961   *Social Life of Early Man.* Chicago: Aldine. 312 pp.

White, Leslie

    1949   *The Science of Culture.* New York: Farrar & Straus. 444 pp.

White, Lynn

    1962   *Medieval Technology and Social Change.* Oxford: Clarendon Press. 194 pp.

Zeuner, Frederick E.

    1963   *A History of Domesticated Animals.* London: Hutchinson. 560 pp.

AGRICULTURAL LANDSCAPES

AUSTRALIAN NEWS & INFORMATION BUREAU

Cattle Station, Northern Territory, Australia

Oasis, Saudi Arabia

SAUDI ARABIAN PUBLIC RELATIONS BUREAU

180

Wet-Rice Fields before Planting, Indonesia

GEORGE HOLTON, PHOTO RESEARCHERS

181

BURT GLINN, MAGNUM

Irregular Fieldscape, Belgium

TOM HOLLYMAN, PHOTO RESEARCHERS

AL LOWRY, PHOTO RESEARCHERS

Duck Farms, Hongkong, New Territories

Field Crops, Arno Valley, Italy

183

P.F.I.

Orchards, Cape Province, South Africa

SATOUR

184

Grain Fields, Southern Scotland

P.F.I.

UNITED FRUIT COMPANY

Banana Plantation, Honduras

185

Coffee Plantation, Brazil

BRAZILIAN CONSULATE GENERAL

Olive Orchards, Central Spain

SPANISH NATIONAL TOURIST OFFICE

Mechanized Chicken Farm, Argentina

IBEC

Wisconsin Dairy Farm, United States

LITTON INDUSTRIES, AERO SERVICE

ALASKA PICTORIAL SERVICE

Pioneer Farmscape, Southern Alaska

Greenhouse Farms, Netherlands

189

P.F.I.

Wheat Landscape, Manitoba, Canada

CANADIAN INFORMATION OFFICE

Wheat Landscape, Kansas, U.S.

190

GRANT HEILMAN

CHAPTER 5

Interregional Contact:
The Discontinuous Patterns
of Regional Expansion and Growth

Previously described briefly as a process of borrowing or copying, diffusion occurs by many different means throughout the earth. The capture of wives in a fight between two Paleolithic hunting bands might well have accomplished a simple form of diffusion when the new women taught other members of their new band another way of processing a slightly poisonous raw food item. The ordinary processes of trade in regionally specialized commodities also spread the familiarities with the products and the manner in which they are used. For many centuries the employment of captured slaves in the labor battalions of the Greeks, Romans, and Arab Moslems produced significant diffusion of knowledge about ordinary mechanical processes throughout the Mediterranean Basin and southwest Asia.

Diffusion as a Cultural Process

Diffusion has operated in a great many ways: by the movements of (1) people; (2) goods or things; (3) ideas. Frequently, all such methods are involved in interrelated fashion. For example, the sugarcane plant was domesticated in New Guinea as a source of a sweet food element, and spread widely throughout southern Asia at an early date (Fig. 5.1). With cane growing went the habit of chewing the peeled stalk as the chief means of getting at the sugar content, and cane chewing still is widely practiced throughout southern and eastern Asia. The Arabs developed the technology of refining sugar from cane in the early centuries of the Christian Era, and itinerant Arab technologists-

traders introduced the relevant procedures from South China to Morocco. Europeans in the fifteenth to seventeenth centuries copied Arab procedures, from the growing of cane by slave labor to the refining techniques, first in the Atlantic islands off the African coast and then in their tropical colonies. Arab word roots (possibly Sanskrit) lie behind our modern English words "sugar," "julep," and "syrup." In our own era the invention of the automobile in the Occident and the corollary developments that followed have created a tremendous complex of culture traits which has become distributed throughout most of the earth: the service station, the garage, the expressway, the traffic ticket, and the traffic jam are now almost worldwide. Not every element in this vast complex operates exactly alike around the world, but the basic ones are present in all cases.

Diffusion seldom pursues a straight line in the distribution of a culture trait or complex. No people take on a whole culture complex without reacting selectively to some element or trait in the new assemblage. Following an evaluation by the new recipients, alteration normally takes place in meaning, form, materials, procedure, function, or technology. Acceptance or rejection may be partial or complete, but totally new applications of some item may significantly alter the whole cultural construct. What is termed *stimulus diffusion* often takes place: no material item is diffused but the idea of something is newly taken on by a given people who render it into a barely recognizable custom, product, technology, or procedure. Be-

191

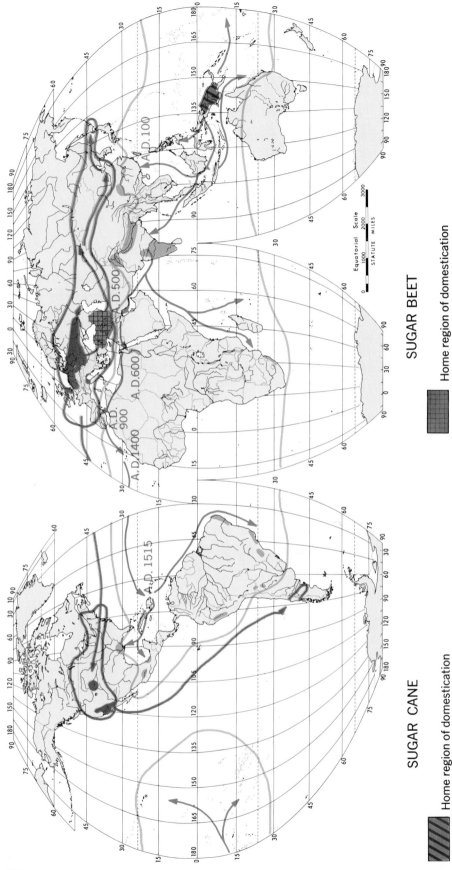

SUGAR CANE

Home region of domestication

A.D.600   Diffusion route and date of arrival

Current outer limits of cane-growing

Current chief production regions

SUGAR BEET

Home region of domestication

Route of diffusion

Current outer limits of beet-growing

Current chief production regions

FIG. 5.1   **THE DIFFUSION OF SUGAR PRODUCTION, FROM CANE AND BEETS.**

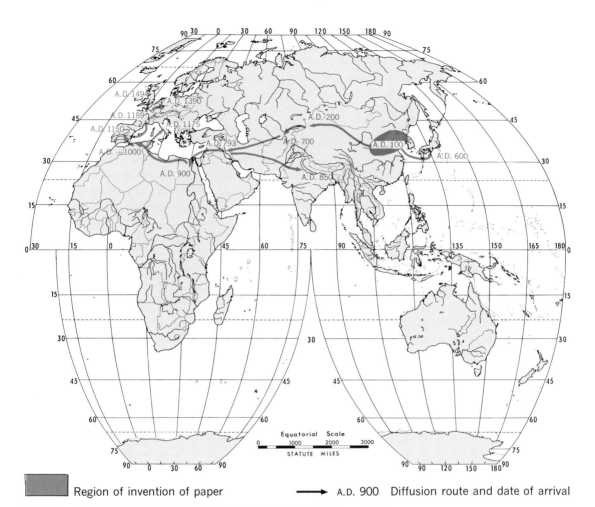

▢ Region of invention of paper	→ A.D. 900 Diffusion route and date of arrival

FIG. 5.2   THE OLD WORLD DIFFUSION OF PAPERMAKING, TO A.D. 1500.

cause the dynamics of diffusion are extremely complex, the consequent formulations of explanatory reconstructions are not subject to rational determination after the fact. Stimulus diffusion probably has been as important as *material diffusion* in the developmental growth of culture among the divergent groups scattered over the earth, for thinking man has always reacted in his own particular ways to things he sees, uses, or experiences. Moreover, the social controls over reaction often introduce divergences by one culture group that may not appear logical, rational, or constructive to members of another.

The dynamics of *innovation*, the technical changes in the function of an activity or operator, are closely bound up with the dynamics of diffusion of materials, ideas, customs, technologies, and procedures. Geographers need to be vitally concerned both with the practical causes and functioning processes involved in the dynamics of innovation and diffusion, and with the resultant localization,

territorial variation, and regional distribution of cultural phenomena over the earth (Fig. 5.2). The routes, time chronologies, and obvious operational processes of culture changes through diffusion, innovation, evolution, discovery, and invention are critical to an effective interpretation of the human occupance of any inhabited region of the earth, and the comparative operation of these processes is essential to attaining regional variation in humanly occupied territories. One of the theoretical concerns of modern geographers lies in the construction of diffusion models and their testing with adequate and accurate empirical data on the interaction of people and ideas.

Since any one region may have been inhabited by different cultural groups, from the Paleolithic Age to the Urban-Industrial Age, the landscape itself and the modes of occupance are normally a regional variant of the total assemblage of culture in the hands of man. Chronological discontinuities in occupance may mask many earlier patterns, just as a stratigraphic discontinuity may conceal the physical processes and results to the geomorphologist seeking understanding of the development of landforms. When a strong disconformity appears in the occupance chronology of a region of the earth, the historical record is broken, and it may be futile even to speculate on what took place earlier. However, wherever the archaeologic record extends the historical record backward in a fairly continuous line, broken only by small unconformities, a reconstruction of the prehistoric diffusion of culture complexes may be a significant element in helping to understand the evolutionary patterns of landscape occupance.

Exploration, Migration, and Regional Conquest

The several direct varieties of human movement over the face of the earth constitute a special case-series in the broad processes of diffusion. Man has moved about the earth for many different kinds of reasons, but a series of these reasons may be grouped under the headings of exploration, migration, and regional conquest. Each variety results in diffusion through the direct transfer of patterns of culture, but each is also an element in the development of regional differentiation.

Exploration

Satisfying a basic human curiosity about "what is it like, there?" exploration is an educative process both for individuals and for culture groups. Exploration has always been carried out with different objectives in mind which, historically, have become more numerous through time. Simple curiosity about an unknown territory may inspire exploration, with an intent to return home once the curiosity is satisfied, or exploration may be carried out with the aim of finding a new home territory more satisfactory than the present one. Exploration may derive from a conceived specific need, and be a planned procedure, carried out to procure a material that will fill that need. All forms of exploration result in expanded human awareness of conditions on the surface of the earth, providing man with options of sites for residence, sources of raw materials, varied ways of living, and potentials for altering human situations.

Earliest man often explored adjacent territories out of a vague sense of curiosity which, when undirected, frequently led him afield into the unknown far country and a very different way of life. In early Pleistocene time and down until the more recent stabilization of world environmental conditions in postglacial time, environmental stress often caused exploration for a more satisfactory home territory less beset by cold, drought, storminess, or excess precipitation. With the growth in human stresses, through local overpopulation, exploration often became the search for a new home territory less beset by human pressures. Once knowledge of technologies and raw materials developed, exploration became a search for specific natural resources, a process still actively being carried on today. Within any given population the factors of curiosity, unease, and specific search have varied markedly, and there have always been those quite willing to throw over the accustomed life to go exploring. In fifteenth-century Europe exploring became a profession; in the twentieth century there is a lament that there is nothing left to explore on the earth, but the adventurous now are eager to explore other planets. Since the beginning of human time exploration has been both an additive process of broadening human knowledge and a factor in the spread of human ways to the far ends of the earth.

Migration

Migration properly refers to the phenomenon of transfer from one territory to another—seasonally, annually, periodically, or as a onetime movement. Among many birds and animals migration is merely a seasonal routine totally normal to life habits. Man long ago learned the principles of *transhumance*, a seasonal migration between the varied life zones within a regional environment. Normally man went up into cooler mountain country in the summer and then came back down to lower country in quest of milder winter conditions; transhumance has long been practiced by animal husbandmen. Man also learned what may be termed labor transhumance, the seasonal migration of labor between areas of seasonal labor scarcity. In modern, affluent society a sort of seasonal transhumance goes on in the movement to the winter resorts and summer resorts, often involving long distances and shifts of large numbers of people. The more significant application of migration, however, has been the one-way movement of permanent settlement over relatively long distances.

Migration is usually a subtle and complex process. Man is neither everywhere sedentary, remaining fixed until he is moved by some force, nor does

TABLE 5.1 CLASSES AND TYPES OF MIGRATIONS

Class of Migration	Type of Migration	
	Conservative	Innovating
Ecological — Ranging	Ranging	Flight from the land
Ecological — Wandering	Wandering	
Socially — Forced	Displacement	Slave trade
Socially — Impelled	Flight	Contract labor
Free	Group	Pioneer
Mass	Settlement	Urbanization

From *The Politics of Population*, by William Petersen. Copyright © 1964, by William Petersen. Reprinted by permission of Doubleday & Company, Inc.

he migrate because of wanderlust. The essential question is: Why do some men migrate and others not? Some migration is *innovating*, as a means to achieve a new mode of existence; other migration is *conservative* as people seek a new location in which to preserve what they have. The distinction is important, since the latter challenges the modern notion that people universally migrate in order to change (improve) their way of life. Within these two kinds of migration, four broad classes can be distinguished: ecological, socially forced or impelled, free, and mass (Table 5.1).

Ecological Migration. Oldest in the human story are the ecological migrations, as when Pleistocene man moved away from regions that grew colder or drier during periods of active environmental change. Men with rudimentary technology, hence limited ability to cope with natural forces, continue moving because the food supply that they are able to obtain from a given area is inadequate. Most ecological migrations have been conservative, with the goal of seeking a familiar environment in which to continue the established way of life. Some migratory peoples (gatherers, collectors, herders) have been *ranging* within established territories in a short-distance migration: back and forth, circulatory, or haphazard (see Fig. 4.10). More distant ecological migrations are *wanderings*, in which whole peoples move intentionally, through fear, natural disasters, or to avoid famines induced by damage to the home territory. Only in modern times have ecological migrations usually been innovating: *flight from the land* has been to towns and cities with abrupt changes from former agrarian livelihoods.

Socially Forced and Impelled Migration. Migrations also can be activated from social causes; policy is formulated and action taken, with the migrants largely passive. *Impelled* migrations are those in which people retain some choice over whether to emigrate; *forced* migrations are those in which people have no such power of decision. Such migrations can be either conservative or innovative (as decided by the activating agent) depending on whether the migrants are simply to be removed or whether their labor is to be used elsewhere. Impelled migration can be further subdivided into *flight* and *contract labor*. The former results either from the driving of a weaker people out of a territory or from population transfers between adjacent countries (e.g., partition of India, with the creation of Pakistan). Contract labor is typified by the indentured servants in British colonies of the eighteenth century or the "coolie" trade of Indians, Chinese, and Javanese to tropical plantations during the early twentieth century. Forced migrations may be either *displacement* (e.g., Soviet Russia's deportations to Siberia after 1939 of more than a million potentially dissident Poles) or *slave trade* (e.g., the eighteenth- and early nineteenth-century capture and overseas shipment of Africans and Melanesians).

Free Migration. Best known of the *free migrations*, in which the will of the migrants is the decisive element, were the overseas movements from Europe during the eighteenth and nineteenth centuries. Only relatively few individuals were adventuresome enough or sufficiently motivated by their intellectual ideals to be *pioneers*. But such innovators blazed trails for others to follow. *Group migration* increased the numbers involved, as communities were transplanted under their own leadership or individuals banded together for mutual assistance and protection.

Mass Migration. Given sufficient prior emigration, some cultures establish the process as approved social behavior. Once begun, *mass migration* is semiautomatic, as long as there are people to migrate. Two subclasses of mass migration are distinguishable: *settlement*, as a conservative reestablishment of rural ways (as in the infusion of northern Chinese into Manchuria after 1890); and *urbanization*, as an innovating solution seeking a new way of life in a large town or city. What requires emphasis is that mass migration (as of Europeans to the New World) is not the whole of the migration process. When this class of migration declined after World War I, largely because of more restrictive limitations imposed on individuals by countries of both emigration and immigration, the usual interpretation was that significant human migration had ended altogether. However, the principal change since 1914 has not been a decrease in individual propensity to emigrate, but rather an increased control by nation-states over international migration.

Whatever the reason and the type and class of migration, the end results of human movement have been *colonization* of regional units on the surface of the earth by peoples born and raised in other culture regions. Colonization may be conservative in its reproduction or partial replication of an older homeland, but more commonly it establishes breaks with the past in that a new way of life is sought or results. Colonization, at the earliest instance, was a spontaneous development; historically, it became a more formal procedure, with recruitment, planning, rules, and government direction. But in all its forms, from the early Paleolithic to the twentieth century, migration and colonization have been chief factors contributing to the differentiation among regional ways of human living on the earth.

Regional Conquest

A special category of human activity, often combining elements of exploration, migration, and colonization, is the phenomenon of regional conquest. Such activity has involved the use of concerted power by a group; the stronger has conquered the weaker. As an expression of group culture the obvious elements of military technology and political organization normally receive primary attention, for the story of regional conquest usually focuses on the action by which hegemony is achieved. In historical terms the process of regional conquest has resulted in the elaboration of spheres of influence, zones of occupance, tributary regions, zones of cultural dominance, satellite regions, political states, culture regions, and other forms of territorial expression of group ways of living. Regional conquest generally results in alteration of some of the ways of living, both among the conquered and among the conquerors. The addition of a territory, by regional conquest, may create a zonal distinction in the culture of the conquerors; the old home territory may continue certain patterns, whereas in the conquered territory a somewhat different way of life may be the final result.

Regional conquest normally has resulted in the establishment of boundaries, divisions, territorialisms, sectionalisms, march lands (militarily occupied frontiers), and other regionalisms in which the hand of man places overlays upon the designs created by nature in the formation of environmental sectors. Such conquest normally institutionalizes these territorial patterns through the exertion of administrative controls. In Paleolithic time regional conquest often resulted in wiping out hunting bands and culture groups as separate entities, although the captured were amalgamated into the new unit to maintain the technologies and elements of culture. In such cases the territorialisms were informal and noninstitutionalized. The Neolithic tribal territorialisms became somewhat more formalized, but could not become highly expressed on the landscape other than through occupance patterns of a basic sort. Appearance of the political state, with its elements of formality, began to institutionalize territorialisms, and regional conquests then began to be demarcated and perpetuated as significant territorialisms often impressing marks upon the landscape. The increasing formality of the political boundary line set up by regional conquest is an item in political historiography permanently adding to the differentiation of the spatial units of the earth.

Exploration, migration, colonization, and regional conquest have all been elements of human differentiation of the face of the earth. The complex interworkings of the four specific items have been going on since at least late Paleolithic, and have been repeated again and again. The critical archaeologic site normally discloses successions of culture that range from Paleolithic upward toward more recent occupance. Although we may read the progress of technologies in the artifacts recovered, often we can tell little of the peoples involved. We presume diffusion of traits, whereas we may often be dealing with diffusion and rediffusion of peoples themselves who were the carriers of the traits. The numbers of people involved in the early patterns were small, but as the population of the earth has grown, the numbers of explorers, migrants, and colonists have grown too. Regional conquest replaced initial occupance as mobile man ever increased his pattern of mobility.

In this complex interworking a simple Paleolithic culture devised by primordial man was spread to the far ends of the earth to be differentiated in the regionalisms created by nature. However, ever more cultured man has added to the differentiation by his constant movement and development of regionalisms of his own making. The patterns of man's movement, therefore, became a cultural tool in his hand, constantly adding to the variety of ways of living that have come to characterize the humanized earth.

The Lengthening of Transport on Land and on the Sea

Man can walk longer and farther than he can swim, and the inference for transport is that land transport is older than water transport. The simple basics of transport, routes, packaging, and movement utilized human muscle and a wide variety of devices that allowed early man to handle volumes of materials. The lengthening of transport on land and sea, however, is a story of the developing of technologies in the packaging of materials and the utilization of motive power other than human muscle. We cannot be certain as to the comparative dates of the first pack animal–pack saddle and the first forms of rafts, dugout canoes, paddles, and simple sail rigs, but they may be roughly contemporaneous. The two types of transport involve different mechanisms and require separate treatment.

Land Transport

There are five physical aspects to the development of an efficient system of land transport: the route surface, the motive power, the mechanism of carriage, the packaging of materials, and the terminal at which materials are handled. In the growth of land transport man has been slow to coordinate all these separate facets, and only in the twentieth century was a truly effective solution reached in a few places on the earth. Attention was first directed to the mechanism of carriage, with the wheel as the first significant transport invention (Fig. 5.3). The war chariot and the sacred carriage apparently preceded the secular cart and wagon, the routeway for passage of the sacred carriage becoming a paved roadway within the precincts of the palace-to-temple zone, whereas the chariot first went cross-country and the formal roadway developed slowly.

Some kind of formal road building must have occurred in southwest Asia, where the wheel was invented, beyond the confines of cities and towns. However, the evidence is very scanty until about 1200 B.C., long after the invention of the wheel.

The great "commercial roads" of ancient southwest Asia were chiefly pack-train routes along which the troops rode cavalry animals. The formally administered "post roads," equipped with guard stations, rest houses, military patrols, and remount stations, were chiefly administrative and for the use of official personnel, but the road surface itself often was unimproved. Even the famous roads of the Roman Empire were often unusable for wheeled traffic above the flat lowlands. The use of stone paving for the "imperial roads" of both the Persian and Chinese road systems facilitated the movement of pedestrians, cavalry, mounted messengers, and pack trains, but such road systems often ignored the issue of gradient, contained steps in the steeper sections, and were not designed for wheeled traffic. In portions of North China where the terrain permitted, roads could be traveled by wheeled vehicles but, for China as a whole, the stone-paved, step-road remained the basis for the Chinese road system until the twentieth century! Not until the mid-nineteenth century was effective attention given to the nature of the road surface itself for the routes between cities and towns, and land transport in the hinterlands remained costly, troublesome, and hazardous.

Pack trains needed no more preparations of the route surface than did man himself. We do not know the full story of pack-animal evolution, but a group of domesticated animals loaded with small units of material first gave man the ability to move things in volume over long distances. In this process the Old World, with its several kinds of large animals in the different regional environments, had a very distinct advantage over the New World, where only the llama-alpaca were available as domesticated animals for development into minimally effective agents of transport. For motive power, although many animals were tried, the ox proved most satisfactory and became the most widespread source of draft power in the Old World. Ancient oxen were not very powerful, were slow, and needed considerable care, but they provided better power than man could. Harnessing the horse as effective motive power was a slow business, for the yoke, used as on oxen, worked poorly and other rigs tended to strangle the horse until the horse-collar was devised. There were numerous variations in animal power, and harnessing and teaming show much variation in time in different parts of the Old World, but the old patterns persisted from about 2500 B.C. well into the nineteenth century

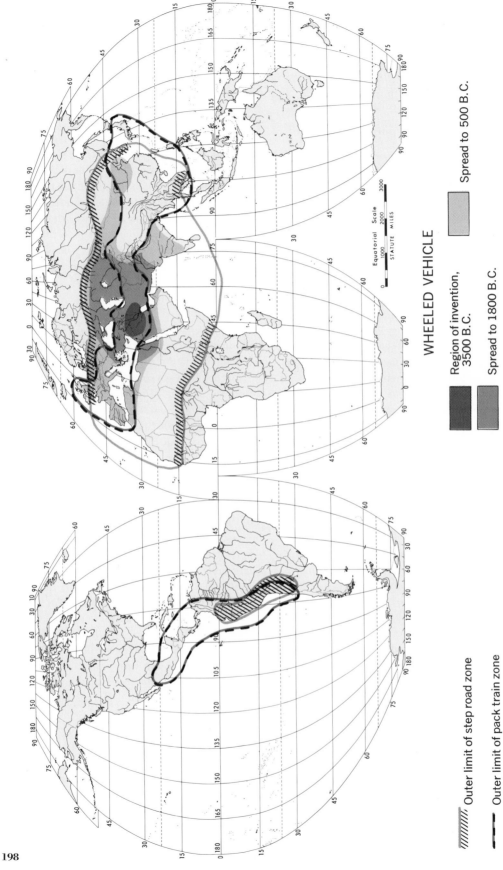

WHEELED VEHICLE

Region of invention, 3500 B.C.

Spread to 500 B.C.

Spread to 1800 B.C.

Outer limit of step road zone

Outer limit of pack train zone

Equatorial Scale

0   1000   2000   3000

STATUTE MILES

FIG. 5.3 THE EARLY DEVELOPMENT OF LAND TRANSPORT.

with only gradual improvement through breeding stronger animals, better teaming, and better harnessing devices.

The simple travois, sled, skid boat, mud way and other elements of simple transport by push-pull-sliding were in existence in varied forms from the tropics to the Arctic prior to the domesticated draft animal. Animal power pulling wheeled vehicles was more efficient. Cart and wagon styles varied regionally over the Old World, with different craftmanship and stylistic trends, but the two-wheeled oxcart remained standard in many regions. The development of the wagon beyond the simple small device appears to relate to northwestern Europe and the powerful breeds of horses developed there, but this came only after the Middle Ages.

The packaging of materials made little progress so long as the vehicles remained small and motive power was limited. Hand loading and unloading at terminals, fords, and break-in-bulk points, meant that man-manageable parcels were the largest possible units for most materials. The terminals required little elaboration other than to serve the needs of travelers and their animals so long as other elements of land transport developed no further than they did.

The history of land transport appears to have made significant progress at a rather early date and then to have stood still, technologically, until well into the nineteenth century. It is a near truism that land transport was almost as costly in A.D. 1820 as it had been in 1820 B.C. Nevertheless, in the diffusion of animals, pack-train systems, carts, wagons, animal harness, and other related features, the intervening period is one of marked spread of the basic elements of land transport over the Old World. There were regional distinctions of particular sorts, in the invention of the wheelbarrow in China (center-wheeled and capable of handling loads up to a thousand pounds) and in the breeding of heavy and powerful horses in northwestern Europe.

Water Transport

We know very little of the chronology of watercraft for the earliest periods, but the simple raft, dugout canoe, catamaran, reed boat, skin coracle, pottery float, and the outrigger certainly derived far back in time. The shores of the oceans, lakes, marshes, and rivers are so extensive that, however the initial efforts began, man early devised a whole series of different traditions for constructing watercraft (Fig. 5.4). There are basic similarities among these traditions in many of the broad types of far-flung sectors of the earth. Similarly, in the evolution of sails, paddles, oars, steering arrangements, and other boating devices there are both several traditions and rough similarities in far parts of the waters of the earth. We derive our first datable and accurate understandings of water transport from particular regions with rather special environmental conditions, in which the traditions of boatbuilding were already fairly advanced, but from which it is difficult to generalize for other portions of the world. For example, the Egyptian watercraft were developed for linear traffic on the Nile River where the prevailing wind blows upstream, so that the stepped mast set forward, the square sail, the paddle system, and the steering mechanisms formed a specialized system. Watercraft evolution, in general, shows more localized regional evolution to fit particular conditions than does land transport.

Whatever the origins, boatbuilding had developed a degree of maturity in several parts of the earth perhaps as early as 3000 B.C. Water transport shows the same variation in aspects as pertain to land transport, in that the medium of navigation, the motive power, the mechanism of carriage, the packaging of materials, and the terminal are significant to the efficient development of the system. The boatbuilding traditions in some regions concentrated chiefly on the mechanism of transport, so that we see many kinds of boats in terms of style, build, material, and waterproofing technology. Many "boats" were wanted for fishing or for aquatic resource extraction, so that these craft tend to confuse the picture where proper transport is concerned. The ease of interchanging use of small craft lends additional difficulty to the problem of unraveling the full story.

Only in a relatively few places did watercraft for significant cargo or passenger traffic develop at a really early date. The Mediterranean Basin, the Arabian Sea, Southeast Asia, and the China littoral appear to be the more significant regions of water transport in the true sense. The southwest Pacific Ocean is perhaps another such region; its boatbuilding tradition is, however, linked to Southeast Asia. It is in these regions that significant shipbuilding traditions appear to center. In each of these regions craft of considerable size developed, each with its technological accompaniments in sail

200

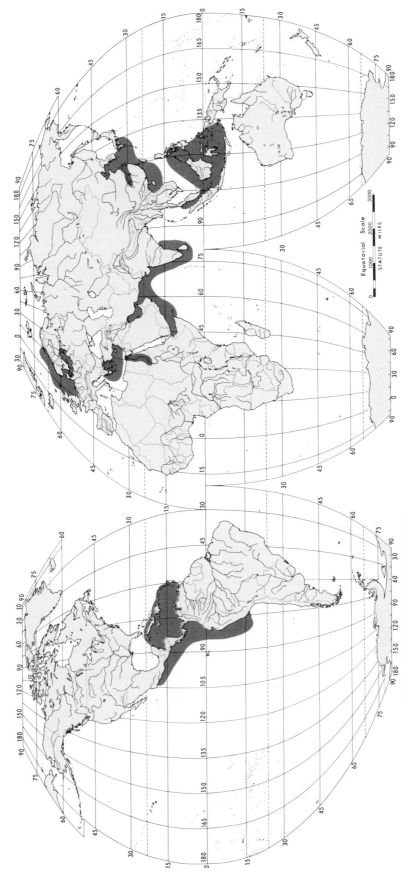

FIG. 5.4 THE ANCIENT PRIMARY TRADITIONS OF SHIPBUILDING.

Equatorial Scale
0   1000   2000   3000
STATUTE MILES

system, hull construct, and other particularly applicable features. Whereas the Nile River tradition involved particular sail systems, there developed in China the tracking system by which gangs of men pulled large craft upstream on rivers lacking a prevailing upstream wind.

Although a water surface is not directly comparable to the land surface in terms of a specific route, there are distinct problems in navigation and the application of power. Nile River craft could not work the Arabian Sea, so that rivercraft, oceangoing craft, and coasting craft did have differing problems regarding the routes they followed. The stormy North Atlantic sailing route was a far different thing from the Mediterranean Sea. The working out of specific sailing routes was a slow matter.

In handling cargo the limitations of manpower, lifting devices, and stowage situations meant that only small units could be taken aboard ship except for special circumstances, such as those surrounding the Nile River barges used for hauling monumental stone.

For watercraft the shore forms a terminal point in cargo-handling, and what today is termed a port was neither needed nor developed until relatively recently. Safe harbors in the event of a storm became a necessity only after ships were built too large to be beached easily or safely. Chinese native watercraft are still built with flat bottoms and square prows so that they may simply nose up on the shore margin.

As we review the history of water transport it is evident that marked progress came very early in particular regions in boatbuilding, in sail rigging, and in evolving special patterns to fit special environmental conditions. In A.D. 1500 it seems clear that southern China ships were the largest, the most seaworthy, the fastest sailers, and the best ships on the seas; they ranged regularly from Korea to the east African coast. As with land transport, the history of water transport suggests limited accomplishment in geographical diffusion of early technology and in the linking of distant regions into transport regions. Again, it is likely that the cost of water transport changed little from perhaps 1000 B.C. to about A.D. 1700. No concerted attack was made on the whole assemblage of water-transport technology until the modern era, and the rather small sizes of ships employed on the open ocean by the fifteenth-century European navigators-explorers attest to the courage of man.

The Linking of Transport Regions

The gradual extension of transport orbits, on land and on water, took place in individual terms around regional centers of limited confines (Fig. 5.5). That is, land transport very early linked together the several portions of the Fertile Crescent, and the lower Nile Valley was linked by water transport to Upper Egypt. Similarly, one can see other early regional linkages: North China was linked by land transport to Chinese Central Asia, the China coast and the lower Yangtze Valley formed a water-transport cell, the island-peninsular world of Southeast Asia was linked by water, the shores of the Arabian Sea were linked by coastal water contact, the "amber trade" linked the Baltic (by land and river) with the Mediterranean, tin from England was shipped to the Mediterranean, and parts of the New World tropics were tied into a water-transport cell. Slowly, during historic time, several of these separate transport cells were interlinked by extensions of the land and water cells. The interlinkage of the Old World was effected, in fact, several times only to be broken apart repeatedly. Within the New World the Andean Highlands were tenuously interlinked with the southern Mexico-Guatemala cell and the Caribbean cell. The final interlinking of the transport cells of the whole earth came permanently only after the Columbian Discoveries, although there is ground for suggesting intermittent interlinkages of the Old World in earlier periods. Such linkages expanded the contact of cultures in a great many different ways.

The Evolution of Exchange, Value Systems, and Trade

The word "trade," in all Indo-European languages, has reference to routes, commodities, occupations, and human movement. This complex includes a large number of different but interrelated elements which now have built into them a group of rather intricate concepts. Today, we normally think of trade as a sophisticated matter determined by objective criteria subject to economic laws. For example, if iron tools are known to be superior to stone tools, one buys or trades for them if they cannot otherwise be made. It is almost better to approach the subject of trade in the vein of two small boys who swap a live frog, a length of nylon string, and three rare bottle caps for a knife with one broken blade, a cracked plastic whistle, and a card picture of a favorite football

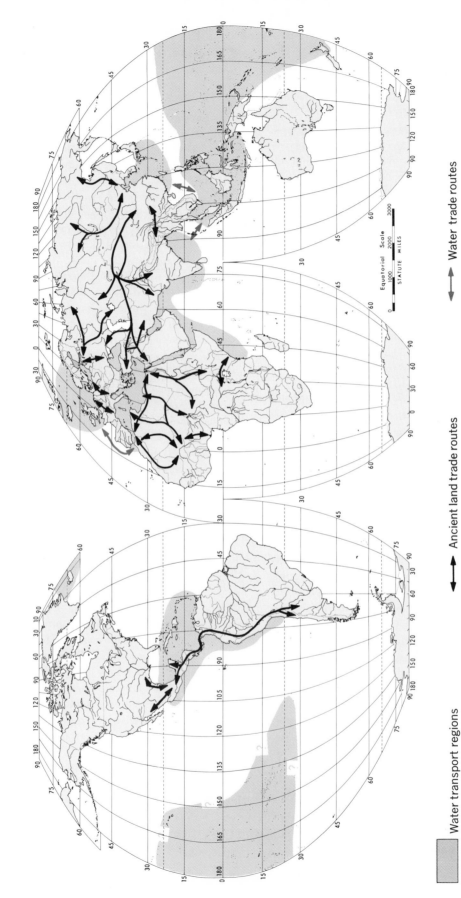

Water transport regions

Water trade routes

Ancient land trade routes

FIG. 5.5 THE LINKAGES BETWEEN TRANSPORT REGIONS IN THE ANCIENT WORLD.

player. What values attach to what, and why does the exchange really take place? The point is that commodity exchange is basic to human nature. Dealing between friends need not be on a formal basis, and value systems are what societies make them. The first boy was tired of playing with the frog anyway, the second got scolded for blowing the whistle in the house too often, and the other items were thrown in as a good deal between friends. Commodity exchange serves the desires of the moment; man is generally acquisitive, gift giving is a human social pattern, and finite and abstract value systems express the mental workings of a sophisticated and cultured society. Paying twice the price for a purse with a Paris label, compared with an equally useful domestic product, when the salesman compliments milady on her beautiful skin, has little more rationale than the exchange between the two boys.

Gift giving is a basic human trait stemming from early human history, and since it operates between friends to establish reciprocal allegiances and social indebtednesses, it functions as a form of exchange. In many societies gift giving is normally conditional and dependent on the return presentation of a gift having the approximate social value. Gift giving often became institutionalized in a particular society within a distinctive social framework in which it was surrounded by ceremony and perhaps tied to particular calendar intervals. Although some highly advanced societies have altered the original framework, the activity has continued to the end that considerable secular trade is needed to maintain the custom.

Strictly secular trade rests on social interaction without necessarily involving friendship. Any and all kinds of products and commodities may be involved, according to the level of culture, and the pattern of demand and supply for secular trade serves the purpose of economic redistribution. Such trade early began to acquire some notions of fair levels of exchange, leading eventually to the formulation of value systems. A value system normally focuses upon some common denominator material that comes to serve as a medium of exchange; many kinds of items, whether cowrie shells or metal coins (with a stamped guarantee of worth), have served as media of exchange. Secular trade varies according to the level of culture. It is small in the simple society living close to nature, but becomes great in the advanced society that has surrounded itself with occupational specialization, a large range of raw materials, and a great variety of commodities created and produced by manufacturing technologies. In the former society the regular level of living may proceed without significant trade, but in the latter even the simplest daily dietary requirements are met through trade.

There are two basic varieties of exchange that apparently have been present from Paleolithic time. One is the exchange of raw or natural products which are the monopoly of particular regions and which are traded outward to all other regions, to be taken in exchange by all kinds of peoples of all levels of culture. Salt, tool stone, free gold, jewel stone, and exotic aromatic plant and animal extracts long enjoyed such monopoly status, and of this list only tool stone has dropped out, even today. Historically, the discovery of many a natural resource has created a regional monopoly until the same item is searched for and found in another place. Economic history discloses that every people holding such a natural monopoly has valued it once comprehending its worth; a corollary is that those peoples not possessing that resource have sought to break the monopoly control over the product by developing alternative sources of supply. The second variety of exchange occurs in manufactured goods and commodities which are known as to utility, purpose, and appeal. Extensive trade in technologically complex and expensive manufactured goods operates chiefly between peoples of comparable culture traits; for example, one can sell automobiles only to peoples who have roads and who know and use wheeled vehicles. Conversely, the variety and amount of trade goods are very limited between peoples of great cultural disparity (e.g., steel knives and cotton cloth for such jungle products as rattans and bird feathers). The spread of trade in manufactured goods must be preceded by the spread of patterns of culture within which the goods have meaning. New inventions and new technologies may create monopoly manufactures; the spread of ways of using them produces a valued export trade, but the later dispersion of the manufacturing technology breaks the monopoly.

Several kinds of exchange systems are utilized in carrying on trade of all kinds. Versions of *silent barter* may operate between enemies, cultural unequals, or peoples who cannot communicate with each other, in which case volumes of commodities are accepted or rejected at a meeting place to which each side resorts in turn. Simple *barter* of commodity for commodity on a bargained basis may serve all the requisites of trade between friendly groups, acquainted peoples, or unfriendly peoples in agreed-upon circumstances. *Tribute* between politically superior and inferior groups, or between militarily unequal groups, may not supplant all needed trade but may form the most significant exchange between the particular groups. *Normal commerce,* so labeled to designate what we customarily think of as peaceful trade, is the more common and voluminous exchange between culturally comparable peoples, between friendly peoples occupying different environments, and between distant regions, but normal commerce is an attribute of a culturally advanced set of peoples who have, make, and produce large volumes of commodities ranging from raw products to complex manufactures.

In the long history of the growth of exchange, there developed a variety of aids, props, and organizational facets that have facilitated trade. Such features as the agreement upon the place at which exchange occurs have developed the marketplace, present in many forms throughout the world. The timing for exchange, be it seasonal, annual, or at short-term intervals, takes numerous forms, ranging from the daily early morning market to the annual postharvest trade fair. Systems for the arrangement of credit are many, but some such system has been required in all significant kinds of trading activities. Casual barter exchange may take place without there being a somewhat formally organized supply system, but regular trade involves the guaranteed availability of commodities at all or known times, so that the organization of supply systems came about in different ways among varied societies. What we know today in the American supermarket as brand-name certification is actually very old and is the guarantee of the producer that his product is of a specific quality. Original brand certification was developed by the skilled artisan who produced manufactured items and placed his sign on his product to make known his guarantee.

In the unfolding of exchange through historic time regional variation in exchange habits and cultural differences in commodities and trading systems have always been a mark of the regional culture. The kind and volume of exchange have grown steadily as human culture improved upon the products of nature by adding manufactured goods to the list of exchangeable items. Diffusion of these cultural systems has been irregular but continuing, both in time and in place. As the Neolithic level of living became dominant over the world, only to be replaced in turn by the Bronze and Iron ages, the systems of trading also spread, increasing the regional variety in trade systems.

A World Drying Out: Mobility and the Maturing of Pastoralism

The domestication of crop plants and animals did not, in itself, produce agricultural systems, as suggested in the previous chapter. On the drier or colder margins of the humid subtropics, where crop growing in early times could not succeed in establishing a base of support, animal husbandry presented an alternative base, trending toward transhumance of either vertical or horizontal proportions. Pastoralism may be described as a system of economic production in which animals convert grassy and shrubby plant growth not directly digestible by, or usable to, man into products he can consume and use, in the form of meat, milk, blood, tallow, hide, skin, wool, horn, or bone. In the working out of regional animal economies, from western Manchuria to the Senegal coast of Africa, the elements of pastoralism began to take shape. The total region was very large, environmental conditions were extremely varied, the human occupance was also varied, and the specific systems differed greatly. There is no standard definition of pastoralism around a fixed set of criteria, but critical to all systems were marked mobility of the culture groups, specialization upon given animals or animal combinations, militant relations with surrounding sedentary societies, participation in caravan trading, and some symbiotic relationship with sedentary peoples whence came those necessities of life not produced through animal husbandry and to whom went such surpluses of animal products as the pastoralist chose to trade. The early Mongol pastoral system differed markedly from the Arabian system, and both varied from that of the Afghans or the Berbers.

Some early versions of pastoralism involved seasonal crop growing in warmer arid lands, either upon seasonally moist tracts of land or in permanent oases; some pastoral groups maintain their cultivational activities even today. Most early versions of pastoralism were less mobile than certain later versions, for the acquisition of riding animals, such as the horse, camel, or reindeer, and the internal development of a mobility system were evolutionary features within particular culture groups.

The term "pastoral nomad" is a common one, but pastoralism and true nomadism, or roving, have not always been joined; pastoralism may, and did, operate without true nomadism, and the extreme mobility of the militant elements of some culture groups was normally bulwarked by the relative immobility of the flock-herd tenders. Seasonal mobility of flocks-herds, and their tenders, normally operated within very specific territorial limits according to grazing ecology. Such seasonal mobility varied from intraregional to interregional transhumance, so long as a given group could control its territorial range. Strict nomadism was sometimes a result of a culture group's being forced out of its home range and was the expression of search for another such range.

Both mobility and the competitive struggle for territory increased among many pastoral peoples under the changing conditions within the whole dry zone as the earth dried out after the last glacial era. As the waning upland ice fields melted away, the lessening of runoff dried up piedmont plains, shrank rivers, reduced the extent of oases, and failed to replenish some of the general reserves of groundwater. The changing fortunes of many agricultural peoples, on whom pastoralists depended, disturbed the symbiotic relationships between the settled and the mobile. As the drier sections of the arid zone grew larger in extent, formerly agricultural groups either took to pastoralism or migrated to stay within the reduced zones of crop growing. Pastoralists themselves sometimes moved in this same direction, but sometimes competitive struggles evicted the holders of regional ranges, who then became homeless peoples searching for a region they could take and hold. Out of these competitive struggles perhaps came the earliest patterns of invasion into North China, Northwest India, Mesopotamia, the Levant, eastern Europe, the Nile Valley, the Mediterranean fringe of Africa, and the southern Saharan fringe throughout central Africa.

We still are uncertain of the precise regional chronologies of the waning Ice Age, the onset of crop domestication, the domestication of animals, and the migratory movements of man in the Old World. We cannot be too certain about the actual evolutionary history of pastoral nomadism within the whole zone that has become our modern Eurasian-African dry zone. It does appear fairly clear that the drying-out process affected the northern, continental interior sectors earlier than the southern sectors, and that the Tarim Basin and parts of the Gobi became inhospitable country prior to the same development in parts of southwest Asia and the Sahara.

As some of the glacial fringes dried out fairly thoroughly, other sectors appear merely to have dried out to the point at which they no longer were so heavily flooded. Such sectors included the Yellow River zone of North China, the Indus River plains, the Euphrates-Tigris Valley, and portions of Transcaspia. Other smaller sectors of the Old World also may have gone through a relative drying out which reduced them into less flooded lowlands occupiable by man. Periodic swings in climatic elements sufficient to alter regionally surface precipitation, runoff, and groundwater supplies accompanied the earlier periods of the postglacial era and can only have added to the complications of many early groups who were trying to stabilize a new way of living.

We can be even less certain, so far, of the chronology of events in some of the New World regions in which plant domestication and crop growing were developing, such as southern Mexico-Guatemala, the Peruvian coast–Andean Highlands. In the New World, with its sparsity of domesticated herd animals, no real animal husbandry became fully elaborated as an alternative to crop growing, and thus pastoralism did not become a distinctive way of aboriginal life.

The changing environmental ecology that accompanied the human accomplishments of the Mesolithic and the early Neolithic added to the patterns of regional mobility of man by requiring migration patterns to evolve. In the late Neolithic many of these movements were in full force in and around the dry zone of the Old World, and they continued into the historic period, giving rise to the appearance of new peoples within the zones of developing sedentary cultures. The very success of life in these regions of sedentary cultures attracted those peoples having difficulty within and around the dry zones.

As the struggles between the steppe and the sown continued, history records the evolution of new forms of military tactics. Pastoral cavalry tactics improved steadily through time, to be capped by the organizational system evolved among the Mongols in the tenth century, a system that made the militant Mongol pastoralists a scourge from North China to well within eastern Europe.

Some view the development of pastoralism as a source of many of the sedentary peoples of the humid margins who became central figures in later history. One view holds that the drying out of the postglacial world exerted such stress upon the peoples within and on the dry margins that the resulting mobility and constant flux is the spark around which civilization kindled in a number of selected or favored regions. Whether this can be an acceptable thesis for the origin of civilization depends on the interpretation of chronologies and events not yet clearly identified.

The Civilizing Processes:
The Import and Export of Culture Complexes

There is no doubt that man was significantly on the move in both the Old World and the New World in the three-thousand-year period after about 7000 B.C., whether the drying-out process was or was not the critical stimulus that motivated large-scale movements of culture groups. The Mesolithic Age had set in motion a large series of developmental cultural processes during a period of active environmental change. The Neolithic Age was a period during which the cultural processes matured sufficiently so that man could begin to make his own choices in ways of living and places of residence. Active migrations and regional shifts were man's responses to environmental change, the procedures developed and utilized, and the places selected to execute them, being decided by human choice. Many of the primary choices were those of powerful ethnic and cultural groups, making it necessary for smaller, less technologically able, and weaker groups to accept the best of second, third, or fourth choices as to location and procedure.

In an inhabited world in a state of flux the cultural processes of invention, discovery, evolution, and diffusion of culture traits and complexes were tremendously furthered by the very patterns of human migration, regional contact, competitive struggle, splintering off and rejoining, alliance and separation, confederation and dissociation, coalescence and disruption, conquest and rebellion. Particularly notable must have been the processes of diffusion, by which most of the then known cultural complexes were spread throughout broad regions. It was at a time such as this that crossroad location (a central place or node in a transport system) provided a very great advantage to the human occupants of a particular regional site. Cultural contacts, friendly or belligerent, afforded such occupants the maximum exposure to human knowledge, technological skills, materials, and procedures. The converse, of course, held true that the secluded refuge site far from a crossroad position could remain untouched by almost all cultural excitement and human contact. Our concern, here, is for the progressive elements of change rather than those of stagnation. Were there data adequate to the renderings of modern geographical theory (in such aspects as network analysis, graph theory, information theory, grouping theory, central place theory, and diffusion theory), patterns and systems could be shown to be in process of development as organizational dynamics in the evolution of civilization. At present the data are inadequate to such demonstrations, but the issues present many challenges that ultimately may be worked out when the archaeologic record becomes more complete.

There is little doubt that the whole of southwest Asia from northwest India to Transcaspia to the eastern Mediterranean Basin (the classical Near East) formed the key zone within which cultural excitement occurred at particular regional crossroads. Moving through this zone, or available to peoples in this zone, were the wide ranges of Old World plants, animals, technologies, economic procedures, ideas, social constructs, political concepts, religious beliefs, tools, exotic materials, labor resources (as people in some form of social bondage), and forces of leadership.

There were other crossroad zones of lesser importance. The eastern end of the central Asian corridor, in North China, centering on the loess highlands, was such a zone, for here joined several routeways across eastern Asia. The western Mediterranean Basin lay athwart African-European routeways and not too distant from Southwest Asia. Southern Mexico–Guatemala was another such zone, although this region lay more at a constriction in several routeways rather than on a literal crossroad, unless one subscribes also to ideas of transoceanic movement. Although, in the physical sense, it is possible to suggest that the Bering Sea passage zone was also a constriction of routeways, this case corresponds more to a high mountain pass than to a favorable crossroad, since its environmental conditions were too rigorous for exploitation by man at the time involved.

What we suggest, essentially, is that the key zone in southwest Asia must have become exposed to the largest sum of human developments, whether or not any one item was fully applicable locally to an ecologic niche or humanly acceptable to a people. For the historical result of comparative regional accomplishment during the Neolithic it is of no critical import as to where in the Old World a particular culture trait originated, no matter in what ecologic niche a specific procedure was devised, and no matter where the first incisive insight into a human organizational manipulation was conceived. In terms of probability, the regional units of the key zone most fully open to the movements of men and human practices stood the best chances of gathering up the best combination of both. However, regional contrasts in the qualities of the environment within the whole of southwest Asia were such that not every local region was equally useful to man at his then level of cultural ability. The hand of man, equipped with a goodly share of the sum of human practices, could turn the best local regions (at that time) into areas of outstanding accomplishment. In this the qualities of environment were important, but the processes of import and export of cultural procedures were crucial.

The Growing Organization of Earth Space: Regionalism and the Expansion of the State

Earliest man, starting from simple concepts of territorialism, could neither conceive of nor organize a large region, and nothing in the previous section should be construed to mean that the whole of southwest Asia was a single regional entity by the time active migration of groups took place and culture complexes diffused. Far from it! At the onset of the activities yielding civilized societies in specific regions, the elements of territorial organization had only slightly developed. The critical spatial element in the growth of civilization was the ability to organize territory into effective combinations. The genesis of this process took place in the appearance of the city and in the rise of the concept of the God-King. Around each city there was territory utilized for the production of food, fuel, animals, water, and such other natural resources as were conceived important to the particular group. The implications of the earliest historical records of these city-states suggests that they were quite small in total areas and in total populations, whether they lay in a large river valley or in a smaller regional tract. There was considerable competition between some of them for control of territory, control of the routeways to distant

regions, and, in some zones, control over water supplies. The sequence of developments, both spatially and chronologically, was not fully alike in all areas.

The expansion of a city-state, the hegemony of its God-King, and the effectiveness of its administrative bureaucracy, depended in good part on the effective appeal and the dynamic style of the religious system, the particular sociopolitical construct, the ethnic composition of the region at large, and the accessibility of the separate portions of the regional environment. It is unclear which of these and other factors may have been the most critical, or whether one alone was indeed critical. Insistence upon specific favorable qualities of the environment at this juncture does not hold in all cases, for Crete, Meso-America, and the Peruvian coast–Andean Highlands were lacking in great river valleys in which volumes of water seasonally flooded areas of rich soil, and not all regions had the same rich resources of domesticated plants and animals. The growth and expansion of such a phenomenon as the regional state depended, essentially, on elements of human creativeness expressed in a dynamic fervor of proportions new to the earth. Given a reasonably good environment possessing some useful combination of resources, the creative human construct enlarged the small city-state into a regional state.

Once the essential framework of the construct of the regional state was put together as a combination of area, peoples, and organizational system, then the creative, the evangelical, the revolutionary, and the dramatic elements appear to have relaxed their intensity, to be followed by a pattern of rational, calculated, opportunistic, and competitive enlargement on historical experience. Leadership among invading and newer ethnic elements, rebels, opportunistic younger sons, or ambitious families visualized new ways of utilizing socioeconomic-politico-military combinations, appealing to the masses of the ruled, capitalizing upon weaknesses in a regional system, or appealing to the unifying cultural factors among particular ethnic elements of the older state. Sargon of Akkad, in an ancient country north of Babylonia, may well have been a leader of this sort (ca. 2300 B.C.) who both rebelled and enlarged his city-state, but his procedures for control over a large territory were significantly personal. By the time of Hammurabi of Babylon (ca. 1900 B.C.) both political structuring and military organization had been perfected to the point that an administrative system could command allegiance at a distance, and a code of laws became operative for at least some social levels of citizenry regardless of their ethnic stock and city of residence. The leaders of the Chou (ca. 1100 B.C.) set up their dynastic reign over a large part of North China by capitalizing upon political and military constructs to take over and enlarge the previous city-state system in force under the Shang and the Yin. At a later time came the imaginative attempt on the part of Alexander the Great to construct an extensive multiregional state too far ahead of the administrative systems yet organized for governing an extensive empire.

Regionalisms, in these early efforts, had numerous bases in both physical geography and in cultural patterns of peoples resident in broad areas. The physical geography of the earth was, by about 3000 B.C., fairly well stabilized into its postglacial patterns of climate, glacial wastage, vegetation, animal distribution, and the like, although minor swings in climatic elements, groundwater wastage, and vegetative shifts continued to take place from time to time. Physical regionalism, therefore, became a fairly fixed pattern which, in its own terms, no longer imposed upon man conditions that motivated regional residence. Cultural regionalism, and particularly the political regionalism of the state, became a matter that man could arrange on his own terms. The ability to envisage the organization of various kinds of physical territories into one unit, the political state, lay within the creative ability of leadership, tempered by the circumstances of competitive and disruptive action on the part of other human groups who might envisage a different regional construct.

In the large zone from northern India to North China to the Mediterranean Basin and in the zone from southern Mexico to northern Chile we see similar kinds of constructs, each varying in detail. Whereas in Egypt the King was also God, without much challenge, in North China the Chou rulers were intermediaries between Heaven and man. The specific civil administrative systems varied, as did military systems; tax systems differed, the specific gods and their worship systems operated variably, social constructs had differing numbers of classes having different obligations and privileges, cropping systems varied according to the crop staples, and other economic constructs showed separation. The broad outlines of each political state, however, showed similarities. Political states could not be self-contained and isolated, for two reasons. First, each state was dependent on resources beyond its borders, so that some kind of orderly relations among states, and between states and less organized regions, were needed. Second, there almost always were challenges to the patterns of power, either from within the state or by peoples from the surrounding regions wishing to share in or take over the state. The state system had developed as a human system of organizing people, territory, and ways of life, but since it was a human construct, the state system was subject to decline, rearrangement, and reconstitution.

The Evolution of Regional Culture Hearths

The precise chronology of each of the regions to be discussed in this section is still somewhat in debate, but precision of dating is not material, since our concern is for comparative regional development in a broad sense. The roots of these developments lie behind the written historical record, and archaeologists have not yet completed a full reconstruction of regional settlement of the prehistoric sequence. Therefore, the order of presentation and the implications of timing are subject to rearrangement with improvement in the record. We know most about those regions in which cultural successes were spectacular, such as the large river valleys of the Nile, Euphrates-Tigris, Indus, and Huang. We know less about the courses of events in many of the other regional landscapes, and this lack of knowledge makes us wary of ascribing too much early success to human efforts in some of these other locations.

Man's impact on many of the regional landscapes has been so strong for five or six thousand years that it sometimes is hard to conceive how he ever could have succeeded in building a cultural structure upon some of the now barren, rocky, arid, and seemingly inhospitable landscapes. The glare of insolation, the lack of vegetation, the sheer barrenness of the light-colored landscapes, the accumulations of sand, the discomfort of the heat, the dust storms and, in some areas, the bitter winter cold rebuffs us, modern residents of the verdant midlatitude lands, when we look at some of the landscapes in which man supposedly made his start in development of high civilization. It is hard to make the effective comparison as to what the *poor* lands were like, if these now barren wastes were the *good* lands, for we have little basis for judgment. Our summary of where and how man achieved civilization, and in what kinds of regional landscapes, is therefore subject to our not knowing the whole story and to our looking at these regions long after man had disturbed the conditions which then existed. For example, much of the erosion and deforestation of the Mediterranean Basin and southwest Asia may well owe to subsequent misuse during the declines of civilizations there.

In the early clustering of culture groups, in particular regional landscapes, there were the successes in which technologies, latent resources, and human effort became combined. Success resulted in population growth of two kinds—the natural increase within the region and the in-migration by others from localities in which peoples could do less well. In these regions of success have accumulated the technologies, traditions, ambitions, growing populations, and new insights, and the ingenious solutions to problems. In a sense success perpetuated success. Such regions became repositories of human traditions, sources of populations that could tap the resources of regions at a distance, and creators of the successful ways of living. They became *culture hearths*, in which cultural traditions became stabilized and in which the human way of living defined the standard of what human living ought to be. Out of these hearths went the rules of living, the technologies, the traditions, and the human systems that denoted the civilized society when members of the region ventured beyond their home territory for whatever reason. The culture hearth was at once the cultural repository and the source of its own perpetuation into the future and outside the homeland.

Within the broad Old World zone there were several major and minor culture hearths significant to the later growth and spread of Old World culture, and within the New World there were also several of them. In this section we review the growth and crystallization of the most significant of the Old World hearths (Fig. 5.6).

Mesopotamia

The term Mesopotamia here stands for the two valleys of the Euphrates and the Tigris rivers, the filled estuary of the two, the surrounding fringes of hill country on the east and north, and the margins of the Arabian Desert on the west and south. Although a geographical unit in comparative world terms, there is a great deal of variety

within the landforms, local climate, and plant cover of the whole region, and even the zone of the river valleys varied markedly from north to south. The estuarine fill of the two rivers has added a significant region to the southern end of the lowland since Mesopotamia began to be a much sought-after homeland. The physical contrasts between north and south are reflected in the sociopolitical history of the two sectors, and a single way of life cannot be presumed always to have been the rule in all localities.

The earliest peoples are not fully relatable to modern ethnic divisions of humanity, nor are some of the in-migrants clearly identifiable. The region is situated athwart perhaps the most frequented crossroads of them all, and its cultural-trading relationships stretch out along the routeways to include the eastern shores of the Mediterranean Sea, the hill country of Asia Minor, the hill margins of Iran, and the littoral of the Persian Gulf. This larger zone is the region termed the Fertile Crescent and, although not all of its portions shared in the early experiences of Mesopotamia, the cultural and historic linkages throughout the larger region are almost inseparable from the patterns within Mesopotamia itself. By its very accessibility the Mesopotamian lowland received a steady stream of militant in-migrants during the fifth and fourth millennia B.C. There were a considerable number of centers of local settlement, and a very active period of competitive struggle between the city-states which delayed the achievement of hegemony by any one. The result was that the large regional state did not appear here quite as early as it did in the Nile Valley, although there seems little doubt that cultural diffusion from this region through Palestine to the Lower Nile River country was one of the elements in the maturing of Egyptian civilization. By about 3000 B.C. the Mesopotamian region had become a bright and shining light of culture to an outer world of barbary.

Accessibility of the Mesopotamian region to peoples round about was a two-way proposition. Diffusion of culture traits and complexes took place outward in all directions from this regional center, although not all of these features derived from within the lowland itself. Over the centuries Mesopotamia received many in-migrating peoples, some of whom came as conquerors, some as settlers seeking a home, some as slaves to do the work of society, and some merely as traders. Although ruling

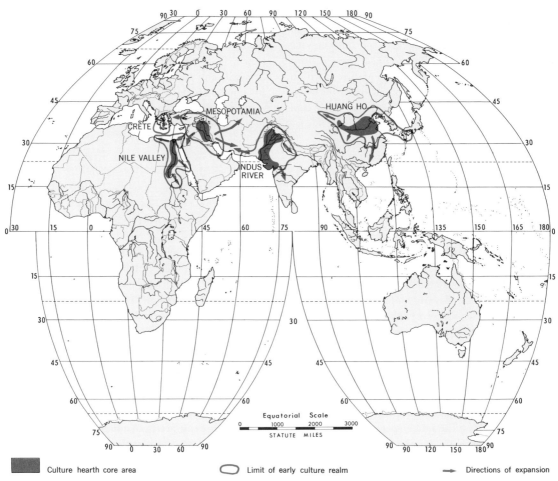

Culture hearth core area   Limit of early culture realm   Directions of expansion

FIG. 5.6   THE EARLY OLD WORLD CULTURE HEARTHS AND CULTURE REALMS.

lines perished, capitals were moved, internal patterns of administration were altered, new elements of culture entered, and old ones dropped out, there was a continuity of ways of living in this irrigated lowland which clearly marked the region, regardless of the identity of the ruling house of the moment. The barbarian in-migrants absorbed the culture of the hearth and became part of it; the professional priesthood, the professional army, the civil bureaucracy, and the merchant-traders evolved their own social structures and their own technologies suited to the land and the changing circumstances, which insured a continuity of life against continued politico-military struggle for control of the rich lowland.

Occupance of sectors of the lowland certainly had occurred prior to the onset of the drying-out process, most likely by both crop growers and animal followers. The earliest archaeologic evidence suggests rather sparse and scattered occu-

pance by sedentary folk in linear patterns which, along the piedmonts, became a branchlike distribution according to the dispersion of water courses on great piedmont fans. The later archaeologic record suggests both increases in population and shifts in locality over time; and the appearance and the growth of formal irrigation facilities were gradual. A peak in both areal occupance and population patterns seems to relate in some areas to the era of Sargon-Hammurabi (2300–1900 B.C.). The distribution of abandoned canal systems and the ruins of settlement suggest considerable variation in occupance, irrigation, and population through historic time. The all-time peak in historic population density may have come only very late, perhaps A.D. 1000–1200, well after the cultural significance of the Mesopotamian hearth had declined.

The conquest of Mesopotamia by the rising power of the Assyrian and Persian kings after about 800 B.C. moved the centers of political power away from the heart of Mesopotamia. No longer so clearly the center of culture in a vast zone of barbarians, Mesopotamia, as merely one sector of a series of new empires, suffered from maladministration. The ancient culture had been passed on, new evolutionary forms of human organization and new technologies were rising, barbarian lands were becoming cultured, and the old hearth lapsed into decadence, decline, and ruin, to become again a land of agrarian villagers struggling to maintain a way of living in a riverine lowland in which the ruins of great cities became mythical marks of the past.

The Nile Valley

The Nile Valley is a watered strip of shallow canyon extending through and standing out in sharp contrast to the bleak and near-barren desert country atop the canyon cliffs on either side. In the fifth millennium B.C., the Nile Valley had something of a gallery forest along its margins, on the natural levees and along tributary canyons entering the main valley. The plant cover of the zone beyond the valley was not then so slight as it has been in more modern time, but it probably was never more than open shrub-scrub parkland away from the wadis, the spring seeps, and the ephemeral lake basins. The drying-out process has accentuated the contrast between the Nile Valley and the desert, and man has scavenged the useful plant cover to its near extinction. Although not inaccessible from any point, the Nile Valley is approached by natural and frequented routeways only from the Sudan and through the delta littoral, so that much of the valley has a relative degree of freedom from invasion. After the drying-out process stimulated movement of the inhabitants of the open country toward the river valley, the upper and middle sections of the Nile enjoyed relative solitude. Near the delta head and along the coastal littoral, on the other hand, the Nile region remained open to access, and there is a greater history of continued contact here than farther south.

Within the region we know as Egypt, centering on the Nile River valley, the advanced beginnings appear to relate to the lower, or northern, region between the head of delta and the first cataract, between about modern Cairo and Aswan. Here there bloomed a culture at an early date which matured into a regional political state even before that event took place in Mesopotamia. There were fewer contending city-states in the Nile Valley, so that the local struggle for hegemony was simplified. Within the delta zone, enjoying contacts with outside regions, appears to lie the real culture core of the Nile region, although much of the evidence for this must lie buried under the sediments of the delta. Writing, art forms, and much of customary culture derive in good part from the north, whereas architecture and politico-religious administration derive from the upper river sector. The union of the linear region into one political state brought into focus a series of culture patterns scattered over an elongated region in a burst of creative brilliance.

As distinctive and as spectacular as it was, the Nile River culture hearth never reached the heights achieved in Mesopotamia over the broad front of civilization as a whole. In early times the Nile River culture region diffused relatively few culture complexes far beyond its own broad African region, including the eastern shores of the Mediterranean. However, in later Greek and Roman times the Nile region was the source for many aspects of Mediterranean life. Enjoying relative solitude in the early period, the Nile Valley was invaded repeatedly from about 1700 B.C. on, and numerous peoples came and went through its lower portion and the delta country.

We actually know very little about the evolution of control over land and water in the Nile Valley, for the archaeologic record is scanty and hard to get at on the Nile River floodplain. The irregularity of volume of flow has long been great; a heavy runoff could have flooded the whole plain, cut new subchannels, filled shallow depressions, reduced gallery forest strips grown since the last heavy flood, and left behind new silt fills in some areas and temporary ponds and marshy tracts in the current low spots. A scanty runoff might never have wet down the whole floodplain and might have affected only the very margins of the main stream. If one assumes for the Nile regular heavy runoff during the last glacio-pluvial, then early man could not have occupied the floodplain at all during the flood season; the drying-out sequence probably introduced the new pattern of irregularity in which the drier years resulted in sequences of insufficient volume to wet down the whole plain.

Earliest occupance must have been patchy, scattered, and centered about the localities having the best year-long conditions. In time crop growers could have devised techniques of bunding, levee building, land leveling, and water channeling that could have extended the semicontrollable areas, everything being subject to the seasonal vagary of runoff patterns. Extensive land leveling, clearing of gallery forest, and reduction of seasonal marshland must have gone hand in hand with increased bunding, water channeling, and seasonal measurement of flood levels for ritualistic-religious purposes. Once certain patterns of skills and knowledge accumulated, significant advances could have been undertaken, resulting in the extension of semicontrollable land areas. However, real control over Nile waters never developed sufficiently to protect against heavy runoff nor to compensate adequately for scanty runoff. Political control of territory and labor force, through the medium of the political state, must have facilitated the extension of measures making for increased cultivability of floodplain land, but exactly when these came about, and when maximum cultivability of the Nile floodplain occurred, is still quite uncertain.

Much of the distinctive Egyptian culture gradually became so stylized that people in the later centuries sought chiefly and slavishly to maintain the traditions and the forms of the past. When colonies of Greeks, Hebrews, and Romans were resident in Egypt, these aliens learned what they could understand of an aging culture that had no spirit left, and to this extent the Egyptian culture hearth served as a source for the diffusion of many things. Well before the onset of the Christian Era, Egypt became a political pawn or a colony of outside power, and the Nile Valley again became a land of agrarian villagers living out an annual cycle of life framed around the seasonal pattern of the Nile River, to which students, travelers, and tourists came to see the architectural glories of the past or to study at a few remaining libraries in which were preserved aspects of southwest Asian, Egyptian, and Greek cultures.

The Indus Valley

The country of the Indus River today seems well separated from Mesopotamia by the rough, high, and rugged country of Baluchistan-Afghanistan-Hindu Kush which ranges from very dry desert along the Arabian Sea littoral to alpine in the Hindu Kush. On its other fronts, the Indus Valley is relatively open to the east and south. The difficulty of travel between the Indus country and

Mesopotamia, and the infrequency of such travel, has been accentuated in modern literatures and has been made more difficult by Anglo-Indian frontier policy. In much earlier time, before the uplands dried out toward their present state of aridity, the high area was well populated, the passes were well known, and the patterns of contact were more frequent. The archaeologic record, far from complete, suggests a Neolithic continuity of occupance from the Indus lowland across to the Mesopotamian lowland, with both crop growing and animal economies widely distributed. Inability of the diggers to get to the bottoms of the Indus great city sites, such as Mohenjo-Daro and Harappa, hampered by alluvial filling and a high water table, precludes establishment of the presence or the lack of evidence suggesting an age of development roughly parallel with the most ancient sites of Mesopotamia. Interpretation, however, tends to conclude that cultural contact and settlement by town-dwelling, city-state, advanced peoples came into the Indus country from the north and west relatively suddenly at a point in time after which the basic steps in the advancement toward civilization had been taken in Mesopotamia.

The Indus Valley was another great alluvial lowland heavily flooded by runoff of melting glacial waters. This valley was not easily occupiable by the Neolithic hill country folk to the west or the Neolithic occupants of peninsular India to the southeast. Changeable river channels were bordered by gallery forest along natural levees, seasonal alluvial fill altered the microforms of the landscape, and shallow, seasonal marshes were scattered. With the drying-out process went significant shifts in river channels, seasonal flow patterns, sedimentation, and the like, accompanied by increasing local aridity of the discontinuous piedmont on the west and encroachment of the Thar Desert from the east. The Indus Valley lowland changes markedly from the Arabian Sea littoral into the foothill country of the Himalayas, but the local contrasts are gradual from place to place.

About 3000 B.C. the Indus country was apparently taken over by in-migrant peoples familiar with the general outlines of basic cultural patterns operating in Mesopotamia, and trade contact between the two regions became significant. We know little of specific political historiography for the region beyond what can be interpolated from the presence of fortified palace-citadels, ritual sites, and the apparent sizes of settlements. The elaboration of a similar culture pattern eastward along the foothill zone did not carry far beyond the drainage of the tributaries of the Indus, but southward the distribution ranges into Kathiawar, southeast of the Indus Valley.

The end of Indus civilization is often stated to have been caused by militant invasion, but Mohenjo-Daro is the only city in which such evidence appears. Other evidence suggests a rather steady decline for Indus culture in the main core zone, with preservation as late as 1000 B.C. on the southern margin in Kathiawar of elements of classic Indus style. The record does not indicate depopulation but rather the reduction of high levels of art, architecture, technology, and land control to a rather crude level more characteristic of towns and villages than of the creative city. Alternatively the decline may indicate the influx of a barbarian people, the Aryans, who put little value in the maintenance of those high levels.

The records of trade between Mesopotamia and the Indus suggest a westward flow of many materials and commodities, and the records of the workshops of the Indus cities suggest the passion for town planning and the practical functioning of a large settlement. The latter may have been a chief cultural contribution, for the grid-plan city became more characteristic of northern Indian city building than it did farther west. The impact of Indus Valley culture lay significantly to the east and south and, as the later outlines of Vedic Indian culture took shape, there was the continuation and spread of a great many of the elements and patterns developed in the Indus Valley culture. Although similar in many respects to that of Mesopotamia, Indus Valley culture exhibited a good deal of regional specialization which makes it unlike the cultures of the Mesopotamian lowland and the Nile Valley.

North China

The basin of the Huang Ho (Yellow River) is less clearly a great alluvial lowland framed by distinctive physical marker features than are the Mesopotamia, the Nile, and the Indus regions. The drainage basin of the Huang has a headwater section clearly demarcated within structural landforms, but its midsection cuts across these elements, and its lower section is a composite alluvial fill produced by the combined actions of several small river systems merging their sediments with the larger volume carried by the Huang. Pleisto-

cene loess blankets much of the pre-Pleistocene surface of the Huang's midsector, so that the post-Pleistocene landscape is one developed on, within, or through the loess cover. The hard-rock outlines of the major structural elements were never fully covered by loess; landscaping processes continued during the height of loess deposition, and both dissected the loessal deposit and transferred the sediment removed to the North China Plain. A regional landscape resulted in which there is a master stream system, several series of master hill and mountain ranges, a huge flat piedmont alluvial plain, and a soft-earth cover of loess. The last has been increasingly etched by natural denudational processes and also by soil erosion induced by human occupance. This regional landscape, therefore, presents distinctly local conditions in different sectors. The eastern margin of the North China Plain littoral, and its southern flank, still present the wet littoral and the seasonally marshy landscapes. Major tributaries of the Huang are separate river valleys on their own, the loess uplands and the hard-rock hill-mountain country often in juxtaposition, the sandy northern fringes of the loess zone grade into outright desert wastes, and the northwestern fringe of the loess shades into a great alluvial piedmont forming a corridor between the high mountain fringe of the northern ramparts of the Tibetan Highland and the open steppe-desert of the rolling Mongolian Gobi.

Throughout the Pleistocene and, particularly, during the closing glacial period, the Huang Basin was heavily beset by flooding of major proportions which, in addition to removing glacial scour products from the headwater zone, picked up large amounts of loess in the midsector to dump the whole load into the shallow waters of the North China Sea. In its lower sector the Huang often shifted its course, appropriating for the flood season the channel of some minor stream flowing from the mountain front into the North China Sea, thereby spreading the fill over a broad range to create what became the North China Plain. Low islands in the North China Sea were covered over completely, middle-height islands remain today as low hard-rock hills on the plain, and the Shantung Uplands, a cluster of large, high islands, were flanked by fill to tie them to the land area as the Shantung Peninsula. At its debouchment on the North China Plain the Huang built up its bed well above the plain, alternately breaking out to reach the sea north of, or south of, the Shantung Peninsula. It is the continuation of this erratic behavior that turned the North China Plain into "China's Sorrow" during historic and modern time. As the flooding volume gradually decreased, with the onset of the Holocene, the contemporary pattern of climatic aridity and variability set in, in which the Huang still may flood enormously in any given year in which there is a moderate to heavy summer rainy season. In such years, the removal of loess from the midsector creates almost a liquid mud flow onto the North China Plain.

The hand of man has rested heavily upon North China during the Holocene period and it is difficult to separate primordial natural landscape conditions of the waning period of loess deposition from the culturally produced conditions of the protohistoric and historic periods. In the closing phases of loess deposition it is not clear what kind and amount of plant cover may have been able to maintain or establish itself both on the loess uplands and the actively sedimenting North China Plain, but man was active in altering that plant cover in the same period throughout the loess uplands, the river valleys, and the alluvial lowlands. Clearly many mountain highland zones of forest have been turned into barren hard-rock expanses within early to late historic time, but we can be less certain of plant and animal ecological conditions on the alluvial lowlands, on the loess uplands, and in the foothills sectors of the mountain country. However, in the widely varying local conditions and the strong juxtaposition of regional ecological environments in early North China there were situations that offered early man many options in ways of living. That the central Asian corridor opens into this regional complex is significant in the drying-out period during which the Old World Paleolithic and early Neolithic living systems were in flux. North China presented a set of situations and conditions conducive to the trial-and-error growth patterns that made the Huang Ho and its tributaries and associated smaller streams a useful region.

The archaeologic record clearly indicates the long occupance of eastern Asia. We are not concerned with *Homo erectus* (Peking Man) but with late Paleolithic and Neolithic distributions of settlement in North China. Although the archaeologic record is not yet well rounded out, there are thousands of known and reasonably well-studied Neolithic sites within the Huang basin. The region clearly constitutes a zone in which village-dwelling, crop-domesticating, animal-using, culture-developing patterns matured. One traditional view holds all this as diffused into North China from western sources, but the increasing record throws steadily greater doubt on the outside origins of many basic elements. The nuclear region appears as the southern loess area surrounding the great elbow bend of the Huang Ho, where it turns eastward, and its tributary streams such as the Wei, the Lo, the Fen, and the Chin, from west to east. The record of the growth of the Yang-shao culture and its Lung-shanoid expansion is not yet completely understood, but evident are its spread eastward onto the North China Plain and its expansion westward into the central Asian corridor, on both margins touching other cultures which set in motion further elements of development.

The broad patterns appear clear, even though there remains debate over the resolution of chronologies, the rise of regional institutions, the origins of cultural complexes, and the correlation of folk-history with the archaeologic record. Shang China evidently shows a growth of the city-state system, the emergence of a regional variant of the God-King, the functional maturing of domestic and palace architecture, the inventive-evolutionary development of manufacturing, and the growth of other culture complexes entirely comparable with those systems and group complexes now well catalogued for Mesopotamia, the Nile, and the Indus regions. The timing is still to be settled but the broad chronology appears to be a little later here than for the Indus Valley and, therefore, subsequent to the chronology of the Mesopotamian culture hearth. The functioning of diffusion, either as material-technology or stimulus diffusion, appears clear. However, there are regional specializations that lend distinctiveness to the appearance of the North China culture hearth. The walled settlement, the Chinese language system, pounded-earth construction and the patterns of domestic and public architecture, both technology and forms in bronze metallurgy and pottery, and other features all have clear continuity with the Chinese Neolithic in too many ways to permit description of the North China culture hearth as built wholesale on a base of diffusion.

The Chou dynasty's attempt to create the large regional state in North China (eleventh century B.C.) followed similar attempts in western centers, but the multiregional environment proved too large for mastery by the organizational concepts employed and in time North China slipped back to a situation dominated chiefly by small regional states and city-states. It was only with the inward diffusion of added new culture complexes in the several centuries B.C. that the large regional state concept was successful. The entry of iron technology, the animal-powered agricultural tools, and organized regional irrigation practices were one side of this pattern of change, but equally important were concepts in military and political organization and institutions of territorial administration normally associated with the rise of the Ch'in empire in the third century B.C. The success of these patterns owes partly to the spread of basic culture complexes out of the North China hearth southward into China, and to the counterflow of barbarian ideas and traits absorbed.

Unlike the cases of Mesopotamia, Egypt, and the Indus Valley, there is clear historical continuity between the North China culture hearth and the later Chinese regional culture area, and between early Chinese culture systems and those of historic China. The Chinese culture hearth remained the center of culture growth and the center of regional power as the Chinese state expanded, whereas in the other cases the later flowering of culture and the appearance of the large regional state came outside the hearth areas, thus causing the discontinuities in culture patterns and the dying out of culture systems within the hearth areas. The most specific illustration of this lies in the dying out of the language systems of Mesopotamia and Egypt, but other elements are also involved.

The Minor Hearths

Neither through archaeology nor history can a clear story yet be completed of certain other regional developments of advanced culture in the Old World. Here we only make brief reference to these minor regional patterns which form part of the larger picture. These include the insular pattern within the eastern Mediterranean Sea and the regional units within Asia Minor-Syria-Palestine. Once the basic Neolithic production systems were established across southwest Asia their more local regional application through diffusion and local development became possible. On this basis any reasonably good local region possessing exploitable resources of soil, water, wood, and tool stone could become a center of Neolithic settlement and local development.

The Island of Crete is such a local regional entity and the record begins as early as 4000 B.C. with early Neolithic crop-growing clusters of villages on the small plains having good soil, local drainage basins, and other requisites. The appearance of culture complexes from the Egyptian Delta zone is matched by those from the eastern sector of the Fertile Crescent, but the resulting blend of features, procedures, art forms, settlements, and other higher aspects of culture denote a local evolutionary sequence. Perhaps peoples from both areas were involved. Sea trading and the spread of Minoan culture forms from Crete to Aegean islands are part of the record and the means of transferring Minoan culture to the earliest of the Greek peoples (Mycenaeans) coming into the Aegean Peninsula. On Crete, the intermontane plains villages were complemented by towns built along the coast to accommodate a significant population increase. Whereas the beginnings of higher Minoan civilization date from shortly after 3000 B.C., the high period comes about 1800 to 1500 B.C. at a time when both Mesopotamia and Egypt were disrupted by invasion. The centralization of political, religious, and administrative power turned the island into one functioning unit, and the record of the archaeologist and the first glimpses into the deciphering of Minoan script reveal an astonishing level of living. There are suggestions that the Cretan "state area" comprised both the island and the waters of much of the eastern Mediterranean, and that significant state revenues derived from levies on sea trade. Around 1450 B.C. Crete lost its power to the Mycenaean Greeks in what probably was militant contact and, though we cannot be sure of the sequence, Crete again became chiefly a region of villages and petty sea trading, exerting little influence on the conditions of Mediterranean life.

The eastern shores of the Mediterranean are backed by a strip of hill country, tapering off in the south but joining the uplands of Asia Minor in the north, as a western border to the Mesopotamian lowlands. Here good lands of winter rain, forested uplands, small river valleys, and a coastal plain form a set of local regions within which Neolithic crop-growing, village-dwelling populations were numerous as the advances toward higher civilization were taken in the Mesopotamian lowland and the Nile Valley. As the drying-out process progressed, there pushed into this region a series of ethnic groups from several origins, each struggling with elements of culture derived from the Mesopotamian hearth and blended into their own basic patterns. Competitive struggle for territory was frequent, if not continuous, in all parts of the region, among Hebrews, Hurrians, Aramaeans, Phoenicians, Hittites, and others from late Neolithic times onward in a succession of attempts to arrange unity between ethnic groups and regional territories.

Mesopotamian basic culture complexes not always being applicable to particular mountain and coastal regions, there came about differential combinations of technologies, economic systems, religious constructs, social formations, military tactics, and political structures. We make no attempt to set down chronologies for precise areas, but between about 2000 B.C. and the beginning of the Christian Era this whole region witnessed a succession of regional cultures elaborating some specific construct in such territory as each could take and hold. The steady ferment of territorial constructs never totally disturbed the flow of ideas, trade goods, the evolving of specific culture systems, and the broad diffusionary processes by which culture spreads. It was within this region that many specific discoveries, inventions, and creative formulations of technologies took place and, for all its turbulence, the zone played a significant part in the development and westward spread of Old World culture complexes.

The Formation and Dominance of Early Regional Culture Realms

The impact of each early culture hearth became felt over a wide range of territory through diffusion of its elements in space and to other peoples as the hearth population settled adjoining territories or as new peoples moved within the orbit of a hearth and acquired elements of its culture. This process did not operate in exactly the same way in each case, but the broad pattern was sufficiently similar that one may speak of the gradual formation of a *culture realm* as resulting from the diffusion of cultural elements from each given hearth area. Four primary and two minor culture hearths for the Old World were centers of the growth of regional civilizations. From these, three primary culture realms evolved: the Mediterranean, the Indian, and the Chinese.

The primary diffusionary movements from the Mesopotamian culture hearth were westward to the marginal territories of the Fertile Crescent, reaching into Egypt on the south and the fringes of southeastern Europe on the north. The primary diffusionary movements from the Egyptian hearth were into the lands around the eastern Mediterranean Basin in the earlier period and westward through the Mediterranean at a later date. In and around the Mediterranean lands the two sets of cultures became repeatedly intermixed, interwoven and, to a degree, synthesized by the peoples who adopted elements and complexes of each. It long ago became customary, in western Europe, to speak of the Greek origin of much of European culture, and many occidental historiographers still use this frame of reference. But the Greeks were an immigrant people who began to move into the Aegean Peninsula shortly after 2000 B.C., from a prior location in the barbarian world, where they possessed a pastoral culture on the economic level and a tribal variety of political structure. Slowly filtering south into the peninsula, the earliest and southernmost groups came into contact with Minoan culture in the island fringes; their rapid adoption of Minoan culture led to the period known as the Mycenaean Age (ca. 1400–1200 B.C.), during which Greek pastoralists turned into militant conquerors, builders in stone, and sea traders in the Aegean and eastern Mediterranean.

The later arrival of the Dorian Greeks, about 1200 B.C. may have provoked the downfall of Mycenae, but it led to the Dorian adoption of much of the prevailing culture and the eventual construct of what we know as Greek Civilization. The political structure of these Greek immigrants never produced a great regional empire, although Alexander of Macedonia later attempted one, but it did result in a strong concern for political theory, within the Greek world, which evolved many elements of the political theory that matured in the Occident.

The evolutionary translation of culture elements from Mesopotamia, Egypt, Crete, and the Levantine shores into Greek culture created a new and broad cultural form which then spread throughout the Mediterranean Basin, back into southwest Asia (with Greek traders, artisans, and soldiers) to create, in the end, a pattern of culture broad enough, and varied enough, to characterize a whole realm rather than a regional culture hearth.

As the Vedic pastoral immigrants into Northwest India overwhelmed the local populace still resident in the zone of the decadent Indus culture hearth (ca. 1500 B.C.), there began another regional case of a culture hearth providing the bases for a broad regional plan which matured into an Indian culture realm. Here territorial expansion eastward and southeastward out of the Indus country was combined with the gradual absorption of a good deal of Peninsular Indian culture. Starting with small regional states and city-states, the larger regional empires sought territorial limits of greater extent, and became more concerned with religious mores, social structures, a new kind of agricultural economy based on rice and other tropical crops, and the inclusion of non-Aryan peoples into their overall scheme. A quite different culture realm became elaborated. Its eventual spread southward to Ceylon and eastward around the shores of Southeast Asia to Indonesia broadened its regional impact in the same way that the southwest Asian culture patterns spread westward.

Migrations of population out of the North China hearth began taking place before the full expansionist thrust of the large political state came about, but the two processes went hand in hand thereafter. The Chinese culture complex was more unified and specific in definition than either that of the Mediterranean or India, and the Chinese were more aggressive in spreading it as a specific way of life. The southern barbarians either became Chinese, in culture, or they had to fight for their way of life. Some of the stronger fought for periods of time, but many of the weaker culture groups and ethnic stocks began emigrating southward, thereby populating upper Burma, upper Thailand, and the Laotian high country with immigrant refugees, a process that, in lesser numbers, still continues. The result was the expansion not only of Chinese culture but also of the Chinese political state into an ever-larger and more comprehensive entity. In this long growth there were absorbed a host of barbarian traits, complexes, ways of living, and non-Chinese peoples. Adoption of basic Chinese ways of living, however, turned one into a Chinese in the fullest sense of the term.

The Chinese hearth exerted its influence northeastward also into southern Manchuria and Korea and, a little later, Chinese culture began to spread to the Japanese islands. Northwestward and westward Chinese culture went only where it could go in terms of village settlement and the agrarian way of life. This choice prohibited its expansion into the Tibetan Highland, and limited its entry into Mongolia and Central Asia to those oases locations in which the settled life was possible. These limita-

tions both proved strong ones, so that the Chinese political realm remained confined along the cold north and arid west, whereas the Chinese cultural realm expanded to include Japan and Korea, and on the mainland it extended principally southward into the humid tropics, as far as Tongking and northern Annam.

We have here suggested the regional formation of three Old World culture realms, which largely dominated the Old World by the start of the Christian Era. Around the fringes on all sides lay lands of the "barbarians," those peoples who continued Paleolithic or Neolithic cultural practices lacking in the elements, or bits, of culture from each of the realms; and their traits and complexes diffused back into the several culture realms to be adopted as intrinsic features. Here and there, on the margins, a people formerly "barbarian" took on enough of the elements of civilization that regional offshoots and satellite entities formed. Sometimes putting together something of political organization and military structure such regional units were able to create sizable and significant regional entities. More common, however, was the blunt and forceful assault upon the border regions of the particular realm by a group of "barbarians," either seeking entry into the territory of the realm or seeking to acquire the goods and commodities of its culture.

The Late Blooming of Other Culture Realms

The physical changes in the nature of the earth's regional environments that stimulated the early efforts of man culminated in a few spectacular regional accomplishments in cultural development, characterized in the preceding sections. This had been a development unique in time, kind, and place, and it set the style of regional culture for large sectors of the Old World. Other regional accomplishments in cultural development followed, somewhat later in time and of similar or related nature, which added greater variety, further distribution in space, and additional depth to the structure of human culture on the face of the earth. This section deals with these later regional systems.

The New World Amerindian Hearths

Recent archaeological work has adequately disproved the older theories of the extreme recency of man in the New World. Nevertheless, there is a strong and emotional variety of disagreement as

FIG. 5.7   THE NEW WORLD CULTURE HEARTHS
AND CULTURE REALMS.

Culture hearth core area

Limit of early culture realm

Directions of expansion

melt, but there are regional basins, smaller valleys, karst platforms, and alluvial piedmonts, many of which are separated from one another by hill country tracts and mountain systems, and there are two long strips of coastal littoral. Climatically the whole region ranges from rainy tropics to mountain alpine to desert fringe; the north and west, where precipitation is seasonal, is a land of summer rains. The whole region is rich in plants of the sort useful to Paleolithic peoples, and it had a varied animal population although one lacking the kinds of domesticables found in the Old World.

Meso-America shows the sequence of development familiar in the Old World—Paleolithic, Mesolithic, Neolithic, and Chalcolithic—although the time span now customarily employed shows evidence of compression into shorter periods, as though early man made rapid progress from the end of the Paleolithic onward. The Neolithic in Meso-America now seems to have begun here at about 5000 B.C., but further research may require shifting this date to earlier centuries. Agricultural villages, irrigation systems, the first formalization of religious systems, the beginnings of monumental architecture, and other features characteristic of the Old World Neolithic show up in formal sequences. Prior to 1000 B.C. complexities of cultural patterns begin to appear in the spread of the community center-temple complex. The ruined city, as a formal urban settlement, does not turn up frequently as an archaeologic artifact, as in the Old World, but clustered settlements around temple-complex sites are clearly evident. The appearance of systems of writing, astronomy-calendars, public works, and other features unmistakably denote the rise of civilization. There are regional differences in many of the features, eastern Maya showing dominance in some and northwestern Olmec-Toltec in others. Specifically the patterns of formal urbanization do not show up as Mayan, but this undoubtedly is related to the tropical forest ecology of the Mayan lowlands, and to the forms of agricultural economy followed, which probably involved the continuance of cyclic shifting cultivation. In contrast the structural basins of the upland northwest disclose the specialized crop-producing economy based on the *chinampa* (raised planting surfaces surrounded by drainage canals on the basin floor). Diffusion contacts with northern South America are evident in the appearance of metallurgy. A few centuries B.C. individual regional en-

to how early was man's arrival in the New World, what Old World culture complexes were diffused to the New World at what times, and how much independent invention of culture took place in the New World. We are unable to adjudicate this quarrel, but hold an open position and a median view, although our leaning is toward more, rather than less, pre-Columbian diffusion of Old World culture by several routes and to several regions (Fig. 5.7).

The Meso-American Zone. The region of central-southern Mexico, Yucatan, and Guatemala forms another of the broad environments in which significant change took place during the late Pleistocene and the early Holocene, and the results were somewhat similar to those of the Old World regions in that a drying out took place, with changes in plant-animal ecology, water supply, and human living conditions. The whole region is extremely varied in landform areas, locality environment, living situation, and local ecology. There is no great river valley suffering heavy flooding from glacial vironments of the whole area had certainly arrived at an equivalent of the city-state level of the Old World, and there followed in the centuries prior to the Columbian Discoveries a succession of regional shifts in power, invasions, elaborations of territorial empires, and growth of trade contacts on interregional bases. These developments parallel those of the Old World, although specific ones were sometimes different in kind and in territorial expression.

As a hearth region the influences of Meso-America were felt chiefly to the north, with cultural diffusion extending as far as what today is the Southwest and the eastern woodland of the United States. The culture systems of Meso-America have been perpetuated into the modern era in all lands south of the United States.

The Peruvian Coast–Andean Highland Zone.
The Peruvian zone of the west coast of South America, ranging from the coast into the highlands, comprises still another region in which human development progressed strongly beyond the patterns of Neolithic crop growing and the development of settled life. This is physically a complex zone ranging from desert on the coast to equatorial temperate highland and mountain alpine climatic conditions, and from a narrow coastal littoral to intermontane valleys, basins, and plateaus separated from each other. Cutting transversely across the zone are snow-fed rivers whose drainage basins possess tracts of moist and cultivable soils. Ecological environments vary markedly with elevation and location and, although there is no great region of uniformity, there is parallelism of environmental conditions between stream basins located relatively close to each other to provide considerable areas of similarity.

Recent research has delimited a new chronology for Peru, though even these dates may eventually prove too recent. On the coast a cropping economy dates the Neolithic at just prior to 3000 B.C. The growth of settlements, expansion of cropping technologies, domestications of the guinea pig-llama-alpaca, growing formalization of religion, appearance of towns and ceremonial centers, development of fortifications, and regional political organization all came prior to 1500 B.C. Irrigation perhaps predates 1200 B.C., and metallurgy was in evidence by 800 B.C., followed quickly by specialization in manufacturing. Highland occupation was only slightly later than lowland development. Between 1500 and about 200 B.C., there

came the maturing of cropping economies, flowering of urban civilization, integration of interregional trade, and the rise of the regional political state. Associated, after about 900 B.C., was the spread of the highland Chavín cultural style over northern Peru, which lies at the base of later Peruvian cultural styles. Political empires appeared in the early centuries of our era as the two highland states of Huari and Tiahuanaco preceded the Inca by some centuries.

In Peruvian life there was no development of systems of writing to provide a specific chronology of record, but there did develop a system of statistical notation (employing the *quipu*, a device of variously colored and knotted cords) which served administrative and governmental ends. There also was almost no development of astronomy-calendar systems, and none of "science" in the Old World sense. During the early centuries of our era the development of road systems, as step-roads (the wheel being known only as a toy), and the growth of proper cities were accompanied by the considerable extension of the political state and its regional administration. These features brought shifts in political power and in centers of influence. At the time of the arrival of the Spanish, the Inca Empire was certainly a large and complex political region, with a high degree of interregional productive economy, population concentration, and economic wealth, and a high level of living. There were clearly connections with Meso-America by land, and possibly by water, and there had occurred the outward spread of cultural influences both southward and northward along the Andean Highlands.

Secondary Old World Hearths and Realms

In the interplay of human events in the Old World there was the steady shift of emphasis among three different forces:

1. *People* as population units having societal constructs,
2. *Culture* as a human-created combine of material and social technologies.
3. *Region* in the sense of territory possessing resources that can be utilized and manipulated.

Earliest man lived in small groups and had little culture by which to elaborate a way of living through manipulation of a particular region, the quality of the region being the critical element. By contrast, later man selected and defined culture hearths possessing bodies of culture by which he could manipulate regions to his own ends and territorial design, the quality of the culture now being the critical factor. That territorial design did not always coincide with the regions of nature reflects the differential powers of human groups in either enforcing their own wishes and desires as to ways of living or establishing such territorial designs as their strengths could impose. We have expressed the viewpoint, common among anthropologists and historians, that in creating civilizations in culture hearths, and in expanding these into culture realms, historic man established several broad centers of cultural influence which played dominant roles in the widespread and further regional development of the earth.

The history of the diffusion of culture indicates that discrete populations in particular regions never retain total monopolies over human ways and technologies, for thinking man watches his fellows for new and different elements of culture and ways of living. Admittedly, depending on the social value systems of different societies, there are variations in rates of adoption of newer ways. Our aim is to suggest that around the primary hearths and within and around the primary realms there was operative the process of creating secondary hearths and culture realms by groups of peoples not active in the life of the primary hearths and realms. Both variably later in time, and variably in territorial appearance (Fig. 5.8), these secondary manifestations stemmed from a combining of complexes diffused from primary realms with complexes of territorially localized origin which were either very old or newly developed. Secondary hearths may involve populations not originally concerned or may include descendants of primary realm populations. However they come about, wherever they are located, and whatever culture systems ensue, such secondary activities are part and parcel of the human tendency to organize earth space for the use of man.

The African Sudan. South of the Saharan dry zone a broad zone stretches across Africa ranging from steppe to tropical forest and from flat lowland through hilly upland into rough mountain country. In this large region many different local environments possess markedly different plant, animal, soil, and water resources. The region is almost unexplored archaeologically, and our tentative version of its development is certain to be altered as research uncovers the past story. It is clear that this whole area has undergone changes since the height of the last glacial period, but the Pleistocene-Holocene physical record is little more understood than the human record. The Saharan drying out must have been accompanied by other changes in regional ecology, and we infer something of a drying out throughout the savanna zone with possibly a southerly shift in several zonal patterns on the lowlands. At least three nuclear areas of significant human creativity may be identified (see Fig. 5.8). One is the hilly upland inland from the coast on the southern bulge of western Africa, a second is the lowlands of the upper Congo basin–Lake Chad region, and the third is the Abyssinian–eastern African high country.

The Abyssinian high country was one of the key regions of plant domestication whenever it came. Across the whole savanna-forest margin, Neolithic living systems gradually matured in which crop growing, village dwelling, regional trading, and handicraft manufacturing were characteristic. Diffusion of technologies may be significant but, by about 4000 B.C. crop domestication was under way in some parts of the zone. Village-dwelling crop growers in a Neolithic context must date not far from 1800 B.C. in at least the Abyssinian sector; and by about 500 B.C. a simple Neolithic pattern must have extended from the Arabian Sea to the shores of the Atlantic. The introduction of some domestic animals into the eastern portions of the dry margins as early as 2500 B.C. brought about the evolution of simple pastoralism, probably through the drying out of the main Sahara, but extensions of pastoralism westward and southward cannot be well dated. Neither can precise dating be given to the extension of crop growing into the southerly zones of heavy forest cover, but it certainly took place. The whole zone is too large, too varied, and too little known to permit inferences of uniformity throughout, and there must have been regional contrasts and local anomalies. The three nuclear areas may well have been subcenters of local dispersion. One can only set a tentative date as just prior to the start of the Christian Era for the late Neolithic across Africa, and this date marks the kinds of changes that advance beyond the Neolithic for all of sub-Saharan Africa. The introduction of metallurgy and some other manufacturing technologies apparently have a dating pattern just prior to and after the start of the Christian Era. Little known archaeologically as yet is the growth of towns, but the process appears

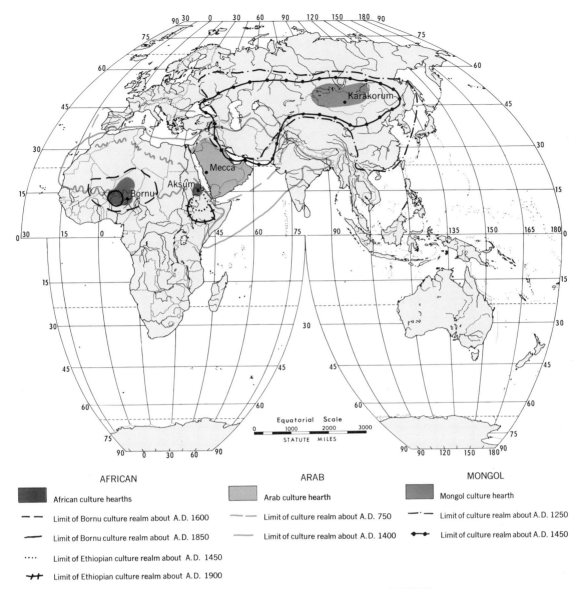

AFRICAN	ARAB	MONGOL
▰ African culture hearths	▰ Arab culture hearth	▰ Mongol culture hearth
– – Limit of Bornu culture realm about A.D. 1600	– – Limit of culture realm about A.D. 750	– · – Limit of culture realm about A.D. 1250
—— Limit of Bornu culture realm about A.D. 1850	—— Limit of culture realm about A.D. 1400	●—●—● Limit of culture realm about A.D. 1450
···· Limit of Ethiopian culture realm about A.D. 1450		
⊢⊢ Limit of Ethiopian culture realm about A.D. 1900		

FIG. 5.8 THE LATER OLD WORLD CULTURE HEARTHS AND CULTURE REALMS.

to be late, about the start of the Christian Era for eastern Africa and somewhat later in the west. Progress beyond the early Neolithic came slowly to Africa south of the Sahara; many of its elements rested upon inward diffusion; and in the early period no primary culture hearth evolved and no culture realm surrounded this zone as a positive force.

The further development of sub-Saharan Africa moved more rapidly, based chiefly on the diffusion of political and economic organization derived from north of the Sahara or from Arabia. We really know but little of trans-Saharan trading traffic other than that its beginnings are very old, but in the last centuries B.C. a series of trading towns appeared across the northern margins of the savanna belt. These towns evolved into city-states and then into territorial kingdoms, perhaps first organized by outsiders from the north but soon dominated by local leaders and upper classes. Through the centuries the shifts in regional control in this broad zone continued to take place according to the importance of trade routes. The widespread introduction of the camel after about A.D. 400 led to expansion of the trans-Saharan trade routes and, later, to the introduction of Islam and the southward diffusion of Arab cultural influences. In the Abyssinian sector this was balanced by the influx of southern Arabian peoples and culture, the Rome-India trade routes, and the adoption of Christianity, followed by the introduction of Islam. There gradually matured a distinctive Arabized-Negro civilization in the central-to-western Sudan and an Arabized-Amharic civilization in Abyssinia. Although there were steady shifts in political controls, social culture, and regional influences, this sub-Saharan zone constituted a culture realm quite separate from that north of the Sahara.

The Moslem Realm. Whereas Christianity chiefly spread throughout the Mediterranean Basin to enter into the Mediterranean culture world, Islam found its early adherents chiefly among populations neither fully part of the Mediterranean realm nor evangelized by Christian missionaries. Originating in a religious revival among and for Arabs (early seventh century of our era but incorporating many Judaic religious ideas and Semitic culture traits), Islam rapidly assumed authority beyond the religious creed alone, to take on a militant political and economic role, initially alienating most non-Arabs. Military and political union of the Arabs resulted, but is was a unity based largely on antipathies, and it thrived on militant economic expansion into non-Arab territories. Islam derived from a regional territory neither highly developed in agricultural terms nor possessed of other outstanding resources. Islam derived much of its social strength from its tolerance of monotheistic minorities and its granting of special privileges to those who joined its ranks. A chief source of economic strength became the tribute levy upon non-Moslems and the conquest of regions outside the homeland. The leadership of Islam came to be centered on a charismatic Caliph who embodied the Prophet-force of Mohammed and the absolute temporal power of the King, in a revival of the concept of the God-King.

Within two centuries the territorial spread of the Islamic Arabs had carried them to political hegemony in lowland Southwest Asia, across northern Africa into Spain, and northeastward into the Transcaspian lands. Moslem armies raided beyond these borders and Moslem fleets raided the northern shores of the Mediterranean. It is not our purpose, here, to recount the detailed expansion of the Moslem Empire. During this early period of expansion Arabs were busy, first in formulating the Qur'ān from the spoken sermons of Mohammed and, later, in interpreting the Qur'ān and in translating its strictures into a workable body of law, social code, economic doctrine, and religious system. So encompassing were these codes of religious law that they came to govern all aspects of life, from architecture to economic activity, thus becoming the handbooks for a whole system of culture. The submission to Islam by any people was a strong force in remolding their earlier culture into an Arabized pattern.

The later spread of Islamic conquest continued northeastward into central Asia and southeastward into India, eventually reaching the equator and the islands of the Indies and the southern Philippines. Failing to make much headway in a Christianized Europe, except in Spain and the Balkans, Islam spread southward into sub-Saharan Africa. The later spread of Islam was no longer by Arabs in all cases, and it was Indian Moslems who carried the will of Allah east to the Indies. Nevertheless, Arabs followed the militant conquerors as theologians (*Imam*) to teach, interpolate, and adjudicate the Qur'ān, even as far as Mindanao in the southern Philippines.

The all-pervading reach of Islam, complemented by the establishment of the tradition of the pilgrimage (*hadj*) to Mecca and by the practice of daily prayers to Allah while facing toward Mecca, provided a bond that united all kinds of peoples into a cultural realm of its own. Although there have been many territorial versions of the Islamic World, with the political and economic rise and fall of units of that world, the formulation of the Islamic culture world was a lasting one which had a tremendous impact upon world history. The widespread travel-trading range of the Arab and Persian members of the Moslem realm, their interests in science, technology, and the arts, and their role in preserving and diffusing early knowledge was highly significant to mankind in almost all parts of the Old World. But, lastly, the rise of Islam was the addition of a permanent culture realm to the spectrum of regional culture on the face of the earth. This was entirely a human product created whole in the mind of man, and not the product of a set of nature's resources enclosed in a superior region.

The Mongol Realm. Just as the Moslem development of a religious culture realm and its expansion into a regional realm did not represent the normal accrual of a culture hearth around a sedentary people operating an agricultural society, neither did the Mongol culture realm express that slow and stable pattern of origin. The Mongol case represented the sudden fashioning of significant political and military bonds among the pastoral peoples of Central Asia by the leaders of the Mongols, originating in the genius of Genghis Khan. Born in the latter part of the twelfth century into a situation in which Mongol tribes held grassland ranges in Outer Mongolia southeast of Lake Baikal, as just one of a series of territorial pastoral ranges, Genghis Khan united all the Mongol tribes into an effective political group able to work together in a program of territorial expansion. Through personal diplomacy, psychological warfare, and interregional struggle Genghis Khan brought the Mongols to the leadership of all the pastoral peoples of Central Asia. The fashioning of superior elements in military strategy and operational horse cavalry tactics resulted in military power which could be focused upon particular objectives in capacity superior to that of any of the defensive strategies and tactics of the surrounding lands. Genghis Khan himself participated in operations from North China to Afghanistan, A.D. 1211 to 1225. Mongol power swept to conquest from China to eastern Europe and to the banks of the Indus, resulting in political hegemony over a large share of Asia. The appeal of religious fervor attached to a charismatic leader had little to do with the case, since Genghis Khan remained an animist and religious activities never became significant in Mongol ascendancy.

Whereas military conquest resulted from superior strategy and tactics, subsequent political control rested on sound military administration based on the procedures and bureaucracies of the conquered territories, with the Mongols holding themselves above and apart from the conquered. The establishment of routes of communication throughout the realm, and lines of continuous contact between its parts, permitted more complete integration of a larger territory than ever before achieved, with effective operational orders getting to the far limits in two to three weeks. Genghis Khan's concept of the state was a simple one, consisting of the pastoral, political elite in the steppe drawing tribute from all surrounding lands, in which each outer region continued its own ways of living in tune with its physical and cultural environment, the whole surmounted by the military power of the mobile Mongol armies. So simple a construct depended too highly on leadership and the continuance of political unity in the absence of firm institutional patterns of a common nature. Its weakness lay in the lack of means of perpetuating the simple concept and in the very multiplicity of ways of living in the settled lands over which the Mongol armies needed to maintain control.

In bringing political control over a huge territory under one leadership, Mongol hegemony necessarily operated an "open-door" empire. Ideas, procedures, commodities, and people were free to move from one margin to another. That an Italian, Marco Polo, could become a civilian government official in China under a Mongol emperor is expressive of a tolerance of culture seldom seen in the tight social and regional controls within the agricultural culture hearths. The simple conceptual basis for the Mongol culture realm proved ephemeral, as it could only be, since little intrinsic permanent or institutional development took place in the pastoral homeland itself. However, the cultural results for the Old World were significant, since the elaboration of the ephemeral Mongol culture realm produced diffusionary effects perhaps even greater than those of any single regionally concentrated and tightly bonded culture hearth. The Mongol "open-door" realm offered the broad regional interchange of ideas, peoples, and commodities at a rate and in a volume never before achieved in the Old World. That Marco Polo, to cite a single example, could later spread in Europe the knowledge of how Chinese lived is the sort of diffusion that promoted the ways of man upon the earth.

The Marginal Satellites of the Old and New Worlds

We have now reviewed the kinds of culture hearths and the centers of their origins in the development of several quite different living systems in both the Old World and the New. We have indicated the expansion of these concentrated living systems into culture realms affecting large territorial sectors of the earth. We have not, of course, completed a discussion of all inhabited portions of the earth or of all the different ways of living thus far devised.

Our account may seem incomplete in that we have not made the Roman Empire the focal point of a major discussion, that we have not listed the great Khmer Empire of mainland Southeast Asia as one of the key formulations, that we have not mentioned Japan, and that we have neglected the

Pueblo culture region of the southwestern United States. From the standpoint of deriving new systems of human living in units of earth space, none of these regional combinations originated basically new systems. Each took the combines of culture devised elsewhere and applied them to a region or regions and, in that application, improved on many of the earlier applications to produce living systems of greater complexity, greater human population, greater wealth and prosperity, or greater artistic heights in limited patterns than obtained in the original culture hearths. From this point of view the Roman Empire was a practical application of the living systems of two culture hearths, Mesopotamia and Egypt, as synthesized in the eastern Mediterranean while tapping some of the resources of northwest Europe. The Roman Empire thereby reached heights, population totals, territorial limits, and levels of prosperity not achieved by either Mesopotamia or Egypt. Koreans, Japanese, and Viet-Namese elaborated the patterns of the Chinese culture hearth in somewhat the same way in more restricted regions. The Khmer Empire synthesized the Brahmanic and Buddhist cultures of the Indian culture hearth in a way never quite achieved in India. And the Hohokam and the Pueblo of southwestern United States-northern Mexico constructed out of Meso-American hearth living systems some new twists in quite unlike regions.

The regional application of hearth-devised living systems to distant and previously lightly developed environments has been occurring throughout the historic human occupation of the earth. The archaeologist describes this even for Paleolithic cultures operating on rather simple bases, but we cannot read the whole record from the artifacts alone. Within the historic period we see the application of the principle again and again. Some of the satellite regions achieved results that seemed to overshadow those of the original hearth. There is disconformity between the Mesopotamian culture hearth and the height of the Roman Empire's application at a distance. In other cases, however, the satellite region remained an incomplete application which did not achieve outstanding results, and the record remains shadowy and not fully understood. World histories seldom include the total panorama of regional development by which nearly the entire earth came to reflect the evolution of human systems devised in regional hearths.

In the foregoing sense the region of northwest Europe achieved what might be termed minor satellite status only during the earlier historic periods. What occidental history describes as the Renaissance was the beginning of regional development that has flowered into the dominant culture realm of modern time, and the Industrial Revolution was a significant chapter in that flowering. The most emphatic material blooming of the European culture realm has lain in the United States and Canada, which not only took the ideas of Europe but also exceeded the Mongol "open-door" policy to make these countries the recipient and applier of culture from the earth as a whole.

As historic time passed and diffusion carried regional cultures to far territories, the total variety of human living systems increased steadily, as it had done during the late Paleolithic. Within the historic time span, however, there has been regional dominance by the culture systems of a relatively few hearths, each expanding territorially to lesser or greater degree to affect a smaller or larger sector of the earth. Whereas, at 3000 B.C., we could clearly itemize only a very few hearths and culture realms, by A.D. 1400 the number of culture realms had increased, and their reach had been extended to a relatively large portion of the earth (Fig. 5.9, pp. 226–227).

The Corners of the Earth and the Regional Balance of High, Median, and Low Cultures

The diffusion of elements of culture is not, per se, dependent on organized transportation systems or purposeful programs for spreading culture, for the very nature of man tends to stimulate him to watch over human beings, to copy their ways, and to try to improve upon their artifacts. Systems of transportation, communication, and purposeful spreading of culture, however, facilitate the distribution of culture over the earth through the bringing of peoples into increased degrees of exposure to one another. The friction of distance, damping the waves of diffusion, applies to the spread of culture traits and complexes, so that fewer elements reach from centers of origination into the far corners of the earth. There are also those corners of the earth inhabited by peoples who resist new ideas and culture change, through the application of their own social and political controls, to prohibit the infiltration of new ways of living. In that several scattered regional locations became creative centers of cultural development, developments spread from these hearths to regional zones around them. In that ways of living varied from one hearth to another, the regional spreads perpetuated different living systems in different major zones of the earth. To the degree that hearths became connected by lines of trade and communication, interchange occurred between major sectors of the earth. Since some late regional developments, derived from particular hearths, achieved greater practical application of principles of culture, the regions they affected reached levels of living strongly contrasting with the levels maintained in far corners of the bases of old and simple living systems.

As we survey the earth at any given date after the end of the Paleolithic Age we see the regional interplay of cultural development. Such a survey, at the end of the Neolithic Age, would have disclosed a few thriving centers around the earth in which notable advance had taken place in productive living systems. Beyond these centers would have been zones in which these productive ideas were in some stage of application and beyond these zones large sectors of the earth still living by systems normal to Paleolithic time. Close to the centers, and throughout the zones of improvement, would have been exclaves within which Paleolithic patterns also continued. If we repeat this survey at about the start of the Christian Era, we would note greater contrast between the most advanced regions of the earth and those "far corners" still living under Paleolithic systems. We would see several outstanding centers of civilization, such as North China, Northern India, the Mediterranean Basin at the time of Roman control under Augustus, southern Mexico-Guatemala, and the lifting level of Peruvian culture. We would also see that Mesopotamia and Egypt were in a state of political and technological eclipse, though the agricultural lowlands were well populated in each

case, and we would be struck by the greater contrasts that existed in levels of culture around the earth.

Were we to conduct still a third survey, perhaps about A.D. 1400, the regional patterns of the development would have afforded greater contrast than at any other time (see Fig. 5.9). We would see both continuity and disconformity, for North China was still the center of influence in eastern Asia, whereas the heavily populated Mesopotamian lowland led a life far lower in level than it had in earlier time. We would have seen in the New World two strong centers in Meso-America and in the Peruvian Highlands. And we would have seen numerous satellite regions depicting the patterns of living systems out of particular hearths. But now the "far corners" were smaller in extent, less numerous in number, and marked by small populations in contrast to the numbers resident in the regions of greater development. The farthest of the "far corners," however, was still living under a system quite typical of the late Paleolithic. It is hard to say what inhabited region of the earth we might have nominated as having the least development of human culture, but it is entirely likely that we would have voted China to have had the most advanced and most satisfactory human system to be found on the earth. Perhaps the most notable feature of all would have been our realization that there were extremely few corners of the earth, save Antarctica, that did not then bear the distinctive marks of man upon the landscape. Some of those marks would have been interpreted as ruins, and we would have attributed them to the failure of systems of living, whereas others were the preliminary marks being made by culture groups growing in strength and still elaborating their systems of productive development of their regional landscapes.

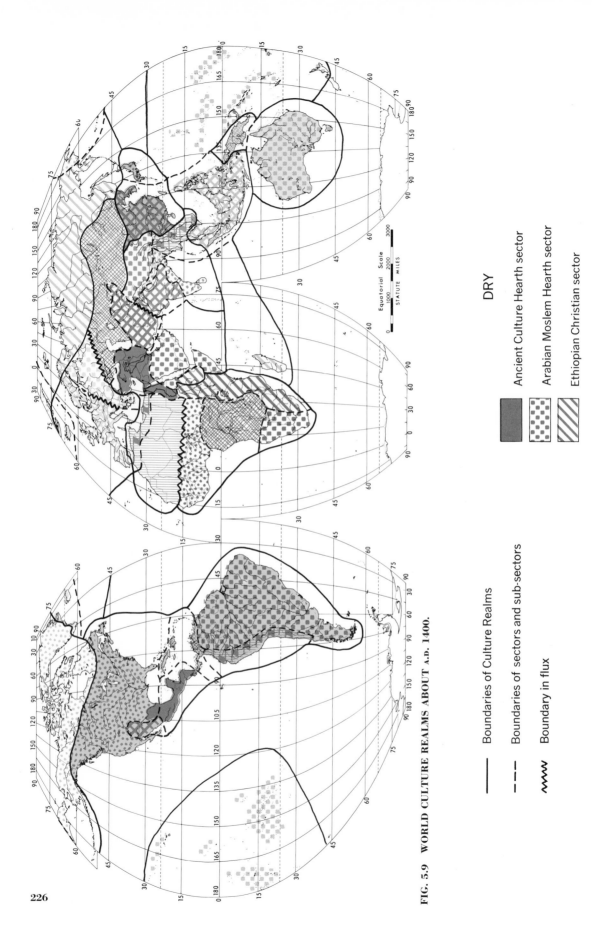

226

FIG. 5.9 WORLD CULTURE REALMS ABOUT A.D. 1400.

Equatorial Scale
0   1000   2000   3000
STATUTE MILES

——— Boundaries of Culture Realms

- - - Boundaries of sectors and sub-sectors

vvvv Boundary in flux

DRY

Ancient Culture Hearth sector

Arabian Moslem Hearth sector

Ethiopian Christian sector

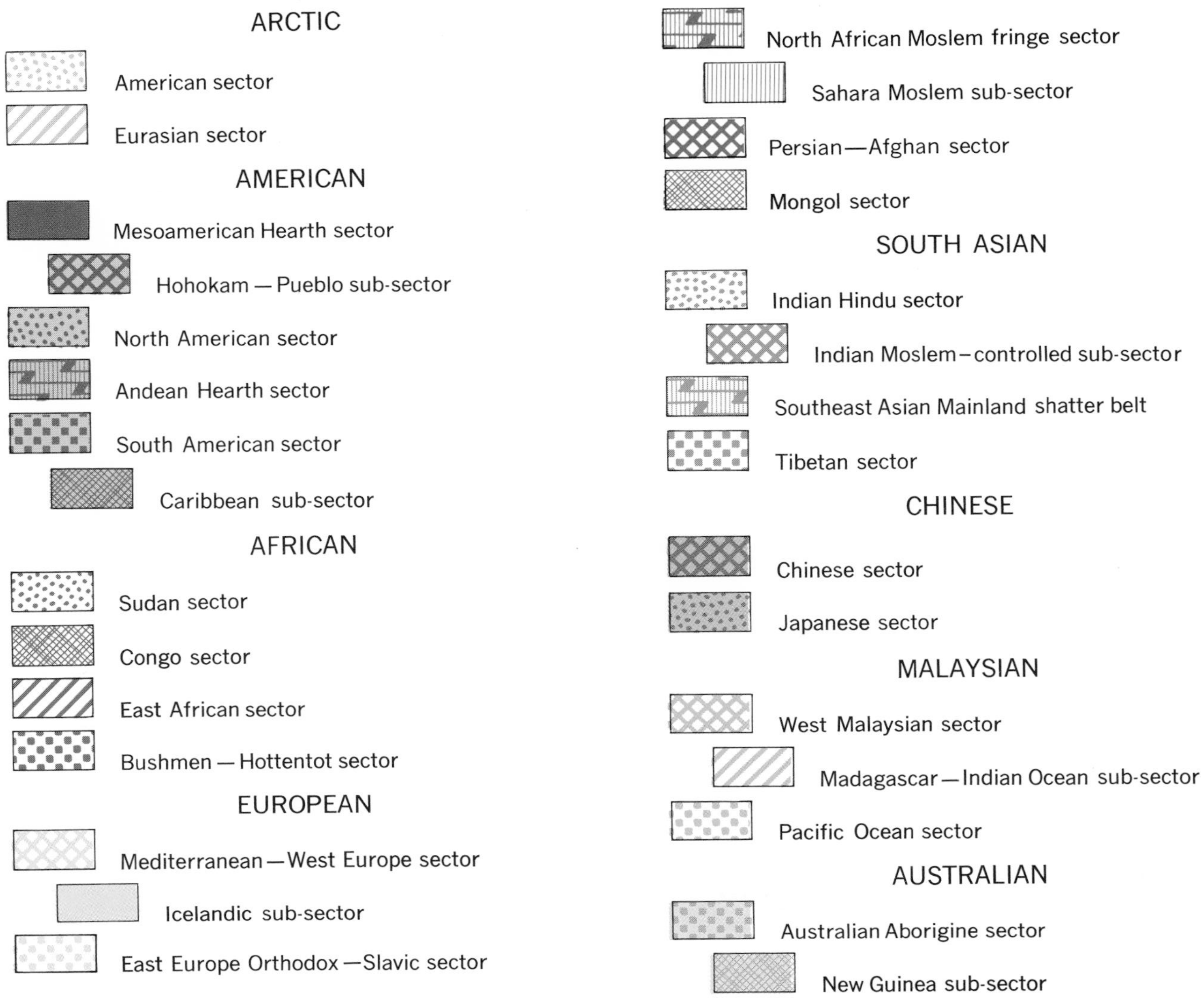

ARCTIC

 American sector

 Eurasian sector

AMERICAN

 Mesoamerican Hearth sector

 Hohokam—Pueblo sub-sector

 North American sector

 Andean Hearth sector

 South American sector

 Caribbean sub-sector

AFRICAN

 Sudan sector

 Congo sector

 East African sector

 Bushmen—Hottentot sector

EUROPEAN

 Mediterranean—West Europe sector

 Icelandic sub-sector

 East Europe Orthodox—Slavic sector

ARCTIC

 North African Moslem fringe sector

 Sahara Moslem sub-sector

 Persian—Afghan sector

 Mongol sector

SOUTH ASIAN

 Indian Hindu sector

 Indian Moslem—controlled sub-sector

 Southeast Asian Mainland shatter belt

 Tibetan sector

CHINESE

 Chinese sector

 Japanese sector

MALAYSIAN

 West Malaysian sector

 Madagascar—Indian Ocean sub-sector

 Pacific Ocean sector

AUSTRALIAN

Australian Aborigine sector

New Guinea sub-sector

FIG. 5.9 (*Continued*)

SELECTED REFERENCES

Adams, Robert McC.
    1965   *Land Behind Baghdad.* Chicago: University of Chicago Press. 187 pp.
    1966   *The Evolution of Urban Society.* Chicago: Aldine. 191 pp.

Anene, J. C., and G. N. Brown
    1966   *Africa in the Nineteenth and Twentieth Centuries.* London: Thomas Nelson & Sons. 555 pp.

Belshaw, Cyril S.
    1965   *Traditional Exchange and Modern Markets.* Englewood Cliffs, N.J.: Prentice-Hall. 149 pp.

Bhargava, K. D.
    1961   *A Survey of Islamic Culture and Institutions.* Allahabad, India: Kitab Mahal. 280 pp.

Braidwood, Robert J., and Gordon R. Willey (eds.)
    1962   *Courses Toward Urban Life.* Chicago: Aldine. 384 pp.

Brainerd, G. W.
    1954   *The Maya Civilization.* Los Angeles: Southwest Museum. 93 pp.

Caldwell, Joseph R. (ed.)
    1966   *New Roads to Yesterday.* New York: Basic Books. 546 pp.

Chang Kwang-chih
    1963   *The Archaeology of Ancient China.* New Haven, Conn.: Yale University Press. 346 pp.

Cheng Te-kun
    1959–
    1963   *Archaeology in China.* Cambridge, England: Heffer. Vol. 1, 1959, *Prehistoric China,* 250 pp.; Vol. 2, 1960, *Shang China,* 368 pp.; Vol. 3, 1963, *Chou China,* 430 pp.

Coedes, Georges
    1967   *The Indianized States of Southeast Asia.* Honolulu: East-West Center Press. 384 pp.

Cottrell, Leonard
    1958   *The Anvil of Civilization.* London: Faber and Faber. 288 pp.

Coulborn, Rushton
    1959   *The Origin of Civilized Societies.* Princeton, N.J.: Princeton University Press. 200 pp.

Crombie, A. C. (ed.)
    1963   *Scientific Change.* New York: Basic Books. 896 pp.

Firth, Raymond, and B. S. Yamey (eds.)
    1964   *Capital, Saving, and Credit in Peasant Societies.* Chicago: Aldine. 399 pp.

Forbes, R. J.
    1950   *Man the Maker.* London: Constable. 355 pp.

Gibb, H. A. R.
    1962   *Studies on the Civilization of Islam.* London: Routledge & Kegan Paul. 396 pp.

Goitien, S. D.
    1967   *Studies in Islamic History and Institutions.* Leiden: Brill. 390 pp.

Gordon, D. H.
    1958   *The Prehistoric Background of Indian Culture.* Bombay: Tripathi. 199 pp.

Grousset, Rene
    1966   *Conqueror of the World. The Life of Chingis-Khan.* New York: The Orion Press. 300 pp.

Gufstavson, Carl G.
    1955   *A Preface to History.* New York: McGraw-Hill. 222 pp.

Helm, J. (ed.)
    1965   *Essays in Economic Anthropology Dedicated to the Memory of Karl Polanyi.* Seattle, Wash.: University of Washington Press, for American Ethnological Society. 143 pp.

. Hornell, James
    1946   *Water Transport, Origins and Early Evolution.* Cambridge, England: The University Press. 307 pp.

Hottinger, A.
    1963   *The Arabs, Their History, Culture and Place in the Modern World.* Berkeley and Los Angeles: University of California Press. 344 pp.

Kroeber, A. L.
    1952   *The Nature of Culture.* Chicago: University of Chicago Press. 437 pp.
    1962   *A Roster of Civilizations and Culture.* New York: Wenner-Gren Foundation for Anthropological Research; Chicago: Aldine. 96 pp.
    1963   *An Anthropologist Looks at History.* Berkeley: University of California Press. 213 pp.

Landau, Rom
    1958   *Islam and the Arabs.* London: George Allen & Unwin. 299 pp.

Lanning, Edward P.
    1967   *Peru Before the Incas.* Englewood Cliffs, N.J.: Prentice-Hall. 216 pp.

Lopez, Robert S., and Irving W. Raymond
    1955   *Medieval Trade in the Mediterranean World.* New York: Columbia University Press. 458 pp.

Majumdar, R. C., and A. D. Pusalker (eds.)
    1951   *The History and Culture of the Indian People.* London: Allen & Unwin. Vol. 1, *The Vedic Age.* 565 pp.

Manners, Robert A. (ed.)
    1964   *Process and Pattern in Culture.* Chicago: Aldine. 434 pp.

Mason, J. Alden
    1957   *The Ancient Civilizations of Peru.* Middlesex, England: Harmondsworth. 329 pp.

Mason, Stephen F.
    1962   *A History of the Sciences.* New York: Collier Books. 638 pp.

McNeill, William H.
    1963   *The Rise of the West.* Chicago: University of Chicago Press. 829 pp.

Moscati, Sabatino
    1960   *The Face of the Ancient Orient.* Chicago: Quadrangle Books. 328 pp.

Murdock, George Peter
    1959   *Africa, Its Peoples and Their Culture History.* New York: McGraw-Hill. 456 pp.

Nash, Manning
    1966   *Primitive and Peasant Economic Systems.* San Francisco: Chandler. 166 pp.

Needham, Joseph
    1954–
    1965   *Science and Civilization in China.* Cambridge, England: Cambridge University Press. Vol. 1, 1954, 318 pp.; Vol. 2, 1956, 692 pp.; Vol. 3, 1959, 874 pp.; Vol. 4, Part 1, 1962, 434 pp.; Vol. 4, Part 2, 1965, 759 pp.

Oppenheim, A. L.
    1964   *Ancient Mesopotamia.* Chicago: University of Chicago Press. 433 pp.

Planhol, Xavier de
    1959   *The World of Islam.* Ithaca, N.Y.: Cornell University Press (English edition). 142 pp.

Polanyi, Karl, Conrad Arensberg, and Harry W. Pearson (eds.)
    1957   *Trade and Market in the Early Empires.* Glencoe, Ill.: The Free Press. 382 pp.

Redfield, Robert
    1956   *Peasant Society and Culture.* Chicago: University of Chicago Press. 162 pp.

Roolvink, R.
    1957   *Historical Atlas of the Muslim Peoples.* Cambridge, Mass.: Harvard University Press. 40 pp.

Roux, Georges
    1964   *Ancient Iraq.* London: George Allen & Unwin. 431 pp.

Sarton, George
    1959   *A History of Science.* Cambridge, Mass. Harvard University Press. 554 pp.

Shinnie, Margaret
    1965   *Ancient African Kingdoms.* London: Edward Arnold. 126 pp.

Singer, Charles, E. J. Holmyard, and A. R. Hall
    1954–
    1956   *A History of Technology.* London: Oxford University Press. Vol. 1, 1954, 827 pp.; Vol. 2, 1956, 802 pp.

Smith, W. C.
    1957   *Islam in Modern History.* Princeton, N.J.: Princeton University Press. 317 pp.

Starr, Chester G., et al
    1960   *A History of the World* (Vol. 1). Chicago: Rand McNally. 630 pp.

Taton, Rene
    1963   *Ancient and Medieval Science.* New York: Basic Books. 551 pp.

Thomas, William L., Jr. (ed.)
    1956   *Man's Role in Changing the Face of the Earth.* Chicago: University of Chicago Press. 1193 pp.

Towle, Margaret A.
    1961   *The Ethnobotany of Pre-Columbian Peru* (Viking Fund Publications in Anthropology, No. 30). New York: Wenner-Gren Foundation for Anthropological Research. 180 pp.

Turner, Ralph
    1941   *The Great Cultural Traditions.* New York: McGraw-Hill. 2 volumes, 1333 pp.

von Grunebaum, G. E. (ed.)
    1955   *Unity and Variety in Muslim Civilization.* Chicago: University of Chicago Press. 385 pp.

von Hagen, Victor Wolfgang
    1957   *The Ancient Sun Kingdoms of the Americas.* New York: World Publishing Co. 617 pp.

Welch, Galbraith
    1965   *Africa Before They Came: The Continent North, South, East, and West Preceding the Colonial Powers.* New York: Morrow. 396 pp.

Wheeler, Mortimer
    1959   *Early India and Pakistan to Ashoka.* New York: Praeger. 190 pp.
    1960   *The Cambridge History of India,* supplementary volume, *The Indus Civilization.* Cambridge, England: Cambridge University Press. 106 pp.

Willey, Gordon R.
    1956   *Prehistoric Settlement Patterns in the New World* (Viking Fund Publications in Anthropology, No. 23). New York: Wenner-Gren Foundation for Anthropological Research. 202 pp.
    1966   *An Introduction to American Archaeology.* Vol. 1: *North and Middle America.* New York: Prentice-Hall. 526 pp.

Wilson, John A.
    1951   *The Culture of Ancient Egypt.* Chicago: University of Chicago Press. 344 pp.

Wolf, E. R.
    1966   *Peasants.* Englewood Cliffs, N.J.: Prentice-Hall. 116 pp.

HOUSE TYPES

PATRICK MORIN, MONKMEYER

Pastoral Tent Camp, Iran

Yurt, Mongolia

GEORGE HOLTON, PHOTO RESEARCHERS

232

Clay Houses, Aleppo, Syria

E. BOUBAT, PHOTO RESEARCHERS

MARC AND EVELYNE BERNHEIM, RAPHO GUILLUMETTE

Single-Family Compound, Togo, Africa

ALASKA PICTORIAL SERVICE

Eskimo Sod House, Northern Alaska

234

Stone and Straw Thatch, Lake Titicaca, Peru

BERNARD SILBERSTEIN, RAPHO GUILLUMETTE

CARL FRANK, PHOTO RESEARCHERS

Board and Palm Thatch, Surinam

235

Log Cabin, Canada

RON WINCH, PHOTO RESEARCHERS

Pueblo Indian Village, New Mexico

AMERICAN AIRLINES

236

Sundried-Brick Village, Iraq

DIANE RAWSON, PHOTO RESEARCHERS

Fronted Cave Homes, Granada, Spain

GEORGE HOLTON, PHOTO RESEARCHERS

UNIROYAL

Estate Manager's Bungalow, Indonesia

Bamboo Pile House, Cambodia

238

FREDERICK AYER, PHOTO RESEARCHERS

Batak Pile Dwelling, Sumatra, Indonesia

239

INDONESIAN INFORMATION OFFICE

LOUIS GOLDMAN, RAPHO GUILLUMETTE

240

Stone and Straw Thatch, Dorset, England

Victorian Town Houses, London, England

Farmstead, Ruhr, Germany

GERMAN INFORMATION CENTER

GEORGE WHITELY, PHOTO RESEARCHERS

Town Row-Housing, Wales

241

GERRY CRANHAM, RAPHO GUILLUMETTE

Rural Farmstead, Central China

J. E. SPENCER

Town House, Central China

242

J. E. SPENCER

J. E. SPENCER

Malay Wood Pile Dwelling, Malaysia

W. L. THOMAS, JR.

Rural Gentleman Farmer's Home, Northern Philippines

243

Cape Dutch Farmhouse, South Africa

SATOUR

COLONIAL WILLIAMSBURG PHOTO BY GEORGE BEAMISH

Powell-Waller Colonial, Williamsburg, Virginia, U.S.

"Dunleith," Mississippi, U.S.

BRUCE ROBERTS, RAPHO GUILLUMETTE

CONSULATE GENERAL OF THE PHILIPPINES

245

Upper-Class Urban Home, Manila, Philippines

Squared Log-Shake Roof Farmhouse, Yugoslavia

ANGELO LOMEO, NANCY PALMER

CONSULATE GENERAL OF FINLAND

Old-Style Farmhouse, Finland

J. ALLEN CASH, RAPHO GUILLUMETTE

246

Modern Fishermen's Housing, Southwest Sweden

ROBERT MOTTAR, PHOTO RESEARCHERS

Trailer Park, Tor Bay, Devon, England

247

Corbusier House, Apartment Block, Berlin, Germany

GERMAN INFORMATION CENTER

Urban Apartment Block, Hongkong

INGER McCABE, RAPHO GUILLUMETTE

CHAPTER 6

The Earth Becomes Global:
The European Explosion

In the modern development of the earth one blossoming surpassed all others that had preceded it. This was the explosion of the European culture realm, often termed the Rise of the West or the Rise of the Occident. It came late, took place in a region well removed from any of the early cultural hearths, and created a culture realm that bid for expansion over the entire planet. Although its final burst came rather suddenly and with tremendous vitality, the growth and development of the culture hearth was slow and drawn out. This chapter traces the rise of Europe, the spread of its culture over the whole of our inhabited globe, and the creation of scattered subcenters of occidental culture in different portions of the earth.

The Mediterranean Heritage:
Greece, Rome, and Christendom

Behind the growth of Europe lies the history of development in the Mediterranean culture realm: Greece, Rome, and Christendom. We have suggested that Greek civilization was built on the evolutionary blending of traits and complexes derived from the Mesopotamian, Egyptian, and Minoan culture hearths which were original sources of elements of civilizations. The Greeks themselves converted many patterns of stimuli into culture complexes unknown in the three earlier hearths, and both Greeks and Phoenicians spread those features throughout the Mediterranean Basin and beyond. From the lesser regional developments in the subordinate hearths of the classical Near East came added technologies, social concepts, and religious ideas which, when blended with Greek

patterns, formed the Roman world of Christendom. Although trade and culture contacts between Greek and Phoenician Mediterranean regions had linked northwest Europe with some of these developments, the latter region remained on the fringes of the barbarian world until the military, economic, and religious power of Rome brought northwest Europe within the influences of the Roman realm (Fig. 6.1). The diffusion of improved agriculture, trade, formal town settlement, architecture and engineering works, military government, manufacturing, the use of Latin, and the Christian way spread new levels of achievement and new ways of living throughout what are now Spain, France, England, and the Low Countries, in western Europe; stimulus diffusion was more significant throughout the Balkan region of southern Europe and southern Russia, Poland, and the southern Baltic sectors in the east. Not all elements of culture proved practical or were fully accepted in the cooler, more humid northern lands, but adaptive blendings occurred between new ways and old to yield evolutionary patterns of culture distinctive to the marginal regions on the northern side of the Roman World.

The crop-growing, animal-keeping, village-dwelling, and rural-oriented basic culture of Europe traces its ancestry to the Neolithic of the third millennium B.C. However, changes steadily occurred in the ethnic patterns of peoples in particular regions over the centuries and in their agricultural-handicraft economies. Changing environmental conditions in northern Eurasia, plus the productive output of both pastoral economy

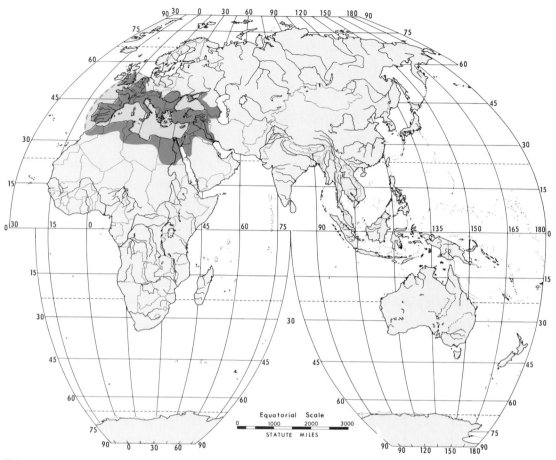

FIG. 6.1 THE MAXIMUM EXTENT OF THE ROMAN EMPIRE, A.D. 117.

and northern-margin crop-growing systems, resulted in regional surplus populations of barbarians who began a period of migratory invasion of the better regions to the south, from China to the Atlantic. The barbarian invasions of the early Christian Era disrupted the political structure of the Roman Empire (Fig. 6.2), but they brought in new peoples who gradually settled down to European ways of living. Western Europe suffered more from these invasions than did either the Eastern Roman Empire or China. There was some militant depopulation, but regional populations were replaced by immigrant, mobile barbarians who steadily looked to settled ways of living. From the time of Constantine onward, the increasing political power in the hands of the Roman ruler, combined in the uniting of the Church and the State, became the model for the new barbarian Kings of Europe. This was a return to a system reminiscent of Mesopotamia, Egypt, and early Persia. Tribal chieftains had often shucked off the bonds of confederacy to fight one another in the outer barbarian world. As kings of budding European states, they continued to fight one another inside the civilized pale.

Medieval Europe: Forest Clearing, Agriculture, Crafts, and Society

Roman occupation of portions of western Europe had introduced a market-oriented economy centered in growing towns, a road system of sorts, and the interregional linkage of basic trade regions, which involved significant changes in agricultural-handicraft economy. Late Roman features included increasing taxation under more intensive military rule and the accumulation of land in the hands of landlords of various types. The so-called fall of the Roman Empire reversed these trends. It lessened the flow of trade, depopulated the towns, destroyed interregional linkages, and pushed the populations back into rural agricultural and handicraft self-sufficiency. This trend, however, was not a return to Neolithic patterns.

Out of the late Roman social changes and the new barbarian social system, there sprouted the seeds of the later feudalism which arose under the development of Frankish military strategy involving professional mounted soldiery who were granted fiefs of land in return for their vassalage. Although local anarchy and the lack of central authority were widespread, the Dark Ages were not so bereft as often depicted in the older literature, albeit life was simpler and not topped by great doings in art and literature in urban settings. By A.D. 500, perhaps, the worst of the barbarian invasions slackened and a significant resurgence began in rural agricultural economy in scattered portions of Europe, from the Atlantic to the Black Sea.

The highly competitive regionalism of the growing political states of Europe occupies the historian, for its picture was one of continual change. The sixth century saw the supremacy of the Christian Church bring the development of West European monasticism whose stability tended to counter the changing political strife in the rural countryside. Under the superstructure of feudalism and monasticism, with their knights and bishops, castles and abbeys, fiefs and church lands, lay the manorial (seignorial) system by which a nearly self-sufficient rural life operated in many portions of Europe. In the turbulent times of the sixth to thirteenth centuries, the independent, small landholders possessed neither the economic resources nor the effective sociopolitical structures to cope with the problems of life. The manorial system represented a grouping that offered protection, resources, cooperation, and economic security. It was only the revival of trade, markets, towns, and interregional linkages in the thirteenth century that offered a real alternative.

In part the manorial system was related to politico-military feudalism, but in part it was related to agrarian economic technology in an underpopulated region. For all the lack of signifi-

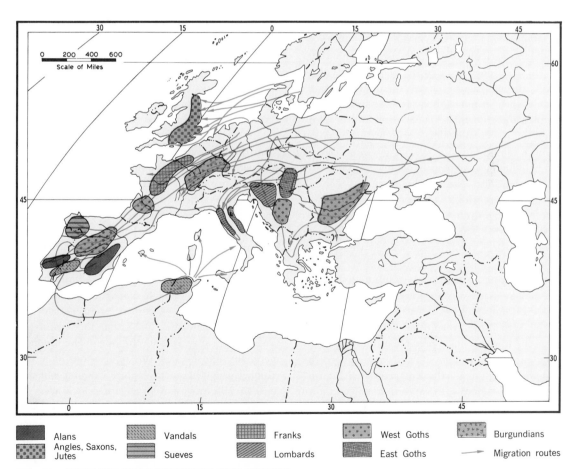

FIG. 6.2 THE BARBARIAN INVASIONS INTO EUROPE.

cant art and literature during the Middle Ages, there began, about the sixth century, an agricultural revolution that altered the face of Europe. The manorial system provided the socioeconomic framework within which these changes could take place. This revolution is more properly termed a regional, agrarian evolution, for it developed slowly, with regional inequality, in the hands of rural, village-dwelling, agrarian folk who were working out new systems of agricultural technology. Involved in these developments were the new types of plows, cultivators, and seeding systems, the rise of the field-rotation systems by which pasturage and cropping would be alternated in infields and outfields, and the solving of the problems of shoeing and harnessing the horse for agricultural draft labor. The new tools made for relatively easy cultivation of wet and heavy soils that could not be handled by Neolithic systems. Field-rotation systems brought cattle to dominance over the Neolithic pig. And the heavy, powerful horse, when properly shod and harnessed, provided draft power with greater daily productivity than the lighter, slower ox.

Complementary features in the growth of a more productive agriculture were the rise of iron mining in central to northern Europe and of the village smith, through whose efforts the feudal knights derived their armor and the farmers and artisans got plentiful iron tools. There were also developments of newer and better crop varieties suited to more humid lands of shorter growing seasons, and field-drainage systems by which to drain clays and bottomlands. Many of these items of technology were the result of westward diffusion of traits and technologies new to Europe in the sixth to tenth centuries. Their evolutionary adaptation to local ecological conditions provided tremendous variety in agricultural economy; field systems, plow-cultivator types, crop combinations, and seasonal land-use systems were extremely varied across Europe.

The agricultural revolution altered the landscapes of Europe, made possible a doubling of its population between A.D. 700 and 1400, moved the center of strength northward, promoted internal migration within the European world, and provided the increased productivity in basic commodities that fed and clothed a population beginning to grow. It was the agricultural revolution that produced the growth of population and the improvement in dietary and living systems which

buttressed the Renaissance. Without it, no improvement in European life could ever have been brought about. The agricultural revolution of this period has been slighted by the general historian, for the peasant life of medieval Europe seemed only full of hard labor and dull rural affairs.

Part and parcel of the process was the steady clearing of brush, gorse, and woodland which had overgrown many formerly Roman-cultivated lands. There was also a more widely distributed direct attack upon the regions of forest that had covered many useful tracts since the first Neolithic clearings had been achieved by shifting cultivation. The old place-names of Europe reflect the era of clearing, with their many names for burning, clearing, digging, and cutting of wild growth. Medieval Europe was not static. Change was constant, but the change lay in the rural countryside in which the regional peasantries were building their village communities, shaping their landscapes, forging their productive systems, and increasing their numbers. Inheritance systems often tended to preserve the sizes of medium and small farms, and younger sons often were forced off the land into nonagricultural callings. Here lies the growth of artisanship, institutionalized into the craft guilds which were divided into apprentice, journeyman, and master.

The buildup in local populations in western Europe did not produce marked surpluses until the ninth century. Until then, open space was plentiful, the drain of military personnel had been adequate, and regional mobility remained high. In eastern Europe this level of regional population growth was reached a little earlier. In the late ninth century many well-settled regions no longer possessed large areas of open lands, and there began a small accumulation of people in the towns. Towns, to this date, had been chiefly fortified points, castles, monastery seats, and administrative centers with only enough supporting personnel to carry on the appointed duties. Surplus persons did not become parasitic, but began to expand the range of artisanry, initiate the role of the itinerant merchant, and manage the applications of power which Europe began to explore in water wheeled and animal-powered mills of different kinds.

Once started, the growth of towns, the expansion of artisanry, the beginning of trade, trade fairs, and markets, expanded steadily. Following the cessation of Norse piracy in the tenth century in northwestern Europe, this town pattern spread northward into Britain and Ireland and the associated coastal lands of the North Sea and the English Channel. The Scandinavians in eastern Europe had been less addicted to piracy and more given to carrying on trade and organizing trading empires, so that a Baltic Sea-Black Sea active trade zone appeared in the eighth century. Integral elements in this increasing prosperity were the slow evolution of new cultural institutions and new spatially administrative institutions. These were needed to handle the larger populations and the increased proximities of settlements. There is involved a pattern that might be termed circular ecologic causation. Each new development induced new ecologic forces applicable in numerous directions, each in turn requiring cultural adjustments and further ecologic change. By the thirteenth century all Europe was again beginning to resemble a thriving and prosperous region, productive in agriculture and active in manufacturing and trade.

The West and the East in Europe

There were, of course, differences in the social history and political evolution of Europe's west and east, the two sectors north of the Mediterranean Basin, related to physical environment and ethnic composition, and to matters derived therefrom. Northwestern Europe in the Neolithic Age was already a Celtic tribal Europe, whose descendants still occupy sectors of the region. The Neolithic occupants of eastern Europe are not yet identified, but they formed mixed groups of several cultures. At least as early as 700 B.C., Scythian-Mongolic invaders poured across the open plains of southern Russia and, following them, numerous other ethnic components filtered in or swept in as militant invaders. Whence came the original Slavic tribes we are not sure, but Slavic stocks have been present in the zone between the Carpathians, the upper Vistula River, and the Don River since at least 500 B.C. Despite other invasions of the open lands of southern Russia, eastern Europe was to become Slavic Europe.

In the west the influence of Hellenistic culture penetrated less far north, but the power of Rome spread farther and earlier and then declined more fully. In the east the Hellenistic influence was greater, and the continuing strength of the Eastern Roman Empire, seated in Constantinople after A.D. 330, preserved a modicum of order along the Black Sea littoral for several centuries. As the Germanic invaders overran western Europe to settle

down as local occupants, only several units of the Goths ventured into eastern Europe, to settle in the valleys of the Vistula and the Dnieper. From the fourth century onward, when the Turkic Huns and their confederates swept across eastern Europe out of Siberia, the eastern sectors of Europe were subjected to repeated, discontinuous invasions by Turkic-Mongol people such as the Avars, the Khazars, and the Mongols proper. Scandinavian thrusts into northern and western Russia were frequent, chiefly in the guise of furthering trade with southwest Asia, and ending in formation of the first city-state, centered around Kiev, in the ninth century. The conversion of the southern Slavic peoples to the Eastern Roman Catholic faith began in the ninth century, to start a formal distinction with western Europe. The development of the Cyrillic alphabet, by one of the early Christian missionaries, formalized the written elements of Slavic speech patterns when Latin still was the chief medium of writing in western Europe.

Enmities over settlement lands between Germanic and Slavic peoples erupted as early as A.D. 700 to set another kind of distinction. Slavery, for example, never truly became a part of the socioeconomic structure of northwestern Europe, whereas it was an old element in eastern Europe. When the growth of feudalism took place in western Europe, there could only be an approximation of this organization of society in eastern Europe because of the continuation of slave institutions. The broad and open physiography of eastern Europe always allowed more widely sweeping patterns of invasion than was true in western Europe, whereas the heavily forested lands of the northeast were more slowly opened by clearing and agricultural settlement than the northern sectors of the more temperate west.

In the broad currents of culture development the whole European world showed considerable similarity, but in the detailed workings of culture complexes, and in the chronologies, there were significant differences. Many of the Asian traits diffusing westward actually came into eastern Europe long before they arrived in the west, but as always, peoples react differently to new ideas. One example of this is the impact of the stirrup as a piece of riding equipment. Coming into use in the Slavic lands in the seventh century, the stirrup reached western Europe only in the early eighth century. But it was the Franks of northern France who saw in the stirrup the meaning for horse-mounted troops and who then began the alterations in military tactics that led to the armored knight and feudalism.

Changing Europe: Towns and Trade

Moslem control of three sides of the Mediterranean Basin after about A.D. 800 thrust the peoples of the northern shores back into Europe, in a sense. It often has been said that barbarians and Moslems blocked the trade routes beyond the Mediterranean, whereas after about 700 much of the failure of trade lay with the Christian southern Europeans. Europe became landlocked, in a sense, since outside Scandinavia the Europeans had not yet taken the sea into proper account. This reflects the growth of an agrarian, rural, village-dwelling Europe little concerned with the waters surrounding it. To some extent eastern Europe maintained trade with Asia Minor through Constantinople. However, it was the Italian town of Venice, which had been engaged in fishing and coastal trade, that reestablished firm contacts with both Constantinople and the Moslem Levant. Gradual expansion in this trade zone turned Venice into a community of traders, handicraft manufacturers, and processors of trade goods. Other north Italian towns also became aggressive again, and by A.D. 1100 the whole Mediterranean was open once more to interregional trade, with goods beginning to move northward across the Alpine pass-routes into the heartlands of Europe.

The evolution of new towns and their collections of traders and craftsmen across the breadth of Europe is a complex story. From Flanders in the Low Countries, woolen textiles had begun to be traded in the ninth century, and by the year 1000 Flanders wools were widely available. Although, in terms of decades, the process of growth of trade and towns seems slow, viewed historically, the process actually was a rapid one. Involved were peasant markets around monasteries and castles and at river fords and water gaps; new towns were created for trade and free of seignorial controls; the availability of surplus primary commodities increased; local population surpluses accumulated in agrarian situations; the Scandinavians shifted from piracy to fishing and peaceful trading. The Low Countries became a northern hub of trade movements complementing the north Italian towns, and a strong process of growth and development set in during the late eleventh century all over Europe.

With ample food supplies and near-plentiful agrarian primary raw materials, with local surpluses in agrarian population, and with human ambitions beginning to express the desire for change, the economic revival of Europe affected many other aspects of life. In the growing towns came the lightening of the old agrarian, feudal, socioeconomic restrictions. The new contact with the Moslem world began the provision of intellectual stimulus. A liberalizing rejuvenation of the Christian Church began. Some towns began to grow into cities and to forge new political and socioeconomic institutions. The collections of inquiring individuals began to create the first universities, and in the north the Hanseatic League began to formalize patterns of interregional trade. The social, political, economic, and intellectual life of Europe began its upward spiral of growth which steadily gained momentum. It brought to an end the economic, urban, and cultural "dark ages" that had dominated Europe for centuries. These developments, broad in range and widely distributed through space, prepared the peoples of Europe for even greater humanistic efforts in the centuries to come.

Regionalized Europe and the Rise of Nation-States

From the fall of Roman political power to well into the eleventh century the peoples and leaders of Europe struggled for territorial integrity and the development of political regionalism of a lasting sort. Looking through a historical atlas of Europe one is struck by the steady patterns of change, by the inconstancy of zonal demarcations, by the rise and fall of particular political territorialisms, and by the frequent reflection, on the political map, of religious territorialisms of some type (Fig. 6.3). The modern national histories of Europe devote much space to the "struggle for freedom" of the numerous ethnic stocks, language communities, family systems, and religious communities. But just as it reflects the stubborn will of particular ethnic-cultural communities to ward off political assimilation into particular territorial combines, the historical atlas reflects the ambitions of the seeker after power, the inheritance of feudal right to lands, and the political expression of intermarriage between high-ranking families. The growth of tribal institutions into political states was a slow process after Roman power declined under the barbarian invasions. The Christianizing

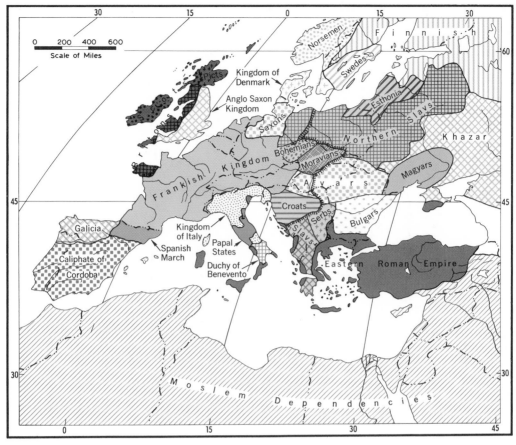

_____ Tributary limit of Frankish Kingdom

FIG. 6.3   THE EARLY EUROPEAN REGIONALISMS.   A. Early Regional Patterns, about A.D. 800.

of the barbarians was involved in these political shifts.

Just as one is impressed by patterns of change, one should be impressed with continuity. The persistence of a division of some sort across the Spanish-French Pyrenees, the recurrence of a northern boundary zone around the northern front of the Alps, the emergence of a line between Norway and Sweden, the perseverance of some boundary not far from the Rhine River, and the zonal similarity of a north-south line extending southward from near the eastern shores of the Baltic are among the elements of continuity in the developing regionalisms of the European world. Whereas the elements of change are humanly derived on landscapes open to such variation, the zones of constancy express some physical environmentalism either very useful to, or insurmountable by, the physical and political technology of human groups.

Just as there grew to be a regional political state of England, there began to emerge a France, a Norway, a Sweden, a Poland, and a Russia (Fig. 6.4). None was the state of any single culture group; in the history of Europe too many things had become too mixed. France of the twelfth century was not a whole France, for Henry II of England inherited title to more than half the territory of modern France, and he married his sons and daughters off in such a way as to extend his royal rights to added lands. Underneath this superficial political map of royal rights, however, the peoples of France were not becoming English, but French. Even though small territorial divisions continued a wide range of institutions, customs, and laws, and the peoples of the region had come out of several ethnic molds, they all shared certain antipathies and came to express certain common preferences through time. That they shared less freely than the English delayed the uniting of

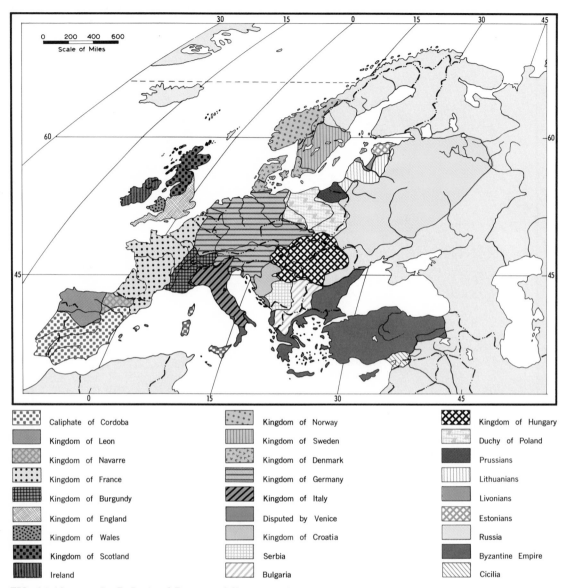

	Caliphate of Cordoba		Kingdom of Norway		Kingdom of Hungary
	Kingdom of Leon		Kingdom of Sweden		Duchy of Poland
	Kingdom of Navarre		Kingdom of Denmark		Prussians
	Kingdom of France		Kingdom of Germany		Lithuanians
	Kingdom of Burgundy		Kingdom of Italy		Livonians
	Kingdom of England		Disputed by Venice		Estonians
	Kingdom of Wales		Kingdom of Croatia		Russia
	Kingdom of Scotland		Serbia		Byzantine Empire
	Ireland		Bulgaria		Cicilia

FIG. 6.3 (*Continued*)   B. Regional Patterns of Change by about A.D. 1000.

France for a century or more behind the emergence of an England, but the seeds were there and sprouting.

Our concern, here, is less for the political map as the expression of the territorial rights of kings than for the broad regional patterns of cultural bonding that were becoming shared by separated masses of villagers and townsmen. Although the Italian peninsula seldom looked like an Italian state between the fall of Rome and the late nineteenth century, and though Sicilians never could agree about much with those living in the Po Valley, both sets of peoples shared ways of living that were to make them Italians. In this, there was, of course, a long period of environmental influence, expressed through such elements as the timing of the rainy season and the crop-growing calendar, but there was also the purely human and cultural tradition of centuries of living in the same broad region with its unending daily minutiae of expounding the ways of life in a particular context.

The Crusades, Travel, the Far Countries, and Exotic Products from Afar

In the middle of the tenth century the Seljuk Turks swept into Southwest Asia in a pattern of conquest that reached and enveloped most of Asia

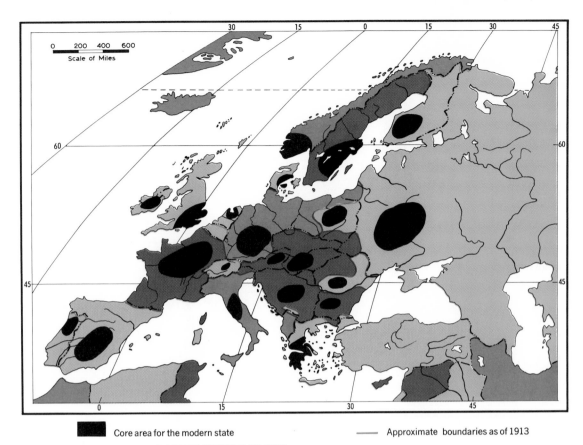

██ Core area for the modern state	—— Approximate boundaries as of 1913

FIG. 6.4 THE RISE OF EUROPEAN NATION-STATES.

Minor. This caused the ruler of the Eastern Roman Empire to appeal to western Europe for help. The appeal came at a time when religious fervor was sweeping Europe and, under Papal exhortation, the First Crusade took shape in A.D. 1096 as a move to repulse the Turks, free the Holy Land from the Moslem infidel, and gain such glory and booty as Christian knighthood could win by force of arms (Fig. 6.5). The time was ripe for change; had not the Turks precipitated it, some other happening would have done so. Although few came back, of the more than fifty thousand men who went on the First Crusade, there did result a Christian foothold in the Levant to which replacement troops continued to move to man the ramparts of the Holy Land. Several other crusades followed before the Moslems took all territory again just prior to 1300, but the significance of the operations lay elsewhere. Many thousands of west Europeans traveled to and returned from a far and unknown country having different ways of living and different products, and western Europe heard about them all. The eyes of Europe

were opening, and the fanciful stories were entrancing, whetting the appetite for more.

Representatives of the Church, and of Mediterranean trading families, had been probing the eastern, outer margins of the eastern realms of Christendom since the tenth century. Before 1300 a number of these succeeded in getting all the way through, or around, Asia to China. The Polos, of Venice, were merchant traders working through Constantinople, who traveled in the East for business and pleasure. In the late thirteenth century a son, Marco Polo, not only went on such a family journey, but also became a civil official in China under the Mongols. By the early fifteenth century all manner of Europeans were active in such travel, from northern Asian overland routes out of Russia to southern partly water routes (via the Red Sea or Persian Gulf) into India, and the news accumulating in Europe only whetted the appetite further.

The era of an agrarian, village-dwelling, quietly rural Europe was coming to an end. The growth of towns, cities, trade, and secondary occupational

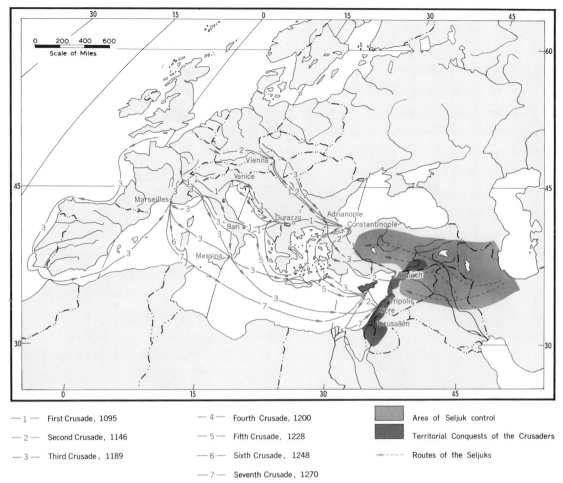

—1—	First Crusade, 1095	—4— Fourth Crusade, 1200
—2—	Second Crusade, 1146	—5— Fifth Crusade, 1228
—3—	Third Crusade, 1189	—6— Sixth Crusade, 1248
		—7— Seventh Crusade, 1270

Area of Seljuk control

Territorial Conquests of the Crusaders

Routes of the Seljuks

FIG. 6.5 REGIONAL MOVEMENT DURING THE CRUSADES.

activity was creating new attitudes in homeland-minded Europeans. Freedom of movement permitted by changing socioeconomic structures, and supported by much more substantial economic resources, began to turn into patterns of mobility on the parts of large numbers of people everywhere in Europe. However, this mobility was quite unlike that of the earlier migrating peoples who were looking for homelands. It was a mobility sparked by curiosity about the far countries outside Europe, and it fed upon the new and strange kinds of products that came from those distant places. There were new kinds of textiles, such as cottons, muslins, and silks; new kinds of food additives, such as the peppers, sugars, and other spices*; old kinds

of incenses and perfumes known to have accompanied early liturgies but now available as actual products; woods of various kinds; jewelstones of many sorts; and many kinds of consumer products in leather, metal, enamel, and porcelain fabricated in fascinating styles and motifs totally unfamiliar to the European world.

Some of these items were not more useful than those already made in Europe, but their shapes, stylings, and motifs were wondrous to behold. Some, like the spices, relieved a monotony of routine diet for those who could afford them. Others, like the cottons, provided utilities not served by the old textiles of Europe. But the

*We cannot, here, detail the consumer demand in Europe behind every wanted product, but the roles of the peppers and cloves are both significant and exemplary. Following calving in the spring, surplus cattle were slaughtered in numbers in the autumn, since European agricultural technology had not yet devised measures adequate to provide sufficient winter fodders for all livestock. And since no adequate technology yet existed to preserve meat during the long winters, peppers and cloves became popular as spices, for they overcame the taste of spoiling meats.

knowledge gained from these included much more. Europeans learned of many new technologies of fabrication and material handling, technologies that never had diffused into Europe during the previous eras but that could be put to use in many productive ways.

Out of the Crusades, the Papal missions, and the free travel to lands outside the home territory the eyes of Europeans were opened, their acquisitive moods enlivened, their imaginations stimulated, and their minds activated. Europeans studying the lore, the knowledge, the technologies, and the products of far countries became dissatisfied with their own ways of living, to the ends that they had to go farther to find out what lay beyond the home territory. The Era of World Exploration was being born.

World Exploration, Ships and Navigation; Stimulus and Results

Getting to China from western Europe by walking and riding a camel was slow; the Mediterranean-Red Sea-Indian Ocean routes were not always open to Europeans; surely there must be some better way! Such was the feeling of many; but the small boats and primitive ships of the early Europeans were unsuited for navigation of the open oceans. During the thirteenth to fifteenth centuries the art of shipbuilding developed conspicuously along the coasts of Europe and harbors evolved into ports. By the middle of the sixteenth century, tough and seaworthy, if uncomfortable and small, ships were coming off the ways. Almost from the start these sound, high-freeboard European sailing ships were built as floating cannon platforms. The knowledge of navigation, of world wind systems, and of the physical geography of the seas was extremely slight, and it was by raw courage, ignorance, and avarice that Europeans set out upon the open oceans to find ways to the far countries (Fig. 6.6).

In the somewhat innocently smug belief in Christendom, sixteenth-century Europeans almost universally looked down upon other peoples as heathen savages or as accomplished and skilled folk misguidedly or wickedly infidel and idolatrous, undeserving of Christian treatment. The militarism of Europe, possessing the tradition of knighthood and the zeal of the Crusades, ranked foremost among the peoples of the world at the time. The acquisitiveness of Europeans had sharp-

ened into an avarice for goods and products unequaled elsewhere. It is little wonder that the Europeans surged around the world in an unprecedented and militant era of linking together the routes and trade realms of the earth. Although there can be little doubt that the oceans had been crossed repeatedly during earlier millennia, these sporadic efforts had never linked the earth in continuous terms. It was the European Columbian Discoveries, and the consequent explorations, that once and for all time brought the whole world within the realm of the trader, the religious missionary, the traveler, the migrant, and the territorial conqueror.

Every returning voyager who could tell a story of visiting strange lands proved again that such travel could be accomplished, and as a result more trips were planned. Every ship bringing back stores of goods from a far country stimulated other merchant traders to try likewise. By the time Sir Francis Drake had looted a Spanish treasure ship (the treasure having been exacted by the Spanish from their conquered domain in the New World), used some of the precious metal to buy spices in the Indies, and returned to England with a cargo that yielded several thousand per cent profit to the financier of the expedition, the patterns of European interregional and international contact had been well established. Armed ships for cargo-hauling came to be built better, bigger, and faster than those built for exploring. Contact was wider. Competition for the spoils was militant. The traders of Europe staked out competitive domains of peoples and their territories in far countries for the enrichment of the homelands and vied for control of the seas with floating gunnery platforms.

If there was not sheer creativeness to this European effort, as there had been in early Mesopotamia or in Greece, the new Europe excelled tremendously at a game previously best played by the Romans. The European version of these events is written by Europeans, with understandable pride in their accomplishments, but an Inca version, or a Javanese version, would be written differently. It was with stubborn and militant response that the British reacted to the Chinese disdain in the late eighteenth century for extensive contact with the "dollar-grinders" of uncouth and uncivilized manner, and it was with a misguided sense of Christendom that the Spanish converted the heathen American Indians while exploiting them. But, for all the rough and militant activity,

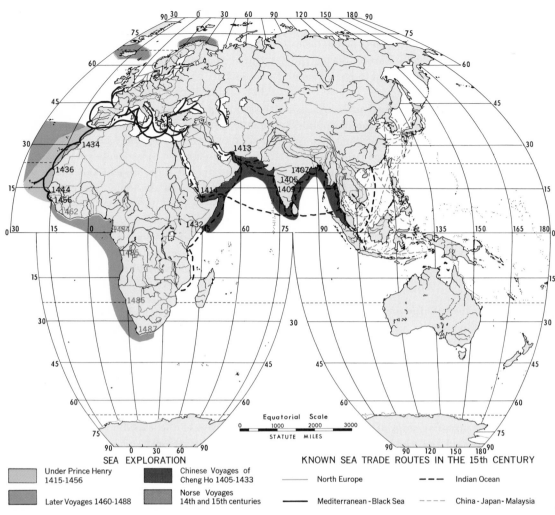

FIG. 6.6   THE COURSE OF SEA EXPLORATION, 1300 TO 1490.

the European accomplishment stood. The world
had been linked into one great trade realm enabling peoples and goods to move from any European homeland to any far country, and for all
goods to start flowing toward Europe from all far
countries. An unprecedented territorial dominance
had been achieved by a major geographical region
on a single and, now, linked-together human
earth.

Trade Commodities, Colonization, Migration, and Early Economic Concepts

Once the Europeans had found their way around
the world (Fig. 6.7), they set out to acquire portions of the goods of the earth. Europe of that
day did not produce many commodities useful to
the civilized parts of the world. Its own manufac-

turing technologies were only slightly developed,
and its products found no ready sale in the markets
of India, China, the Indies, or even the Moslem
realm. Europe's rather simple manufactures did
appeal to the simpler cultures of the world, but
such cultures did not always produce the things
Europeans wanted. The Europeans gradually
worked out procedures of trading that substituted
regional products for other products until suitable
patterns of exchange could work in most places.
It was not long before British and French traders,
for example, regularly began looting Spanish treasure ships to gain the gold and silver with which
to buy pepper in the Indies, to sell to Germans
and Scandinavians in exchange for fish, which
could then be sold to Spaniards for more gold with
which to buy pepper. A little later, after the
colonial settlement of what is now New England

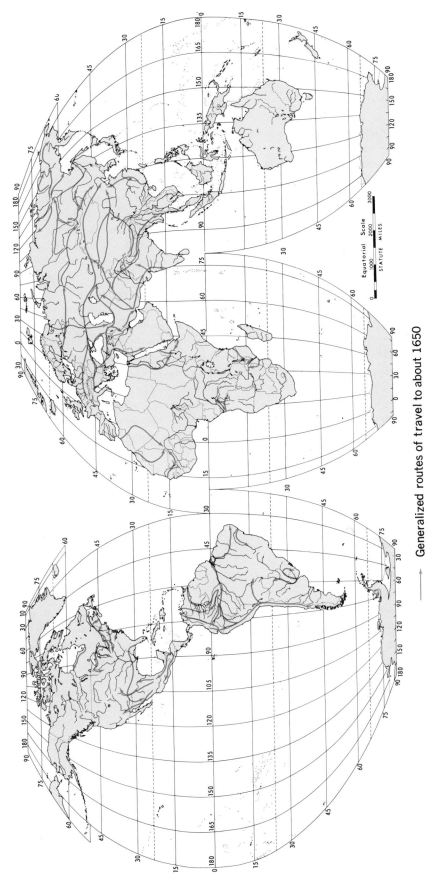

→ Generalized routes of travel to about 1650

FIG. 6.7   THE COURSE OF LAND EXPLORATION, 1100 TO 1650.

Equatorial   Scale
0   1000   2000   3000
STATUTE   MILES

261

had taken place, ginseng and furs could be carried from North America to China in exchange for silks, tea, and porcelainware. Most of the silks and porcelain and a share of the tea were taken home to England and France, and the surplus of tea was pushed off on the American colonists for more ginseng and furs.

This crude interpretation is perhaps not suitable to current economic theorists, but it expresses the interregionalism of early modern trade. European mercantilist economic theory clearly held that a country had to sell more than it bought to prosper and, until the manufactures of Europe became acceptable around the world, a bartering process had to obtain. In response to economic theory some countries of Europe began to renovate their manufacturing activities to suit their trading programs, and the industrial revolution finally yielded the kinds and grades of products acceptable in all far countries.*

The linkage of regions of the earth through transport made possible another new kind of activity. This was the migration of Europeans abroad in the start of a pattern of colonial settlement in any land empty enough to afford sites and weak enough in military power to be unable to repel the colonial effort. Political hegemony over the colonial lands was assumed, without question, by the migrating Europeans. Village-dwelling, agrarian Europe had not been totally lifted out of the era of feudalism, the manorial system, and the tight control by the Church, so that many Europeans sought many kinds of freedoms in such ventures. This was a unilinear kind of movement, however, for neither Chinese, Javanese, nor Mayans sought similar freedoms in Europe or the other far countries of the earth.

The colonial settlement by small groups seeking their freedoms became a pattern that initiated larger-scale movements out of almost every European country. By about 1750 both the trading programs and the colonial migration programs (the word "plantation" first referred to a planting of people) had assumed both significant proportions and those rather distinctive patterns that were to spread ships, merchants, political flags, and colonial settlements of Europeans around the world in the following decades.

*We do not here ascribe the whole origin of the Industrial Revolution to this cause, of course, but there is a relationship.

The Spreading Europeans and Cultural Interaction

With the map of the lands and seas of the earth established by the explorer-cartographers, and the routes worked out by the sailing ships, Europeans began a pattern of migratory exodus from their homelands more varied than any pattern of human migration since the early Paleolithic spread of man over the earth. In the guise of "exploration" Europeans ventured into every land around the earth, and sailed every sea, running their ships into every harbor, bay, gulf, and river mouth. On land they crossed and recrossed every continent and large island with few exceptions, until the map of the earth no longer could leave large blank spots which had to be labeled "unexplored" (Fig. 6.8). What were they looking for? Anything they did not know about. The European curiosity about the earth had mounted steadily until it had become an infatuation with exploration, until the profession of "explorer" had become an honored one. By the opening of the twentieth century only the interiors of the two islands of New Guinea and Borneo, and the vastness of Antarctica, remained relatively unknown to the Europeans, and the passion for exploration began to turn into a program of climbing high mountains "because they are there" as a substitute for the exploration of unknown countries. Parenthetically, we may note that many a young man of European ancestry, in the twentieth century, has bemoaned the fact that there was nothing left to explore.

The wake of the explorers, extending from 1600 to about 1910, carried a veritable flood of adventurers, colonists, settlers, refugees, soldiers of fortune, mining prospectors, fur trappers, timber cutters, Christian missionaries, itinerant traders, commercial travelers, company agents, and inquiring scholars. Each class of migrant was intent upon its own purposes; colonists sought to establish the flag and territorial rights of their motherland; settlers sought land and release from traditional socioeconomic bonds; refugees fled political and religious persecution; missionaries carried the message of Paul the Apostle; commercial travelers sought knowledge of products and markets; European sojourners lived abroad until they acquired sufficient wealth to retire to their homelands; and the scholars sought the knowledge by which to organize the masses of information brought back by all other Europeans about the places, peoples,

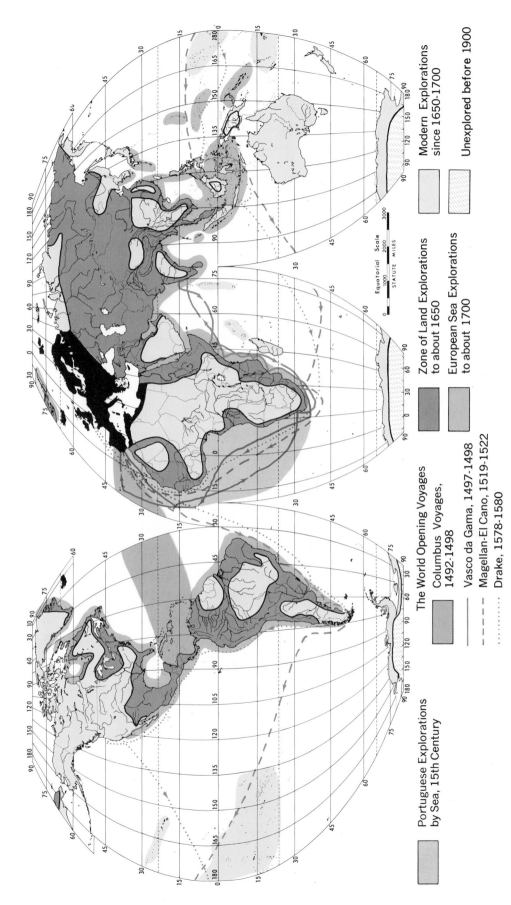

Portuguese Explorations
by Sea, 15th Century

The World Opening Voyages

Columbus Voyages,
1492-1498

Vasco da Gama, 1497-1498

Magellan-El Cano, 1519-1522

Drake, 1578-1580

Zone of Land Explorations
to about 1650

European Sea Explorations
to about 1700

Modern Explorations
since 1650-1700

Unexplored before 1900

Equatorial   Scale
0   1000   2000   3000
STATUTE MILES

FIG. 6.8 WORLD EXPLORATIONS.

and conditions of the earth. We may note, parenthetically again, that in the twentieth century the "tourist industry" is built upon this European concept of "explore the earth" in the personal sense; persons of European descent do more traveling about the earth than do all other ethnic stocks combined.

Although a great many people made round trips to the ends of the earth and back, far more ventured forth not to return, so that the European dispersal over the earth became the most widespread of any (Fig. 6.9). In the nineteenth century the account of almost any country included a listing of Europeans resident in the land. For such a region as the United States, of course, the listing became a statement of primary population (and the original population turned into an appendix item), but in Thailand or Japan the listing included almost every European nationality in a "foreign community" in which Scot lived neighbor to Portuguese and Greek.* It finally became commonplace to say that more Scots were scattered over the world than resided in Scotland, and that there were more Irish in New England and New York than in all of Ireland.

Cultural interaction followed. The European brought with him his own ways of living, taught the inhabitants of his place of residence the basic elements of these ways, built a house in his own style, brought plants and tools from his homeland, dressed in his own style, and insisted in eating by his own cuisine. In New England, this diffusion planted the culture of Great Britain in a mixed pattern, whereas Pennsylvania and Quebec reflected the cultures of Germany and France, and California acquired a Mediterranean-styled culture modified by Mexican experience. However, to China, India, the Indies, Brazil, Chile, Hawaii, and the "South Seas" there was brought an amalgam of many varieties of culture from Europe as "the European way." This was cultural diffusion on a grand scale. Yet it was only one side of the matter, for, since the European objective for going abroad was to acquire the strange goods of the world, the homeward flow of commodities to Europe, and to all areas of significant European settlement,

*Even in the 1930s the senior author and family were members of a "foreign community" of about 200 non-Chinese in a large city of interior China in which American, Canadian, Scot, English, Welsh, Dutch, Belgian, Danish, Swedish, Russian, German, French, Italian, Czech, and Portuguese "nationalities" were represented.

brought a tremendous range of new ways of living and new ways of doing things. When applied to specific patterns in the dual movement of culture traits, diffusion theory can make clear the comparative rates, amounts, and flow lines of many interesting culture complexes among sectors of the earth.

In time, although in lesser numbers than Europeans, peoples of other lands around the earth became part of the human movement system. The so-called Chinatown turned up in London, Paris, San Francisco, New York, and Havana, and such cities as London, New York, and Paris began to acquire colonies of nationals from all over the earth.

The Conquest of Places and Peoples, and Comparative Socioeconomics

Europeans did not go forth upon the earth as humble refugees, seeking asylum and the sufferance of residence in strange lands at the will of their sovereign inhabitants. They went forth in the full confidence of the superiority of their own ways and cultures, holding high their own egotisms, senses of dominant status, concepts of social structures, and ideas about comparative economic values of earthly goods. In the lands of simpler cultures, slightly developed politico-military organizations, and nonaggressive peoples, Europeans quite naturally, and to them logically, claimed hegemony in all terms, on behalf of the home country and God, so that civilization, trade, and Christianity might then be brought to these uncivilized and heathen places. In many of the lands of more highly developed cultures the European came peacefully as a trader, but he was quick to take to managing things when the patterns of events went against the expansion of trade. Calling upon the home government for military and political assistance became routine operations. In relatively empty lands possessing regional environments similar to European homelands, traders found little of value, but colonists-settlers found inviting circumstances. They were followed by increasing flows of Europeans who proceeded to take over the territory. In lands in which the superiority of the European was contested in any way, the resort to forceful measures was quick, and Europeans were involved in skirmishes, fights, military campaigns, and wars in steady succession, from the time of Pizarro and Cortez to the Zulu Wars.

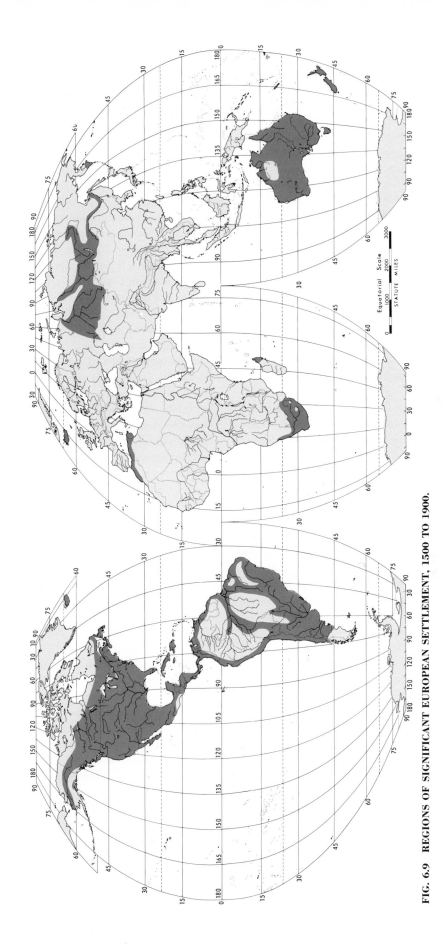

FIG. 6.9 REGIONS OF SIGNIFICANT EUROPEAN SETTLEMENT, 1500 TO 1900.

Equatorial Scale

STATUTE MILES

0   1000   2000   3000

This whole set of developments was merely a variant of the perennial struggle among human groups for territoriality, but a variant on a scale not previously experienced in human history. It resulted, of course, in the establishment of sub-territorialisms, politically labeled colonial empires, by every European country which could carry through the operation. Some of the colonial lands, heavily settled by Europeans, sought their independence of Europe in various ways, but this only resulted in the full-scale extension of the world of Europe to such places; North America, for example, is properly an extension of the European culture realm. Some territories, already well populated at the advent of the European, experienced somewhat different histories; most of the Latin American territories became independent states during the nineteenth century in different stages of "Europeanization," whereas Asian and African territories remained in some specific political position of a colonial nature, with Europeanization relatively variable.

Some economists have insisted that "Eastern economics differs from Western economics," really meaning that economic thought of the European world is basically unlike that of non-European culture realms. Although this conclusion is not properly tenable, it is clear that the early acquisitive habit of the European world introduced a novel element into the traditional, non-European systems of local and interregional exchange. Europeans sought new and different commodities everywhere and began to think in worldwide terms of import and export on a grand scale (compare Fig. 5.5 with Fig. 6.10). However, economies in other parts of the world were not amenable, rather suddenly, to total world trade, and the new European economic activity amounted to a cultural revolution.

Faced with this and other economic developments from about 1300 onward, Europeans began to evolve economic theory. Out of the monopolistic patterns of feudal economics arose such theoretical constructs as those of the Physiocrats and the Mercantilists, the latter dominating the economic contacts of early modern Europe with the whole earth and directed to monopolistic controls by the rising European states. Under the impact of Adam Smith's *Wealth of Nations*, European economic thought continued to change. Nevertheless, European economic thought and its practical applications were both rather different from,

and more highly developed toward, interregional trade than the economic thought and systems of other portions of the world during the centuries down to the present.

Accompanying the settlement of some regions and the conquest of others, Europe first, and the whole European culture realm later, pushed economic utilization of every resource its culture could comprehend, its technology could process, and its transport system could move, everywhere on the earth. From the standpoint of the European this became economic *development*; from the standpoint of the colonial land and the raw-materials-producing region it became economic *exploitation*. As the European Industrial Revolution bore fruit, Europe gradually turned from importing finished handicraft manufactures of fine workmanship and paying however it could be done, to importing only cheaper raw materials and paying with goods of standard quality turned out by its new factory system. These goods, in unending volume, undermined the handicraft manufacturers of the rest of the earth, along with rendering non-European economies unstable, and ended by upsetting the economies and the economics of most non-European portions of the world. Much of this trend was not wickedly intentional but, under the pressures of European-expressed superiorities, the use of military pressure, and the revolutionary productivity of a European economic world, it has become customary around the world to accuse the European culture realm of economic and political exploitation of the worst order.

The Opening Up of the Midlatitude Forests and the Grasslands

The European system of occupance evolved in a midlatitude region of humid climatic conditions. Here forest growth with perennial grasses interspersed throughout old clearings, and perennial water supplies, were everywhere available. Particularly in early modern Europe, with the northward shift of occupance patterns, was this so. Whereas the European Explosion carried Europeans all over the earth, and whereas they tentatively tried settlement procedures in all kinds of environments from the tropics to the polar margins, they succeeded best in those midlatitude forest lands that had previously been lightly occupied by gathering and collecting cultures or by hunters-gatherers who practiced a minimum of crop growing. Around the earth this meant chiefly

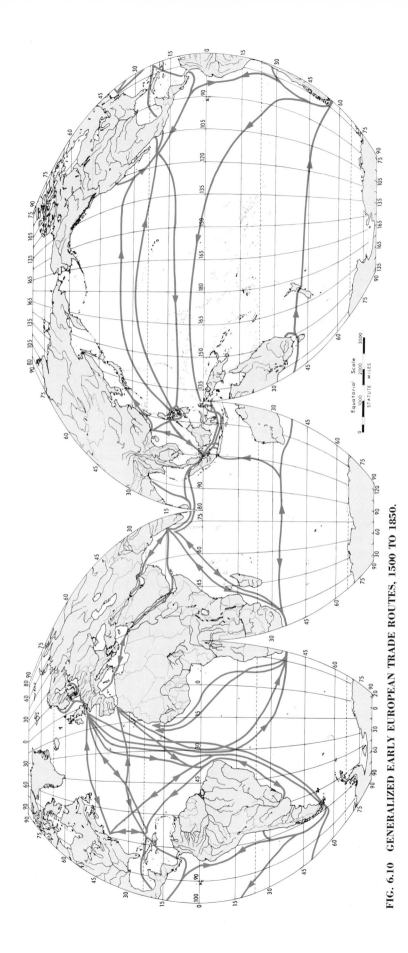

FIG. 6.10 GENERALIZED EARLY EUROPEAN TRADE ROUTES, 1500 TO 1850.

the broad territories of the United States and southern Canada and eastern Russia-Siberia, for only small sectors of the world's midlatitude forest lands lie in the southern hemisphere. Only relatively late in time, during the nineteenth century, did European settlement perfect effective technologies for significant occupance of the warmer subtropics (Fig. 6.11).

Essentially, European colonial settlement occupied lands of small population and slight economic development, using occupance patterns standard to Europe of the time. Relatively self-sufficient economies, in local regional terms, depended on combinations of crop growing and animal husbandry. As pioneer settlement took place, the participants could at first produce only small surpluses, could not man much secondary economic activity, and remained dependent on Europe for manufactured goods. Settlement became extensive, spreading throughout the range of territory occupiable by the technologies in use. This continued to be true for the Russian-Siberian sector until the appearance of Communist political reorganization of Russian life.

In the Anglo-American zone, however, life followed a different sequence. Westward from the seaboard starting point, small farm settlement ran out of forest country as it proceeded, coming up against the drier grass country of the Midwest of the United States and Canada. Here Europeans were at first at a loss for suitable technologies, since their traditional concepts of good agricultural country were attuned to humid, forested landscapes. Gradually in the moister sectors of the Midwest (the prairie country) a grain farming–cattle raising system evolved, initially dependent on driving the grain-fed animals to eastern markets. In the drier sectors, to the west, a livestock economy began to develop on the open grasslands and cattle and sheep began to replace the wild buffalo of the plains. Some sedentary farmers leapfrogged to the West Coast, but those on the Great Plains slowly pushed westward, as technologies advanced, displacing the earliest cattle and sheep ranges and employing extensive land-use procedures, animal-powered mechanization, and the new rail-transport facilities to market both the grain crops and surplus livestock. The integration of grain farming, livestock raising, increasing mechanization, and commercial exploitation of distant markets by rurally dispersed families on farms of a few hundred acres each, developed a new kind of agri-

cultural system and created a new form of cultural landscape in turning the prairies and plainslands into farmlands. The cattle and sheep raisers progressively retreated to the westernmost drier and rougher sectors of the Great Plains in which crop cultivation was hazardous under the existing technologies.

Faced with constant labor shortages in their ever-expanding settlement patterns, the North American Midwest started the European cultural realm, and eventually the whole earth, on another agricultural revolution, that of mechanization and the application of power in large volumes to the primary production of food commodities. Although the specific inventions came from several parts of the European cultural realm, it was the American-Canadian farmer who turned crop growing into an industrial pursuit. This particular revolution has not yet run its course in its own homeland.

The European occupance of the midlatitude forest and grassland country began humbly, but coupled with inventive technological evolution continued occupance added a totally new dimension to settlement of the earth by productive man. The European home region has been variably caught up in this developmental procedure, which, in the twentieth century, has been changing the traditional occupance of the Soviet zone. Elsewhere around the earth, in the forest margins–drier grassland ranges something of the same sort has begun to take place, chiefly in the twentieth century. Australia notably began in the late nineteenth century to develop the mechanized grain-farming system on the dry margins, with cattle and sheep raising in the drier country beyond and the integration of the economic systems taking place. The Argentine pampa shows a similar, but not identical and not strictly contemporary, kind of evolutionary economic development. And, somewhat slowly in our terms of time, adaptations of the mechanization and industrialization of agriculture are diffusing to other ecological and cultural realms around the world.

The Redistribution of Life-Forms

As man learned to travel the whole world over, and initiated the great patterns of resettlement, he simultaneously set in motion a vast series of transplantations of all kinds of life-forms. Man not only took with him his decorative-crop plants and his domestic animals, but also the common weed

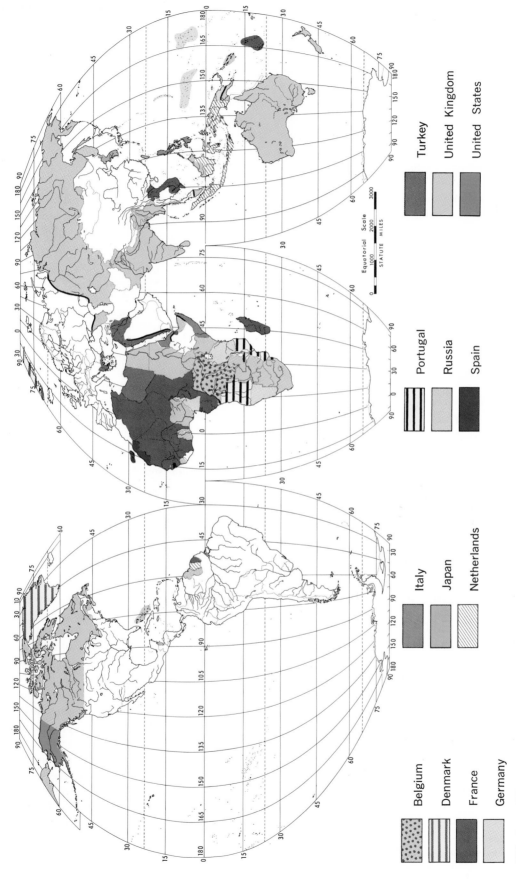

Belgium

Denmark

France

Germany

Italy

Japan

Netherlands

Portugal

Russia

Spain

Turkey

United Kingdom

United States

Equatorial Scale
0   1000   2000   3000
STATUTE MILES

FIG. 6.11   THE SPREAD OF COLONIAL CONTROLS, 1900.

plants and the animal pests. An even more numerous class of life-forms were the microorganisms that travel about with man. Man is a disturber of natural and established ecologic conditions, creating situations in which other life-forms are provided with fresh opportunities. The plants and animals that follow man around the earth do not necessarily prefer the physical conditions of man-created, open, disturbed, ecologic niches, but often they can tolerate and exploit them. Purposeful or accidental introduction of an organism into a new environment through human action is often possible only because the existing habitat has been greatly altered in terms of its previous ecologic balance. This pattern refers not only to the crop plants and the domestic animals, and to the weeds and the animal pests, but also to the microorganisms that provoke disease among all other forms of life. Although these changes had, of course, been an integral part of the systems of ecologic change on the earth ever since life first began, the volume and rapidity of change that started with the Columbian Explorations exceeded in rate and scope the changes of any previous human period.

Disease

The spread of man has served to disperse his own parasites, whether through infectious diseases or diseases transmitted by vectors or alternate hosts. Nearly all the more deadly epidemic diseases were transported from the Old World to the New World following the Columbian Discoveries. There had been no devastating smallpox, measles, malaria, or yellow fever, perhaps no typhus or typhoid, almost no tuberculosis. From the Old World came the greatest transport of disease to new and susceptible peoples, the most striking example of the influence of disease on history. The worldwide distribution of contagious diseases is clearly a consequence of post-Columbian intercontinental contacts (Fig. 6.12).

Yellow fever and malaria were both spread from the Old World to the New. The common vector of yellow fever, the mosquito *Aedes aegypti*, presumably traveled with the slave ships from tropical West Africa across the Atlantic to the Americas. The malarial parasite was not present in the Americas until the arrival of the Spaniards, who brought it from the Mediterranean region. Thus the unhealthiness of the lowland tropics of the New World is a post-Columbian phenomenon.

The unconscious dispersion of man's own viruses

has had a catastrophic effect in contact situations, especially between Europeans and other peoples who lacked either immunity or cultural experience in methods of treatment. The decimation of the New World populations was significantly a result of introduced diseases. Throughout the Pacific Basin and in Australia both Old World and New World diseases took terrible tolls during and immediately after voyages of exploration or the initiation of settlement programs.

Plants

Accidental introductions of plants probably outnumber purposeful introductions by man. Dispersal, especially of seeds, can be effected by a number of means:

1. By adhesion to moving objects such as a person's clothing, mud on cart wheels or boots, dust in cars or trains.
2. By inclusion of seeds among crop seeds or among other plant materials, used for fodder or for packing, and in fecal matter.
3. By inclusion among mineral matter, such as soil, ship ballast, or road metal.
4. By carriage of seed intended for purposes other than planting (as of seeds for food or medical use) that somehow escape, become established, and reproduce.

The plants purposefully dispersed by man are the crop plants (major and minor), the ornamentals, and the landscape modifiers (reforestation, erosion prevention). The major crop plants have been very drastically changed by the domestication process, for the most part being completely dependent on man for dispersal and reproduction. In some cases, then known as cultigens, they no longer have the capacity to produce viable seeds and thus depend on man-controlled propagation. Most cultigens simply cannot compete with wild vegetation. They do not escape from cultivation successfully to form part of the wild vegetation and disappear when man ceases to intervene on their behalf. Among the crop plants and the ornamentals, however, some readily escape to join with the weeds or the native wild vegetation. Plants used for reforestation and erosion protection frequently include species alien to a locality.

The changes in flora and fauna in many parts of the world, which resulted from the spread of Europeans overseas, reflected the replacement of native plants and animals by exotics. Europeans sometimes greatly transformed landscapes, as in

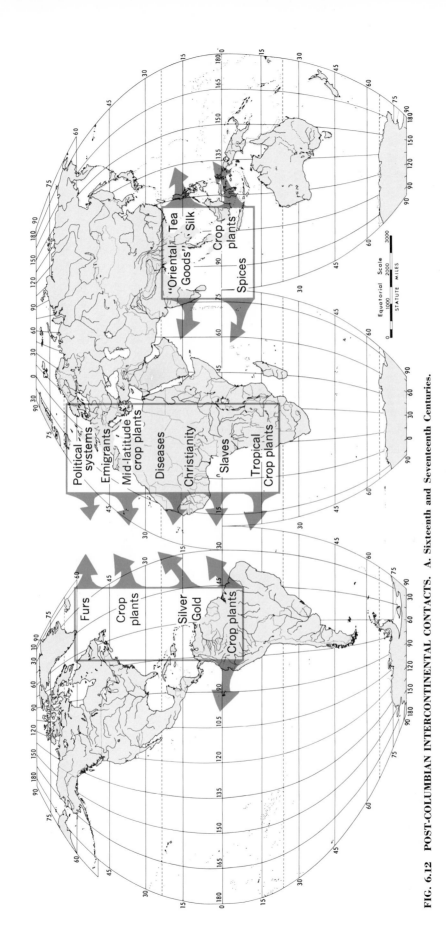

FIG. 6.12 POST-COLUMBIAN INTERCONTINENTAL CONTACTS. A. Sixteenth and Seventeenth Centuries.

271

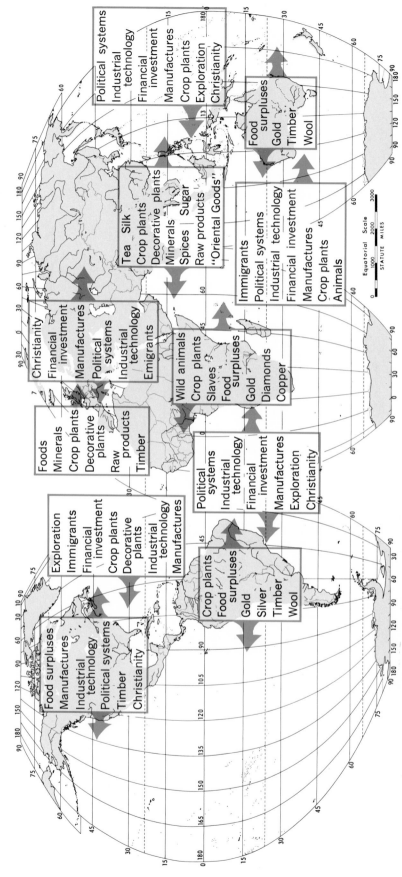

Political systems
Industrial technology
Financial investment
Manufactures
Crop plants
Exploration
Christianity

Food surpluses
Gold
Timber
Wool

Tea Silk
Crop plants
Decorative plants
Minerals
Spices | Sugar
Raw products | "Oriental Goods"

Immigrants
Political systems
Industrial technology
Financial investment
Manufactures
Crop plants
Animals

Christianity
Financial investment
Manufactures
Political systems
Industrial technology
Emigrants

Wild animals
Crop plants
Slaves
Food surpluses
Gold
Diamonds
Copper

Foods
Minerals
Crop plants
Decorative plants
Raw products
Timber

Exploration
Immigrants
Financial investment
Crop plants
Decorative plants
Industrial technology
Manufactures

Political systems
Industrial technology
Financial investment
Manufactures
Exploration
Christianity

Crop plants
Food surpluses
Gold
Silver
Timber
Wool

Food surpluses
Manufactures
Industrial technology
Political systems
Timber
Christianity

Equatorial Scale

STATUTE MILES

0   1000   2000   3000

FIG. 6.12 (Continued)   B. Eighteenth and Nineteenth Centuries.

272

parts of New Zealand, Australia, South Africa, and North and South America, by creating human habitats remarkably identical, in ornamentals, domestic animals, weeds, even wild birds, with the landscapes of their European homelands. Since the end of the fifteenth century man has been the greatest single force for extending the ranges of plants.

Animals

With man's habitations have gone the animals who live there with him: the household mice and rats, the roaches, silverfish, and ants, fleas, lice, and bedbugs, and two mosquito forms—*Aedes aegypti* and *Culex fatigans-pipiens*—that, outside of their native Old World habitats, breed only in man-made accumulations of water. As the predominant terrestrial vertebrate, man has domesticated and spread only a very few of the millions of species of the dominant terrestrial invertebrates, the insects. Wild insects, however, are constantly being moved about by modern man, with his automobiles, trains, ships, and airplanes. The airplane, with its speed, is the most potent of man's new agencies for insect dispersal. Fortunately, the establishment of an insect in a new region is not always easy, and only a small fraction survive. Nevertheless, nearly half of the major insect pests of any particular region will be found to be species accidentally introduced by man.

Man's major role as an agent of dispersal of invertebrates has been primarily with the thousands of species that he has incidentally transported with his travels and shipping, such as the appearance of the American oyster drill across the Atlantic into oyster beds in England. Man also has been involved in the dispersal of such other invertebrates as ticks, mites, household spiders, earthworms, and other soil inhabitants. There have been several deliberate introductions of crustaceans for food purposes, such as Chinese crabs and American crayfish into Europe. Mollusks have been moved about a great deal, mostly accidentally, but occasionally introduced into new regions as human food. The most notorious case of the latter type was the dispersal of the African snail, *Achatina*, to many tropical Pacific islands by the Japanese.

In the spread of the vertebrate animals man's role almost always has been deliberate and purposeful; the only vertebrates accidentally dispersed are probably rats and mice, lizards and burrowing snakes, and fish—the latter as a consequence of man's canal-digging between previously unconnected watersheds. The deliberate introductions of vertebrates have been for one of four reasons: as domestic animals, for sport, food, or fur, to control a pest, or for sentimental reasons. Although the domestic animals, in general, have become directly dependent on man for survival, there are striking examples of domesticates escaping to go wild. Such animals include dogs, cats, swine, goats, horses, camels, and cattle. The grazing domesticates have been a very powerful instrument for landscape change in many parts of the world, the goat being an outstanding example in its worldwide transfer from the Mediterranean.

Transfers of wild animals for sport are usually attempts to recreate the familiar sport of the remembered homeland and represent human reluctance to change established sporting habits to include a new fauna. Successful introduction of exotic animals may bring unprecedented, unfortunate consequences, if in the absence of natural enemies the new animals increase overly rapidly and become nuisances or destructive agents. One is reminded of the cases of carp or starlings in the United States, deer in New Zealand, or rabbits in Australia.

Europeans at the Ends of the Earth: Globalism Becomes Fixed

During the nineteenth century European influence became so solidified around the earth that it apparently fixed the habits of globalism for foreseeable historical time (Fig. 6.13). Exploration became almost terminal in searching out the remaining, possibly productive parts of the earth. Settlement rounded out occupance of such sectors as it could find useful. Political control almost reached its final expansion, trade procedures solidified in all parts of the earth, industry turned out products superior to those elsewhere which were in good demand everywhere, and the European technological revolution was running at an increasing pace. Facilitating the diffusion of the new technologies, societies outside the European culture realm reacted progressively to the systems of European culture. Japan started on a program of transforming its Chinese-style agrarian society into a Western-style industrial society including colonial territory and extensive foreign trade, the economies of numerous countries shifted their orientation to the provision of many commodities useful only in foreign trade, and European industrial tech-

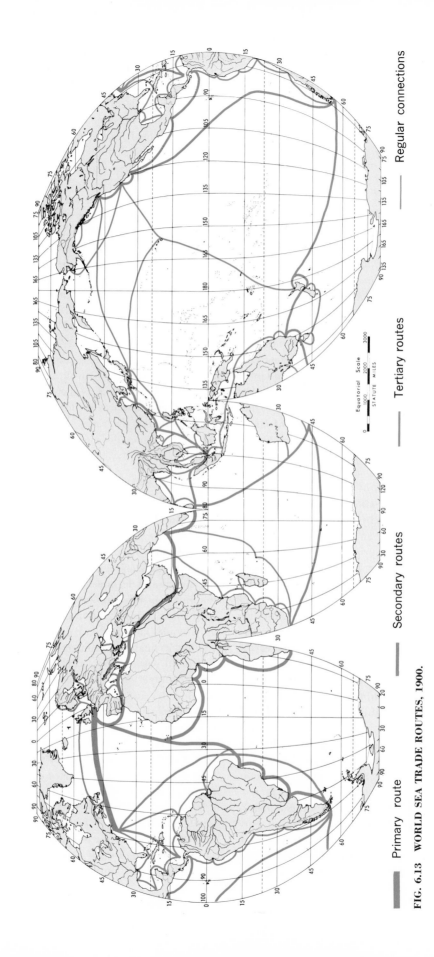

Primary route ——— Secondary routes ——— Tertiary routes ——— Regular connections

FIG. 6.13 WORLD SEA TRADE ROUTES, 1900.

274

nologies invaded many cities around the world.

Prior to the establishment of worldwide linkages, the collapse of life in a culture hearth meant decline for a very large region. In the nineteenth century the decline of China meant the lessening of satisfactory ways of living for Chinese, but it meant less in comparative terms for the progress of life over the earth, since other regions could replace China as a producer, as a market, and as a contributor to ways of living everywhere. By 1900, European culture systems were so widely spread around the earth, with so many regions contributing to production, trade, cultural expansion, and general productive growth, that never again could the earth relapse into separate regionalisms of a lesser sort. Evolutionary changes had begun to take place in almost every culture which were only to grow in rate of change, depth of penetration, and acceptance by peoples. So many local culture traits and complexes had been diffused around the earth, and so interrelated in evolutionary change, that particular foods, particular clothing, specific tools, and operating procedures were now worldwide in distribution. It could be said that, in some respects, the peoples of the world were beginning to converge in their ways of living. The humanized earth had become one world.

SELECTED REFERENCES

Armytage, W. H. G.
    1961   *A Social History of Engineering.* London: Faber & Faber. 378 pp.
Baker, J. N. L.
    1931   *A History of Geographical Discovery and Exploration.* London: G. G. Harrap. 543 pp.
East, W. G.
    1962   *Historical Geography of Europe* (4th ed.). London: Methuen & Co. 492 pp.
Eco, U., and G. B. Zorzoli
    1963   *The Picture History of Inventions from Plough to Polaris.* New York: Macmillan. 360 pp.
Forbes, W. J.
    1950   *Man the Maker, A History of Technology and Engineering.* London: Constable & Company. 355 pp.
Friis, Herman R. (ed.)
    1967   *The Pacific Basin, A History of its Geographical Exploration.* New York: American Geographical Society. 457 pp.
Glacken, Clarence J.
    1967   *Traces on the Rhodian Shore: Nature and Culture in Western Thought from Ancient Times to the End of the Eighteenth Century.* Berkeley and Los Angeles: University of California Press. 763 pp.
Gutkind, E. A.
    1964   *International History of City Development,* Volume I, *Urban Development in Central Europe.* New York: The Free Press of Glencoe. 491 pp.
Hale, John R.
    1966   *Age of Exploration.* New York: Time, Inc. 192 pp.
Lach, D. F.
    1965   *Asia in the Making of Europe,* Vol. 1, *The Century of Discovery.* Chicago: University of Chicago Press. 1040 pp.
Lach, D. F., and C. Floumenhaft (eds.)
    1965   *Asia on the Eve of Europe's Expansion.* New York: Prentice Hall. 211 pp.
Lewis, A. R.
    1958   *The Northern Seas: Shipping and Commerce in Northern Europe,* A.D. *300–1100.* Princeton, N. J.: Princeton University Press. 498 pp.
Mason, S. F.
    1962   *A History of the Sciences.* New York: Collier Books. 638 pp.
McConnell, J.W.
    1947   *Basic Teachings of the Great Economists.* New York: Barnes and Noble. 347 pp.

McNeill, W. H.
  1963   *The Rise of the West*. Chicago: University of Chicago Press. 829 pp.
Myres, J. L.
  1943   *Mediterranean Culture*. Cambridge, England: The University Press. 51 pp.
Ogilvie, A. G.
  1957   *Europe and Its Borderlands*. Edinburgh: Thomas Nelson & Sons. 340 pp.
Parker, John (ed.)
  1965   *Merchants and Scholars* (Essays in the History of Exploration and Trade). Minneapolis: The University of Minnesota Press. 258 pp.
Parry, J. H.
  1961   *The Establishment of the European Hegemony: 1415–1715, Trade and Exploration in the Age of the Renaissance*. New York: Harper and Row. 202 pp.
Penrose, B.
  1952   *Travel and Discovery in the Renaissance, 1420–1620*. Cambridge, Mass.: Harvard University Press (reprinted as an Atheneum paperback, 1962). 463 pp.
Starr, C. G., *et al.*
  1960   *A History of the World*, Vol. 1. Chicago: Rand McNally. 630 pp.
Taton, R.
  1963   *Ancient and Medieval Science from the Beginnings to 1450*. New York: Basic Books. 551 pp.
Thomas, W. L., Jr. (ed.)
  1956   *Man's Role in Changing the Face of the Earth*. Chicago: University of Chicago Press. 1193 pp.
White, L.
  1962   *Medieval Technology and Social Change*. Oxford: Clarendon Press. 194 pp.
Whittlesey, D. S.
  1949   *Environmental Foundations of European History*. New York: Appleton-Century-Crofts. 160 pp.
Wren, M. C.
  1958   *The Course of Russian History*. New York: Macmillan. 725 pp.

CHAPTER 7

The Convergence of Humanity: Cultural Variations Decrease as the Entire Earth Becomes Man's Resource Base

The explosive spread of Europeans over the whole of the known world in the four centuries after about A.D. 1500 was an historical shock to the rest of mankind. As an event it was both unforeseen and without precedent; the rest of the world was not in any way prepared to react to, to accommodate to, or to resist such a phenomenon. Along with the Europeans came a complex of goods, processes, and ideas that set in motion a series of irreversible social and cultural changes: colonization, Christianization, commercialization, industrialization, and new aspects of urbanization, as well as wholly new concepts in public health and preventive medicine, public education and the emancipation of slaves and women, and new political systems such as democracy, socialism, and communism. European expansion, with all of its ramifications, exploded across a world that, for all the previous 11,000 years since the close of the Pleistocene, had known only the civilizing force of men out of Asia.

In the second part of the nineteenth century, the cultural development of Western mankind was pointed to by Europeans with great confidence, as exemplifying the law of human progress. Evolution, as a process, was both physical (biological) and cultural (technological and moral). The conditions of the past had evolved into the present and would improve into the future. The idea of the inevitability of human progress was an article of faith during the European age known as "The Enlightenment."

We know much more now than we did then.

The global wars and revolutions of the twentieth century have destroyed the myth of continuous progress. Vastly increased archaeological knowledge of previous societies and civilizations reveals that specific cultures have experienced both progression and retrogression and that some cultures were expanding at the same time that others were collapsing. The cultural evolution of mankind since the Upper Paleolithic has never been unilinear, but multilinear—the abstract totality is the result of a series of simultaneous positive and negative increments, fluctuating like a changing bank balance. Progress in some cultures in some times and places was offset elsewhere by stagnation, retrogression, or extinction of other cultures. But never before was man able to compare the cultures of the whole earth, to use consciously the advances of one positive zone for the purposeful advancement of a negative and lagging sector.

In this chapter we examine the proposition that a multifluctuating system of variant, isolated cultures is no longer possible. Rather, as a result of Europe's demonstration that the entire earth has become man's resource base and one intercommunicating system, a trend toward cultural convergence has set in. Men in every continent are engaged at present in establishing, maintaining, and expanding a vast urban-industrial society of extraordinary complexity. It is easy to demonstrate that the many traditional cultures, those enormously varied patterns for human living which previously evolved in partial isolation from one another, are disintegrating under the impact of the modern urban-based industrial society. The clear trend is that those who live in a large city or its suburbs anywhere, whether Cadiz, Cairo, Calcutta, Canton, Caracas, Chicago, or Christchurch, despite certain functional and social differences, are coming to have more in common in their ways of life than they have in difference. The faith and hope of those striving to achieve in the modern urban-industrial society is that they, too, can share in demonstrated benefits of increased longevity and improved material well-being.

Man as a Single Interbreeding Unit

In the past several centuries, more people have moved, or have been moved, across longer distances than ever in human history. One of the predictable results of contacts among human groups is that, given the opportunity, interbreeding will take place. Human breeding populations have always been open systems, but they have been rendered far more open over the past few centuries than heretofore. The modern "melting pot" countries such as the United States, Canada, and Brazil clearly attest to this point. A trend toward biological convergence has been established in the modern world, furthered by the vast increase of travel for business, education, recreation, and military operations.

The spread of prehistoric man over the earth created numerous opportunities for small groups to exist in partial-to-full isolation from one another. The formation of human varieties was a gradual process of divergence among breeding populations, each occupying different territories. Much of human history reflects the adaptation of small units of population to the circumstances of local regions: the climate, vegetation, soils, disease, transportation routes, cultural contacts and conflicts with neighboring groups. Biological divergence was inevitable, owing to sexual selection, genetic drift, and differential cultural adaptation as a result of the limitations imposed by reproductive isolation during the past. The larger societies that emerged in historic time consisted of somewhat expanded regional associations of overlapping and crisscrossing mating groups, whose members were likelier to intermarry among themselves than with members of other populations. Man came to recognize the results of biologic variation; the idea of "race" was a social invention of the seventeenth and eighteenth centuries.

The races that "count" are all those that are socially recognized. The biological significance of visible differences in skin color, stature, or hair form is meaningless, unless made meaningful in cultural terms. For example, definitions of "beauty" may enhance the chances of perpetuating the preferred forms over others by increasing their probabilities in sexual choices. Highly visible differences in physical appearances among men and women have been used in various cultures as signals for prompting culturally conditioned responses in behavior toward strangers (those recognized or believed to be members of other cultural systems). Beliefs in racial differences become social myths and serve as culturally learned excuses for perpetuating or elaborating social, nationalistic, religious, or economic differences. Racism, based on myths of racial superiority, is self-defeating: it alienates particular groups of people from all other peoples; it denies opportunities for personal fulfillment; it is economically wasteful of possibilities for human achievement; it perpetuates ignorance and fosters fear and hate. As a cover for motives grounded in self-interest, racism denies the reality of universal values of the dignity of an individual and is a culturally imposed barrier toward establishment of any system of equality, respect, and cooperation among mankind. The reality is that no one racial group is in the ascendancy; each is outnumbered by all the others. In the world as a whole we are all minorities.

The trend in recent human evolution has been an increasing amalgamation. Civilization enables race convergence caused by genetic exchange to outrun race divergence. The earlier pattern of a world divided into relatively small, isolated populations, each undergoing separate biological and cultural evolution, is rapidly breaking down. Boundaries among most breeding populations are not so much blurred as in flux, shifting in both time and space.

In modern times we have seen whole tribes and peoples disappear after their lands had been invaded by Europeans and other culturally dominant strangers. The native Tasmanians are gone, and so are the Indians of Baja California, the ten tribes of the Great Andaman Islands, and the Yamana of Tierra del Fuego. The Ridan Kubu of Sumatra were decimated by two epidemics of smallpox in 1905 and 1908. Many others are on their way out. These sad cases of ethnic oblivion give us a feeling that human history is a long record of utter extinctions, but this is not true. Just as Neanderthal man was not so much exterminated by *Homo sapiens sapiens* as absorbed by him, so the Tasmanians were absorbed by the Europeans who replaced them on their islands. A mixed Tasmanian-European population survives today, although the last individual Tasmanian culture bearer died in 1876. Eventual elimination of a distinctive localized population most commonly implies only the gradual absorption of a small population's gene pool into that of a larger one. The merging of gene pools from varying populations is producing larger populations different from earlier more localized ones by showing more individual variations. This is the process now occurring in many complicated ways at varying speeds all over the world. Given sufficient time, many locally identifiable populations will disappear as such, yet each affected locality will have a population with greater variability among its members than now exists.

Biological mixing among humans is regarded as advantageous as it is among domesticated plants and animals. The resultant offspring exhibit "hybrid vigor" and, given appropriate cultural circumstances, tend to exceed their parental groups in vitality, stature, and fertility. Human evolution becomes more and more irreversible as the different forms that it takes become increasingly dependent on the conscious actions of men in creating new biological possibilities. The most important thing about the biological convergence of the modern era is that it serves to maintain the unspecialized character of man. If the genetic systems called *races* had ever been isolated long enough to become closed, man would have become biologically divergent into different species. The modern convergence of humanity, by keeping open the channels for gene exchange among all human races, has been a great force for human unity.

The Blending of Cultures

The simplicities of the ways of life of our ancestors of thousands of years ago are mostly gone; we are facing instead the complexities of a quite different age. The remaining thousands of preliterate, noncultivating peoples are relics of the past, surviving by sufferance, almost by accident, in refuge areas not yet preempted by civilization.

Between the years 1958 and 1967, an International Committee on Urgent Anthropological and Ethnological Research set down in its *Bulletin* brief notes about racial groups, tribes, cultures, or languages on which research was particularly urgent

in order to save for science data that otherwise might be irretrievably lost. The obvious assumption was that numerous tribes, cultures, and languages, never before investigated, were fast disappearing and that data about them would soon be forever beyond the power of recording for subsequent analysis and critical study. The reason why this condition existed was equally obvious: very few cultures still exist that have not been more or less altered by the influence of modern technological civilization.

Various reasons were presented for considering certain situations as urgent:

> The tribe is small in numbers and may soon die out.
> The tribe will soon be absorbed by its neighbors (through intermarriage and hybridization) and lose its identity.
> The tribe's culture is in process of change (e.g., giving up its language) and will soon lose its separate identity.

The Committee, as part of its endeavors, attempted to list all existing tribes of food gatherers and collectors (hunters-fishers); that is, a roster of all contemporary noncultivators (Fig. 7.1). The list, though incomplete (e.g., in New Guinea and the Arctic) reveals the existence of many widely scattered remnants or relict cultures. Despite their apparent simplicity, these cultures differ from one another as a result of long and varying cultural developments, of adjustments to the environment, and of contacts with other peoples. Present-day gathering and collecting (hunting) groups do not necessarily live as did early man. They are, of course, the closest contemporary analogy, but they are not living fossils of the Paleolithic. For example, there are not many groups left today where stone is still being used for toolmaking. One must be very careful of the conclusions about prehistoric life drawn from the study of living gatherers and collectors, because the latter have also been changing over the long span of time. After all, they are our contemporaries, with a longevity equal to our own.

There were perhaps 500 relatively separate social and political units, or "tribes," in Aboriginal Australia prior to European occupation of the continent. Some have disappeared; some that were few in membership are now but remnants. Those that are left range between two extremes—the traditionally oriented or the predominantly Australian-European. No Aboriginal group remains

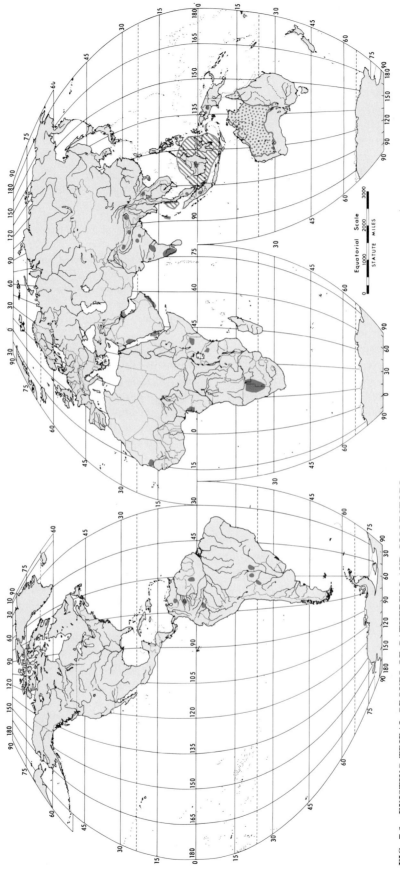

FIG. 7.1 EXISTING TRIBAL GROUPS OF GATHERERS AND COLLECTORS.

uninfluenced by the urban-industrial society of modern Australia. The Northern Territory, in the Kimberleys, and the central desert are virtually the only areas in Australia where some traditional life is still continuing. In another generation or two, most of it will be gone, its disappearance accelerated by the impact of white settlement, mining exploitation, pastoral expansion, the effects of governmental policies of assimilation, and the general downgrading of what has come to be called the "old way." All Aborigines are moving in the direction of closer identification with the dominant society, and typically aboriginal traits are receding. The experience of alien impact has not been uniform among the societies; in some urban, suburban, and country areas, part-Aborigines have lost their aboriginal identity and become completely absorbed. The direction of cultural change is clear; the only variety in the occurring changes is in the differing rates.

More important than the extinction of cultures has been the process of acculturation. Whereas significant evolutionary changes in human biology require time intervals of a much greater length than the span of a human life, cultural changes can be effected ever so much faster. Through learning, men can acquire the characteristics of several or many cultures in their single lifetime. The economic opportunities that the Europeans opened up for the modern world provided plentiful opportunities for cultural contact, on plantations, in mines, in farm settlements, and in commerce and industry. The commercial frontier, especially, brought together people whose tribal and kinship identifications had been largely destroyed and provided opportunities for new cultural amalgams. Conditions of potential economic equality were fostered between participating groups, as the marketplace, and the town life around it, were relatively freer of moral and political restraint. Urban commercial centers have been focal points for worldwide cultural change in that they afford greater ranges of socioeconomic opportunities and greater freedom for individuals to achieve social mobility.

Whereas the European-established plantations and the mines began as economic systems using slave and other forms of compulsory labor, they evolved patterns of contract and free labor based upon a caste, class, or racial social structure. Modern industrial societies are developing both biracialism and cultural pluralism to accommodate peoples of different racial and cultural origins. But both systems have tended to break down under the increasing mobilities of populations. Where peoples of different cultural origins enjoy complete social mobility, blending has occurred into a common national heritage, as in Brazil where a new culture, is evident in the fusion from Europe, America, and Africa.

The cultural impact of the European was the strong impetus for increasing the rate of cultural change around the world. Modifications of existing cultures took place everywhere, with a clear trend toward incorporation of European traits, often referred to as the "modernization process." The traditional cultural patterns were uprooted to greater or lesser degree depending in part upon the population ratios of Europeans to non-Europeans, whether Europeans were settlers or sojourners, and the receptivity of the non-Europeans to the new ways. Selectivity is the keynote in the acculturation processes; some European ways are deemed acceptable, others modified, yet others rejected. For example, modern China has ejected Christian missionaries, yet adopted Marxian ideology, political nationalism, and nuclear weapons, all Western creations, in order to become a world power.

On a worldwide basis, cultural blending is taking place. The emergent cosmopolitan culture is neither European nor American, neither Asian nor African, but a fusion of elements in varying proportions. Most cultural studies have been analytical, sorting out the component parts of the new cultures as to their derivations; more important is the conception that the phenomenon of acculturation has been global and that new values and ideas and personalities are emergent. Hawaii and Japan are avid proponents of the new vision of an open, cooperative world, whereas Alabama and South Africa temporarily have adopted antiacculturation policies and, through restrictive legislation and police power, seek to stem the tide.

The Spread of Technological Civilization

Technological civilization emerged upon the world from the eighteenth-century industrialization of Northwest Europe. Both were based originally upon a factory system that was coordinated by clocks and powered by the burning of coal in steam engines. This system manufactured products with interchangeable parts and employed labor that flocked to the factory towns and adopted urbanization as a way of life.

The American system, interpreting that of Northwest Europe, dwelt on breaking the components of manufacture into a sequence of standardized tasks that an unskilled laborer could easily be trained to do. Imagination and talent were invested in invention of improved machinery and managing the organized tasks and men. Wage labor was supplied by European immigrants, most of whom had been peasant-based and tradition-oriented; as new Americans their families rather abruptly became urbanized, factory-organized, market-oriented, and literate as a result of public schooling. The process spread slowly, taking firm hold only after 1865 and gaining momentum by 1880. But the result was that, during the late nineteenth century, the United States was completely transformed from a regional, agrarian-based society into an urban technological civilization.

After 1870, the new civilization spread, in some form, to other lands so that, today, all lands and peoples have felt the impact of technological civilization. Invention of machinery and the harnessing of inanimate energy are only parts of the story; also involved have been changes in human thought and habit: in concept of efficiency, in social organization, and in personal self-confidence that made possible greater productivity.

We here take issue with the commonly expressed belief that traditional cultures must disappear or remain relics of the past in order that a technological civilization can begin to develop. The most successful growths of industrialization and urbanization have occurred in precisely those areas where industrialization long coexisted effectively with traditional culture, and the blending of cultures has been harmonious rather than disruptive. Japan is the outstanding example, proving that acceptance of the new technological civilization has no one-to-one correlation with either Caucasian racial stocks or European cultural values. Japan is the most fully industrialized country in Asia: today the world's largest producer of cameras, rayon, ships, and transistor radios, and the greatest exporter of cement, ceramics, textiles, and toys. That such leadership was achieved within 25 years after total defeat in World War II amply proves the thesis. For all this modernization, however, the Japanese have not surrendered their own cultural mores, as any Japan Airlines advertisement will indicate, and the Japanese are synthesizing

world culture while blending it into their own culture system. To societies of traditional culture, but without some development of material technological traditions, the transition to modern technological civilization requires a little more time and a greater amount of experimental practice. The international nature of contemporary corporate industrialization provides a wide variety of learning mechanisms to such societies as choose to take advantage of it.

Intercommunication and Cultural Interchange

The spread of technological civilization has been enhanced by its own products, the new facilities for transport and communication that increased speed and quantity with greater reliability at lower costs. These improvements have made possible greater worldwide intercommunication and trade, and have established a permanent network for cultural interchange. The world's peoples have been tied into a single interlocking communications system of shipping routes, postal services, telegraph cables, telephone lines, railroad lines, newspaper and magazine publications, airline routes, radio and television networks, and communication satellites.

No longer are government offices (foreign offices, defense departments, intelligence sources) the principal agencies concerned with world events. Current knowledge of world affairs is vital to international news services, banks and industrial corporations with wide-flung branches and affiliates, entrepreneurs in sports and the arts, scientists and scholars, foreign students and travelers of all nations. The flow of knowledge is stupendous, whether measured in the bulk of international mail, the numbers of simultaneous channels used in cable transmissions, or in the numbers of overseas publications received in a sizable and active library. Consider two examples only,—the magazine *Science*, the weekly journal of the American Association for the Advancement of Science, and the *Geographical Review*, published quarterly by the American Geographical Society. *Science* had a circulation, in June 1965, that included 9804 paid subscriptions to 130 countries and territories outside the United States; eleven countries received more than 200 copies, another ten more than 100. The *Geographical Review*, as of June 1964, was being sent to 105 countries, including seven countries (Cameroon, Canary Islands, Congo, Macao,

Paraguay, Uganda, and Upper Volta) not reached by *Science*. That current interest in scientific development is indeed worldwide is best demonstrated by the single copies of *Science* being sent to such places as Aden, Cambodia, Gambia, Malawi, Monaco, Nepal, Tanzania, and Western Samoa. More than a million articles appear each year in the 50,000 periodicals in the world devoted solely to the natural sciences. Scientific knowledge flows more freely from nation to nation than any other commodity.

Cyclic growth and decay in cultures, as in the lives of individuals, had a kind of accidental appropriateness in the past when empires, differentially involved in the governing of less organized groups, were highly dependent on resources and a technology they alone commanded. In previous ages of slow transport, natural disasters were suffered locally, recurring famines were impossible to relieve, and wars could be won or lost before becoming known to others. In the modern intercommunicating world, however, the analogy of growth and decay of individualistic cultures ceases to be relevant or productive. (Admittedly, the peoples of the earth have not yet learned the comprehensive use of all of our modern systems to the end that mankind does not yet collectively act to prevent extensive suffering in a particular region of the world during a specific time period. There remain political, social, and economic inhibitions which, so far, prevent full-scale and worldwide application of technologies reducing human need and suffering. This suggests that there is a widespread cultural lag in the applications of technological systems and that material technologies have developed more rapidly and extensively than have political, social, and economic systems.) In the practical sense, however, each society is now clearly part of a worldwide network, a single intercommunicating system, that could be self-renewing and self-perpetuating, even though we may feel less than confident that it is reliably self-preservative.

Two brief examples illustrate that the cooperative, coordinated nature of communication in our modern world has created wholly new circumstances.

The International Telecommunication Union (ITU) has existed since 1865. It began in Europe to make possible the sending of telegraph messages across national boundaries (for many years telegrams had to be handed across political frontiers).

As new technologies in communication were developed, in telephone calls, cables, radio broadcasts, television, communication satellites, and messages through outer space, the responsibility for their international coordination also became tasks for the ITU. Among the now 124 member states of ITU, there are international agreements, for example, on the routing and transmission of telegrams, the leasing of telephone circuits, the assignment of broadcasting frequencies, and standards for radio messages of distress, urgency, and safety. Plans have been made that allocate telephone numbers to individual countries, thus taking a long stride forward to the day when telephone subscribers throughout the world will be able to dial one another directly.

International cooperation in postal matters also had its origin in the 1860s. The Universal Postal Union (UPU) was established in 1874, and now its work is all but taken for granted since the world has become a single postal territory for the reciprocal exchange of correspondence. One postal law governs the exchange of mail among the UPU's more than 120 member countries. The "routine" postal arrangements have established some important matters of principle: freedom of transit by the best means available is guaranteed for mail exchange between countries; each country retains the charges collected on "letter mail," thus enormously simplifying accounting operations; parcels, money orders, and cash-on-delivery items are handled separately. Recently, all member countries of the UPU were asked to standardize the sizes of letter envelopes to facilitate automated procedures for stuffing, sealing, stamping, and sorting.

No cultural group that has access to the totality of knowledge of all other human groups, across the chasms of space and past human time, can ever again be truly isolated. Much of the demand for increasing the speed of cultural change has come from the underdeveloped parts of the world, where people have come to know that they need to know more, and, through various programs of scientific exchange and technical assistance, they have discovered the ways to ask.

The Example of Public Health: Organized Combat Against Disease

One of the most praised, and praiseworthy, agencies of the United Nations is the World Health Organization (WHO). It is a towering symbol of the modern trend toward the convergence of humanity, epitomizing the unity of thought by men of all political persuasions on mankind's need for a common defense against infectious disease. As world population has grown and as people in their daily living and working have been herded closer and closer together, the opportunities have increased for the transmission and outbreaks of contagions. Greater vigilance on a worldwide scale is vital today for continued human survival in our present complex world.

What is now realized is that war, conquest, and other upsets of the equilibrium of civilization set the stage for more powerful agents of human tragedy. Machine guns and high explosives are far less deadly than the typhus louse, the plague flea, the yellow-fever mosquito, the plasmodia of malaria, the cholera spirilla, and dysentery and typhoid bacilli.

The need for international cooperation in health matters is now obvious; disease knows no frontiers. International cooperation in health had its origin when the first International Sanitary Conferences met in Paris in 1851, to encourage international efforts in limiting the spread of cholera, plague, and yellow fever, and to speed international trade and travel. In 1902, a regional body, the Pan American Sanitary Bureau, was established in Washington, D.C., and, in 1907, an international office of public health was created in Paris to report on the spread of quarantinable diseases, on methods for combatting them, and to harmonize quarantine arrangements in the participating countries. The Health Organization of the League of Nations took over many of the previously developed arrangements and considerably expanded them, carrying on many active programs directed to combatting plague, cholera, sleeping sickness, yellow fever, and related diseases.

The idea of a single international health agency gained expression with the founding of the United Nations in 1945. The World Health Organization (WHO) was created in 1948, taking over the services of international quarantine, epidemiology intelligence, biological standardization, and assisting individual countries in strengthening national health services. WHO has helped coordinate medical research, adapted international standards for biological substances in medicine, applied health controls to air, land, and sea traffic, studied comparable health statistics from as many countries as possible, and exchanged scientific information.

Two examples will indicate the international work carried on with WHO assistance. The malaria eradication campaign launched by WHO in 1955 is the largest health campaign ever undertaken on a worldwide level. The various national "armies" of health workers total more than 190,000 persons—doctors, engineers, entomologists, microscopists, spraymen, and supervisors—in more than 85 countries inhabited by over 740 million people. Malaria illnesses are reported to have dropped from 250 million in 1955 to 140 million by 1963.

The International Sanitary Regulations adopted in 1951 serve to prevent the spread of such diseases as cholera, plague, relapsing fever, typhus, smallpox, and yellow fever. The regulations cover all forms of international transport—ships, aircraft, trains, and road vehicles. They deal with such matters as vaccination certificates, the sanitary conditions to be maintained at seaports and airports open to international traffic, and measures to be taken against disease in these ports. Maximum protection against the spread of disease is combined with minimum disruption of trade and travel. Under the regulations, governments are obliged to inform WHO when cases, or suspected cases, of the quarantinable diseases occur. WHO promptly reports this information in a daily radio bulletin, broadcast from its Geneva headquarters and retransmitted throughout the world. The bulletin then appears in printed form in the *Weekly Epidemiological Record*, which was begun by the Health Committee of the League of Nations in 1925 and has been published without interruption ever since.

The worldwide struggle for the control of disease can have no foreseeable end because evolution is continuous: no living form is permanently stabilized. On evolutionary grounds, therefore, it is logical to suppose that infectious diseases are also changing. New ones are in the process of developing just as old ones are being modified or disappearing. New diseases have come from two sources: (1) through modifications of parasitisms already existing in man by gradual adaptive changes in their mutual relations; and (2) through the invasions of man by parasites from other animals as a result of new contacts with animals and insects to which man was not previously exposed. An example of the latter is tularemia, transmitted from infected animals by bloodsucking insects such as wood ticks and horseflies. It has become a menace to man only since the early part of the twentieth century.

Developed Legal, Religious, and Learning Systems

A section of Chapter 4 discussed the beginnings of human systems for political organization, religious concepts, and the appearance of writing, leaving the evolution of each category incomplete. Each subject displays its own particular variety of growth, each plays a role in the evolution of advanced historic and modern civilizations, and the systemic and spatial aspects of each are interwoven into the broad patterns of cultural convergence that characterize the modern world. The growth of variety in intrinsic beliefs and practices was notable in the earlier time periods and aspects, whereas it is the applications of conceptual principles in specific spatial systems that have marked the modern era. Each theme can be dealt with in the contemporary sense as the separate geographies of political systems, religious systems, and educational systems.

The World's Legal Systems

What we commonly term law is really codified custom of behavior. Each human society has developed a body of normative principles designed to govern interpersonal relationships as a means of social control, backed by sanctions that enforce punishments to those who act in defiance of accepted social custom. In simple societies there usually has been little separation of the body of custom into sectors, whereas in the advanced society the separation of the whole body of law into specific categories has been normal, wherein each category pertains to a fairly specific body of custom. Such categories as criminal law, civil law, commercial law, and maritime law are exemplary. Any body of law includes two aspects, the substantive (which defines the norms of behavior) and the adjective (which prescribes the procedures and the agents of enforcement). Said in another way, there are three elements to any body of law: (1) the regularizing of behavior in the specific customs, laws, and statutes, (2) the elements of official authority that interpret the laws, and (3) the applications of sanctions against transgressions. In any society, therefore, one can distinguish the law as a body of custom, the institutional forms developed for the interpretation and adjudication of the law, and the institutional forms and systems of punishment developed to carry out the law.

Among simpler societies it is often hard to differentiate all the foregoing aspects, elements, and institutional forms. Theft is not really common among the simpler societies, punishments are correlative ("an eye for an eye, a tooth for a tooth, a life for a life"), imprisonment is chiefly absent as a sanction against transgression, and the legislation, adjudication, interpretation, and administration of custom and sanctions lie largely in the hands of kinship groups, ritual chiefs, headmen, or tribal councils. The evolution of the political state produced the evolution of the concept that transgressions of custom were breaches of the god-king's peace and laws. In the organized political state there occurred the codification of laws, along with the development of agencies that interpreted the law and administered the sanctions. In time the latter agencies became the legislators, judges, courts, assessors, prosecutors, record keepers, bailiffs, sheriffs, police, and jailers, and others of the government bureaucracy who administer the law in all its varied forms in the advanced society. Around this whole set of constructs, for the whole body of world law, each society has developed its own specific legal institutions designed to make the law, to interpret the law, and to enforce the law.

As private property in land became an accepted principle, for example, there not only was the simple expression of law to this effect, but there also developed the institutional forms of the deed recorder, the tax assessor, the tax collector, the official treasurer, the financial controller, and the title guarantor. As a body of mineral law came into being there developed not only the laws concerning rights to minerals, but also the institutional forms and agencies designed to interpret mineral law, administer mineral law, and effect sanctions for transgressions. In the modern era in the United States the whole body of corporate law has developed not only the specific statutes governing corporate behavior, but also all the legal institutions that are required to interpret and administer the laws created.

In one sense law is the same everywhere throughout the earth, the statement of societal behavior norms. It is the institutions of law that vary most among societies. The body of law, of course, has grown infinitely from the early Paleolithic Era to the present, as man has created his varied and more complex cultures, but the spatial and regional differences among bodies of societal law are best seen in the variation of the legal institutions. The law, everywhere, says that this is right and that is wrong. In New Guinea, among a given culture group, the kinship group and the ritual chief are makers, interpreters, and administrators of the small, oral, and uncodified body of operative custom. In the United States the body of codified law is immense and highly categorized, and we have a host of legal institutions by which the law is made, interpreted, adjudicated, and administered.

The rules by which men are governed apply equally to all inhabitants of a single political territory but differ from one political territory to another. The law embodies the whole story of a nation's development, what it has been, what it is, and what it is tending to become. As Justice Oliver Wendell Holmes, Jr., wrote: "The life of the law has not been logic: it has been experience." We are here concerned with the spatial attributes of legal systems, because they are the touchstone by which to identify the means men use to organize and administer political territories on the earth's surface (Fig. 7.2).

In the Western world, legal systems are customarily divided into two groups: (1) the *civil-law systems*, as on the Continent of Europe, in Quebec and Louisiana, throughout Latin America, and, by extension, in much of Africa and Asia; and (2) the *common-law systems*, developed in England and diffused overseas into its colonies, now become nation-states, hence almost coextensive with the English-speaking world. In civil law, which was strongly and variously influenced by Roman law, large areas of private law are codified, a matter not typical of common law. Nevertheless, both systems share many values and both are products of Western civilization.

The essential difference between the two systems derives from the creation in England, earlier than on the European Continent, of a national, efficient, and centralized administration of justice. After A.D. 1066 the unified law of the royal court of the Norman kings became the one law common to all the realm. The centralization of justice produced an organized class of lawyers, the English bar, which established its own tradition of teaching law, in contrast to the dominant role in legal education held by universities on the Continent. A basic reason why Roman law was never fully utilized in England may well be the existence of an independently organized bar with a vested interest in the law as administered in English courts. Bench and bar came to defend the law, which they had

created from the encroachment of later English kings.

The adoption in civil-law countries of codes of law that revised and unified diverse local laws almost always followed historic periods that were sharp breaks from past traditions, as in France after 1789 or Germany after 1870. The few great exceptions are in Scotland and in the Roman-Dutch law of South Africa, which operate with modified civil law systems. Codification always implies something of a new start (e.g., the French Civil Code, or Code Napoléon, became effective in 1804; Austria's in 1811; the German Civil Code in 1900), the conscious creation of something that replaced all that had preceded.

A third legal system in the world is that of the Communist bloc, extending from Central Europe to North Korea and North Viet-Nam in easternmost Asia. Law is essentially the means whereby the political leadership exercises control over society. Civil law elements in the legal institutions of Communist countries have been reduced almost to the vanishing point. Expropriation and planning measures, backed by criminal sanctions, have made almost all law public law. Nevertheless, there remain some significant differences between the legal tradition of the Peoples' Democracies and their Soviet model, as well as the divergences discernible in the independent countries following their own "road to socialism."

A fourth legal system is that of Islam, based upon the Qur'ān and other religious sources. It reflects traditional religious views in dealing with family and inheritance law and preserves the jurisdiction of religious courts in such matters. Saudi Arabia and Yemen are examples of Arabic countries where Islamic law has been least influenced by Western concepts.

The traditional Chinese body of law and legal institutions forms a fifth system, derived from folk customs of Chinese and non-Chinese people of China and its borders, modified by various early legal philosophers from Confucius to Hantzu, and eventually codified into Confucian state doctrine that provided the governance of China to about 1900. The Chinese legal system strongly reflected the pragmatic social views of the ruling classes, by which peaceful relations were established and maintained throughout the empire among the great family that composed Chinese society. Civil institutional forms became highly developed in the Chinese codes, and it is from these that the rest

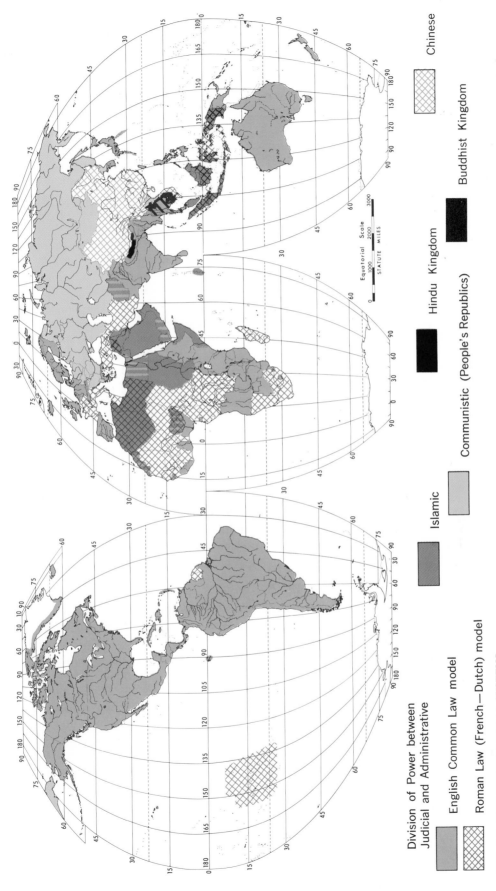

Division of Power between
Judicial and Administrative

English Common Law model

Roman Law (French—Dutch) model

Islamic

Hindu Kingdom

Communistic (People's Republics)

Chinese

Buddhist Kingdom

FIG. 7.2 THE WORLD'S LEGAL SYSTEMS.

of the world has taken the concept and the forms of the modern civil service. To variable degree the Chinese legal system became the framework for the evolution of the localized regional legal systems of Tongking-Annam, of Korea, and of Japan. The Communist take-over of North Korea, China, and North Viet-Nam substituted much of Communist law for the traditional systems.

In other parts of the world, the interpenetration of common, civil, Islamic, and indigenous law has produced mixed systems. Latin American countries have a fundamental civil-law character, yet the impact of common law has been felt through incorporating provisions of the United States Constitution into Latin American constitutions. Puerto Rico, Louisiana, and Quebec are civil-law enclaves in a common-law world; commercial law in Quebec, for example, reflects English influence. In Ceylon and Guyana, common law has widely replaced the former Roman-Dutch system. The new nations of India, Israel, and the Philippines have followed common-law methods, turning to British or American solutions to meet some of their problems. Liberia's legal system is almost entirely patterned after its nineteenth-century United States model, with the interior of the country still partly governed by customary tribal law.

Civil-law systems have spread into many parts of Asia and Africa. The main structure of the German civil code was adopted by Japan and Thailand, and strongly influenced both Greece and pre-Communist China. Austrian models were influential among the Balkan nations, prior to their absorption into the Communist orbit. Turkey copied the Swiss Civil Code and the Swiss Code of Obligations, was German-influenced in its Commercial Code and Code of Criminal Procedures, and used an Italian model for its Penal Code. The Code Napoléon has influenced most of the Islamic nations in North Africa and southwest Asia (e.g., Civil Codes of Egypt, 1949; Syria, 1949; and Iraq, 1953), which synthesize Islamic law with a Western civilian-style commercial code in the law of obligations and in commercial law. The Islamic Republic of Pakistan, on the other hand, has synthesized British common law.

Scandinavian legal systems occupy a special position, with characteristics of both common-law and civil-law systems. Most statutes are not organized into comprehensive code systems, yet many uniform statutes have been enacted to be effective throughout all the Scandinavian countries, governing such matters as marriage, sales, checks, insurance, trademarks, air traffic, and social security. A model for coordination and cooperation among sovereign nation-states has been created.

Evolution of Political and Administrative Organization

The most cosmopolitan institutions in late medieval Europe were its universities:—at Bologna, Paris, Montpellier, and Oxford—each of which attracted students and masters from all the Western world. Europeans, with eagerness, studied the past in the search for new wisdom, and did not stand forever in awe of its commands; they used their present to exercise choices for action rather than remain compliant with preordained ways of life, and they imagined a future as a time of promise and achievement rather than the unfolding of a preestablished certainty. The foundations of the modern secular nation-state were set down in the reformation of Roman law by the medieval law schools at the universities of Europe, and the system of conducting international relations derives much from the principles used for governing these academic communities, as self-governing faculties divided initially into recognized national groups.

The great contribution of Europe to political organization is the concept of the nation-state. Nationalism arose in the later Middle Ages in those kingdoms that were unified within defined and defensible borders and enclosed people who spoke the same language and identified their interests with that of the political territory they inhabited. Ethnic consciousness among a group, as a stimulus to solidarity, was a vital part of the nation-state idea. England was among the earliest of the consolidated states, followed by France and others, as rival kings created national realms, each out of fear of the others. Nationalism, as expressed in monarchy, was the unifying force that created Europe's fragmented territorial units which have tended to persist into modern times.

Each new state, as it emerged in Europe, was built upon local custom and institutions, but within a bounding framework of a common legal system modified from Roman law. Most early states of the thirteenth and fourteenth centuries were the work of law-minded kings and citizens. The cortes, diets, parliaments, and states-generals all were representative assemblies. The concepts of despotic rule and representative government are contradictory, but what evolved in Europe was the modification of absolutism into constitutionalism supported by new legal institutions. The idea of the state shifted from its initial meaning, that of an extension of the ruler's personality and interests, and came to stand for a conglomeration of individual people who had political rights and obligations. The transformation of sixteenth-and seventeenth-century Europe into a plethora of separate sovereignties was established in the Treaties of Westphalia (1648), which recognized that states, as distinguished from governments, were members of the society of nations, that states were secular political organisms, and that all states were sovereign, independent, and equal.

Western Europe, at the end of the fifteenth century, no longer possessed any vestige of an international state, such as the Roman Empire had been for its known world, but was an international community of separate and equal states. In their voyages of exploration, Europeans were amazed to discover that there existed ways for solving the problem of administering a territory and its people of which they had not yet dreamed. In its areas of different size, shape, population, and character, the world was found to be even more diverse than the fragmented Europe of the sixteenth century.

It must be remembered that all of men's ways for governing other men derive from a time when almost all the world's peoples were illiterate and were expected to remain so. Except for the Mongols, the great imperial designs in existence in the sixteenth century—Chinese, Indian, Ottoman (Islamic), Turk—were linked inextricably to a religious (the God-King) or quasireligious-ethical (Confucian) orientation that had scant attraction for a secular Europe which was beginning to cope at home with the impact of the printing press and the rise of science.

The discovery that there were other continents beyond the Atlantic and that their pagan inhabitants were rational human beings, as set down by the Dominican friar, Bartolomé de Las Casas, put a great strain on Europe's image of a world community composed solely of European national states. From sixteenth-century Europe there emerged the ideas of a "collective will of mankind" or "law of nations"; the idea that a world community existed, composed of lands and peoples that differed from one another; the idea that a single superstate, created by military conquest, was impossible of achievement; the idea that the world could not be held together by any single creed in which all peoples would believe.

The logic of these ideas that emerged from the European discoveries was not immediately comprehended. The fervor of saving the world for Western Christendom sent many Spanish and Portuguese overseas to spread the gospel and the territorial extent of European empires. Periodically, the dream of world empire burned fiercely, as among the French under Napoleon, the English during the "Pax Britannica" of the nineteenth century, the Germans under Bismarck and Hitler. To cite but one other example, the Russian national state began its independence when Moscow was emancipated from the Mongols. When Ivan III married the niece of the last Byzantine emperor, Moscow, as capital of the new Russian state, became the new center of Eastern Christendom, the successor to Constantinopole, the "Third Rome." The Russians inherited the claim to be the leading Orthodox state, with the sacred mission of saving mankind. Linked with the power of the nation-state and the ambitions of autocratic rulers, a messianic kind of imperialism emerged. The Russians, like the Byzantines, accepted a political organization of government absolutism and professed the supremacy of their own state among the nations of the world. Russia, from the seventeenth to twentieth centuries, was successful in transforming the state of Muscovy into an expansive multinational empire stretching across northern Asia to the Pacific. The revolutionaries of 1917 fell heir to the territory of the world's largest nation-state and substituted the orthodoxy of Marx and Lenin as the new creed.

The twentieth-century's worldwide political structure bears the unmistakable imprint of its European origin, and the diffusion therefrom of the idea of nationalism. Most of the new states that have arisen in the Americas, Asia, Africa, and the Pacific have been formed in the image of a European model, or at least use a European political vocabulary: self-determination, nationalism, independence, self-government, human rights, democracy. The important point about the political organization of the contemporary world is not that it is fragmented into so many units, but that almost all of these units are now of the same kind, the independent nation-state, 122 of which are equal members of the community of states, the United Nations. Much guidance toward the choice of a European model for government derived from tutelage while colonial territories of European powers, and more recently from the United Nations as the responsible agency for the future of nonself-governing territories. At the end of World War II there were still some 800 million people who were not self-governing, that is, were being ruled by other peoples of different cultures and usually of a different race. But in today's world these peoples of Asia, Africa and the Pacific have mostly emerged and are making their presence felt in world affairs; there are now less than 100 million people still subject to colonial rule, mostly in Portuguese Africa and in New Guinea, and the trend is toward achieving the end of the colonial era. And note that the transition from subjugation to independence for most peoples during the past quarter century generally has been made in a peaceful and orderly way, by negotiation rather than by force, a process of evolution not revolution.

The diffusion and transplantation of Western political concepts into non-Western societies, including many nonliterate cultures, has resulted in great incongruities, however. The concept of the political community has been widely accepted, but not the idea that an individual has inalienable political rights. The newly emerged states of the mid-twentieth century have focused upon achieving independence and nationhood, with national identity equated with select groups of individuals as power elites, not the totality of the new nations' citizenries. Libya, for example, is an independent state, whose charter indicates that it is a representative, democratic, constitutional monarchy, federating the former territories of Fezzan, Tripolitania, and Cyrenaica. However, most Libyans are nonliterate, largely nomadic tribesmen of the Sahara, whose wishes toward adherence to a nation-state are unknown. Libya has an internationally generally accepted ideal form of political organization, but does it conform to North African realities?

Varieties of Political Territories

Every human being lives under, or in contact with, a political system. It is a measure of the degree of cultural convergence, or integration, in the modern world that the vast majority of the earth's people are in touch not only with their own system and its subsystems, but also with one or more outside systems. For example, a citizen of Wisconsin may be, and likely is, actively concerned with a school district, a town government, a conservation district, a county, the Wisconsin state government, and the federal government of the United States. Because he is a citizen of the United States, many political systems impinge upon his life indirectly, as in alliances such as NATO, SEATO, the United Nations, or as in relations with foreign governments, such as Canada, Great Britain, India, or South Viet-Nam.

Every political system is characterized by identification with some area on the earth's surface. The concept of a nation is unthinkable apart from association with specific territory, since every state is part humanity and part land. There are thus two intertwined relations in a political system: the organizational process by which it functions and the territory over which it exercises jurisdiction. Political processes are the succession of actions or operations that man conducts to establish and maintain a political system. Every political process has a territorial area uniquely associated with it and no territorial area escapes some relation with a political process. Since political processes have spatial distribution and spatial relations, they are relevant subjects for geographic study. The political territory has various political features, such as boundaries, capitals, administrative subdivisions, exclaves and enclaves, that can be studied, and political processes, such as internal disunity or cohesion, expansion, regional attitudes or voting characteristics, and management of resources, whose spatial characteristics can be analyzed. There is still a great deal to be learned about the various ways in which man organizes space for political purposes.

The politics of historic empires, of tribe and ethnic community, and of colony have given way to the politics necessary to produce an effective nation-state that can operate successfully in a system of other nation-states. A nation-state has at least six characteristics: an expanse of territory delimited by boundaries, an effective administrative system that controls the area, a specific set of legal institutions, a resident population, an economic structure or source of livelihood, and systems of transport and communication. A nation-state has three basic functions to perform: maintain its internal cohesion, finance its cost of operations (government, international obligations, social welfare), and guard its territorial security. Some communities, however, are nation-states only in form and by international courtesy. We continue to overextend our use of such optimistic expressions as "developing," "emerging," or "transitional" when discussing some countries with gloomy futures: barely viable nations with shaky and archaic governments and with peoples that are growing faster in numbers than in well-being. Some seem to have little capacity for maintaining public order, for mobilizing resources, or for making and upholding international commitments. Nationalism as a diffuse and unorganized sentiment is not enough; public institutions are needed to control and operate the society, and translate into policy and programs the aspirations of nationalism and citizenship. The state-idea involves, then, an effective organization and management (the application of space-adjusting techniques) to territorial space on the earth's surface.

Table 7.1 lists the political territories into which the entire earth's land surface, except Antarctica, is divided. Each of these political units has a central governmental structure, and each is separated from its neighbors by political boundaries. Yet not all are independent, or self-governing. Figures 7.3 and 7.4 portray the changes in distribution in self-governing and nonself-governing units between 1887 and 1932, whereas Figs. 7.5 and 7.6 portray the contemporary (1967) distribution.

As the table and maps indicate, there are vast differences among the world's political units in matters of size, location, and shape and in the physical attributes that derive therefrom—climate, landforms and drainage, soils, plants, animals, and mineral resources. Note, for example, that as yet no strong and cohesive nation-states lie wholly or primarily within the equatorial and tropical regions and that relatively few states, none of great size, are completely landlocked, without frontage on any sea or ocean (Table 7.2). The breakup of the colonial systems has seen the number of independent states nearly double during the past quarter century. This proliferation of nations has introduced many small, weak, and poor nation-states into the world system. More than 60 nations have fewer than 5 million people each, and 31 have fewer than 2 million each. How can these small countries maintain their economic and political posture as equals within the international community if their territorial viability is in doubt?

Most nation-states have internal subdivisions (see Fig. 1.9a), either as regional units or special-purpose subsystems (e.g., school districts, port authorities, soil conservation districts, judicial districts, development authorities, and others). The study of spatial distribution and spatial relations thus can focus upon such territorial phenomena as (1) domestic-regional political systems (provinces, states, counties), (2) urban-community or other densely settled areas, and (3) local or regional special-purpose districts.

A major problem area in man-land relationships is concerned with resource management and land planning in various forms. We apply spatial analysis to adjust the political disequilibriums caused by nonconformities between changing land occupance (e.g., changes in population densities and distributions, and in technologic capabilities) and the existing legal system. Since political decisions have an impact upon the use of land (e.g., Israel's frontier areas as quasimilitary districts; the organization of Canada's northern territories), there are an unending series of problems in a developing world.

The Roles and Spatial Patterns of Religions

In Chapter 4 the basic role and fundamental concepts of religious beliefs were set forth, to suggest the formative and organizing impact of religion in human cultures. Out of the thousands of small culture groups operative in small environments during, let us say, the early to mid-Neolithic, there have emerged only a small number of discrete and organized religious systems in which codified beliefs became highly systematized and structured. In these systems there evolved the dynamics and mechanisms able to perpetuate the religious elements apart from the integral content of the culture of the group among whom the system developed. This is to say that in most cases a set of religious beliefs were inseparable from the whole body of culture of a particular culture group; when that group lost its individual culture, the religious beliefs were also lost. For example, in a sense, the religious beliefs of the Tasmanians perished along with the specific culture of the Tasmanians, as the Tasmanian culture group died out. In a relatively few cases, however, a dynamics and a set of mechanisms were created that allowed the religious beliefs to be spread among peoples of other cultures. Thus certain sets of religious beliefs have tended to diffuse around the world, to become accepted by many kinds of peoples possessing quite varied systems of culture. In these cases, religious beliefs have become integrated into the separate bodies of culture to greater or lesser

(continued on page 297)

TABLE 7.1   POLITICAL TERRITORIES OF THE EARTH, 1967
(Numbers identify the places on the maps, FIGS. 7.5 and 7.6)

Place	Possession of (Where Applicable)	Area (in Thousands of Square Miles)	Population (in Thousands)	Density of Population (Persons per Square Mile)	Capital (Population in Thousands)
AFRICA					
Western Africa					
1. Cape Verde Islands	Portugal	1.56	220	141	Praia (6)
2. Dahomey		45	2,300	51	Porto-Novo (65)
3. Gambia, The		4	330	81	Bathurst (29)
4. Ghana		92	7,740	84	Accra (492)
5. Guinea, Republic of		95	3,420	36	Conakry (113)
6. Ivory Coast, Republic of		124	3,750	30	Abidjan (212)
7. Liberia		43	1,310	30	Monrovia (81)
8. Mali, Republic of		465	4,576	9.9	Bamako (135)
9. Mauritania, Islamic Republic of		419	900	2.1	Nouakchott (6)
10. Niger, Republic of		459	3,250	7	Niamey (42)
11. Nigeria, Federation of		357	56,400	158	Lagos (675)
12. Portuguese Guinea	Portugal	14	549	39	Bissau (20)
13. St. Helena (incl. dependencies)	United Kingdom	0.047	4.7	100	Jamestown (1.6)
14. Senegal, Republic of		76	3,490	46	Dakar (383)
15. Sierra Leone		28	2,450	87	Freetown (128)
16. Togo, Republic of		20	1,660	83	Lomé (80)
17. Upper Volta, Republic of		106	4,882	46	Ouagadougou (100)
Eastern Africa					
18. Burundi		11	2,780	253	Bujumbura (70)
19. Comoro Archipelago	France	0.8	212	265	Dzaoudzi (2.9)
20. Ethiopia		395	22,590	57	Addis Ababa (505)
21. French Somaliland	France	8.9	81	9.1	Djibouti (41)
22. Kenya		220	9,376	43	Nairobi (315)
23. Malagasy Republic (Madagascar)		230	6,180	27	Tananarive (299)
24. Malawi		37	3,900	105	Lilongwe (22)
25. Mauritius	United Kingdom	0.72	741	1,029	Port Louis (125)
26. Mozambique	Portugal	298	6,956	23	Lourenço Marques (184)
27. Réunion	France	0.97	387	399	St. Denis (65)
28. Rhodesia		150	4,260	28	Salisbury (314)
29. Rwanda		10	3,018	302	Kigali (4.2)
30. Seychelles Islands	United Kingdom	0.16	46	290	Victoria (11)
31. Somali Republic		246	2,500	10	Mogadishu (121)
32. Tanzania, United Republic of		342	10,514	31	Dar-es-Salaam (129)
33. Uganda		80	7,551	93	Kampala (123)
34. Zambia		290	3,780	13	Lusaka (122)
Northern Africa					
35. Algeria		952	12,300	13	Algiers (884)
36. Ifni	Spain	0.74	54	73	Sidi Ifni (13)
37. Libya		679	1,559	2.4	Tarābulus (Tripoli) (213)
38. Morocco		171	13,323	78	Rabat (262)
39. Spanish North Africa (Ceuta and Melilla)	Spain	0.012	8	13,167	
40. Spanish Sahara	Spain	103	48	0.47	El Aaiun (4.5)
41. Sudan		967	13,733	14	Khartoum (135)
42. Tunisia		48	4,565	95	Tunis (680)
43. United Arab Republic (Egypt)		386	29,600	77	Cairo (3518)

TABLE 7.1 (*Continued*)

Place	Possession of (Where Applicable)	Area (in Thousands of Square Miles)	Population (in Thousands)	Density of Population (Persons per Square Mile)	Capital (Population in Thousands)
Middle Africa					
44. Angola	Portugal	481	5,154	11	Luanda (225)
45. Cameroon, Republic of		182	5,150	28	Yaoundé (93)
46. Central African Republic		238	1,352	5.7	Bangui (111)
47. Chad, Republic of		496	3,300	6.7	Fort-Lamy (92)
48. Congo, Republic of		132	865	6.6	Brazzaville (136)
49. Congo, Democratic Republic of		905	15,627	17	Kinshasa (403)
50. Equatorial Guinea (Rio Muni and Fernando Pöo)		7.5	267	36	Santa Isabel (37)
51. Gabon, Republic of		103	462	4.4	Libreville (31)
52. Sao Tomé and Príncipe	Portugal	0.37	64	173	Sao Tomé (3.2)
Southern Africa					
53. Lesotho, Kingdom of		12	745	62	Maseru (9.5)
54. Botswana, Republic of		275	559	2	Gaberones (12)
55. French Southern and Antarctic Territories	France	8.5	—	—	
56. South Africa, Republic of		472	18,298	39	Pretoria (423)
57. South West Africa	United Nations (until 1969)	318	574	1.8	Windhoek (36)
58. Swaziland		6.7	292	44	Mbabane (9.9)
NORTHERN AMERICA					
59. Bermuda	United Kingdom	0.021	49	2,333	Hamilton (2.8)
60. Canada		3,560	19,785	5.5	Ottawa (468)
61. Greenland	Denmark	840	37	0.044	Godthaab (1.3)
62. St. Pierre and Miquelon	France	0.093	5	54	St. Pierre (3.5)
63. United States of America		3,554	200,000	56	Washington, D.C. (2250)
LATIN AMERICA					
Tropical South America					
64. Bolivia		424	3,702	8.7	La Paz (361)
65. Brazil		3,286	82,200	25	Brasilia (131)
66. Colombia		439	17,787	41	Bogotá (1662)
67. Ecuador		176	5,238	30	Quito (368)
68. French Guiana	France	35	36	1	Cayenne (19)
69. Guyana		83	647	7.8	Georgetown (148)
70. Peru		496	11,854	24	Lima (1730)
71. Surinam	Netherlands	55	350	6.4	Paramaibo (123)
72. Venezuela		352	8,722	25	Caracas (1590)
Middle America (Mainland)					
73. British Honduras	United Kingdom	8.9	106	12	Belize City (33)
74. Canal Zone	Administered by United States under treaty with Panama	0.36	54	150	Balboa Heights (3.1)
75. Costa Rica		20	1,474	74	San José (322)
76. El Salvador		8.2	2,928	357	San Salvador (281)
77. Guatemala		42	4,438	106	Guatemala City (573)
78. Honduras		43	2,284	53	Tegucigalpa (154)
79. Mexico		760	40,913	52	Mexico City, D.F. (3193)
80. Nicaragua		57	1,655	29	Managua (275)
81. Panama		29	1,246	43	Panama City (359)

TABLE 7.1 *(Continued)*

Place	Possession of (Where Applicable)	Area (in Thousands of Square Miles)	Population (in Thousands)	Density of Population (Persons per Square Mile)	Capital (Population in Thousands)
Temperate South America					
82. Argentina		1,080	22,352	21	Buenos Aires (3876)
83. Chile		286	8,567	30	Santiago (2314)
84. Falkland Islands (incl. South Georgia)	United Kingdom	4.6	2.2	0.48	Stanley (1.1)
85. Paraguay		157	2,030	13	Asunción (305)
86. Uruguay		72	2,715	38	Montevideo (1204)
Caribbean					
87. Antigua—Barbuda	United Kingdom	0.17	63	371	St. John's (21)
88. Bahamas	United Kingdom	4.4	138	31	Nassau (55)
89. Barbados		0.17	244	1,435	Bridgetown (12)
90. Cayman Islands	United Kingdom	0.1	9	90	George Town (2.7)
91. Cuba		44	7,631	173	Havana (1463)
92. Dominica	United Kingdom	0.29	65	224	Roseau (13)
93. Dominican Republic		19	3,619	190	Santo Domingo (529)
94. Grenada	United Kingdom	0.13	93	715	St. George's (27)
95. Guadeloupe	France	0.69	306	443	Basse-Terre (12)
96. Haiti		11	4,660	424	Port-au-Prince (250)
97. Jamaica		4.4	1,779	404	Kingston (126)
98. Martinique	France	0.42	310	738	Fort-de-France (61)
99. Montserrat	United Kingdom	0.032	14	438	Plymouth (3.5)
100. Netherlands Antilles	Netherlands	0.38	207	545	Willemstad (45)
101. Puerto Rico	United States	3.42	2,703	790	San Juan (452)
102. St. Kitts—Nevis—Anguilla	United Kingdom	0.15	62	413	Basseterre (16)
103. St. Lucia	United Kingdom	0.24	99	413	Castries (35)
104. St. Vincent	United Kingdom	0.15	86	573	Kingstown (21)
105. Trinidad and Tobago		1.98	950	480	Port of Spain (94)
106. Turks and Caicos Islands	United Kingdom	0.17	6	353	Grand Turk (2.4)
107. Virgin Islands	United Kingdom	0.059	9	153	Road Town (0.89)
108. Virgin Islands	United States	0.13	41	315	Charlotte Amalie (13)
ASIA					
East Asia					
109. Bonin Islands	Japan	0.04	0.22	5.5	
110. China (Mainland)		3,759	716,000	192	Peking (5420)
111. China (Taiwan)		14	12,651	904	Taipei (1028)
112. Hong Kong	United Kingdom	0.4	3,804	9,510	Victoria (675)
113. Japan		143	98,560	689	Tokyo (10,687)
114. Korea (North)		47	11,800	251	Pyongyang (940)
115. Korea (South)		38	28,816	758	Seoul (3376)
116. Macao	Portugal	0.006	174	29,000	Macao (174)
117. Mongolia		604	1,050	1.7	Ulan Bator (218)
118. Ryukyu Islands	Administered under military government by the United States	0.85	935	1,100	Naha City (247)
Southeast Asia					
119. Brunei	Protectorate of United Kingdom	2.2	97	44	Brunei (38)
120. Burma		262	24,732	94	Rangoon (1530)
121. Cambodia		70	6,200	89	Phnom Penh (404)
122. Indonesia		736	103,100	140	Djakarta (3318)

TABLE 7.1 (Continued)

Place	Possession of (Where Applicable)	Area (in Thousands of Square Miles)	Population (in Thousands)	Density of Population (Persons per Square Mile)	Capital (Population in Thousands)
123. Laos		91	1,960	22	Luang Prabang (45), royal capital Vientiane (162), administrative capital
124. Malaysia		128	9,395	73	Kuala Lumpur (316)
125. Philippines, Republic of the		116	33,193	286	Quezon City (398)
126. Portuguese Timor	Portugal	7.3	547	75	Dili (52)
127. Singapore		0.22	1,865	8,477	Singapore (831)
128. Thailand		198	30,591	154	Bangkok (1608)
129. Viet Nam (North)		63	18,400	292	Hanoi (644)
130. Viet Nam (South)		66	16,124	244	Saigon-Cholon (1400)
South Asia					
131. Afghanistan		250	15,227	61	Kabul (450)
132. Bhutan		18	750	42	Thimphu (1.0)
133. Ceylon		25	10,965	439	Colombo (511)
134. India		1,263	498,900	395	New Delhi (295) (Delhi—2298)
135. Maldive Islands		0.12	98	817	Male (12)
136. Nepal		54	9,920	184	Katmandu (220)
137. Pakistan		366	102,885	281	Rawalpindi (340)
138. Sikkim	Protectorate of India	2.7	176	65	Gangtok (12)
Southwest Asia					
140. Bahrain		0.23	182	791	Manama (62)
141. Cyprus		3.6	598	166	Nicosia (103)
142. Iran		628	23,428	37	Tehran (2317)
143. Iraq		172	8,262	48	Baghdad (1307)
144. Israel		8	2,615	327	Jerusalem (181)
145. Jordan		37	1,935	52	Amman (311)
146. Kuwait		5.8	468	81	Kuwait (152)
147. Lebanon		4	2,280	570	Beirut (500)
148. Muscat and Oman		82	565	6.9	Muscat (6.2)
149. Qatar		4	70	18	Doha (45)
150. Saudi Arabia		927	6,630	7.1	Riyadh (170)
151. South Yemen		60	868	14	Al Ittihad
152. Syria		72	5,467	76	Damascus (545)
153. Trucial Oman		32	111	3.5	Dubai (55)
154. Turkey		296	32,050	105	Ankara (902)
155. Yemen		75	5,000	67	San'a (100) Ta'iz (80)
EUROPE					
Western Europe					
156. Austria		32	7,255	227	Vienna (1634)
157. Belgium		12	9,499	792	Brussels (1058)
158. France		213	49,157	231	Paris (2790)
159. Germany (West)		96	59,313	618	Bonn (142)
160. Liechtenstein		0.06	19	317	Vaduz (3.8)
161. Luxembourg		1	332	332	Luxembourg (77)
162. Monaco		0.0006	25	41,667	Monaco-Ville (2.4)
163. Netherlands		13	12,387	953	's-Gravenhage (599)
164. Switzerland		16	6,080	380	Berne (167)
165. West Berlin	Germany (West)	0.185	2,200	11,900	

TABLE 7.1 (*Continued*)

Place	Possession of (Where Applicable)	Area (in Thousands of Square Miles)	Population (in Thousands)	Density of Population (Persons per Square Mile)	Capital (Population in Thousands)
Southern Europe					
166. Albania		11	1,814	165	Tiranë (153)
167. Andorra		0.19	11	58	Andorra la Vella (2.2)
168. Gibraltar	United Kingdom	0.0025	24	9,600	Gibraltar (20)
169. Greece		51	8,550	168	Athens (1853)
170. Holy See (Vatican City State)		0.00016	1	—	Vatican City (1)
171. Italy		116	52,520	453	Rome (2455)
172. Malta and Gozo		0.12	330	2,750	Valletta (18)
173. Portugal		35	9,199	263	Lisbon (816)
174. San Marino		0.024	17	708	San Marino (3)
175. Spain		195	31,737	163	Madrid (2559)
176. Yugoslavia		99	19,632	198	Belgrade (678)
Eastern Europe					
177. Bulgaria		43	8,207	191	Sofia (801)
178. Czechoslovakia		49	14,167	289	Prague (1020)
180. Germany (East)		42	17,012	405	Berlin, East Sector (1071)
181. Hungary		36	10,164	282	Budapest (1935)
182. Poland		120	31,551	263	Warsaw (1241)
183. Rumania		92	19,027	207	Bucharest (1367)
184. Union of Soviet Socialist Republics		8,648	231,869	27	Moscow (6427)
Northern Europe					
185. Channel Islands	United Kingdom	0.075	112	1,493	St. Helier (28)
186. Denmark		17	4,720	278	Copenhagen (1262)
187. Faeroe Islands	Denmark	0.54	36	67	Thornshavn (7.5)
188. Finland		130	4,628	36	Helsinki (482)
189. Iceland		40	190	4.8	Reykjavik (77)
190. Irish Republic (Eire)		27	2,855	106	Dublin (593)
191. Isle of Man	United Kingdom	0.227	48	213	Douglas (19)
192. Norway		125	3,723	30	Oslo (485)
193. Svalbard and Jan Mayen Islands	Norway	25	2.6	0.10	
194. Sweden		173	7,773	45	Stockholm (799)
195. United Kingdom of Great Britain and Northern Ireland		93	54,436	585	London (7949)
OCEANIA					
196. Australia		2,971	11,479	3.8	Canberra, A.C.T. (78)
197. New Zealand		104	2,677	26	Wellington (162)
Melanesia					
198. British Solomon Islands	United Kingdom	12	133	11	Honiara (3.5)
199. New Caledonia	France	7.2	89	12	Noumea (35)
200. New Guinea, Trust Territory of	United Nations, adminstered by Australia	93	1,539	16	Port Moresby (14)
201. New Hebrides	Condominium— United Kingdom and France	5.7	66	12	Vila (3.5)
202. Norfolk Island	Australia	0.013	1	77	Kingston
203. Papua	Australia	91	562	6.2	Port Moresby (14)

TABLE 7.1 (*Continued*)

Place	Possession of (Where Applicable)	Area (in Thousands of Square Miles)	Population (in Thousands)	Density of Population (Persons per Square Mile)	Capital (Population in Thousands)
Polynesia and Micronesia					
204. American Samoa	United States	0.076	23	302	Fagatogo (1.4)
205. Canton and Enderbury Islands	United Kingdom and United States	0.027	0.3	11	
206. Christmas Island (Indian Ocean)	Australia	0.055	3.2	58	
207. Cocos (Keeling) Islands (Indian Ocean)	Australia	0.005	0.62	124	
208. Cook Islands	New Zealand	0.93	20	215	Avarua (10)
209. Fiji Islands	United Kingdom	7	464	66	Suva (38)
210. French Polynesia	France	1.6	86	54	Papeete (20)
211. Gilbert and Ellice Islands (incl. Phoenix Island)	United Kingdom	0.36	53	147	Tarawa (7)
212. Guam	United States	0.21	72	343	Agaña (2.0)
213. Johnston Island	United States	0.0005	0.15	300	
214. Midway Islands	United States	0.002	2	100	
215. Nauru		0.0082	4.9	598	Nauru
216. Niue	New Zealand	0.01	5	50	Alofi (0.96)
217. Pacific Islands, U.N. Strategic Trust Territory of	United Nations, administered by the United States	0.69	90	130	Saipan (8.3)
218. Pitcairn Island	United Kingdom	0.002	0.086	43	
219. Tokelau Islands	New Zealand	0.004	2	500	
220. Tonga, Kingdom of	United Kingdom	0.27	72	267	Nuku'alofa (9.2)
221. Wake Island	United States	0.003	1.1	367	
222. Western Samoa		1.13	122	108	Apia (25)
Atlantic					
223. Ascension	United Kingdom	0.034	0.35	10	Georgetown (0.3)
224. Azores	Portugal	0.89	337	379	Ponta Delgada (23)
225. Canary Islands	Spain	2.8	967	345	Las Palmas (205)
226. Madeira	Portugal	0.31	283	913	Funchal (37)
227. Tristan da Cunha	United Kingdom	0.04	0.26	6.5	Edinburgh (0.2)

degree, acquiring modifications in conceptual systemics and practices, developing institutional elements that permitted the functional aspects of religion to play particular roles in the separate cultures. As such, this selective perpetuation of a relatively few systems of religious beliefs is a part of the broad process of cultural convergence that has taken place in late historic times and during the modern era.

In the modern world we sometimes are impressed more by the sectarian divergence that seems rather recently to have appeared in religious beliefs and practices than by the actually more significant processes of convergence of religious beliefs. That is, we cite the many kinds of Christianity as a symptom of sectarian divergence which has seemed to be an increasing trend in the modern world. This view, however, neglects the fact of the missionary spread of some kind of Christianity which has been replacing the much greater variety of slightly organized religions and the great but variable reservoir of local animisms.

The historic processes by which a set of animistic beliefs becomes "organized" into a formal religious system, or by which a "religious revolt" spawns a new body of organized religion, are both complex and multivariate, and they have operated in many different ways through time. Each successful case involves a complex element of cultural dynamics which is integrally related to the state,

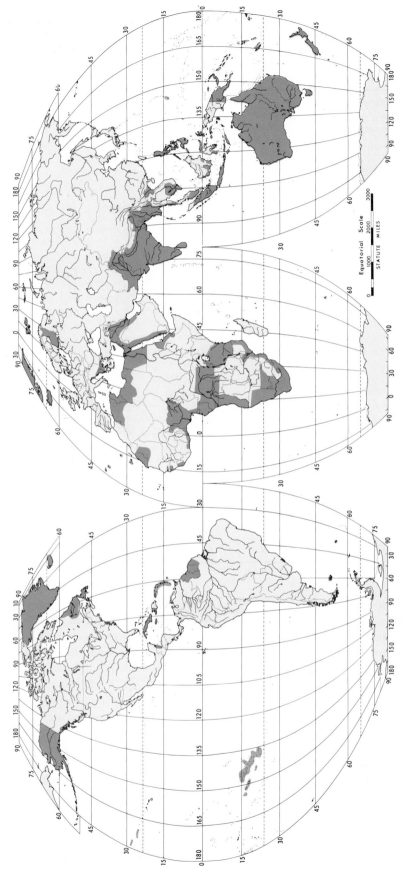

FIG. 7.3 DEPENDENT AREAS OF THE WORLD, 1887.

298

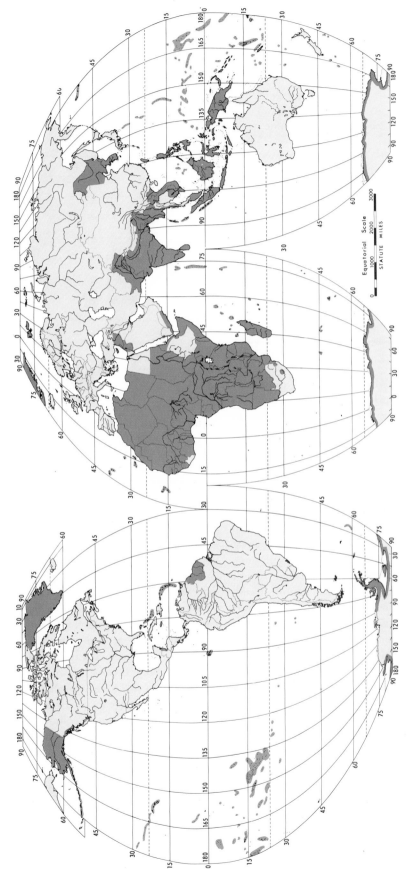

FIG. 7.4 DEPENDENT AREAS OF THE WORLD, 1932.

Equatorial   Scale

0   1000   2000   3000

STATUTE   MILES

299

TABLE 7.2 NATION-STATES WITHOUT DIRECT ACCESS TO AN OCEAN OR SEA

South America	Africa
Bolivia	Mali
Paraguay	Upper Volta
Asia	Niger
Mongolian People's Republic	Central African Republic
Nepal	Uganda
Sikkim	Burundi
Bhutan	Rwanda
Laos	Zambia
Europe	Nyasaland
Luxembourg	Rhodesia
Switzerland	Swaziland
Liechtenstein	Lesotho
Austria	Botswana
Hungary	
Czechoslovakia	
Andorra	
San Marino	
Vatican City	

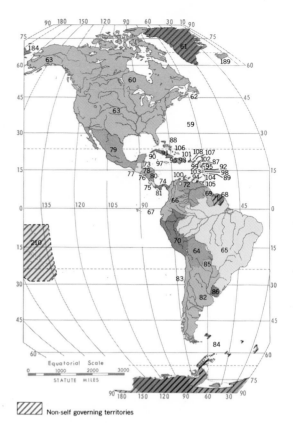

Non-self governing territories

FIG. 7.5 POLITICAL TERRITORIES OF THE WESTERN HEMISPHERE AND THE PACIFIC.

condition, and strength of the body of previously existing culture in which the phenomenon occurred, and which has equally integral relation to the state and condition of the previously existing set of religious beliefs among that culture group. Behind every really new formulation of an organized religious system was a strong and growing body of folk religion (animism) and a significant condition of vitality in the culture of the practicing group. Behind every religious revolt that sparked the formulation of a "reform religion" there must have been a condition of cultural crisis of some sort which provided the dynamic that sought expression in the revitalized formulation of religious beliefs and practices. The processes involved are not only complex; they are also not amenable to casual generalization.

In the development of organized religious systems there are a number of common features, but there are many ways in which these common elements work. Some organized religious systems lack sacred books or priesthoods, and the conceptualization of the supreme power may be expressed in different ways. However, all systems of organized religion seek the establishment and maintenance of cultural norms in regard to morality, the sanctity of marriage, and codes of group behavior, and all have some formulation of the "do's" and the "don't's" for that normative be-

havior. These rules never are absolutes, in reality, but they are the warnings concerning the punishments that result upon transgression of normative behavior, and all organized religions have forms of penitence by which the wrongdoer may regain his status as an honorable member of society. Many organized religions carry the formulation of norms beyond the specifications of social behavior into such matters as dress, diet, housing, and economic practices. Some organized religions contain, either permanently or at some time, the belief that adherents should carry the belief to the nonbeliever; that is, they involve missionary zeal for the spreading of the religious belief. In that all organized religions have asserted some degree of control over the formulation of cultural norms and practices, organized religions have been forceful agents in cultural development and agencies for the perpetuation of culture patterns.

A particular set of religious practices normally tended to be coextensive with the spatial pattern of a particular culture, in the very early and developmental phase. The diffusion of early folk

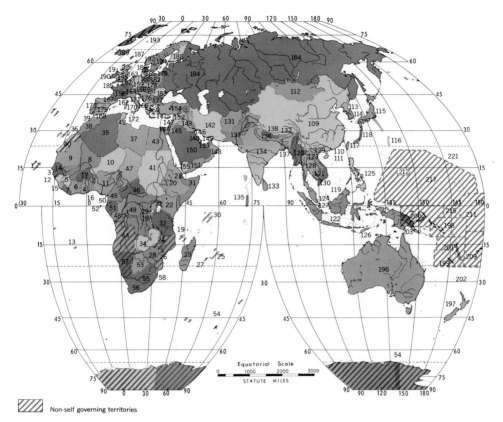

FIG. 7.6 POLITICAL TERRITORIES OF THE ATLANTIC AND THE EASTERN HEMISPHERE.

Non-self governing territories

culture, and the mixing of such cultures, diffused and mixed religious beliefs. Historically, the organizing of formal religious systems seems interrelated to the formulation of organized political systems, and a set of religious beliefs tended, initially, to take the same spatial patterns as accrued to the spatial limits of the political state. In the concept of the God-King, the supreme ruler was both God and King, so that the allocation of political favors, the administration of the state, and the enforcement of political injunctions automatically carried the same elements in religion to the same peoples over the same space. Historically, we see in the expansion of a political state the spread of a particular religious system, and the modern accompaniment by Christianity of European political imperialism is not a new feature. The preservation of the association of political system and religious system has been clearly preserved in the modern era in the continuance of the state religion. Thus with the expansion and contraction of political states there has been a pattern of spatial expansion and contraction of religious systems. However, the spatial dimensions of the political state are subject to rapid and repetitive changes, for the political state as a formal organization under a particular ruler has been a very fragile construct, whereas a religious system that has been deeply integrated into a regional culture is a persistent and durable thing. There is, therefore, no total correlation between the spatial limits of the political state and the spatial distribution of religious beliefs, and there are many cases of the long-term persistence of spatially distributed religious beliefs despite changes in political controls.

In modern times the growth of the concept of the separation of church and state has given rise to secular political systems, in the strict sense, a characteristic which then permits the spatial intermixture of religious systems to a high degree. This secularism in political administration sometimes has led both to the proliferation of sectarianism in religious systems and to the rise of secularism as a personal viewpoint, quite notably in the United States and Canada. Despite such trends, the United States, for example, remains broadly classifiable as a Christian society. In the same sense, however, one thinks of France as not only Christian, but as Roman Catholic Christian, and the separation of the formerly complete bond between the Roman Catholic Church and the political administration of Spain is so recent, and still so slight, that Spain remains a Roman Catholic society. At the other extreme, the total secularism of early Soviet Communist ideology at first attempted to ban all practice of any religion whatsoever.

Beyond the specific role of religion as a formulative and a preservative agent in systems of culture, there are many other varieties of impact of religion on regional cultures. There are large numbers of religiously motivated place-names in all parts of the earth; the calendar systems motivating the divisions of the year into particular segments and the patterns of ceremonial days produce significant variety from place to place through religious establishment; architectural styles that go with religious systems have much wider implications than just the forms of the religious structures themselves; the degree to which religious practice is spread out on the landscape in field shrines, house shrines, sacred groves, and sacred places is a significant manifestation of religion in many parts of the earth; and among some religious systems the whole orientation of the total landscape becomes a matter of arriving at a system of mystical harmonics. To the degree to which a particular religious system perseveres in a particular doctrine, such as the vegetarianism of India or continuance of the prohibition of eating meat on Fridays among Roman Catholics of the Mediterranean Basin, religious beliefs have strong impacts upon the whole orientation of a regional economy. The taboo on the eating of pork, in Moslem lands, has led to the disappearance of the pig as an economic animal in the operative economy. These are but illustrative of the variable role of religion in cultural practice the world over.

The world map of religions displays the diffusionary spread of the several Old World religions as a complicated one in which many specific regions show mixed patterns of religious affiliation (Fig. 7.7). Similarly the world map demonstrates that there remain large islands of simple animism and regions in which folk religions possess distinctive patterns corresponding to ethnic culture systems. China is here mapped as practicing a folk religion, rather than the frequently mapped Confucianism; Confucianism properly was a politico-

ethical state cult practiced chiefly by governmental bureaucracies. Lands now controlled by Communist political ideology are mapped only in the nominal sense that varieties of religious beliefs still are preserved by portions of populations. The world map illustrates clearly the worldwide sweep of Christianity in the modern period, this fact in itself being another element in the trend toward cultural convergence, for, among all the living churches, the Christian Church is most actively on the missionary bent in expanding the scope of the faith, and the Christian Church has been a strong factor in the spread of modern world culture. The tabulation of religious faiths is highly generalized, and makes no effort to separate sectarian elements of particular faiths (Table 7.3).

TABLE 7.3 WORLD RELIGIOUS AFFILIATIONS

Religion		Estimates in Millions
Christianity		
Roman Catholic	590	
Eastern Orthodox	145	
Protestant	235	
		970
Islam		
Sunnite	385	
Shiite	45	
		430
Hinduism		425
Buddhism		
Theravada	75	
Mahayana	150	
		225
Shintoism		70
Taoism		50
Judaism		13.5
Sikhism		7.5
Minor organized creeds		15
	Subtotal	2,206
Ethnic folk religions		500
Tribal and ethnic animisms		175
Secularized descendants from Christianity		250
Secularized descendants from other faiths		70
Unknown		150
	Total	3,351

Language, Writing, and Systems of Learning

A language is a group achievement, an agreed-upon system for attaching meanings to a limited

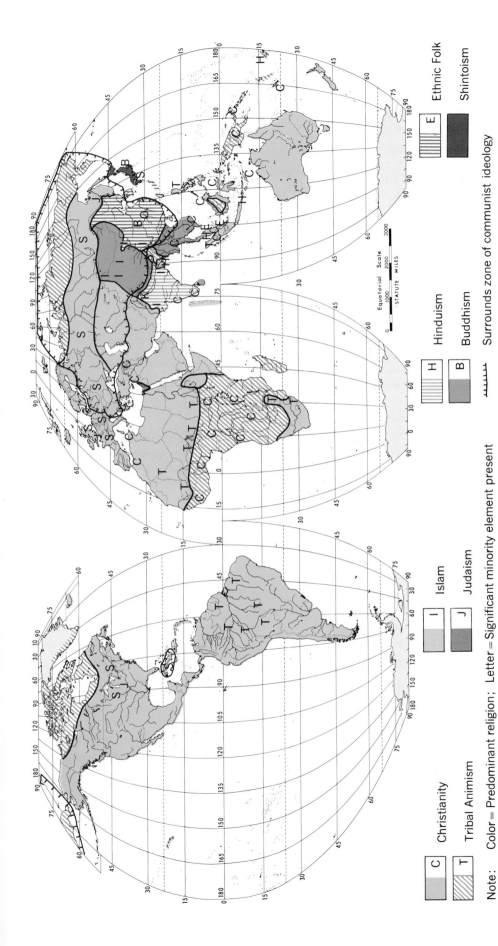

Color = Predominant religion; Letter = Significant minority element present

Other minority elements: K = Sikhism; O = Taoism; S = Secularism

Christianity

Tribal Animism

Islam

Judaism

Hinduism

Buddhism

Ethnic Folk

Shintoism

Surrounds zone of communist ideology

Note:

FIG. 7.7 THE WORLD'S RELIGIOUS SYSTEMS.

303

set of sounds and sound arrangements from the vastly greater number of possible sound combinations and orders. Most spoken languages are extremely old; some cultural groups, however, have lost their original languages and speak borrowed languages. Languages have a dynamic character; some have grown and expanded (for instance, English, which was spoken by not quite 3 million people on less than the whole of just one island in the fifteenth century but now is spoken by hundreds of millions of people the world over), whereas others have remained small, have retrogressed, or have disappeared. Those languages whose internal mechanisms most readily permit of various kinds of changes, such as word borrowings, cultural transfer of meanings, and coinage of new words, are best able to keep abreast of cultural change and are most likely to persist. The language pattern of the twentieth-century world sets bounds upon regions (see Fig. 1.7A, page 20) in which persons speaking the same language can maximize the operation of their cultural processes. Most individuals of the world, including most Americans, are monolingual; many individuals or even whole cultural groups, principally minority ones, are bilingual and participate easily in several cultural realms; fewer individuals and societies (Switzerland is an unusual example) are truly multilingual and more cosmopolitan in their abilities and in their effectiveness to communicate directly with a larger proportion of the world's peoples.

Studies in historical and comparative linguistics had their first successes in the nineteenth century, demonstrating the relationships among the Indo-European group of languages. Our present knowledge of the world's languages is very complex: almost 4000 have disappeared from use in the course of human evolution, whereas nearly 3000 languages are currently in use, some 120 in Europe alone. By considerations of word sounds, word roots, similar sentence structures, use of gender, and words used in common, the living and "dead" languages have been shown to be variously interrelated (Table 7.4). Some, such as Basque or Ainu, seem to defy all efforts at classification, but the others are grouped into "families" and "subfamilies." English, for example, is a part of the Germanic family of the European and Indo-European families, whose many parts, in sum, are now used by about one half of the world's people. Latin, which began as a minor dialect along the lower course of the River Tiber, was spread by Roman conquest over most of the shores of the Mediterranean and Western Europe. When the Roman Empire declined, Latin diverged locally into the several Romance languages. Changes in languages are all an important part of cultural evolution; some, as in Eire and Israel, have even been revived, for political reasons.

The Evolution of Writing

Writing, as a device for communicating by visible linguistic symbols, is a permanent extension of spoken language and a more recent cultural invention. There is no fixed relation between most forms of speech and the writing systems used to record them. There are four basic kinds of true writing: picture writing, ideographs, scripts transitional between these, and phonetic writing. Ideographs are highly developed and conventionalized symbols with accepted definitions of meaning for things or ideas; the characters in written Chinese are ideographic. Phonetic writing uses symbols to represent sounds, not things or ideas. Most of the world's writing systems are phonetic.

Three ancient phonetic systems, with minor variants, are known to have been developed (some "dead" languages may have used other systems, now unknown): the syllabic, the hieroglyphic, and the alphabetic (Fig. 7.8, pp. 312–313). Syllabic writing evolved from pictographic. Groups of signs stood for syllables of sound, compounded for words. The cuneiform writing of Sumer in ancient Mesopotamia is our best known example. Although syllabic writing was in use as early as 4000 B.C., it died out by the beginning of the Christian era and has no known descendants. Hieroglyphic writing also is an early form that died out by A.D. 600. Ancient Egyptians, who used one form on monuments and a cursive form for business and private needs, provide the chief example of hieroglyphic writing. The most advanced writing systems are alphabetic, in which a single symbol identifies a single sound. Only a small number of symbols are needed (various alphabets use from 21 to 40) because they can be combined in various ways to meet phonetic needs. The idea of an alphabet was devised somewhere in the classical Near East prior to 2000 B.C. and spread outward by migration and by idea diffusion (Fig. 7.9, p. 314). There are many variants in the growth history of alphabetic systems, some dying out, some new patterns starting.

One form of alphabet, comparable in place and time of origin to Phoenician and to early Hebrew,

TABLE 7.4 CLASSIFICATION OF THE WORLD'S LANGUAGES

Phylum	Superfamily	Family	Subfamily	Language group	Languages
Indo-Hittite		Anatolian			*Hittite, *"Hieroglyphic" Hittite, *Luwian, *Lycian, *Lydian, etc.
	Indo-European	Armenian			Armenian
		Indo-Iranian	Indic	Sanskrit	*Vedic Sanskrit, *Classical Sanskrit
				Prakrit	Various *Prakrits, *Pali
				Himalayan	Kashmiri, etc.
				Western Indic	Lahnda, Sindi, Gujarati, Marathi, Rajasthani, etc.
				Central Indic	Panjabi, Hindi (written as Hindustani and Urdu), etc.
				Eastern Indic	Bengali, Oriya, Assamese
				Southern Indic	Singhalese
				[other]	Romany
			Iranian	[ancient]	*Avestan, *Old Persian, *Pehlevi, *Soghdian, etc.
				West Iranian	Persian, Caspian dialects, Kurdish
				East Iranian	Baluchi, Pashto, Tajik, etc.
				[other]	Ossetic
		Hellenic			Greek (*Homeric, *Classical, *New Testament, Modern)
	European: South and West European	Italic [Ancient]	Osco-Umbrian		*Oscan, *Umbrian
			Latin-Faliscan		*Latin, *Faliscan, *Praenestian, etc.
		[Modern =] Romanic	East Romanic	Insular	*Dalmatian, Sardinian
				Continental	Romanian, Italian
			West Romanic	Gallic	French, Provençal, Catalan, Franco-Provençal, Rhetic, North Italian
				Iberian	Spanish, Portuguese
		Celtic			*Gaulish
			Gaelic		Irish, Scotch Gaelic
			Brittanic		Welsh, *Cornish, Breton
	North European	Germanic	Northeast Germanic	East Germanic	*Gothic
				Scandinavian	*Old Norse, Icelandic, Faroese, Norwegian, Swedish, Danish
			West Germanic	Continental	*Old Saxon, Low German dialects, Dutch (including Flemish, Afrikaans), German (including *Old High German, Yiddish)
				Anglo-Frisian	Frisian English (including *Old English, *Middle English, Scots)
		Balto-Slavic: Baltic			*Old Prussian, Lithuanian, Lettish
		Slavic	North Slavic: West Slavic		Polish, Kashubian, *Polabian, Lusatian (Upper and Lower Sorb), Czech (including Moravian), Slovak

*Languages no longer spoken.

TABLE 7.4 *(Continued)*

Phylum	Superfamily	Family	Subfamily	Language group	Languages
			East Slavic		Russian, White Russian (= Belorussian), Ukrainian
			South Slavic		Slovene, Serbo-Croatian, Macedonian, Bulgarian, *Old Church Slavonic
	[possibly South and West European]	Thraco-Illyriah			*Thracian, *Illyrian, *Venetic, *Messapic, Albanian
		[possibly Hellenic]			*Ancient Macedonian
		[unclassified]			*Phrygian
					*Tocharian
Afroasiatic		Semitic	East Semitic		*Akkadian, *Babylonian
			North Semitic	Canaanite	*Old Canaanite, *Moabite, *Phoenician (including *Punic, *Carthaginian), *Hebrew, Modern Hebrew, Ugaritic
				Aramaic	*Biblical Aramaic, *Nabataean, *Samaritan, *Mandean, *Syriac, New West Aramaic, New East Aramaic
			South Semitic	Arabic	Classical Arabic, Modern Arabic dialects
				South Arabian	*Mineo-Sabean, Soqotri
				Ethiopic	Gez, Amharic, Tigre, Tigrinya, etc.
		Ancient Egyptian			*Egyptian, *Coptic
		Berber			Tuareg, Rifian, *Canary Islands, etc.
		Cushitic			Somali, Danakil, Sidoma, etc.
		Chadic			Hausa; related languages
				[8 other groups]	[some 50 languages in Nigeria]
Niger-Congo	[Niger-Congo proper]	Atlantic			Wolof, Temne, Fulani; many languages spoken in Senegal, Guinea, Sierra Leone
				Mandingo languages	Mende, Malinka, Bambara, Dyula, etc.
		Voltaic		Senufo languages	[several languages]
				Gur languages	[many languages in Volta, Ghana]; More, Mossi Dagomba, Dogon
		Kwa		Akan languages	[in Ivory Coast, Ghana]
					Fon [in Dahomey], Gan [in Accra, capital of Ghana]
				[other]	Yoruba, Ibo, Nupe, Bini
		Benue-Niger		Bantu	Swahili, Zulu, Xhosa, Pedi, Sotho, Chwana, Thonga, Shitswa, Nyanja, Sbona, Bemba, Kikuyu, Luganda, Nyaruanda, Rundi, Umbundi, Kimbundu, Luba, Kikongo, Lingala, Mongo-Nkuda, etc.
				[Non-Bantu]	Tiv, Jukun, Efik, etc.
					Ijo
				Adamawa	[languages in Nigeria and Cameroons]
		Eastern			Zande, Banda, Sango

TABLE 7.4 (*Continued*)

Phylum	Superfamily	Family	Subfamily	Language group	Languages
				Kordofanian	[languages in Nuba hills, in Sudan]
Sudanic	Chari-Nile	Eastern Chari-Nile		Nubian languages	[Nile Valley, Kordofan, Darfur]
			Nilotic	Western Nilotic	Shilluk, Dinka, Nuer, Lango
				Eastern Nilotic	Masai, Bari, Turkana, Lotuho
				Southern Nilotic	Nandi-Suk
		Central Chari-Nile			Mangbetu
				Sara-Bagirmi languages	[in Chad]
	Saharan				Kanuri, Teda, Daza
				Maban languages	Wadai
				Furian	
					Songhai [in Timbuktu]
				Koman languages	[at Sudan-Ethiopian border]
Click languages		Khoisan		Northern	
				Central	Hottentot
				Southern	
					Sandawe
					Hatsa
[Affiliation unknown]					*Meroitic
Ural-Altaic	Uralic	Finno-Ugric	Finnic		Mordvinian, Cheremis, Permian, Komi, Udmurt
					Finnish, Estonian, etc.
					Lappish
			Ugric	Ob-Ugric	Vogul, Ostyak, etc.
					Hungarian or Magyar
		Samoyed			Tawgi, Yenisey, Samoyed, etc.
		Turkic		East Turkic	Altai, Uigur, etc.
				West Turkic	Kirghiz, Bashkir, Kazakh, Karakalpak, etc.
				Central Turkic	Kashgar, Uzbek, Nogay
				South Turkic	Turkmenian, Azerbaijanian, Turkish
					Yakut
					Chuvash
		Mongolic			Mongol, Buryat, Dagur, Oyrot, etc.
		Tunguzic			Manchu; Tunguz languages of Manchuria
Paleoasiatic [a geographical group, not known to be a single phylum]		Yukaghir [=Odul]			Kolyma, Tundra, Khuvantsy
		Chukchean			Chukchee [=Luoravetlan], Koryak [=Nymylvan], Kamchadal [=Itelmen]
					Gilyak [=Nivkh]
					Ainu
				Yeniseyan	*Ket, *Kott
Caucasic [not proved to be a phylum]		Kartvelian			Georgian, Mingrelian, Laz, Svan
	North Caucasic	Checheno-Lesgian			Chechenian, Ingush, etc.
		Awaro-Andi			Awar, Andi, etc.
		Abazgo-Kerket			Adyghe, Ubykh, Abkhaz, etc.
					[other languages]

TABLE 7.4 (Continued)

Phylum	Superfamily	Family	Subfamily	Language group	Languages
[Mediterranean?]					*Sumerian [Caucasic?— Ural-Altaic?]
					*Elamite [unknown affiliation]
					*Etruscan [pre-Indo-Hittite?]
					Basque
					Burushaski [pre-Indo-Hittite?]
					[Other ancient extinct languages]
		Dravidian			Tamil, Malayalam, Kanarese, Badaga, Kota, Toda, Telugu, Brahui, etc.
				Andamanese	[Several closely similar languages]
Malayo-Poly-nesian		Malayan	Western		Malagasy, Formosan, Chamorro, etc.
				Philippine languages	Tagalog, Bisayan, Ilocano, Igorot, Bataan, Magindanao, etc.
					Malay, Bahasa Indonesia, Sumatran languages, Javanese, Balinese, etc.
			Eastern		[eastern islands of Indonesia]
		Melanesian			New Caledonian, New Hebrides, Solomon Islands, etc.
		Micronesian			Caroline Islands, Yap, Ponape, Gilbert Islands, Marshall Islands, etc.
		Polynesian			Samoan, Futuna, Uvea, Tonga, Maori, Tahitian, Marquesan, Hawaiian, Rapanui (Easter Island), etc.
		Austro-Asiatic	Mon-Khmer		Cambodian (Khmer), Cham, Semang, Sakai, etc.
				Nicobarese	[several languages]
					Khasi
			Munda		[Himalayan languages— possibly Sino-Tibetan]
					Chota-Nagpur languages
					Vietnamese, Muong languages
					Papuan [New Guinea] languages, relations not known
	Australian				[many languages]
		Tasmanian			
				Japanese	Japanese proper, Okinawan
					Korean
Sino-Tibetan	Tibeto-Burman	Tibetan			Tibetan proper (Bodish), Sherpa, Sikkim, Lepcha, etc.
		Burman			Kachin
				Burman	Burmese, Arakanese, Karen
		Chinese			North Chinese (including Literary Chinese), Cantonese, Hakka, etc.
		Thai			Siamese, Laotian, etc.
Eskimoan		Eskimo			Greenlandic, Central Eskimo, Alaskan Eskimo, etc.
		Aleutian			Aleutian
Na-Dene					Haida
					Eyak
	Dene				Tlingit

TABLE 7.4 (Continued)

Phylum	Superfamily	Family	Subfamily	Language group	Languages
		Athabascan		Northern	Kuchin, Chipewyan, Sarsi, etc.
				Pacific	Hupa, Mattole, etc.
				Southern	Navaho, Apache languages
Algonkian-Mosan		Algonkian-Ritwan	Ritwan		Wiyot, Yurok
			Algonkian	Eastern	Micmac, Abnaki, Malecite, Penobscot, Passamaquoddy, *Mohegan, *Narragansett, etc.
				Central	Delaware, *Mohican, *Miami, *Illinois, Potawatomi, Ottawa, Algonkin, Ojibwa, Shawnee, Kickapoo, Sauk, Fox, Menomini, Cree, etc.
				Western	Blackfoot, Cheyenne, Arapaho, Gros Ventres
					*Beothuk [relationship not certain]
					Kutenai
	Mosan	Wakashan			Nootka, Kwakiutl, etc.
		Chimakuan			Chimakum, Quileut
		Salishan			Coeur-d'Alene, Kalispel, Belacoola, Tillamuk, etc.
Macro-Penutian	Penutian	Californian Penutian			*Miwok, *Costanoan, Wintun, Yokuts, Maidu, etc.
		Oregon Penutian			Takelma, Coos, Kalapuya, etc.
		Chinookan			Chinook, Wishram
					Tsimshian
		Mixe-Zoquean			Mixe, Popoluca of Veracruz, Zoque, Huave
					Xinca, Lenca, [possibly Chibchan]; Jicaque [Hokan?]
		Sahaptian			Sahaptian, Nez-Percé, Klamath, Modoc, etc.
	Azteco-Tanoan	Uto-Aztecan	South Californian U-A		*Luiseño, *Gabrielino, Tubatulabal
			Hopian		Hopi, Paviotso, Mono, etc.
			Utan		Ute, Paiute
					Shoshoni, Comanche
					Tarahumara, Cahita (including Yaqui)
			Aztecoidan	Nahuatl	Nahuatl proper (=Aztec, Mexicano); etc.
				Nahuatl	[Dialects in Southern Mexico and Guatemala]
				Piman	Pima, Papago
		Tano-Kiowan	Kiowan		Kiowa
			Tanoan	Tiwa	Taos, Picuris, Sandia, Isleta, *Piro, etc.
				Tewa	Santa Clara, San Juan, San Ildefonso, Nambe, Pojoaque, Tesuque, Hano
				Towa	*Pecos, Jemez
[Possibly part of Macro-Penutian]	Mayoid	Huastecan			Huastec, etc.
		Mayan			Maya, Yucatec, Lacandón, Chontal, Chol, Tzeltal, Tzotzil, etc.
		Quichoid			Mam, Quiché, etc.
[Possibly Macro-Penutian]					Totonac

TABLE 7.4 (*Continued*)

Phylum	Superfamily	Family	Subfamily	Language group	Languages
					Zuni [relations not known, probably not Macro-Penutian]
Hokan-Siouan [possibly not a valid phylum]	Hokan-Coahuiltecan	Hokan			Achumawi, Shasta, Karok, Pomo, Washo, etc.
		Esselen-Yuma			*Esselen
			Yuman		Havasupai, Walapai, Yavapai, Mohave, Yuma, etc.
		Salinan-Serian			Salinan, Chumash, Seri
		Subtiaban			*Subtiaba, *Tlapanec
		Coahuiltecan			Tonkawa, Karankawa, etc.
		Yukian			Yuki
		Keresan		Eastern	Cochiti, Zia, Santa Ana, San Felipe, Santo Domingo
				Western	Acoma, Laguna
	Iroquois-Caddoan	Caddoan			Caddo, Wichita, Pawnee, etc.
		Iroquoian			*Huron, *Erie, Iroquois (Mohawk, Oneida, Onondaga, Cayuga, Seneca, Tuscarora), *Conestoga, *Susquehanna, Cherokee
		Siouan [possibly related to Algonkian-Ritwan]			Iowa, Oto, Missouri, Omaha, Ponca, Osage, Dakota, Assiniboin, Winnebago, Mandan, Hidatsa, Crow, *Ofo, *Biloxi, Catawba
					Yuchi
	Gulf [possibly related to Algonkian-Ritwan]	Natchez			Natchez, Taensa
		Muskogean			Choctaw, Chickasaw, *Alabama, *Koasati, *Hitchiti, Creek (=Muskogee), Seminole, etc.
		Waicurian			*Waicuri, etc. [relationship not known]
					*Timucuan [relationship not known]
Macro-otomanguean	Otomanguean	Otomian			Otomi, etc.
		Popolocan			Popoloca, etc.
		Mazatecan			Mazatec, etc.
					Trique
					Chiapanec, etc.
		Mixtecan			Mixtec, Cuicatec, Amusgo
		Zapotecan		Zapotec	[several languages]
					Chatino
		Chinantecan			Chinantec
					Tarascan
[Possibly Macro-Chibchan]	Misquito-Matagalpan				Misquito, etc.
		Suman			[Many languages]
		Matagalpan			
[Unclassified]					Cuitlatec [and some others in Mexico]
[Macro-Chibchan]		Chibchan			[Languages in Central America and Colombia, including: Guaymi, Cuna, Chibcha, etc.]
		Cariban			[*Languages of the West Indies]: "Black Carib" of Honduras, Dominica Island, [languages of northern South America, including some south of the Amazon].

TABLE 7.4 (Continued)

Phylum	Superfamily	Family	Subfamily	Language group	Languages
		Arawakan		Island Arawakan	*Ciboney, *Taino, Arawak, [languages north and south of the Amazon]
	Macro-Gê	Gê			[A number of languages]
		[Several others]			Caingang, Botocudo, etc.
	Tupi-Guarani	Guaranian			[A number of languages]
		Tupian			Tupi proper or "lingua geral"; others
	Quechumaran	Quechuan			Quechua of Cuzco, etc.
		Aymaran			Aymara
[The rest of this part of the list, down to the next heavy line, is of families or languages in South America whose relationships have not been established.]		Catuquinan			Catuquina, etc. [many languages]
		Tucanoan			Tucano, etc. [many languages]
		Panoan			Amahuaca, etc. [a number of languages]
		Macro-Guaicuruan			[several languages]
		Araucanian			Picunche, Mapuche, Huilliche, Chilote
		Chon			Tehuelche, Ona
					Several hundred unclassified languages, including Alacaluf, Yahgan, Chono, Charrua, Bororo, Jivaro, Witoto, Puelche—to list a few languages that have been reported on in linguistic journals.
					Pidgin languages: *Lingua franca (based on medieval Romanic); Pidgin English—Chinese, Melanesian (=Neo-melanesian), Taki-Taki (in Dutch Guiana); Haitian Creole (French), French pidgin in Pacific, and in West Africa; Papiamento (Spanish—in Curaçao); *Chinook Jargon (Chinookan—NW United States); Russenorsk (Russian-Norwegian), Russian-Mongolian; etc.
					Constructed auxiliary languages: Volapük (based chiefly on Germanic), Esperanto (Romanic and Slavic), Ido (Romanic), Novial (Romanic and Germanic), Interlingua (Latin), etc.

Source: George L. Trager, "Languages of the World," Collier's Encyclopedia, Vol. 14, pp. 305–310, 1967.

*Languages no longer spoken.

was Aramaic. Important derivations of Aramaic were the Classical Hebrew, Arabic, and Brahmi scripts. The Arabic scripts became the forms of writing adapted by the Persian, and later the Ottoman, Empire; Arabic was spread as the language of Islam and the writing of the Qur'ān, the sacred book, from North Africa through western, southern, southeast, and central Asia. The Brahmic scripts were the forerunners of all the other scripts of India, some of which in turn spread to southeast Asia.

The linkage of language with writing is a cultural achievement, as a people come to adopt, and adapt, one or more forms of alphabet, numerals, and writing styles that they have received by diffusion from an often nearby source region as a result of

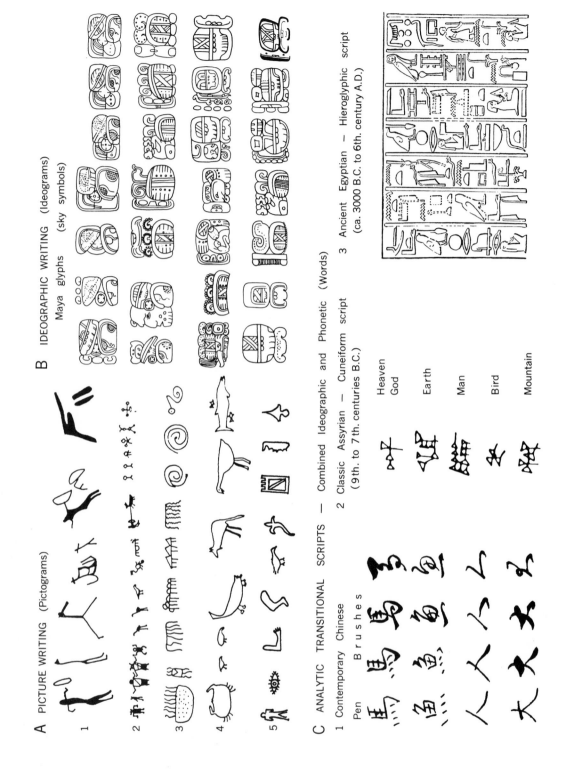

A PICTURE WRITING (Pictograms)

1

2

3

4

5

B IDEOGRAPHIC WRITING (Ideograms)

Maya glyphs (sky symbols)

3 Ancient Egyptian – Hieroglyphic script
(ca. 3000 B.C. to 6th. century A.D.)

C ANALYTIC TRANSITIONAL SCRIPTS – Combined Ideographic and Phonetic (Words)

1 Contemporary Chinese

Pen   Brushes

2 Classic Assyrian – Cuneiform script
(9th. to 7th. centuries B.C.)

Heaven
God

Earth

Man

Bird

Mountain

312

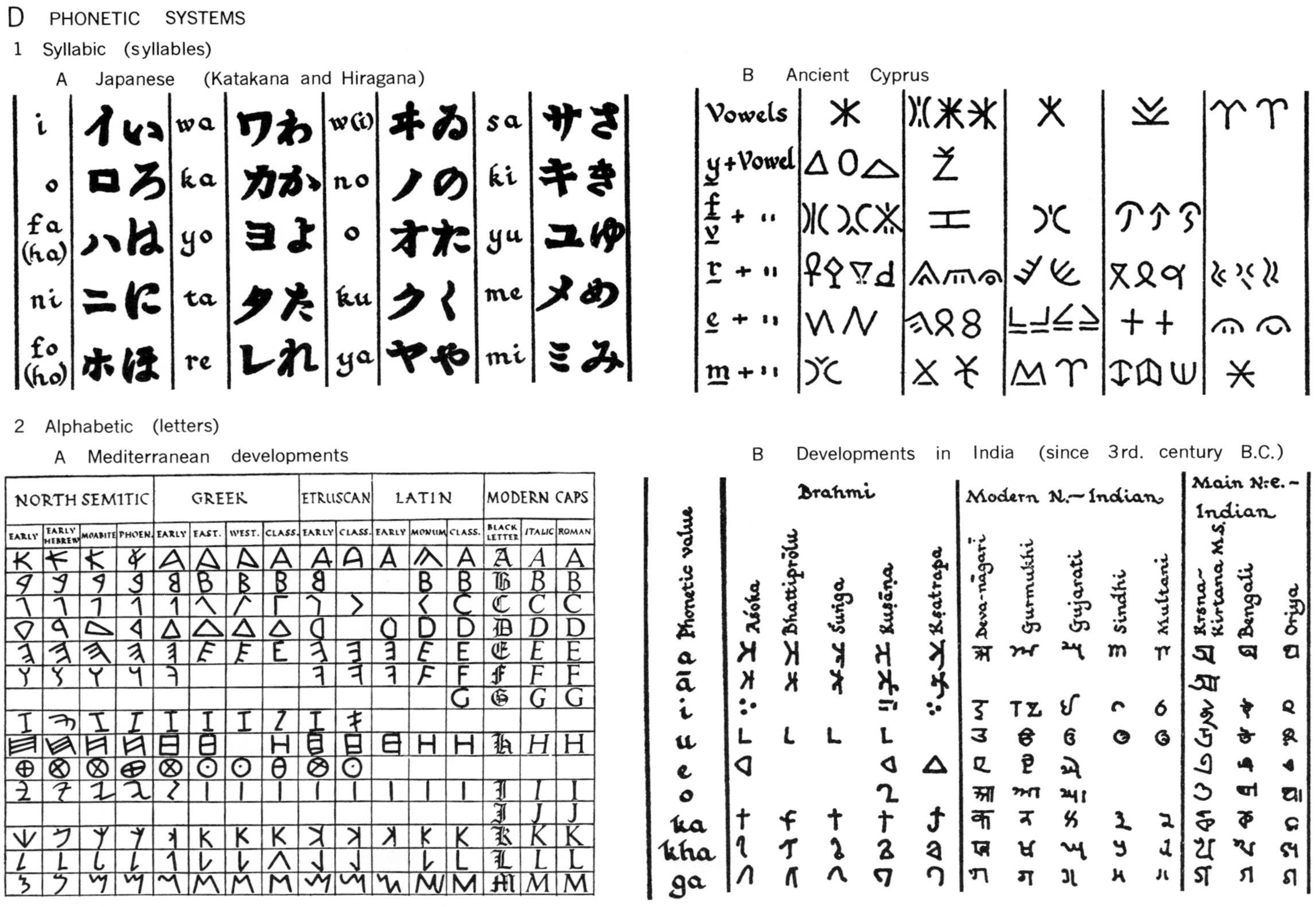

D PHONETIC SYSTEMS

1 Syllabic (syllables)

A Japanese (Katakana and Hiragana)

B Ancient Cyprus

2 Alphabetic (letters)

A Mediterranean developments

NORTH SEMITIC				GREEK				ETRUSCAN		LATIN			MODERN CAPS	
EARLY	EARLY HEBREW	MOABITE	PHOEN.	EARLY	EAST.	WEST.	CLASS.	EARLY	CLASS.	EARLY	MONUM.	CLASS.	BLACK LETTER	ITALIC ROMAN

B Developments in India (since 3rd. century B.C.)

Brāhmī

Developments in India (since 3rd. century B.C.)

Modern N.-Indian

Main Nre.- Indian

FIG. 7.8 FORMS OF WRITING. Sources: (A) From *Writing* (Ancient Peoples and Places Series) 1962, by David Diringer, by permission of Frederick A. Praeger, Inc. (B) From *Maya Hieroglyphic Writing*, by J. Eric S. Thompson. (1960) Copyright by the University of Oklahoma Press. (C) Item 1, From *Beginning Chinese* by John De Francis, (1963) by permission of the Yale University Press; Item 2, From *Writing* (Ancient Peoples and Places Series) 1962, by David Diringer, by permission of Frederick A. Praeger, Inc.; Item 3, Adapted from *The Tomb of the Vizier Ramose* by N. de Garis Davies, by permission of the Egypt Exploration Society. (D) From *Writing* (Ancient Peoples and Places Series) 1962, by David Diringer, by permission of Frederick A. Praeger, Inc.

313

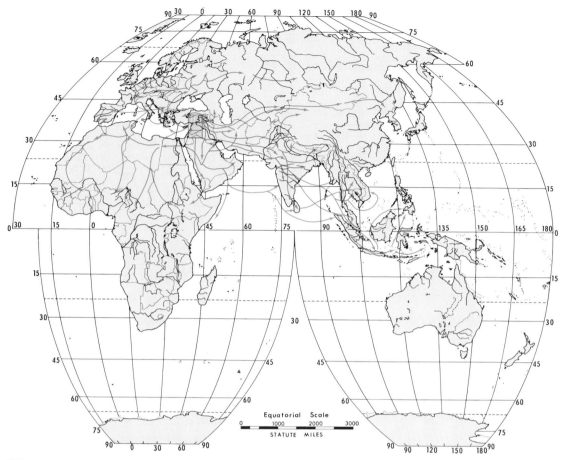

FIG. 7.9 DIFFUSION OF THE IDEA AND USE OF ALPHABETIC WRITING.

cultural contact. Perhaps the best way to illustrate the process and the results attained is to present an unfamiliar example, that of Cambodia (see Fig. 1.7B, p. 21).

Cambodian is the language of the Khmer people, some 5½ million of whom live in the country they call Srok Khmer. The name Kambuja was first popularized abroad by the Portuguese; English-speaking peoples now use the name Kingdom of Cambodia to designate the southeast Asian country. In addition, some 600,000 Khmer live in the Mekong delta region of South Viet-Nam and several thousand around the provincial capital of Pakse in southern Laos, whereas about one million people in eastern Thailand speak a variety of Cambodian dialects. The spoken language is of the Mon-Khmer family of languages, characterized as nontonal and nonpolysyllabic in contrast to the adjacent tonal languages of Thai and Viet-Namese and the polysyllabic language of Indonesian or Malay.

When the Khmer people accepted the civilizing influence of India in the first centuries of our era, Sanskrit terms and writing were taken over and adapted to Cambodian speech; then in the fourteenth to fifteenth centuries, when Theravada (Hinayana) Buddhism diffused by way of Ceylon and replaced Brahmanism and Mahayana Buddhism in Cambodia, the new model became the Pali language and its forms of writing. The Cambodian alphabet and numerals thus derive from southern, rather than northern, India. Modern Cambodian uses two forms of writing (Fig. 7.10): "oblique script," based upon popular handwriting, for most printed works; and "round script," preserving twelfth-and thirteenth-century usage, for religious texts, formal inscriptions, and to provide variation or emphasis (where English uses *italics*, or slant letters, Cambodian uses vertical letters).

The major alphabets of Europe also owe their present distribution to the forces of religion. Adherents of the Eastern Orthodox Catholic Church learned to use the Cyrillic alphabet, as adapted from the Greek, whereas the Latin alphabet (of 23 letters, the J, U, and W being added during the Middle Ages) was used by the Roman Catholic Church in the West. The Latin alphabet thus came to be the one most spread around the world by the expanding Western Europeans. This is the way in which the alphabet and writing system used by Americans was diffused to the New World. We write an Etruscan-Roman variant of a Greek form of an alphabet invented in or near Phoenicia by a North Semitic people on the basis of their adaptation of nonalphabetic writing in still earlier cultures. The Latin alphabet has been used by missionaries and others to create a form of writing for contemporary languages lacking developed scripts of their own (e.g., Karen in Burma) or to effect a change from a previously used form (e.g., Viet-Namese). Governmental reforms have further spread the Latin alphabet (e.g., with slight variations to accommodate phonetic differences, as in Turkey, replacing Arabic in 1928; in Communist China to increase literacy and efficiency in mass communication). As a result, probably more people

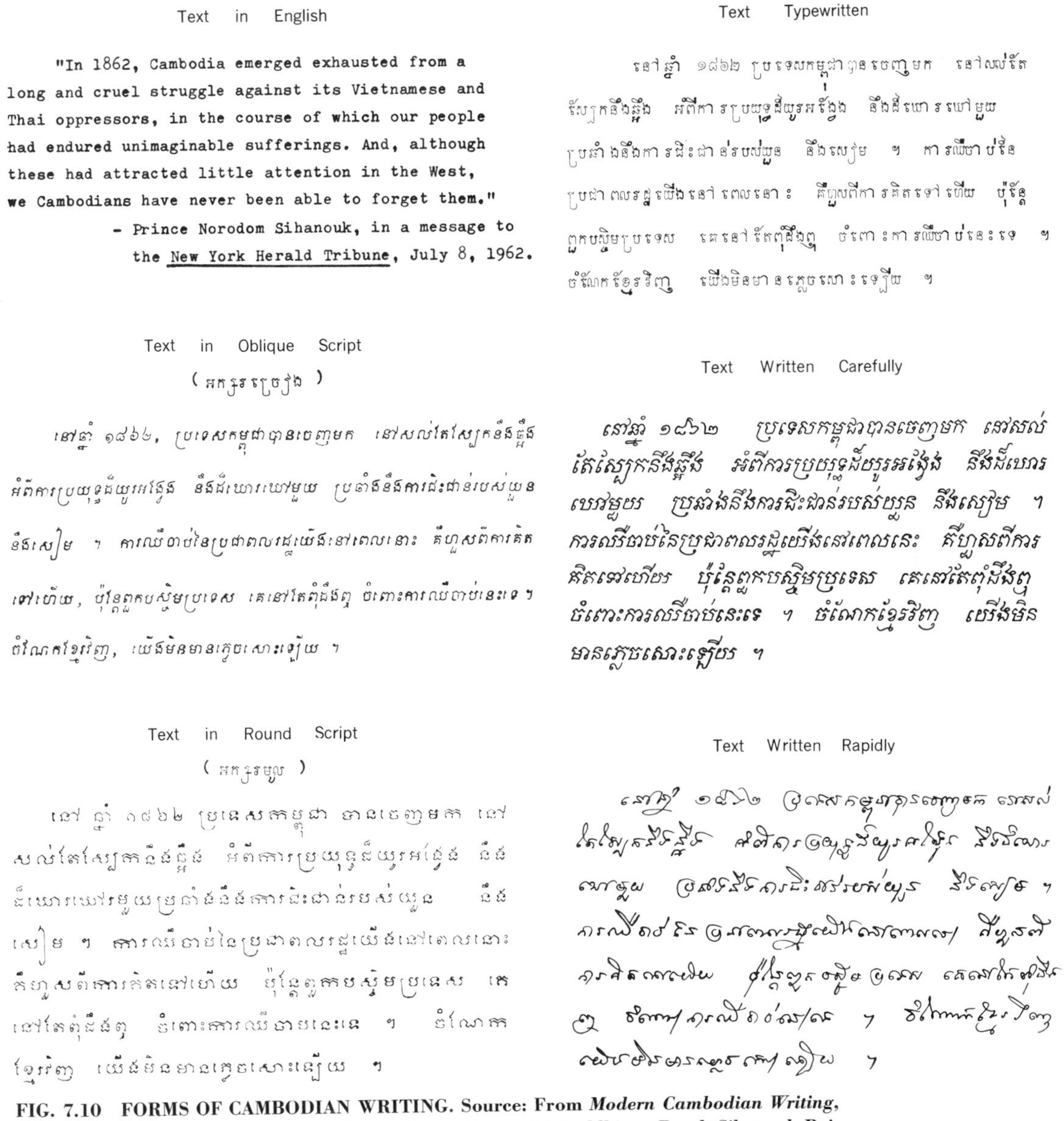

Text in English

"In 1862, Cambodia emerged exhausted from a long and cruel struggle against its Vietnamese and Thai oppressors, in the course of which our people had endured unimaginable sufferings. And, although these had attracted little attention in the West, we Cambodians have never been able to forget them."

    - Prince Norodom Sihanouk, in a message to
    the New York Herald Tribune, July 8, 1962.

Text Typewritten

Text in Oblique Script

Text Written Carefully

Text in Round Script

Text Written Rapidly

FIG. 7.10   FORMS OF CAMBODIAN WRITING. Source: From *Modern Cambodian Writing*, 1962, by Derek Tonkin. Phnom Penh: Université Buddhique Preah Sihanouk Raj.

in the world are familiar with the Latin alphabet than with any other form of writing or printing. The attributes of the Latin alphabet are its simplicity and flexibility for nontonal languages, since it contains both consonants and vowels. Throughout the present-day world, the greatest volume of information and entertainment is disseminated and the most extensive campaigns to reduce illiteracy are overwhelmingly in those languages that employ the Latin alphabet in their forms of writing.

Educational Systems

Systems of education have long been in existence. For a millennium or more, scholars from Japan, Korea, India, and southeast Asia traveled to China, as the center of learning for eastern Asia, and upon return spread the wisdom of Confucius and other sages by means of curricula based upon the Confucian classics. In Western Europe prior to the sixteenth century, the Roman Catholic Church, regarded as the custodian of truth and the proper agent for dispensing it, held a monopoly in education. As an international institution with a highly centralized, hierarchical administration, the Church operated its schools with a uniform curriculum, based upon a single language, Latin. The independent European nations that emerged from the Protestant Reformation created systems of education that were nationally, rather than internationally, focused with instruction based upon local vernaculars side by side with Latin schools and the universities. Prussia, in the eighteenth century, attracted wide attention with its program of universal education, combined with compulsory military training. To these two factors were attributed Prussia's rapid rise to political power, based upon military superiority, strong economy, and efficient organization. In the late nineteenth century, the Japanese government rejected classical Chinese learning, sent hundreds of young men to study in Europe and the United States, and quickly acquired the knowledge needed to industrialize the nation. The Japanese educational system was reconstructed along Western lines, new schools were introduced, and Western scholars afforded positions of honor in Japanese universities.

It would be easy to say that there exist today as many systems of education as there are nation-states and internal self-governing territories. But such a statement would be too easy and would overlook the existence of certain elements useful for purposes of general comparison. We here distinguish three categories of social philosophy (i.e., what the educating society hopes to achieve in educating its young) which serve to establish the social role of the schools (Fig. 7.11). These are:

1. Belief that knowledge of the good and the true is *received* from a supernatural source.
2. Belief that knowledge of the good and the true is *discovered* in nature or in the processes of the natural universe.
3. Belief that knowledge of the good and the true *evolves* out of intellectual processes, derived from the everyday experiences of ordinary men.

The educational significance of each of these three social philosophies is that the selection of societal leaders for each is substantially different and the educational systems supported by each reflect these differences in the opportunities they afford to members of their societies.

There are a number of societies whose members believe they have received, or are continuing to receive, knowledge of the good and the true in some extraordinary way from a source external to the temporal events of day-to-day experience. Differences occur among such societies only in the social means of "receiving" the revealed knowledge. The traditions based upon revelation include the Jewish, Islamic, Christian, Hindu, Buddhist, and Shinto.

Two examples provide a contrast in educational methods. The educational systems maintained by persons of Jewish faith teach children, especially boys, to read the Books of Moses and other prophets as a guide for direction of their personal affairs in daily life. Hebrew schools are created wherever a congregation of Jews exists, or the instruction is given in the home by Jewish parents. Self-sufficiency and independence are the rule, because adherence to the revealed truth does not call for a highly structured social organization or a strong hierarchical system of control. Roman Catholics believe that God has delegated sovereignty and the authority to interpret His will to the head of the Church. In Spain, for example, the Church is recognized as the spokesman for God and is acknowledged as the supreme power by the head of the state and the people. The Church long exercised certain veto rights in civil affairs, priority in education, and a monopoly in religion. Education not only promotes policy made by religious authority but also justifies the existing sociopolitical

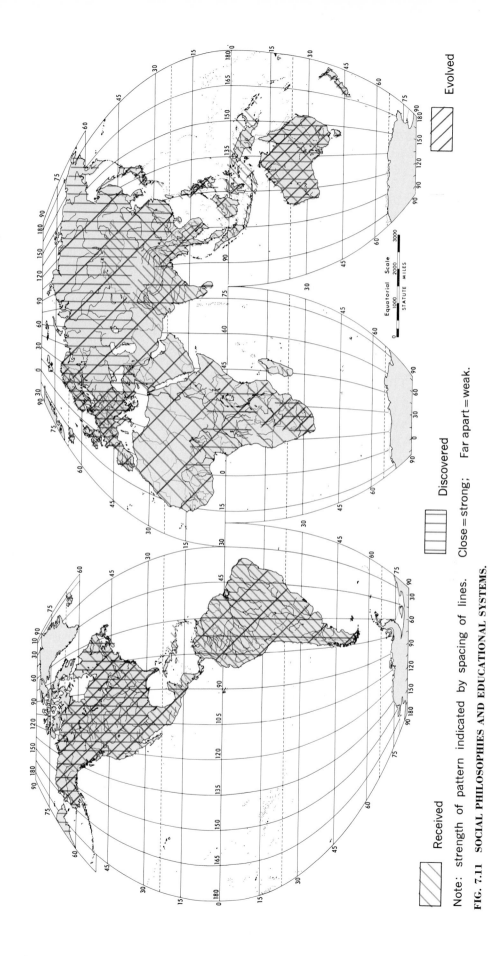

Evolved

Discovered

Close = strong;   Far apart = weak.

Received

Note: strength of pattern indicated by spacing of lines.

FIG. 7.11 SOCIAL PHILOSOPHIES AND EDUCATIONAL SYSTEMS.

Equatorial Scale

317

structure by means of theological argument. Not only is the established Church recognized by the state, but the state also includes a prescribed form of religious instruction in the official system of education. The preamble to the Primary Education Act of 1945 states that the primary schools "must provide first and foremost a Catholic education." In Spain religion and government are intimately interwoven: the Head of State, in effect, is the chief administrative officer of the Spanish branch of the Roman Catholic Church, and, in turn, Roman Catholicism is the proclaimed official and protected religion. Members of clergy have judicial immunity, and the hierarchy reviews, with the privilege of rejection, all appointments to public office. Thus teachers in state schools must be acceptable to the Church and the curriculum and content of specific courses must pass its inspection. The effect is to impose a social and political, as well as theological, orthodoxy. Not until 1967 did some relaxation of restrictions on Protestants occur.

The second category of social philosophy includes those that assume "discovery" through observing objects and processes in the natural universe. The discovery process is a natural phenomenon, whose method can be taught. Proficiency in its use can be developed and the attainment of results can only follow an expenditure of effort in promoting the search for knowledge. Education, under this social philosophy, is a matter of great importance and is usually provided at public expense to those regarded as capable of benefitting from it. Usually only a small proportion of the population is considered intellectually talented, hence, provided with intensive training.

Again, two examples are presented, from France and the Soviet Union. French social philosophy, since the eighteenth-century "Age of Enlightenment," adhered to a rational method for discovering knowledge, whose essence was the absolute dependence on inductive logic. After the Revolution, church control of schools was abolished and a system of public schools under centralized civil control substituted. But these were not for everyone, since the ability to reason was not believed to be equal in all men. After 1870, the secondary schools had the purpose to locate and produce future leaders with the ' best minds" to direct national affairs. The education system was highly selective and a child's future status was determined at age six, when he was entered in school. Private primary schools (*Classes préparatoires*) led to municipal or state secondary schools, thence on to great schools or universities for those who became the intellectual elite. For the masses, public elementary schools prepared for trade and vocational schools, schools of commerce, and the normal schools. Not until 1925 could a gifted public elementary school student, by passing a rigorous examination, transfer to a secondary school and aspire to a university career. The selective "two-track" system existed until their consolidation as part of the reforms of 1959. Now compulsory school attendance has been extended to age sixteen, progress from elementary to the secondary level is automatic, and guidance counseling, rather than a written examination, determines the kind of secondary program to be followed. Since 1960 the French have accepted a new educational ideal: no longer an exclusively intellectual education, but instruction for each student to the extent of his capacities. The French educational system has become more open, yet the highly centralized control insures that the policy-making positions, the higher administrative posts, and the civil service favor those with the best records in the higher educational institutions.

The Soviet Union operates by the method of inquiry known as dialectical materialism. Only those individuals thought to have a special talent for discovering knowledge by this method are given a unique and separate education, accorded special privileges, and elevated to the status of a ruling elite, which decides upon policies affecting the good of all Soviet citizens. The election machinery prevents persons from being appointed to policy-making and executive posts unless they are qualified as members of the expert class, the Communist party. The party organization is centralized and directs its authority downward to the local level; it identifies and trains leaders and makes their control effective at all levels. Education is used as a chief instrument of the state to produce Soviet citizens. Attendance in schools is compulsory and free in accordance with the goal of equal educational opportunity for all; the schools train the masses for socially useful roles through literacy, emphasis upon science and engineering, technical skills, productive habits of work, and Communist theories of society and ethics. However, the identification of potential future leaders and their specialized educational development is left to the party, which operates through its Communist youth organizations.

The third category of social philosophy focuses upon knowledge that has evolved or is constructed from human experiences. Such knowledge is neither complete nor infallible, hence the societal institutions it creates constantly require adjustment and sometimes replacement. Since all men are not alike in their knowledge, experiences, and prejudices, the highest validity lies in group, rather than individual, judgments. Hence, societal authority is held to reside with the people, and societal institutions are created and controlled by society as common endeavors. Communications are facilitated and wide participation in decision making is encouraged, so that all may benefit from the policy of diverse experiences and opinions. The decision-making role is shared by all, and no individual or special interest group is permitted to force its will upon the total group.

The example of Switzerland will suffice as an illustration. The Swiss enjoy one of the highest literacy rates in the world, but no single educational pattern is followed, no central administrative agency for education exists, and there is no uniform set of laws regulating instruction. Educational authority is divided among the 25 *Cantons*, or states, and the local *Gemeinde*, or communities. Elementary education is compulsory and free for eight years; secondary schools of various types charge fees, except in Zürich, but provide grants for needy children. Only seven cantons have universities, but maturity examinations, applied uniformly among the cantons, guarantee admission to the universities to anyone who meets the minimal requirements. Educational opportunities are extended to all classes of students everywhere in the country. Great freedom exists to experiment in educational practices through local self-government. The social role of education is to enable the people to retain their sovereignty and to make the exercise of their powers both efficient and personally rewarding. Schools are expected to encourage social mobility and cultivate special talent wherever found. The Swiss social philosophy attributes dignity to all individuals and values their active participation in decision making in government, education, and other aspects of life.

As the example of France indicates, the world trend in educational systems is a slow change from categories one and two toward category three. Educational programs in such diverse places as Great Britain, Japan, and the newly emerging,

former colonial areas of Africa and Asia are being expanded and revised to afford a greater measure of individual opportunity and self-determination. Provision of industrial, technical, and vocational training is assisting the creation of a middle class in societies formerly divided between a higher class of educated elite and a lower class of workers. National educational systems now being revised or newly instituted inevitably will raise the general economic and cultural levels of their societies and afford opportunities for more children to rise above the economic and social level of their ancestors and parents.

Out of Many: The Trend Toward a Universal Community

Most of the writings about the European colonial period have been studies of the particular, tending to emphasize differences: between white and nonwhite, dominant and subordinate, rich and poor. The differences in policies and behavior among the Europeans, themselves, also have been abundantly emphasized. But the colonial era was only a brief period of human time on the earth which made possible a vast worldwide cultural diffusion quite without precedent. Rather than creating insuperable differences, the European imperialism resulted in making the earth more uniform, because it was the mechanism that spread the great revolution of the West to the rest of the world.

The Occident during the eighteenth and nineteenth centuries, not only expanded its commercial exploitation and political domination, but also sowed the seeds for removal of its dominant controls over the rest of the earth by transmitting its revolutionary ideas: enlightenment and reason, science and industry, organization of human affairs, the dignity and value of the individual person. Concepts of nationalism, self-determination, freedom, and economic development were European ideas. The meanings and implications of American independence, of the French Revolution, of British constitutional history, and of socialist theory about revolutionary action were not lost upon Asians and Africans.

The will of the colonial powers to maintain their empires declined as the economic value of colonies decreased, some to become economic burdens. Once colonial peoples reached critical levels of development they refused to accede to alien government no matter how efficient and enlightened.

The pent-up demand for self-government was triggered by World War II, which collapsed the southeast Asian colonial empires and left the European powers in a much weakened status without either the resources or the will to perpetuate the old colonial systems in either Asia or Africa. The fundamental contradiction was this: how could Europeans fight a war for freedom and democracy, utilizing, for example, a half million Africans in achieving military victory in Europe, then deny these principles to their colonial peoples. A wave of political independence has swept the world since 1945; in less than one generation most of the world's people became independent; only vestiges of European colonialism remain. The world of 1940 was sharply divided between independent nations and their colonies and nonself-governing territories; the world of the 1960s is much more uniform, the concept of self-government for independent nations almost everywhere prevails (Fig. 7.12). Nationalism has become a worldwide phenomenon in this century; in itself worldwide political nationalism is an advance over sectional colonialism, but it possesses built-in inhibitions against the most effective functioning of our single species on our unitary earthly homeland.

Growing quietly in the minds of men is the gradually emerging concept of a world community, even though political nationalism is stronger today than ever before. The idea of our common humanity, the kinship of all human beings, is more widely recognized today by more people than ever in history. All men have a similar origin, live through a cycle of birth and growth, childhood and youth, sickness and health, love and friendship, sorrow and joy, and share the common destiny of death. The oneness of humanity is no longer a philosophical vision but is becoming historic fact and a guiding principle for thought and action in solving the problems of the future.

Over the past two decades a working partnership has been created in which the richer lands have helped the poorer in their efforts to speed economic development. The rich lands have taken the first step toward wisdom by recognizing that they are small islands of privilege among the vast poverty-stricken lands which contain a majority of the brotherhood of man, far different in cultures, ways of livelihood, and physical appearance. Release of the poor lands from the imprisonment of their poverty will enable latent energies to produce not only things of the hand but also things of the mind

and the spirit so to enrich the lives of all men everywhere. Between 1949 and 1964 annual economic aid from rich lands to poor lands almost trebled, from $1\frac{1}{2}$ to over 4 billion. More than a dozen rich countries are now engaged in regular bilateral programs of economic aid. The Colombo Plan was established in 1950; the International Finance Corporation in 1956; the International Development Association in 1960; the Inter-American Development Bank in 1960; the Alliance for Progress in 1961. The first United Nations Conference on Trade and Development was held in 1964.

Science is certainly one of the forces for universal understanding. Earthquakes, sunlight, gravitation, plant growth are studied as processes of significance for all human beings. The weather, the sun, the planets, the stars must be studied cooperatively. The International Geophysical Year of 1957–1958 brought together more than 60 nations for intense scientific cooperation that examined the earth as a planet. Among the resultant accomplishments were the discovery of the Van Allen radiation belt, the first moon-approach rocket, the first man-made satellite, the first trip under the Arctic ice, the most complete exploration of Antarctica. Science knows no borders; it has become a universal language.

A self-imposed ending of the human adventure on earth is now feasible, whether through mechanical, nuclear, or biological warfare or all three combined. At no great cost per capita, wholesale destruction is possible of all that the world has required millennia to build. This challenge has made our differences of race and religion, class and color, nation and ideology irrelevant for grasping the new realities, in which militarism and nationalism have become outmoded. Throughout the evolutionary continuum from the little communities of isolated tribes to the modern nation-states, a self-righteousness about the cultural values of one's society has spawned collective arrogance and selfishness, and men have fought each other again and again to uphold their distinctive ways of life. Nations are not immortal; they are temporary arrangements for organizing particular segments of earth space. Although they seek permanence, their real achievements are to create new life out of old forms and to transmit the great heritage of arts and skills, ideas and ideals on which further cultural evolution can still build.

There are no more closed societies. The new

order that is emerging is neither national nor continental, neither Oriental nor Occidental, but universal. The new realization is that all members of the human family are bound together, and no nation can be hurt without injury to the rest; frontiers are losing their significance. Each nation is but one of many, and each makes its specific contribution to the richness and variety of the world. The old concept of the nation-state, separate, sovereign, absolute, autonomous, with faith in force, is very slowly but surely giving way to the new universal community with its ideals of cooperation, freedom, peace, and justice under law. Although the world is still studded with missed opportunities, great strides have been made toward accepting peaceful means for settling disputes, averting violence by legal solutions, securing minimum economic conditions of well-being and removing grievances of political subjection and racial discrimination. We are all heirs to the cultural wealth and knowledge of the whole world; full access to this heritage is fundamental for the enrichment of human experience for every individual.

The crisis of our time, our recognition that we are in the midst of an immensely complex world revolution, may be looked upon as the birth pangs of a new world civilization. Men are in process of adjusting their sense of scale to the full planetary dimension of human life. The vision is that of a completely viable world civilization, not necessarily unitary, however, either as a world movement, a world religion, or a world economy. The ideas and prophecies of a new worldwide order have come from many kinds of thinkers (historians, philosophers, sociologists, humanists, biologists) and from many countries. Many different, and often opposed, groups, such as Islam, Roman Catholicism, Bahai Faith, Communism, and others have contributed their views of what the future will bring. Most have been partial views, emphasizing politics, or economy, or religion, or social structure, or science. But, significantly, these various world views, however dissimilar, reveal a near-universal awareness of a need to discover new orientations and objectives for human living. One thing is clear: only those who anticipate the future can achieve the capability of bringing it under control. The present era provides the best opportunity that has ever existed for creating an optimally integrated world, a universal community, a world city, a cosmopolis.

Variety in Unity: An Orchestration of Cultures

Science and industry, education and communication are unifying mankind at the physical and intellectual levels. Humanity is a living community united from within by those values that are inseparable from human dignity and freedom. And yet we cannot conceive of a world without national differences, without cultural variety, without various kinds of artistic wealth. Variations in cultural subsystems impart beauty and creativeness. Global awareness and cooperation through science and technology, and linkages of economic arrangements and political forms, do not necessitate a monotonous uniformity in living. An appreciative respect for cultural differences is both possible and necessary. Indeed, an integrated world community can foster the development, by the varied peoples of the world, of their local customs, arts, languages, and literatures without fear of external pressures for conformity, just as the Welsh or the Basque cultures persist in Great Britain or Spain.

Coordination among all the world's various cultures is analogous to the harmony maintained by the various instruments in an orchestra when the musicians are playing a symphony. Harmony of thought is a major asset in the building of a cosmopolis, just as it is for the building of any particular civilization. A solid framework for traditional American culture, it may be recalled, was provided by Protestant North Europeans who, in the New World, initiated all later immigrants and absorbed their further contributions into the expansive American civilization. A world community can only be a balanced synthesis, a dynamic equilibrium of unity and diversity, with its very vitality stemming from the rich diverseness of its oneness. Various cultures have emphasized various aspects of the truth; the more mankind becomes culturally integrated, the more will these various aspects be recognized as valuable contributions to a larger whole.

Technological society is only the preliminary step toward an ecologically holistic world community. The world is growing together most rapidly on the level of communication, exchange of technology and trade, and least rapidly on the level of beliefs, values, and politico-administrative systems. Whereas the major religions have confronted one another many times in the past, have clashed, split, fused, and produced syncretic offspring, there

322

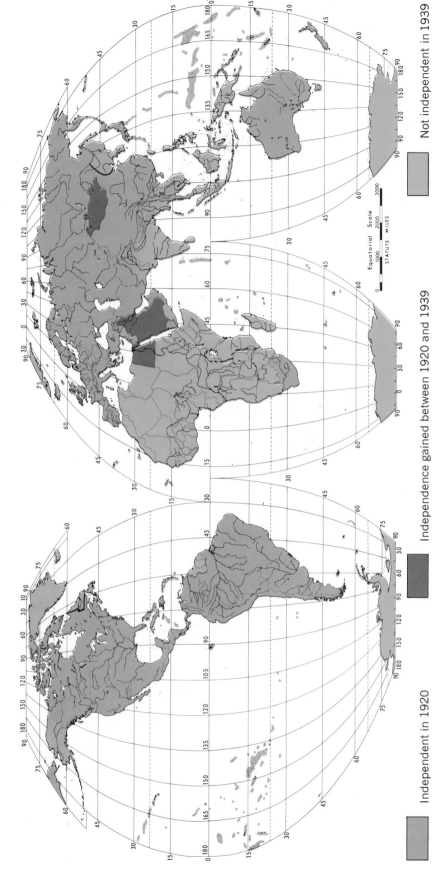

Independent in 1920

Independence gained between 1920 and 1939

Not independent in 1939

Equatorial Scale

STATUTE MILES

FIG. 7.12 THE NEW NATIONS OF THE MID-TWENTIETH CENTURY. A. 1939 Situation.

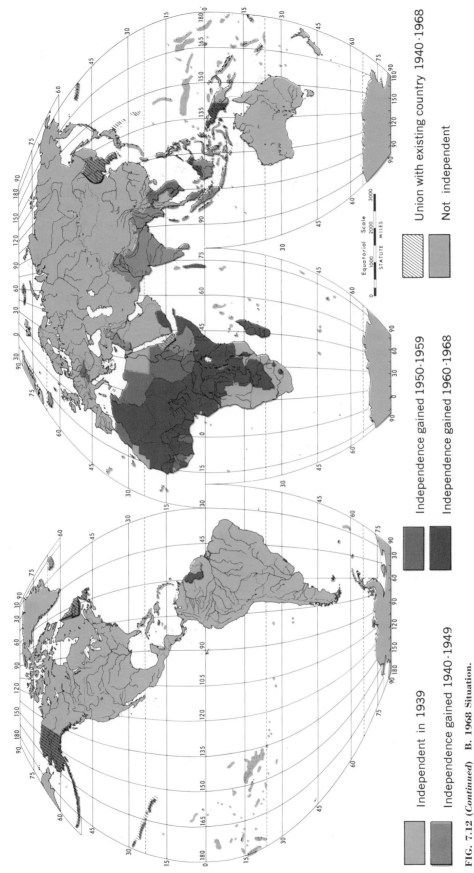

Independent in 1939

Independence gained 1940-1949

Independence gained 1950-1959

Independence gained 1960-1968

Union with existing country 1940-1968

Not independent

Equatorial Scale

1000 2000 3000

STATUTE MILES

FIG. 7.12 *(Continued)* B. 1968 Situation.

323

has never been a time like the present, when all are meeting collectively on a single world stage. The first World Parliament of Religions, with 59 delegates, was assembled at the Chicago Exposition in 1893; the work of synthesis has scarcely had time in which to begin, but recognition of harmony in ethical values has inspired further effort. Full synthesis among the professed universal religions will take a long time; yet, in the twentieth century, forces are at work (e.g., ecumenical movements in both Buddhism and Christianity) to reverse the traditional mode of fission into pluralistic creeds. In the past, each of the higher religions was a product of a particular culture, and its adherents came from that culture and those others to which the religion came to be diffused. Today, in a more open world, the higher religions are freer to appeal across cultural lines to one or more different varieties of human personality. For example, an intuitive Frenchman can become a Buddhist, a Filipino can become a Mormon, or a Black American can be attracted to Islam with its emphasis upon the fraternity of all men regardless of race.

The Immense Journey

Part Two of our volume began with a description of man's Pleistocene inheritance, presented the conditions of man's emergence, and assayed an outline of how man, as a culture bearer, has been able to spread over the earth to become its dominant form of life. The present Part Three began by tracing the effects of cultural divergence in creating regional cultures, to be followed by their partial combination and recombination into a fewer number of regional empires, and ended with consideration of the breakthrough into a global interlinkage initiated by Europeans. Truly, man's journey has been long in distance and immense in scope, as a cultural achievement.

For the greater part of the Pleistocene, the range of man remained restricted to tropical and subtropical Africa. But, by the end of the Middle Pleistocene, a fundamental redistribution of man had taken place: a definitely *sapiens* form of man had succeeded in invading the northern parts of the Old World continents. Once North America was reached, man's expansion progressed quickly, like an irresistible tide, over the New World: only a few thousand years were required to reach Patagonia. The rise out of Africa and the worldwide spreading of *Homo sapiens* was a true humanization of the world.

As a result of this worldwide expansion of Upper Paleolithic man, the human cultures of the Mesolithic were no longer merely tropical and subtropical, but panterrestrial systems of advanced life. Continuous and intensive efforts over many more millennia were required to change a somewhat precarious hold on the earth. Crop growing and protoindustry were cultural inventions of great significance, enabling men slowly to fill the gaps and establish a first network of communications and trade with other groups of men in the several regions of the world.

More than a million years were spent, mainly in Africa, on acquiring the biologic and cultural capacity for a human planetary invasion. Some 30,000 years more were required for the actual occupation of the world's continents. Approximately 11,000 years, the combined Neolithic and most of historical time, until about a century ago, were necessary to affect a consolidation of man's dominance over the earth.

The present process of cultural convergence over the earth's surface is a wholly new experience for the earth and its life-forms. It represents an era of cultural fulfillment for that unusual but ungeneralized primate who created and elaborated culture, became prolific, and made the whole planet his home. Man alone has grasped the concept of evolution. The way is now being opened for yet more astounding achievements, as more and more men are able fully to draw upon the whole of the world's ideas, present and past, and have access to the utilization of the full range of its space, its technology, and its resources.

Such has been the great accomplishment of the human adventure, for which the name "noösphere" (from the Greek *Noös*, "mind") has been suggested to distinguish the human surface of the earth, just as the terms lithosphere, hydrosphere, atmosphere, and biosphere are commonly used to distinguish the earth's other aspects. The evolution of the noösphere has created the conditions necessary to a new transformation of the earth, for such is the nature of the evolutionary process.

SELECTED REFERENCES

Alexander, Lewis M.
  1963 *World Political Patterns* (2nd ed.). Chicago: Rand McNally & Co. 628 pp.
Anene, J. C., and G. N. Brown (eds.)
  1966 *Africa in the Nineteenth and Twentieth Centuries.* London: Ibadan University Press and Thomas Nelson & Sons. 555 pp.
Ayres, C. E.
  1961 *Toward A Reasonable Society: The Values of Industrial Civilization.* Austin: University of Texas Press. 301 pp.
Boulding, Kenneth E.
  1964 *The Meaning of the Twentieth Century: The Great Transition.* New York: Harper & Row. 199 pp.
Bouquet, A. C.
  1962 *Comparative Religion.* Baltimore: Penguin Books. 320 pp.
Chiari, J.
  1964 *Religion and Modern Society.* London: Herbert Jenkins. 215 pp.
Desmonde, William H.
  1962 *Magic, Myth, and Money: The Origin of Money in Religious Ritual.* New York: Free Press of Glencoe. 208 pp.
Fischer, Eric
  1948 *The Passing of the European Age: A Study of the Transfer of Civilization and Its Renewal in Other Continents* (rev. ed.). Cambridge: Harvard University Press. 228 pp.
Frazier, E. Franklin
  1957 *Race and Culture Contacts in the Modern World.* New York: A. A. Knopf. 338 pp.
Hays, H. R.
  1963 *In the Beginnings: Early Man and His Gods.* New York: G. P. Putnam's Sons. 575 pp.
Honnold, John (ed.)
  1964 *The Life of the Law: Readings on the Growth of Legal Institutions.* Glencoe, Ill.: The Free Press. 581 pp.
Huxley, Julian S. (ed.)
  1961 *The Humanist Frame.* London: George Allen & Unwin. 432 pp.
International Union of Anthropological and Ethnological Sciences
  1958–
  1967 *Bulletin of the International Committee on Urgent Anthropological and Ethnological Problems.* Vienna: Committee Secretariat. 8 vols.
James, E. O.
  1965 *From Cave to Cathedral: Temples and Shrines of Prehistoric, Classical, and Early Christian Times.* New York: Praeger. 404 pp.
Nakayama, Ichiro
  1963 *Industrialization of Japan.* Honolulu: East-West Center Press. 73 pp.
Noss, John B.
  1963 *Man's Religions* (3rd ed.) New York: Macmillan. 816 pp.
Parkinson, C. Northcote
  1958 *The Evolution of Political Thought.* New York: The Viking Press. 327 pp.
Pei, Mario A.
  1965a *Invitation to Linguistics: A Basic Introduction to the Science of Language.* Garden City, N.Y.: Doubleday & Company. 266 pp.
  1965b *The Story of Language* (rev. ed.). Philadelphia and New York: J. B. Lippincott Company. 491 pp.
Platt, John R.
  1966 *The Step to Man.* New York: John Wiley & Sons. 216 pp.
Price, A. Grenfell
  1963 *The Western Invasions of the Pacific and Its Continents, A Study of Moving Frontiers and Changing Landscapes, 1513–1958.* Oxford: Clarendon Press. 236 pp.

Pye, Lucien W. (ed.)
    1963   *Communications and Political Development.* Princeton: Princeton University Press. 381 pp.
Rodnick, David
    1966   *An Introduction to Man and His Development.* New York: Appleton-Century-Crofts, 520 pp.
Romein, Jan
    1962   *The Asian Century: A History of Modern Nationalism in Asia.* Berkeley and Los Angeles: University of California Press. 448 pp.
Smith, Huston
    1959   *The Religions of Man* (Mentor Book MD253). New York: The New American Library. 336 pp.   ·
Sopher, David E.
    1967   *Geography of Religions.* Englewood Cliffs, N.J.: Prentice-Hall. 118 pp.
Sorre, Maximilien
    1961   *L'homme sur la terre.* Paris: Hachette. 365 pp.
Thut, I. N., and Don Adams
    1964   *Educational Patterns in Contemporary Societies.* New York: McGraw-Hill Book Company. 494 pp.
Tonkin, Derek
    1962   *Modern Cambodian Writing.* Phnom Penh, Cambodia: Collection dirigée par M. Chau Seng (Culture et Civilisation Khmeres, No. 5). 62 pp.
Wagar, W. Warren
    1963   *The City of Man: Prophecies of a World Civilization in Twentieth Century Thought.* Boston: Houghton Mifflin Co. 310 pp.
Wainhouse, David W.
    1964   *Remnants of Empire: The United Nations and the End of Colonialism.* New York: Harper and Row. 153 pp.
Ward, Barbara
    1966   *Spaceship Earth.* New York: Columbia University Press. 152 pp.
Woodruff, William
    1966   *Impact of Western Man: A Study of Europe's Role in the World Economy, 1750–1960.* London: Macmillan, and New York: St Martin's Press. 375 pp.

TOOLS

CARL FRANK, PHOTO RESEARCHERS

Indian Footplow, Ecuador

ARAB INFORMATION CENTER

328

Traditional Scratch Plow, Jordan

Two-Mule Single Steel Plow, Alabama, U.S.

U.S.D.A.

Malay Steel Share,
Wet-Field Plow, Malaysia

J. E. SPENCER

Plowman, En Route, Philippines

329

W. L. THOMAS, JR.

Rice-Field Hand Tractor, Japan

BOB AND IRA SPRING

EASTFOTO

Traditional Threshing Techniques, China

E. BOUBAT, PHOTO RESEARCHERS
JOE MONROE, PHOTO RESEARCHERS

331

Early Sixteen Horse Reaper-Thresher, Wisconsin, U.S.

STATE HISTORICAL SOCIETY OF WISCONSIN

Modern Wheat Combine, Reaper-Thresher, United States

INTERNATIONAL HARVESTER

Eight-Share Tractor Plow, United States

INTERNATIONAL HARVESTER

333

Powered Corn Picker, Nebraska, U.S.

UNION PACIFIC RAILROAD

American Indian Handloom, Guatemala

TIERS, MONKMEYER

Foot-Powered Loom and Hand-Spooler, Mexico

334

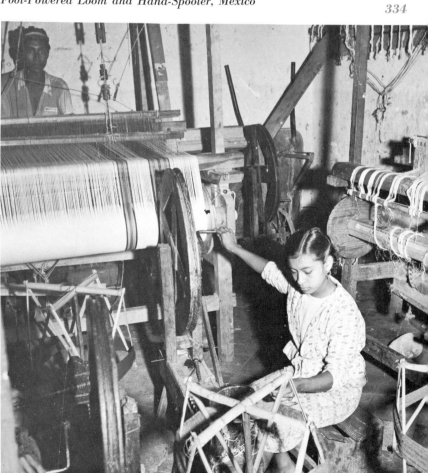

PATRICE HARTLEY, RAPHO GUILLUMETTE

WEST POINT-PEPPERELL

Mechanized Spinning Room, Alabama, U.S.

335

Mechanized Weaving Room, Alabama, U.S.

WEST POINT-PEPPERELL

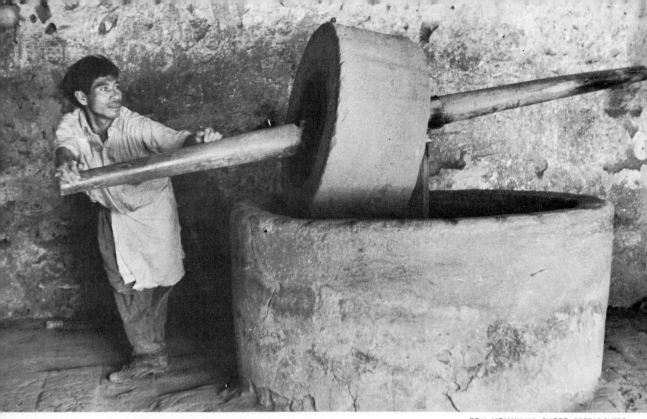

TOM HOLLYMAN, PHOTO RESEARCHERS

Grinding Pottery Clay, Guatemala

336

Animal-Powered Grain Mill, China

J. E. SPENCER

GERMAN LORCA

Semimechanized Egg Boxing, Brazil

337

Electronics Assembly, Japan

JAPAN NATIONAL TOURIST ORGANIZATION

BELL TELEPHONE LABORATORIES

Part of a 7094 Computer System, United States

338

Integrated Steel Plant, Pennsylvania, U.S.

BETHLEHEM STEEL COMPANY

PART *FOUR*

A Closer Look at the Modern World: The Increasing Similarity in Man's Means for Transforming the World's Regions to His Own Ends

---

The Geographical Explorations of the twelfth to sixteenth centuries physically proved that man, anywhere on the earth, could go to any other portion of the earth, and both transport commodities over the whole and observe the ways of men elsewhere that he could apply to his home country. Conceptually, the Geographical Explorations suggested that man at last possessed the potential for using the whole earth. These two patterns of knowledge have for the first time in human history brought about a fundamental transformation in the human outlook upon the world as a whole: the concept of one world as a single productive unit for the good of all mankind, everywhere. The transformation has required time for its practical and complete understanding; even now it remains incompletely realized in many ways. Gradually, however, human societies in all parts of the earth have come to a particular comprehension of the possibilities.

The possible aspects of the "new look" range throughout the spectrum of human culture. A New York or Singapore resident may obtain an item on his dinner menu, a flower for a corsage, a book on an interesting subject, or the latest manufactured novelty from any other part of the world in a regular procedure that he thoroughly understands. In lesser vein, a Borneo Dyak may go only so far as to acquire a new outboard motor for his dugout canoe or buy his wife a bottle of fingernail polish from distant manufacturing sources, but his casually tapped small output of rubber may end up as a tire marketed for a sports car just as far away, and a Greenland cryolite miner may enjoy a new aluminum-cased flashlight from a distant source without further participation in, or understanding of, the role of fused cryolite in electrolytic reduction of alumina into the metallic product he uses. Although a whole range of possibilities is inseparably involved in all aspects of modern life for all societies on all levels of culture, only the most sophisticated persons utilize the possibilities to their fullest extent. Most members of most societies, in their normal routines of living, profitably use only the easily available elements resulting from the preliminary integration of the earth into one operating system. In the mid-twentieth century we are still working at the primary problems of integrating the earth into one operating whole, in a reversal of the long, long historic trend of divergence of the earth's regions into totally separable units; the process of convergence has by no means come to its completion.

Fundamental to the procedure of utilizing the whole earth are two particular sets of processes: those relating to resources and those relating to space. All other aspects of the realization of the unity of the earth are consequent upon the resources-compounding and the space-transforming processes. There are two elements to each of these processes, and human history during the seventeenth to twentieth centuries has been, in a sense, their elaboration in four different ways. These four types of elaboration may be summarized under the following headings:

1. **Resource-extracting techniques,** concerned with the acquisition and production of all kinds of physical and biotic raw materials.
2. **Resource-converting techniques,** focused upon the processing, manufacturing, and fabrication of the physical and biotic raw materials into agents, by-products, and end products for human utilization and consumption.
3. **Space-adjusting techniques,** which shorten the effective distance of travel, transport, and communication, so that various kinds of regions of the earth have been integrated and organized in a basic and primary manner, through the development of transportation, communication, and trade, and through political, economic, and administrative organization of the territorial units of the earth.
4. **Space-intensification techniques,** by which a new and higher order of utilization of earth regions has been achieved, resulting in increased productivity, increased population density, urbanization of much of the earth, improving levels of living, and the maximization of the potential of this humanized earth.

The concern of this part of the book is to deal systematically with each of the four, primarily as each operates in the contemporary twentieth-century world. Each of the four chapters concerns one of four elaborations, and each builds on the patterns of developments sketched in earlier chapters for earlier time periods. Since each chapter deals systematically with its specific technique on a worldwide basis, the discussion is generalized and focuses on the elements of advancing methods. The regional application for each is a part of regional geography and, necessarily, outside the scope of this book.

CHAPTER *8*

Resource-Extracting Techniques and Raw Materials Production in the Twentieth Century

By common acceptance of the concept, a forest is a resource, a thing of value to mankind. Ecologically, of course, one can assert that a forest may also be a resource to a bear or to a beaver; the bear's use of the forest resource differs from that of the beaver, and the different values lie in the different aspects of plant cover. But people now outnumber both bears and beavers, and man thinks in terms of human values. The human values of a forest have varied strongly from early Paleolithic time to the contemporary era. To a gathering-collecting band of Paleolithic men the resource lay in the fruits, berries, and nuts borne on trees and shrubs, in the plants producing fish poisons and string materials, in the grubs found in rotting logs, and in the small animals and birds that lived in the forest; these were the things that Paleolithic man comprehended. The forest also had value as a refuge against enemy hunting bands, but it was a known liability in that predators inhabited it.

To the early Neolithic shifting cultivator in the same forest region, trees were a problem factor; they had to be girdled, cut down, and burned to permit crop growing in sunny clearings. The uncut forest retained its value for its edible products that could be gathered, but predators and enemies lurked among the trees. Wood had some value, for tools, for shelters, and for firewood, but there was far more than enough supply. To the later Neolithic sedentary, agricultural village established in that forest region, the vast number of big trees constituted more problem than resource, for a great deal of labor had to be expended to clear the land, and to get rid of the stumps, to create fields for crop production. A little of the wood was of value for housing construction, for fencing, for tools, and for firewood, but the village was small and the forest extensive. The uncut forest supplied some game and some fruits, nuts, roots, and vegetable greens, as well as a continuing supply of tool wood and firewood. The pigs could be turned into the forest to root for edible items in the ground and to fatten on the fall nut crop, but enemies could use the forest as a screen for an attack on the village, predators still ranged the forest, and children got lost in it. On balance, to the late Neolithic villager, a little forest growth was good, but too much provoked more trouble than it contributed value.

To feudal England the forest posed different values. Wood from the forest had come to have value to townsmen, for firewood, for charcoal, for furniture, for tools, and for construction. The deer were the King's, and commoners caught poaching on the preserves were summarily dealt with. To Robin Hood and to all men fleeing the bonds of feudalism the forest was a refuge from the Sheriff of Nottingham, and the deer were for the taking; the Sheriff must have thought of the forest as a nuisance, but the King valued it for occasional hunting jaunts. Eventually the forest was cleared, in part, to make way for farms that could feed the townsmen; the town grew larger, and today Sherwood Forest is a valued park in the city of Nottingham where children may play.

To early eighteenth-century New England of the seaboard fringe, the forest in the hinterland had great value. Enemy Indians no longer lurked close by, the tall white pines made good masts and spars for sale to English and American builders of wooden sailing ships, the oaks made good ship timbers and planking, the maples could be tapped for maple syrup, and the housewife preserved berries collected from the woods in the summer for the enlargement of the winter diet. The forest supplied construction timber, furniture woods, staves for rum and sugar barrels, hardwoods for tool handles, and hardwoods for charcoal for the smithy. Fur-bearing animals of the forest still yielded a goodly haul to the winter trapper, the autumn deer kill provided meat for the winter months, and cattle could be run in the more open woods during the summers, producing milk for cheese making. Forests were good to have at a little distance away, and they constituted a valuable resource, but the forests close by were eliminated in favor of crop fields and pasture lands.

To twentieth century Americans forests are not plentiful enough, for they are an enormously valuable resource. In the northeast they are wonderful to look at in the fall when the leaves have turned color, and all of our forests are prized as vacation spots during the summers. Local residents may picnic in nearby forests during much of the year, for predators no longer lurk in them. Today forests are valued because they protect the surface of the land from erosion and serve as watersheds for the accumulation of water supplies for cities. Many of nature's forests no longer are very good ones, owing to careless human exploitation of them in the past, but the conservationists are desperately afraid the industrialists will lay barren the whole face of America in their eager efforts to produce wood pulp for papers, plywood and construction wood for housing and for use as forms in building in concrete and steel, paperboard for cartons and boxes, cellulose for plastics, resins for glues, and supplies of wood for the thousand and two needs of modern technological living patterns. Wood in bulk is the great resource of the forest today, and wood producers are no longer content to let nature replace the growth on cut-over lands. Rather, they have taken to planting and growing trees on farms in selected species to yield the largest possible returns of assorted woods designed to meet the range of needs.

The hollow-log grub, the fruit-and-nut, and the refuge values of the forest no longer count, few predators and enemies lurk in the forest to be a liability, game hunting has now become a luxury sport for city dwellers, and firewood is an expensive luxury to most city folks. Nature's scenic beauty has become a prime recreation resource to the contemporary city dweller; other economic values of the forest today lie in the realm of cellulose, resin, and wood in many forms and sizes, and in the realm of watershed and erosion control. Twentieth-century wood consumption per capita far exceeds that of even late Neolithic man, and the largely cultural landscape of the contemporary earth demands tighter and tighter control. The Paleolithic forest resource is incomprehensible to contemporary Americans, but the contemporary resource of the forest could not have been comprehended by Paleolithic man. The change in culture has redefined the resource. What constitutes a resource is a matter of continuing cultural reappraisal.

Similarly, there have been different levels of comprehension for all other things normally termed "natural resources," such as air, rock, sand and gravel, soil, water, minerals, and the fossil fuels. The value of air and natural water as resources has been fully comprehended only very recently in some of the more heavily populated portions of the earth. No product, natural or created, properly becomes a resource until its utility is fully comprehended, its technology of manipulation becomes mastered, and its output becomes in some way consumed by people somewhere on the surface of the earth. The bauxite-rich soils of the island of Jamaica served its farmers poorly in the past; the bauxite was no resource and the soils formed upon it were poor. It little matters that Jamaican farmers today still do not understand aluminum technology on our single-region economic earth, so long as someone does somewhere else. The current mining of bauxite on Jamaica has started to tap what is now a resource for both Jamaica and the aluminum-manufacturing countries, and the reconstitution of Jamaican soils on the mined-out bauxite ranges will turn the soils into a resource of a quality they did not previously possess. For many regions, the geographic unity of the earth, as one operational economic super-region, today enables the listing as resources of many things that could not have been termed resources even a century ago, and the earth itself possesses things that cannot be listed as resources for any region today. We cannot list these because we do not yet comprehend them, but Science asserts that this is so; recent developments in materials technology through new additions to culture, in scientific knowledge and procedure, lend credence to the assertion.

Forest Products, Wild Harvest, and Tree-Farm Production

Actually, today, we can comprehend the whole range of utilities inherent in a forest, but man's cultivated landscapes have spread so widely, cultural preferences have developed so highly, and the forest regions are now so diminished in extent that the wild gathering of grubs, fruits, roots, leaves, and nuts no longer contributes a dominant element to the human diet for the population of the earth. Whereas all the ecologically humid areas of the earth once possessed forest growth, today not more than 10 per cent of the surface of the earth is in productive wild-forest growth wherein reproduction is a matter of purely natural development (Fig. 8.1). Only two great zonal sources of large volumes of forest products remain: in the northern latitudes of the northern hemisphere (United States, Canada, and Eurasia) and in a few portions of the humid tropics and subtropics (chiefly in Brazil, the Congo, and Malaysia-Indonesia). Another 10 per cent of the surface is now in despoiled, fractionated, and poorly managed "forest" which is quite unproductive. Still another 5 per cent of the surface of the earth today carries forest growth chiefly planted or managed by man in such a way that plant reproduction is stimulated, restricted, or controlled to the end that these are specialized cultural forests. It is commonly said that forests should be kept intact, and the conservationist and nature lover advance all sorts of reasons therefor. But forests grow old, their great trees die, insects and diseases attack them, and their ecological balance changes through time by invasion of new species or through the dominance of particular species when slight changes in environmental circumstances take place through purely natural processes. A forest left entirely alone does not go on endlessly increasing in economic value, although natural forests may increase in aesthetic value to urban populations of the earth even as the forests decline in area and distribution.

It is common to say that all tropical forests are hardwood forests, that high-latitude forests are softwood forests, and that the temperate forests contain mixed softwoods and hardwoods. Such generalizations are convenient but inaccurate, as are the generalizations that coniferous forests are easy and cheap to log because all the trees are alike, whereas tropical forests are difficult and costly to log because a given sector will contain only a few representatives each of innumerable species. It is true that far northern hemisphere forests contain few species of trees, whereas there are many hundreds of species of trees in tropical forests, but the alleged difficulties of logging off a forest are no greater in one zone than in another, for they are purely matters of cultural technology in both instances. It is perfectly true that the rather primitive technology of searching out and cutting the very soft matchwood trees in tropical forests today may involve the selective cutting of one or two trees per square mile only, and that the seeking out of burls developed on old "English walnut" trees in former orchard remnants in Southern California (valued for their irregular grain patterns and exported to Italy for use in expensive veneers in thicknesses of one-thirty-second of an inch) may involve the cutting of only a hundred trees per year. It is also true that some heavily populated portions of the earth depend heavily on wood fuels as a source of energy; for example almost 40 per cent of the energy consumed in India during the mid-1960s was derived from wood. However, in the twentieth century we should acknowledge that these procedures are more reminiscent of Neolithic forest utilization than of modern forest technology. Such exotic procedures of procurement of wood will continue to have a place in the modern world, but the best in modern forest technology no longer resembles the Neolithic gathering procedures for the great volume of its products.

The managed forest and the tree farm today are part and parcel of production in all areas of progressive forest development over our earth. There are many regions that lag in these procedures, and there are still zones in which the cutting of naturally reproduced forests is still taking place. The latter, however, are being replaced by cultivated farm landscapes in many parts of the earth or by managed cultural forests. The government forest preserve and the private tree farm are becoming the effective way to grow wood products in a volume adequate to the needs of a huge population possessing increasingly demanding systems of consumption. Sustained-yield forestry both on lands held by local to national governments and on private holdings is only beginning to reach an

344

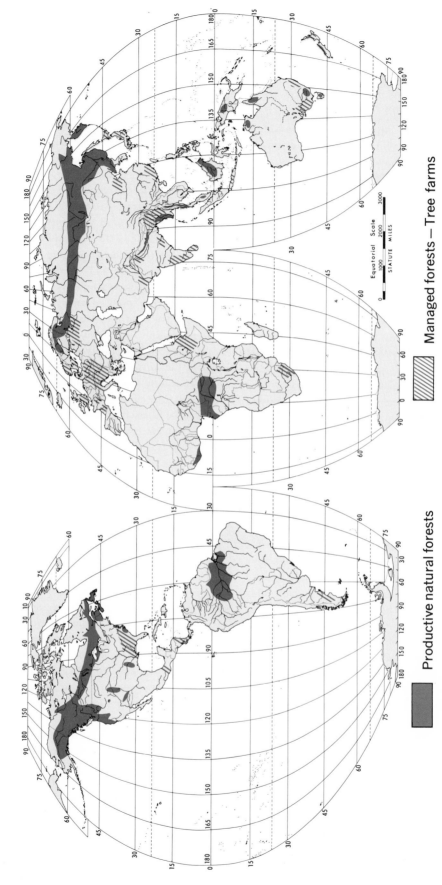

Productive natural forests

Managed forests – Tree farms

Spread of tree farming.

FIG. 8.1 REMAINING PRODUCTIVE NATURAL FORESTS AND THE SPREAD OF TREE FARMING.

effective level in parts of the earth, but such systems now are widely scattered and will increase rapidly in the near future (see Fig. 8.1).

The utilization of forest products ranges even more widely today than ever, owing to the technological changes in modern industry. Beyond wood in bulk sizes, and the fruits and nuts, man has sought hundreds of varieties of gums, pitches, resins, tars, waxes, oils, saps, tannins, and sugars from the fluid components of growing trees, shrubs, herbs, and grasses. The Paleolithic technique was to gather natural exudations. A later technique became that of slashing trees heavily to cause them to bleed out the desired product, or to cut the whole living plant into bits to permit reduction of the desired extract. Neolithic-style collecting of wild rubbers is very old; the late nineteenth-century start of the natural rubber industry employed slashing of scattered wild forest trees and the inefficient collecting and boiling down of the latex; the twentieth-century technique is the growing of rubber trees in continuous stands of farms (plantation estates and small holdings) and the systematizing of tapping, collecting, and reducing the latex. The latest development is the selective breeding of high-yielding trees that produce over 2000 pounds per acre per year; the Neolithic yield rate must have been less than an ounce per acre. The gathering of wild rubber from the Amazon Basin in 1900 produced about 50,000 tons, or about four ounces per acre for the whole region in which the *Hevea* rubber tree grew. The early "rubber plantation," about 1910, produced something over a hundred pounds per acre, the Malayan smallholder recently has produced just under 400 pounds per acre from his casually handled small planting, and the 2 million acres of carefully managed, large Malayan corporate farms (when all planted to the new high-yield stock) can perhaps average 1500 pounds per acre per year. The processes involved have been those of intensification of production. There are many other types of forest extracts that may be grown on tree farms, with the same proportionate patterns of increased production as shown for rubber.

Within the twentieth century it is predictable that man can almost rearrange the "forests" of the earth into planted, controlled "farms" which not only will produce the wide range of forest products required, but also will produce them more efficiently than nature ever did. As of the 1960s there still is a good way to go in the achievement of

this end, but the cultural processes of change are actively at work in all parts of the world.

Minerals, the Mining Cycle, and Comparative Technologies

By about 1000 B.C. man had learned to deal, in practical terms, with the mining, smelting, and fabrication of many of our known metallic minerals, although he failed to comprehend either the chemistry or the use potential of most of them. By the beginning of the Christian Era, most of our currently well-known minerals of all types were being mined, smelted, fabricated, or otherwise used. The miners learned to mine, and the smiths to smelt and fabricate, on rule-of-thumb bases that did yield metal products and mineral compounds of wide range in very small quantities. The failure of the traditional alchemists to solve the complex problems of industrial chemistry prevented the use of many types of ores and the enlargement of manufacturing procedures. As late as 1850 England turned out only 40,000 tons of steel, although the annual output of pig iron had risen to 3 million tons, and finished steel sold at about five times the price of traditional wrought iron. The procedures then employed were basically similar to those used in India or China, none of them having advanced very far beyond the procedures devised in southwest Asia in the first production of iron as metal. Until the latter half of the nineteenth century man had made few advances in minerals technology beyond the levels achieved by the start of the Christian Era. Although we use the terms Copper Age, Bronze Age, and Iron Age in historical chronologies, the true age of minerals, for consumption by the mass of mankind, belongs to the nineteenth and twentieth centuries.

The Distribution of Minerals

Minerals occur all over the earth, both in the solid crust and in the oceans and seas. Some occur as single elements, such as free (pure) gold or native copper, but most minerals are compounds of elements, such as sodium chloride (table salt), hematite (an iron ore, as ferrous oxide), bauxite (an aluminum ore, as aluminum oxide), or malachite (a copper ore, as copper oxide, perhaps the first copper ore mined and smelted). The natural occurrences of many minerals relate closely to geophysical and geochemical processes acutely bound up with the physical history of the earth, such as the episodes of vulcanism and mountain building. Other minerals are related to past or current denudation and alluvial deposition; some minerals occur in zones of dehydration of water bodies, whereas still other minerals are the results of accumulation of chemical compounds in shallow water bodies.

Every country on earth possesses stocks of minerals of some kind. Around 1500 B.C. about 120 common minerals had been classified as to properties, uses, and worth, whereas today about 2000 minerals have been identified and classified, the larger share of this number, and most of the rare minerals, having been added to the list in the last three centuries. In terms of human history most minerals, except those that are direct products of vulcanism (sulfur, for example) or obtained from the sea, constitute a nonreplenishable stockpile of potential natural resources. The value of these mineral stockpiles has depended quite directly on the cultural technologies of the populations controlling the territories of occurrence. Naturally, some regions possess large stocks of minerals whose technologies are now known and understood by the populations, and we speak of such regions as mineral-rich. Other regions actually possess more rock, or alluvium, and fewer ores, but often such regions are inhabited by peoples not interested in mineral technologies; no extensive searches for mineral resources have been carried on, so that such regions have often been described as mineral-poor. Our modern technologies have been demanding, and searches recently made in areas formerly labeled mineral-poor now turn up stocks of ores where none had been known. Also, as in the cases of uranium, petroleum, and natural gas, earlier judgments about potential resources were quite faulty, since the minerals were little known and the finding techniques only imperfectly elaborated. Quite recently we have begun to turn to the sea, or to the sea bottom, as a source of minerals, with totally new technologies, although we cannot yet go very far in this direction. Actually, since the whole earth forms one finite stockpile region for minerals, the wealth or poverty of any particular region is dependent not only on its physical makeup but also on the cultural awareness and the technologies mastered by its populations (Fig. 8.2). Because the distribution of actual mineral resources, therefore, involves an element of culture, the very concept of "mineral resource" is far from static. For example, the nineteenth-century addition of petroleum to the list of major

natural resources altered the whole construct for the whole earth, and the twentieth-century additions of the uranium minerals repeated the alteration.

The Mineral Cycle

Although in the ultimate sense no replenishment of mineral resources is possible, there is clearly a cyclic pattern to man's historic production of minerals in any one region and for the earth as a whole. This cyclic aspect has been almost wholly a matter of cultural technology, in practical terms. The mineral cycle is a compound affair, for it involves both the comprehension of values in minerals not previously mined in a given region and the application of new technologies to revive a mining region in which the older methods of locating and extracting a particular mineral had been inadequate, and the region perhaps even abandoned.

When Paleolithic man first stripped a surface vein of its jadestone, for the making of tools, he passed the malachites by, since he could not see in them anything more than pretty stones, perhaps, and he similarly paid no attention to the ferrous oxides nearby. Later, when copper smelting had become possible, miners worked the malachites, but ignored the jades and iron ores. Still later, the iron-ore miner concentrated on the ferrous oxides, and perhaps only plucked a charmstone from the jade or malachite deposits. The nineteenth-century iron-ore prospector noted the occurrence of all three minerals in a local region but passed them by because the deposits were "worked out." The contemporary geophysical prospector for petroleum paid no attention to the three minerals in his excitement over a deep-set field of petroleum. This kind of thing has been going on steadily, since the Paleolithic, so that mining has been carried out and given up in many a region time and time again, leaving behind numerous mining "ghost towns" in all parts of the earth.

The first copper miners (let us say about 3000 B.C. on a specific site) mined copper which they found in the pure state, and they hacked it out from surface occurrences until their mines reached depths beyond their technological capacities. They then abandoned the mining area in favor of some other surface deposit, totally ignoring the high-grade cuprite ores nearby. At a later date copper miners returned to work the cuprites for smelting into metallic copper, but they abandoned the mine

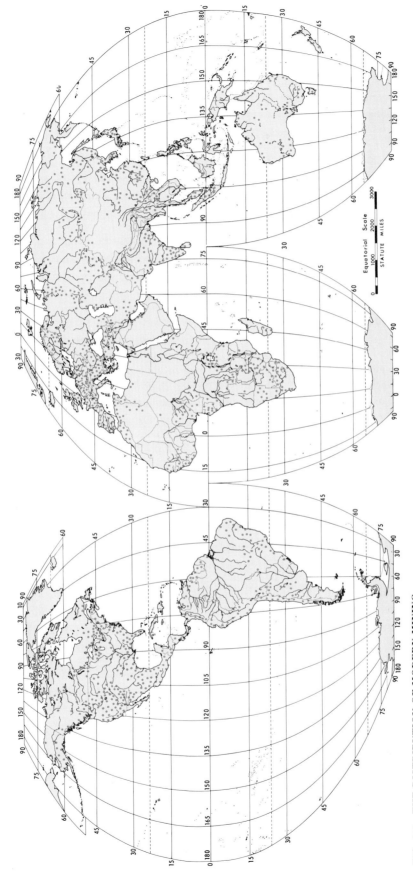

FIG. 8.2 THE DISTRIBUTION OF MODERN MINING.

347

when the ores became lower in grade deep in the ground and when water accumulated too abundantly. Still later, when miners had learned to sink shafts, bail out water, and lift the product to the surface, miners returned to work the pure copper deposits, but they ignored the low-grade cuprites. The early nineteenth-century copper miner assayed the low-grade cuprites at 10 per cent copper and well worth extraction, for mine water-pumping, air-ventilating technology, and ore-smelting techniques had improved to the point that they could handle such deep-vein ores, but mining ceased when the ore grade dropped below 4 per cent; a great slag pile marked the abandoned mine. By 1920 smelting technology had again improved, and miners returned both to work the slag pile and to sink a new shaft into the cuprite ore body for mining ore just over 2 per cent copper. Today copper miners accept as "copper ore" any rockpile that contains at least 0.5 per cent copper, and they often work over the slag heaps abandoned in earlier endeavors. And so it has gone: mine to the limit of mining or smelting technology and abandon; return when an improvement in technology judges the mineral occurrence to be a resource, but abandon when the technologic limit is reached; return again with a new technology that permits processing of ore too low in grade for the earlier smelter.

Within the last 20 years the definition of "iron ore" has changed markedly for the first time in centuries. Formerly, iron ore of under 40 per cent iron was too poor to work, and steel producers became worried that the world's iron ore supplies were approaching exhaustion. New processing technologies for beneficiating iron ores (meaning a process of mechanically eliminating the barren rock from the iron-bearing rock) produces concentrates from ore as low as 20 per cent iron of a quality better than that formerly mined from higher grade deposits. A few years ago many Americans were about to declare that coal no longer was a valuable natural resource to the United States. New mining technology, new transport technology, and new consumption technology now affords new opportunities for the use of coal.

Volume of production is another element in the mineral cycle which, when graphed, produces an irregular curve steadily ascending in amplitude. The copper miners of the whole earth, in 1500 B.C., probably handled a few hundred thousand tons of rock material to get at a hundred thousand tons of copper ore, from which they produced a few thousand tons of copper. Today, working with ores ranging from about 0.5 per cent to about 10.0 per cent copper content, world production averages about 4 million tons of metallic copper per year; such production involves handling hundreds of millions of tons of rock and low-grade ores, and it involves complex technologies that can be carried out only on a very large scale.

A copper miner, in 1500 B.C., often smelted his own copper ores, working alone or with a helper or two. Today, working with the lower grade ores constituting the mineral resource, the mining of many minerals has become a corporate affair, since no single person can cope with the problems of labor, technology, and total costs in the required orders of magnitude. In many of the rarer minerals the ore mining is the least significant element in the whole set of procedures, for the total ore volume may run only a few thousand tons per year, but the smelting technology requires complex and costly installations, and the resulting mineral yield may be sold at many dollars an ounce. There are fewer than a dozen lithium mining operations going on in the world today, although there soon may be more, and one concern produces from its North Carolina mine over half the world production of lithium oxide. The price of iridium, in 1965, was $80 per ounce in bulk lots, and total world production was only a few tons.

Thus, the mineral cycle has involved not only the spread of mining in repetitive patterns all over the earth, but also the repeated shift to larger and costlier kinds of operations in which greater numbers of people are involved and in which the technologies have periodically increased in complexity. The lone prospector still operates as a searcher and finder of ore bodies, though most prospecting is technologically organized, but the application of the resource has now become an operation that requires both large amounts of capital and the association of persons of highly varied and accomplished skills. In some cases, such as petroleum prospecting, even the lone searcher no longer functions very effectively. Basically, this condition exists because the easy-to-find, pure-to-rich ores, the surface-to-shallow depth resources of most portions of the earth, have been exploited fully. The solid crust and ocean volume of the earth still contain huge quantities of even the common minerals but no longer are they so casually available. Although there is a conceivable limit to the potential mineral resources of the earth, expanding technologies will be able to cope with the problems of retrieval of minerals for quite some time to come; the pessimistic view places the limit at something over a century, whereas the optimistic view puts it much further in the future.

The Mineral Groups

It has been customary to group the mineral resources of the earth into several different kinds of categories, and the economic discussion of mineral production, distribution, and trade normally employs such categories. We acknowledge these categories in the brief discussion that follows, but an extended treatment of their economic aspects is beyond the scope of this book. Brief comment must suffice for this subject.

Iron and Its Alloys. The mainstay of the modern world has been iron which, in the form of steel, still holds the leading position despite the increasingly common use of the light metals. Iron normally occurs only as an ore, which must be smelted at a fairly high temperature. There is a group of other minerals that can be blended with iron to improve its characteristics and properties. Such blending was accidentally done in earlier time, even to producing stainless steels, but control over this technology dates only from the late nineteenth century. The ores of iron and the ferroalloys take many forms, and the number of such alloys steadily increases with expanding metals technologies. Manganese is needed to turn iron into steel, but can be used, in further amounts, to create a steel with particular, desirable qualities. Tungsten, chromium, molybdenum, nickel, vanadium, titanium, and cobalt are the primary alloys used to impart toughness, hardness, strength, stainlessness, magnetism, or other properties to steels, but such other metallic minerals as copper, lead, zinc, and tin are employed to coat or finish particular steels for specific uses.

The mining of some variety of iron ore is almost worldwide today, as is the mining of the whole group of the ferroalloys. Specific iron ores and particular alloys have more restricted distributions and mining, although the search still goes on for added sources in each case. The flow of the iron and ferroalloy ores today is worldwide in the regular trade pattern, for modern technologies call for blending of ores, and the comparative economics of mining and transport makes this possible. During periods of war such flow patterns are interrupted, of course, but the trend is toward worldwide integration of ore fields and smelting centers.

The Nonferrous Metals. Copper and tin, among the very early common minerals mined and used, remain critical to modern technology. Lead and zinc are somewhat later additions to the common minerals list but are also critically used at present. Aluminum and magnesium, on the other hand, are elements whose technologies were learned only in the nineteenth century, and they form the basis for the "light-metals" aspect of modern metals technologies. Gold and silver are among the ancient minerals whose mining continues today, but it may be that exhaustion of these mineral-bearing ores is becoming more critical than that of any of the others; a breakthrough in technologies seems needed to provide adequate volumes for the future.

A number of other minerals in this broad category are almost modern in their recognition, mining, smelting technology, and use. Such are beryllium, lithium, iridium, and osmium, mined and smelted today but not yet well known as to possible uses. Even the potential volumes of supply of the latter group are little known, since the distribution of ores, and the mining of them, is quite restricted today.

The Nonmetallic Minerals. A large group of minerals is nonmetallic in nature. This group is customarily subdivided into subgroups according to the mining-use systems. Economic discussions of the nonmetals often categorize them in different ways, such as the building materials, the fertilizers-chemicals, the precious stones, the industrial agents, and so on.

The building materials group of nonmetallic minerals includes the building stones, such as marble, granite, basalt, limestone, sandstone, laterite, and others. Also included are such prosaic materials as sand, gravel, and crushed rock. These last three are economically of very great significance in the modern era of steel-and-concrete construction of buildings, bridges, roads, canals, and other such manifestations of modern technology.

The fertilizers and chemicals range from ordinary common salt through the more complex salts and the potassium, phosphorus, sulfur, and nitrogen compounds that occur naturally in sedimentary strata scattered over the face of the earth. The jewel stones involve the whole range of precious and semiprecious stones, a great many of which not only retain their traditional values and usages, but today have significant industrial applications. The industrial agents include a long list of items from the rare earths (one use is to impart better color in a television picture tube) through the refractory minerals employed to line modern industrial furnaces to the radioactive minerals employed throughout modern industrial activity.

Some nonmetallic minerals, such as the pottery and porcelain kaolins, are of long use, technology, and value, though somewhat prosaic in their mining and processing. In general these minerals are widely distributed over the earth, though particular items may be highly restricted as to occurrence. Others are greatly affected by cultural habit and fashion, such as the jades. Jade stones no longer are mined for weapons and tools, but particular jades are mined as jewel stones. Chinese jewel jade of the pre-Christian era was whitish in color (known as "mutton fat"); only since the sixteenth century has the green-colored jade come into fashion. Green jade abounds around the world, but the particular shade of "jade-green" jade is both recent in terms of fashion and restricted in distribution; thus California or Wyoming jades rate only as poor-grade and semiprecious. The Chinese fashionable green jades are now getting scarce, so that a color shift may again occur, with Wyoming jades carved in China becoming fashionable and valuable.

The Power Minerals. Much of the world's population has not yet adopted any one of the fossil fuels as a source of heat for power, since many people still cook and heat by wood or charcoal, or by straw, leaves, grasses, or dried cow dung. Nevertheless, coal is not only the dominant power mineral at present, but also its mining and use is older than often thought, for coal was mined in pre-Columbian America and at several places in the Old World at an early date. The industrial usage of coal seems to have started in China prior to the Christian Era, and to have diffused westward into northwestern Europe by the seventeenth century. Coal mining, and industrial application, spread around the world in the late eighteenth and early nineteenth centuries, and most of the earth's coal supplies are now quite well known. Irregular distribution of coal has made for a large coal trade today.

Marco Polo commented on the use of petroleum as a mange cure for camels, and some kind of petroleum-seep product has been widely gathered and used for centuries. Burmese dug holes to get at a petroleum that could be burned as a lighting fuel long before the modern petroleum well appeared and uses of petroleum developed in the United States in the nineteenth century. Throughout the earth for many uses petroleum has been steadily replacing coal because liquid petroleum is easier to handle in world transport. Whereas the estimates, during the 1920s, of the world petroleum reserves foresaw the exhaustion of the resource by the 1950s, the application of geophysics to prospecting has tremendously enlarged the recognition of petroleum-bearing situations, and the resource seems available for a considerable period despite the greatly increased consumption of the product as a power fuel. In addition to petroleum, the volume of power reserves of natural gas resources has been greater, so far, than its expanded consumption.

The uranium minerals as power sources are so recent that their distribution is not yet well known, and the total significance of the resource cannot be stated simply. This is one of the most exciting phases of the growth of human culture, and it is probable that by tapping this energy source, human technologies may be expanded, in the future, far beyond ordinary understanding.

The technological growth of rocketry has developed into fuel components a number of formerly prosaic minerals which seemed to have only restricted usage in industrial application. This again, is one of the exciting cultural developments of the mid-twentieth century which promises a degree of intensification of power development greater than any found so far. It is far too early to project any datum with regard to potential. Although the mixture of prosaic minerals such as sulfur and saltpeter in the making of gunpowder is an old technology to produce power, the technologic application of such procedures to truly productive activity has been a function of the mid-twentieth century only, and the potential limits of such cultural attainments can only be estimated.

Summary Notes

For all that the term "Iron Age" is used to pattern an historic chronology, and for all that metallurgy constituted a revolutionary step forward in human ability, only the simple aspects of metallurgy characterized the second and third millennia B.C. Beginning very hesitantly in the late eighteenth century, the large forward steps in the recognition of the value of minerals, in their mining and smelting, and in their application, took place only in the late nineteenth century and these steps have become huge strides in the twentieth century as human intellect applied itself to the problems and possibilities. The increase in mining and extraction of resources has been revolutionary, with a consequent change in the daily life of people in those regions in which the activity has been foremost. In the course of a year, the average United States citizen today has the use of a greater volume of metals, nonmetallic minerals, and other mineral resources than did about 50,000 Mesopotamians during the life of Hammurabi and more than 10,000 Romans during the life of Julius Caesar. It is true, of course, that the American citizen, during the 1960s, also has the use of more such products, by perhaps 50,000 times, than some native resident of present-day western highland New Guinea, but the world trade routes and the world spread of cultural technology give to the residents of New Guinea a hopeful prospect never possible to Mesopotamians in the time of Hammurabi. The diffusion of modern technologies, and the productive and consumptive patterns that go with them, is moving at a rate never accomplished in earlier millennia. The expectation is that the rates of diffusion, cultural acceptances, selectiveness of elements, and productive abilities will increase even more rapidly in the future.

Aquatic Products:
The Fisheries, Sea Hunting, Fishing Systems, and the Growth in Regional Technologies

Among the world's peoples there probably always have been fishermen, and it is likely that there always will be, because fishing can be done both for economic gain and for pleasure. The line between the two is often hard to distinguish. Fishing, in the broadest sense, can be a lazy man's recourse to gain and to pastime, or it can be one of the earth's most arduous engagements, whether for survival or sport. It may be a residual occupation for the poor of a region, and it can be the calculated activity employing a costly and complex technology of a complex variety. If carried to excess in a region, fishing must decline owing to depletion of the resource, whereupon regeneration may occur to permit increased fishing at a later time. In the drying out of the earth, after the last glacial era, the natural distribution of aquatic life-forms became somewhat restricted; man has permanently fished out the naturally maintained stocks of aquatic life-forms in many freshwater territories; but man can grow and transplant aquatic life-forms from one region to another, and he now knows enough about this procedure to "farm" aquatic products on chosen sites, either as a technology in economic production or in the furtherance of fishing as a vacation sport. If the modern economic pursuit of aquatic products can be restrained within the ecological balance of the natural generation of an economic good, fisheries can be a permanently productive component in any regional system (Fig. 8.3). If such restraint cannot be maintained, man could alter the whole technologic approach from a system of "taking" a resource to "farming" it; the practice of "farming the oceans" is now discussed rather often, but only a few steps have yet been taken in this direction.

The whole broad zone of fishing and sea hunting is one wherein the conservationist often raises his voice. The fear of extinguishing forms of life is fairly real in quite a few cases, from the odd species of minnowlike fish in some desert remnant lake or stream, possessing no significant economic value in the strict sense, to such high-value forms as some of the whales or the salmon. Human activity in altering the ecological habitat of many aquatic life-forms may unwittingly extinguish them, and the continued ruthless pursuit of other life-forms, such as some of the whales or some of the seals and their relatives, may literally kill off the natural populations before man learns the proper ways of maintaining them in controlled waters.

Beachcombing, as a Paleolithic occupation, is still with us on many shores. Hook-and-line fishing is still practiced and, though the equipment itself may be of strictly modern manufacture, the technique is Paleolithic. The hand throw-net is of the same cultural stage, as are the restraining weir and the fish trap. Of the fishing nets now in use only the trawl is modern, perhaps dating from the eighteenth century. Pond planting of fish, shellfish, and aquatic plants appears to be Neolithic in ultimate derivation, but only in the last few centuries has it been turned into true economic production. Sea hunting, for the whales, the seals, otters, walruses, and some of the larger fish, certainly derives from the Neolithic at the latest.

What is modern about the continued employment of these ancient techniques is the use of modern materials to make them more efficient, and the application of power to the operation of the boats and the gear, the new technologies in handling the take and the catch, and the processing of

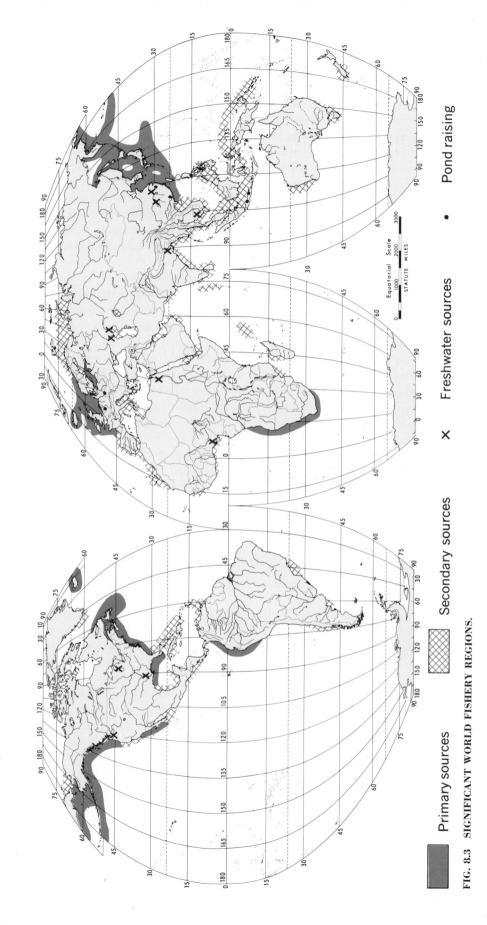

Primary sources   Secondary sources   Pond raising

           X   Freshwater sources

FIG. 8.3   SIGNIFICANT WORLD FISHERY REGIONS.

the yield. The actual fish-catching techniques of the modern salmon and tuna fisheries resemble the ancient ones, but the modern powered tuna fleet, with its freezing equipment, and the cannery for disposal of the catch, are creations of the twentieth century. The modern whaling combine, consisting of a floating oil-and-meat preserving factory and a group of powered catcher boats equipped with harpoon guns is a far cry from the eighteenth-century New England whaling ship, and its very efficiency threatens to destroy its own resource. Edible fish and the decorative goldfish have been raised in ponds for about two millennia, but the twentieth-century estuarine fish pond assembly linked with a cannery and a quick-freeze plant promises a kind of controlled economic production which could revolutionize, finally, the whole fishery industry. Controlled-water, shallow-sea "farming" of many kinds of aquatic products is not yet in extensive practice, but the technology is ready for widespread development.

Fishing has long been worldwide, in the simple sense. Certain ways of fishing have been restricted, out of physical or ecological conditions and the nature of the life-form distributions. The human interest in fishing has varied among the societies of the earth, and some peoples have declined to fish though they have inhabited regions with potential resources. Beachcombing has been restricted to seashores having tidal ranges. Some interior regions, dependent on freshwater resources, long ago exhausted them by exploitation or, more recently, extinguished them through creating physical conditions inimical to aquatic life. Western China is exemplary of the first pattern, and northeastern United States recently approached the second through the dumping of excessive volumes of heated water and industrial wastes into water bodies. The dietary consumption of fishery products has been culturally implemented. The Roman Catholic lands have been once-weekly consumers of fish, the Hindus of upper caste levels in India never ate fish, Americans lowered their consumption of "fishy taste" fish products to a markedly low level. On the other hand, Scandinavians, Eskimos, and Filipinos eat large amounts of fish in many forms, and the Japanese eat more kinds and larger volumes of fishery products, including aquatic plants, than any other people.

Fishery activity, therefore, has varied greatly around the earth, both according to physical conditions and human interest. It commonly has been said that tropical lands have seen little fishing, but this is quite untrue for the Southeast Asia–Western Pacific Islands zone. Pearl, coral, sponge fisheries, and related activities have been restricted to biological zones of occurrence. Demersal fishing of the shallow offshore banks apparently first became significant in the waters off Northwest Europe and off Korea–Japan–North China. Northwest Europeans extended it to the Newfoundland offshore banks, and began significant interregional trading in salted, smoked, and dried herring and cod in the fifteenth century. European trading of fish toward the tropics did inhibit the growth of commercial fisheries in low-latitude regions. European-American whalers and seal hunters did roam the world's oceans exclusively until the Japanese entered the game and developed the floating factory. Antarctic waters now remain the only really active zone of whaling.

The four great continental shelves of Eurasia and North America, for several centuries, were the chief potential commercial fishery zones owing to their excellent ecological environments. Although Northwest European countries began the modern pelagic fishery-trade pattern, this spread to the New England-eastern Canadian colonial region rather early in the seventeenth century and to northwestern North America and to Japan in the late nineteenth century. More recently Peru has become the chief fishery nation, exploiting the great offshore resource, which had been there all along, through the use of modern equipment and technology. Russian fishing trawlers have roamed the world's oceans in recent decades. American technologies in equipment and Northwest European-American fishery practices are now diffusing around the world. Fishery-waters resource surveys, the introduction of power equipment, refrigeration, canning, and freezing are improving fisheries on all oceanic margins, and improved transport systems are moving fishery products both interregionally and inland from coastal zones around the world. The annual fishery product catch and take now approaches 50,000,000 tons per year for the earth as a whole, and the way is open for further increasing this annual haul.

The chief accomplishments in the whole broad fishery field, thus far in the twentieth century, have lain in the modernizing of the equipment for catching, handling, and processing and in the improvement in the knowledge of when and where to fish. Early man fished fresh waters and the edges of the sea by guess and by intuition; ninth-century fishermen began working the demersal and pelagic waters offshore by the accumulation of trial-and-error experience; modern fishing fleets hunt by sonar devices through the open oceans. Nevertheless, of the perhaps 50,000 species of fish, shellfish, sponges and related forms, and the aquatic plants, only relatively few are really utilized by man. The revolution in world fisheries has barely begun.

Water Supply: The Realization of a Resource

Around the subject of fresh water there has been a curious dichotomy of thinking throughout human history. Man has known its values in the arid lands of the earth, for all kinds of uses, whereas in the humid lands water has been taken for granted in ordinary times; and everywhere the sudden surplus of water has been more of a problem than an asset. Potable, nonsaline water for man, for animals, and for plants has been considered a free good, in economic terms, over all the earth throughout most of human history. As the earth dried out, at the end of the last glacial era, man learned to value water and to conserve it in the dry zones, and the migrations toward perennial water supplies were part of the story of the growth of civilization. In the formerly too-heavily flooded zones man was relieved at the lessening of those floods, for he could now occupy territories in which living was easier. The storage of water for domestic purposes and the accumulation of water for irrigation in the dry regions taxed human ingenuity to devise many different kinds of procedures for storage and accumulation. Thus the cistern, the qanat, the well, the windmill, the irrigation ditch, and the agricultural terrace all attest the recognition of the value of water. These devices were inventions of man struggling with water problems in the dry zones of southwest Asia, and they came into use at different historic dates. Special rules were devised for the control and apportioning of water, so that a body of specialized water-right law evolved, and the "watermaster" became an important administrative officer in most dry land societies of the Old World. Around the dry margins and throughout the humid zones, on the other hand, ingenuity and energy went into the procedures for diverting water surpluses and for preventing floods. The dike, the dike system, the floodgate, the drainage canal, the field drain,

and the relatively late pumping systems all attest the effort to get rid of surplus water. The "dike watch" replaced the "watermaster," and no specialized body of water-right law evolved; rules were devised about rights to water, but they were comparatively simple and proceeded on quite separate assumptions. In the dry regions untimely surpluses, and floods, were suffered through, as were the unseasonal droughts in the humid regions; in each kind of region the untimely happening seldom received much concerted attention.*

At an early historic date man learned to utilize the waterwheel for the creation of power and for lifting water. He learned to transport by boat and by barge economic goods on the free-flowing streams, and he has long used that free flow to carry away the refuse he dumped into water bodies. In time man learned to canalize streams and to dig canals in the creation of a waterline transport pattern. He also learned to move water, through aqueducts and crude piping systems, from source areas to areas of concentrated use. In modern time water has become a tremendous source of power, through the hydroelectric installation, utilizing a device for accumulating water, the storage dam. The storage dam is a relatively late Old World device now being used for all sorts of water-control purposes all over the world in a rather sudden burst of technological applications, the potential ramifications of which were best characterized in the western United States in the early twentieth century. But for all that, man has really known the value of water for a long time, and the traditional dichotomy of thinking about water has persisted.

For the world as a whole the following generalizations still held at mid-twentieth century. In the humid lands water is cheap, there is lots of it at all times and often too much, the seasonal flood is more serious than the unseasonal drought, water is the ever-present free economic good, no special systems of control over it are required, other than flood prevention, and no care need be taken to keep it clean. In the dry lands water is dear, there really is never enough of it, concerted efforts are needed to ensure its continued adequacy, untimely

*We must recognize, of course, that diking procedures did spread to some of the arid land regions, and that, after the Crusades, the windmill became a device for pumping out water surpluses in some humid regions; the broad generalization holds despite the diffusion of specific devices and procedures into the opposite zone in the course of time.

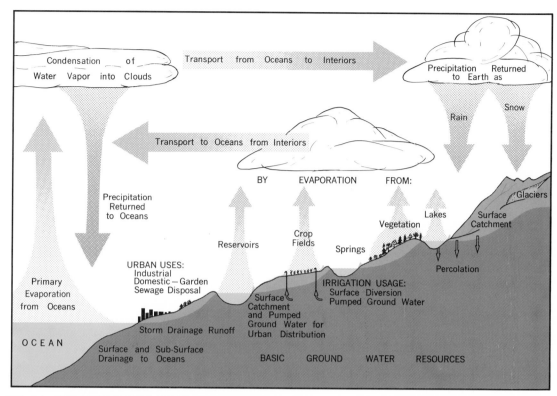

FIG. 8.4 THE HYDROLOGIC CYCLE IN CULTURAL USAGE.

flood is feared but not really guarded against, water is a free economic good, but special systems of control over it are required, administration of its usage is specially arranged, and great care is taken to maintain the purity of water supplies.

Out of a somewhat sudden rash of water problems, however, man is becoming aware of his past misconceptions and the dangers of his past carelessnesses. This is nowhere more dramatically illustrated than in the drastic water shortages for New York City during 1964–1965, a great city in a humid region of free and plentiful water, as compared with the continued relative adequacy of water supplies for the city of Los Angeles, a rapidly growing great city in a dry region of valuable and scanty water. What is more, the waters of portions of the humid northeastern United States were terribly polluted through the casual dumping of wastes, so that many free-flowing streams almost resembled sewers in the early 1960s, whereas wastes are almost never dumped into the scarce water bodies of the dry lands. The American situation provides more startling contrasts than many other portions of the world, but it is clear that a wholesale revolution in thinking must take place about the control of fresh water in the cultural landscape. Fresh water is a free economic good that may be taken casually and without much care in only a few portions of the earth today; in most places fresh water is a valuable resource to the large world population but it must be handled with the care appropriate to its value. What may be termed the technological revolution in modern living systems demands a revolution in the thinking about fresh water, in the storage and handling of freshwater supplies, and in the whole attitude toward groundwater and water in lakes and free-flowing streams.

Water as an Agent and as a Commodity

As a resource, fresh water now has value in several different ways, as it has always had such values (Fig. 8.4). In some cases this value has lain in water's use as an agent, but in other situations water has been a commodity. In streams and in canals water retains its value as a transport agent. In agriculture water is both an agent and a commodity used in greater quantities than ever, for irrigation procedures have spread out of the very dry lands across the semiarid zones and into the humid regions. In its domestic garden and public park application, water is both an agent and a commodity used in ever larger quantities in growing the decorative plantings that surround homes, dot the open green spaces, and line the freeways. For domestic drinking and cooking purposes water is a commodity, and its use rises with population increase. As an agent, water in much larger volumes now is being used to transport wastes than heretofore, as piped sewage systems expand their coverage of urban and semiurban settlements. As an agent, furthermore, water is becoming ever more frequently used in the many kinds of cleansing operations that are carried on in and around urban settlements, from the laundering of clothing through street cleaning and the "car-wash" operations, to the daily shower bath for the members of the population. All of these usages are somewhat traditional, in one sense, but today they require far greater quantities of water for a far larger population than was true in an earlier era.

The industrial use of water, both as an agent and as a commodity, has a traditional background also, in the strict sense, but in both purposes and volume the industrial use of water in the modern world has increased at an exponential rate as compared to most of the other consumption systems. Many modern industrial procedures require huge consumptions of water for the output of comparatively small tonnages of finished products. From the washing of the iron ores onward through the several processes of the iron and steel industry the total consumption of water reaches the figure of about ten gallons of water to every pound of steel; expressed summarily, the iron and steel industry of the United States uses roughly $4\frac{1}{2}$ billion gallons of water per day, or about 1600 billion gallons per year. By comparison, New York City uses about $1\frac{1}{2}$ billion gallons of water per day for all uses. Although the iron and steel industry is the largest single industrial user of water, paper manufacture and the chemicals industries are also large consumers.

The largest single use of water, of course, is biological, for the growing of crops; more than half the total annual consumption of all water supplies (snowfall, rainfall, and irrigation water) in the United States is for agriculture. Western United States was long the big user of water brought to the land as irrigation water. More recently, irrigation has become much more widely practiced for many kinds of crops grown in regions traditionally thought of as humid. As intensification of agricultural production spreads through all parts of the country, it is likely that the agricultural usage of water will continue to increase.

The "use" of water in streams, canals, and lakes, as an agent for transport, is not properly consumption at all, for such water is merely moving through a particular stage of the hydrologic cycle en route to the oceans. Similarly, the "use" of water in hydroelectric power production is not a consumptive pattern, save of kinetic energy. Much of the water employed as an agent is not fully consumed but is cycled back into the ground or into streams and lakes. Many of the industrial uses of water, and those in the cleansing and waste-removal operations, do not consume the water, but channel it back into natural watercourses. Unfortunately much of the water employed in these uses is heavily contaminated by sewage and industrial wastes or highly heated when it returns to the natural watercourses, thus creating ecological problems for downstream users in the same drainage basins. Even much of the water employed in agriculture finds its way into the groundwater zone, although in general it is customary to say that irrigation water is consumed rather than merely employed as an agent. It is difficult, therefore, to differentiate among the several kinds of uses of water as to employment as an agent or as a commodity. Excluding the water utilized in flowing water bodies for transport and for hydroelectric power production and, thereby, defining as consumption all water that enters culturally developed water systems of any type, the consumption of water in the United States in the mid-1960s had reached the figure of about 1700 gallons per capita per day. This is one of the highest of the world's figures at present, but in other portions of the world where increasingly technological industrial operations and advancing levels of living are to be found the increase in the per capita water consumption is striking.

What is so notable about the contemporary patterns of water consumption has been the rates of increase and the widespread distribution of modern processes for handling water in large volumes. Although the storage dam was a device invented well back in the pre-Christian era, as were aqueducts and pipe systems, it is only within the last century that such systems have begun to come into their own around the earth. The artificial lake created by the huge masonry and steel dam, serving many kinds of purposes, properly belongs to the twentieth century, as does the piped water system providing domestic water supplies and the piped sewage system for the removal of wastes. Every large city in the world today has its piped water and sewage systems, and countless villages and rural homesteads have easy access to piped domestic water derived from controlled sources.

The Costs of Water Technology

Although traditionally water has been thought of as a free economic good, in the sense that water is a natural part of a physical environment, the growing population of the earth and the growing complexity of cultural practices involving water, have made the procurement, transport, treatment, and distribution of water increasingly expensive in all parts of the earth. Although it is free rainwater and snowmelt water that is piped long distances to semi-arid Los Angeles, the handling procedures are rather expensive. Institutions of urban government vigorously tackle all the problems involved, the citizenry is kept conscious of these problems, and the water meter and the periodic water bill are significant elements of daily life. Abundant free rainwater and snowmelt water surround New York City, but the humid-zone tradition has persisted; most New York water is not metered, the citizenry has been less concerned, and the urban institutions have worked from year to year only, to the end that New York's water problem is greater than that of Los Angeles. Water as a free economic good is employed, through the hydroelectric installation, for the creation of electricity, but the procedure of development is really costly. Most of the cheap sites have already been exploited to their full capacity, and the additional satisfaction of demand faces steadily increasing cost. Water, as a free economic good, is sought for industrial purposes, and many industrial concerns establish their own water systems. However, in the volumes demanded in contemporary industrial technology, the adequate presence of clean, fresh water becomes an important locational factor, and the sheer costs of providing these volumes of the free economic good become considerable. In the same way, the continued provision of larger volumes of the free economic good for the expansion of agricultural irrigation practices involves steadily heightened costs.

The concept of the watershed and its disciplined control have become truly effective in only a few regions within the last century. The current spread of this concept around the world today is part of a cultural process of the comprehension of a significant environmental resource. The problems of pollution of freshwater resources in most humid parts of the earth had not been faced squarely even in the 1960s. Water supply in most such regions has remained a local matter, seldom highly organized, with little thought for other users within the same drainage basin. It is inevitable that cultural practice must improve tremendously in many humid regions, and around the arid margins, as the population of the earth increases. The traditional view of water as a free economic good, without liability, must be replaced by the view of water as a valuable environmental resource to be employed carefully for the good of all.

In the view of water as an economic resource, users who seek clean water supplies must learn the cultural habit, and evolve the cultural technology, of processing that water after use, and of discharging it into transport channels (rivers, lakes, canals, or the ground) as clean water; the alternative is the ubiquitous sewer in which no one may find clean water, but only hazards to health and technological processes.

The primary developments in the whole field of water supply have become technologically mature within the last few decades. Since 1900 man has learned how to handle water in huge volumes in almost all of the ways needed. Even the desalination of nonfresh water is technologically under control although it may yet cost more than we like to pay for water. It is human thinking and human practice that have not recently kept pace with human technological ability. In too many regions of the earth cultural practice still smacks of the Neolithic system, and it remains for the revolution in cultural practice of water control to spread throughout the whole earth in all its ramified aspects.

Agriculture: Global Interchange, Specialization, and Industrialization

One of the more significant results of the Columbian Discoveries was the hemispheric and continental transfer of crop plants, domestic animals, and crop-growing technologies (see Chapters 6 and 7). Although it does appear that a few such transfers did actually predate Columbus, the wholesale manner in which elements of agriculture were moved about during the centuries following Columbus finds no historic comparison. The basic grain, fiber, root, and fruit crops of the Old World were moved about and transferred to the New World and to Australasia, New World crop plants became basic staples in parts of the Old World, domestic animals as draft power and meat producers were scattered over the earth, and agricultural technologies were transplanted in mass. The interplay of these several elements of agricultural practice was a continuing operation, as new and relatively empty lands were put under crop, old cropping systems were renovated, trade movements in basic commodities began to expand into a worldwide pattern, labor and power shortages slowly began to be compensated by increasing mechanization, and crop growing gradually shifted from subsistence and local barter to distant market-oriented commercial patterns. The role of the plant explorer became a specialty as botanists and agronomists searched out the far countries for crop and decorative plants that could be put into production in homelands and other regions. Increasingly the accent became heavier upon the innovator in technology who could increase the productive yield from the farms of many parts of the earth, and agriculture began that developmental trend toward the industrial production system that marks the most advanced regions of the world today.

The basic and elemental concepts of the soil as a medium of production are quite old in several parts of the earth, and crop-breeding practice is not new. Concepts of fertilization became basic in a few regions at a very early date, the utility of irrigation water has long been known in the dry lands, the realization of utility of nonhuman power in land preparation came a long time ago, and a glimmering of the value of intensification of production technologies is not modern. However, the accumulation and pyramiding of knowledge and technological skill implicit in the occupational specialties of soil scientist, agronomist, horticulturist, plant hybridizer, geneticist, irrigation engineer, land reclamation engineer, and agricultural engineer represent qualitative improvements derived from the late nineteenth and twentieth centuries only. The continuing revolutionary development has not yet reached its maximum even in the most technologically advanced agricultural regions, just as the spread of contemporary knowledge has not yet reached the far countries of the earth. The rural peasant farmer who operated on the basis of traditional farmer's lore is still being replaced by the highly trained technician who keeps an eye, simultaneously, on the weather forecast, the cost-accounting book, the commodity market newsletter, the machinery catalogue, the government agricultural agent, and the plant hybridizer's booklet. As this kind of farmer becomes numerous in some regions of the world, it becomes increasingly necessary for farmers elsewhere to follow suit, and the industrialization of crop growing will continue apace.

By the 1960s crop transfer had not been fully completed to all possible regional environments of the earth but, between the northern and southern hemispheres and among the separate continental sectors in each hemisphere, repetitive regional production zones for most of the now significant crops and animals have been fairly well worked out (Fig. 8.5). Wheat, for example, is grown in many regions where it does well, and from which it flows to consumption regions around the earth. Wheat is being exported from some production region toward a consumption region in every month of the year in a fairly well-articulated system. Cotton, beef, butter, vegetable oils, oranges, tea, coffee, and other products are produced in many regions, consumed the world over to some degree, and move in an articulated series of systems motivated by seasonal production cycles, competitive price structures, and seasonal demand frequencies. Volumes of production increase, volumes of consumption both increase and change, and trade patterns alter in detail as to direction and volume, but the basic structure of world trade in raw materials continues, and the really notable thing is that the resource-extracting techniques have been tremendously improved, by any kind of measure.

Within the broad zonal patterns of the world's cropping systems there are some clearly discernible elements of regionalism that have characterized the historic expansion of agriculture (see Fig. 8.5). Among the oldest of the plant fibers there has been the dominance of the tropical and subtropical regions. Jute, abaca, kapok, ramie, hemp, the henequen sisals, and the cottons have been in this group. Some of these plants have been hard to transfer to other regions; some, such as hemp and the cottons, have been quite amenable to transfer to the lower midlatitudes in relatively recent time. Nevertheless, the chief centering of most of the significant plant fibers has remained within the subtropical margins, where the fiber plants constitute an important element in more localized regional agriculture. Jute remains chiefly a product

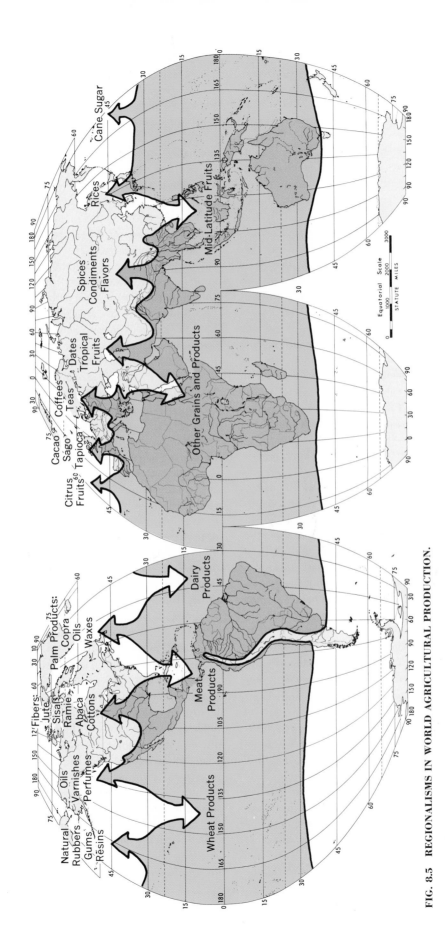

Cane Sugar
Rices
Spices
Condiments
Flavors
Mid-Latitude Fruits
Teas
Dates
Tropical
Fruits
Coffees
Cacao
Sago Tapioca
Citrus
Fruits
Other Grains and Products

Fibers:
Jute
Sisal
Ramie
Apaca
Cottons
Palm Products:
Copra
Oils
Waxes
Oils
Varnishes
Perfumes
Natural
Rubbers
Gums
Resins
Dairy
Products
Meat
Products
Wheat Products

Equatorial Scale
1000   2000   3000
STATUTE MILES

FIG. 8.5 REGIONALISMS IN WORLD AGRICULTURAL PRODUCTION.

of the Ganges Delta, abaca chiefly of the Philippines, and the sisals largely of southern Mexico, although some success has attended intratropical transfers, such as sisal to Tanzania. Modernized cultural technologies in home regions have not kept pace with those in the newer regions to which some of the fiber plants have been moved. Thus cotton production within the United States has significantly shared in the recent agricultural revolution by which mechanization has greatly altered the production and cost patterns.

The animal fibers, on the other hand—wool, mohair, and camel's hair in the Old World and llama-alpaca-vicuna wool in the New World—have been the product of cooler climates in the higher latitudes or the high mountains. Intercontinental and interhemispheric transfers have found new regions of production which have edged into the dry subtropics of the world, thereby altering the production patterns in traditional homelands. Silk is a slightly anomalous member of the animal fibers, long restricted to eastern Asia. Historic transfers of the silkworm and the mulberry tree have been made to many parts of the tropical and subtropical world, with little success.

In the historical development of plant domestication (see Table 4.1 and Fig. 4.8A) we noted that there were a number of regional centers which, out of their wild-plant assemblages, yielded significant groups of crop plants, and that the Old World, particularly, yielded groups of animals (see Fig. 4.8B and Table 4.2). As man has worked with these plants and animals, to improve them in quality and to move them about as producers, he has rearranged the assemblages into distinctive groups in different regional environments around the earth, according to his ability, the nature of the environments, and his cultural choices. This has been a process steadily taking place, and one which has changed the nature of the particular assemblage from century to century (Fig. 8.6 and see pp. 179–190, 327–338). It is a process that is actively taking place at the present time in most parts of the earth. In the 1960s economic geographers refer to the American Corn Belt as a distinctive agricultural region. Involved in the annual production cycle in the Corn Belt are corn (maize) from Middle America, soybeans from North China, wheat, barley, and oats from southwest Asia, leguminous and grassy forage plants from several regions, a number of vegetable plants from both the Old World and the New, the pig and cattle from the Old World, the

chicken from Southeast Asia, and a few other crop plants and animals-birds from many sources as minor items. This assemblage is integrated in a highly efficient manner to use land alternately and to produce particular outputs of crops or animals according to market demand. This is a highly mechanized agricultural system, employing rotation systems, fertilizers, new hybrids, and watchful attention to the market, to form one of the earth's most productive agricultural regions in this century.

Elsewhere around the earth, the same kinds of selective assemblages have been compounded, although the degree of productive efficiency seldom approaches that of the American Corn Belt. One more illustration must suffice. In its own way the Chinese agricultural region of the Szechwan Basin is both distinctive and productive. There, rice from South China, wheat from southwest Asia, the sweet potato from Middle America, a variety of soybean from Central China, sugarcane from New Guinea, sorghum from India, cotton from Ethiopia, rape (*Brassica napus*) from southwest Asia, corn from Middle America, the tung oil tree from Southwest China, several citruses from South China, the pig and the chicken from Southeast Asia, the water buffalo from southern Asia, the goat from central Asia, and a few minor crops and animals have been put together into a very distinctive regional assemblage that makes the region one of the most productive sectors of China. That there is much less mechanization, much less employment of fertilizers, and fewer new hybrid varieties prevents its yielding the huge surpluses that come out of the American Corn Belt, since per capita yields are lower.

It is obvious, today, that traditional pastoralism in several portions of the Old World is being turned into a kind of industrialized livestock raising, and the extensive range-cattle pattern so dear to the Hollywood western movie is being intensified into a more productive livestock raising industry in other parts of the world. It is equally obvious that synthetic production of numerous commodities is replacing the natural production patterns of a former era in a series of shifts not yet fully refined. The economic geography of world agriculture remains both a complex and a changing thing, as the agricultural revolution continues to spread spatially and to increase its qualitative efficiency. Simultaneously with these changes in the production systems changes are taking place in consumption systems, as Filipinos increase their liking for wheat and dairy products in a regional environment traditionally a rice producer and nondairy-product oriented, as Americans shift from natural silks to synthetic fibers and as the European Common Market rules alter regional trade movements of particular commodities. Such changes in the flow of agricultural commodities will continue, just as the broad zonality of production patterns will remain in force while altering their specifics.

Certain sectors of the earth can still be described as in the Neolithic, so far as their agricultural systems of production of primary commodities are concerned. Much of the interior of New Guinea remains, in the 1960s, at the Neolithic level in agricultural terms, although it may not remain there much longer. Such a sector as Mesopotamia, in terms of rural agricultural system, is little removed from the era during which the ox-drawn plow first began to change Neolithic crop growing; the rural agricultural scene no longer is Neolithic, but even less is it twentieth-century. In selected rural farmscapes of Europe, Japan, Peru, or American Appalachia the agricultural system employed is still descriptive of the late eighteenth century. These are not the regions of the world that feed the large populations of urban residents now living in twentieth-century manner. Only the North American Midwest can afford, today, to ship abroad in a year about a year's United States consumption total of wheat to feed regions in which population has grown faster than agricultural production. Resource-extracting technology has been altered fundamentally; technology is today available to the whole earth. Unless the peoples of the earth adopt similar technologies there will be greater hunger in the crowded lands of the earth 'ere long.

The Regionalisms of Supply in Raw Materials, Power, and Food

Economic geography is concerned with the regional distribution of production of primary commodities and their movement to consuming centers. Out of the earth's environmental regionalism certain patterns emerge as natural conditions which man has accepted without undue opposition. Although, technologically, bananas could be grown in Antarctica today, it seems not worthwhile to pay the price to do so when there are so many tropical localities in which bananas will grow easily and cheaply. Man normally has sought the easier ways of accomplishing ends he comprehended, although on many occasions he has stubbornly insisted on doing things his way regardless of the price to be paid.

In the realm of primary production there are several axioms worth stating that affect the spatial distribution of production. In the area of mineral commodities the normal sequence has been to begin with the richest sources processable by the easiest and cheapest means, and to proceed to utilize less rich sources only when a new technology has been developed through expansion of human culture. In the zone of power production, theoretically, man has always sought to shift labor from his own muscles to some other source of power. Here man has often been controlled by cultural habit. It may be a bit incomprehensible to the twentieth century American that in the Chinese Szechwan Basin no wheel turned in transport until the 1930s and that no one used other transport when a man could pick up an item and carry it (in Yunnan, in Southwest China, no man carried what could be loaded onto a horse). In the production of agricultural commodities it is an axiom that the largest volume and the highest quality of crop yields are often not in the aboriginal ecological home of the crop plant, but somewhere out toward its ecological margins, where man has improved the plant and bred varieties that will tolerate conditions not tolerable in the homeland. Here man often has to play nursemaid to the crops to secure that maximum yield of high quality. Thus the "Sunkist" orange grown in Southern California, by growers who pamper their orange trees and protect them from frost, is produced both in larger volume and in better quality than in its Southeast Asian homeland. For the United States, the saying, "there must be a better way to do it," is virtually an axiom. It is this persistent search which, combined with European cultural trends in the realm of rewarded inventiveness, has sparked the current technological revolution.

It is also a notable axiom that man has capitalized upon the natural regional monopoly in minerals, technological skills, and crop-animal products when he could. Thus China long kept the source of silk secret, and Brazil forbade the export of the seeds of the *Hevea* rubber tree. However, there is a corresponding axiom that men in other regions break a natural monopoly at the first possible opportunity, be it in mineral resource, technology,

A.D. 1800

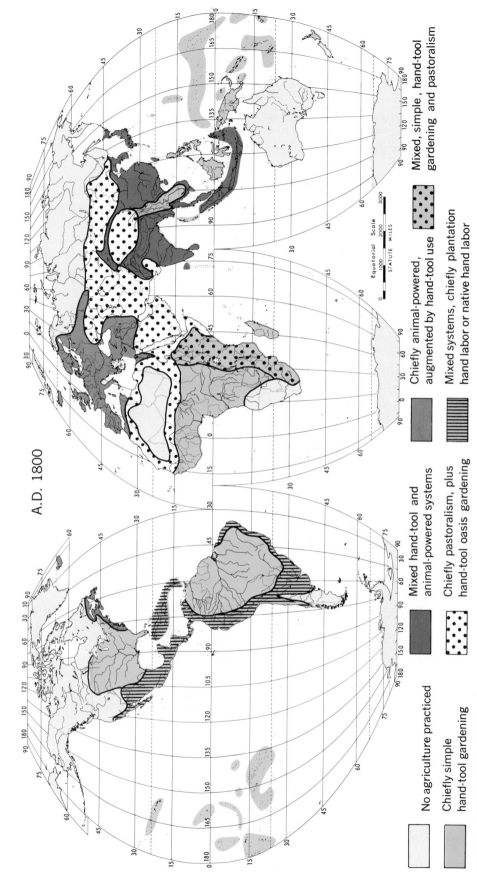

No agriculture practiced

Chiefly simple
hand-tool gardening

Mixed hand-tool and
animal-powered systems

Chiefly pastoralism, plus
hand-tool oasis gardening

Chiefly animal-powered,
augmented by hand-tool use

Mixed systems, chiefly plantation
hand labor or native hand labor

Mixed, simple, hand-tool
gardening and pastoralism

Equatorial Scale
1000 2000 3000
0 1000 2000
STATUTE MILES

FIG. 8.6 SYSTEMS OF AGRICULTURAL TECHNOLOGY. A. In A.D. 1800.

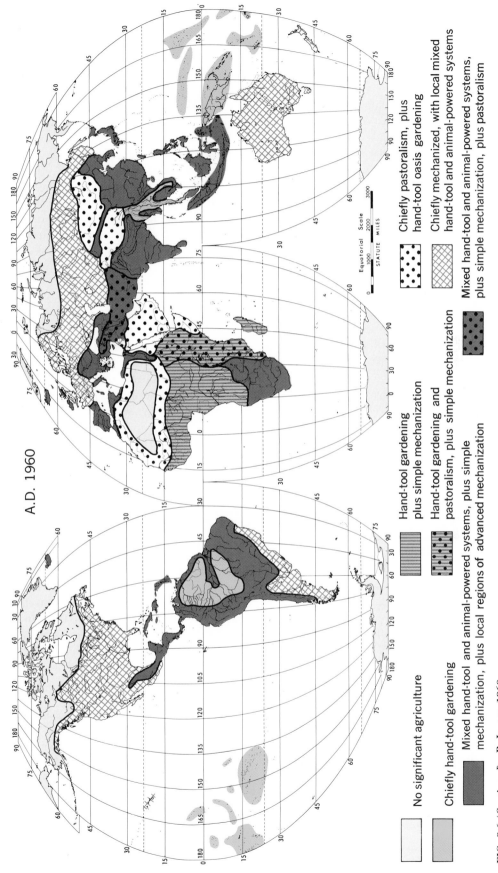

A.D. 1960

Equatorial Scale

1000   2000   3000

0   STATUTE MILES

No significant agriculture

Chiefly hand-tool gardening

Mixed hand-tool and animal-powered systems, plus local regions of advanced mechanization

Hand-tool gardening plus simple mechanization

Hand-tool gardening and pastoralism, plus simple mechanization

Mixed hand-tool and animal-powered systems, plus simple mechanization, plus local regions of advanced mechanization

Chiefly pastoralism, plus hand-tool oasis gardening

Chiefly mechanized, with local mixed hand-tool and animal-powered systems

Mixed hand-tool and animal-powered systems, plus simple mechanization, plus pastoralism

FIG. 8.6 (Continued) B. In A.D. 1960.

crop product, or manufactured product. Thus an Englishman spirited *Hevea* seeds out of Brazil, spies steal technologies for their motherlands, and many formerly nonsteel producing countries search out iron ore and erect steel mills. The progressive culture group that finds itself dependent on outside sources for certain commodities, technologies, or products, in the long run, seeks its own internal sources of supply or expands its region to include those resources. Acceptance by man of certain axiomatic rules of procedure, the persistences of doing things in willful and culturally determined ways, and the cultural technologies devised to improve on nature all have affected the spatial patterns of the supply of raw materials, the sources and locations of power supplies, the centering in production of food resources, and the very technologies of resource extraction from the earth. The breaking of natural monopolies in the last few centuries has led to the almost worldwide diffusion of the resource-extracting techniques, and such diffusion conditions the spatial distribution of the production and use of these techniques.

In the realm of plant and animal raw materials the post-Columbian transfers had not been completed and ecologically regionalized when modern industrial chemistry began to make inroads on production schemes, trade patterns, and consumer use. Some of the items had a short boom period as natural products, only to be almost totally replaced by the synthetic products. Industrial chemistry has not yet run the gamut of the long list of plant raw materials, and it is likely that many of them will continue in production in their traditional homes under their traditional culture systems, either for localized use or for world trade.

Power Supply

Here the term power [units of energy per second, expressed as the standard kilowatt (kw)] is interpreted very broadly as any means of performing work. At the highest level of technology man has come a long way from the point in time at which human muscle was the only applicable power source; however, in many parts of the earth culture groups and societies have yet to apply much of the available power technology. The sources of power are many, but the problems of utilizing some of these sources are cultural in that technological procedures are involved. Power-creating technologies now range rather widely, but most

of those in use are still rather elementary, and the problems of widespread application are somewhat involved (Fig. 8.7). Man uses solar energy as converted by plants, but the means of turning plant materials into suitable forms of power have been only slowly developed and still are not very efficient. Man uses solar energy as expressed in the planetary wind systems, but the range of applications has not developed very widely on an efficient basis. Similarly, the power of moving water has only recently been harnessed in other than the most inefficient of applications. There is internal earth energy available, but the problems of application have not been dealt with satisfactorily in other than a few isolated cases. The nuclear reactor has recently been added to the list of sources, but the normal work accomplishment procedures are still undergoing perfection.

This historical human approach to the development of power began with man himself as the source of power. The application of fire was perhaps second in the sequence, burning common combustible materials. Through wood, charcoal, peat, coal, petroleum, natural gas, and such plant wastes as bagasse, the fire technology for power production has grown more efficient and taken over more and more of the world's work load. The application of fire to plant or fossil plant products today remains the chief source of power. Through the domestication of the larger animals man gained another power source, and animal power still is a much used source in many parts of the world, but it is destined to decline in importance. Through the windmill and the sail the winds were tapped for power for a period of history, and in the West there remains the recreational use of wind power in the sailboat. The high-level application of wind power has remained beset by technological problems and is little used today. Through the waterwheel cultural technology has progressed to the modern hydroelectric sequence and, today, electricity is the chief medium of energy throughout the world, procured through both the fire and hydro sequences. From the first crude "gunpowder" mix of combustible materials compounded in China through the various "dynamite" compounds to the contemporary endothermic and thermonuclear mixtures, the work potential of the "explosive" variety and the jet thrust has steadily increased, both in ability and in efficiency, and perhaps we are on the verge of a revolution in power development.

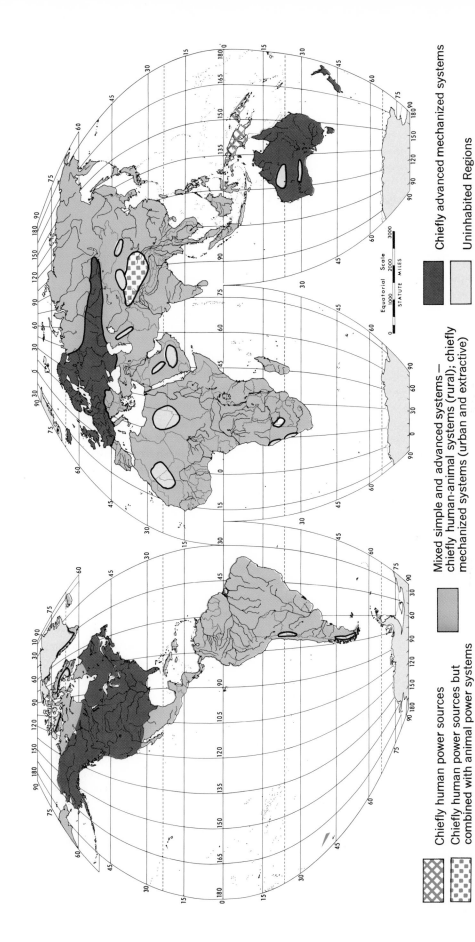

Chiefly human power sources

Chiefly human power sources but combined with animal power systems

Mixed simple and advanced systems — chiefly human-animal systems (rural); chiefly mechanized systems (urban and extractive)

Chiefly advanced mechanized systems

Uninhabited Regions

Equatorial Scale
0   1000   2000   3000
STATUTE MILES

FIG. 8.7   SYSTEMS OF POWER PRODUCTION.

365

None of the applications of power so far utilized has achieved very high efficiency, and it is often estimated that we are wasting as much as 80 percent of all the energy potential in our older forms of power development. Particularly for the fossil fuels it is high time that some greater efficiency in technology were obtained. Even though the present known fossil fuel resources are greater than ever, they are being used infinitely more rapidly than they are being created, and the supply will become exhausted eventually.

In distributional terms of total power potential, power is available to every sector of the earth through some medium, but the cultural technologies are unequally distributed. In more conventional terms the northern hemisphere has far more than half the total of the fossil fuels, the hydroelectric potential, and the combustible plant materials. Within the northern hemisphere the United States, Canada, the Soviet Union, and China are points of concentration. For the United States and the Soviet Union this becomes a matter of both the resources themselves and the cultural technologies by which they handle the conventional sources of power and the newer and more complex endothermic and thermonuclear media. For much of the rest of the earth the present basic canvass of power resources is still quite incomplete, and the development of the technologies of application is sketchy. Experiment with advanced techniques on solar machines, for example, is fairly far advanced in India, although the practical application still has far to go to make the medium available to the population. Although China still appears rather short of the petroleum form of power source, the survey is inadequate and the technologies of application are restricted.

Food Products

The zonality of world food agriculture in the modern period (see Fig. 8.5) is compounded of three different factor complexes. There is, first, an environmental and regional centering of production related to the broad climatic zonation of specific plant tolerances to temperature and precipitation, and to the zones of occurrence of wild plants that were turned into domesticated crop plants. Domesticated in southeastern Asia, rice has dominated the regional agriculture of this sector of the world ever since. Maize is a New World subtropical domestication and it has been traditionally dominant in sectors of the New World.

Some of the *Brassica* cabbages came into domestication in Northwest Europe so that the large, flatheaded cabbages are as naturally a part of European agriculture as the various cabbage food preparations are a part of European diet. On the other hand, some of the *Brassica* cabbages were domesticated in Eastern Asia, and the tall, nonheaded cabbages are naturally a part of Chinese and Korean agriculture and cookery. These traditional patterns have been preserved in basic agriculture in many different ways, and it is this kind of design that associates wheat, barley, and oats as crops of European agriculture, and the breadstuffs, scotch whiskeys, and oatmeals as parts of the European dietary-beverage complex, whereas the taros, yams, and pigs are part of the agriculture of the South Pacific, and poi, roast yams, and barbecued pork are thought of as typically Polynesian.

Second, there is the transfer of crop plants about the earth, from ecological homelands into analogous regions elsewhere. This has produced a repetitive zonation of agricultural regionalisms around the earth. Thus the olive, vine, stone fruit, winter grain, summer vegetable agricultural complex of the Mediterranean Basin, with its irrigation systems and other technological attributes, was translated into Southern California, Central Chile, South Africa, and southern Australia. The North European agricultural system spread across the central to northern sectors of the United States and across southern Canada, as well as to southeastern Australia, complete with crops, animals, processing systems, and dietary complexes. The tropical elements of agriculture similarly were transferred between the New World, the Asian, and the African tropics, so that coffee, coconut, sugarcane, and other crops find repetitive production regions.

Third, there has been the tendency by man to push crops into nonanalogous ecological environments by breeding new varieties of old crops that possess new tolerances, or by finding crop plants that naturally possessed high ranges of tolerance to specific environmental conditions. Thus, in time, some of the wheats have been transformed from a crop of the subtropical margin to a high-latitude crop, and wheat growing has pushed northward in both Eurasia and in Canada. Citrus fruits have been taken out of the humid tropics into the drier subtropics to the very margins of frost and moisture tolerances. In exploiting both the adaptabilities and the tolerances of crop plants man has both broadened and duplicated traditional ecological regionalism in crop growing.

By the 1960s, under the impact of the three trends, there have been produced both duplication and heterogeneous mixture in world agriculture. The mixing of crop systems has been subject to both human preference and human willfulness, so that the matters of transfer have not always been entirely logical in terms of environmental ecology. Europeans settled in the New World took to corn as a crop plant and spread it widely, also eating it in many forms as a regular item in their dietary. Europeans remaining resident in Northwest Europe, on the other hand, still consider corn a product only good for feeding livestock. Although the white potato can be grown over most of China, the Chinese have not taken to it willingly, and the crop is grown only in those highland or northern margins in which other, preferred crops cannot be grown well. The Philippines lie within the traditional rice-growing zone of Eastern Asia, and rice has been the traditional staple food crop. Within the Central Philippines, in the Visayan Islands, the coralline limestone soils are often too dry for rice growing. Here in the late eighteenth century corn began to be an acceptable food, and corn growing began to expand. Within the Visayan Islands sector today corn is the staple food, rather than rice, and corn dominates the regional agriculture.

Despite such historic changes in the traditional regional patterns of crop plants, there remains a broad zonality in world agriculture. This zonality is less continental or hemispheric than world climatic zonation in design. The world's tropics still yield agricultural products not produced elsewhere. The humid subtropics still produce particular commodities not found in the dry subtropics. The high-latitude regions yield crop assemblages that can only be duplicated in high-mountain country in the low-latitude areas of the earth.

Although the sixteenth and seventeenth centuries were periods of rapid and extensive change in the regional patterns of world crop growing, the process has continued right into the twentieth century, and it will continue into the future as man keeps up his experimentation with crop plants in different ecological environments of the earth, to test the adaptability and the transformability of particular plants. Thus it is that in Southern California, in recent decades, active production of avocados has been instituted, with a crop tree domesticated in Middle America. Careful plant selection and breeding and equally careful ecological siting for orchards in frost-free and wind-sheltered localities have produced a significant crop that adds variety to the American diet. Similarly, the Chinese tung-oil tree now is being grown in southeastern United States to produce a domestic source of a paint-lacquer ingredient, which both expands American agriculture and breaks a Chinese monopoly.

The food agriculture of the earth, today, presents a broad but complex pattern of duplication and regional specialization (Fig. 8.8). Crop surpluses are available to move into the routes of trade to all parts of the world, but many food items are regionally available in many parts of the earth with only short-haul transport required. There is every indication that the duplication will increase to the end that many items will be available to people everywhere. On the other hand, regional agricultural specialization remains an attribute of many particular sectors of the earth owing to inherited traditional preferences, per the dietary, to the difficult problem of transferring certain crop plants to other ecological analogues, or to the increasing ease and declining costs of modern transport.

The Have and the Have-Nots: Development and Underdevelopment

Some regions of the earth are described as wonderful in living qualities and rich in resources, whereas others are often described in less bountiful terms. There can be no questioning of regional inequalities in the compounding of total physical-biotic environments on our changing earth. Not all parts of the earth are alike, man can never make its innumerable separate regions into fully similar or equivalent entities, and there will always be some regions considered better than others by some collective human judgment. Human values of quality, or satisfactoriness, have always varied and, presumably, they always will vary to some extent owing to psychosocial outlooks of men in groups. In the present brief era of emergent political colonialism and strongly contrasting sociopolitical systems it has become popular in some quarters to describe advanced cultures as malignant exploiters that have preyed upon the regions and the peoples of the less advanced sectors of the earth. This procedure is an old one, often repeated in specific circumstances of the past, adapted to

368

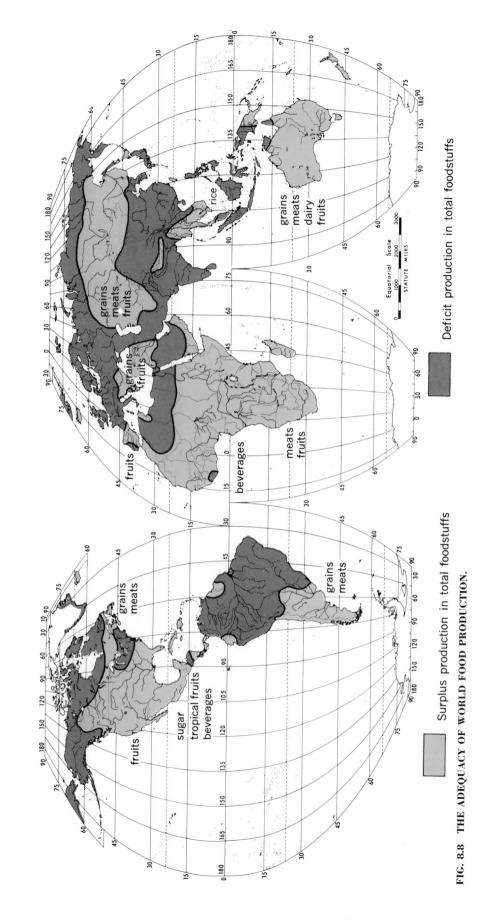

Surplus production in total foodstuffs

Deficit production in total foodstuffs

FIG. 8.8   THE ADEQUACY OF WORLD FOOD PRODUCTION.

the settings and crises of the times, and expressed in the language and thought of the era. Such a procedure is easily adopted, for it shifts responsibility for human development, initiative, and progress from the shoulders of the exploited and places it wholly on the shoulders of the exploiters. However, this procedure disregards both the physical-biotic environmental differentiation of the earth and the very nature of cultural evolution.

There now can be little doubt that mankind is a part of a broadly irreversible evolutionary development of the organic aspect of life on earth. Man came onto the scene as an element in that organic development. Culture has been the means of bringing about the dominance by man within the organic world. Culture has also been the means by which certain groups of men, in more or less organized societies, speeded up and differentiated the cultural evolution of mankind, so that marked inequalities have resulted in the living systems to be found in different regional environments on the earth's surface (Fig. 8.9). Although there has been no real doubt that the linkage of the inhabited regions of the earth would produce a "one-world" condition at some time, the variable use of culture by human societies has created extreme regional and qualitative differentiation along the route, as discussed in earlier chapters. The "one-world" stage, or phase, has been approximated only within the last two centuries, through the selective employment of culture by certain groups of men in more highly organized societies (rather than in less organized ones). But is it within the current or future prospect that the generally irreversible evolution of human culture may now be stabilized and stopped, to diverge upon a tangent course in which the end result could be the making of life totally equal for all of mankind? Would such stabilization be progress or stagnation? Is true equivalence in human living systems, probabilistically, the outcome of an evolutionary process on an earth which possesses basic physical inequalities? Would it be possible for mankind to stabilize the organic and cultural evolutionary processes at a point at which literally everyone has an equivalence of everything and possesses the same degree of psychosocial satisfaction? This simply does not seem possible. One may ask whether cultural evolution has now reached that point at which mankind, singly, in societal combines, or collectively, may be able to stay its further development at any chosen point, to make cultural achievement

for every society of mankind equivalent in every region of the earth. This, too, does not seem very possible.

In the time of man on the earth there have been obvious differences in the rates of embracement of new cultural advances and in the purposeful pursuit of human living systems that would provide the maximum comfort, prosperity, and psychosocial satisfaction. In former times some societies took residence in regions not affording strong opportunity for the adoption (by diffusion) of cultural progress. There can be only one comparative result at any point in time when, on a nonuniform earth, there are variable potential patterns of opportunity and when different societies pursue human comfort and prosperity at different rates. This result is that there must be qualitative differences in the patterns of human achievement in terms of progress, comfort, prosperity, and psychosocial satisfaction. The conclusion is inescapable: there always have been the haves and the have-nots, the leading and the lagging.

Unless the evolutionary aspects of human cultural development are to be stopped, stabilized, or controlled, the leading will be achieving some new advance while the lagging are moving toward the former status of the leading. This is a qualitative matter and it must not be construed as a territorial one. Rates of human progress have not been the same in all parts of the earth at all times, and the leadership in cultural progress has shifted from one society to another, but the qualitative differential in human living systems between the leading and the lagging has been growing greater through time, at least to the present. We still have lagging societies constrained by the patterns of the Paleolithic, the Neolithic, and the early metal ages resident on our one earth at the time during which some societies have entered the edges of the Nuclear Age. It is the latter, rather than the former, who are pressing for further growth, an action that can only increase the differential in quality of living systems.

The foregoing discussion must not be construed as condoning unjust exploitation of the weak by the strong (the lagging by the leading), but how does mankind decide what is exploitation? Can there be a single standard of rightness in such matters? What value should be attached to an earth substance which is deemed a resource by one society but is not comprehended in any way by another? Shall its utilization be prevented until

370

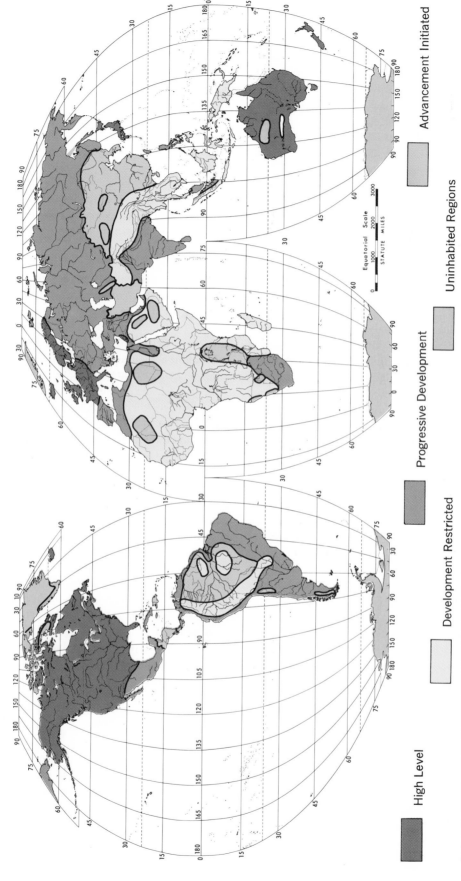

High Level

Development Restricted

Progressive Development

Uninhabited Regions

Advancement Initiated

Equatorial Scale
1000   2000   3000
0
STATUTE MILES

FIG. 8.9   COMPARATIVE CULTURAL DEVELOPMENT OF EARTH RESOURCES. (Technology, Resources, Organization and Perception of Environmental Possibilities.)

the time that the lagging possibly may use it? Can the "profits" of utilization of resources be more equitably shared? Mankind is now living through an era during which such questions must be faced in some way. But what is the way? The past history of mankind indicates only the competitive evolutionary struggle for a living system more satisfactory than mere biological survival, in which separation of the whole of mankind into societal units has involved the competition between some of those units for space, resources, and tools of culture. The definition of a utopia that would permit a kind of total equivalence in living systems on a nonuniform earth is not only beyond the comprehension of the authors, but is also beyond the scope of the present volume.

The Reduction of Wild Habitats

The year before man became man the causes of physical change in the nature of the earth could be ascribed to natural processes. The year after man became man the causal equation needed to take man into account, albeit slightly at that point. As culture has been expanded by man the role of human activity has increased steadily. An old saying was that man could not control the weather, but man now is able to create so much smog in many environments that the weather and climate are being altered in those regions. The issue is the ability of man, as a causal agent, to alter natural processes. Clearly man has become quite able to alter natural processes in different ways, and to alter the face of the earth.

Perhaps the most significant form of human alteration accomplished so far is the reduction of the so-called natural habitat of the face of the earth (Fig. 8.10 and see pp. 115–124, 179–190). Formerly the reduction was in small ways, at low rates, to small significant result. Tremendous changes by man through time have been wrought in the prehuman natural landscapes of the face of the earth but, until recently, any landscape in which the plant and animal life could be described as "wild" was often termed a natural landscape. Within the last two centuries the ability of man to effect change in the natural landscape has increased tremendously by virtue of his greater numbers, his more powerful tools, and his ability to go anywhere on the face of the earth. The result is that the wild habitats are either being totally transformed into cultivated and settled landscapes or the acts of transient man are becoming so significant that the wild habitat is altered substantially. Who has not returned to some geographical site remembered as lacking an agricultural landscape or a settlement, only to find farms or settlements thereon? Who has not climbed a mountain, or found a secluded spot in a forest, a desert, or on a stream bank, only to find a human artifact already there?

Within the last two centuries, during which the rates of population growth have been trending upward, there have come to be so many people and so many human requirements for forest, marine, mineral, and agricultural resources, or just for living space, that the rates of reduction of the wild habitat have increased greatly. The ability of man to procure these resources is far greater than it was, for his tools now give him a collective strength never before possessed and enable him to go greater distances than ever with the product. At the present rates of change, says the pessimist, the last truly wild habitat will have vanished before the end of the present century! Such is man's dominance of the face of the earth.

This does not mean, of course, that crop fields, village settlements, or the high-rise buildings of cities will soon be everywhere. The reduction of the wild habitat involves the rearrangement of the surface of the earth into man-controlled patterns. As the tree farms increase in number and area, better forests will grow where "natural" ones now grow. As parks replace native woodlands, there can be better recreational sites than before. As dams rise at narrows, the number of lakes is increasing steadily, particularly in arid lands. Chosen "wild" plants and animals will be kept, fostered, grown, and cared for. Recreational landscapes ordered to human dimensions and type will replace old bits of "wild" country, even as the golf-course architect orders the arrangement of fairways, roughs, and greens. The conservationist will decry this loss of the "wilderness" and will prevent it when possible. However, the dominance of man in ordering the face of the earth will continue as human requirements for ordered living space continue to grow.

The largest component in the man-ordered landscape, of course, will be crop fields and animal pastures for at least the foreseeable future. It is primarily the increasing demand for added food supplies that lies behind the current expansion in the cultivated landscapes of the earth. Rates of current population growth indicate that, despite the greatly improved agricultural production technology of a few parts of the earth, the added

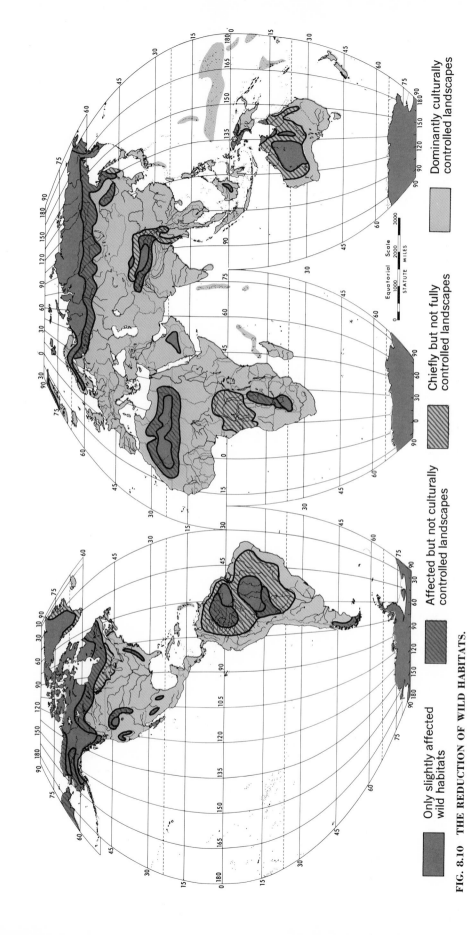

Only slightly affected
wild habitats

Affected but not culturally
controlled landscapes

Chiefly but not fully
controlled landscapes

Dominantly culturally
controlled landscapes

Equatorial Scale

0   1000   2000   3000
STATUTE MILES

FIG. 8.10 THE REDUCTION OF WILD HABITATS.

increased consumer demand will, within the very near future, require the expansion of agriculture to just about all the potential agricultural lands. Further expansion in consumer demand will then have to be met by increasingly efficient production technology in all the lands of the earth unless even more population elements are to grow hungry.

The Continuing Spread of Production Patterns

The traveler to the fairytale town in the folklore province of the far country is not shocked by what he often actually sees today, although emotionally he may react that it really was nicer in the old days when one could go to a really different land in which all this modern trend had not yet begun. The visitor to the tropical rain forest can watch the mechanized log loader, and he will need to watch for the careening logging truck speeding down the roadway bulldozed into the forest primeval. That forest may soon be converted into a new tree farm if it does not become a heavily populated farmscape. The steel mill is erected on a landscape that was being cropped by shifting cultivators only a generation ago. The trunk highway may have followed the forest trail to the site, but the new rail line cuts an alien element across the only partly forested region. The hydroelectric dam now creates a lake in a wild river canyon, and the transmission towers snake across hill and valley toward a city which a generation ago was but a quiet agricultural village. In a society in which people formerly were chiefly concerned with a modestly productive agricultural economy, the national economic plan now places a priority upon a steel industry, and the top priority for graduates of the expanded educational system lists the engineer and the skilled technician. The large construction firm today headquartered in an American or German city has employees scattered around the world busily engaged in building the producing artifacts of the industrial society. The agricultural equipment manufacturer who formerly sold chiefly to American farmers may now sell nearly half his mechanized equipment abroad, and his sales sheet lists most of the countries of the earth.

These examples are not fanciful; they are out of the field notes of the authors of this book. The present is an era of extensive and intensive change in production patterns all over the earth, as the pace of upgrading of production technology spreads around the world. It is a pace that can only increase in tempo as formerly conservative societies grasp the opportunities for culture change at a rate seldom witnessed earlier. In some countries American engineers compete with Canadian, English, French, German, Italian, Japanese and Russian engineers for the installation of the most productive plant, and the government aid systems proffered may range through the list of occidental countries for particular elements of modernizing technological change. The critical point is that modern technologically formulated production patterns are diffusing rapidly to all parts of the earth, as the processes of cultural change affect political, social, and psychological change.

The two decades of the 1950s–1960s saw the wholesale onset of the processes of change. There naturally are errors, inefficiencies, incompatibilities, and contradictions involved as totally new technologies come in to replace old ones, for the new technologies also require compatible cultural and psychosocial changes in old culture systems. Integration in these matters cannot be achieved in a single generation in the formerly underdeveloped lands of the earth, for it required more time to produce these changes in the originating homelands. Often there are contradictions that arise out of the inability of the installation builders to fit the new elements to the old economy or situation, owing to a fundamental ignorance of culture patterns, psychologic viewpoints, or cultural mores. This is one of the prices of cultural change at forced-draft speeds, and it is but a diagnostic feature of the very rates of change.

The processes of spread in production patterns, in one sense, become a race to catch up. When Japan decided to modernize its production economy in the 1860s, electricity had not yet become a major element in industrial procedures anywhere. Before Japan had achieved a modest coal-powered industrial development, the electrical industries had been born, and further advances had to encompass that growth, too. Change in production systems around the world may need to involve almost all of the varied subsystems, but such change may skip over particular segments or subsystems to modernize with the latest and most productive. Some countries, therefore, may never go through the animal-powered expansion of agriculture as did the United States, but may update directly with mechanized motive power. There can be no one solution to these kinds of problems, but it is certain that there is taking place the continuing spread of new and more productive means of resource-extracting techniques.

The Future of Known Resources

Every discussion of natural resources, including this one, is constrained by several sets of assumptions. Perhaps the most basic of present assumptions relates to where the mineral resources are located and what societies control them, for tables of resources are compiled by political status and resources are still regarded as near monopolies reserved for economic, military, and political control by the state in which they lie. Another set of assumptions relates to the qualities of resources and whether the several resources are economically workable by currently known technologies. A third set of assumptions relates to the issues of geologic and other kinds of resource survey. This pattern of assumption normally considers finite what we now know, and it does not take into proper account the incompleteness of our knowledge of earth resources. The present discussion disregards all these assumptions, since the earth is now linked into one operating whole with regard to technology and transport. This discussion makes the assumption that the earth's resources will be available to those who can process them into usable products desired by the whole world's population. The basic issue is whether the earth's critical resources are predictably exhaustible within a finite period.

There is little merit, for this discussion, in arguing that source A is about to become exhausted and that we must strictly conserve it, when sources B and C possess enormous quantities of the resource in question at present economic and technologic levels. Similarly, there is little merit in arguing for the utmost care regarding source E because sources F and G cannot now be utilized by economic and technological standards now applicable. Future technological advances surely can find a way to make sources F and G economically available when there is need for the advance. There is not much merit in arguing that resource H is absolutely vital to the future of the economic world and that its present source must be controlled very tightly, when modern Science can find a way around this problem. The last few decades demonstrate the futility of this approach.

For all of the thousands of different materials that are utilized as resources in some manner in the present world of complex technology, the really critical items come down to a relatively small number. Most of our resource materials are replaceable by substitutes to some degree; the matter of "irreplaceableness" is attached to customary and habituated technology, by habituated economics, or by the fact that no alternative technology and usage system has been necessary in the traditional past. If the most advanced modern cultural technology is to be restricted by the traditional limits of the past, then the conclusion is rapidly reached that the future of the population of the earth is very dim indeed. There are many materials, resources, items, and things that man could do without in the future, in a limited austerity. There are many materials that now can replace others, but for economic habits which maintain present usage. Science has not really exerted itself, as yet, to find replacements for some kinds of materials, because the present sources seem inexhaustible and it would not be worth the effort to replace them. In the future, when such technologic replacements become necessary, it is within the present capacity of technology to turn to replacement sources for many of our present customary resources.

The list of basic resources is as short as it is because it is a list of rather fundamental items, the ingredients of which can be combined in many separate ways in different mixtures, and because several of the items are chemical elements, as given, whereas others are natural-product mixtures of several chemical elements. Probably no two lists would set down the same absolute number of really critical items needed by our present level of economic technology, but ours is presented in Table 8.1. We would agree that the most basic list of all would merely be a selective list out of the total roster of chemical elements, leaving it to scientific technology to find the ways of combining these into whatever is necessary. On the other hand, we have not totally disregarded the traditional issues of cultural systems, economic technology, and practicality. There is no merit in starting with simple chemical elements when coal, petroleum, and cellulose are so plentiful in already complex mixtures.

The first three items on our list are natural products of the past and present earth. The coals (anthracites to peats, chiefly plant carbons and hydrocarbons), celluloses (chiefly plant carbohydrates), and the petroleums (including natural gas, chiefly plant and animal hydrocarbons) are the mainstay of our economic world, because they

TABLE 8.1 MATERIALS CRITICAL TO MODERN INDUSTRY[a]

Coals	Sulfurs
Celluloses	Sodiums (chiefly chloride)
Petroleums–natural gases	Glass sands (chiefly quartzes)
Radioactives	Kaolins
	Gypsums
Irons	
Manganeses	Coppers
Tungstens	Tins
Nickels	Leads
	Zincs
Nitrates	Aluminums
Phosphoruses	Mercuries
Potashes	Golds
Calciums	Silvers

[a] Stated as generic compounds, with specific combinations occurring in numerous constituent forms, chiefly as ores.

combine many elements into forms easily reduced, compounded, recombined, and processed. The earth's total volume of the carbons and hydrocarbons is sufficient that the reserves should last for hundreds of years even at increased rates of consumption. It is true that most of these resources now appear to lie in the northern hemisphere, that France, or Chile, possesses only a very small fraction of the total, that Guyana or Monaco may possess almost none, and that the United States has the largest reserves of any political state. Applied to coals the above is even more true than for the celluloses. We really are not certain of the condition of the petroleums. In terms of exhaustibility it is probable that the petroleums will become exhausted much earlier than the coals and the celluloses, the last of which can be grown in future forests, but it may well be that over the long run of time the release into the atmosphere of the smog-producing hydrocarbons will be more critical than the problem of conservation of reserves of the petroleums.

The next group of items, iron and its basic alloys, presents no significant problem. There is a tremendous volume of iron in the earth's crust, and ample supplies of manganese, tungsten, and nickel. Other ferroalloys are useful but they merely gild the lily. Iron compounds are critical to the continuance of life as we know it today, despite the light minerals, and a fundamental reorganization of civilization would be required were iron to be removed from the list of commodities.

The third group of items forms the primary elements of the agricultural fertilizers. This group is critically important to the future health and very subsistence of the earth's population, and the problem lies not in their scarcity but in the habituated neglect of their use by crop growers in most parts of the world. Although the easily derivable sources are not plentiful for the potashes and the phosphoruses, the earth's total volume is adequate for a period of centuries. Modern chemical technology is perfectly able to produce sufficient volumes, and it is economic undertakings that have lagged.

The fourth group of resources comprises somewhat nonglamorous and unspectacular items that are so common and widespread that they do not get much discussion. However, these resources are critical to civilization as we know it. Sulfur is a primary agent in a large number of industrial processes, glass in some form is basic to much of modern living, the limestones provide the cements in which the modern world builds, and the clays go into a huge number of economic products deeply entrenched in ways of modern living. The total reserves of each are so large that there is no problem surrounding any of them.

In the last group of items is a set of metals variably significant to modern industrial technology, entrenched in cultural custom, widely usable in many different ways, or prized for other than economic purposes. The last two items, gold and silver particularly, have nonindustrial significance but probably are critical to our patterns of life. Of this last group it is very possible that gold and silver may present some serious problems in the near future. The mining industry insists that it is an economic cost problem involving the arbitrary politically established price on the two metals. However, it does appear true that the easily and cheaply mined gold and silver stocks have been about mined out, and that no technological process of refining has been devised sufficient to extract the two metals from other existing sources at present price levels.

It would be possible to make a case for other specific resource items, but the basic conclusion is that the earth's resources are plentiful for a long time to come. It is not that the resources do not exist. It is, in part, that cultural technology has not sought the solutions potentially possible in all cases. More significant, however, has been the habituated political attitudes which have made territorial monopolies of particular resources, attitudes that must change if the earth is to operate properly as one economic world in the future. We shall return to this topic in a later chapter.

Admittedly, the foregoing presentation of the issue of resources is not derived from the standard literatures on natural resources as written from the nationalistic viewpoint, nor is it derived from the traditional literatures on the conservation of natural resources. Nothing said by us should be taken to condone wasteful usage of resources, for that is simply uneconomic, culturally immature, and technologically inefficient. The presentation is made from the standpoint that the whole earth constitutes one resource base for the support of mankind. Wise, forward-looking, and technologically efficient considerations of fundamental resources, with currently-known technologies and those advances understood by Science, suggest that man can live comfortably on the present earth for a long time to come, provided he is equally wise, forward-looking, and technologically efficient about his own numbers. But as to the simple matter of resource adequacy, this entire section was written in consideration of the attitude expressed thus:

"Simple calculations show that the Earth can probably provide comfort and convenience for upwards of fifty billions of persons—if the surface of the tropical oceans were to be exploited. Such a possibility does not suggest that this is a desirable pattern for the future, nor does it say anything about the feasibility of getting from where we are now to a general worldwide state of adequacy, regardless of ultimate numbers. A procedure or strategy for development has therefore been sought that attempts to introduce these new technologies to best advantage. From this exercise it appears that even the promised, but as yet unproved, technological achievements are likely to be insufficient. However, they miss the mark by much less than any known alternative approach."*

Our presentation has been made on the triple assumption that man will never let his total numbers reach 50 billion, that human culture (and, therefore, cultural technology) has not yet reached its maximum potential capacity for resource extrac-

*R. L. Meier, *Science and Economic Development*, New York: Massachusetts Institute of Technology and John Wiley & Sons, 1956, p. 236.

tion and resource conversion on our earth, and that political monopoly will not always stand in the way of resource development.

Cultural Technology and the Future Concept of Resources

What we have perhaps belabored as the comprehension of a resource is really a rather complex set of interactions, conceptually and technologically. It would appear that the early historic interactions were empirical in nature, by which experience resulted in a limited comprehension not fully accompanied by adequate conceptual theory. In terms of human cultural development the early achievements, remarkable as they were, were immature and incomplete. The history of metal smelting, down to the nineteenth century, would suggest this pattern (see Chapter 4, under the heading "The Age of Metals, Mining, Ores, and Smelting"). In the contemporary Age of Science, however, conceptual theory often leads the way, with the invention of the means being an experimental and consequent result, followed still later by the evolution of efficient productive machinery. Such is the history of nuclear reaction and space rocketry, with early theorizing by Max Planck and Albert Einstein and the later conceptualizing by Enrico Fermi, all of which preceded the experimental building of the effective instruments, whereas the perfecting of the hardware was still going on during the 1960s. What is today termed basic research is a combination of theorizing (including following up on educated guesses and hunches) and laboratory experimentation, and it normally has little to do with practical application in everyday life. The empirical knowledge that accumulates is the result of building and operating working instruments, machinery, and other devices. As satisfactory experimentation concludes, there follows the elaboration of an engineering technology and the development of the effective hardware by which the routine operation may be undertaken as an economic endeavor. As the economic endeavor increases in scope, the pool of labor skills accumulates and the engineering refinements multiply. All of this is, relatively, the reverse of the procedures involved in the Mesolithic and Metal Age developments.

Out of this twentieth century research-to-production sequence the concept of resources is being probed and expanded in a way never before within the grasp of man. Conceptualization of chemical processes, physical reactions, and the essential nature of materials is far ahead of laboratory experiment, and both are well ahead of the empirical engineer, the hardware builder, and the organized entrepreneur. The linkage between these several stages, however, is much closer than it formerly was. Where Democritus (concept of the atom) and Archimedes (engineering theory and some application) of pre-Christian Greece, and Leonardo da Vinci (engineering design) of Renaissance Italy could but theorize, experiment, or fill notebooks with engineering ideas, the large contemporary corporation may integrate the several aspects of basic research, experimentation, design, applied research, engineering, and production into a continuous sequence. Although it may still take some years for a research conceptualization concerning telephonic communication to reach the home user of a telephone, or for a conceptualization in organic chemistry to reach the department store as a new textile, the integration present in such series is far beyond the level of accomplishment of any earlier society, and the ultimate reach of this cultural combination can only be estimated. The total eventual impact of university, corporation, and government research endeavor may, today, be such that we stand close to the threshold of astounding sequences of advancement, as some proponents of Science assert. In the terms we have employed in this book, this means that cultural development in this sector of human endeavor may be about to reach a degree of maturity.

If any share of this projection be approximate, the very nature of resources-in-general may be expandable for at least the whole of the human era. In the ultimate sense, the finite resources of the planet Earth have a limit, but man is not restricted to the use of the traditional forms of resources known and used in the past. So long as there are supplies of the necessary and known chemical elements available in the whole of the earth's crustal sector, or in the oceans, and so long as solar energy remains available, human intelligence is free to find a cultural technology sufficiently capable to extract the materials and energy in new ways for the production of ultimate consumer goods in any style that culture may define. This, in a sense, is the real meaning of the dominance of the earth by cultured mankind. The realization of the potential in extracting and converting the organic and inert materials of the earth into commodities and products usable by man knows only those limits set by man's own culture.

The reach of such conceptual theory, of course, poses problems, and some of these will be dealt with in a later chapter. Here, however, questions arise out of the previous remarks. To whom do the oceans belong, as raw materials resource? Who may endlessly withdraw water from the ocean volume, through desalinization, to humidize a desert a thousand miles from the nearest seashore? There is more oxygen in the crust of the earth than in the atmosphere. What country in the world is entitled to draw a supply of oxygen from the crustal sector of the earth under the central Pacific Ocean? Which society is entitled to withdraw supplies of heat from the deep interior of the earth to serve as a source of power? Which country is entitled to use that heat to rearrange its sector of the terrestrial wind systems' air-mass flow to improve its own climatic system? In the 1960s these, and others, may be academic questions, but how long will this be so? If Science achieves any proportion of the success demonstrated in the first half of the twentieth century, the questions may become very real not too far in the future. Then the question of to whom do the earth's resources belong will raise the qualitative regional differential of culture to a new problem level, for the specter of the haves and the have-nots will become more acute. The richness of the resources of a society will then be measured not by the possession of territorial space on the surface of the earth, but by the cumulative level of culture expressed as resource-extracting and converting techniques applicable at the time. From the standpoint of earth resources there arises the ultimate need for a one-world kind of economic compact phrased in such a way that the modern-era problem of destructive economic exploitation does not stand in the way of further cultural development of mankind as a species owning the earth.

SELECTED REFERENCES

Alderfer, E. B., and H. E. Michl
    1957   *Economics of American Industry* (3rd ed.). New York: McGraw-Hill. 710 pp.
Alexander, John W.
    1963   *Economic Geography.* New York: Prentice-Hall. 661 pp.
Bateman, Alan M.
    1955   *Economic Mineral Deposits* (2nd ed.). New York: Wiley. 916 pp.
Bauer, P. T., and B. S. Yamey
    1957   *The Economics of Underdeveloped Countries.* London: Nisbet; and Cambridge, England: Cambridge University Press (1965 printing). 271 pp.
Berry, Brian J. L.
    1967   *Geography of Market Centers and Retail Distribution.* Englewood Cliffs, N.J.: Prentice-Hall. 146 pp.
Boesch, Hans
    1964   *A Geography of World Economy.* Princeton, N.J.: Van Nostrand. 280 pp.
Coale, Ansley J., and Edgar M. Hoover
    1958   *Population Growth and Economic Development in Low Income Countries.* Princeton, N.J.: Princeton University Press. 389 pp.
Cottrell, Fred
    1955   *Energy and Society.* New York: McGraw-Hill. 330 pp.
Darling, J. Fraser, and John P. Milton (eds.)
    1966   *Future Environments of North America.* Garden City, N.Y.: The Natural History Press. 767 pp.
Estall, R. C., and R. O. Buchanan
    1961   *Industrial Activity and Economic Geography.* London: Hutchinson University Library. 232 pp.
Firth, Raymond, and B. S. Yamey (eds.)
    1964   *Capital, Savings and Credit in Peasant Societies: Studies from Asia, Oceania, The Caribbean, and Middle America.* Chicago: Aldine. 399 pp.
Ginsburg, Norton D.
    1961   *Atlas of Economic Development.* Chicago: University of Chicago Press. 119 pp.
Graubard, Stephen R. (ed.)
    1966   "Tradition and Change," *Daedalus,* Vol. 95, No. 3, pp. 713–915, of the Proceedings of the American Academy of Arts and Sciences.
    1967   "America's Changing Environment," *Daedalus,* Vol. 96, No. 4, pp. 1003–1223, of the Proceedings of the American Academy of Arts and Sciences.
Gruber, Ruth (ed.)
    1961   *Science and the New Nations.* New York: Basic Books. 314 pp.
Jarrett, Henry
    1966   *Environmental Quality in a Growing Economy.* Baltimore: The Johns Hopkins Press, for the Resources for the Future. 173 pp.
Kindelberger, Charles P.
    1958   *Economic Development.* New York: McGraw-Hill. 325 pp.
Manners, Gerald
    1964   *The Geography of Energy.* London: Hutchinson University Library. 205 pp.
Meier, Richard L.
    1956   *Science and Economic Development.* New York: Massachusetts Institute of Technology and John Wiley & Sons. 266 pp.
Mountjoy, Alan B.
    1963   *Industrialization and Underdeveloped Countries.* London: Hutchinson; and Chicago: Aldine, 1966. 200 pp.
Myrdal, Gunnar
    1957   *Economic Theory and Underdeveloped Regions.* London: Duckworth. 168 pp.
    1960   *Beyond the Welfare State.* New Haven, Conn.: Yale University Press. 287 pp.

Nef, John U.
  1958   *Cultural Foundations of Industrial Civilization.* London: Cambridge University Press. 163 pp. (Republished as a Harper Torchbook by Harper & Brothers, New York, 1960, 164 pp.)

Samuelson, Kurt
  1957   *Ekonomi och religion.* (Published in the United States under the translation title *Religion and Economic Action.*) New York: Basic Books, 1961. 156 pp. (Harper Torchbook by Harper & Brothers, New York, 1964).

Schonberg, James S.
  1956   *The Grain Trade: How It Works.* New York: Exposition Press. 351 pp.

Schultz, Theodore W.
  1964   *Transforming Traditional Agriculture.* New Haven, Conn.: Yale University Press. 212 pp.

Seidenberg, Roderick
  1950   *Post-Historic Man.* Chapel Hill, N.C.: University of North Carolina Press. 246 pp. (Beacon Press paperback edition, Boston, 1957).

Smith, J. Russell, M. Ogden Philipps, and Thomas R. Smith
  1955   *Industrial and Commercial Geography* (4th ed.). New York: Holt. 689 pp.

Thirring, Hans
  1958   *Energy for Man; Windmills to Nuclear Power.* Bloomington, Ind.: Indiana University Press. 409 pp.

Thoman, Richard S., and Edgar C. Conkling
  1967   *Geography of International Trade.* Englewood Cliffs, N.J.: Prentice-Hall. 190 pp.

Van Royen, William, et al.
  1952   *The Mineral Resources of the World.* Englewood Cliffs, N.J.: Prentice-Hall. 181 pp.
  1954   *The Agricultural Resources of the World.* Englewood Cliffs, N.J.: Prentice-Hall. 258 pp.

Whittaker, Edmund
  1960   *Schools and Streams of Economic Thought.* Chicago: Rand McNally. 416 pp.

Woytinsky, W. S., and E. S. Woytinsky
  1953   *World Population and Production.* New York: Twentieth Century Fund. 1268 pp.
  1955   *World Commerce and Governments.* New York: Twentieth Century Fund. 907 pp.

CHAPTER 9

Resource-Converting Techniques: Processing, Manufacturing, and Industrialization in the Twentieth Century

During the Paleolithic era it would have been difficult to distinguish between different stages of manufacturing activity. At what point could one distinguish between processing of raw materials and the manufacturing of end products? There was little of the specialization in resource conversion such as we commonly describe today. The very word "manufacture" signifies operations carried on by hand to improve the quality of a raw material, but the meaning of the term has been extended so that, today, it includes all of the many and complex operations carried on in turning raw materials into end products, even up to the computer-controlled industrial plants in which machines of some kind perform all the sundry operations. However, very few materials are directly converted today into end products by a single operation. It is necessary, therefore, to distinguish stages in industrial activity and to distinguish separate levels of use for many of the materials that enter into the whole of industrial activity.

Economic geographers and economists employ several terminologies and grouping systems in their discussions of industrialization. With regard to the materials themselves, it is possible to distinguish primary raw materials, secondary agents, and end products. The operations involved can be discussed under the headings processing, manufacture, and assembly; two pairs of terms often employed for the operations are primary and secondary manufacturing, and light industry and heavy industry. Another pair of terms often employed for the products are producer goods and consumer goods. Whatever the organization and terminologies used,

discussions of industrialization consistently point out the increased efficiencies that derive from the multiple procedures of resource conversion in the twentieth century.

In the Paleolithic, had one man specialized in crudely shaping stone blanks for arrow heads, another specialized in cutting and peeling arrow shafts, a third specialized in gathering and cutting the feather, a fourth in making the string for ties, and a fifth in gathering and melting down a kind of pitch or gum, we could have isolated the processing activity. Could we then have seen other men finishing the arrowheads, polishing the shafts, shaping and sizing the feathers, softening and sizing the string, and purifying the pitch, we could have labeled the manufacturing operations. Could we then have watched the specialists assemble the stone, wood, feather, string, and pitch into the completed arrow, we would have identified the assembly operation. From the record it seems extremely doubtful that Paleolithic man ever developed such division of labor. This level of economic activity was carried on, from beginning to end, by the same individual in what has been termed primitive household industry. Specialization of operation and division of labor did appear, however, in some patterns of community workshop industry in early historic Egypt, Mesopotamia, and China, and it did characterize manufacturing operations in Greece, Rome, and medieval Europe. Community workshop industry, with highly specialized skills and division of labor, is still frequent in the twentieth-century assembly aspects of manufacturing, but such activity now is only a residual or relict element in our complex industrial system.

Out of the Industrial Revolution has come both the application of power, derived from inanimate sources of energy, to manufacturing and the separation of manufacturing operations into many different levels with regard to the handling of raw materials. The wastes and impurities of many primary raw materials, for one sequence of operations leading to a "product," become the processed raw materials for an entirely different sequence, and many of our "products" are, in reality, only agents in some further processing of a different raw material at some particular stage in manufacturing. For example, much of the phosphates that enter into the manufacture of commercial fertilizers are the impurities of iron and ferroalloys processed in the steel industries, and sulfur production is chiefly carried on to yield the "product" sulfuric acid, whose use in turn is principally as an agent in further manufacturing. Much primary manufacturing no longer produces an end product of consumer utility. For example, steels of many shapes and compositions are turned out by the steel industry to become the "raw materials" in further manufacturing processes which shape them into particular products. But even these "products" have only selected utility, a utility in the final assembly of some compound product. Examine an automobile, a refrigerator, or a television set from this point of view. Each is composed of hundreds of "products" grouped together into a final "consumer product"; but not one of the three will work all by itself, for each needs power, power that is the result of another whole sequence of operations. No single workman, in the twentieth century, working by the Paleolithic system, could ever produce an automobile, a refrigerator, or a television set from their ultimate raw materials. It is not that the workman is unskilled, but that the things he would need come from hundreds of primary raw materials, processed through hundreds of operations requiring intricate equipment, and subjected to hundreds of manufacturing processes by complex machinery before sufficient end products can be finally assembled into a "consumer product."

The Regional Heritage of the Industrial Revolution

The shift from the empirical to the conceptual approach in the cultural development of the earth applied to both resource-extracting and resource-converting techniques and was neither worldwide nor parallel in the beginning, but centered in Western Europe, from Italy to Poland to England. It began as a revival of secular learning that fed on the body of ancient science, but it was greatly stimulated by the Geographical Discoveries' production of new knowledge, new materials, and new equipment gathered from the ends of the earth. In the late sixteenth century secular learning began to look forward, rather than backward, encompassing in its broad sweep the craftsmen, the merchants, the scholars, and the educated leadership of society. One of the most notable aspects of the growth of secular learning was the interest in quantitative measurement and accuracy, as evidenced by the changeover to the Gregorian Calendar, the introduction into European usage of the Arabic number system, the development of such instruments as the slide rule, the interest in accurate timekeeping that led to precision mechanics in clock and chronometer making, and the origination of mathematical aids such as the modern calculus, the table of logarithms, and the use of the decimal point in arithmetic. A second aspect, and one difficult to pinpoint, was the beginning of the growth of the interest in experimentation, by which the innovator began to be approved rather than restricted.

Many late sixteenth- and seventeenth-century Europeans interested in all kinds of things were both craftsmen and scholars, able to think conceptually and to translate their thoughts into instrumentation, experiment, measurement, and the projection of potential conclusions as to significance. The European universities, the growing number of scientific societies, and many of the engineers and advanced craftsmen of the era were linked by common concerns and interests. Mercator (Gerhard Kremer, 1512–1594) was a well-educated Dutch copper engraver, instrument maker, surveyor, cartographer, and mathematician who served several noble families as a "consulting scientist" besides being a commercial producer of maps and atlases. John Wilkins (1614–1672) was a Puritan clergyman who was educated at Oxford and was later Bishop of Chester. But he also wrote on astronomy and how to get to the moon, was much concerned with engineering mechanics, and produced a treatise on engineering mathematics related to the transportation of coal from mines. For some years he was Warden of Wadham College, Oxford, and a chief founder and first secretary of The Royal Society for the Improvement of Natural Knowledge (1660), the concerns of which included ". . . all useful arts, manufactures, Mechanick practices, Engynes, and Inventions by Experiment. . . ." Most of our modern scientific societies are descended from this Royal Society. Thomas Newcomen (1663–1729), an ironmonger and toolmaker for the Devonshire tin mines, took off from Thomas Savery's original papers presented before the Royal Society and Savery's first experiments with a steam engine, and from the work of Italian and French engineers-scholars, to produce a workable engine useful in pumping water from mines. James Watt (1736–1819) studied commercial instrument making as an apprentice craftsman, and in 1757 took a post as instrument maker (skilled mechanic) at the University of Glasgow, where he was asked to repair a broken-down Newcomen engine used in the practical physics course. Working in succession with professors and manufacturing engineers, Watt finally produced improved engines which, by 1781, were sufficiently efficient to be copied widely and increasingly put to work. This kind of interlocking relationship among scholars, engineers, mechanics, manufacturers, and merchants in the early modern European world led directly into that revolution of the resource-converting technologies which is called industrialization.

The place was Europe, but the ideas and the materials were from the world at large, as Europe began its modern industrial revolution. The coal-powered cotton mill, first integrated in 1785, was located in England. Coal as a fuel derived its ultimate technology from China, elements of the spinning and weaving devices came from Egypt and China, cotton was from the Middle East, the cotton textiles desired were those of India (madras, calico, muslin), the steam engine was European in experimental motivation if English in final perfection, the labor was English, and the market that made the whole thing go was world-scattered. It had fallen to Europeans first to travel the world over and to bring back to their homelands ideas, mechanical procedures, and raw materials, to which Europeans added creative thinking, labor, and other raw materials, but it was the world as a whole that finally accepted the products of these activities to make the whole worth doing. The heritage of the Industrial Revolution, therefore, involved a Europe-centered integration of concepts, technologies, product desires, and raw materials drawn from the then-known world.

Increasingly, as the decades wore on after the end of the sixteenth century, every decade saw some further development in technology, use of raw materials, application of labor, new product, and new market. A spiraling advance in material cultural development had begun in which every success led to two more new beginnings. Although these remained centered in Western Europe, for the most part, until after 1800, the nineteenth century was the period during which not only the industrialization procedures gathered strength, but also Europeans began the diffusion of industrialization around the world into the colonial lands settled by their emigrants. They also carried this diffusion into the far countries to which they voyaged and from which they sought the increasing volumes of raw materials demanded by the industrial machine they had created in their homelands.

Although this chapter is chiefly concerned with the growth of the processes that created industrialization in Europe and spread it around the world, we must recognize that those very processes were significant to the modification of landscapes all over the world. Mining landscapes, tree farms, urban industrial complexes, and industrial ports have created new kinds of forms and patterns on the surface of the earth. The Ruhr Valley of Germany appears very different today from what it was three centuries ago, and the island of Singapore is changing its very shape and surface under the impact of growing industrialization. Portions of northeastern United States have almost been physically made over as industrial landscapes have matured. It is not only the physical removal of ore bodies that changes landscapes, as in northern Minnesota's iron ranges, but the differing kinds of economic systems that have evolved along with industrialization, as seen in the wall separating East and West Berlin. Ultimately it is these changing and differing landscapes to which the geographer returns for the characterization of different parts of the earth.

Elements of the Industrial Complex

Our concern, as geographers, is essentially with those economic processes that integrate capital, labor, equipment, raw materials, and organization into productive systems. However, we are not concerned with the theoretical bases for the functioning of any single economic system, but are interested in the economic processes by which modern industrialization is able to intensify the systems of resource conversion as compared with the structures operative in the preindustrial era, or in a contemporary nonindustrial society such as, let us say, the Chimbu peoples of highland New Guinea. The latter are primarily an agricultural people who live by a complex system of shifting cultivation, a simple handicraft-household system of manufacturing, and a socially institutionalized form of trading. The comparative generalizations attempted here concern different economic elements for the purpose of demonstrating the superior productive efficiency that has resulted from modern industrialization. In other words, this presentation does not attempt an analysis of complex economic theory, but describes the technological mechanisms functioning in the twentieth century among advanced societies that operate by complex economic theory. For our purpose certain elements must be treated differently from the treatment given by the economist engaged in a theoretical analysis of modern economics.

Elements of Technology

Manufacturing began in campsites, working sites, individual homes, and such spots as men chose to carry on their individual operations on stone, bone, wood, fibers, and other materials. The general term often applied to such simple manufacturing operations is *primitive household industry*. As simple technologies evolved and man learned to harness simple sources of power, such as the waterwheel, the windmill, a draft animal, or a group of human laborers, newer and different kinds of raw materials could be processed in greater volumes in what often has been termed *simple-powered household industry*. As technological processes and labor skills evolved still further, without development of large power volumes, men often worked in groups to achieve a given end. Specialized division of labor in such activities was common. The volume output was greater than when men worked alone, and the site of operations often became a specialized building or working site. *Community workshop industry* is the term often applied to such activities. All three modes were common in the more advanced regions of the world, the early civilizations, by the start of the Christian era, and they generally prevailed until the time of the Industrial Revolution. In 1600, some regions around the world could have

been described as still carrying on only the simplest of operations equivalent to primitive household industry. Other regions found the first two patterns operative, and a few could be described as possessing all three (see pp. 327–338).

What the early phase of the Industrial Revolution did, in one sense, was to add (not substitute) a fourth category to the possible systems applicable to the conversion of raw materials into consumer products. There are three aspects to this development, all three involving elements of advanced technology. There is, first, the employment of huge amounts of inanimate energy to the end that labor becomes the manipulator of power rather than its source. Second, there is the involved technology in the processing of raw materials by which many kinds of physical, chemical, and manipulative changes are made in the raw materials. Third, there is the development of the physical plant, the "factory building," which became a specialized instrument for specific purposes. By the late nineteenth century the evolution of industrial procedures had produced what could be designated *energy-powered-factory industry*. In mid-twentieth century there is being added a fifth level of industrial operations, one that may be termed *corporate, powered production-line industry* in which machines take over more and more of the operations, with skilled labor now tending to become machine managers, as the whole set of processes grow both in complexity and in volume output. Our modern kind of industrial operation differs from that in earlier times by its innate complexity and in that man uses power and technology to do what he formerly did himself. The automated factory in which a computer controls the whole set of procedures according to a program established by a few engineers will have made it possible for man to accomplish work not only more easily, but also with greater efficiency, in greater volumes, and on a wider range of operations than heretofore.

Not all work in an industrial society is done by complex, powered, factory industry. Still at work, in his garage, workshop, or the backyard is the individual, sometimes carrying out his operation by the simplest of tools and human labor. But if he succeeds in making a good new product, his next procedure is to apply simple power to some stage of the operation. Men still gather in community workshops to carry on industrial processes in which the largest single component may be the human labor input. The industrial society today has the choice of five different systems: primitive household industry, simple-powered household industry, community workshop industry, energy-powered factory industry, and corporate, powered production-line industry (as here itemized—the series can be classified into more or fewer). It is significant that in highland New Guinea the Chimbu still can apply only the first system, whereas in Japan, England, Germany, or the United States any of the five deemed most useful can apply. That modern industrial society is able to supply the level of technology required to accomplish what it wants to achieve means that the capacity of the industrial society to convert raw materials into end products is tremendously increased. The diffusion of industrial technology has proceeded to the end that it is now widely dispersed around the world. This means that man, widely throughout the earth, is able to accomplish work, make things, and produce goods in a way never previously achieved. The patterns of diffusion will continue until that day when mankind, everywhere, has at its command the technological capacity to do almost as it chooses with raw materials.

Economic Elements

The mainstay of a productive society is its capital resource, as comprehended, formalized, organized, and employed. In traditional preindustrial societies living by cultivation, land was the chief economic good and the primary capital resource; among a pastoral people capital lay in the grazing range and in the stock of animals; and among a gathering society "capital" of a sort lay in the productive trees, shrubs, herbs, roots, and small animals forming the wild habitat. Since the sixteenth century there has been both a striking comprehension of, and a marked accumulative diversification in, the nature of the capital resource. Capital today may be considered to comprise land, manufacturing plant, machinery, raw materials, finished products, money, and credit-debt-goodwill. The contemporary entrepreneur manipulates these in various ways so as to yield the largest possible flexibility toward productive output. The comparative ratios of capital involved in economic undertakings vary from one society to another, and the several elements may take various forms, but the large and diverse capital resource is the hallmark of the modern industrial society.

Organization is only partially an economic element in modern industrialized society, but diversification and intensification are significant here too. The one-owner, one-operator, economic undertaking still exists, but modern industrial society has added many more organizational forms. Most of these take some aspect of the corporate structure, but they range from the private single corporation through the worldwide publicly owned holding company with an intricate substructure of subsidiary corporations, and to the joint endeavor organized as a separate company by two corporations with related product interests. The compound form of most modern economic organizations permits scale-efficiency and integration returns of various kinds, and makes for productivity far beyond the capacity of simpler organization (Fig. 9.1A,B,C).

In the modern industrial system the patterns of labor mobility, specialization, range of technological skills, and sheer numbers constitute a significant economic element. The United States possesses perhaps the most highly productive labor force of any society ever occupying the earth. Although, during past eras, it was possible to organize a massive labor force for a specialized project ranging from building an Egyptian pyramid to repairing a Chinese dike, those earlier labor forces supplied chiefly motive power rather than technological skills. Such labor-force quality and capacity as found in modern industrial societies is far-reaching in its ultimate productivity.

Administrative Elements

Societal controls over productivity have had marked economic significance since well before the formalization of the political state, but the controls operative today are unlike most of those of earlier societies in their impact upon productivity. The use of taxation, tariffs, prohibitory rules, and stimulus rules are not new by any means, but their function has been adjusted so as to permit, augment, and foster industrial productivity in a way never before achieved. Although restrictions in the forms of patent laws and government production quotas do exist, in general there has been relaxation of the rules concerning both quantity and range of production. The feudal and kingly monopoly over production and consumption of particular goods is narrowly restricted today. The Communist state is no exception to this rule, for its chief officer has only a few personal perquisites as such.

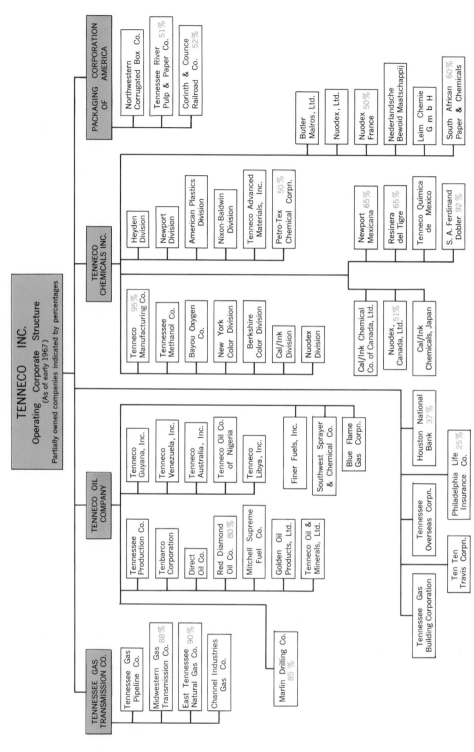

FIG. 9.1 THE ORGANIZATIONAL STRUCTURE OF CORPORATE INDUSTRY. A. Organizational Chart—Tenneco Inc.

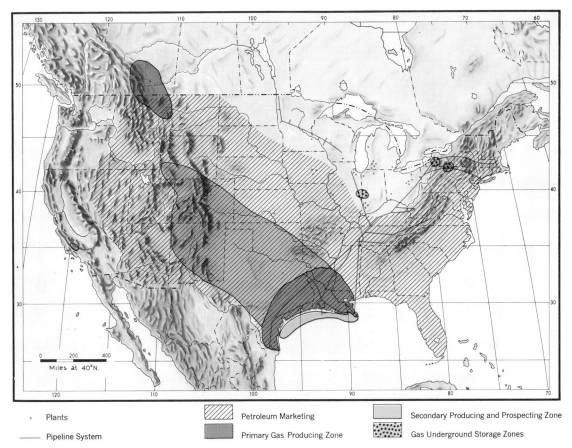

·	Plants	▨	Petroleum Marketing	▧	Secondary Producing and Prospecting Zone
——	Pipeline System	▰	Primary Gas Producing Zone	▩	Gas Underground Storage Zones

FIG. 9.1 (*Continued*) B. Tenneco, Inc. Activities in the United States.

Although the antitrust rules of the contemporary United States can be matched against the medieval European rules against "engrossing" (cornering the market in an economic good), the traditional economic structures of the past are no match for the impact of modern-day patent law protection, internal commercial freedoms within political states, and sundry government services to manufacturers. Particularly are these features notable in the economic structure of such a country as the United States. In the organizational structure of many early political states very rough equivalents may be found for some of our present government administrative offices-departments, but in most early states these bureaucratic agents served chiefly to restrain the power of regional rivals and to maintain the power of the chief ruler. Although it sometimes appears that restrictive regulation is the chief function of American bureaucracy, in actual fact the chief service performed by much of American governmental organization is the facilitating of economic activity. In the famous aphorism of President Calvin Coolidge, "The business of America is business."

Regional and Interregional Elements

The evolution of the kinds of economic activity relating to resource conversion from preindustrial circumstances to modern organization of society has been marked by an ever greater economic and technologic efficiency. In traditional India or China resource conversion was a localized matter, attuned to the local consumer and operator in terms of a localized processing of a raw material through to the finished product. In the Roman Empire it was much the same, and localized resource conversion remained generally true in medieval Europe. Duplicatory operations at a small scale on relatively low efficiency generally resulted. This is the heart of the discussion of the "self-subsistence" theme that runs throughout early economic history. Under conditions of undeveloped transportation, the lack of comprehension of cost accounting and the economies of scale effi-

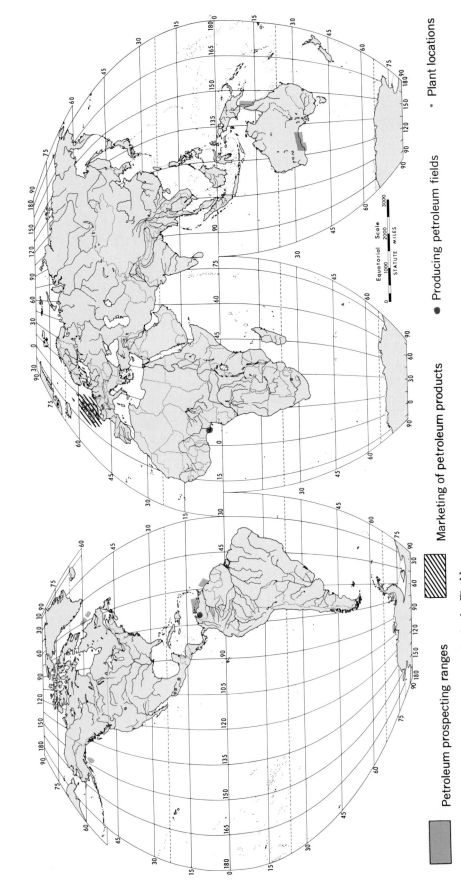

Petroleum prospecting ranges   Marketing of petroleum products   • Plant locations

• Producing petroleum fields

Equatorial Scale
0   1000   2000   3000
STATUTE MILES

FIG. 9.1 (Continued) C. Tenneco Inc. Activities in the World.

ciency, and rather simple technology, older patterns of resource conversion could not become very efficient. Despite the facts that a little silk got from China to Rome, that Italian porcelains moved to India, that Scottish wools were worn in Germany, that Greek olive oil was consumed in southern Slavic lands, and that Baltic amber got to Greece, these small-volume trade movements could only remain small because of the low rates of efficiency in resource conversion that prevailed in the ancient world.

The modern world has witnessed the historical buildup of manufacturing districts in England and the Low Countries, in eastern North America, in southern Japan, in southeastern Australia, and elsewhere. Whether such regional concentrations have followed any particular locational scheme or not, efficiencies of operations have accumulated in the whole of modern industrial undertakings which are significant to the rates of production and to potential output. In the integration of conversion of basic raw materials, in which early-stage by-products become the cheaper raw materials for other industrial operations and semifinished goods become agents in still further procedures, there is accumulated an efficiency never achieved in the preindustrial world. The very scale of resource conversion, in which millions of tons of a raw material flow through a continuous operational sequence, closely calculated by cost, engineered by technologic skills, moved by mass transport, and geared to specific consumers produces a capacity hitherto unattained. Recall that steel products in 1800 were scarce in the United States, costly, and had to be carefully preserved and reused, whereas today the casual junking of automobiles into eyesore accumulations indicates a steelmaking capacity so great that old iron and steel have relatively low value. Actually, this is one point of immaturity in our industrial technology; the efficient salvaging of waste consumer products has not yet caught up with the efficient conversion of basic raw materials.

Critical to the whole complex of resource conversion is the role of mass transport. Through such transport raw materials in huge volumes may be brought where we will, power may be moved where we choose, semifinished elements may be articulated in designed patterns, and final products may be distributed across the whole land. The role of transport in the space-adjusting and space-intensification procedures constitutes part of the subject matter of the next two chapters, and therefore its role in resource conversion is merely acknowledged here.

The articulation of the earth's resource regions is very much a part of the present system of resource conversion, by which both quality and capacity operations are heightened. That coal may move around the earth, that petroleum moves almost everywhere, that iron ore from Venezuela can be mixed with that from Labrador and Minnesota, along with manganese from the Philippines or India, with tungsten from Thailand, nickel from New Caledonia, and titanium from western United States, at any steel plant so choosing is a part of the marvel of contemporary resource conversion. The actual choices made now can be determined in terms of fractional costs per ton in a technological operation never possible to an itinerant European ironsmith of medieval times. The range of sources for the raw materials contained in any multicomponent consumer product today forms a gazetteer of the world's regions.

Economic Institutions

Some elements of modern industrialization were not mentioned in the previous section. Here we survey a few of them, chiefly conceptual-institutional aspects, which are part of the whole politico-cultural development of industrialism. In their basic forms all of these are old elements, but each of them has been transformed under the inventive evolutionary development of the modern industrial societies now functioning throughout the earth. Probably none of these institutional forms has reached the degree of maturity at which it may stabilize for a long era, and each of them is subject to further internal change, as practiced in different countries around the earth.

Private Ownership and Private Initiative

Private and personal ownership of things probably first began in the purely personal belongings of people, and it may have applied to clothing, decorative trinkets, tools, weapons, utensils, and the sleeping place in the family abode. In the evolution of social stratification and political organization private control over elements of the habitat probably attached itself to topmost social strata and to chiefdom. At the opposite extreme personal slavery is very old, and the ownership of a person, as a chattel, may be associated with the early developments of private ownership. Private ownership, in the first kingly state, attached to the God-King alone, but later came to be attached to the temple as apart from the God-King as a person. It may be that private ownership in land evolved through the status of the God-King's family members, and through the temple as personification of its priests. The extension of private ownership, for commoners, to produce gathered, to crops grown, or to animals raised or tamed, came at an early date. The extension of private ownership to land, mineral resources, forests, livestock, and other natural resources came only after the stabilizing of the political state. The concept of private land-ownership was an old development in the Mediterranean Basin, reaching China only shortly before the beginning of the Christian Era.

We are not very clear as to the onset of private initiative beyond the fashioning of purely personal belongings, owing to the long continuation of the habit of ceremonial gift giving. Such customs may actually have evolved as privileges bestowed by a chief-king, but they are old ones in the zones of earliest development of civilization. Privately made goods to be exchanged, and the right of the individual entrepreneur to make and sell goods, are both very old. It is clear, at least, that both private ownership and private initiative are economic traits inherited by the modern world. An approximation of money economies and the regional manufacturing-trading function both appeared in several societies at an early time, but never matured fully. Modern capitalism, however, appears a product of Western Europe at the end of the Medieval Era. Its organizational origins can be argued, as to whether they arose out of a Protestant ethic on the strength of the Protestant Reformation, whether they derive from the family trading ventures of the north Italian city states, whether they derive from the economic activities of the great Catholic merchant families, or whether they owe in part to the early prohibitions on participation in general economic activity by Jews and other particular religious sects, thus forcing these groups to specialize.

The broad view taken here is that classical capitalism was an evolutionary economic aspect of sweeping cultural change in Western Europe and that many forces contributed to the general developmental growth which carried this particular form of economic organization to a more advanced state in Western Europe than did any of the prior motivational forces in other lands at earlier times.

In any case, by the early nineteenth century, classical capitalism had taken shape, embodying private initiative and private ownership of capital resources, the means of production, and the control over many kinds of natural resources. Elements of classical capitalism spread from Western Europe to other parts of the earth, being found in the early twentieth century in some institutional form in much of the earth.

Capitalism, however, is not a static concept nor is it a static economic structure. Both its forms and nature keep changing. Those who deride classical capitalism have spoken, and chiefly speak, of characteristics already out of date; the archetype illustrations of the evils of capitalism no longer show many of these characteristics. Both government participation in and regulation of private enterprise had reached significant proportions in the nineteenth century, steadily increasing during the twentieth century. In the United States, in the 1960s, the ownership of many corporate enterprises was not held by a few "bloated capitalists" but was shared among the more than 20 million citizens owning personal stocks, the insurance companies, nonprofit foundations, university-college endowment funds, and the rapidly growing employee pension and retirement funds. Most Americans receive financial returns from some one of these. The real owners of the General Motors Corporation in 1966 were the 1,350,000 stockholders, for the directors-officers-managers owned less than 1 per cent of the corporation. The "big" owners are the foundations, endowment funds, mutual funds, and the pension funds. The employee pension fund of Sears, Roebuck & Co. (210,000 employees), in 1966, owned 24 per cent of the stock in the corporation, and there were 243,000 other owners of stock in the company. The directors-managers-officers of the General Electric Company, in 1966, owned only 0.1 per cent stock in the company, and the 562,000 stockholders (including the company pension fund for 242,000 employees as a single "stockholder") are spread across the United States and among several foreign lands. In addition to the ownership of industrial and commercial enterprises, public ownership, vested in special territorial units, cities, counties, states, and the federal government is far greater, in the United States, than is commonly understood.

The trend toward public ownership of capital resources and productive facilities has markedly increased since about 1940. American capitalism is rapidly tending toward the situation in which most "private enterprises" will be publicly owned but managed separately from the "public enterprises" managed and operated by some unit of formal government. There is both check and balance in this dual pattern which is now described by economists as a "mixed economy." The most recent trend in private ownership is the huge growth of mutual investment funds, in which individuals hold shares of pooled funds, the funds comprised of very wide and mixed assortments of common stocks, preferred stocks, corporate debentures and bonds, and government bonds ranging from municipals to those of the federal government. The day may soon come when the ownership of capital resources and productive facilities will be held very broadly, with almost every citizen participating in either direct or indirect form.

The modern labor union, deriving from an organization in Great Britain in the very early part of the nineteenth century, was a response to the rougher workings of the classical capitalism. The evolution of the modern labor union roughly paralleled that of modern capitalism, at least in the United States, and is another element in the increased capacity of industrial enterprise. In the United States the head of a large labor union has fully as much economic power as the head of a large corporation. Witness any of the prolonged strikes that have affected the United States in the last decade, whereby whole sectors of economic activity ceased for a time interval. Not only is the United States today a "mixed economy" in terms of the control and ownership of economic enterprise, it is also a "laboristic economy" in the language of economics. There is ground for stating that the American labor union is, in the 1960s, subjected to far less governmental control than the private corporation, and the labor union system has become highly institutionalized, guaranteed by federal statutory provisions, and protected.

The United States often is characterized as the chief exponent of modern capitalism, an island outpost in an increasingly collectivized world. Yet the seeds of modern American economic organization also are diffusing around the world. One of the most notable economic trends in Japan during the 1960s was the "going public" of formerly privately owned enterprises, as increasing numbers of Japanese began to own stock in corporate enterprises, and this trend is now to be seen widely setting in elsewhere. These broad changes in economic organization-structure are part of the changing nature of culture in general. It would seem that the present trends within the United States represent a more satisfactory route toward an improved and advanced economic organizing of capital resources and productive enterprises than do the totally collectivized forms of economic organization.

Collectivized Ownership and Party Leadership

State control of all elements of a society, by Marxian theory, should lead to equal prosperity, rights, and freedoms for all members, and to the lessened role of government. The revolutionary procedures by which the Marxian state replaces other kinds of politico-socioeconomic structures are satisfactory to the overthrowing of those structures, but it was found that the chaos resulting from no governing agencies at all could not be tolerated. In practice, therefore, the Marxian state has operated at the authoritarian level characterized by oligarchic rule of a sort that preceded the development of democratic institutions, even though the oligarchy governs in the name of the whole population, that is, the masses. In the sphere of economic activity no incentive system has been found to replace private initiative. Political and economic theory has run aground against the innate acquisitiveness that human beings possess as part of their biologic-psychologic makeup. The partial overthrow of old cultural institutions has been followed by the invention or evolution of new kinds of institutions, ranging from social stratification through political procedure to economic procedure. The "five-year plan," as a design to stabilize economic activity of a proper sort, aimed at the increase of productivity according to need. The earliest construct of Marxian economics worked extremely poorly; evolutionary change in structure, coupled with more advanced technological practice, has improved its performance considerably, but it remains an inefficient construct from almost every point of view.

The genius of leadership centered in the Communist party was, in theory, to provide both political and economic administration of the Marxian state for the equal good of all. In practice, there is no dispute that the topmost leaders of the Communist party, in whatever country, have lived well and profited from their restricted, but useful, perquisites. It is not so clear, however, that Communist party leadership has benefited all members of a society equally well. Economic decision-making power instituted in committees, bureaus, and other units, has not been able to achieve very high efficiency in planning or in production. Purging committees and replacing the membership is not, of itself, a productive act, and the new membership can only act within the system as designed. Although Soviet Russia has made economic progress, during fifty years, it is at the very least an open question whether that population in that region of the earth could have done better by another system.

Collectivist structure has also diffused over a part of the earth during the last half century, through revolutionary means that have wiped out older cultural, political, and economic procedures. Most other regional patterns of collectivization are much younger than the Soviet Russian pattern: most of them show the high degree of inefficiency that characterized early Soviet Russia. Those groups acceding to power, in the name of the Communist party, all have taken the historical cultural traditions of their own societies into account, so that no two collectivized states operate wholly alike. But in every new collectivized scheme there show up the same general forms of socioeconomic stratification by which leadership lives very well and the bottom elements merely exist. There is no question but that the institution of the collectivized state affords rebellious leadership the opportunity to liquidate the former topmost socioeconomic strata and to install itself in their position. Social and economic mobility, for the membership of the Communist party, has been achieved in every case, and for those who accept and conform the level of living has improved steadily; for the purged there can be no response to the question of better levels of living. It remains unproven that Collectivized Ownership and Party Leadership is amenable to greater economic efficiency and greater economic productivity than Private Ownership and Private Initiative.

Alternate Economic "Isms"

On the world map neither the mixed economies nor the collectivized economies cover the whole of the earth (Fig. 9.2). The present is an era in which in some far country a semineolithic economic system may still operate. In purely internal terms highland New Guinea still fits the case; there are other illustrations in which the fit is not very good. Such regions operate in curious hybridized patterns. In one such country, politically organized as a democracy, a military dictator may hold political and police power. In some rural sectors economic activity may resemble that achieved when plow agriculture replaced hand gardening, and in other sectors agricultural feudalism may obtain, with control over agricultural lands and mineral resources vested in the educated and wealthy classes who could comprehend their economic utilities. In urban sectors partial elements of classical and modern capitalism may be operative. Economic development plans, sponsored by an international agency, may have been initiated, there may be a Peace Corps contingent from the United States just getting under way, attempting to stimulate community economic enterprise, and a Communist cell may be fomenting political and economic revolution. How do we describe such a country, in terms of its economic system? In some variant this is actually the condition throughout much of the earth at the present time, to which the recent term underdeveloped has been applied. Change is in process, but in directions that are often conflicting and at rates that are slow and restricted by cultural tradition.

Other portions of the earth constitute regions standing somewhere between the example of the United States, that of Communist China, that of New Guinea, and that of our underdeveloped case. Great Britain, France, Canada, India, Chile, and Egypt are cases in point, where economic theory, economic practice, and economic institutions are hybridized in some variable but particular degree, bulwarked by particular social systems, political institutions, and psychological combinations. Each of these is actually going through considerable cultural change in respect to the economic system and its economic institutions. There is no question, however, about the increasing evolution of economic constructs that facilitate higher rates of resource conversion.

Power Production and Manufacturing

Just as the introduction of the draft animal altered the basic construct of gardening and brought on the evolution of agriculture, the introduction of large-scale power from inanimate sources altered the construct of older systems of manufacturing and brought on the evolution of

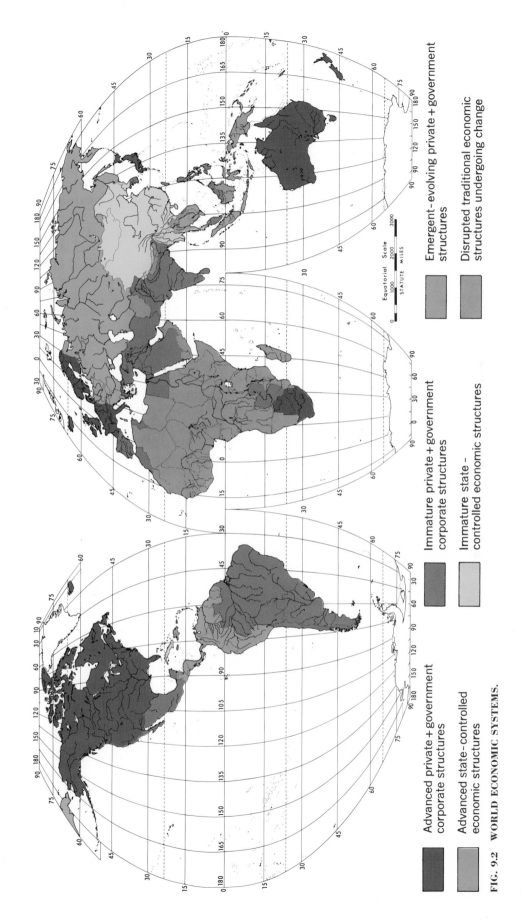

Advanced private + government
corporate structures

Advanced state-controlled
economic structures

Immature private + government
corporate structures

Immature state -
controlled economic structures

Emergent- evolving private + government
structures

Disrupted traditional economic
structures undergoing change

Equatorial   Scale
0   1000   2000   3000
STATUTE   MILES

FIG. 9.2   WORLD ECONOMIC SYSTEMS.

393

corporate, urban, powered, factory industry. The beginnings of such power patterns show slower development than gardening-to-agriculture, coming several thousand years later, but these beginnings also show more tentative starts in fragmentary aspects. The first tentative starts in power application go back of the real onset of the Industrial Revolution, but it is the integration of engineering principles with inventive experimental technology and the use of fossil fuel that characterize the modern steam engine power system. From that point onward, progress in the development and application of power has been relatively continuous, to the end that twentieth-century man has at his command, in the mature manufacturing region, almost unlimited volumes of power. It has been the use of power that has made possible many of the modern kinds of manufacturing operations and the ranges of activities that constitute the high level of living.

In the gross measure of total energy applicable from all sources in any given society, or political state, there is a rough key to the capacity for manufacturing. In that many societies employ part of the total power for other kinds of uses (Americans often go riding in automobiles for the fun of it), the total measure of power is not a direct index of manufacturing, but that total measure of power is an index of sorts to the cultural potential for the whole pattern of living. In that a heavily populated region, such as China or India, derives much of its gross power production from human labor or from nonindustrial production, the total measure of gross power is neither a key to manufacturing nor to the level of living. India, in the 1960s, still derived a significant share of its total power production from wood, charcoal, dried animal dung, and other sources in such small and inefficient patterns that the total volume of power cannot be considered an index either to manufacturing or to the level of living. In terms of mature power development the world leaders today are the United States, the Soviet Union, United Kingdom, Western Germany, France, Canada, and Japan, with the smaller countries of northwestern Europe ranking equivalently in the scale of maturity but lower in terms of total volume (Fig. 9.3). China and India rank high in total production but not in the scale of maturity of power development, although both are raising their levels significantly during the 1960s. A number of other countries, such as Australia, South Africa, Brazil, and Argentina rank relatively high in total production of power.

The revolution in power production by the world leader is demonstrated by figures of startling contrast. In 1800, in the present area of contiguous United States, the probable total capacity amounted to less than 5 million horsepower, most of which was concentrated close to the Atlantic seaboard and was derived from simple waterpower, animal power, and human energy. By 1850, this total power capacity was up to about 35 million horsepower, some 15 per cent of which derived from human energy, about 6 per cent from inanimate energy used in machines of all kinds, and the balance of nearly 80 per cent was provided by animal power. In the early 1960s total power capacity had increased to about $1\frac{1}{2}$ billion horsepower, but its derivation had markedly altered. Animal energy had almost dropped from the list (under 1 per cent), human energy had decreased to under 3 per cent, and the balance came from inanimate energy used in machines of all kinds. Speaking figuratively, to pinpoint the subjective significance of the power volume, each citizen of the United States in the early 1960s had at his ultimate disposal and use the energy that could be provided by about 25 full-grown human slaves working at normal human capacity (calculated as 0.3 horsepower). In simple figurative contrast, the total supplemental energy available to the inhabitant of highland New Guinea could be provided by one teen-age boy per person. These are only crude measures whose finite accuracy is not extremely high, but they do indicate the order of revolution in power development that has occurred. The eventual industrial potential for power development is much greater.

Measurements of per capita power available to members of individual societies, of course, produce some interesting statistical abstractions. As petroleum producers, with small populations, the Bahrein Islands lead this list, and Brunei ranks high. There are various other measures of power that may be extracted from the total power statistics, yielding odd rankings of countries, but the significant aspect is that the leading industrial countries of the earth rank relatively high in any kind of measure, and the United States leads the list in a composite measure of the application of power to daily living. In terms of the rates of growth for power production, it is notable that a number of regions or countries not heretofore

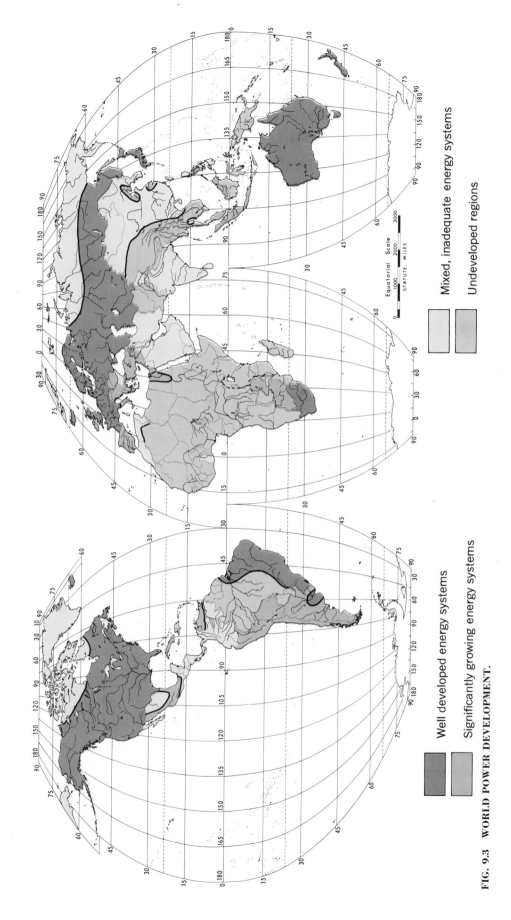

Mixed, inadequate energy systems

Undeveloped regions

Well developed energy systems

Significantly growing energy systems

Equatorial Scale
0   1000   2000   3000
STATUTE MILES

FIG. 9.3   WORLD POWER DEVELOPMENT.

ranked in the manufacturing regions of the world are rapidly increasing their total power production. In terms of increase in rates of power production between the 1930s and the 1950s the 25 or 30 countries achieving the most rapid rates were countries with little previous power and only older-style systems of manufacturing. In comparative terms the United States was not increasing its power production at the same rates. These kinds of measures are, of course, somewhat deceptive in that high rates of increase are characteristic of elementary beginnings. Nevertheless, the conclusion is inescapable that the cultural practice of production of power from nonhuman sources is rapidly spreading around the earth. This can only mean improvement in levels of economic activity and in the levels of living to all participating societies. Systems of power production that take the work load off human shoulders are the means of raising cultural levels from the Neolithic or near post-Neolithic toward the twentieth century in all parts of the earth.

The most direct concern with the production of power is its utilization in work accomplishment, in manufacturing, transport, the provision of water supplies, lighting, and heating and air conditioning. All of these kinds of uses contribute to the lifting of the levels of living. From the standpoint of raising the per capita income of members of less developed societies, it is the application of power in manufacturing and transport that is most critical. The production of power, as a first step in the modernizing of the old systems of manufacture and transport, is the most critical step of all. Although many of the secondary steps in the evolution of modern manufacturing have not yet begun to accrue in many of the developing countries of the earth, it is significant that the spread of power production systems is well under way.

The Cyclic Evolution of Industry

In the history of manufacturing is there any orderly pattern to the appearance and practice of resource-converting activities? Taking the long view it would possibly appear that there is only a very general order of precedence. The need to process food supplies came first, but it immediately brought on the need for tools, utensils, and agents. The biological need for clothing must be counterbalanced by the human desire for adornment, and these "needs" brought about a demand for "textiles" and for cosmetics and jewelry. The near-

contemporaneous need for protection from predators brought the need for weapons and shelter, adding constructional materials and tools for housing. Manufacturing, in that simplest scene, required no factories, and a working site was either where man was or the spot at which he found what he sought. Production was clearly separated in space from consumption. Producer goods, that is, the equipment needed to manufacture other kinds of goods (such as stone tools with which to make other tools), came much later into the sequence, and only when mankind had already developed a conceptual pattern of the repetitiveness of manufacturing.

Once this primordial pattern arose, how did it change and expand? Slowly, by small elements only, by limited exchange, by acquisition of new products that required new ways of handling, or by acquisition of new tools that could process an old product a little differently. At some late juncture, such as the Neolithic Revolution, or the onset of Civilization, there had to be wholesale change and expansion, but one perhaps without particular order or sequence as things then began. Was there an order in the diffusion of industry from the "developed" region to the "underdeveloped" region at such a time? About these kinds of things we really know very little. There is not much that we can apply in transferring our attention to the modern situation which began with the Industrial Revolution. The latter era is one in which wholesale change, invention sequences, and expansion occurred so widely that its cyclic nature is somewhat different from those of older patterns. However, viewing the Industrial Revolution, there are some points to be made about the rise of aspects of industrialization, its regional birthplaces, and about its diffusionary transfer to the underdeveloped region.

The Industrial Revolution began and reached fair maturity in Western Europe, with many of its developments centered in England and Scotland, but with similar beginnings in France and Italy. Both simple-powered household industry (such as grain milling) and community workshop industry (such as the early wool textiles) grew to the point that the critical problem became power to run the machines. This led to the rise of coal mining as a resource-extracting procedure, coal replacing charcoal and other simple power sources. With a power source available, the issue became the means of converting that source into power, leading to the steam engine. Initial development of power found its application in the machine works that produced the engines and the mechanical devices, and in the pumping of air into mines and the water out of mines. This constitutes a feedback procedure whereby the converted power is used to gain more sources of power. Within the same rough time dimensions, however, some of this power began to be applied to the newer spinning and weaving machines that had been invented for the textile industries, to the making of better iron and steel products for the making of more machines, to the grain milling industries, and to the extraction of products from the power source itself, giving rise to the most elemental of the chemical industries. Some of the products of the latter segment we would now call agents, since they became used in further industrial processes. Thus the first resource-converting procedures led to greater productivity in old manufacturing lines, but they gave rise to new kinds of industrialization by creating whole new segments of activity. From this point onward the story becomes a complex maze of explosive nature, as one new twist led to the application in three more, one of which produced a feedback to two older items, which in turn yielded several brand-new features.

Critical to the onset of the industrial cycle and for the later regional development of industrialization in far parts of the earth is the conversion of some source of power into the energy required to do what man (or a donkey, or a waterwheel, or a windmill) cannot do himself. Second, there is the direct application of that power into specific operations that lead to finished products, such as the textiles. Third, there is the offshoot patterns in which a by-product of an elemental stage becomes the agent in some added set of procedures (extracts from coal going into the chemical industries). Fourth, there come the complex phases of industrialization that integrate the resource-extracting and resource-converting procedures into an interlocking chain, in which one feeds upon the other but in which the total activity is always greater than the sum of its parts (isolated and unpowered).

In the growth of industry in the United States, it was not until about 1830 that the simple powered household and the community workshop types of industrial operation began to be replaced by more complex systems. Textiles, chemical industries, iron and steel activities, the machine works activities, and grain milling developed in quick succession, following upon the expansion of coal mining after the 1830s to reach a fair degree of integration by the end of the American Civil War. After that came the dynamic and explosive growth in the industrialization of the United States. If we examine India, we see somewhat the same kind of slow starting sequence in the latter portion of the nineteenth century, but we see a slower approximation of the dynamic takeoff point toward the end of World War II.

There is no specified sequence for all the countries of the world. It is clear, however, that the conversion of a resource into power, the feedback of that power into more resource extraction, and the branching out of resource conversion into many different lines is vital to the process of industrialization. There is a crude cyclic aspect to these simple and elementary stages of industrialization leading to mature development. Coupled into the whole dynamic of industrialization are two other processes, of space adjustment and space intensification, to be considered in the next two chapters.

The Processes of Industrialization and the Classifications of Manufacturing

We have dealt casually with the terminologies employed by the economic geographer and the economist to classify and describe industrial activity. We do not propose, here, to enter into a complex discussion of the whole subject, but some comment is needed concerning industrial activity as an aspect of resource-conversion practice. Earlier, it was suggested that a fivefold breakdown of manufacturing could be distinguished: primitive household industry; simple-power household industry; community workshop industry; energy-powered factory industry; and corporate, powered production-line industry. The countries of the world could have been mapped fairly easily on this basis prior to World War II; in the 1960s there are too many regions making the transition toward the modern factory system to permit easy distinction in regional patterns for the earth as a whole. The value of this classification lies chiefly in its conceptual framework for the long-term historical understanding of the evolution of cultural technologies of resource conversion; it is clear, however, that too much of the earth continues to employ early types of resource-conversion technology. Distinctions have been made between primary and secondary manufacture, between light industry and heavy industry, and between producer goods and consumer goods, as indicating phases of industrial activity. None of these distinctions is very hard or fast, for reasons discussed earlier.

Economic geographers and economists are often impressed by selected characteristics of particular industrial groupings, and they often write of manufacturing according to some distinctive framework adopted to fit an organizational purpose. Coal extraction will be combined with the conversion of coal into power, and with the use of coal as an industrial raw material; there then may be a chapter on copper, which ranges from the geographic distribution of copper mining through smelting technology to industrial fabrication. It is rather normal to separate the power industries from the manufacturing industries, as such, but very often power production is broken down further into chapters devoted to the sources of power; coal, petroleum-natural gas, and hydroelectrics. The modern trend toward conversion of all power into electricity makes difficult the integration of separated discussions. A glance through chapter titles of books on economic geography will disclose mixed patterns of organization for the resource-extracting and resource-converting discussions. Almost all geographic discussions of industrial activity include a chapter on the iron and steel industries as the backbone of modern industrialization. It is common to consider the textile industries under one heading, and the chemical industries logically can be grouped together, but the grouping of manufacturing of machine tools, ships, and agricultural implements suggests that chapter numbering, rather than the nature of industrial activity, is the controlling organizational factor. Recent studies of manufacturing tend to concentrate on one of three aspects: manufacturing regions, general locational factors and forces, or manufacturing by product-process groupings. Collection of statistics and classification of raw data on industry sometimes force the discussion of manufacturing into particular frameworks. We are not suggesting that there is an easy way out of the problem of how to classify modern industrial activity for, by its very nature in maturity, there is an interlocking and integration of all kinds of industrial procedures. Such integration is given particular shape in the United States by the politico-cultural policy of changing government antitrust rulings, to which corporations re-

spond by corporate merger. This results in the blurring of the data concerning different aspects of resource extraction and conversion. In Japan, on the other hand, the long-term holding and manipulation of wealth by particular socioeconomic strata yield patterns by which integration and the blurring of data take a quite different shape. State control of industrial activity in the Communist realm puts another complexion on the whole of industrial organization and data collection.

Historically, mankind evolved manufacturing around several groups of products: tools, weapons, clothing, trinkets-charms-toys-gadgets, utensils, furniture, and shelter materials. So long as primitive household industry and simple-powered household industry prevailed, direct manufacture was the rule, and machine tools (tools for controlling the making of other tools or finished products) remained little-made or embryonic in nature. Community workshop industry, in that it employed only human or simple power, required only simple machine tools in the form of simple lathes, jigs, forms, patterns, vises, and like items. Most of these tools are quite old, essentially developed long before the Industrial Revolution. A distinctive feature of the Industrial Revolution was the invention of new machine tools of many kinds, and the evolutionary development of the older simpler kinds of machine tools. It was this development by the "instrument maker" which, in fact, made the harnessing of power possible on a large scale in the seventeenth and eighteenth centuries in Europe. Machine tools are the basic mechanisms of modern industry, in that they enable the harnessing of large amounts of power to carry on the manufacturing of many kinds of "products" involved in modern semifinished and finished goods. Community workshop industry did not markedly change the basic nature of manufacturing, nor did it greatly increase the range and kind of products. On the other hand, the Industrial Revolution, by its ramifications into engineering mechanics, industrial chemistry, and industrial physics, has altered the range of products manufactured and the nature of manufacturing. The range and nature of manufacturing has also been greatly affected by European inventive-experimental mindedness, and by the plethora of raw materials derived from all over the earth. More recently the Industrial Revolution has been stimulated by certain growing scarcities and price patterns which have led to substitution of raw materials but which have yielded whole new series of segments of manufacturing out of the creation of synthetic products.

The approach to the classification of manufacturing on the earth today, therefore, must take into account the traditional technologies and the traditional systems of manufacturing, incorporating into the classification the socioeconomic-cultural elements of the diverse societal systems around the world. The classification of manufacturing cannot be phrased only in terms of industrial groupings reflected by the United States Census Bureau's collection of data. Something of the itemized fivefold enumeration, or an elaboration of this simple listing, must be employed for both our own do-it-yourself manufacturers working in their garages and hobby shops, and for the simpler systems in other parts of the earth. For the countries of the earth now approaching industrialization of the modern sort for the first time, the regional manifestations of manufacturing (furniture for example) are apt to display types, degrees, and regional distributions quite unlike those now found in the occidental regions in which the modern systems of corporately organized and power-supported manufacturing industries developed. Both combinations of old and new, and hybrids, characterize many of the regions of recent industrialization. In numerous cases the processes of industrialization will skip some of the stages, and the kinds of manufacturing normal to the regions of slow evolutionary development, and there will be lacking some of the interlocking and integration found in regions of mature development. Labor patterns will vary, as will consumer-market orientation, dependent often on cultural habits and customs. No single formalistic classification, description, or analysis may serve the whole earth at the present stage of industrialization.

One last historical element must be introduced. Whereas manufacturing has always ranged over a certain breadth, in terms of the kinds of products turned out, some industrial processes moved out of the domestic residence at a relatively early point. The wetting of plant fibers in water obviously required a special working site at a very early date, but not a formal factory. The smelting of metals could not be done inside the house, whereas spinning and weaving, and the processing of foods, could. Without adducing further illustrations, it is clear that certain kinds of manufacturing, at the onset of the Industrial Revolution, already were amenable to concentration in factories, and the factory has formalized as industrial ability has increased in scope. On the other hand, the food-processing industries long remained within the home, or close by it, and these have been among the last to undergo industrialization in the full sense of the term.

A genetic approach to the issues of modern industrialization suggests that power development and the processing of raw materials go hand in hand, forming initial steps in the conversion of extracted resources. The preliminary processing of minerals (concentration and other such first-stage processes), the processing of forest extracts, and the processing and milling of agricultural products are all related aspects of light industry that provide the raw materials and agents for the manufacturing industries. Light industry, power development, and agricultural processing are often the first aspects of industrialization to develop in a region that is beginning the transition from older systems to the modern powered factory. Hybrid patterns of power development and processing technologies will be present, using some older technologies and labor skills. Involved may be textile manufacturing, the making of semifinished goods, and the final manufacture of consumer products not requiring large amounts of power, highly involved technologies, or the application of complex engineering mechanics or industrial chemistry. Among the consumer products are some of the electrical manufactures, some of the rubber goods industries, and various of the food manufactures. Assembly of finished products from imported manufactured components is a recent significant aspect of light manufacturing in a region undergoing industrialization.

As urbanization occurs or increases, and as technological education occurs, many kinds of other beginnings may follow the development of power production and light manufacturing. The logical developmental sequence would suggest various heavy industries, such as iron and steel, heavy metal fabrication, the manufacture of machine tools, and certain of the chemical industries, accompanied by the continued additive of greater power production. Engineering inefficiencies and the wastage of by-products owing to the lack of integration occur at this stage. There would follow the expansion of the range of manufactures and the regional localization and concentration of industries according to environmental factors and factors of industrial integration in the product and by-product, raw material, and industrial agent. Secondary types of manufacturing would then gradually fit into niches in the industrial picture with variety, range, and duplication of product occurring among the numbers of entrepreneurs. This begins to approach a kind of maturity in industrialization, at least as now defined in the most advanced industrial regions.

However, there are regional and cultural variables to the theoretical genetic evolution of industrialization, as developed in practice, which make the conceptual pattern yield to realism. If the industrialization processes are spontaneously derived from the initiative of the population native to the region, there are apt to be all sorts of hybrid activities, technological combinations, and peculiar production sequences. A "bronze factory" seen in Thailand illustrates this kind of growth pattern. The "factory" occupied three closely spaced former private homes and the area between them, and it had 25 small electric motors in use for cutting, shaping, and polishing, all set on the floor beside which the workmen squatted in traditional style. A traditional-style hand-operated charcoal-fueled forge melted the initial metal mix, and hand filling of the molds continued. Except for the electric motors, this really was community workshop industry.

Within the same urban complex of Bangkok were numerous other factories right out of the American industrial scene. If government planning enters the process of industrialization, once it has begun spontaneously, there are apt to occur contradictions to a logical sequence of growth. Such an undertaking as the development of an iron and steel industry may occur at a stage prior to the evolution of a technological capability and a manufacturing capacity to utilize the output. This was approximately the case of the Philippines in the late 1950s.

A third pattern is that in which government planning initiates the whole of modern industrialization, as took place in Japan in the late nineteenth century. There all elements of industrialization were developed contemporaneously, new forms of industrial activity being inserted into the program as such activity appeared elsewhere around the earth in the course of time.

There is still a fourth kind of evolutionary sequence that can be seen in several sectors of the earth, primarily in the former colonial holdings of European industrial countries. Kinds of manufacturing were set up that did not necessarily integrate locally, but which integrated into the industrial activity of the homeland of the colonial power; another aspect of colonial manufacturing was the kinds of manufacturing set up to facilitate desired economic development of the colonial region. At the termination of colonial periods the regional picture of manufacturing in the new country could only be somewhat fragmentary and nonintegratable at the outset. Further growth then has been rather markedly subject to inexperienced government planning, irregular technological skills, irregular labor systems, inexperienced entrepreneurship, and inadequate capital resources.

Industrial geographers have approached the subject piecemeal, or with eyes too fixed upon certain production aspects of contemporary occidental industrialization. We suggest the utility of some version of our primary fivefold breakdown as possessing value in a world survey. For modern and mature industrial regions, the modern classification system would seem systematically separable into such segments as the power industries, raw materials processing industries, industries concerned with agents, by-products, and manufacturing components; secondary manufacturing of finished goods; tertiary manufacturing assembly of compound consumer goods; and the service industries required by the complex interlocking nature of modern industrialization. Such a systematic grouping of manufacturing activity does not accord with statistical tabulating systems being set up for worldwide use by census takers and economists interested in determining national income components. Such a grouping does, however, have utility in understanding the spread of the processes of industrialization over the earth as resource-conversion systems.

Industrial Location: The Factors and the Complex

Many contemporary economic geographers and economists, as part of their concern for spatial analysis and location theory, are concerned with studying the dynamic processes involved in determining the location of industrial activity in advanced societies. Such problems are discussed here only in broad terms; the recognition of the problem itself involves a significant element in the intensification of industrial processes of resource conversion. It seems doubtful if earliest man had even a glimmer of comprehension as to the significance of locating his working site other than where he happened to be or where he found what he wanted. The archaeologist does record later manufacturing as taking place on the sites of settlements, and he also records manufacturing as occurring on what he terms primary working sites, at which man must have at least camped while doing the manufacturing needed. Such primary working sites normally were located on or hard by sources of raw materials. In the cases of tool-stone processing, even late Paleolithic man probably figured out that it was easier to work a big stone down to at least the rough approximation of the final instrument than to lug a heavy raw stone a long distance to his preferred campsite. If this be taken as true at a rather early date, then an elemental aspect of industrial location can be assumed as operative over the long term. Wherever the processing of bulky or heavy raw materials involves a weight loss (as in cement manufacture or vegetable canning-freezing), the manufacturing is located close to the sources of raw materials. This is a basic rule of modern industrial location theory.

Further reflection leads to such other known simple rules as that easy-to-transport raw materials are brought close to sites of hard-to-transport raw materials when more than one material, agent, or component of industrial activity is involved. Certain light and easily transported finished products may be produced in a few specified centers in which the labor skills are concentrated; the location of such centers may have resulted from original causal factors not directly related to the specific industrial operations. On the other hand, some finished products costly to transport tend to be manufactured close to the sites of consumption, provided the raw materials are available nearby. The former rule has meant that valuable products have been traded far and wide, away from their centers of manufacture, during a long portion of human history; the latter rule has meant that the manufacture of certain kinds of things has tended to diffuse widely over the earth, once the concepts and the technologies were understood and dispersed. In both cases there is a rule involving the ratio of the cost of manufacture to the cost of transport. There are numerous other rules and subrules governing the matters of industrial location which are becoming quite well understood as location theory is amplified and exemplified in studies of industrial location.

Central to the whole issue of industrial location, however, has been the recognition and comprehension of resources, the invention and evolution of technologies, the comprehension and understanding of interrelations between raw materials and cultural processes, and the historic progression of patterns of fabrication of the things we call manufactured goods. Early Paleolithic man may only have worked out the rule of thumb for one or two rules of industrial location, whereas today the complexity of industrial location includes a very large number of factors. Historically, stone-tool manufacture diffused over the earth, being so elemental a kind of manufacturing that it went wherever man went. In England of the thirteenth to sixteenth centuries the smelting of iron ore could be carried on in numerous locations, because both the ore and the charcoal for fuel were widely available; locational factors were simple ones. However, as the forests were cut off in certain locations, iron mining and smelting migrated after the charcoal makers into the hill and mountain country where forests were still plentiful, since iron ore was widely available and the small yield of iron could be transported easily, by comparison. Coal mining and use, in contrast to stone-tool manufacture, did not just go where men went in the early periods. The comprehension of coal as a resource is held to have occurred first in eastern Asia, for the Old World, and a limited independent comprehension occurred in southwestern United States at a late date for the New World. Once coal became a known resource in England, the increasing scarcity of charcoal led to a substitution by coal (as coke, after experiment), resulting in significant changes in the location of iron smelting. It was Europeans who spread coal mining around the earth, with the manufacturing of things by and from coal, in the nineteenth century, changing the basics of industrial location for the world as a whole.

The manufacture of automobiles illustrates another working of the whole cultural complex of factors of industrial location. The automobile was a product of advanced inventive technology in both Western Europe and the United States at roughly the same time. A very few places became the first centers of automobile manufacture by the workings of a relatively simple set of causal factors, some of which were related to the older patterns of wagon building. Today, however, automobiles are manufactured in many countries in all parts of the earth, and assembled in many more, following the diffusion of advanced technologies. Today, also, the locational factors in automotive manufacture have been very intricate, subject to exacting economic analysis, and constrained by whole sets of parameters. Among these are the locations of power sources, locations of resource conversion for the primary materials, factors of labor, transport, consumer demand, national prestige, and pressure on currency reserves, and a group of complicated tertiary factors each of minor but significant nature. Issues of location for industrial operations subsidiary to the automotive industry are also constrained at present by most of these same sorts of parameters in each of several countries of the earth.

The very point of our comment on industrial location has to do with the complex buildup of the factors which, now, do affect industrial location in any of the major regions of the earth. No longer is it a simple matter of the location of the manufacturing process either in the settlement site or on the working site of the basic raw material. Where industrial location may at one time have been a matter of regional isolation, there now is a complicated set of issues that may involve the whole earth for one or a few products. Not all of these issues are strictly modern in their impact —recall that at one time the early Egyptians preferred to import iron products from the Middle East and pay for them with their tribute gold derived from the Sudan. In the modern world, the processes of resource conversion have become infinitely complicated by the very integration of large numbers of resources into complex end products and by the interregional spread of advanced manufacturing over the earth. Resource conversion, itself, has been greatly heightened by these interlocking relationships, and the more carefully these relationships can be analyzed the greater the efficiency in resource conversion can become. Partly, these issues have been complicated by the matter of scale. No longer is it the judgment surrounding the making of one stone tool, or the production of a few dozen items, but the comparative judgment about the cost-to-value ratio involved in making either 2 or 5 million items for a worldwide market, set in the context that there may well be dozens of other entrepreneurs making the same kinds of calculations for the same general market. In these terms the problems of industrial location have become both real and significant, but

by their very acute assessment the whole of resource conversion is rendered far more productive.

The Manufacturing Region

Tierra del Fuego, near the southern tip of South America, is a scantily occupied region, having slight production of economic goods and a low consumer demand. The island of Java is a densely settled region, having a significant production of economic goods of restricted variety, and a consumer demand in food and clothing that is low per capita but large for all of Java, against a demand that is comparatively small for complex manufactured goods. Somewhat inefficient operation of government for some years threw Java back onto its own resources to a considerable degree, and both primary production and manufacturing reverted toward the regional self-sufficient stages characterizing primitive household industry and community workshop industry. Northeastern United States is a heavily settled region in which the primary production of food is far below the high level of consumer demand, in which the primary production of industrial raw materials is strongly developed, and in which the industrial procedures of integrated manufacturing are very highly developed to yield a significant surplus of manufactured goods.

In the theoretical sense, we could assert that all three regions, Tierra del Fuego, Java, and Northeastern United States, could be labeled manufacturing regions. However, a modern industrial geographer would balk at the label for Tierra del Fuego, and would dismiss Java as a region carrying on only an elementary kind of manufacturing in a not very significant total volume. The point of the argument is that wherever man lives, he carries on manufacturing of some kind, at some level, to some measure of output, for the very definition of manufacturing includes all of the human activities of turning raw materials into something else. But in the twentieth-century world the term manufacturing region has been given that special definition which involves large volumes of raw materials, large quantities of power, large volumes of labor possessing varied skills, large numbers of factory establishments carrying on many operations, and large numbers of customers within transportation range (Fig. 9.4). This, essentially, constitutes what has been distinguished as corporate, powered production-line industry. The manufacturing re-

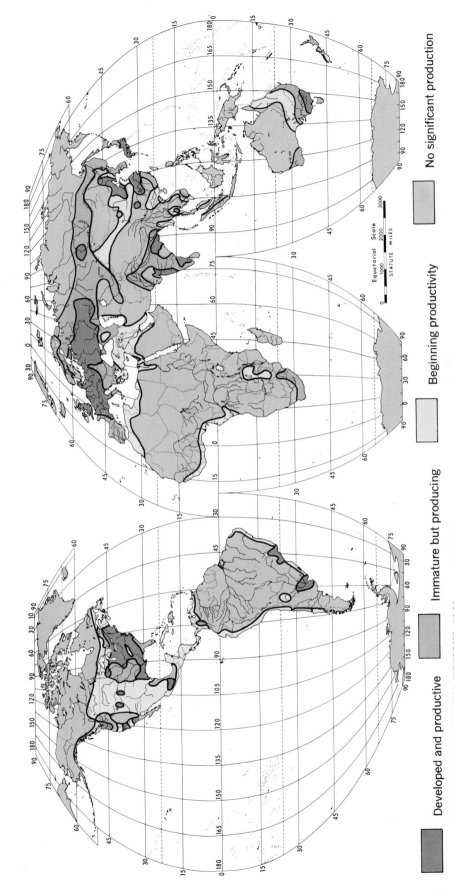

Developed and productive   Immature but producing

Beginning productivity   No significant production

FIG. 9.4 WORLD MANUFACTURING REGIONS, 1960.

Equatorial Scale
STATUTE MILES
0   1000   2000   3000

gion, therefore, is a region in which twentieth-century cultural technology is highly developed for a culturally adapted consuming population. This clearly limits the demarcation of manufacturing regions over the earth; further, such demarcation establishes hierarchical levels of world economic producing activity and consuming habit.

The modern manufacturing region is a product of the nineteenth and twentieth centuries. As first mapped and discussed decades ago, there were but few such regions scattered over the earth. The contemporary discussion of world manufacturing identifies a larger number of mature regions, and distinguishes a number of regions that are increasing their level and tempo of activity (see Fig. 9.4). The modern manufacturing region is a region of significant urbanism, of highly developed cultural habit and custom, of strong food deficiency, and has well-developed transport ties to the rest of the earth. It is characterized by complexity and by integration of its economic activity, and it is a region in which there are concentrated not only diversified labor skills, but also inventive technological skills and the concern for research into resource-converting techniques. A region of this kind possesses complex business organization which facilitates capital accumulation, transfer, and application to manufacturing ends. It is a region in which there are large volumes of varied types of nonhuman power available to do its work. The modern manufacturing region is possessed of advanced cultural habits which are in tune with the technological processes of production—in a slang phrase, the region's population has been brainwashed to consume the variety of products that can be turned out.

Man in the twentieth century, so far, has not discovered all the wealth of the earth, but today's manufacturing region contains significant volumes of industrial raw materials close at hand, sufficiently well tied by transport to other raw materials ranges so that these can be integrated into the whole operation. Environmental factors are operative in the cultural processes of resource extraction and regional establishment of manufacturing, but it is chiefly the cultural factors that have been adduced to turn good resource regions into modern manufacturing regions of high capability. From some points of view, the modern manufacturing region is the clearest mark, so far, of the cultural capability of man to use the resources of the humanized earth for his own benefit.

In addition to the mature manufacturing region, as indicated, there are hierarchical levels of immature, developing, and underdeveloped manufacturing regions, districts, or centers. In configuration such lesser manufacturing regions are often smaller, or irregular in outline, and they are characterized by lesser measures of output, range of manufacture, and labor supply. They may differ in kind by being specialized in products, and they may lack some of the environmental advantages of the larger and more developed regions. From the viewpoint taken in this volume, such immature manufacturing regions have not yet culturally evolved the depth, range, and efficiency in resource conversion that obtains in the mature manufacturing region.

Beyond the manufacturing regions that the industrial geographer is inclined to place on his world map are numerous other regions in which manufacturing of a sort does take place. In these areas, however, it is likely that power is restricted either in volume or in kind, that technology is culturally older and not in step with that of the advanced sectors of the world, and that the whole cultural complex reflects the culture patterns of an older era or of a particular society that has not yet adopted the systems that characterize the most highly advanced sectors of the earth.

The Manufacturing Regions of the Earth

As modern manufacturing commences, in any industrial region of the earth, it is impossible to carry on all the manifold operations yielding all of the processed raw materials, agents, and "products" required to assemble all of the sundry producer goods needed to manufacture the tremendous variety of consumer goods. Manufacturing does not come full-blown to any region. There must be the evolutionary growth of many different kinds of manufacturing, in which there takes place the integration of processes altering primary raw materials into agents, by-products, and semifinished products. Such manufacturing requires the growth of the power facilities, the growth of the producer goods phases, the accumulation of labor skills, the intricate organization of manufacturing units (companies, divisions, branches, sections), the accumulation of capital, the development of engineering-planning skills, and the growth of transportation systems to permit the integration of materials. It further requires the growth of a "market" by which all of the separate "products" have buyers, all the way from processed raw materials to final consumer products. Power production and raw material processing are somewhat fundamental to the whole process. The addition of every new line of processing or manufacture permits the further integration of resource conversion toward a higher efficiency. Raw material processing and light industry are the mark of the early stage of industrialization. The complex integration of raw materials, processes, agents, products, and assembly are the mark of industrial maturity, whereby the efficiency of resource conversion has reached a very high level.

In the twentieth-century world, through corporate and state organization, many of the separate elements in the whole of industrialization are scattered over the earth. Venezuelan iron ore may flow to the United States to be processed and manufactured into the steel parts of motor trucks which may finally be assembled in Malaysia, whereas the copper wiring in those trucks may have been manufactured in the United States from copper mined in Chile, the aluminum parts may have been manufactured in the United States out of alumina reduced in Canada from bauxite mined in Jamaica, and so on. Assembled in Malaysia also may be a Japanese and a British truck, for each of which the integration of raw materials and products was similar, and all three trucks may be fitted with tires manufactured in Malaysia from locally grown rubber. In this case three types of worldwide corporate organization had integrated manufacturing processes involving raw materials from over the earth.

The striking feature of twentieth-century manufacturing, whether light industry in the Philippines, heavy industry in Japan, Germany, and the United States, or final assembly in Malaysia, is that twentieth-century resource conversion has reached a state, and an efficiency, never known in any earlier society. This system of resource conversion does tie the whole earth together into one manufacturing system, the separate sectors of which operate at different levels in many different "manufacturing regions" of the earth. It is this efficiency of resource conversion that makes the modern world so different from the Paleolithic world.

In our context, it is clear that the whole of the earth is now bound into one great compound region of resource extraction and resource conversion which has facilitated the growth of modern industrialization and has greatly improved the quality and levels of living for large portions of mankind. It is equally clear that there are great regional divergences in systems of resource extraction and resource conversion. The concern for the heretofore underdeveloped regions, for the systematic spread of modern industrialization, and for initiating the development of modern systems of resource extraction and conversion, is motivated by the dual desires to lift the levels of resource development and levels of living in all parts of the earth so that those of the maturely developed industrialized sectors may be lifted still further through the increasing employment of technology expressly directed at resource development. It is not likely, however, that all parts of the earth can be brought to the same levels of industrial development within the near future. Regional diversities and regional inequalities will continue to be depicted in present and future maps having to do with resource extraction, and they certainly will be present in maps of resource conversion. The three accompanying maps (Figs. 9.5, 9.6, and 9.7) present several different interpretations of particular aspects of world industrialization. No one of them is entirely original, and aspects of each of them have been presented in other studies. All of them do, however, illustrate some significant facet of industrialization and resource conversion.

No lengthy textual interpolation of the regional presentations of the maps seems required. The position of the United States stands out clearly in every presentation, as does that of northwest Europe, the Soviet Union, and Japan. We have not tried to present the data for every single political state now operative, since such detailed presentation is beyond the scope of this book. The maps are regionalized into commonly recognized sectors of the earth in such a way that the broad picture remains significant.

The Continuing Growth and Spread of the Industrial Revolution

Occasionally one reads a statement which implies that the Industrial Revolution occurred, and that since that time things have been thus and so. The Industrial Revolution cannot be identified as something that happened in the past. The inventive developments began in the fifteenth century, but they began simply, without formal prior plan, and by experimentation not well grounded in physical theory. The revolutionary changes have gathered strength and speed as they have been

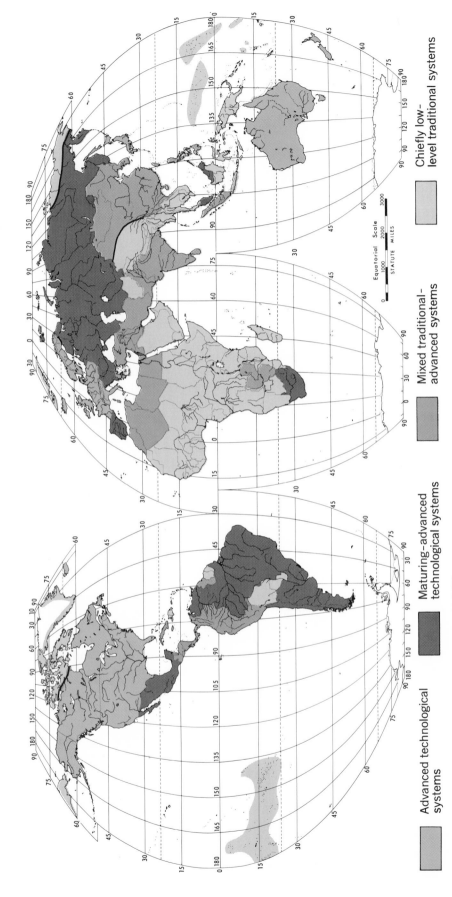

Advanced technological
systems

Maturing-advanced
technological systems

Mixed traditional-
advanced systems

Chiefly low-
level traditional systems

Equatorial Scale

0   1000   2000   3000
STATUTE MILES

FIG. 9.5   MEASURES OF DEVELOPMENT: TECHNOLOGY.

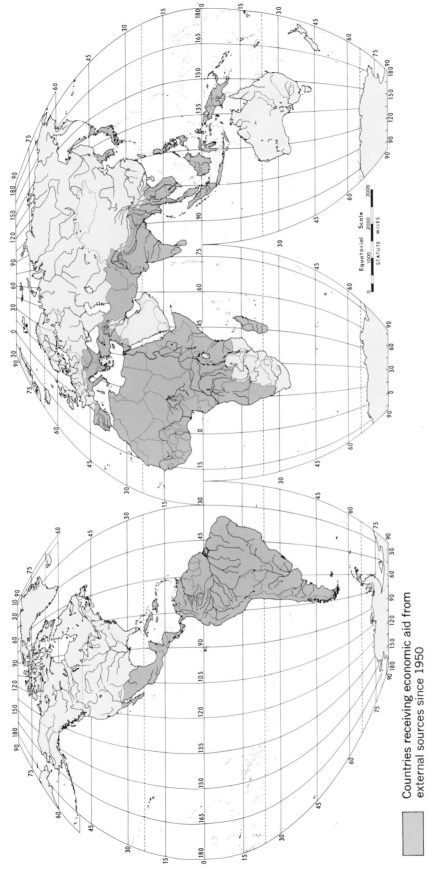

Countries receiving economic aid from
external sources since 1950

FIG. 9.6 MEASURES OF DEVELOPMENT: ECONOMIC AID RECEIVED.

407

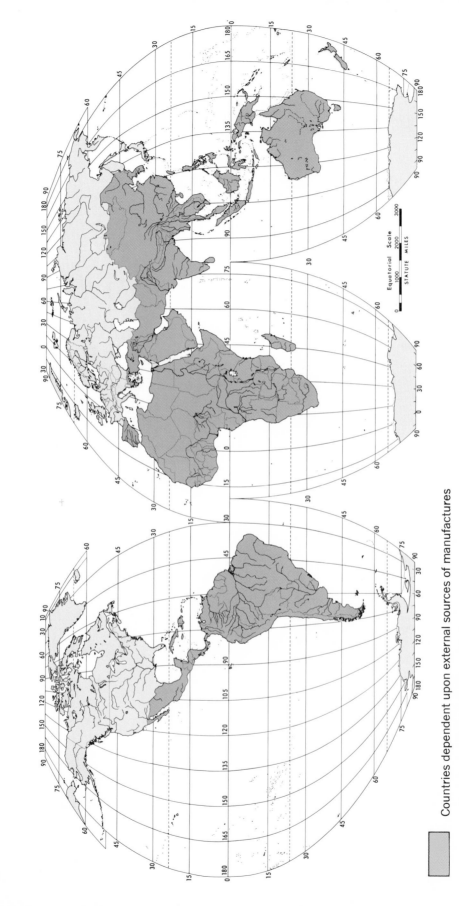

Countries dependent upon external sources of manufactures

FIG. 9.7 MEASURES OF DEVELOPMENT: DEPENDENCE ON EXTERNAL SOURCES OF MANUFACTURES.

bulwarked by developing theory, have broadened the ranges of their impact, and are in good stride at present. If the eighteenth century saw somewhat of a lull in the patterns of progress of the Industrial Revolution, the twentieth century has seen a striking impetus in those patterns, based on the value and emphasis given to technological inventiveness. The lone inventor has given way to the research combines whose whole time is spent on the investigation of new means, new procedures, and new products. The concept has diffused around the world, and no longer do all the new ideas turn up in Western Europe or the United States. Research not only has thought toward new ways of doing traditional work, but has also thought up whole new zones of industrialization never before conceived. The mid-twentieth century sees more effort expended on inventive research and the possible expansion of industrialization than had occurred, possibly, in the whole of human time prior to the sixteenth century. Inventiveness, research on resource conversion, and industrial expansion have become a way of life to a significant share of the population. It may be that, within the United States, for the period 1945–1965, more effort was being expended than in any other single country, but the only certainty is that across the earth the total effort will increase. To the degree that this is as true in the Soviet Union as in Japan, and in India as in Germany, industrialization will continue to be an expanding concept. The Industrial Revolution, thus, is by no means finished; some hold that merely a firm basement for it has been established, with the larger share of progress to come in the future. This view concerns the systematic evolutionary growth of the Industrial Revolution, but it constitutes only one aspect.

The second aspect is the geographical diffusion of the Industrial Revolution over the varied lands of the earth, from the northwest European initiators to a large share of the societies of the earth. That a formerly agricultural and handicraft manufacturing society in a far country now puts a high priority upon the development of an iron and steel industry is an integral part of the continued growth of the Industrial Revolution on the planet Earth. Whereas Siddhartha Gautama (the Buddha) in India, and Lao-tzu in China preached renunciation of the physical world, there arose in northwest Europe a conviction that the physical world should be conquered, and that the material world could be utilized to improve the level of living among mankind. The term Industrial Revolution is given to the complex of movements and processes constituting that conquest. The diffusion of that concept is rapidly maturing throughout the world today. In the words of John Nef, writing about a conference, ". . . it was with surprise that I discovered, at our Washington meeting, that the conquest of the material world is the subject which raises the major issues that concern the leaders and the people of every country."* A cultural concept of the relationship between man and his environment developed slowly through the early centuries of civilization in the Occident, and became explicitly formulated into working procedures in northwest Europe during the period we label the Industrial Revolution; that concept has become a vital concern to man in most parts of the earth today. The Industrial Revolution will only have become geographically complete when all of the peoples of the earth have shared in, and profited by, its processes.

The Industrial Revolution is often held to pertain only to manufacturing and to industry. It has been a concern of the last two chapters to suggest that the new cultural concept of the relationship between man and his physical environment involves recognition of two aspects to the conquest of the material world, namely the extraction of resources and their conversion into products helpful to man. The basic element in that cultural concept is that the earth exists for the use of man, man as its now dominant life-form. It is then up to man to utilize the earth to the greatest advantage possible through the most efficient technological procedures he can devise. Resource extraction, as a set of technological procedures, applies to any and all forms of extractive procedure applying to the interior of the earth, to its surface, and to the atmosphere around it. There are those who would now extend the concept beyond the bounds of our own planet into space within our universe.

The cultural concept involving the conquest of the material world should not be viewed wholly hedonistically. The modern concept does involve altering the ancient dogmas of Buddhism and Taoism, and of early Christianity, that the earth belongs to God and that man is on it to suffer mean and renunciatory existence in the glorification of God. Need one take the view that a God

*John Nef, *The Conquest of the Material World*. Chicago: University of Chicago Press, 1964, p. vii.

of our universe desires that man refrain from inquiring into the physical laws of the universe, that man should restrict his living systems to low levels of efficiency in the utilization of resources present, and that man should pursue the goal of living out a mean, poor, and miserable existence? The exploration of the physical laws of any godly universe, the higher efficiency in the use of resources, and the greater improvement of the life of man can be viewed, holistically, as the greater glorification of God.

Conquest and control of the material world, currently, has outstripped control and arrangement of the social and cultural world, but efficiency on this level, too, is within the reach of man if he chooses to make the effort. After a long period of divergence in human living spaces and systems mankind has not yet systematically integrated the relatively recently instituted processes of convergence which began with the Columbian Discoveries and which have brought our earth culturally toward the one-world circumstance. We shall have more to say on this subject in the final chapter of this book.

SELECTED REFERENCES

Alexander, John W.
1963   *Economic Geography.* New York: Prentice-Hall. 661 pp.
Alexandersson, Gunnar
1967   *The Geography of Manufacturing.* New York: Prentice-Hall. 154 pp.
Alexandersson, Gunnar, and Göran Norström
1963   *World Shipping; An Economic Geography of Ports and Seaborne Trade.* New York: Wiley. 507 pp.
Arensberg, Conrad M., and Arthur H. Niehoff
1964   *Introducing Social Change.* Chicago: Aldine. 214 pp.
Barnett, Homer G.
1953   *Innovation: The Basis of Cultural Change.* New York: McGraw-Hill Paperbacks. 462 pp.
Beadle, G. W., et al.
1959   *Science and Resources: Prospects and Implications of Technological Advance.* Baltimore: The Johns Hopkins Press. 250 pp.
Berry, Brian J. L.
1967   *Geography of Market Centers and Retail Distribution.* Englewood Cliffs, N.J.: Prentice-Hall. 146 pp.
Boserup, Ester
1965   *The Conditions of Agricultural Growth; The Economics of Agrarian Change Under Population Pressure.* London: George Allen and Unwin, and Chicago: Aldine. 124 pp.
Breese, G.
1966   *Urbanization in Newly Developing Countries.* Englewood Cliffs, N.J.: Prentice-Hall. 151 pp.
Brown, A. J.
1965   *Introduction to World Economy* (rev. ed.). London: Unwin University Books. 214 pp.
Clawson, Marion
1964   *Natural Resources and International Development.* Baltimore: The Johns Hopkins Press, for Resources for the Future. 462 pp.
Cottrell, Fred
1955   *Energy and Society: The Relation Between Energy, Social Change, and Economic Development.* New York: McGraw-Hill. 330 pp.
Creamer, D., et al.
1960   *Capital in Manufacturing and Mining: Its Function and Financing.* Princeton, N.J.: Princeton University Press. 344 pp.
Dalton, George (ed.)
1967   *Tribal and Peasant Economies.* Garden City, New York: Natural History Press. 588 pp.

deSchweinitz, Karl, Jr.
  1964 *Industrialization and Democracy: Economic Necessities and Political Possibilities.* New York: Free Press of Glencoe-Macmillan. 309 pp.
Dumont, René
  1957 *Types of Rural Economy: Studies in World Agriculture.* English edition, London: Methuen & Co. 556 pp.
Ellsworth, P. T.
  1964 *The International Economy* (3rd ed.). New York: Macmillan. 550 pp.
Estall, R. C., and R. O. Buchanan
  1961 *Industrial Activity and Economic Geography.* London: Hutchinson University Library. 232 pp.
Finkle, Jason L., and Richard W. Gable
  1966 *Political Development and Social Change.* New York: Wiley. 599 pp.
Firth, Raymond
  1964 *Essays on Social Organization and Values.* London: University of London, The Athlone Press. 326 pp.
Foster, George M.
  1962 *Traditional Cultures and the Impact of Technology.* New York: Harper. 292 pp.
Froehlich, Walter (ed.)
  1961 *Land Tenure, Industrialization, and Social Stability: Experience and Prospects in Asia.* Milwaukee, Wisc.: Marquette University Press. 301 pp.
Garst, Jonathan
  1963 *No Need for Hunger.* New York: Random House. 182 pp.
Gates, Paul W.
  1960 *The Farmer's Age: Agriculture, 1815–1860.* New York: Holt, Rinehart & Winston. 460 pp.
Ginsburg, Norton D.
  1961 *Atlas of Economic Development.* Chicago: University of Chicago Press. 119 pp.
Glass, D. V., and D. E. C. Eversley
  1965 *Population in History; Essays in Historical Demography.* London: Edward Arnold. 692 pp.
Gruber, Ruth (ed.)
  1961 *Science and the New Nations.* New York: Basic Books. 314 pp.
Hagen, Everett E.
  1962 *On the Theory of Social Change: How Economic Growth Begins.* Homewood, Ill.: The Dorsey Press. 557 pp.
Harbison, Frederick, and Charles A. Myers
  1964 *Education, Manpower, and Economic Growth,* New York: McGraw-Hill. 229 pp.
Heady, E. O., and L. G. Tweeten
  1963 *Resource Demand and the Structure of the Agricultural Industry.* Ames, Iowa: Iowa State University Press. 515 pp.
Heilbroner, R. L.
  1962 *The Making of Economic Society.* New York: Prentice-Hall. 242 pp.
Herfindahl, O. C., and Allen V. Kneese
  1965 *Quality of the Environment: An Economic Approach to Some Problems in Using Land, Water, and Air.* Baltimore: The Johns Hopkins Press. 96 pp.
Higbee, Edward
  1963 *Farms and Farmers in an Urban Age.* New York: Twentieth Century Fund. 183 pp.
Hoagland, H., and R. W. Burkoe
  1962 *Evolution and Man's Progress.* New York: Columbia University Press. 181 pp.
How, R. C.
  1959 *The Conservation of Natural Resources.* London: Faber & Faber. 255 pp.
Huberty, M. L., and W. L. Flock (eds.)
  1959 *Natural Resources.* New York: McGraw-Hill. 556 pp.

Jarrett, H. (ed.)
   1958   *Perspectives on Conservation: Essays on America's Natural Resources.* Baltimore: The Johns Hopkins Press. 260 pp.
   1961   *Comparisons in Resource Management.* Baltimore: The Johns Hopkins Press. 271 pp.
Liebenstein, Harvey
   1957   *Economic Backwardness and Economic Growth: Studies in the Theory of Economic Growth.* New York: Wiley. 295 pp.
Martindale, Don
   1962   *Social Life and Cultural Change.* Princeton, N.J.: Van Nostrand. 528 pp.
Mead, Margaret
   1964   *Continuities in Cultural Evolution.* New Haven, Conn.: Yale University Press. 471 pp.
Mudd, Stewart (ed.)
   1964   *The Population Crisis and the Use of World Resources.* Bloomington, Ind.: Indiana University Press. 563 pp.
Nef, John U.
   1964   *The Conquest of the Material World.* Chicago: University of Chicago Press. 408 pp.
Packer, D. W.
   1964   *Resource Acquisition in Corporate Growth.* Cambridge, Mass.: MIT Press. 118 pp.
Potter, N., and F. T. Christy, Jr.
   1962   *Trends in Natural Resource Commodities, 1870–1957.* Baltimore: The Johns Hopkins Press, for Resources for the Future. 568 pp.
Pounds, N. J. G.
   1959   *The Geography of Iron and Steel.* London: Hutchinson. 192 pp.
Rogers, Everett M.
   1962   *Diffusion of Innovations.* New York: The Free Press of Glencoe. 367 pp.
Rosovsky, Henry (ed.)
   1966   *Industrialization in Two Systems.* New York: Wiley. 289 pp.
Samuelson, Paul A.
   1967   *Economics, An Introductory Analysis.* New York: McGraw-Hill, 821 pp.
Shannon, Lyle W. (ed.)
   1957   *Underdeveloped Areas, a Book of Readings.* New York: Harper. 496 pp.
Schultz, Theodore W.
   1964   *Transforming Traditional Agriculture.* New Haven, Conn.: Yale University Press. 212 pp.
Schurr, S. H.
   1960   *Historical Statistics of Minerals in the United States.* Baltimore: The Johns Hopkins Press, for Resources for the Future. 42 pp.
Schurr, S. H., and B. C. Netschert
   1960   *Energy in the American Economy, 1850–1975: An Economic Study of its History and Prospects.* Baltimore: The Johns Hopkins Press, for Resources for the Future. 774 pp.
Smith, J. Russell, M. O. Phillips, and T. R. Smith
   1955   *Industrial and Commercial Geography.* New York: Holt. 689 pp.
Steward, Julian H.
   1955   *Theory of Culture Change; the Methodology of Multilinear Evolution.* Urbana, Ill.: University of Illinois Press. 244 pp.
Thoman, Richard S., and Edgar C. Conkling
   1967   *Geography of International Trade.* Englewood Cliffs, N.J.: Prentice-Hall. 190 pp.
Tostlebe, A. S.
   1957   *Capital in Agriculture: Its Formation and Financing Since 1870.* Princeton, N.J.: Princeton University Press. 232 pp.
Walker, Charles R.
   1962   *Modern Technology and Civilization.* New York: McGraw-Hill. 469 pp.
Wolfe, Roy I.
   1963   *Transportation and Politics.* Princeton, N.J.: Van Nostrand. 136 pp.
Zolschan, George K., and Walter Hirsch (eds.)
   1964   *Explorations in Social Change.* Boston: Houghton-Mifflin. 832 pp.

MARKETS

J. E. SPENCER

Itinerant Peach Peddler, China

Brush Hawker with Tricycle, Singapore

PICTORIAL PARADE

414

Boat Peddlers, River Market, Bangkok, Thailand

TOURIST ORGANIZATION OF THAILAND

BRUCE GOLDMAN, D.P.I.

Outdoor Vegetable Market, Israel

415

Spinning Equipment Shop, Iran

INGE MORATH, MAGNUM

IAN GRAHAM, PHOTO RESEARCHERS

Flower and Fish Markets, Bergen, Norway

Wool Market, Afghanistan

FRITZ HENLE, MONKMEYER

Sidewalk Newsstand, Paris, France

417

SUSAN McCARTNEY, PHOTO RESEARCHERS

RALPH MARDOL, D.P.I.

Retail Stands, Casablanca, Morocco

418

J. E. SPENCER

Periodic Village Market, West China

MARC AND EVELYNE BERNHEIM, RAPHO GUILLUMETTE

Urban Market, Addis Ababa, Ethiopia

Town Market, Saudi Arabia

ARAB INFORMATION CENTER

DORETHEA LANGE, MAGNUM

Interior of General Store, California, U.S.

420

City Market, Frozen-Food bins, Milan, Italy

IBEC

MEXICAN NATIONAL TOURIST COUNCIL

La Merced Public Fruit and Vegetable Market, Mexico City

Urban Supermarket, Mexico City

421

MARC AND EVELYNE BERNHEIM, RAPHO GUILLUMETTE

A Modern Shopping Center, United States

LAWRENCE LOWRY

422

Interior of Yorkdale Shopping Center, Toronto, Canada

CANADIAN NATIONAL FILM BOARD

CHAPTER *10*

Space-Adjusting Techniques:
Transport, Trade, and Communication;
Political and Administrative Organization

Man's sense of territoriality, his identification of life and activity with specific places, has pervaded human history from remotest tribal days to the present, little diminished in its intensity. The flowering of new nation-states, an expression of self-determination by human groups especially marked in the mid-twentieth century, and the fiercely persistent attachment of individual men to private property are examples enough. For millennia, as men worked ever outward from their first confined territorial small-group experience, they depended upon accretions of newly discovered knowledge to widen their concepts, to make something bigger than their earliest territorial instinct. Even into the twentieth century the techniques useful for exploration, discovery, and description of new lands have been essential to leaders in every vigorous society and nation. What began as a rudimentary individual sense of place has been gradually reoriented, in cultural terms, and related to a substantial body of knowledge about the spatial characteristics of the surface of the earth. The early concept of tribal hunting grounds has been replaced in advanced societies by concepts of family landownership, trade routes, the boundaries of the principality, kingdom, or nation, and of the total earth as a sphere. Thus man's conceptions of earth space and of spatial relations have also evolved.

The word "space" obviously has different meanings for an astronomer or astronaut, a newspaper or magazine advertiser, or an interior designer or architect. Geography's concern is with space on the earth's surface, which is quadriscalar: it has the qualities of *extent* (length, area, volume), *location* (a specificity of place, including site and situation), *density* (quantity of phenomena contained per unit area), and *succession* (variations in quality owing to changes that occur during periods of time).

Concepts of Spatial Interchange and of Space Adjustment

If everything existed in the same place, there could be no differentness. Only space makes possible the particular, a sense of dissimilarity or nonconformity from place to place over the earth's surface, and makes areal differentiation, or regional variation, a reality. Just as evolution requires that everything cannot occur at the same time, so a concept of particularity requires that everything cannot be equally near. A corollary of spatial place is the concept of distance; New York and Washington, D.C., are spatially different places spatially distant from each other.

Each place on the earth's surface has a network of spatial interrelations (location, distance, direction) with all other places on the earth's surface. A thing that appears (is born, created, or built) and then disappears (dies or is destroyed) acquires and loses properties of spatial interrelations even though it may never occupy more than one place on the earth's surface. If a thing moves, it occupies one place at one time and another place at another time; this kind of change involves spatial relations just as much as it does relations in time. Things can change their positons in space only through a lapse of time, time being used up in moving from one place to another.

To Aristotle space represented a *relationship* between objects; to Democritus space was a *container* in which objects exist; to Albert Einstein it was a *medium* connecting the objects. In this book we consider space to be one aspect of *motion* (or change); time is the other. Spatial and temporal relations are much alike. Evolutionary change in the phenomena on the earth's surface interweaves both time and space, as reciprocal components of the physical universe.

The concept of spatial interchange evolved from the activities of early man, as he began the differentiation in livelihood from gathering to collecting. In essence, the recognition and acquisition of a local abundance of foodstuffs created the possibility of harvesting (as in seed collecting, hunting, or fishing) more than could be consumed or used upon the spot where gathered. Collecting requires not only abundance but also movement, the transfer of goods from the place where collected to another place (e.g., campsite) where processed and consumed. The separation in space of place of production from place of consumption is basic to the concept of spatial interchange. Various technologies, not present among food gatherers, are necessary to achieve a collecting way of life: a technology of movement of things (transportation) and a technology of processing, as in food preservation and storage (resource conversion).

The space-adjusting techniques include all those culturally invented ways by which man changes the locations of things from where he acquires or produces them to other locations where he desires them to be. Sometimes this calls for the moving of materials; thus trade has evolved. Sometimes this calls for the movements of people: thus travel has evolved. Sometimes this calls for the movement of ideas; thus communication has evolved. Man has repeatedly adjusted spatial interaction by inventing newer technologies that have always tended to speed up movement and carry greater volumes of materials, peoples, and ideas across intervening spaces. The cumulative effects of transport and communication have shortened the effective distance between places on the earth's surface.

The space-adjusting techniques also include all those culturally invented ways by which man changes the ownership of things in the process of moving, extracting, or converting resources. As a good passes from a producer to a manufacturer, it increases in value because of its change of location through trade of a raw material. As a product passes from a manufacturer to a distributor, it increases in value because of its change of location through wholesale trade. As a product passes from a distributor to a consumer, it increases in value because of its change in location through retail trade. Each step effects both an increase in value and a change in location.

The space-adjusting techniques further include all those culturally invented ways by which groups of men acquire access to and manipulate control over territorial spaces and the resources these contain. Men have organized the highly diversified space accessible to them on the earth's surface into a set of compartments, partitioned for different purposes. The long-term trend has been to create uniform sets of conditions, within each compartment, applicable to the people who come under the jurisdiction of the particular compartment or territory. Because of cultural diversities (allegiances, sets of beliefs, communal spirit, concepts of identity), human attempts to establish political regional uniformities have created further differences in the space on the earth's surface. These culturally imposed differences further complicate the operations of spatial interchange.

The Ease and Difficulty of Moving Materials, People, and Ideas

In Chapter 8 we learned that both the identity of resources and their relative scarcity or profusion are culturally determined. The long-term trend has been to add ever more items to the storehouse of man's useful raw materials as the technologies of resource-extraction and resource-conversion improved. For example, aluminum has been a resource only since its identification as a chemical element and the discovery in 1886 of the electrolytic process for extracting the metal from bauxite, a hydrous alumina silicate. In Chapter 9 we learned that it is the culture of a given people that determines the uses to which all things shall be put: upon ignorance or skill, whether they shall be used at all; and upon technologies for resource conversion, the various ways in which they can be used. In this chapter, we focus upon space-adjusting techniques, for these help determine in what circumstances and in what amounts the various members of a community can have access to and use of the world's resources.

Since man evolved on land, we may assume that movement on land began earliest and has always, save for such exceptions as falling off a cliff, involved the deliberate use of a motive power. For most of human time this power came from man's own muscles, until in the Old World the domestication of animals added a new source of energy for transport. Again, a long time span was spent using animals to carry, pull, and push loads, and adapting such inventions as the wheel, chariot, cart, horseshoes, stirrups, harnesses, and light vehicles (wagon, carriage) to extend the range, in volume, weight, and distance, of transport for things and people.

Somewhat later man discovered that transport on water was easier than on land. A favorable current can move a ship of any size. Rivers, which are moving belts of water, became the world's first great highways after boats were invented. The earliest civilizations were chiefly potamic (river-oriented). In any era, ships have always been larger in capacity than the land vehicles of the same era. For most of the time that men have moved in ships, they used sails to catch the power of wind. The difficulties of erratic wind flow (absent or contrary) were overcome by having oars available so that a crew, or slaves, could apply their muscles to move the ship, as a temporary reversion to an earlier source of energy.

The transportation "revolution" came upon man only relatively recently. Until well into the nineteenth century regular travel over long distances could not exceed ten miles per hour. A mail coach, with good weather and relays of horses and drivers, could cover no more than 225 miles per day; the fastest of the "Yankee clipper" sailing ships set a record of 436 miles in one day. Now the world has mostly shifted its energy for transport from living organisms to the fossil fuels (coal, petroleum, gas) and is beginning further to change to nuclear energy. A burst of creativity brought the steam-propelled ships, cars, and trains; the bicycle; the electric streetcar and locomotives; the automobile and its big brothers, the truck and bus; the diesel ships, trucks, and trains; the airplane, first propeller-driven then jet-powered; and finally the several-man orbiting satellite. The results have been astounding: the land-speed record, with great effort, has been pushed to a fraction over 600 miles per hour, but anyone with the price of a ticket can travel faster, and with ease, in a commercial jet airplane; the astronauts and cosmonauts move at over 18,000 miles per hour.

Until the last century, there was little distinction to be made in the movement of materials, people, or ideas. All moved at about the same relatively slow speeds. There were some exceptions in the transmission of signals over limited distances through the use of human sounds (e.g., the whistling of the Canary Islanders, the yodeling of the Swiss), or drums or church bells, or even lanterns, beacon fires, and smoke signals. But the content and number of such speedier messages were very limited. The distinction in speed between communication and transportation came with the telegraph: the French system of optical telegraph stations in 1794 between Paris and Lille; then the Chappe telegraph network in France in 1844 connecting 29 cities through 500 stations; the first international telegraph cable of 1850 between Calais, France, and Dover, England; and, most significantly, the successful laying in 1866 of the transatlantic cable.

The "revolution" has been even more dramatic in communications than in transportation. Only 20 years separated the invention of the telephone (1876) and of the wireless telegraph (1895); only 17 years between the first radio broadcast (1906) to the first transmission of television pictures (1923). The current range and speed of communications is phenomenal! Since 1963, Europe and the United States have maintained telephone and television contact through the Telstar and Early Bird satellites; radio contact was established across a distance varying from 30 million to 206 million miles with the space probe Mariner IV; and a computer has the capacity to transmit the entire contents of the 26-volume *Encyclopaedia Britannica* in three minutes.

In the present world it is easiest to transmit ideas (words, pictures, sounds) electronically; complicated ideas for instruction, persuasion, and decision making can be sent quickly by people who travel by air; valuable or vitally needed or perishable goods can be sent by airfreight; but most goods, as freight, are transported by land, sea, or both at slower speeds. As a general rule, the greater the bulk and weight and the lesser the value of the goods to be moved, the lesser in cost and slower in movement will be the means of transport chosen.

Shortening the Effective Distance of Travel and Transport

The study of transportation enables one to analyze the interconnections between regions or places: the location of routes; the volume, value, and directions of flow of traffic; the influence one region has upon the economic activities of all other regions to which it is interconnected. Without means of transport for the exchange of regional surpluses, there could be no economies other than at the subsistence level.

In Chapter 5 explanatory reference was made to the five elements involved in any kind of transport: route surface, motive power, mechanism of carriage, packaging of materials, and terminal facilities at route-ends. Only in the nineteenth century did human inventiveness revolutionize transportation, by attacking problems around some one of the elements of the complex. During the twentieth century there has been coordination of the procedures for all five elements in many parts of the world; however, the revolution in transportation is still not complete, owing to the widespread lack of attention paid to some one of the five elements. The current attention being given the "parking lot" problem for the automobile, the "air terminal" problem for the airplane, and the "containerizing" solution to the packaging of materials for sea transport are examples of contemporary lack of full coordination in elements of transport.

Land Transport

The first of the means by which man achieved the ability to travel faster than any other animal was the railroad (see pp. 459–477). For decades, during the nineteenth century, the railroad was supreme, but in the twentieth century, automotive transport has been overwhelmingly successful, contributing to the mid-twentieth century decline of railroads.

The great caravan routes of Asia and Africa were but well-marked trails for animal traffic. Travel during the Middle Ages, by courier or individual, was mostly on horseback, and goods were carried on packhorses, until an efficient method was devised for harnessing horses to vehicles. In England road engineering began with John Metcalfe in 1765; then, in 1815, the Scottish engineer John Loudon Macadam substituted for the cumbersome Roman system of road construction a tough, resilient, tight mixture of uniformly small broken stones, in a layer about ten inches thick on a well-drained subsurface; the essential conditions were a smooth surface and a durable foundation. The term macadam has been used ever since; only later did asphalt or oil become added to the process to form an all-weather seal. Extensive and durable roadway systems for surface transport are principally products of the nineteenth century; efficient and well-maintained systems are twentieth-century phenomena and are still being extended, as witness the present-day construction, mostly in reinforced concrete, of the United States Interstate Highway System (Fig. 10.1).

The concept of laying tracks to form a smooth roadway began with the tramroads of the coal mines, in which trucks were drawn along wooden rails by men or horses. Tramways were used principally to bring coal, stone, and iron ore downslope from the pit heads to the edges of rivers or canals, as links to barge traffic. But tramroads could have only partial success until something other than horsepower was employed.

The first cross-country railway began operations in England in 1825, using a locomotive engine rather than horses, at a speed of 10 to 15 miles per hour. Competition, once begun in the 1820s between canals and railways, was won by the latter, because of the advantages not only of faster and cheaper transport but also of certainty and regularity in shipments during winter-frozen periods or periods of low water. Railway lines mushroomed in England; by 1840 there were 76 companies and 2235 miles of track; and England's entire system of internal transportation had begun its change. Many canal companies were taken over by the railroads; the number of roadside inns and turnpikes declined; additional railroad traffic developed, consequent upon reduced costs and increased speeds for all classes of society; land adjacent to railroads increased in value, both for commercial gardening and for industrial purposes; and stagecoaches adjusted from competing with railroads to serving them as feeder lines for collecting and delivery. An expanded railroad network thus made possible the urban-industrial transformation of nineteenth-century England, one element of which was the increase in speed of movement.

The diffusion of the steam-powered railroad to other countries was extremely rapid: Spain and the United States (the Baltimore and Ohio line), 1830; Belgium and Germany, 1836; France and Russia, 1837; Italy, 1840; Switzerland, 1852. The United States, in part because of its sheer size and vast

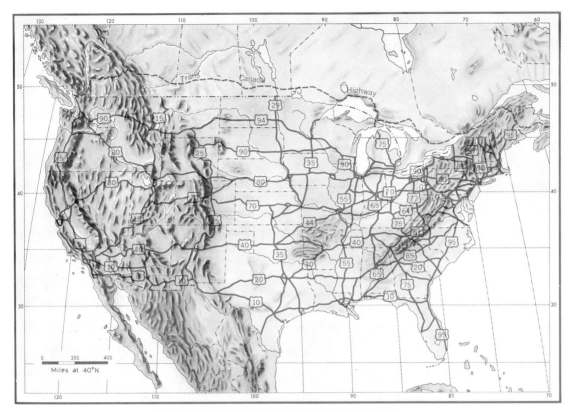

FIG. 10.1   THE INTERSTATE HIGHWAY SYSTEM OF THE UNITED STATES.

distances, almost at once seized the lead; by 1850, it had 9283 miles of track to England's 6521, Germany's 3726, and France's 2484. The United States affords an unparalleled example of transport development in a new country undergoing rapid economic growth.

The era of American railroad expansion lasted from 1830 to 1916, with a peak period in the 1880s when more than 70,000 miles of railroad were constructed. The maximum single-track construction totaled 254,307 miles in 1916 (although multiple tracking enabled track mileage to expand to 410,364 miles by 1930). A continuous decline has been the experience ever since (Fig. 10.2). Modernization has included the replacement of steam by more flexible and efficient diesel electric locomotives, in both passenger and freight service. By 1963 some 394 different railroad companies operated over 374,522 miles of track; consolidation of companies and discontinuance of unprofitable passenger-train services have become an increasing trend in the 1960s. The United States' railway system is unequally distributed; it is thickest in the northeastern quadrant, thinner in the southeast, and sparsest in the western half of the

country, in direct correlation with the distribution of population.

Different modes of land transport developed at different times, giving rise in regions of early urban-industrial development to problems of adjustment of the older forms to accommodate the new. In the United States, railroads began in 1830, pipelines in 1865, automobiles in 1893, intercity trucking in 1918, commercial airlines in 1926. The development of motor vehicles and improved highways seriously affected railroad passenger and freight traffic; the airlines' intercity passenger mileage came to exceed that of the railroads' owing to the diversion of much long-distance passenger traffic (Table 10.1). The new modernizing nations do not have to suffer through such problems of sequential readjustments but are free to choose among, or to coordinate, the several existing transport forms: railroads, pipelines, motor vehicles, as well as water and air transport. Whatever their problems of capital formation and investment, the new nations are better able to plan wholly integrated transport systems taking advantage of all existing forms of transport with a minimum of costly duplication of services.

1860

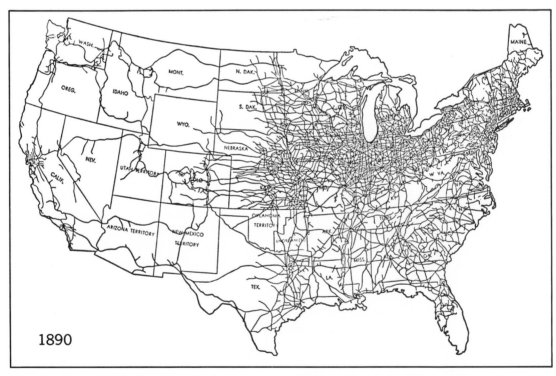

1890

FIG. 10.2   THE EXPANSION AND CONSOLIDATION OF RAILROADS IN THE UNITED STATES.

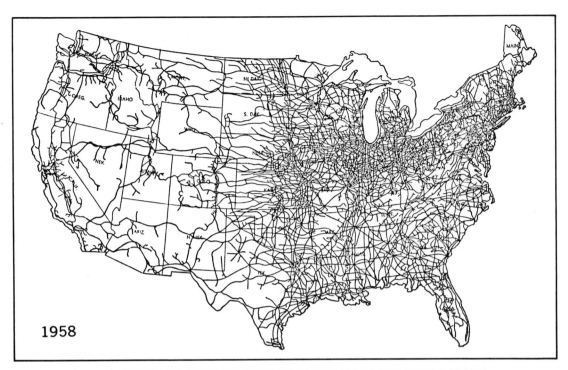

1958

FIG. 10.2   THE EXPANSION AND CONSOLIDATION OF RAILROADS IN THE UNITED STATES.

TABLE 10.1   COMPARISONS OF IMPROVED TRANSPORT FACILITIES FOR INTERCITY MOVEMENT IN THE UNITED STATES

A. MILEAGE (AS OF 1963)

Agency	Mileage
Highways, intercity (high-type surface)	442,918
Airways (with very-high-frequency facilities under control of FAA)	342,502
Railroads	214,387
Pipelines, oil	204,064
Waterways, improved (excluding ocean and Great Lakes)	25,260
Other Intercity highways (lesser surface)	2,702,587
City streets	474,952

B. FREIGHT TRAFFIC (AS OF 1963)

Agency	Millions of Ton-Miles	Per Cent of Total
Railroads	629,337	43.02
Highways	347,865	23.78
Pipelines, oil	250,319	17.11
Waterways, inland (including Great Lakes)	234,172	16.01
Airways	1,296	0.09
Total	1,462,989	100.00

C. PASSENGER TRAFFIC (AS OF 1963)

Agency	Millions of Passenger Miles	Per Cent of Total
Highways		
Buses	21,917	2.63
Private Automobiles	748,467	89.69
Airways	42,765	5.12
Railroads	18,632	2.23
Waterways, inland (including Great Lakes)	2,763	0.33
Total	834,544	100.00

D. FREIGHT AND PASSENGERS (PER CENT)

Agency	1940 Ton-Miles	1940 Passenger Miles	1950 Ton-Miles	1950 Passenger Miles	1960 Ton-Miles	1960 Passenger Miles
Railroads	61.34	8.71	58.69	8.12	43.51	2.86
Highways	7.91	90.46	12.39	89.57	22.50	92.37
Pipelines, oil	11.62	—	12.70	—	17.18	—
Waterways, inland	19.13	0.46	16.19	0.30	16.76	0.27
Airways	<0.01	0.37	0.03	2.01	0.06	4.50

Many formerly colonial territories owe their transport network to European-introduced technology. Route patterns, however, were often dictated by military strategy and governmental needs; many colonial transport systems were never economically self-sustaining. Railroads were built to connect mining centers and agricultural areas with ocean and river ports, hence designed to facilitate exports; or to connect an inland capital with an import city; or to assure national hegemony by linking isolated regions; or to circumvent unnavigable portions of rivers. Yet the inherited systems have benefited the new nations in their subsequent economic development programs.

The country placing most emphasis upon railroads is the Soviet Union, with its long distances and nearly flat terrain. Its 75,000 miles of track carry an annual load of two billion passengers and two billion tons of freight; this is 90 per cent of the U.S.S.R.'s intercity freight and 75 per cent of its intercity passenger volume. The Soviet objective is to intensify production at the least cost; the higher the rail volume, the more efficient the operation, and the lower the freight rates and passenger fares. Truck performance, on the other hand, is low-level, mostly within cities over short distances. In 1960, there were 3,345,000 trucks but only 638,000 automobiles—one car for every 330 people. The choice to date has been to concentrate freight movements on railroads rather than invest in a vast highway network for long-distance trucking, extracting as much service as possible from a minimal capital investment.

The automobile, truck, and bus, using internal combustion engines burning gasoline or diesel fuels, have become the most ubiquitous transport vehicles in the world. A jostling stream of about 120 million cars moves about the earth, nearly two thirds in use in the United States. World production is about 12 million annually, nearly two thirds in the United States. Cumulatively, the United States automobile industry produced its 200 millionth motor vehicle in December 1962. The gasoline engine in all forms is, however, a great contributor to air pollution; the private motorcar seems all important for the twentieth-century way of life, but is it likely that its present form will survive the century of its dominance?

Pipelines are a specialized transport system, based on the principle of continuous, as contrasted to vehicular, flow. Many pipelines are privately owned and operated, and principally serve to move natural gas and a host of liquids: crude oil, gasoline, and other petroleum products. Many city-owned pipelines move water, sewage, and gas. Experiments with transporting solid articles in capsules through pipelines are under way; moving pulverized coal, ores, and other solids in suspension in water is already being done on a limited scale. Pipelines can now be built to whatever diameter is required; limits on size are those of market demands because it is most efficient to operate a pipeline at near capacity. The development of pipelines has permitted a locational shift in petroleum refining. The earliest pipelines were crude-oil lines, connecting to seaboard, to railroads, or to refineries, the latter located at great distance from the oil fields but close to large consuming markets. Many of these pipelines have since been converted to product lines, transporting gasoline from refineries located near oil fields to markets, however distant. As Fig. 10.3 indicates, natural gas lines now span the North American continent, but this form of transport is so different that it is not really competitive with any other method. A pipeline can move one ton of oil 1000 miles for about $2.00; the advantage of pipeline transport is so impressive that 20 per cent of all land freight (measured in ton miles) in North America is moved by pipelines. However, pipeline transport is still restricted by national political controls in other parts of the world.

Transmission of electricity, however generated, is less a form of transportation than a substitute for it, as the transport of fuel (coal, petroleum, natural gas) is minimized or eliminated. Electrical transmission is, however, a fabulous space-adjusting technique, enabling man to disperse energy from the point of production (e.g., a waterfall) to many points of consumption.

Water Transport

This topic heading is ambiguous. But whether it is water itself that is being moved, as in irrigation canals, flumes, aqueducts, piped water, or piped sewage systems, or whether it is goods and people being transported in vehicles on or in water, the effect of space adjustment (a change in location) is the same.

Transportation forms that use water in which to move are customarily divided into foreign (ocean shipping between countries), coastwise or intercoastal (ocean shipping between domestic ports), and inland waterways (lakes, rivers, naviga-

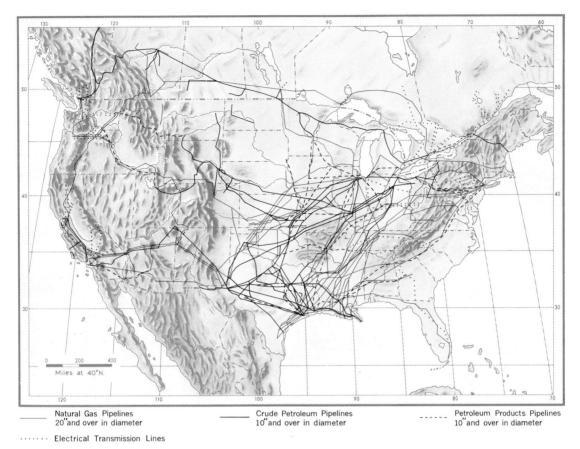

_____ Natural Gas Pipelines   _____ Crude Petroleum Pipelines   - - - - - Petroleum Products Pipelines
20″and over in diameter   10″and over in diameter   10″and over in diameter

· · · · · · Electrical Transmission Lines

FIG. 10.3   LONG-DISTANCE PIPELINES AND ELECTRICAL TRANSMISSION LINES IN THE UNITED STATES.

tion canals). For the United States, coastwise transportation monopolized the trade between ports in the colonial period; all intercoastal (Atlantic-Pacific) shipping was around South America, until construction of the Panama Railroad in 1854 made possible a shorter ocean-rail-ocean route; the opening of the Panama Canal in 1914 stimulated an increase in intercoastal traffic until World War II; but since the mid-1940s neither coastwise nor intercoastal shipping has regained its earlier importance, owing to railroad and truck competition.

The inland waterways of the United States (Fig. 10.4) consist of five systems: New York Barge Canal, Atlantic and Gulf Intracoastal waterways, coastal rivers, Mississippi River, and the Great Lakes. The improved waterways of the first four of these total 25,260 miles, of which 15,228 are nine or more feet in depth, hence suitable for accommodating modern barges. The most traffic is carried, and the largest vessels are used, in the Great Lakes system, moving grain, iron ore, and coal. Inland water transport was greatly revived during the early twentieth century to create cheap freight transport, to relieve traffic congestion, and to keep railroad rates down. Waterways are improved and maintained by the federal government, but considered as "public highways" open to use by anyone; tolls are collected only at the Panama Canal and the St. Lawrence Seaway. The disadvantages of inland water transport are its slowness, its seasonal character in the north owing to frozen waterways in winter, the interruption of service during floods or droughts, as in the Mississippi River, and the cost of freight transfer from land to barge or ship and back to land.

Ocean transport has always included both economic and military objectives. One must distinguish naval from merchant vessels; among the latter are passenger or passenger-cargo carriers, freighters (scheduled liners and tramps), and industrial carriers (tankers and ore carriers). The largest of the merchant vessels are the supertankers; the most numerous are the freighters.

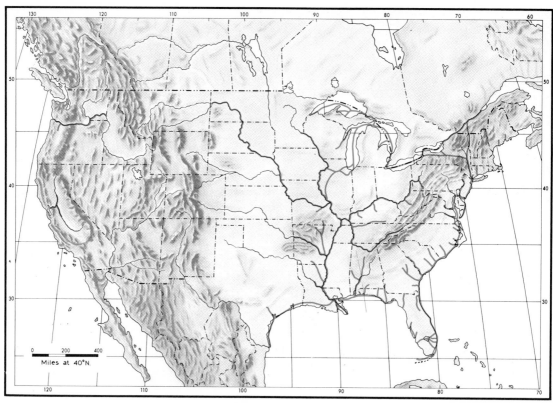

FIG. 10.4   INLAND WATERWAYS OF THE UNITED STATES.

At the opening of the twentieth century, the gross tonnage of the world's merchant fleet was 29 million tons, of which 6.5 million were sailing ships and barges and the majority were coal-burning steamships. The sailing ships all but disappeared in the early years of this century. Coal as fuel has now been all but replaced by oil; but the use of oil-burning steam turbines in very large high-speed vessels has enabled steamships to hold their own (Table 10.2). In 1961 there were 130 million gross tons of steamers and motorships, despite the loss of 34 million gross tons during

TABLE 10.2   CHANGING PATTERNS OF MOTIVE POWER IN THE WORLD'S MERCHANT FLEET

Power	Percentage of Merchant Fleet Tonnage		
	1914	1939	1961
Coal-burning steamships	96.6	45.3	4.1
Oil-burning steamships	2.9	30.0	50.5
Motorships	0.5	24.7	45.4

World War II. The greatly expanded shipbuilding activity since 1945 has produced a new class of larger, faster, and more efficient ships, essentially tankers, that can produce more ton-miles per year than older ships.

Until World War II, tramp steamers dominated the world's merchant fleet. These did not follow fixed routes or time schedules and sought cargoes wherever they could find them, shipping and trading being parts of the same business with decisions on buying and selling being made in distant ports. The twentieth-century decline of tramp shipping has been the result of several factors. The improvement of worldwide communications enabled the functions of shipping and merchandising to be separated, with decisions on buying and selling being made in a headquarters office and sailing instructions being given accordingly. The liner trade expanded; rather than carrying whole shiploads of bulk cargo (grain, cotton, coal), the newer liners carry general cargo (in bags, bales, special containers) or passengers, often both, on regular schedules and routes at higher speeds than do tramps. The industrial carriers have taken on the former role of tramps for specialized cargoes; a commercial or industrial firm owns and operates its own ships for moving large volumes of raw materials (crude oil, iron ore, refrigerated bananas). In the 1960s, shipment of grains and fertilizers by tanker has become common. The speeds of movement may be compared as follows: older tramps, including World War II Liberty ships, have speeds of 10 to 11 knots; new large tramps, about 18 knots; modern cargo liners 18 to 24 knots.

Ocean transport involves not only the carrying of people and goods, but also the connections at particular ports. Loading and unloading (terminal operations) incur 50 to 75 per cent of the total costs of ocean shipping. In the United States, there are 237 improved commercial seaports, but the traffic, whether foreign, coastwise, or intercoastal, is concentrated at 20 principal ports (Fig. 10.5). There is an obvious pattern of relationships between port locations and the spatial locations and developments of cities, the growth patterns of industrial regions, and the spatial networks of transportation in many parts of the earth.

Air Transport

The first successful flight by a heavier-than-air powered machine at Kitty Hawk, North Carolina, on December 17, 1903, was the culmination of experiments made by men of many nations during the previous centuries. The airplane was not the creation of any single culture. Today, only two thirds of a century later, the worldwide character of air transport is self-evident, since the world is laced by a network of air routes (Fig. 10.6).

The development of the airplane into a major means of transport gave rise to problems far beyond the capacity of individual governments to solve. The need for safety and regularity in air transport involved building airfields, setting up navigation aids, and establishing weather reporting systems. Standardization of operational practices for international services was of fundamental importance, in order to avoid errors caused by misunderstanding or inexperience. Establishment of standards—for rules of the air, for air traffic control, for personnel licensing, for air safety—all required more than national action.

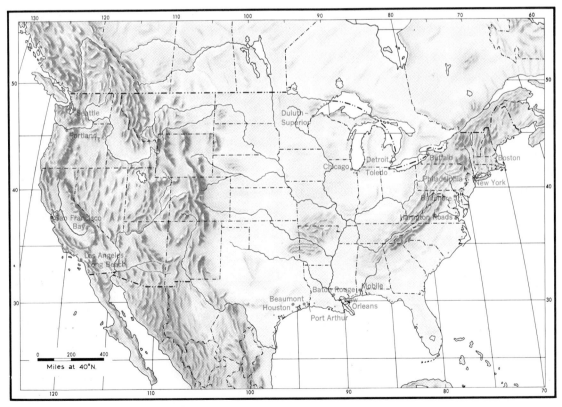

FIG. 10.5 COMMERCIAL SEAPORTS OF THE UNITED STATES.

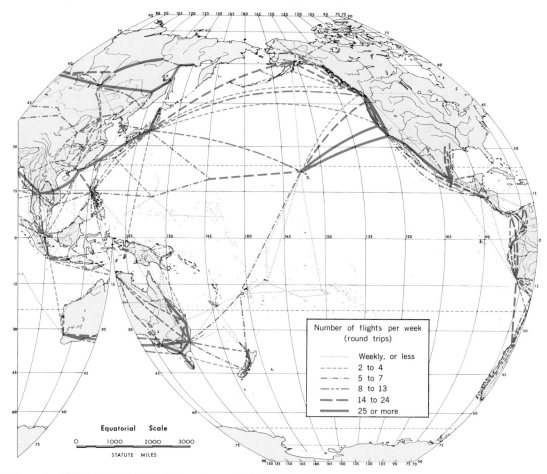

Number of flights per week
(round trips)

.... Weekly, or less
– – – – – 2 to 4
–·–·–·– 5 to 7
–··–··– 8 to 13
━ ━ ━ 14 to 24
━━━━━ 25 or more

Equatorial Scale

0   1000   2000   3000

STATUTE MILES

FIG. 10.6   SCHEDULED COMMERCIAL AIRWAYS OF THE PACIFIC BASIN, 1960.

Commercial air transport began in 1926 in the United States, coincident with the letting of the first government contracts to private companies for the transportation of mail. Airmail carriers were required, by such contracts, to provide passenger facilities, as a means of reducing the cost of transporting mail. From such a federal stimulus, the present massive air transport system had its beginnings (Table 10.3). Commercial aviation has literally "taken off" since World War II. The amazing expansion has resulted from the combination of a host of factors: the availability of skilled flight crews; the expansion of route mileage by the main trunklines; the establishment of numerous feeder or local lines, including helicopter "commuter" services; the launching of airfreight service; the expansion of nonscheduled services and all-cargo airlines; and the institution of "air-coach," "tourist," and "economy class" services by regularly scheduled airlines. Technological advances in capacity and speed of turboprop and turbojet aircraft

have created new opportunities for rapid expansion in transport services. Quick movement across long distances has been the hallmark of air transport with which other forms of transport cannot compete. Not only has traffic been diverted from

TABLE 10.3   GROWTH OF SCHEDULED DOMESTIC AIR TRANSPORT IN THE UNITED STATES (*after Federal Aviation Agency*, FAA Statistical Handbook of Aviation, *1966*)

Year	Passenger Originations	Express and Freight Ton-Miles
1930	385,000	—
1935	763,000	1,098,000
1940	2,523,000	3,476,000
1945	6,541,000	22,175,000
1950	17,468,000	152,223,000
1955	38,221,000	229,966,000
1960	52,375,000	386,933,000
1965	84,467,000	943,126,000

surface transport carriers, but also much new traffic has been generated (e.g., business commuting, vacation trips to far places, shipment of perishables such as cut flowers). A large passenger jet also carries a truckload of freight; a jet freighter can carry the equivalent of one railway freight car.

Aircraft may not move indiscriminately through air space. In the interests of safety, airways are prescribed; lanes are designated along which an aircraft is guided from airport to airport. The present airway system of the United States, maintained and operated by the Federal Aviation Agency, is an elaborate set of navigational aids, consisting of radio signal stations (very-high-frequency omnidirectional transmitters), beacon lights, weather-reporting service, auxiliary landing fields, air-route traffic-control centers, traffic-control towers, radar and instrumental approach systems, and route levels (low, to 14,000 feet; intermediate, from 14,500 to 24,000 feet; and high-altitude jet-route, above 24,000 feet). A nation's airways are used, of course, not only by commercial carriers and by private operators, but also by the military establishment.

The equivalent for aircraft, of the coastal port or harbor for ocean shipping, is the airport, where flights originate and terminate. In 1964, according to the F.A.A., there were 8814 airports in the United States. Most of these are "general aviation airports." The most important, for our consideration of space adjustment, are the 715 "air-carrier" airports, which primarily serve the scheduled airlines. Airports are generally provided by cities which seek their benefits (that is, to possess a "harbor of the sky"); municipal ownership is usually necessary since few airports are profit makers and partial federal aid for their construction is available only where the land is publicly owned.

The principal advantage of air transport is speed, which is greatest on long distance nonstop flights for which the proportion of time spent in land transport to and from the airport is minimized. Other advantages are frequency of schedules and ability to move in any direction to remote places. An airplane, even the very largest, is still small compared to an ocean liner or a train. Since large loads, such as ships or trains require, do not need to be concentrated, loaded, and unloaded, frequent flights can be scheduled. A flight once per week to a remote Alaskan outpost may be considered "frequent," compared to the surface transport

alternatives. A further advantage is that, given an airport of adequate size, an airplane may travel to a remote area not otherwise provided with transport facilities. The airway requires not as large an investment in route "rights of way" as do roads, railroads, or canals. Alaska, the Amazon Basin, Australia, Borneo, and New Guinea all are served by one or more local airlines which link their sparsely settled areas to the worldwide network of commercial air services. Again, there are clear spatial relationships between the locations of air terminals and the regional economic development patterns of regions in all parts of the world.

Evolution of Trade

The exchange of goods and services among peoples separated across great distances on the earth's surface has been a continuing process since prehistoric times. Reference was made in Chapter 5 (The Lengthening of Transport on Land and on the Sea) to the historic processes of linking the very old trade cells of the ancient world. The Columbian Discoveries finally linked all the world's trade cells together, although the linkages were tenuous and not highly productive of movement of goods of comparatively low value. Improvements in transport were made during the seventeenth and eighteenth centuries, but the most spectacular advances in expansion of trade have come about during the past century, resulting from the impetus of the Industrial Revolution. Every increment to man's resource-extracting techniques made possible an increase in raw-materials production. Similarly, every addition to man's techniques for resource conversion made possible a great increase in the kinds and numbers of new products available for human use. The "feedback" effect was fully operable, in that the improvements in land and water transport introduced an era of flourishing international trade.

Increasing Volumes and Increasing Distances

The modern expansion of trade is so intimately linked with technological developments in production and transportation that it is difficult to separate cause from effect. The harnessing of inanimate energy to industrial machinery has made possible a vast increase in the volume and variety of manufactured goods. Such commodities no longer are consumed only locally, but, in varying ways, receive worldwide distribution. The increases in size and speed of railroads, trucks, ships, and planes enable a more effective distribution of goods in ever larger quantity and variety, whose sale makes possible the construction and operation of new manufacturing plants, including the cost of the machinery and purchase of inanimate energy to run them.

Mass transport now moves raw materials in huge volumes, often over great distances. Partly, this has been made possible by technological progress: in the 1860s a 3000-ton ship carried only 800 tons of cargo and needed 2200 tons of coal; by 1899 the volumes were reversed. The first cargo ship over 3000 tons was launched in 1899, a far cry from today's 150,000-ton supertankers. Increases in train capacities, expansion in truck haulage limits, and the growth in aircraft capacities all reflect the same sorts of technological progress, and the volume flow by pipeline introduces still another medium of movement. There is no technological limitation today on man's ability to move anything he chooses from one place to another across the earth's surface. The limitations on space adjustment are cultural rather than physical. There must be sufficient reasons for undertaking projects of space adjustment, plans laid, engineering and administrative decisions made and orders given, financial feasibility determined, and perhaps political agreements entered into among states or nations. The logistic problems of supplying the military forces in World War II, in Korea, or in South Viet-Nam, and the sending of the "wheat fleet" to India are indicative of mid-twentieth-century capabilities.

Economic Specialization by Production Areas

Trade among peoples in different regions within a country, or among countries, involves the exchange of goods or services produced in one region or country and desired in another. A farmer, who has planted and raised a sizable apple orchard, sells his apples, and with income purchases other articles, such as shelter, food, and clothing, that he needs. He might even decide to buy some other variety of apple for eating or cooking that he himself does not produce. By specializing in the production of a good that has a market elsewhere and engaging in its marketing or trade, the farmer and his family are better off than if he attempted to be self-sufficient and produce on his farm all the materials needed for his shelter, food, clothing, etc.

Trade among nations is essentially similar to this

"apple farmer" analogy. By producing in quantity those goods for which they have a special advantage or capability, nations or their people can exchange their products for other needed goods. There are many reasons for areal specialization: the nature of the resource base; existence of a supply of skilled labor; existence of tools and machines (capital investment); government assistance; proximity to markets.

All of the factors of production combine in various proportions to create special advantages or handicaps for regional productivity. Clearly, the factors of production are distributed unevenly over the world. If this were not so, all regions could produce equally, and there would be no need for trade. However, there would still be the cultural preference for the "import." The flow of trade, then, is to be explained largely in terms of the relative abundance or scarcity of the different factors of production, and in terms of cultural preferences of consumers in different regions of the earth. The principle of comparative advantage thus applies. Regions and nations specialize in the production of goods for which they have the least comparative disadvantage.

Regionalisms of Markets

The ultimate basis of trade is that it serves to adjust the spatial differences between places of production and places of consumption. Most trade is bilateral, between individuals or corporations who buy and sell, import and export. Geographers have tended to emphasize the routes and movement of transport facilities and the volumes, routes, and flow of goods in trade. But equally important is an understanding of the multilateral and regional systems of methods of payment. When foreign exchange can be freely bought and sold in order to undertake transactions, a network of trade can extend widely over the world. Countries can then fully specialize in their best or most profitable products, if not both, and use the foreign exchange earned by their exports to buy imports from many other parts of the world.

Over the past century, the world's economy has passed through a number of distinct phases. Between 1850 and 1928, there existed a stable multilateral system of world trade, led by Great Britain as an industrial power, as a main source of foreign investment, and as banker to the world, and facilitated by the remarkable improvements in communication and transport. It was a period of economic internationalism, operating under the gold standard, in which exchanges were free and every country's economy had to be adjusted to the international equilibrium.

The stock market crash of 1929 meant an abrupt, if temporary, end to American private investment overseas. As the shock of the depression spread around the world, every country moved to protect its domestic economy from the reverberations in the international economy. The gold standard was abandoned and currencies were depreciated in order that each country's value of exports would maintain a proper balance of payments. Price stability had to be restored and the level of employment increased. Political factors replaced wholly economic forces during the 1930s in shaping the pattern of world trade. Bilateral trade agreements negotiated between countries became the prevailing consideration that arranged the direction and the commodity composition of world trade flow. Economic nationalism was the rule, marked by a resurgence of trade among the members of the British Commonwealth and by closer ties of all European colonial powers with their possessions overseas.

World War II shattered the "normal" patterns of world trade and affected the participating nations quite differently. The United States and Canada, for example, vastly increased their industrial potential, while the industry of Western Europe was all but destroyed or worn out. The American economy provided the foodstuffs and capital goods imports for the rebuilding of postwar Europe, but in the process Europeans became aware of the competitive superiority of manufacturing "know-how" possessed by the United States and sensed the danger of becoming too greatly dependent upon one country.

The spread of the industrialization process around the world has now changed the relative proportion of commodities entering world trade; industrial products are increasing and the percentage of raw materials is decreasing. Over the past several decades there has been rapid economic growth in such nations as Argentina, Brazil, Mexico, Australia, India, South Africa, Yugoslavia, and Finland. All of these countries are now processing much larger quantities of their own locally extracted raw materials than ever, thereby reducing the volume of raw materials that formerly entered the export trade.

The countries of Asia, Africa, and Latin America, many of which depend on a single commodity for export earnings (Fig. 10.7), have steadily been losing ground in world trade. Their main foreign exchange earnings—tropical agricultural products, petroleum, and minerals—have not increased in value as fast as prices on the manufactured goods that these countries have purchased from abroad. In spite of increased local productivity, many countries are exporting more volume of goods but earning less income than they formerly did. The "trade gap" between export earnings and import needs is increasing. To cite a few examples: if the market price of coffee drops by one cent (U.S.) a pound, it costs Colombia $7 million a year. In Malaysia, a drop in natural rubber prices means a halt in the rise of level of living that a smallholder was expecting from his improvements in crop practices. Ghana, which derives 60 per cent of its national income from cacao, had to reduce its economic plans drastically following a crop-price decline.

The most successful example of regional organization for the promotion of trade comes from Western Europe. In 1947, the Organization for European Economic Cooperation (OEEC) was established to distribute United States aid efficiently under the European Recovery Program (the Marshall Plan). Beginning as a program for economic recovery, the idea of cooperative unity persisted and, after American aid ended in 1951, the Organization continued as a coordinating agency for its 18 member states. The European Coal and Steel Community was founded in 1951, with headquarters in Luxembourg, to pool basic industrial production and take the first step toward economic cooperation. The first common market for coal and iron ore, scrap, and steel was opened in 1953 among the six participating nations: Italy, France, Germany, Netherlands, Belgium, Luxembourg. These six nations in 1957 formed a union setting up a European Atomic Energy Community (Euratom) and a European Economic Community (EEC), better known as the Common Market. A customs union has gradually removed all obstacles to the free movement of goods, people, firms, services, and capital among the member countries. Greece, Turkey, and 18 independent African countries have been made associate members. The EEC is now well on its way to becoming a political federation with a greater population and economic productivity than either the Soviet Union or the United States.

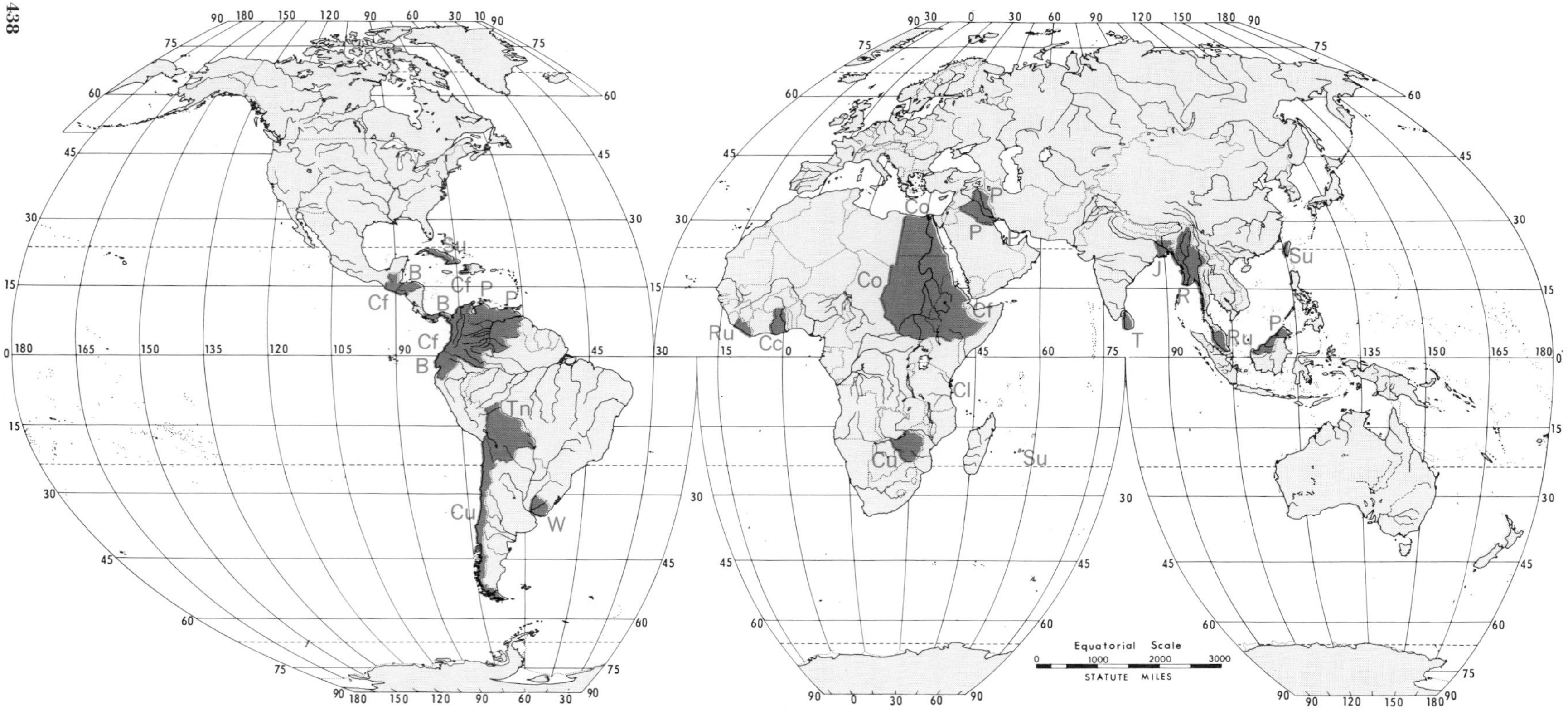

438

FIG. 10.7 COUNTRIES CHIEFLY EXPORTING A SINGLE COMMODITY.

B   Bananas
    Ecuador
    Honduras
    Panama

Cl   Cloves
    Zanzibar

Cc   Cacao
    Ghana

Cf   Coffee
    Colombia
    El Salvador
    Ethiopia
    Guatemala
    Haiti

Cu   Copper
    Chile
    Rhodesia

Co   Cotton
    Sudan
    United Arab Republic
    (Egypt)

J   Jute
    East Pakistan

R   Rice
    Burma

P   Petroleum
    Brunei
    Iraq
    Kuwait
    Netherlands Antilles
    Qatar
    Venezuela

Ru   Rubber
    Liberia
    Malaysia

Su   Sugar
    Cuba
    Mauritius
    Taiwan

T   Tea
    Ceylon

Tn   Tin
    Bolivia

W   Wool
    Uruguay

Equatorial Scale

0   1000   2000   3000
STATUTE MILES

The very success of the European Economic Community, or "Inner Six," prompted the formation in 1960 of the European Free Trade Association (EFTA), associating the "Outer Seven": Great Britain, Portugal, Austria, Switzerland, Denmark, Norway, and Sweden. Its purpose is to achieve free trade of industrial products within its area; it is not as vigorous as the EEC in striving for fuller social and economic integration. Should Great Britain be admitted to the Common Market, the other members of the EFTA will seek to join, to create a full European community. Europe's assets for integration in developing its regional economic organization were many: a developed industrial base, good transport and communication facilities, and a common purpose.

Other regional economic development and trade associations have been formed, on the European model, but not possessing all of Europe's assets. In Asia, the earliest formed was the Colombo Plan, a loose cooperative system that mixes economic assistance from six donor nations (Australia, Canada, Japan, New Zealand, Great Britain, and the United States) with mutual help from 18 largely recipient nations. In southwest Asia, Turkey, Iran, and Pakistan have formed a loose union called Regional Cooperation for Development (RCD); a joint shipping line is in operation. The most effective organization for economic cooperation in Latin America is the Central American Common Market (CACM), formed in 1960, to include Costa Rica, El Salvador, Guatemala, Honduras, and Nicaragua. The ten-member Latin American Free Trade Association (Mexico plus all the countries of South America except Bolivia, Guyana, Surinam, and French Guiana), created in 1960, has been less effective because of political instability and competitive economies. In 1962 some 29 newly independent nations of Africa formed the *Organisation Commune Africaine et Malgache* (OCAM), linking former French and Belgian colonies into a common organization for economic cooperation and development.

The new and striking idea of regional economic integration clearly has been spreading outward from Europe, with a variety of kinds of stimulus and assistance from different international agencies. Ways are being paved toward further regional political groupings of individual nation-states, with widespread benefit to be derived from increased efficiency.

Currency Blocs and Government Barter Agreements

Despite these trends toward regional cooperation, political controls over trading systems through the several currency systems blocs have, in the twentieth century, tended to confine trade within restricted channels, according to several groupings: the Sterling area; the European Common Market of Continental Europe; the Dollar area, grouped around the United States; and the Communist ruble bloc (see Fig. 1.12). More than half of all exporting and importing of each bloc occurs among the countries of that bloc. This results in trade compartmentalization, because it is easier to make payments within such groupings than between blocs. The means by which world trade is made to balance, in goods moved and payments transferred, is by having some important trading countries, such as Japan, the Union of South Africa, and the oil-rich countries of southwest Asia, remain outside of any bloc, trading freely with most or all of the others.

Such politico-economic constructs as the Commonwealth (British) not only form a currency bloc, but also have had exchange arrangements for all kinds of products. Sometimes these have been characterized by particular tariff systems giving preference within the group, as with the Commonwealth, or as the pattern operative between the United States and the Philippines.

There was a time when the regional interchange of raw materials, commodities, and products was entirely private; the trading parties reached independent agreements concerning the exchange. More recently there has come into being the barter trade agreement negotiated between governments acting as economic intermediaries for the entrepreneurs, be they government-operated or privately controlled. Cement, steel products, a fertilizer factory, and chemicals may flow one way in an agreed monetary volume, whereas rice, tea, copra, and cottons may flow in the other direction in a corresponding monetary volume.

Such manipulations of economic institutional patterns have increasingly replaced the older and simpler economic linkages of separate sectors of the earth as the need for increased volume movements has characterized recent resource-conversion programs. None of these forms, patterns, or systems is stable, for all of them are subject to renewal, cancellation, alteration, replacement, and developmental cultural change. As the Bank of International Settlements, the International Monetary Fund, and other such combines work to facilitate truly worldwide economic activity, contemporary national and international economic institutions continue to attain greater economic enterprise. Increasingly, such agreements cut across zones of divergent political organization and grouping.

Economic regionalism is supplanting economic nationalism as the main characteristic of contemporary world trade. The larger scale of activities within a trade region (greater production, consumption, and trade) create opportunities for specialization among countries, enhancing overall efficiency and reducing costs of production. The regional blocs, as means for a wider sharing of complementary resources and for access to a greater population of consumers, may be considered as long-term transitions toward the ideal of worldwide integration and optimum allocation of resources for all. Fig. 10.8 illustrates the twelve trading regions that now characterize the world trade pattern. An analysis of trade, region by region, reveals a number of significant changes in the trade of each region since 1928. Note that all comparative statements are in terms of changes in *percentages of total value* of exports and imports.

Continental Europe. This region, because the multitude of its nation-states calls for a high volume of international trade, has consistently been the world's leading region in its value of international exports and imports. Exports to Great Britain and the U.S.S.R. have declined by half since 1928, whereas Asia, Africa, the United States, and the Middle East have become more important markets. Imports come principally from the United States, Great Britain, Africa, and Latin America; there is increasing dependence of Europe on oil supplies from southwest Asia. Continental Europe, as a whole, is a net importing region with all regions of the world, except for Asia, with emphasis upon an increase in the import of raw materials.

United States. As the second most important trading area of the world, the United States now conducts most of its foreign trade within the Americas. Almost as much is exported to Canada as to Continental Europe; more is imported from Latin America than from all of Europe and Africa combined. The percentage of food imports has been

rising, whereas the percentage of raw materials imports has decreased. Two thirds of American exports consist of manufactured goods.

Great Britain. The relative share in world exports has declined substantially, owing to the effects of World War II. Exports declined to the Soviet bloc, Asia, and Latin America, whereas those to Africa and southwest Asia increased. In order to obtain food and raw materials from other than the dollar area, imports have increased from Africa, Australia–New Zealand, southwest Asia, and Canada. Great Britain has consistently been a net importer of raw materials and food from other regions, paying for them with earnings from capital, transport, tourism, insurance, and other "invisible" earnings. Textile exports have declined drastically, but fortunately have been offset by the rise in exports of machinery and vehicles.

Latin America. Trade patterns have become more closely integrated with the United States, largely as a result of trade diversion from Western Europe. Fluctuating trade policies have produced marked instability in some countries: for example, Brazil had an import deficit of $110 million in 1952, followed by an export surplus of $379 million in 1953. Much of Latin America's instability is the result of fluctuations in the world prices for the five commodities (coffee, petroleum, sugar, wool, and cotton) that contribute more than 60 per cent of Latin American exports.

Asia (except for Japan and mainland China). This area has changed in this century from a net exporter before World War II to a net importer since 1945. Population growth has outrun food production; rice exportation has declined; and many foodstuffs have been imported, mainly wheat from the United States and Canada. More intensive use of raw materials is being made locally to supply the newly established industries of the recently independent nations. Trade with mainland China was never strongly reestablished after World War II, whereas, despite the hostilities of the war, a strong trade relationship has now been established with Japan. The rise of imports from the United States has been spectacular, and, perhaps surprisingly, the economic ties of former colonies have mostly increased with their former metropolitan countries in Europe (France, Great Britain, Netherlands).

Canada. The trade pattern of Canada is closely tied to the United States, to whom Canada sends 60 per cent of its exports and from whom it

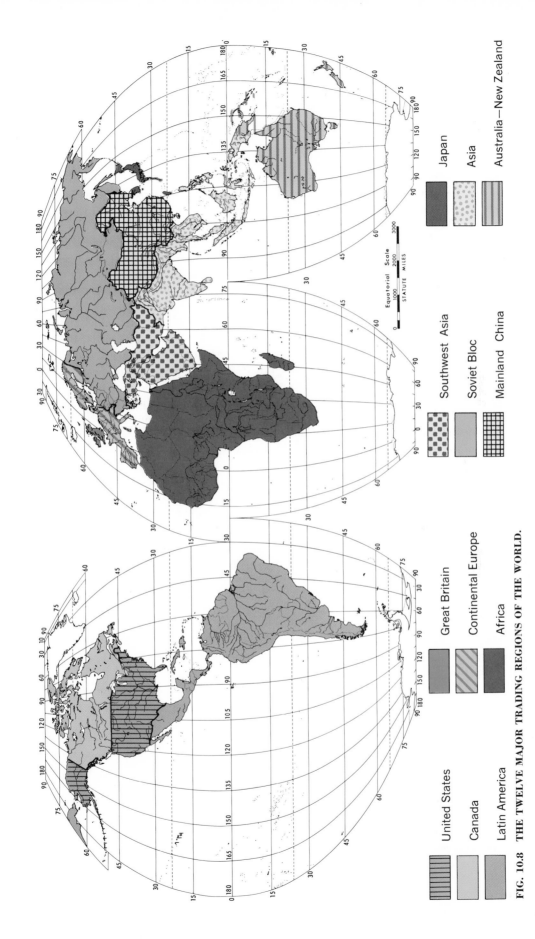

	United States		Great Britain		Southwest Asia		Japan
	Canada		Continental Europe		Soviet Bloc		Asia
	Latin America		Africa		Mainland China		Australia—New Zealand

Equatorial Scale

0   1000   2000   3000
STATUTE MILES

FIG. 10.8   THE TWELVE MAJOR TRADING REGIONS OF THE WORLD.

441

receives nearly 75 per cent of its imports. The Canadian economy is rapidly industrializing, but to accomplish this, nearly two thirds of its manufactures, including capital goods, are imported.

Africa. The share of Africa in the world's exports and imports has increased appreciably. Continental Europe and the United States are receiving more African exports, principally of raw materials, such as copper, lead, zinc, and uranium ore, as well as coffee and cacao. Only the Union of South Africa, by virtue of its revenues derived from exports of gold and diamonds, has a strong industrial base.

Southwest Asia. The relative increase in world trade by the countries of southwest Asia results from the phenomenal growth of oil production since World War II. For example, the combined exports of Kuwait, Aden, and Saudi Arabia leaped from $27 million in 1938 to $1476 million in 1953 and to $3390 million in 1964. Oil provides more than one-half the total value of southwest Asian exports, followed by agricultural products such as cotton, dates, barley, and citrus fruits. Only Israel exports manufactured goods. Export ties are closest with Continental Europe and Great Britain. This region is unique in that it has export surpluses with all other regions except mainland China and the United States.

Japan. For nearly a decade after World War II, Japan survived only on the basis of United States subsidies during the Occupation, followed by the industrial stimulus provided by its role as a staging area and producer of food and supplies for the United Nations forces in Korea. Since ratification of the Peace Treaty of World War II, however, Japan's industrial and trade resurgence has been remarkable, as normal trading relations were resumed. Rapid changes took place in both the regional distribution and the commodity composition of its trade. In 1965, North America remained the principal trade region, exceeding the whole of Asia. Japan is absolutely dependent on the import of food and raw materials (85 per cent of imports) whose cost is met by the export of manufactured goods (80 per cent of exports). Since Japan does not belong to any regional bloc or monetary arrangement, the country's position in the network of world trade and payments is somewhat unstable.

Australia and New Zealand. The trade of Oceania has fluctuated considerably. Trade balances closely correlate with world demand and the rise and fall in prices for the principal goods: large quantities of wool, meat, and dairy products. Ties have always been close with the Sterling bloc, especially Great Britain, although an increasing share of exports is being sent to the United States and to Asia, including Japan. At least 75 per cent of imports are manufactured articles, with increasing preference for those from the United States.

Soviet Bloc. The external trade of the Soviet bloc is negligible. As a result of the "Iron Curtain," the regional trade of Continental Europe with the Soviet bloc dropped to about 4 per cent of Europe's exports and imports. Some 4 to 6 per cent of Asia's trade is with the U.S.S.R.; less than 3 per cent of Great Britain's or Japan's trade is with the Soviet bloc; less than 2 per cent of Latin America's, Canada's, and Australia–New Zealand's; less than 1 per cent of the United States'. Recent purchases of wheat from Canada, the relaxation of the embargo on shipments from the United States to the U.S.S.R., and the extension of Continental Europe's trade and tourism to eastern Europe, will slightly increase the Soviet bloc's share of trade with North America and Europe.

Mainland China. The external trade of mainland China, except with North Korea, North Viet-Nam, Burma, and eastern Europe is small in volume. Contacts with the outer world through Hong Kong and Albania provide mechanisms for the remittance of funds from overseas Chinese to relatives in their homeland. Such are a source of valuable currencies for use in the trade relationships that exist outside the Soviet bloc. The much-heralded and politically inspired trade missions of the early 1960s into Cuba and the new nations of Africa invariably turned sour or backfired, to China's detriment so far.

Channels for the Distribution of Goods

In contrast to railroads, canals, and paved roads, the air and the oceans are free highways over which planes and ships can roam. But most vessels and planes, save for private planes and boats, and tramp steamers, follow rather well-defined routes, whose locations and directions are linked to their terminals, the seaports and airports they connect. Most of the world's trade and air traffic is funneled through a relatively few terminals, capable of handling and servicing the large modern transport vehicles and having sizable productive hinterlands.

The world's leading sea-lanes are shown in Fig. 10.9. Clearly shown is the fact that trade moves

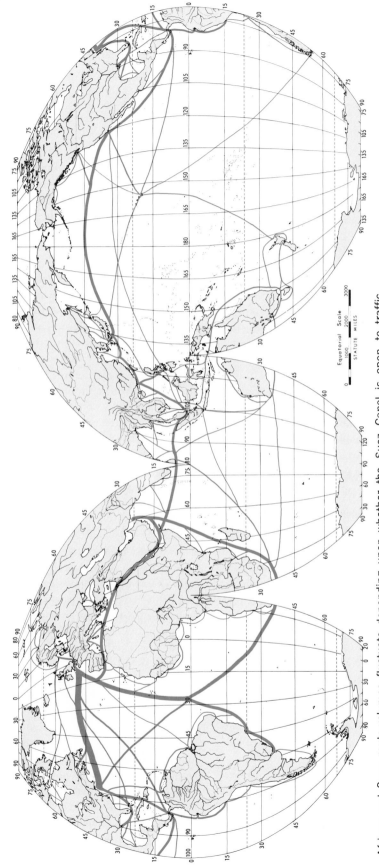

African and Suez route-volumes fluctuate depending upon whether the Suez Canal is open to traffic.

FIG. 10.9 THE MAJOR COMMERCIAL SHIPPING LANES OF THE WORLD.

in channels, shaped by the transport routes and by the communications network. The pattern of ocean transport routes of the eighteenth century would have looked greatly different, as sailing ships followed the earth's wind system and the world's regions of production and consumption required fewer and different commodities than now. Prominent, for example, would have been the New England shipment of fish and ice to the West Indies and the return voyages with cargoes of rum and molasses. The nineteenth century brought the clipper ships and the tea and wheat trades. In the late nineteenth century, London became a great world port, outstripping Hamburg, Rotterdam, and Antwerp, and such countries as Denmark and Sweden began to buy Australian wool, Canadian wheat, United States tobacco, and Argentine leather not directly overseas, but all from the entrepôt of London.

International trade has become vastly complex. The merchant trader, the merchant banker, the freight forwarder, the import house, the national corporation are commercial institutions that have developed at each end of the channels of trade. Organized markets to serve growing populations called for greater and greater volumes of standardized goods; and, where standardization and grading could not be accurately achieved, as in wools, furs, and diamonds, there evolved international auctions with competitive bidding taking place after inspection.

Widening the Resource Sustenance for Ever More People

In consequence of the Industrial Revolution and worldwide trade, a way of life has been evolving in which it is possible for an entire community to enjoy comforts and even luxuries, such as previously were accessible only to a small minority. Our freedom is virtually synonymous with the fullness of life as it has been realized by technological society. The greater the number of industries and occupations and the more abundant the consumer goods, the greater is the freedom of choice in employment or business and freedom of choice to buy whatever one pleases. Such conditions are now more available than ever to more of mankind.

To illustrate how widespread are the present-day sources of production and manufacture of the commodities we use and consume in our daily living, let us examine the first hours of a "typical" American's morning.

Our solid American citizen awakens in a bed built in North Carolina from a variety of woods, including imported paneling such as Philippine mahogany. He throws back covers made from synthetic fibers processed from West Virginia coal, or of cotton from Texas, or linen from Ireland, or wool from Australia. These materials may have been spun and woven in Pennsylvania, or Hong Kong, West Germany, or Canada. He slips into his moccasins, made in Massachussetts of leather from India and Argentina, and goes to the bathroom, whose fixtures were manufactured in Indiana and Los Angeles. He takes off his pajamas, made in France, and washes with soap manufactured in Cincinnati. He then shaves with a stainless steel blade made in England of steel from Sweden.

Returning to the bedroom, he removes his clothes from a chair made in Denmark of teak from Thailand and proceeds to dress. He puts on his garments, all made in the United States, of wool from New Zealand, cotton from Egypt and the Sudan, buttons from Fiji, and puts around his neck a silk tie from Italy. Before going out for breakfast he glances through the window, of glass made in Illinois, and if it is raining puts on overshoes made in Taiwan of rubber from Malaysia, and takes an umbrella, made in Japan. Upon his head he puts a hat made in New York of felt from Uruguay or Iran.

On his way to breakfast he stops to buy a newspaper, printed on paper from Canada, paying for it with coins made of copper from Arizona, Utah, or the Belgian Congo. At the restaurant he uses a plate made of a plastic from Ohio; his tableware is of stainless steel from Sweden, his glass from Belgium. He begins breakfast with a grapefruit from Arizona or bananas from Honduras or perhaps a papaya from Mexico. With this he has cocoa from Ghana or coffee, blended from products of Brazil and Colombia, with cream and sugar. The milk was produced in, and delivered by tanker-truck from, Wisconsin, whereas the sugar was grown in Hawaii. The coffeepot was made in Japan of iron from Australia, chromium from the Philippines, and nickel from New Caledonia. After his fruit and first coffee he goes on to waffles, made of wheat from North Dakota, processed in Minnesota. Over these he pours maple syrup from Vermont. As a side dish he may have an egg from Delaware or Maryland, or a strip of bacon produced in Iowa, Canada, or the Netherlands.

When our friend has finished eating, he settles back to smoke a cigarette from Virginia or a cigar from Spain or the Philippines. While smoking he reads the news of the day, printed in his town from wire-service reports of events in nearly 100 countries around the world. As he absorbs the accounts of foreign troubles, he might, if he is a good conservative citizen, express the thought that this world would be a better place in which to live if all peoples "stayed in their own backyard" and had as little as possible to do with each other, and that he, for one, was a firm advocate of the policy of "Buy American."

The Private Corporation as an Organized Space-Adjusting Force

The twentieth century has witnessed the culmination of a new era in international trade. Numerous private corporations, as organizing and administrative devices, have burst the bounds of individual countries to become exceptionally large interterritorial operational units, thus practicing worldwide systems of space adjustment. The international corporations use the worldwide networks of travel and communication and can administer complex affairs with appropriate speed at reasonable costs. Within minutes, ships, trucks, and planes can receive orders that send them to distant places, expanding trade in some directions, perhaps curtailing it in others. The international corporation is able to allocate a variety or a "mix" of its resources—capital, administrative capacity, and technology—in order to achieve its goals. In so doing, existing spatial interchanges may take on new patterns; for example, a new assembly plant in a new country may substitute the import of raw materials for former shipments of finished products. Indeed, the movement of men and money may result in the full stoppage of physical movement of commodities, as a corporation branch plant in a foreign country becomes productive for a foreign market and imports cease.

For example, General Motors Corporation today operates in 18 countries. Established in 1908, the corporation has grown fantastically, now assembling annually more than 7 million cars and trucks throughout the earth. It spends $9 billion each year for goods and services from 26,000 suppliers, scattered over the earth. Its annual payroll of about $5.2 billion is disbursed in many parts of the world. Its dollar sales ($20.7 billion for 1965)

are greater than the annual gross revenue of 118 of the 122 countries that are members of the United Nations.

Some 750 United States corporations engage in significant foreign operations. Investments in plants and facilities overseas now exceed $60 billion and represent more than one fourth of all capital investment by United States companies. Europe is the area of prime interest, slightly exceeding Canada, with Latin America rated third. Such endeavors have meant investment opportunities, jobs, and new products for peoples of other lands.

The leadership in world business has been captured by the diversified multinational corporations. Although many of these are United States-based, there are also many with headquarters elsewhere around the world. There were 185 industrial companies outside the United States whose sales in 1965 exceeded $250 million. The leader, by far, is Royal Dutch/Shell, a joint British-Netherlands corporation that produces gas and chemicals and operates almost around the world.

For a full comparison of the world's greatest industrial corporations, defined as those with 50 per cent or more of sales from manufacturing or mining, Tables 10.4 and 10.5 list 81 companies, each with assets of more than $1 billion in 1965, and Fig. 10.10 locates all their headquarters. The headquarters of the 49 major United States corporations are distributed among 12 states: New York City is the world's "capital" with 21, followed by Pennsylvania with six, Ohio five, Michigan four, Illinois three. The northeastern industrial zone of the United States clearly predominates. Western outliers in California, Oklahoma, and Texas are all petroleum corporations. The 32 leading industrial corporations outside of the United States are all located in the northern hemisphere, 24 of them in Western Europe, six in Asia, and two in North America.

Trends Toward Interdependence

The space-adjusting techniques of transport, trade, and communication have all been used on an increasing scale of frequency, distance, and volume to create interlocking worldwide networks that serve one another. No one of the techniques could have been developed to its present order of magnitude without the existence and support of the other techniques. The end result is that the

TABLE 10.4 WORLDWIDE COMPARISON OF THE LEADING INDUSTRIAL CORPORATIONS IN THE UNITED STATES (*Assets of over $1 Billion in 1965*)[a]

World Rank In Assets	Company[b]	Headquarters	Industry	Assets	Sales	Net Profit	Number of Employees
1	Standard Oil (New Jersey)	New York City	Petroleum products	$13,073,437,000	$11,471,529,000	$1,035,675,000	148,000
2	General Motors	Detroit	Autos	12,586,170,000	20,733,982,000	2,125,606,000	734,594
4	Ford Motor	Dearborn, Mich.	Autos	7,596,834,000	11,536,789,000	703,049,000	364,487
5	United States Steel	New York City	Iron and steel	5,451,740,000	4,399,590,000	275,476,000	208,838
6	Texaco	New York City	Petroleum products	5,342,903,000	3,779,406,000	636,698,000	56,960
7	Mobil Oil	New York City	Petroleum products	5,212,380,000	4,907,504,000	320,116,000	80,600
8	Gulf Oil	Pittsburgh	Petroleum products	5,210,833,000	3,384,742,000	427,233,000	55,200
9	General Electric	New York City	Electrical equipment, appliances, electronics, machinery	4,300,440,000	6,213,595,000	355,122,000	300,000
10	Standard Oil of California	San Francisco	Petroleum products	4,165,825,000	2,442,453,000	391,225,000	44,434
12	General Telephone & Electronics	New York City	Communications, electronics	3,783,488,000	2,035,621,000	166,750,000	121,935
13	International Business Machines	Armonk, N.Y.	Machinery, electronics, publishing	3,744,918,000	3,572,825,000	476,902,000	172,445
15	Standard Oil (Indiana)	Chicago	Petroleum products	3,514,102,000	2,471,988,000	219,272,000	41,158
19	Chrysler	Detroit	Autos	2,934,488,000	5,299,935,000	233,377,000	166,773
20	DuPont (E.I.) deNemours	Wilmington, Del.	Chemicals	2,847,762,000	3,020,758,000	407,229,000	109,336
22	Shell Oil	New York City	Petroleum products	2,671,464,000	2,562,209,000	234,031,000	34,548
23	Tenneco	Houston	Diversified, incl. packaging	2,659,540,000	1,037,916,000	95,317,000	18,064
24	Bethlehem Steel	Bethlehem, Pa.	Iron and steel	2,609,869,000	2,579,384,000	150,028,000	130,000
26	Western Electric	New York City	Communications	2,303,354,000	3,362,149,000	168,288,000	168,846
27	Union Carbide	New York City	Chemicals	2,282,828,000	2,063,901,000	226,917,000	60,900
29	Phillips Petroleum	Bartlesville, Okla.	Petroleum products	2,029,064,000	1,450,702,000	127,716,000	29,873
30	International Telephone and Telegraph	New York City	Communications, electronics	2,021,795,000	1,782,939,000	76,110,000	199,000
33	International Harvester	Chicago	Machinery, trucks	1,814,491,000	2,336,719,000	100,574,000	111,980
34	Monsanto	St. Louis	Chemicals	1,784,109,000	1,468,147,000	122,967,000	56,227
36	Union Oil of California	Los Angeles	Petroleum products	1,758,516,000	1,233,993,000	119,214,000	17,416
37	Aluminum Co. of America	Pittsburgh	Aluminum	1,743,069,000	1,165,596,000	75,587,000	48,159
38	Westinghouse Electric	Pittsburgh	Electrical equipment	1,711,516,000	2,389,909,000	106,903,000	115,141
41	Sinclair Oil	New York City	Petroleum products	1,694,519,000	1,275,472,000	76,673,000	18,926
43	Continental Oil	New York City	Petroleum products	1,679,473,000	1,449,674,000	96,151,000	21,261
44	Goodyear Tire and Rubber	Akron, Ohio	Rubber products	1,637,812,000	2,226,256,000	109,228,000	103,664
45	Cities Service	New York City	Petroleum products	1,635,417,000	1,200,772,000	104,118,000	21,000
48	Dow Chemical	Midland, Mich.	Chemicals, magnesium	1,526,761,000	1,176,228,000	108,130,000	33,800
51	Eastman Kodak	Rochester, N.Y.	Photographic equipment and supplies	1,445,325,000	1,463,485,000	247,625,000	55,500
52	Celanese	New York City	Diversified; synthetic fibers	1,418,563,000	862,290,000	64,950,000	36,804
55	Procter & Gamble	Cincinnati	Soap; cleansers	1,337,195,000	2,058,594,000	133,191,000	36,600
56	Republic Steel	Cleveland	Iron and steel	1,334,612,000	1,374,541,000	77,302,000	55,888
58	Anaconda	New York City	Copper	1,324,068,000	993,855,000	79,476,000	42,813
59	Radio Corporation of America	New York City	Communications	1,269,370,000	2,042,001,000	101,161,000	100,000
60	Allied Chemical	New York City	Chemicals	1,268,595,000	1,121,289,000	84,347,000	36,600
61	Firestone Tire & Rubber	Akron, Ohio	Rubber products	1,259,975,000	1,609,756,000	86,667,000	88,383
62	Armco Steel	Middletown, Ohio	Iron and steel	1,222,609,000	1,188,545,000	93,508,000	38,006
64	Sun Oil	Philadelphia	Petroleum products	1,205,783,000	925,243,000	84,835,000	21,154
65	Reynolds Metals	Richmond, Va.	Aluminum, magnesium	1,192,714,000	739,796,000	52,643,000	30,300
66	Grace, (W.R.)	New York City	Diversified	1,170,592,000	1,003,070,000	45,348,000	53,400
70	International Paper	New York City	Paper products	1,150,442,000	1,303,741,000	88,545,000	51,435
72	Reynolds (R.J.) Tobacco	Winston-Salem, N.C.	Tobacco products	1,111,987,000	1,004,037,000	133,357,000	16,320
73	National Steel	Pittsburgh	Iron and steel	1,089,449,000	1,107,227,000	87,497,000	29,753
78	American Can	New York City	Containers; packaging	1,026,961,000	1,265,062,000	62,109,000	48,081
79	Olin Mathieson Chemical	New York City	Diversified; chemicals	1,007,781,000	874,244,000	50,481,000	43,000
80	Caterpillar Tractor	Peoria, Ill.	Construction and farm machinery	1,006,500,000	1,405,300,000	158,500,000	52,924

[a] After Fortune, July 15, 1966.
[b] Listed in order of assets.

world's people now have available more frequent, faster, and more voluminous means of, communications, travel, and transport than ever existed. For example, Hawaii as a native kingdom a century ago, linked by slow sailing ships to other ports of the world, was a far cry from the present American state linked by telephone, radio, and communication satellite to the rest of the world; just one among the many airlines, an international corporation selling transportation, connects Hawaii to 127 cities and 87 countries on 6 continents.

Increasing the Speed and Efficiency of Operation of Cultural Processes

Man today has the capacity to send and receive in countless ways both intended and unintended messages. The flow of communications sets the direction and pace of social change. Message sending has been a universal problem for all cultures, but the problem has varied with different cultural levels. All had the drum, smoke-signal, knotted-string, carved-stick, wampum-belt variety of techniques at the start, with the courier as a critical component. Those cultures that developed writing very early went ahead of the nonliterate cultures. Literacy improved the accuracy of communication, and regionally, as in Rome, India, China, the Maya Empire, the courier systems were highly organized, as regional administration depended on a regular volume and flow of messages.

The "communications revolution" has been almost concurrent with the revolution in transportation. Regular communication over long distances could not exceed the speed of a messenger on horseback (e.g., the "pony express") until less than two centuries ago. It now seems appalling to contemplate that for most of human time on earth the process of communication was undifferentiated from other social processes. The flow of information was in accordance with traditional hierarchies. Status relationships determined who received, evaluated, interpreted, and responded to communications. Customarily only the members of small elites were literate; not until the late nineteenth century did the majority of the people of any nation possess such a capability. The concept of "mass media," now so commonplace, depends upon "the mass" being able to read, to understand, to afford, and to be receptive to, new forms of communication. Modern-day achievements in increasing the speed of operation of cultural processes and in economic and political development

TABLE 10.5 WORLDWIDE COMPARISON OF THE LEADING INDUSTRIAL CORPORATIONS OUTSIDE THE UNITED STATES (Assets of over $1 Billion in 1965).[a]

World Rank In Assets	Company[b]	Headquarters	Industry	Assets	Sales	Net Profit	Number of Employees
3	Royal Dutch/Shell	Netherlands-Britain	Petroleum, natural gas, chemicals	$12,107,276,000	$7,180,975,000	$628,387,000	186,000
11	British Petroleum	Britain	Petroleum products	3,855,880,000	2,408,000,000	225,680,000	60,000
14	ICI (Imperial Chemical Industries)	Britain	Chemicals	3,696,840,000	2,284,520,000	207,760,000	170,000
16	Finsider (Società Finanziaria Siderurgica)	Italy	Iron and steel	3,360,736,000	979,424,000	26,282,000	76,380
17	Unilever	Britain-Netherlands	Food, detergents, paper, chemicals	3,105,262,000	5,100,578,000	178,413,000	294,000
18	National Coal Board	Britain (gov't-owned)	Coal	2,967,720,000	2,464,675,000	185,000	477,281
21	Philips' Gloeilampen fabrieken	Netherlands	Electrical equipment, electronics, chemicals	2,728,397,000	2,084,358,000	110,241,000	252,000
25	ENI (Ente Nazionale Idrocarburi)	Italy (gov't-owned)	Petroleum, textiles, engines, machinery	2,451,200,000	937,760,000	960,000	56,521
28	Edison Group	Italy	Chemicals, synthetic fibers	2,147,200,000	732,480,000	39,840,000	51,956
31	Mitsubishi Heavy Industries	Japan	Machinery, autos, ship-building, aircraft	1,925,333,000	1,091,692,000	15,775,000	86,443
32	Charbonnages de France	France (gov't-owned)	Coal, electricity, chemicals	1,908,018,000	942,059,000	−65,424,000	184,356
35	ERAP	France (gov't-owned)	Petroleum products	1,771,905,000	691,302,000	35,953,000	13,595
39	Hitachi	Japan	Electrical equipment, appliances, machinery	1,703,650,000	1,149,489,000	26,336,000	129,133
40	Hindustan Steel	India	Iron and steel	1,702,898,000	433,163,000	4,505,000	85,000
42	Montecatini	Italy	Chemicals, minerals	1,690,162,000	580,725,000	27,518,000	47,890
46	Yawata Iron and Steel	Japan	Iron and steel	1,569,598,000	926,085,000	22,367,000	59,140
47	British-American Tobacco	Britain	Tobacco products	1,547,543,000	1,000,000,000	118,158,000	90,000
49	Alcan Aluminium	Canada	Aluminum	1,521,871,000	823,543,000	57,765,000	60,130
50	August Thyssen-Hütte	West Germany	Iron and steel	1,471,769,000	1,724,651,000	26,958,000	94,207
53	Siemens	West Germany	Electrical equipment	1,401,200,000	1,794,750,000	45,325,000	257,000
54	Tokyo Shibaura Electric	Japan	Electrical equipment	1,389,164,000	822,758,000	6,061,000	111,830
57	Fiat	Italy	Autos, tractors, aircraft, engines	1,330,397,000	1,528,486,000	39,405,000	123,109
63	Fuji Iron and Steel	Japan	Iron and steel	1,208,850,000	766,133,000	13,525,000	38,289
67	Pemex (Petróleos Mexicanos)	Mexico (gov't-owned)	Petroleum products	1,169,881,000	674,423,000	19,060,000	53,973
68	Farbenfabriken Bayer	West Germany	Chemicals, pharmaceuticals	1,165,339,000	1,575,250,000	66,875,000	99,800
69	Farbwerke Hoechst	West Germany	Chemicals, pharmaceuticals	1,156,574,000	1,309,000,000	63,949,000	72,918
71	Volkswagenwerk	West Germany	Autos	1,136,750,000	2,316,875,000	93,750,000	125,517
74	Courtaulds	Britain	Fibers, textiles, chemicals, packaging	1,070,611,000	953,436,000	66,979,000	110,000
75	BASF (Badische Anilin-Soda-Fabrik)	West Germany	Chemicals	1,051,495,000	1,012,500,000	70,666,000	47,840
76	Salzgitter	West Germany (gov't-owned)	Iron and steel, machinery, coal	1,044,780,000	842,150,000	0	80,127
77	Petrofina	Belgium	Petroleum products	1,030,342,000	639,480,000	26,934,000	16,600
	Not included in ranking, above, since assets and profits are not reported:						
?	Friedrich Krupp	West Germany	Iron and steel, machinery, electrical equipment	Not available	1,251,750,000	Not available	112,029

[a] After *Fortune,* August 1966, pp. 148–151.
[b] Listed in order of assets.

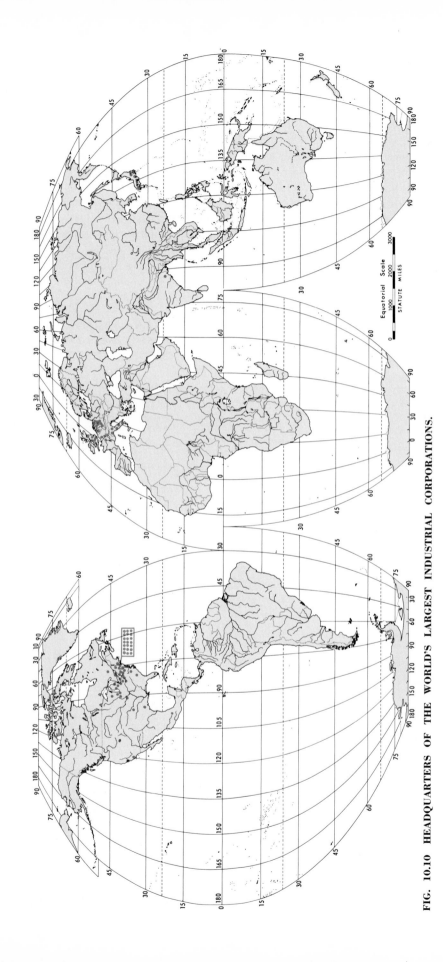

FIG. 10.10 HEADQUARTERS OF THE WORLD'S LARGEST INDUSTRIAL CORPORATIONS.

Equatorial Scale

STATUTE MILES

0   1000   2000   3000

are all intimately tied to advances in the use of languages, in writing, in printing, in education, and in the technologies of our "electrical age."

A modern communications system is capable of transmitting a massive flow of uniform messages to a wide audience. In contrast, a traditional system handles only a very limited volume of messages, at very uneven rates of speed, and with great variety in repetition. Today much of the function of informal, person-to-person level of communication in a modern society consists of screening out and evaluating specialized information from the mass flow. Opinion makers exist, in government, business, the professions, and other endeavors, who invest time and energy in "keeping up" on special subjects and being "fully informed." Others who may need their information are dependent on them for their detailed knowledge, as reported in lectures, articles, books, or memoranda. The problem for most people in the world is to gain access to the flow of communications: through knowledge of one or more of the world's great languages, through education to literacy, through regular contact with one or more of the mass media. For others, who so possess these resources that they are taken for granted, there is the further problem of controlling and keeping in proportion the volume, speed, and consistency of the flow of communications, sifting the messages, and deciding what is relevant and significant.

A government-supported educational program is one of the cultural devices now widely practiced by modern societies as a way to increase the speed of their cultural processes in an efficient manner to as many persons as possible at an early age. Educational systems and their agencies are formal means by which societies seek to fulfill their highest aspirations, by transmitting and transforming their cultures and maintaining and upgrading their social systems. Educational systems are space-adjusting techniques, since they seek to create cultural uniformity and continuity over all the territory occupied by the society operating the educational system.

Communications: Eliminating Many Needs for Movement

All forms of communications are tools to be used for human purposes. One overriding purpose has been to bridge space and time. Ideas, today, can leap around the world in a matter of seconds; they are also stored (e.g., books in libraries, action on film, speech on tape) so that the present generation can learn about and profit from the experiences of its predecessors. The processes of communication include more than the transmittal of sounds as speech or the transfer of symbols as writing or printing. In addition to language, man has used gestures, facial expressions, dances, and pictures to convey meanings, often in effective combinations, as in the theater or motion pictures. Our concern with communications lies in the effectiveness of such means of space-adjusting techniques, for through communications many needs are eliminated for the movement of people or of goods.

All of our means for communicating directly with other people at a distance represent technological advances, because the need for more costly and time-consuming transport or travel (the movement of vehicles to convey messages or to bring people together) can be reduced. Our present-day forms of mass communication—telegraph or teletype, telephone, radio, teletypesetting, wirephotos, phonograph, motion pictures, television—are all dependent on electricity to accomplish transmission across distances.

The "electrical age," which has rendered our modern era so different from any previous period of human existence, began just a century ago. Developments of wireless telegraphy ran ahead of the extended use of the telephone. The telephone has become a necessity of life, both in the home and in business, in the United States and many other countries. Although telephone systems have been introduced to most other countries, access to the use of telephones is as yet unequal where telephones are few (Fig. 10.11). While the telephone was being spread around the world, its use vastly intensified in the United States and northwest Europe. The continued demand for more available circuits led to the development of the transcontinental microwave (radio relay) system. Direct distance dialing, which became operational in the early 1960s, permits anyone to dial directly to almost all other telephones anywhere in the United States. The newest development which will solve the problems of intercontinental distance and heavy traffic (thousands of simultaneous messages) and make possible a truly worldwide linkage of telephone systems is the communications satellites. Whereas four million overseas calls to and from the United States were made in 1960, 100 million would be possible in 1980, at much lower cost than

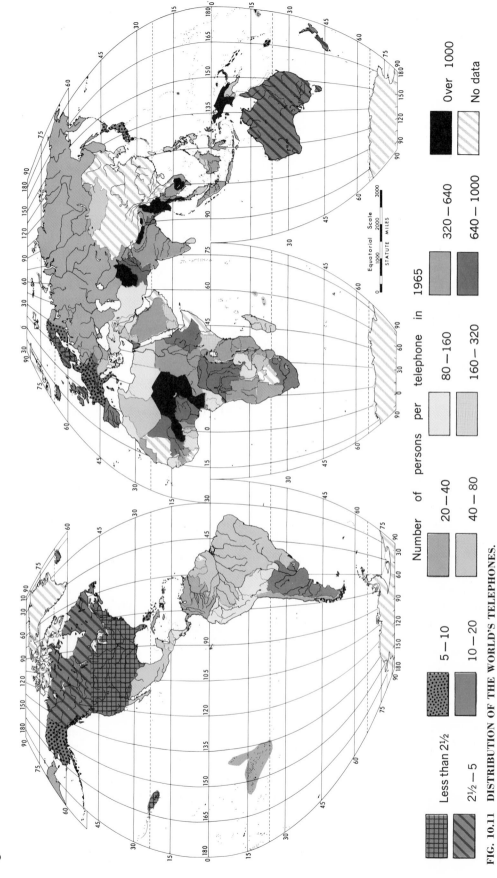

Number of persons per telephone in 1965

Less than 2½

2½ — 5

5 — 10

10 — 20

20 — 40

40 — 80

80 — 160

160 — 320

320 — 640

640 — 1000

Over 1000

No data

Equatorial Scale

STATUTE MILES

FIG. 10.11 DISTRIBUTION OF THE WORLD'S TELEPHONES.

laying additional submarine cables. Great progress in space adjustment (long-distance person-to-person communication) has been made since the first telephone exchange was opened in New Haven, Connecticut, in 1878.

In fashioning the first medium of instant mass communications, the new science of electronics led the way. World War I put the wireless to use for military communications; the postwar boom of the 1920s put the radio into private homes as a means of mass communication for entertainment and education. The phonograph, based on Thomas A. Edison's device of 1877, was rendered practicable in 1927 by electronic amplification. The transistor, a minute solid-state component, has replaced the vacuum tube, and in so doing has ushered in an even newer "electronic age" of rapid mass communications based on the electronic computer. The speed of operations of cultural processes has taken a revolutionary jump forward, unknown to any previous era, not only in the incredibly rapid actions of computerized programs and machines, but also in the worldwide spread of inexpensive, portable radio receivers—the transistorized radios of pocket size that have reached nearly all the world's peoples and brought them into touch with the world's civilizations. The fascimile, a device for photographic transmission, the laser light for long-distance transmission in 1960, and other inventions are making possible the transfer of vast amounts of data at fantastic speeds.

Motion pictures and television, first in black and white, then in color, followed by tape-recording of sounds and kinescopes of both pictures and sounds, are all part of twentieth-century technology that has revolutionized the worldwide communications to reach mass audiences. For many new nations, television is a "status symbol" and there are more television receivers than telephones (Fig. 10.12).

Channels for International Communication

Most people receive the bulk of their ideas about other parts of the world from the same media that bring them local news. These domestic media rely principally on national and international wire services. The "big five" of these are: Reuters (serving 110 nations), Agence France-Presse (outlets in 104 countries), Tass (for Communist countries), the Associated Press (7600 outlets in 80 countries), and United Press Interna-

tional (6500 subscribers in 111 countries). In addition there are some 178 national or specialized news services. More than 80 per cent of foreign news in United States newspapers comes through the two major United States agencies, A.P. and U.P.I. Daily newspapers are heavily concentrated in Europe, North America, Japan, and Australia. In 1962, Great Britain had 112 with a daily pressrun of 26 million copies; by contrast, Pakistan had 99 with a 600,000 circulation, Indonesia had 95 with a circulation over one million, and the United Arab Republic had 37 with a total circulation of 500,000.

A second major source for information from abroad is radio and television. In 1962 there were some 12,500 radio transmitters and 400 million radio receivers throughout the world, with the greatest rates of increase in Africa and Asia as inexpensive battery-powered transistor radios have become widely distributed. Television is spreading widely also; between 1950 and 1962, the number of television receivers outside the United States increased 80 million (served by over 3400 transmitters in 83 countries) and now outnumber those in the United States. The airwaves are truly international, since it is easily possible to tune in on programs originating in neighboring nations. Most nations of the world now have some form of international broadcasting service, by shortwave. The most recent trends in international communications consist of regional, continental, and intercontinental linkages. Eurovision, for example, links the television networks of Western European countries with those of Tunisia, Yugoslavia, and Israel. Intervision includes the Soviet Union and six East European countries and exchanges some programs with Eurovision, and the Asian Broadcasting Union and the African Radio Television Union became operative in 1964. Satellite relays promise that worldwide "live" television will become common in the next decade. The world will certainly be a more communications-linked community when an important event, on television, can be witnessed simultaneously by 1 billion viewers.

Books and magazines travel widely, either in their original form or in translation. More than a third of all translated books are from English to other languages, followed, in decreasing ranks, by Russian, French, and German titles. Many popular magazines have many overseas subscribers; the *National Geographic Magazine* each month

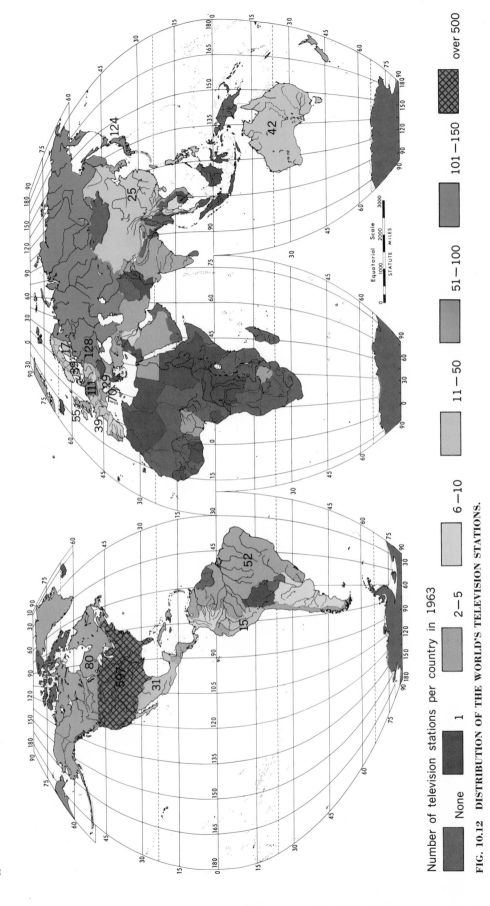

Number of television stations per country in 1963

None   1   2—5   6—10   11—50   51—100   101—150   over 500

FIG. 10.12   DISTRIBUTION OF THE WORLD'S TELEVISION STATIONS.

sends over $\frac{1}{2}$ million copies abroad. Others, such as *Time* and *Reader's Digest*, print special overseas or international editions. The United Nations and its agencies publish more than 50 periodicals, many in several languages.

Most countries rely heavily on foreign-produced films for their many theaters. Films are second only to radio as the most widely available mass medium. Japan is the world leader in film production, followed by India and Hong Kong, with the United States a poor fourth. Other significant producers are Italy, the Soviet Union, France, Great Britain, Republic of Korea, and the Philippines. The United States, India, and the Soviet Union show mostly their own films, but other countries have more cosmopolitan tastes: Great Britain and Italy show mostly American films.

There are many other forms of international communications: trade fairs, sporting events, cultural exchanges, travel, international education, private businesses, government intelligence, and diplomatic reporting services. The means and the opportunities for learning about the rest of the world are exceedingly diverse, yet all are interlinked and serve to correct or to reinforce one another.

The Role of Purposeful Invention

Science, technological change, and societal institutions are parts of a single pattern of development in which each part reinforces the others. Changes in one element bring subsequent changes in the other aspects. For example, organized scientific research is essentially a social invention, begun in the fifteenth and sixteenth centuries and elaborated in the nineteenth and twentieth centuries, which has resulted in an enormous increase in the pace of technological change. This exuberant growth in the production and dissemination of knowledge has stimulated an unprecedented rate of societal development.

The expansion of knowledge has been one of the most irreversible forces known to mankind. Scientific method has become the most productive way, both in rate and in amount, for man to acquire new knowledge. Science has made possible technological developments that could not possibly have been achieved in the past: a dynamo, aluminum production, an internal combustion engine, release of nuclear energy. And science, through the extension of men's senses through the telescope and radio astronomy, has also made possible a

self-consciousness of time and place: Man is aware that he is a temporary occupant of a rather small and obscure planet revolving around a minor sun in a remote part of an ordinary galaxy, perhaps one of a billion or so in the universe. And similarly, through the social sciences, man has achieved a social self-awareness: that every culture is but one of thousands of subsystems or possibilities in the world for ordering human life and interpersonal relations. Self-awareness of a social system can produce conscious efforts toward changes in the system.

Science and technology are inseparable, and both have evolved in unbroken continuity throughout the life process of mankind, as a continuation of the efforts of man to manipulate his physical-biotic environment. Scientific knowledge is part of man's cultural heritage. Technological society is the most successful way of life that man has ever known. We now have more widespread and useful knowledge about the uniformities of nature and about the interdependence of all human activities than men have ever had before, as well as a capacity for achievement that expands as knowledge and skills increase. Knowledge and skills accumulate because they are objectified in tools and symbols, which in turn are combined to form new cultural traits that take their place in culture and are available to others for further combinations. The Wright brothers were successful in achieving human flight, whereas Leonardo da Vinci was not, because they enjoyed the advantage of coming later in a developmental process and had more information and new materials available for their use.

By the sixteenth century, printing had become an industry and publishing a business, with characteristics that were forerunners of the modern day. Cheaper paper, automatic typesetting, rotary presses, and lithography all helped fulfill the needs of the new mass education. Fundamental for the development of the modern world has been the concept of widespread public literacy; to achieve this, books, periodicals, and newspapers were needed in large quantities for distribution at low cost to all classes of people all around the world. That libraries were collections of books or depositories of knowledge has long been understood. The revolutionary idea of the modern era is that libraries should change from being preservers of books to facilitators of the use of books by the general public.

In his book, *The Step to Man*, John R. Platt indicates that an "optical limit" library is now technically feasible. A page of print can be reduced in area by as much as one million times, by photographing it at the smallest size at which a high-powered optical microscope can resolve the individual letters. A microlibrary is now possible; an exhibit at the New York World's Fair in 1964 displayed the whole of the Holy Bible in less than two square inches. At this scale reduction, a library of all the world's books could be stored on one wall of an office, or in a desk or cabinet, attached to a selective device for reading (projection upon a well-lit, well-focused screen in front of a comfortable chair) and a "print-out" device for enlarging and recording whatever was needed, whether a map or sketch or photograph, for prolonged study, comparison, or revision. If electronic scanning is preferred, pages of anything one desired in the world's literature could be projected onto any television screen of any classroom, or any room of a home.

Our obviously impressive scientific achievements too often tempt us to believe that the solution of all our problems and our ultimate salvation lies in the direction of a constantly improving technology. Whatever the benefits of science and technology, it is still man who determines how the new material, machines, and techniques are to be used, and for what purposes or goals. Men are sometimes slowly, sometimes rapidly, expanding their bounds of knowledge. The modern extension of life expectancy affords individual men more expectations for maturing, for learning, for accomplishing what was "not possible" prior to the twentieth century.

Let us look a 100 years ahead, to a time when our children's children will be grandparents late in the twenty-first century. Is it conceivable that the pace of dramatic change that has characterized the twentieth century can be continued? The speed of travel, the near instantaneity in communications, and the power of nuclear weapons would seem to have reached points of diminishing returns. The time required to cross the American continent has been reduced, during the past century, from three months to three hours. Will Americans of the next century continue this pace of change and think it necessary to expend effort and energy to reduce the time to three minutes? What more is there to do in this aspect of cultural change?

What seems far more likely is that the pace of change will become slower in the innovating centers of technological civilization and that more attention will be given to the diffusion of knowledge, wealth, and technology to all the rest of the world in order to create a truly global habitat for modern civilization. This process, of course, is already well launched. Its symbols are the steel, glass, and reinforced concrete skyscrapers, the jet airports, the supertankers, the economic development programs, the communications satellites, the solid-state computers, and automation. The world does not jump from an undeveloped scientific and technological society to a fully developed one everywhere at once. As in adolescence, growth in stature slows down in order to complete the more complex secondary changes or adjustments in other parts that characterize maturity. And these, too, are space-adjusting techniques.

Modern means of communication have made the earth a unity, but they have not created uniformity. The discovery that the earth is "global" does not change the fact that peoples are first of all a part of their local culture pattern, each with its own interdependent relationships of man to man and man to nature, its own traditions, preferred institutions, and ways of making a living.

Trends Toward Interdependence

All communities seek to preserve their ancient traditions, hence resist domination by other peoples and absorption into their cultures. This behavior, throughout the ages, has sustained the conception of freedom as a condition—the absence of coercion—a principle embodied in Woodrow Wilson's phrase, "self-determination of peoples." The principle of self-determination for colonial peoples grew out of (1) the Mandate System of the League of Nations in which colonial powers agreed to serve as trustees for the former German colonial territories, and (2) the Russian Revolution and its support for agitation against colonialism.

In the Atlantic Charter, in 1941, the position of the United States, as one of the signatories, was expressed in Article 3 which declared "the right of all peoples to choose the form of government under which they will live" and that it wished "to see sovereign rights and self-government restored to those who have been deprived of them." Winston Churchill's interpretation was that the Atlantic Charter had applicability only to the nations of Europe under Nazi control, whereas the colonial peoples saw the statement as a proposal to give them the right of self-determination of their political affairs. In any event, the Atlantic Charter was signed at a time when Asia was in open revolt and Africans were voicing opposition to colonial rule, and the principle of "self-determination" therein expressed was carried into the United Nations, when formed in 1945, and set down in its Charter. Application of the doctrine of "self-determination of peoples" thus has given rise, in the mid-twentieth century, to a political fragmentation of the world; logically, there is no stopping point short of the individual. The realities of the cultural and political fragmentation of mankind would appear to stand quite in opposition to the recent processes of cultural convergence and to the ideal of the unification and harmony of mankind.

Certain values, however, have been idealized by all the great world religions as the highest of which mankind is capable: loving kindness, gentleness, nonviolence, brotherly helpfulness to all others. These values express the essential cooperativeness or sense of mutual aid that is fundamental to the life process. Awareness of the contemporary hazard of mutual destruction is more intense and widespread than ever before. Nuclear fission and the atom bomb did not cause international hostility; it is the other way around. International (inter-culture group) hostility has long existed among mankind. But nuclear fission and warheads have made international hostility a hazardous and out-moded concept for furthering human existence; more men than ever now understand that war is incompatible with continuance of a technological (that is, urban-industrial) way of life predicated, as it is, upon uninterrupted high productivity, intricate means of communication and transport, and dense concentrations of population.

There is emerging an enlarged view of social responsibility, involving concern for and loyalty to mankind rather than to nation-states, and a conception of the latter as subsystems of a larger whole. Differences among cultures and individuals are to be valued as subsystems, both as ends and means. A genuine system of world integrative relationships need not be predicated upon the elimination of conflict, but calls for the use of increased skills in conflict management without overt violence, emotions of violence, or undue tension.

The creation of voluntary, multiterritorial associations of separate sovereignties, or federations,

began early in modern Europe. Two examples were the commercial-oriented Hanseatic League (twelfth to sixteenth centuries) in northern Europe, and the Council of Constance (1414–1418), which assembled the representatives of all European powers for deliberation on the peace of Europe as a whole. Both were instruments for reconciling the varying points of view of their participating members and both utilized familiar legal concepts and procedures to make their achieved syntheses work.

The trend toward interdependence clearly set in during the nineteenth century, beginning with the Congress of Vienna after the Napoleonic wars. International conferences, organized as *ad hoc* parliaments, became more and more frequently utilized to coordinate conflicting policies. Inter-governmental agreements created agencies for a host of transnational tasks: joint administration of international rivers; operation of postal, telegraph, and cable services; promotion of public health and sanitation. Multilateral treaties were concluded: legal customs, codes of international law, regulation of commerce and finance, control of the slave trade. Concurrently, individuals participated in nongovernmental voluntary associations that held periodical international congresses and formed international unions. By the end of the nineteenth century, the European nation-states were bound by a vast network of international organizations: unions, tribunals, commissions, bureaus, congresses, each of which had limited functions, but which, in sum, expressed a felt need for international peace and order.

The twentieth century has continued the trend toward interdependence and greater integration, expanding its regional focus from Europe to the entire world. Aspects of this trend can be considered as separate, even competing, movements; but, for our purpose, it is sufficient to realize that the extension of international constitutionalism and the concept of organized unity among nations has been furthered by different, interlocking, and concurrent movements. We need here only mention the political and economic integration of Western Europe and North America that ensured the recovery of Europe's economy after two devastating wars, the worldwide agreement that led to the formation in 1944 of the International Civil Aviation Organization (ICAO) to coordinate the facilities and service for air transport, and the establishment of the United Nations in 1945 as a world organization for the maintenance of global peace and collective security.

The essential thing about our world is the vast amount of cooperation that exists, even between countries that are opposed to each other in political ideology. Much more publicity is given to conflicts and disasters than to the achievements in cooperation; but why should this be so, when our evolving world depends on cooperation and not on conflict? The network of cooperation among nations both in technical and political fields continues to be more widely spread and more closely woven than ever. More than a hundred nations have now adhered to the Moscow Treaty banning nuclear weapons tests in the atmosphere, in outer space, and under water. An even more important symbol of increasing international trust is the 1968 Nuclear Non-Proliferation Treaty.

The "knowledge" that we are moving closer and closer to "one world" is part of the mythology of our time. Is it true? Will the future produce one world or many? Phrased thusly, as an "either-or" question, we simply pose a false issue, for the world already is a "mixed community," solving some of its problems in terms of worldwide co-operation (e.g., postal systems, health quarantine, weather data exchange), and handling many other problems on a different basis (e.g., regionally, government to government, by separate countries, locally). The concept of many-leveled culture worlds, like the layers of an onion, presents possibilities of operational freedom and potentialities for new discoveries scarcely conceivable in a monolithic "one-world" system. All nation-states are making surrenders of sovereignty every time they conclude an international agreement or join an international organization. To do so, there must be sound reasons that the results will be beneficial and the ends incapable of being achieved in isolation, by unilateral action. The United States, for example, has been engaged in making bilateral treaties since the very first years of its existence, and with most other nations since, as these have come into existence. Not all international problems can be solved in such manner, and the United States has also joined many regional blocs and international organizations. Through agreement on mutually desirable, if limited, goals, coexistence of divergent groups not only has become possible but also, and more importantly, fruitful.

Coalescence of power into larger aggregations than nation-states has been the true achievement of the late twentieth century. Populations are no longer isolated, ideas and goods readily cross old political boundaries, cultural principles and prejudices can be changed. For example, as the concept of national sovereignty has been surpassed by concepts of higher order, the nation-states no longer exist all by themselves as wholly separate units.

Man's Manipulation of Space: Two Summary Examples

In his book, *The Hidden Dimension*, Edward T. Hall reports on his consulting the pocket Oxford dictionary and extracting from it all terms referring to space or having spatial connotations, such as together, distant, over, under, away from, linked, enclosed, wander, level, adjacent. He concluded that nearly five thousand terms could be classified as referring to space; this is 20 per cent of the words listed in the pocket Oxford dictionary. More than an individual realizes, man continually is using and manipulating space.

In creating the total world in which he lives, man is constantly changing his concept of space on the earth's surface, and this is reflected in human accomplishments in space adjustment that create ever-fresh possibilities for spatial interchange. Several well-known examples will suffice to demonstrate that, in reality, all of the space-adjusting techniques—transport, trade, communications, and political organization—are intimately interwoven.

The idea of a canal to pierce the 100-mile wide Isthmus of Suez and connect the Mediterranean Sea and the Indian Ocean through the Gulf of Suez and Red Sea, was considered by Venetians as early as 1504. All earlier canals, whether of Pharaonic Egypt or Roman Egypt, or after Islamic conquest, served for navigational connections between the Nile delta and the Red Sea during seasons of high water in the river. A Suez Canal became technically feasible only following the development of steam navigation. Only the passage of large cargo vessels would make such a canal profitable, and large sailing vessels were too difficult to manuever in the narrow confines of the Red Sea against the prevailing strong winds from the north. The Suez Canal was opened in November 1869. The canal, in one quick stroke, changed the spatial relations of the Old World. It shortened the distance from Liverpool to Bombay by about 4500 nautical miles over the former ocean voyage around the Cape of Good Hope, and also deflected the new route from the high seas.

A second, and very recent, example of the interaction of all space-adjusting techniques consists of the various international tunnels of Europe. Tunnels are symbols of the changing attitudes of nation-states toward transport linkages with foreign countries on their borders. The idea of a tunnel beneath the English Channel (*La Manche*) at the 22-mile wide Straits of Dover (*Pas de Calais*) linking Dover, England, and Calais, France, was proposed as long ago as 1802. But the insistence of the British that their country was an island, a fortress-home blessed by a moat supplied by Providence, prevented completion of all attempted proposals until, in the early 1960s, Great Britain decided that it was a part of Europe and should have a fixed connection, by land transport, to the continent. Recognition that existing transport (sea and air) is an economic bottleneck had much to do with the decision; more than eight million passengers, 400,000 vehicles, and 11 million tons of merchandise cross the channel each year, nearly one-half the passengers and one-fourth the vehicles by air. A joint venture of France and Britain, the tunnel under the channel is now under construction. The great Alpine tunnels are nearly as significant in facilitating all-weather vehicular movement between territorial spaces: Italy and Switzerland are connected by a highway tunnel, the Grand St. Bernard, opened in 1964; France and Italy by a two-lane highway through the seven-mile long Mount Blanc tunnel, completed and opened to traffic in 1965.

Not only are all the space-adjusting techniques intricately interwoven, but they also contribute to a further aspect of space, the intensification of its use. The previously mentioned "optical limit" library is but one example of a space-intensification technique. Chapter 11, which follows, considers many more.

SELECTED REFERENCES

About Travel and Transport

Alexander, John W.
  1963   *Economic Geography*. Englewood Cliffs, N.J.: Prentice-Hall. 661 pp.

Alexandersson, Gunnar, and Göran Norström
  1963   *World Shipping, An Economic Geography of Ports and Seaborne Trade*. New York: Wiley. 507 pp.

Fabre, Maurice
  1963   *A History of Land Transportation* (The New Illustrated Library of Science and Invention, Vol. 7). New York: Hawthorn Books. 112 pp.

Jackman, W. T.
  1962   *The Development of Transportation in Modern England*. London: Frank Cass & Co. 820 pp.

Lansing, John B.
  1966   *Transportation and Economic Policy*. New York: The Free Press. 409 pp.

Locklin, D. Philip
  1966   *Economics of Transportation* (6th ed.). Homewood, Ill.: Richard D. Irwin. 882 pp.

Marlowe, John
  1964   *World Ditch, The Making of the Suez Canal*. New York: Macmillan. 294 pp.

Pawera, John C.
  1964   *Algeria's Infrastructure: An Economic Survey of Transportation, Communication, and Energy Resources*. New York: Praeger. 234 pp.

Wolfe, Roy I.
  1963   *Transportation and Politics* (Searchlight Book #18). Princeton, N.J.: Van Nostrand. 136 pp.

About Trade

Belshaw, Cyril S.
  1965   *Traditional Exchange and Modern Markets*. Englewood Cliffs, N.J.: Prentice-Hall. 149 pp.

Berry, Brian J. L.
  1967   *Geography of Market Centers and Retail Distribution*. Englewood Cliffs, N.J.: Prentice-Hall. 146 pp.

Berry, Brian J. L. and Duane F. Marble
  1967 *Spatial Analysis: A Reader in Statistical Geography.* Englewood Cliffs, N.J.: Prentice-Hall. 512 pp.
Boesch, Hans
  1964 *A Geography of World Economy.* Princeton, N.J.: Van Nostrand. 280 pp.
Brown, Robert T.
  1966 *Transport and the Economic Integration of South America.* Washington, D.C.: Transport Research Program, The Brookings Institute. 288 pp.
Ellsworth, P. T.
  1964 *The International Economy* (3rd ed.). New York: Macmillan. 550 pp.
Fryer, Donald W.
  1965 *World Economic Development.* New York: McGraw-Hill. 627 pp.
Kindleberger, Charles P.
  1962 *Foreign Trade and the National Economy.* New Haven, Conn.: Yale University Press. 265 pp.
McCreary, Edward A.
  1964 *The Americanization of Europe.* Garden City, N.Y.: Doubleday. 295 pp.
Thoman, Richard S.
  1962 *The Geography of Economic Activity, An Introductory World Survey.* New York: McGraw-Hill. 602 pp.
Thoman, Richard S., and Edgar C. Conkling
  1967 *Geography of International Trade.* Englewood Cliffs, N.J.: Prentice-Hall. 190 pp.
Thorbecke, Erik
  1960 *The Tendency Towards Regionalization in International Trade, 1928–1956.* The Hague: Martinus Nijhoff. 223 pp.
Ullman, Edward L.
  1957 *American Commodity Flow.* Seattle, Wash.: University of Washington Press. 213 pp.
Young, John Parke
  1963 *The International Economy* (4th ed.). New York: The Ronald Press. 795 pp.

About Communications

Davison, W. Phillips
  1965 *International Political Communication.* New York: Praeger. 404 pp.
Fabre, Maurice
  1963 *A History of Communications* (The New Illustrated Library of Science and Invention, Vol. 9). New York: Hawthorn Books. 112 pp.
Pye, Lucian W. (ed.)
  1963 *Communications and Political Development.* Princeton, N.J.: Princeton University Press. 381 pp.
Zilliacus, Lawrin
  1965 *From Pillar to Post, the Troubled History of the Mail.* London: William Heinemann, Ltd. 217 pp.

About Political Territories and Organization

Alexander, Lewis M.
  1963 *World Political Patterns* (2nd ed.). Chicago: Rand McNally. 628 pp.
Apter, David E.
  1965 *The Politics of Modernization.* Chicago: University of Chicago Press. 481 pp.
Jacob, Philip E., and James V. Toscano (eds.)
  1964 *The Integration of Political Communities.* Philadelphia: Lippincott. 314 pp.
Parkinson, C. Northcote
  1958 *The Evolution of Political Thought.* New York: The Viking Press. 327 pp.
Robinson, E. A. G.
  1960 *Economic Consequences of the Size of Nations.* New York: St. Martin's Press. 447 pp.
Van Vorys, Karl (ed.)
  1965 *New Nations: The Problem of Political Development* (The Annals of The American Academy of Political and Social Sciences, Vol. 358). Philadelphia: The American Academy of Political and Social Sciences. 270 pp.
Wainhouse, David W.
  1964 *Remnants of Empire: The United Nations and the End of Colonialism.* New York: Harper. 153 pp.

TRANSPORT

DE WYS

Human Transport, Canal Excavation, Indonesia

INGER McCABE, RAPHO GUILLUMETTE

LONDON DAILY EXPRESS, PICTORIAL PICTURE

Human Transport, Shoulder Pole, Macao

Cart Transport, Communist China

460

Human Transport, Four-Man Sedan Chair, India

RAGHUBIR SINGH, NANCY PALMER AGENCY

RENE BURRI, MAGNUM

Pedicab Transport, Communist China

PATRICK MILLER, D.P.I.

J. E. SPENCER

Motorized Pedicab, Thailand

Ricksha Transport, India

Dogsled, Alaska

ALASKA PICTORIAL SERVICE

462

Llama Packtrain, Peru

BERNARD SILBERSTEIN, RAPHO GUILLUMETTE

VAN BUCHER, PHOTO RESEARCHERS

Horse Taxi,
Calcutta,
India

463

FRANCES MORTIMER, RAPHO GUILLUMETTE

Oxcart,
Indonesia

BAHNSEN, MONKMEYER

Horse-and-
Buggy Era,
Missouri, U.S.

APSA, PERUVIAN AIRLINES

Reed Boats,
Lake Titicaca,
Peru

464

River Junk, Bound
Downstream, China

J. E. SPENCER

Motorized Ferry, Niger Republic

KAY BRENNAN, D.P.I.

*Powered Ocean
Transport, 1857*

ILLUSTRATED LONDON NEWS, COURTESY OF NEW YORK PUBLIC LIBRARY

LORD, MONKMEYER

Modern Barges on the Mississippi River, United States

Finnish-Built Oil Tanker, 1950s

CONSULATE GENERAL OF FINLAND

Quincy Railroad
Passenger Coach,
1820s, United States

NEW YORK PUBLIC LIBRARY

The "De Witt Clinton" 1831, United States

NEW YORK PUBLIC LIBRARY

Passenger Train, Early Twentieth Century, United States

NEW YORK CENTRAL RAILROAD

UNION PACIFIC RAILROAD

Diesel Freight Train, 1960s, United States

JAPANESE NATIONAL RAILWAYS

Tokaido Electric, 125 mph, 1964, Japan

UNION PACIFIC RAILROAD

CALIFORNIA DIVISION OF HIGHWAYS

Four-Level Freeway "Stack," Los Angeles, California, U.S.

◀ *Freight Yard, Los Angeles, California, U.S.*

469

The New and the Old, Egypt

RENE BURRI, MAGNUM

UNIROYAL

Rubber-Belt Sand Conveyor, United States

KAY BRENNAN, D.P.I.

Wooden Waterwheel Feeding Aqueduct, Syria

470

IBEC

Mechanical Warehouse Stacker, Venezuela

INTERNATIONAL HARVESTER

Power Loader and Truck, Anywhere Today

AMERICAN FOREST PRODUCTS INDUSTRIES

Power Log Loader, California, U.S.

The Airplane Goes Anywhere,
Greenland East Coast

DE WYS

Pipeline Control Point, Saudi Arabia

472

ARAB INFORMATION CENTER

PORT OF NEW YORK AUTHORITY

Power-Loading a Freight Plane

GENERAL ELECTRIC COMPANY

Denison Hydrofoil in Action

473

Kennedy Air Terminal, New York, U.S.

DOUGLAS AIRCRAFT CORPORATION

The Planes Grow Larger, 1967

PORT OF NEW YORK AUTHORITY

474

Moving People with Power Equipment

CROWN, MONKMEYER

CHAPTER 11

Space-Intensification Techniques: Increased Production and Urbanization

The space-intensification techniques include all those processes that permit an increase in the use of space beyond that made possible by nature on the earth's surface. For example, the arts of civil engineering, architecture, and city and regional planning are major contributors of techniques for concentrating human activities in relatively small spaces. A modern city is thus a great engineering work which, by adding levels and further usable area over the same land surface, permits an astonishing intensification of space utilization. Our objective in this section is not a full discussion of urban geography, but a pointing up of the role of modern urbanization as a key element in the processes of space intensification.

Intensified use of space involves great concentration. Not centrifugal forces, but rather centripetal action and centralization become dominant in order in achieve high densities. Space-intensification techniques focus upon particular sites and expand outward from such points to others. In intensifying available earth space, emphasis is placed upon a new kind of relationship in man's ties to the earth: the view is now vertical rather than extensive. The objectives of space intensification are to improve upon or "do better" than nature, either by increasing the rates of productivity for raw materials (fish, furs, forests, farms) beyond those previously achieved or by creating more usable surface area than previously existed.

This chapter is the last of the four that analyze the varying techniques by which modern man is able to transform the world's regions to ends of his own choosing.

Cities as Concentrations

Cities are the end products of forces for concentration of specialized human activities and vast numbers of people. As Chapters 4 and 5 indicated, cities have been in existence for a long while, a time span of an order of magnitude of at least 5500 years. However, beginning shortly after A.D. 1750, urbanization, as a process, has created a wholly new situation. Urban agglomerations are today not only very much larger than ever previously attained but they are also more numerous. Only recently has it become possible to have the *majority* of the people of any country living in urban concentrations. From about 1850 to 1920, this was characteristic only of Great Britain; today all industrial nations are highly urbanized and a third of all the world's peoples live in urban places. Furthermore, the process of urbanization is rapidly accelerating: at the present rate of growth, more than half the world's people will live in urban areas with populations of 100,000 or more by the year 2000. With the appearance of urbanized societies, the twentieth century is experiencing a new and fundamental change in man's social evolution.

Urbanization is the rise in the *proportion* of a total population that is concentrated in urban settlements, as distinct from rural dispersion. As a change in a ratio, urbanization should not be confused with absolute growth; it results from the growth of both the numbers and sizes of cities, but is not the same as the growth of cities. Urbanization, an increase in the urban/rural proportion, has a beginning and an end, whereas cities may continue to grow in size as a result of general population increase with no change whatsoever in a stabilized, high-level urban/rural balance

Human populations have been forming into cities of various kinds for almost six millennia, but at no time before the nineteenth century did the urban areas in any country contain more than a small fraction of the total population. Many cities, city-states, leagues of cities, even city-based empires flourished, but never an urbanized society.

Any reasoned discussion of the population sizes of ancient cities inevitably founders upon the shoals of inadequate data. For those sites that have been archaeologically restored, who knows the average number of residents in their households? Population figures put forth by earlier writers have been described as exaggerated, according to more recent work by archaeologists and demographers. It now seems unlikely that the largest of the cities of 2000 B.C. in Mesopotamia or the Nile Valley exceeded more than 10,000 to 15,000 people, even including part-time farmers living on the outermost city fringes.

Historic cities cities may have reached the million mark (e.g., Chang'an about 1800 years ago, Rome in the second century of this era, Hangchow and other Chinese cities as described by Marco Polo at the end of the thirteenth century), but only in special situations, since it is unlikely that existing technologies for producing surplus food and the limited means of transporting it for any appreciable distance could long have supported centers of over a million people. By conservative estimates, Rome at its largest had about 300,000 inhabitants, Constantinople about 200,000, Baghdad before A.D. 1000 about 300,000, Edo (Tokyo) some 500,000 during the Tokugawa era. Teotihuacan, as the largest urban site in the New World, in the vicinity of modern Mexico City, may have had a population well over 100,000 during the first millennium of our era. It seems clear that, until the eighteenth century, cities of more than 100,000 were sparse, centers over 25,000 were uncommon, and that most cities of consequence ranged between 5000 and 15,000 persons. Size of population did not necessarily correlate with a city's historic importance.

The introduction of gunpowder early in the fourteenth century made it impossible for cities to rely any longer for their defense upon the simple wall and moat. The building of larger, more complicated, and more expensive fortifications, in reality considerable works of engineering skill, consumed much labor and capital in Continental Europe, during the sixteenth and seventeenth centuries. English towns, on the other hand, were free from this drain on their resources and thus gained an advantage in their quest for commercial supremacy.

As cities became appendages to military fortifications, building went on only within the city's protective walls: open spaces were rapidly built over, and further growth could take place only vertically. Overcrowding in the capital cities began in the sixteenth century. In London four and five-story buildings replaced two-story ones; and buildings with heavy stone walls were replaced by less-space-consuming ones with wooden frames. In the seventeenth century these practices were widespread, in the form of high tenements: 5 or 6 stories in Paris and Geneva, to 8 or 10 in Edinburgh. As competition for space provided the pressure that forced a rise in land values in the political capitals, slum housing became the rule for most seventeenth-century cities.

The straight-line military avenue, the square, the parade ground, and the barracks became symbols of the new city. Also, in the sixteenth century, more manipulable, lighter carts and wagons came into more general use as the old-fashioned solid wheels were replaced by ones with hub, spokes, and rim. Pedestrians, who ruled the narrow twisting lanes of the medieval city, gave way to men on horseback and in carriages on the avenues. Forever after, pedestrians were shunted out of the center of the broad ways, to the *side*walks, or became casualties to the new vehicular traffic.

After the sixteenth century, the largest cities were those in which the royal court was located. Paris in 1594 contained 180,000 residents, London had 250,000, Naples 240,000, Milan over 200,000, Lisbon, Seville, Antwerp, and Amsterdam over 100,000, and Palermo and Rome 100,000. In the eighteenth century, the cities of Moscow, Vienna, St. Petersburg, and Palermo each held over 200,000 people, and Warsaw, Berlin, and Copenhagen were in the 100,000 class. Toward the end of the eighteenth century Naples had 433,930 inhabitants, Paris around 670,000, and London over 800,000, whereas the trading cities or the industrial cities for the most part remained with less than 50,000.

In 1800 only about 3 per cent of the world's people lived in the 750 urban areas of more than 5000 inhabitants; there were but 45 cities of over

100,000 population. Asia had the largest total population in urban agglomerations; Edo (Tokyo) was probably the largest single concentration the world had yet seen. In 1800, London was Europe's most populous city, yet with fewer than one million people, whereas Paris had little more than half a million. Twenty-one European cities with a population of 100,000 or more contained only about one thirty-fifth of Europe's people. By contrast, in 1900 there were 147 European cities each over 100,000 whose 40 million people composed one tenth of the European population, whereas in the world there existed 11 great cities of over one million inhabitants each, London and Paris being joined by Berlin, Calcutta, Chicago, Moscow, New York, Philadelphia, St. Petersburg, Tokyo, and Vienna. By 1930, there were 27 cities in the "million" class headed by New York; and by 1950, 49 surpassed the million mark, with 875 of more than 100,000 and 27,600 of more than 5000. By 1961, the world's 21 largest cities, each over $2\frac{1}{2}$ million population, included well over 85 million people, nearly 3 per cent of the world's total.

Cities also are concentrations of human activities. In modern cities one expects to find political parties or factions, chambers of commerce, credit associations, labor unions, factories, churches, schools, newspapers, welfare agencies, humane societies, fraternal and civic associations, museums, art galleries, zoos, auditoriums, parks, playgrounds, business districts, residential areas (including slums), sanitation plants, and public transportation. The impress of high population densities creates a tremendous increase in demands for special services: streets, public water supplies, public sewage systems, garbage and trash disposal, police protection, fire protection, civic centers, schools, libraries, parks and playgrounds, transportation systems. Complicated administrative systems arise to handle the interrelated, complex problems of engineering, law, finance, education, and social welfare (see pp. 120–124 and 505–514).

The Bounds of City Growth

Not until about 100 years ago did the proportion of the human population concentrated in cities begin to increase significantly. The earliest cities were the products of societies that relied principally upon animate sources of energy: the muscles of men and animals, the burning of wood, straw, and dung, and the forces of wind and falling water.

Although possessing metallurgy and such devices as the plow and wheel, the earliest cities were preindustrial, supported by social surpluses in food production that could be collected, stored, and redistributed.

A literate elite has always been an essential part of urban life, because a written tradition was necessary to create the complex religious, administrative, and legal systems and to provide the basis for systematic and cumulative organization of knowledge (e.g., mathematics, astronomy, land measurement, records of ownership, and taxation of production and trade; and the secular laws and the sacred edicts). The city as a form for concentrating activity and settlement focused upon the God-King at its center, the location of the most imposing buildings of religion and government, and the cluster of residences of the elite and their servants. The urban nucleus was normally surrounded by the shop-dwellings of craftsmen who served the elite; at the outskirts were the poor, and the part-time and full-time farmers. Cities concentrated (continuously or seasonally) a large number of different specialists in a small area; the intensity of the resultant human interaction encouraged cities to become focal points for social and technological change.

Preindustrial cities were characterized by distinctive complexes of interrelated phenomena:

1. An agrarian base producing a food surplus that supported a superordinate ruling class, bureaucrats, and many specialists (the surplus may have been a socially exactable one, not necessarily an absolute one in modern secular economic terms).
2. An upper class that was hereditary and that
   (a) controlled the state through theocratic sanctions and military power;
   (b) exacted tribute from the peasants;
   (c) received luxury items produced by craft specialists;
   (d) commandeered produce from surrounding areas and trade routes;
   (e) had complete authority over the lower and outcaste groups;
   (f) maintained status through conspicuous consumption;
   (g) was trained in literacy in special schools;
   (h) practiced arranged marriages.
3. Men were dominant, women remaining in the background.
4. Lower-class artisans were organized in kin-based guilds, lived in special districts within the cities, and marketed their goods without fixed prices. Lower-class culture was a culture of poverty.

5. Record-keeping was present, but its form or style (e.g., writing may be absent, as in Inca and some African societies) was less important than whether it functioned to record produce, taxes, historic events, sacred happenings, and other administrative matters.

6. Monumental and ceremonial architecture formed the physical functional core of the urban entity and served to house the ruling classes and the theocratic apparatus that operated the state.

There are important variables within the great category of preindustrial city; not all are alike (a regular plan may have been absent, and a fully functional urban core may often have been lacking, as in centers remaining largely sacred, religious, or ceremonial), but neither is each unique. The concept of preindustrial describes the only type of city that existed throughout all but the last few centuries of historic time and affords a base line for measuring the changes in urban form and function of our modern era. Many present-day cities in various parts of the world are still preindustrial in character, and most are in transition, evincing many characteristics of their preindustrial past while struggling to become more fully industrialized.

The growth of the preindustrial city has always been limited by internal and external restrictions. Travel within the city had to be mostly on foot, supplemented by movement in boats, on the backs of men or animals, or in animal-drawn vehicles. Communications had to be made by person-to-person contact or carried by messenger. Such situations limited the extent of a city's functions of personal interactions to areas that measured only a few square miles. The preindustrial city was also limited in its vertical extent by the height of its "walk-up" buildings. Sometimes intensity was achieved by covering every square inch of available space, crowding offices, residences, factories, and shops close together around the administrative center. The result was a fantastic rise in the locational value of land near the city center compared with the cost of the structures that could be built upon it. The concept of a congested "downtown" or "central business district," with its particular structures, street patterns, and institutions, is a heritage from the preindustrial city in which secular urbanization became advanced.

Other limitations to city growth were functional or technological. There were limits on the amounts of food and fuel that could be acquired from a rural hinterland by purchase, taxation, or conquest; limits of distance and travel time for bringing bulk items from source regions; and limits on how much fresh water could be acquired and distributed. Preindustrial cities were generally unhealthy, for congestion insured the rapid spread of diseases and fires while presenting difficulties for the removal of wastes (sewage, garbage, trash, animal dung). Death rates almost invariably exceeded birthrates in preindustrial cities; population growth was possible only by the city's attraction of migrants from rural areas.

Evolution of the Industrial City

The stimulus for change from the preindustrial to the industrial city derives from commercial forces (not necessarily private secular forces only): the merchants, financiers, and landlords. The trading cities that changed most under a moneymaking economy were those in which private investment had the greatest freedom to accumulate private profits. Merchant adventurers expanded production, widened markets, furthered technological change, and brought raw materials and finished products from afar. In the emphasis on profit-making speculations, more and more of the economic life lay outside the control of the traditional towns and cities, which became ever less self-sufficient.

The great achievement of the market economy was the production of goods that required safe and speedy distribution. This was the modern incentive for technological exploits that gave successive rise to stagecoaches, canal systems, docks and warehouses, railroad lines, and streetcars. Mass transportation moved not only goods but also workmen, so that, for the first time in history, walking distances between homes and places of work no longer set the limit to a city's dimensions. The expansion of public transportation made possible a vast horizontal extension of the nineteenth-century city, although not necessarily any decrease in the time required for the journey to work.

Space was money; that is, land had a market price. Urban congestion, represented by the close-packed erection of tenements four and five stories high, resulted not from efforts to provide residences for people but to create sources of sufficient rents to correspond with the income demanded by high-cost land. After it was discovered that there were even higher profits to be obtained from industry than from trade and rents, the nineteenth century saw the rise of industrial cities, generated by the mines, the factories, and the railroads. Coal and iron were the basic raw materials; the steam engine supplied the steady output of inanimate energy. Industrial cities were built so rapidly that their basic improvements over preindustrial cities were few: usually incomplete and inadequate systems of water pipes, gas mains, and sewers. Once the concentration of factories began, the increase in urban populations was overwhelming: Manchester in England had about 6000 people in 1685; about 40,000 in 1760; a population of 72,275 in 1801; and 303,382 by 1851.

The steam engine changed the scale of activity. Industries were both large in size, to effect economies, and concentrated in form, to draw power from the central source. More labor was needed in the large factories, and more people thus lived in residences close by. New population centers settled around industrial sites located on or near coal areas, along the railroad lines, in the transport junctions, and at the ports. Factories, railroads, and residential slums were the prime constituents of the industrial cities. Factories occupied the best sites, near water for transport, boiler supply, cooling agent, or solvent, and also for the discharge of wastes. Factories and railroads became formidable concentrations; the city's residential area consisted of the jumbled sectors left over among the railroads, switching yards, dump heaps, and factories. Utilities and government, police and fire protection, hospitals and schools, plumbing and sanitation, were often belated additions. Smoke, fumes, dirt, and noise were omnipresent and affected masses of people, who had to accept these conditions as inevitable concomitants of city life.

The breaking of the bounds of city growth was an achievement of trade and transport. But in the realization of increased size the industrial city fed upon its own products. Public hygiene or sanitation was a nineteenth-century achievement. New standards of light, air, and cleanliness were made possible by the molding of large glazed drains and the casting of iron pipes for use in bringing fresh water from distant sources and disposing of sewage. Provision of such services became a city responsibility, and for the first time the sanitary improvements known only to the palaces and the elite of preindustrial cities were extended to entire populations.

The Rise of Urban America

Most European and many Asian cities are centuries old, whereas comparatively few American cities predate the nineteenth century. The starting point of a newly founded city is inevitably a simplified version of some existing city or cities. Early American cities derived from the forms current in England at the time of their founding (Washington, D.C., an exception, followed a Baroque style designed by a French engineer). In America, establishment of the nation-state preceded the formation of all but a few cities; at the beginning of the nineteenth century only 4 per cent of the population lived in urban agglomerations of more than 8000 population.

In 1860, less than one fifth of the United States' population lived in urban places of more than 2500 inhabitants. There were 34 cities of over 25,000, nine of which each had over 100,000 inhabitants. Eight of these nine largest cities were thriving ports, as a result of commercial expansion in an age of rapid land settlement. The rise of urban America was dramatic during the half century from 1860 to 1910. The number of cities of over 25,000 population increased from 34 to 228; and cities over 100,000 from nine to 50, eight of which exceeded a half million. Westward expansion, the extension of the railroads, the discovery and exploitation of natural resources added to the flow of commerce, but the rise of new factory towns was the principal means of transforming the United States into an industrial nation.

The existence of large cities became possible only after the achievement of farm surpluses and the development of the means to transport such surpluses to consumers in cities. Such concentrations of consumption are the result, of course, not the cause of city building. Most American cities originated where a break in bulk occurred in the transport of goods and where storage and commodity processing occurred. The interaction of transport and city growth is clearly understood in the United States and is easily demonstrated (Fig. 11.1). The Northeastern urban-industrial core region of the United States is markedly dominant: it has the greatest volume of transportation, and, as the great market, aligns the routes of the rest of the country. Raw materials in great volume are shipped to it, and lighter-weight, higher-value finished products are shipped out. This concentration has resulted in 68 per cent of the nation's

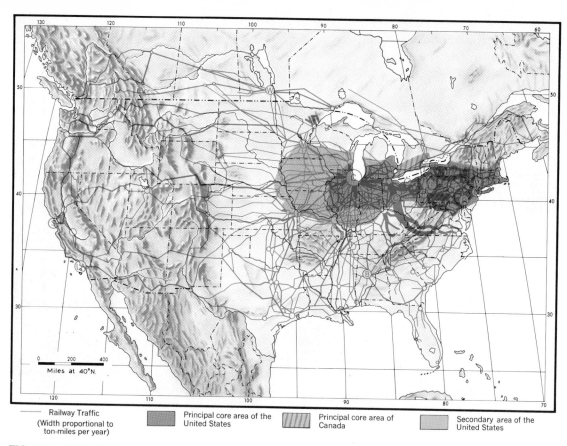

Railway Traffic
(Width proportional to
ton-miles per year)

Principal core area of the
United States

Principal core area of
Canada

Secondary area of the
United States

FIG. 11.1   THE CORE AREA OF THE UNITED STATES AND CANADA, 1960. (After Edward L. Ullman, *American Commodity Flow*, 1957, with permission of the University of Washington Press.)

industrial employment, 52 per cent of its income, and 43 per cent of its people being located in about 8 per cent of its area. The industrial development of the United States, which began using coal for the generation of steam and in the manufacture of steel, by coincidence occurred close to the eastern coal fields. Once the concentration began, it generated its own momentum; its very existence was, and is, an important factor for the location of other activities.

The concentration has been described in the form of a single area or core region. But within the region there are further points of internal concentration—the urban areas (Fig. 11.2). Urban areas in the United States have been growing in population, expanding even more in their areal extent, and thus declining in overall density. Several factors have made possible this expansion and rearrangement of our urban areas: the larger centers attract more in-migrants; these centers provide a greater range of interdependent facilities and services; automobiles and trucks provide short-haul

access, hence an easy expansion of urban transport (larger and more varied journeys to work); industrial activities are shifting from resource extraction and resource conversion toward more processing and service activities, hence are less localized.

Assuming access to external sources of food and raw materials, the larger the urban area the more it is self-contained. Towns of 10,000 population have only about one third of their employment serving internal needs; cities of 500,000 are about evenly divided (one half of the labor force serving internal needs, one half external). According to this measure, the more populous the city the more self-supporting it can be, and perhaps more efficient, since more of its trade can be hauled internally, resulting in a saving of transport costs to and from more distant places.

Improvement in transport and communication changed the nature of urban space by allowing not only greater distances to be covered but also the development of favored sites. Streetcars and mass transit focused upon one large center—the "downtown" or central business district (CBD)—and cities expanded outward along radial transit corridors. The automobile made the intervening spaces accessible. As urban transport improved, the urban areas not only expanded in area, but the range of location choice also widened. The monopoly quality of close-in urban locations was weakened, and the more desirable sites were reached and developed according to their intrinsic advantages.

Urban Areas, Suburbs, and Metropolis

In contemporary thinking and popular speech we generally consider urban areas and cities synonymous, but they are not identical, for the following reasons:

1. Urban settlements can be, and are, variously defined from country to country (political status, population size, population density).
2. Cities are densely settled separate entities of considerable population size, with important, often multiple, functions. Not all urban areas are cities, since urban areas range downward to smaller and smaller places in a transition across an urban-rural continuum. Cities are dominant urban areas, whereas there are many more lesser urban areas.

3. The modern definition of a city must include more than size and density of population, functions, or areal extent. Cities are also legal entities; they are incorporated and have status under state laws. Not all urban areas, however, choose to become cities.
4. Legal or corporate cities have names, unitary governments, and boundaries fixed by law. Built-up areas, however, may extend beyond a city's boundary line, with little visible change, so that the corporate city may form only a part of a much larger contiguous urban area.
5. The legal city is usually the main body, but not the whole, of the physical city. The latter is the total built-up urban area extending in all directions until interrupted by farms, forests, mountains, deserts, or water bodies. Mostly, the physical city is composed of a variety of governmental units, frequently one or more smaller incorporated cities plus outlying portions of the built-up area remaining as parts of a county. Most urban areas thus include a central city or several cities, spoken of as *underbounded*, plus a contiguous urban fringe (Fig. 11.3). In the United States there has arisen the concept of the SMSA (standard metropolitan statistical area) as a unit of urban settlement, for which data can be manipulated at will.
6. There are many exceptions, of course, to the foregoing rule. A legal city may annex dozens or hundreds

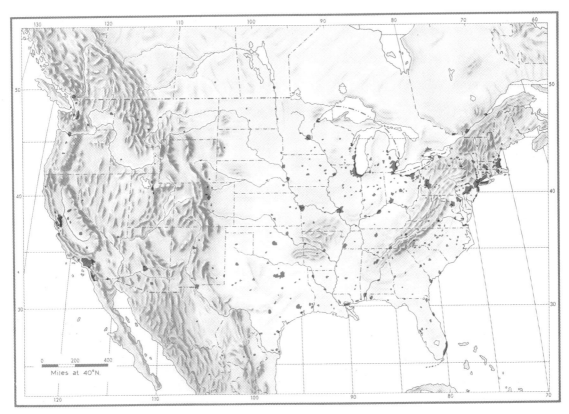

FIG. 11.2 URBAN AREAS OF NORTH AMERICA, 1960.

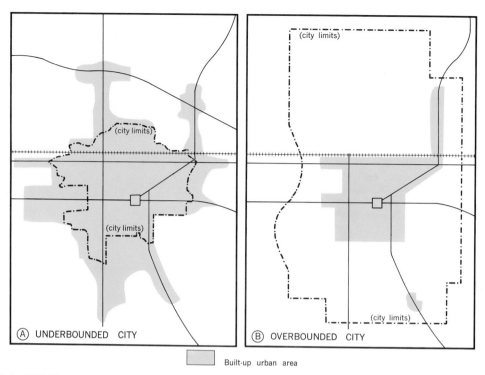

FIG. 11.3   UNDERBOUNDED AND OVERBOUNDED CITIES.

of square miles of rural or desert or mountain land (e.g., Oklahoma City spread into five counties, encompassing 620 square miles, as of 1962; many Philippine cities legally include large rural agricultural zones in order to secure an enlarged taxable area; the Chinese city of Peking is over 6000 square miles in area). In such cases the boundary of the legal city may not reflect the true shape or areal extent of the urbanized, or built-up area, and the city is spoken of as *overbounded*. However, the population total of the urbanized area is the most realistic figure available to indicate the pattern of agglomerated settlement in the United States. The concept of urban area (physical city) is certainly more realistic than the legal city, which is an administrative area.

Suburbs

Suburbs are not at all new. Country villas existed in classical time and, after the twelfth century, many medieval monasteries were situated outside city walls. During the Renaissance, country houses in park-like settings served aristocrats from Italy to England for reasons of health, quiet, privacy, recreation, leisure, and the aesthetics of open space and greenery. Suburban living was the proper antidote for the crowded city, but available only to those few who could afford it.

What is new since the latter part of the nine-

teenth century is the popularity of suburbs and their ease of accessibility, first by railroads (1850–1920), then by streetcars (1895–1940), and (after 1920) by private motorcars. But the rise of suburbia really began in the late 1930s, with the reduction in length of the workweek (from an average of 60 hours per week in 1910 to 40 in 1933) and easier and cheaper home financing based on government-insured, long-term mortgages at low interest rates. The worker had both the time to commute and a suburban home he could afford.

As rapid transport and an extensive road system became necessities, much of the attractive qualities of suburbs began to disappear. Rising land values, rising densities of homes per acre, and increased demands for city services (utilities, protection, schools) tipped the scales in the original compromise between rural and urban. What began as a retreat from the city resulted in the spread of the city outward from its central core. Suburbs tended to become segregated, one-class dormitory communities attached by private means of locomotion to a city for those productive enterprises, creative activities, and intellectual stimuli that the suburbs lacked. The suburbs achieved a transitional improvement in physical environmental form only to create a socially deficient environment, lacking in a pedestrian sense of scale, a sense of community, and civic responsibility.

Expansion to Metropolis and Megalopolis

The urban settings of the Middle Ages and the Renaissance, and even until the eighteenth century, were generally self-contained entities walled off from their surroundings. The modern city is essentially different from its predecessors. The world's great cities indeed have characters all their own yet are inextricably linked to, and dependent upon, their relations to the rest of the world (Fig. 11.4).

There are many other reasons for city growth in addition to favorable situation (coastal or river port, railroad center). There is always the role of accident, of personal decision, of the local invention of a new technique, or of deliberate action by planning. Especially important is the action of a nation-state. It may select the biggest city as its capital (e.g. London) or, more commonly, the capital city becomes the largest city because it is the capital (Madrid, Berlin, Tokyo, Djakarta, St. Petersburg). Not all of the world's great cities are political capitals, however; many are economic centers (Milan, Sydney, New York). And not all political capitals are excessively large; some are wholly created according to plan (Canberra, Brasilia), others are nineteenth-century restorations (Athens, Rome) or European creations for colonial rule (Rangoon, Lima). Contemporary central place theory, concerned with the location and spatial ordering of cities and towns, is developing a significant body of knowledge concerning urban location, growth, and hierarchical status which, in the modern world, may do much to explain the worldwide developing patterns of urbanization.

The impulses that have generated modern city growth were not those from within: the merchants, artisans, and city officials. Rather, the modern city is the result of three interrelated sets of external forces: the centralized nation-state; the rational, capital-using, and ultimately mechanized economy; and the vastly improved communications that permitted the organized deployment of great numbers of men and materials.

Some cities grew to become regional centers, each with its satellites and subsidiaries, and towns arose on the outskirts as former crossroad hamlets suddenly acquired vitality when industrial promoters chose their sites for new factories or an enterprising builder perhaps backed by a transit company developed the nucleus of a residential suburb. The new communities were functional offspring of the major urban centers, as colonies under the control or influence of a mother city. Urban areas were more than single cities and became instead a metropolitan sprawl. The word "metropolis" literally means "mother city."

Urban growth concentrated large population densities in major towns; improvements in transport facilities often only spread congestion into new areas. As commercial and other functions increasingly occupied the downtown business district, the numbers of residents declined in the city's central wards, only to be replaced by even higher daytime populations at work in the city's soaring skyscrapers that marked every metropolis by 1915. Factories grew in size and were relocated on more spacious sites outside central business districts, often beyond the city limits where taxes and land costs were lower, as soon as high-voltage electric power and surface transportation became available. Factory suburbs and dormitory communities appeared as functional subsidiary neighbors to the great core cities, which assumed the character of regional capitals.

One solution to metropolitan living is the formation of new satellite towns around the great centers. Reston in Fairfax County, Virginia, and Germantown and Columbia in Maryland, are appropriate American examples, all some 18 to 25 miles from Washington, D.C.; Petaling Jaya, adjacent to Kuala Lumpur in Malaysia, Letchworth in England, and Cumbernauld in Scotland, are examples of a worldwide trend. Yet most future urban developments will not start afresh with complete new settlements, but build upon the existing communities, with populations of 50,000 to 500,000, that have already appropriated the most favorable sites for economic viability. Around such nuclei, attempts are being made to create clusters of well-ordered, vigorous, attractive, and satisfying environments able to accommodate man's requirements for a life of fulfillment and offering continuous and easy access to the recreational opportunities and quiet harmony of the open countryside. There is emerging a concept of regional urbanism shorn of the conceit that bigness of itself equates with excellence.

If one avoids the either-or argument of city versus the suburb, a level of awareness can be attained recognizing that each has its respective advantages. But then, a further image emerges, a wholly new concept of regional "cities" covering hundreds of square miles. Urbanization has already created several vast agglomerations of varying texture (metropolises or megalopolises), in which farms and pastures so intermingle with intense developments, factories, and shopping centers that to distinguish the individual patches as city, suburb, or country is a meaningless exercise; there will be many more such in the future. The present interlocking complex has produced great urban conglomerates in which few people live on farms but in which almost everybody commutes to work in factories, shops, and offices throughout the urbanized region. The rhythms of life in our urban regions are becoming more diverse and less precise in their patterns of ebb and flow, as the dividing line and spatial separation between work and nonwork loses its sharpness. (See frontispiece photograph and some of the illustrations following p. 119).

Vertical Intensification of Space Use

The symbol of verticality in space use is the multistoried skyscraper. An immediately conjured image is that of New York's Empire State Building whose 102 stories reach 1250 feet high and which has reigned supreme since 1931 as the world's tallest building. Chicago will argue that its John Hancock building of 100 stories, part skyscraper, part apartment house, is higher; skyscrapers around the world are showing one trend of the future.

The intensification of space utilization achieved by the Empire State Building is extreme. Built upon a surface area of about two acres, the office building houses 900 business firms employing 16,000 people (a density equivalent to approximately 5,100,000 persons per square mile); the maintenance and cleaning staff alone numbers 400. The building contains 10 million bricks, 50 miles of radiator pipes, 3500 miles of telephone and telegraph cable, 6500 windows, and 18,000 telephones.

Many materials have been used in high-rise construction; brick, flat limestone, steel, glass, aluminum, all have their advocates, and the steel skeleton closed in by curtain walls is now worldwide in use in large cities, but perhaps nothing is as symbolic as concrete. More architects have used concrete with greater freedom and imagination since 1950 than in the previous 100 years, thanks to major developments in structural design and

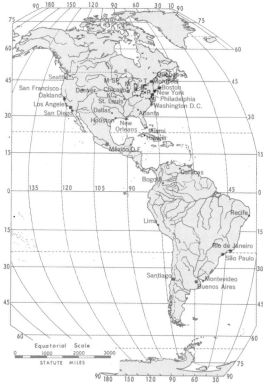

METROPOLITAN AREAS
- 1 to 2 million people
- More than 2 million people

FIG. 11.4 METROPOLITAN AREAS OF THE WORLD.

new methods of fabrication and construction. Until 1871 cement was produced from ingredients taken as they naturally existed; what is known as Portland cement requires care in the proportions of clay and limestone and in subjection to intense kiln heats. The use of concrete reinforced with iron beams came into widespread use after the late 1870s. The invention in 1911 of a machine to make standardized concrete blocks provided a cheap and convenient unit of construction that soon became widely used; prestressing of concrete with high-tensile steel began only in 1951. Expansive cement, used in concrete panels, points the way to a new era in concrete construction, since design need not take into account the phenomenon of drying-shrinking-cracking.

The means toward verticality in space use include the elevator (or lift) and the escalator for rapid passenger and freight transport. With safety devices added, elevators came into widespread business use during the 1870s, at the same time that typewriters made office workers productive. After electricity, substituted for hydraulic power in 1889, simplified their operation, the use of

Equatorial Scale

0   1000   2000   3000

STATUTE MILES

METROPOLITAN AREAS

•   1 to 2 million people

▪   More than 2 million people

FIG. 11.4 (*Continued*)   B. The Old World.

elevators was extended to hotels and apartment houses. Elevators, which enabled top floors to command premium rents, were but one element in high-rise construction. Taller buildings required cast-iron and steel-frame construction, sheathed in fireproof materials.

The larger buildings were made practicable by the transport facilities that brought crowds of people to the downtown shopping districts and office centers. They stimulated improvements in interior heating and lighting, in sanitary facilities, and especially in telephone communications to improve business efficiency, all advances of the 1880s. The first moving stairway, or escalator, was installed in 1892. Now, of course, the standard practice is to combine the use of power ramps and escalators (the capacity to move 8000 persons per hour is almost 30 times that of a single elevator) for continuous traffic flow at the lower levels with

"local" and "express" elevators to the upper floors of tall buildings. The self-monitoring electronic devices installed in elevators since 1953, to work automatically without attendants, can be programmed to adjust elevator locations in anticipation of expected changes in traffic flows. Through such control systems, vertical transportation no longer has any need for human supervision.

Vertical intensification of space use results in the greatest concentration of people in urban areas that the world has ever experienced. Unfortunately the customary census enumerations record where people reside (sleep) rather than where they work. Thus the central core (The Loop) of Chicago in 1950 reported 11,000 residents, whereas 275,000 persons were employed there in the daytime. Residential densities in cities are considered low if they fall below 5000 persons per square mile, yet this figure is higher than the greatest recorded rural densities for Java, a most congested island by rural standards. In the zone immediately surrounding Chicago's Loop and extending two to three miles from the center, residential densities are over 30,000 per square mile. Beyond, at distances from four to six miles, densities are about 15,000, and in the eight-to-ten-mile zone average about 12,000 per square mile.

Complexity of Internal Differentiation

Commerce and industry after the seventeenth century submerged the city with speculative and competitive planlessness. Merchants, financiers, and landlords favored urban expansion. The ideas of the marketplace became pervasive in every part of the city, augmented in the nineteenth century by various mechanical inventions and the rise of large-scale industrialization. The separation of home and workplace began as a privilege of rich merchants. By the nineteenth century the practice had spread almost over Europe, as the functions of producing, selling, and consuming were separated into different kinds of buildings located in different parts of the city. Traffic and the geometry of streets took precedence over all other urban functions. Quiet, self-contained neighborhood quarters where people could congregate and meet were subordinated to the "block" and its houseplots, whose size and shape were determined by the arrangement of the widened and heavier-paved avenues that facilitated vehicular movement.

Great cities need not have long histories or fantastic settings, although Rome and Rio de Janeiro are an example of each. Yet, Copenhagen is unhistoric in its significance, Amsterdam rose upon a marsh, and Shanghai grew out of an undistinguished county seat town located on a small tributary stream near the Yangtze River mouth. In functional terms, a great city today possesses an attractively varied downtown with a large middle-class population living in or close by to sustain its shops, theaters, museums, and to taste regularly of its range of services.

Inner city land increasingly is becoming too expensive to warrant low-density development; so the trend is to build to high densities at high rental prices (or with government subsidies for low-income housing). Cores of some of the world's cities have been in decline over the past several decades, but this is not yet certainly a worldwide trend—it may be a regional trend common to the United States only in this era. Retail sales may lessen "downtown" because of the competition from shopping centers that have evolved in the suburbs where their customers live. Former central cores in many cities are no longer the most important, but merely one of several business districts with different specializations. However, in many old European cities the old city cores continue to be prime residential zones, and there is no single trend that can be described for all the world's urban places.

A symbol of urban complexity, or economic perverseness, is the transportation tangle. Industry shifts more and more of its manufacturing and warehousing activities to roomier plants built on cheap land in the suburbs, while central business districts are increasing their concentrations of administrative professional and clerical jobs. Cross-commuting is the result, as blue-collar workers leave the city in which they live for work in the outlying districts, and white-collar workers travel even farther from their residential suburbs across the ring of the industries and warehouses to their downtown offices and businesses in the central city.

Some functions locate near the outlying airport; regional shopping "centers" decentralize the retail trade; large factories are on large tracts of land at the outskirts; educational, recreational, and entertainment functions are rather widely dispersed. The present-day city often has no single center, but is a federation of multiple "centers" for general and special purposes. Problems of travel times, congestion, and site utilization are diffused (and equalized) among all the town's citizenry.

Problems Created by Human Concentration

The geographer, of course, is greatly interested in the effects on the physical and biotic landscape of man's wholesale modification of his environment. For example, water-control structures alter the regimen of streams and thereby produce significant changes in water quality, channel morphology, and vegetation in both upstream and downstream reaches of natural channels. Changes resulting from large-scale construction operations on the land produce initially large concentrations of sediments in streams. Following completion of construction, large areas are covered by impermeable surfaces, whereupon streams are starved of sediment. This sequence of briefly more and thereafter much less sediment causes decreased channel conveyance, increased flooding, vegetative growth in channels, reduced oxygen in bottom waters, and changes in populations of fish and microbiota. Later runoff from parking areas, roads, and streets varies in both quality and quantity from its former conditions.

Lewis Mumford, in his *The City in History*, contends that, whereas cities are the "containers" of civilization, resulting from implosion or the drawing together of creative interacting forces within a city's walls, they also subject men to depersonalizing regimentation and occupational specialization. Today's cities, he feels, make men the creatures rather than the masters of technological development and expose them to a full range of increasing hazards, from pollution of air and water and exposure to communicable diseases to mass extermination in biological or nuclear warfare.

Two and one half million people live in Harlem but not really out of preference. Few buildings are over six stories, so Harlem is truly a crowded place to live. If all of Manhattan Island were as densely populated as Harlem, it could house the whole population of the United States. In the late nineteenth century, New York City undertook a massive building program to supply housing for its immigrants. Thousands of five- and six-story walk-up tenements were constructed; some 43,000 of those built before 1900 are still occupied, along with another 15,000 built before 1920. At an average of 15 apartments per building, a total of 870,000 apartments are in need of repair or replacement.

Low density of settlement, in itself, can be attractive. Yet suburban sprawl (which is just as much a part of American life today as urban blight), with its commercial street-ribbons, removal of trees, and growth of junkyards, usually is not. Helter-skelter shelters and their ugliness owe largely to the unrelated individual efforts by people with interests other than aesthetics and lacking the desire to create immediate personal environments responsive to changing needs for living, learning, and evolving. Suburban sprawl can also be inefficient. Installation of utilities—sewers, water, electricity—is more costly on the urban fringes.

The physical and functional problems of building and maintaining large cities began to be resolved less than a century ago. The problems of cities have been changing, growing along with their populations. It is easier to pile up people and to stack up buildings in a shapeless and formless mass than it is to give civic structure to this mass. By current projection, by the year 2000 about half of the United States population will be living in about 41 huge metropolitan areas of over one million population each; as of the late 1960s it was not certain that the existing socioeconomic rules of management would suffice to administer such enormous settlements.

For the bulk of their citizens, urban areas are evidently satisfactory and attractive places in that they provide the stuff of daily life that improves upon that which their fathers and grandfathers enjoyed. The urbanization process has resulted from the migration of persons seeking a better life, from country to small towns, from towns to cities, from cities to metropolises. The cities attract the finest of engineers and artists, and the most adventurous youngsters; and cities also have slums and the poor, probably now on a larger scale than did cities in the past. The problems that cities pose are not new but they are susceptible to human resolution.

Urban areas are in ferment. There is an aroused interest in local government owing to many factors: reapportionment of state legislatures, rising costs of local government and education; acute awareness of pollution to land, air, and water; the development of new local governmental organizations such as regional planning boards and water and sewage authorities; the adoption of new local taxes on income and sales. This interest is related to the greatly increased expectations that a well-educated citizenry have of the services produced by government within a federal system.

The problems of governing metropolitan areas are not to be resolved easily. There are intense rivalries, rooted in politics, between city and neighbor city, between cities and their suburbs. Fragmentation of power and jurisdiction frustrate efforts to build regional decision-making processes. The problem of governing is to maximize the opportunity to experience regionalism and partake of regional decisions. Given substance and incentive, the mechanisms of regional government will in time evolve.

The great city (particularly the American city) has been so vast, so varied, and so much in flux that it has provided its critics with an overwhelming list of things to dislike. It has been described as too big, too noisy, too smelly, too commercial, too crowded, too full of immigrants, too artificial, too pushy, too heartless, too grimy, too wild, too vulgar, too ostentatious, too uncontrolled, too gaudy. But the essential, and higher, criticism has been of the city's deficiencies: in society, in civilization, and in brilliance—deficient in organic social organization and elevated conversation. Cities have been found wanting principally because they are not civilized enough; complicated centers for living they may be, but they have not yet fully realized their potentialities in fostering fundamental values of education, individuality, and easy communication among men. The places of the past were the wilderness, the isolated farmstead, the plantation, the self-contained village, the small town, and the detached neighborhood. But all over the earth these are going, as the world is evolving into a cluster of urbanized regions, and it is in just these regions that the further achievements of civilization are to be realized.

Urbanization as a Worldwide Process

Beginning with nineteenth-century England, but now proceeding apace over the world is the transition from urban-based civilizations to urbanized societies. The urbanization of society is the most comprehensive, profound, and unprecedented social change affecting the present world. What was described as the process of cultural convergence is taking place in the context of gigantic regional cities in which most human beings soon will be living. They already are in existence in much of Europe, Japan, Australia, Canada, India, and the United States (Fig. 11.5). Tiles in the twentieth-century mosaic are in process of overlapping themselves; the process of urbanization has not yet diffused worldwide, for there remain scattered, though declining, pockets of non-industrialized societies. Meanwhile, the creation of predominantly urbanized societies is spreading outward, principally from the United States and Europe under the guise of economic or technological development, to engulf former city-based civilizations in a wholly new, higher-level arrangement and organization of mankind. The countries already urbanized are distributed widely over the globe. Australia and Great Britain have over 80 per cent of their population living in urban areas; West Germany, the United States, Canada, Denmark, and Japan are in the 70 to 80 per cent category; Belgium, the Netherlands, Argentina, and France are in the 60 per cent group,

and Sweden and the U.S.S.R. are over 50 per cent urbanized. Across the world six extensive urbanized regions are clearly evident: northwest Europe, northeastern North America, the Pacific coast of Anglo-America, around the mouth of the Rio de la Plata, central to southern Japan, and southeast Australia. The urbanization process is unfolding in other smaller zones, with big cities appearing all over the world, as local regional developments. Although the mass of world population still consists of rural, village, or town dwellers (see Fig. 1.4), such a clear trend toward city life has set in that one may well speculate what the pattern of clustering of world population will be, say, for the year 2000 or 2500.

What does it mean for an urbanized society when all of its food, drink, clothing, and housing— all of its subsistence commodities, that is—can be produced by between 10 and 15 per cent of its work force? Such a society's economic life will become largely a matter of providing personal services; its organization will be different from that which is presently familiar. There are several existing circumstances that are indicative of the new order: the disintegration of the industrial-based city as a well-coordinated social entity, and the inability of the nation-state to insure the defense and security of its concentrated settlements, since missiles have simultaneously extended destructive forces to a fully worldwide range and lowered their cost of transport. By a time when 90 per cent of a nation's population live in urban areas, will the earlier concept of "city" really have any meaning?

Space Intensification in Resource Extraction

Discussion in the latter part of Chapter 8 left off with mention of the technological inroads being made by the application of industrial products to the processes of resource extraction. Hybrid varieties, industrialized crop raising, synthetic production of fibers, tree-farm forests, all were identified as symbols of the increased productivity made possible by the new agricultural revolution. Other examples of technological progress can be illustrated by such processes as the concentration of magnesium metal from the sea and of nitrogen from the atmosphere into fertilizers. Modern high-level productivity, an intensification of use of existing earth space, has become possible only because of the existence of urban-industrial economies and their products, including their abilities to harness inanimate energy.

Space Intensification in Agriculture

As late as 1800, production technology had not begun to quicken markedly, although many of the intercontinental crop and animal transfers had taken place, and the processes of ecological accommodation and attunement to new environments were well under way. A single farmer could not then feed many persons beyond his own family, whereas today in the more advanced agricultural regions of the earth less than 10 per cent of the labor force is required in the industrialized agriculture of the 1960s. In 1800 it was possible to look around the world (see Fig. 8.6A, p. 362) and differentiate strongly the regions of European root-grain-animal agricultural systems, the Mediterranean-type agricultures with their irrigated summer crops and winter rain-grown grains, the Oriental hoe cultures with their manicured wet-rice fields and intensive garden cultures, the tropical plantation systems with their large labor forces, selected commercial crop-subsistence food patterns, the arid-land systems of nearly self-contained pastoralism, and the many localized cropping-culture complexes, for there were traditional systems slowly matured in ecological balance with regional environments and regional cultures. Today, of course, there still are regional systems of agriculture that differ in many respects, for there are many regional environments in which the traditional technologies have barely begun to transform, and there are still the significant culture-crop-farmscape variations to be seen on the land (see Fig. 8.6B). However, there is increasing similarity in the industrialization of the tropical plantations, the mid-latitude grain farms, the Mediterranean dry-margin irrigated fruit and vegetable farms, and the livestock farms in all parts of the earth in that advanced mechanization, complex crop hybridization, advanced economic organization, and complex technologies are being employed to heighten productive capacities and to achieve greatly improved efficiencies.

The evolution of crop growing and animal raising began with the technological advances of domestication and cropping systems, as a dimly seen system of improvement in living. These technologic improvements stimulated sociocultural changes of many sorts in the many separate regions to which the new technologies spread. However, the new production systems were subject to sociocultural controls in varying degrees among the different culture groups of the earth, and technologic advance could go no further, in a sense, than permitted by cultural controls. The production systems also remained subject to the broad controls of the physical environment in that Neolithic man could not successfully move humid-tropical or seasonal-subtropical crop plants to alien environments. The fusing of crop-growing and animal-raising technologies into agriculture represented another era of technologic revolution during which cultural controls yielded to technological advancement. During much of subsequent agricultural history the sociocultural, political, and physical environmental influences have remained dominant, generally governing the operation of agricultural systems. What is so often termed "peasant agricultural system" was really a way of life in which agricultural technology was subject to sociocultural definition of general aims, seen most clearly perhaps in the traditional Chinese agricultural system and in the village agricultural life of Medieval Europe. In such developments the particular agricultural system placed strong physiognomic and morphologic imprints upon the face of the earth, to create regional variation around the world and to constitute spatial variation among culture systems and regional environments. Technological change in agriculture has been subject to both the cultural and the environmental sets of influences, but it would now appear that, historically, the cultural control has been the more significant in the restriction of agricultural economic productivity, for agriculture was always but a part of a broad regional system of culture.

It was in the turn-of-the-century United States–Canadian Midwest, among the mixed immigrant populations only loosely articulated into culture systems, where labor shortages were marked and continuing, that economic technology became somewhat released from restrictive cultural and environmental controls to set the farmer on the path of technologic revolution in agricultural production. In American-Canadian agriculture today one can have the reaction that it is scientific production technology that is almost dominant in the control of agriculture operations, and that the American-Canadian cultures are adjusting to this technology rather than subjecting agriculture to traditional cultural aims. It is perfectly true, of course, that changes in American social outlook are

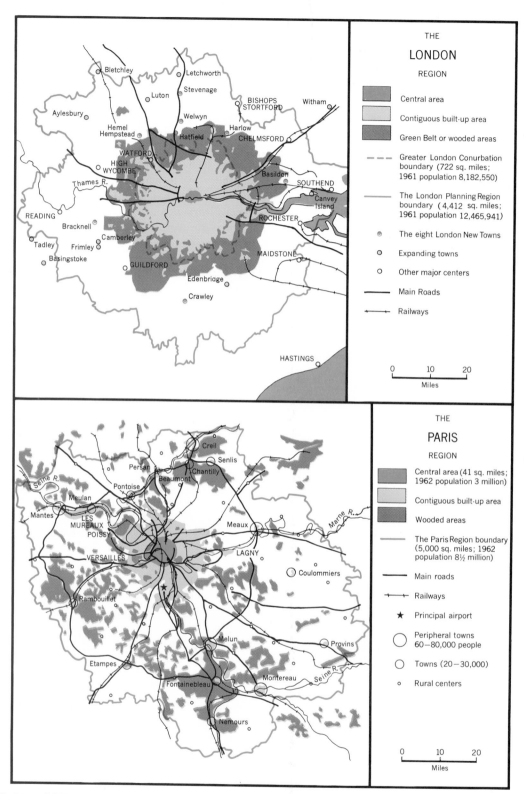

FIG. 11.5 SOME GREAT WORLD METROPOLISES. A. London. B. Paris.

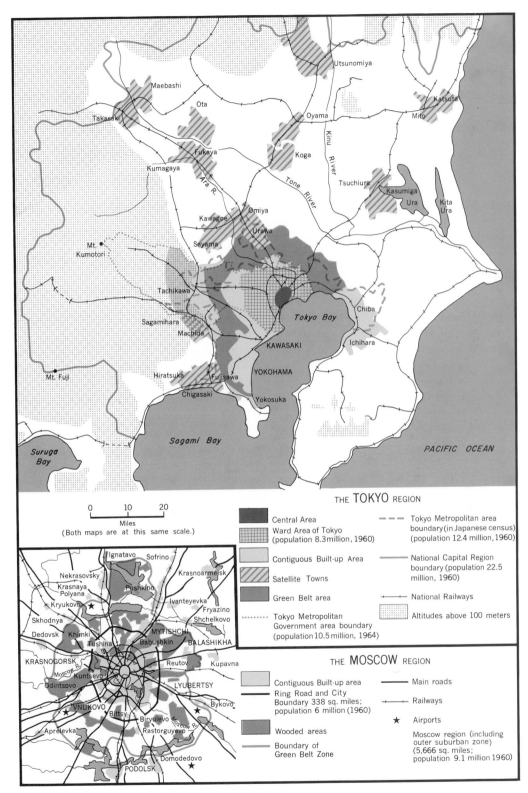

THE TOKYO REGION

Central Area

Ward Area of Tokyo
(population 8.3 million, 1960)

Contiguous Built-up Area

Satellite Towns

Green Belt area

Tokyo Metropolitan
Government area boundary
(population 10.5 million, 1964)

Tokyo Metropolitan area
boundary (in Japanese census)
(population 12.4 million, 1960)

National Capital Region
boundary (population 22.5
million, 1960)

National Railways

Altitudes above 100 meters

THE MOSCOW REGION

Contiguous Built-up area

Ring Road and City
Boundary 338 sq. miles;
population 6 million (1960)

Wooded areas

Boundary of
Green Belt Zone

Main roads

Railways

Airports

Moscow region (including
outer suburban zone)
(5,666 sq. miles;
population 9.1 million 1960)

0   10   20
Miles
(Both maps are at this same scale.)

FIG. 11.5 *(Continued)*   C. Tokyo. D. Moscow.

Space-Intensification Techniques: Increased Production and Urbanization | 491 aiding and abetting such technological change and improvement, but in the American scene of the twentieth century this almost becomes the classical question of the chicken or the egg. (See the agricultural tools among the illustrations following p. 330.)

From the incubator on the North American continent these twentieth century technological changes have been, and are, diffusing around the world. The Argentine, Australia, the Soviet Union, Japan, and varied sectors of the humid tropics and subtropics, each in its own time and system, are all following the lead of the nineteenth and twentieth-century agricultural revolution in which mechanized and scientific technology are changing sociocultural patterns and economic relationships throughout the realm of agriculture. This is another era of marked impingement of technology upon systems of social culture, and the social unrest and economic turbulence of many parts of the world are the manifestations of the strength of modern scientific technology.

Consider the impact of scientific knowledge and technological capabilities in modern agriculture when applied to the problems of those regions in which at least half of the world's people obtain more than 60 per cent of their bodily energy from rice. If more than 30 per cent of all human energy derives from this one species of plant, ponder the disastrous consequences of a rapidly spreading rice predator, or the rice equivalent of the chestnut or elm blight. On the other hand, what an opportunity for improving human living conditions if rice yields could be appreciably increased.

About one quarter of the world's total cereal production is rice, and over half of it is grown in the tropical and equatorial regions, mainly in Asia where yields are deplorably low by modern production standards. Average yields for tropical countries seldom exceed 1800 pounds per acre: the average Indian yield is about 1350 pounds, that of Thailand about 1450, and of the Philippines about 1100 per acre. By contrast, temperate zone countries, as Japan, Australia, and in the Mediterranean, have rice yields that range from 3600 to 5400 pounds per acre, partly as a result of better water control, land preparation, weed and pest control, and other practices. The quest for higher rice yields is proceeding in just those tropical regions where the food problem is most acute.

Most rice varieties can be classified loosely into either *indica* or *japonica* types. Indica types are typically those of the tropics: tall and weak-stemmed, with a profusion of long, drooping, pale-green leaves, and late-maturing habits. The grain usually remains dormant for a period following maturity, an important trait in the tropics where high humidity can cause grain to germinate before harvest. The tropical varieties of rice evolved through selection by many generations of farmers who required plants that would thrive under conditions of low fertility, poor water and weed control, and a rudimentary agricultural system. Improvements in cultivation practices produce disappointing yields; nitrogen application, for example, leads to taller and leafier indica rice plants but little or no additional grain.

By recent modern, scientific breeding programs, a new and more desirable short-statured plant type has been achieved, combining the virtues of the traditional indicas with additional desired characteristics of high yield, nitrogen responsiveness, lodging resistance, and short growth duration. As first publicly announced in July 1966 by the International Rice Research Institute, one such selection IR8–288–3, has produced astounding yields wherever tested, ranging from 5000 to 9000 pounds per acre. These are yields from three to seven times the national averages for Southeast Asian countries. Without fertilizer, the new IR–8 produces at least as well as the commonly grown varieties, but for the first time the contemporary Asian farmer has a food plant able to respond to high levels of nitrogen and attain rice yields that are astounding for the tropics. Consider the possible impact on the Asian food situation. If 15 per cent of the rice lands of India could yield 1800 pounds per acre more than at present, then India's annual 10 million ton food-grain deficit would be eliminated. In the Philippines an extra 900 pounds per acre from 10 per cent of the rice lands would render that rice-importing country self-sufficient.

There are many other examples of the application of modern technology to intensify agricultural production. The first practical use of growth-regulating chemicals, for example, was to stimulate root formation. Commercial production of plant-regulating substances, mostly to control plant behavior rather than stimulate growth, has expanded tremendously since 1945. By mid-1966, the United States Department of Agriculture had approved 34 growth-regulating chemicals for 92 different uses in crop production to make crops better suit our needs. For example, practically all table grapes of the Thompson Seedless variety now are sprayed with gibberellic acid to improve their size and quality (loose clusters of large, long berries). Acceleration of fruit and bud growth is also being achieved in raisin grapes, tomato plants, and white potatoes. Flower initiation and development has been controlled on apple and pear trees to achieve an even volume of annual production. Retardant chemicals have modified the flowering seasons of such ornamentals as azaleas, rhododendron, and holly. Plant regulators make such fruits as apples and pears remain on the trees until the appropriate harvest period, increasing yields and reducing the labor. The high cost of thinning by hand stimulated use of chemical thinners. But the greatest amounts of regulating compounds are used to control weeds.

Plant geneticists have made tremendous strides by selecting characteristics from one species and passing the genes that carry those characteristics to a closely related species. Hybrid corn, nematode-resistant soybeans, and rust-resistant and short-straw wheat are among the more important results. Frequently, the gene-passing must be accomplished through a third, or intermediate, species. Rust resistance, for instance, was passed from a wild grass to wheat through emmer, a feed grain.

Progress in animal genetics, however, has been slower, primarily because animals are immensely more complicated organisms than plants. One of the research objectives is to enable animal breeders to transfer desirable characterstics, such as disease resistance, from wild birds to domestic poultry. Crosses between Dark Cornish roosters and Japanese quail, by artificial insemination, have produced intermediate offspring, chicken-quail hybrids. The next objective is to induce fertility in these offspring and then backcross them with their parent species to stabilize a new species intermediate between quail and chickens. Obviously, new species production would be a significant step in man's control and direction of evolution.

Space Intensification in Mineral Resource Extraction

The technological "feedback" that permits intensification in resource-extraction techniques is nowhere better illustrated than in prospecting, exploration, and mining of ores. Magnetics and electromagnetics are the two principal geophysical methods adapted for airborne surveys, with induced polarization the most popular ground method. For example, by 1970 the Canadian Geological Survey will have completed a million-mile aeromagnetic survey of the entire Canadian Shield; already the British have completed an aeromagnetic map of England, Wales, and part of the Irish Sea, and the Russians have reportedly flown the entire U.S.S.R.

The continually growing shortage of skilled underground miners coupled with the escalating costs of labor, supplies, and equipment are catalysts for improvements in underground mining. The objective is an economic, automated continuous excavation method that would produce rock at the mining face in sizes suitable for automated transportation directly into the grinding mills.

Ocean mining is already under way: tin ore is being dredged from 90-foot depths off Thailand, iron ore off the Japanese coast, coal from undersea tunnels off England, Nova Scotia, and New Brunswick, aragonite off the Bahamas, and diamond dredging off South Africa. But truly large-scale operations are as yet only in the research and development stage.

Most mining, however, with coal the major exception, is from open pits (82 per cent of United States metal ores and almost 92 per cent of nonmetals). Bulk-handling techniques are on a gigantic scale. In Arizona, 200 million tons of overburden are being removed to reach a copper ore body 460 feet below the surface; 54-cubic-yard scrapers, 60-inch-wide belts $1\frac{1}{2}$ miles long, and 100-ton trucks are doing the job. In Illinois the world's largest mobile land machine operates in strip coal mining, lifting 270 tons in a single bite; an even larger machine, capable of lifting 550 tons, is being built. A three-scraper tandem, 200 feet long, on 10-feet-high tires, loads 360 tons in $1\frac{1}{2}$ minutes. Technological achievements of a high order are not exclusive to the United States. In Japan, the world's longest conveyer belt system moves rock 10 miles from a limestone pit to loading docks at Nagato. West Germany has the world's largest mobile rock crusher, weighing 440 tons and capable of processing as much as 1000 tons per hour of hard rock; by following the shovel, it can increase shovel production and feed onto conveyor belts, thus lowering transport costs.

Secondary recovery is the term used to describe the variety of processes that are used to push petroleum out of rock after the decline of natural pressure, hence extend the life of costly-to-explore-and-drill oil wells. Natural pressure and pumping (primary recovery) were all the extractive processes available in the early days of the oil industry; but these were inefficient, leaving behind between 65 to 80 per cent of the oil. The pushing techniques now in routine commercial use directly displace oil from the rock by water or natural gas. This can accomplish a 50 per cent level of extraction, adding about one third to the petroleum produced. Further research is directed at improvements in extractive efficiency, by increasing the area swept out by the pushing fluid (higher viscosity) and increasing its oil-recovering efficiency (better solvent or heating). By 1980, secondary techniques are expected to account for about one half of domestic United States petroleum production. The result would be a doubling of proven oil reverses without a cent of cost for further exploration and drilling.

Intensification in Resource Conversion

Key developments that changed production processes early in the twentieth century were the *assembly line* and the concept of *mass production.* The former disintegrated a total task into its smallest elements of sequential activity (the *line*), then regrouped them (the *assembly*) to create a total product. The role of the individual worker (pride in craft-skill) was subordinated to efficiency (time and motion study) in production. Mass production requires that like parts in an assembly line be interchangeable, and that all parts (even workmen) be replaceable in order to permit continuous maintenance and flow of the line for maximum production of goods in least time with least unit costs.

The assembly line and mass production were techniques that enabled production to increase markedly and twentieth-century industrial firms to expand at an unprecedented rate. Unlike the "entrepreneurial" or "one-man rule" of the early stages of the Industrial Revolution, one man could no longer maintain a constant vigil on daily events, formulate managerial decisions, and initiate action. As a consequence, the first half of the twentieth century was marked by the growth of organizations whose managerial structures were pyramidal or hierarchical, as responsibility and authority were delegated to subordinates and enterprises were divided (dispersed) for purposes of management and control. Such an organization most effectively limits the flow of information between levels in the hierarchy, transmitting only a small fraction of the information that is created or becomes known at each level to the next higher (or lower) level (although, it is to be hoped, all that is needed by these other levels).

The early 1940s witnessed the emergence of the electronic computer, with its near-infinite capacity for storing data and its near-instantaneous capacity for manipulating and retrieving them. A computer can handle all tasks that are "programmable," that is, those that can be precisely defined in structure and procedures, and can do so more quickly, more accurately, more completely, and more economically than can human beings. (See the photograph of the computer room on p. 338.)

Electronic data transmission and computation are capable of analyzing minute-by-minute activities of production and summarizing the analysis to management with a minimum of error and time lag. Centralized electronic decision making is widely practiced today: witness the airline and the hotel reservation systems, signature-validating systems, police-record files, air-defense command, the satellite-tracking systems, and others, already in existence. Once again it is possible for one man (the manager) or a small group of men (the executive board) to possess all the information necessary for production control.

The centralization of information and decision making made possible by electronic data transmission and computation systems is reversing the trend toward specialization that prevailed in the earlier part of this century. Former individual or semiautonomous units are being made into larger ones; and what were single-purpose companies are able to expand rapidly into diversified activities. This explains the remarkably similar patterns of expansive growth among the world's largest business corporations during the mid-twentieth century. Whereas, former activities were fragmented and artificially compartmentalized, a production system (the interactions among various components) can now be studied as a whole. Of course, this means that the responsibilities of top-level management are increased, as the area of impact of decisions is greatly enlarged. The performance of a manager is still measured by the results he achieves, but he now has more refined tools for reaching rational decisions.

Electronic computer-based production systems are effecting a "second" industrial revolution, based on the techniques of systems analysis, which is still in the making. In part, the computer is a new tool that enables us to do familiar tasks more accurately and quickly (e.g., addition, replacing desk calculators); but, more importantly, the computer can be applied to fundamentally new tasks as components to control such complex activities as air traffic patterns and petroleum refining. These latter are the truly new space-intensification techniques, because they have never existed before or never have been capable of being performed before. By speeding intercommunication among a large number of activities, by rapid and error-free calculations, and by rapid compilation and reporting of data, an almost unlimited range of choice is possible in designing control systems wherein the computer monitors and adjusts production to achieve explicitly stated objectives.

A fully effective computer-using production system integrates the design of the product, the design of the process by which the product is made, and the design of the control system that monitors and adjusts production to achieve set objectives. Fully automated factories are now in existence (machine tooling of engine blocks, petroleum refineries) in a few cases. They represent a radical departure from conventional techniques, but provide sufficient outstanding examples of what can be accomplished, as the approach becomes more widely adopted.

Automation is a new way of analyzing and organizing work, not a mere extension of mechanization. New machines, such as electronic computers, numerical tool controls, massive transfer machines, and the instrument panel of an oil refinery, have been made possible by the new concept. Automation links production, information-handling processes, or both into an integrated system, by applying the principle called "feedback" in the design of machines that can control their own operations and be free from the limitations (reaction time; powers of perception, concentration, and discrimination; height; tolerances of heat and cold; manipulation of two arms and ten fingers; ability at coordination) of their human operators. The idea of automation is not new; what is new is its widespread application. The fundamental importance of automation is the ability to create automatic information and control systems that both multiply productivity and efficiently distribute commodities to insure guaranteed minima of life, and also to free men to undertake new tasks not previously possible.

Chemistry, Nutrition, and Food Production

The application of scientific knowledge in the United States has converted food processing into a gigantic chemical industry. Take breadmaking as a case in point. Dietary habits of the nineteenth century created the demand for refined white bread. This fitted with prevailing milling practices, because the marketing of whole-grain flour was impracticable owing to hazards of spoilage. Beginning in 1923, bakers began to improve the nutritive value of white bread by including skim milk solids in the bread mix. Between 1919 and 1926 the national production of ice cream increased 45 per cent, and an enormous quantity of skim milk was being thrown away since there was no organized marketing system for selling it or getting it back to farms for animal feeding. But the proteins and vitamins of skim milk made up for the deficiencies of white flour, and commercial bread began to contain 6 per cent nonfat milk solids. After 1940, bread began to be enriched by the inclusion of thiamin, riboflavin, niacin, and iron, the vitamins being available from chemical synthesis at low cost. Much of the prepared foods of the United States today are "fortified" or "enriched"; read the label on the next package, carton, or can that you open.

There are vast international differentials in nutritional levels, per capita food intakes, and availability and distribution of food supplies. The emphasis in the United States has been upon increased variety in the diet. Since 1940 per capita consumption of wheat, cereal breakfast foods, and potatoes has been cut by 30 per cent, while intake of meat, fish, poultry, dairy products, and fruits and vegetables has increased by about 20 per cent.

Further dramatic advances have resulted from experimental inquiry. In 1900, the accepted view was that the complete nutrition of man or animal depended upon protein, potential energy in the form of carbohydrates and fats, and an ill-defined list of inorganic elements, especially those deposited in bones. By contrast, at present the known number of elements considered essential to an adequate diet totals 51. These are water, oxygen, 16 inorganic elements, 10 amino acids, 17 vitamins, triply unsaturated linoleic acid, glycine, serine, proline, hydroxyproline, and glutamic acid.

It is a far cry from the idea of "eating in order to live" to the quantitative concept of furnishing all the necessary nutrients in balanced proportions without excess of calories for each individual through the experiences of a lifetime. But the mass of humanity has not been benefited by nutritional studies; only a limited proportion of the world's population has been helped. The national diet of China forms a remarkable contrast with that of the United States with its overemphasis upon meat. For millennia, China has focused attention upon intensive agricultural production based on effective water control (irrigation and flood protection) and intensive labor to obtain the greatest number of calories per unit of cultivated land. The consequence was a preponderance of small farms and a dense population, with land too valuable for human-food production to be used as pasture for cattle. Attention was concentrated on the growing of plants (wheat, millets, soybeans, and rice) rather than the raising of herd animals. The traditional Chinese diet derived over four-fifths of its calories from the seed-grains, from legumes 7 per cent, from potatoes 4 per cent, and less than $2\frac{1}{2}$ per cent from animal products, mainly pork.

Essentially vegetarian and based mainly on cereals, the traditional Chinese diet was lacking in certain nutritive elements, especially minerals and vitamins. The extemely low consumption of such products as milk (considered culturally abhorrent), eggs, green leafy vegetables, and fruits results in a deficiency in protective foods: protein derived from vegetables is much less easily digested than animal proteins. Chinese traditions of light-milling of grain and quick-steaming of vegetables offset these handicaps, but the vegetarian diet means an excess of roughage. Grains are bulky, digestive organs are overworked, and the body is more susceptible to intestinal diseases. Under Communist rule new ways of handling food have appeared along with new ways of handling men: agricultural production through bureaucratically directed labor brigades instead of individuals or family teams, food distribution through state planning instead of farmstead budgeting, consumption through public canteens instead of family tables. The available evidence indicates a lessening of per capita consumption of pork and a substantial rise in per capita consumption of sweet potatoes—the effect is the greatest peacetime worsening of nutrition in modern times.

Mechanization in Agriculture: Chickens and Eggs

A significant change in American habits of food consumption is clearly demonstrated by the 250 per cent increase in chickens and a 350 per cent increase in turkey consumption per capita that has occurred since 1930. The poultry industry has become big business; factories of 30,000 laying hens are not uncommon; and average annual production of eggs per hen has increased from 121 to 217. The twin goals of maximum meat and maximum egg production have been realized through improvements in breeding, feeding, disease control, and mechanized management. Production is concentrated upon only four or five commercial varieties of chickens fed to laboratory specifications with an omnibus mixture in the form of mash or in pellets. A modern hen lays a pound of eggs for each three pounds of feed consumed; young fryers generally yield a pound of body weight for each two pounds of feed eaten. Fowl plague has been eradicated and many formerly catastrophic diseases have been controlled by improved sanitation, vaccination, and medicated feeds.

Most striking has been the standardization of processes and the increase of scale in operations through mechanization. The hatching and rearing of young chicks is entirely by artificial devices. From egg laying to market delivery, almost no human handling is involved. Poultry houses are enclosed so that light, temperature, humidity, and ventilation can be precisely controlled. Two or three laying hens are closely confined in a cage with $1\frac{1}{2}$ square feet of floor space; multilayered banks of such cages suspended from above contain thousands of hens to facilitate mechanical feeding in time-regulated moving troughs, mechanical cleaning, and egg collecting on moving belts. A mechanized egg factory is a sizable operation: each day 60,000 hens consume $7\frac{1}{2}$ tons of feed and produce more than three tons of droppings; a minimum of 40,000 eggs per day would be required for commercial success. For such an operation, the human labor averages three tenths of a man-hour per hen per year. Owing to labor efficiency, fresh eggs, chickens, and turkeys are now available as everyday staples throughout the year, and poultry production operates without any government protection in the form of price supports or production quotas.

Applications from Microbiology

The importance of microbiology has become recognized only in the twentieth century. From near nothing in the 1930s, the United States production of antibiotics has expanded mightily:

to 3632 tons in 1963, valued at $338 million. The modern era draws upon its discoveries of the antibiotics to (1) combat infectious diseases that attack man and his domesticated animals, (2) combat many plant diseases not previously subject to control, (3) improve the nutrition of animals by supplying certain antibiotics to their nutrients, and (4) gain additional means of conserving foodstuffs never dreamt of before. Antibiotics are able to exert a stimulating effect upon animal growth. Penicillin and the tetracyclines (bacitracin and neomycin) occupy an important place in the feeding of poultry, pigs, and young ruminant animals, and increases in the growth response and food conversion are of the order of 5 to 50 per cent. Antibiotics are also used in the preservation of foodstuffs, including fresh and processed foods. Fish and poultry are usually preserved by immersion in ice, or in a solution, containing the antibiotic. Nystatin applied to the skin of bananas controls spoilage by fungi. Virus preparations and human and animal semen can be preserved by the use of certain antibiotics. Shortly it may be expected that microbes, such as algae, yeasts, and certain molds, will be economically feasible food sources.

Iron into Steel

The extraction and processing of iron ore is undergoing a quiet revolution, marked by global competition, giant ore carriers, tailored pellets, prereduction, and decentralization of steelmaking. Ore production and steelmaking are becoming more closely interlocked as increased technological capabilities are being used by giant corporations to achieve economic efficiency. All the world's sources of iron ore are economically available to steelmakers; at ocean freights of 50 cents per ton per 1000 miles, transport costs from Africa, South America, or Australia can be figured at $3 to $6 per ton. The future, however, lies not with low-grade ores, but with the use of tailored (prereduced) pellets of high iron content (ratio of iron to silica) that improve the pig-iron yield of blast furnaces with minimum coke consumption and lower labor costs. The trend is for prereduction to be accomplished at the mine sites, to save transport costs. Oxygen steelmaking is on the way to replacing open hearth furnaces. By 1970 an experimental continuous-flow steelmaking plant is expected to be in operation; raw materials will go in one end and out the other will come slabs or billets. Continuous production would supersede

the up-to-the-present batch process of steelmaking. (See the photograph of the integrated steel plant on p. 338.)

New Sources of Water

The need for developing unexploited sources of potable water is well understood. Analyses of United States water reserves from conventional sources (i.e., underground aquifers, flowing streams, or lakes) indicate that the nation's water use now exceeds, or soon will exceed, locally available water supplies. Conservation and improved use of existing sources, although helpful, will be inadequate to meet the projected increase in need. The practical alternatives in seeking new sources of water are the following:

1. Develop untapped conventional sources, including interbasin transfer.
2. Collect, process, and reclaim sewage or effluent waters.
3. Exploit a source of saline water (brackish or seawater) by construction of desalting facilities.

The first of these alternatives extends the conventional means of resource extraction; the latter two alternatives, through their application of modern technology, are examples of space intensification in resource conversion.

Water renovation, to meet drinking water standards, requires full treatment, an absorption process involving activated carbon plus chlorination. To approach a full recycle system would also require inclusion of a desalting process. If treatment of effluents sufficient to permit their discharge are considered as sewage costs, and only the final steps of renovation are charged as water-supply expense, production costs would approximate 36 to 40 cents per thousand gallons. Presumably much of this renovated water would be used to recharge existing underground aquifers, particularly in areas where groundwaters are approaching the upper limit of salinity tolerable in potable water supplies. The high-purity level of the renovated water will reduce the salinity level of the total mixed waters and make additional, now marginal, sources immediately available as usable supply without the expense of developing entirely new sources.

Of all the earth's water, 97 per cent is in the ocean. Desalination is a proven and feasible technology: shore-based commercial plants have been producing fresh water from the sea since the 1940s. The conversion of seawater to high-quality fresh water is an extraordinary achievement in the application of space intensification to resource conversion. The largest desalter in operation in the late 1960s produces 1.5 to 1.7 million gallons per day at costs of 85 cents per thousand gallons. The high quality of product, the full-year seasonal reliability, and potentially close physical relationship of source to point of use are factors favoring desalination processes. A conceptual design and cost analysis of a large dual-purpose seawater conversion and nuclear power generation plant for the Metropolitan Water District of Southern California calls for the creation of a man-made island to be built about one half mile off the coast of Bolsa Chica State Park (Orange County in Southern California) in about 30 feet of ocean depth, as a site for using nuclear power to produce both electrical energy (San Diego and Los Angeles systems) and desalted fresh water, the latter at the rate of 150 million gallons per day at an estimated cost of 22 cents per thousand gallons. At an additional cost of five cents per thousand gallons, the water is to be delivered to the nearest inland location (Yorba Linda) for entry into the existing Metropolitan Water District aqueducts and reservoirs.

Space Intensification in Space Adjustment

New technologies of miniaturization and microminiaturization involving radical new techniques that encapsulate components in ever-tinier packages but with multiplied powers, are being applied to communications, transport, industrial processes, and to living spaces.

Satellite communication represents a vast extension of man, because communication is possible almost without regard to distance. That is, unlike the costs of messages sent by telegraph cable, telephone cable, and microwave relay, the cost of satellite communication is nearly independent of distance. By 1967 extensive use already was being made of the Relay, Telstar, Syncom, and Early Bird communications satellites to bring events and programs of foreign origin, as they were happening, to television screens in the United States. Future communications satellites will be larger, will cover nearly all areas of the world, and will be capable of broadcasting directly into the home.

Electronic films are being used increasingly to reduce further the space requirements of television equipment, computer logic and memory circuits, two-way communications systems, missile and spacecraft controls, and pocket radios. As distinguished from photographic film, electronic films are delicate tattoos of electronically active material which have been condensed from hot vapors onto cold, hard insulating surfaces such as glass. Such thin films can act singly or in combination as whole electronic circuits or as components thereof. Uses of such films may eventually lead to a television camera only half an inch square, a hand-held battery-operated computer, a superconductive computer memory capable of storing 250,000 bits of information on a glass slide five inches square, videotape that can store pictures optically for later readout by an electron beam, and integrated circuiting for all forms of electronic equipment.

Computers promise a millionfold increase in man's capacity to handle information. Already familiar is their use in solving business problems and in increasing the efficiency of industrial operations. But computers are finding other applications as well—in medicine, the library, education, and in credit and finance. Tape-recorded and processed cardiograms, scoring of personality tests, and automated simultaneous testing of blood samples are being accomplished at various medical centers. Evaluation of information, its programming onto tape, and its instantaneous retrievability by computer are the bases for the building of centers of scientific information exchange from which those to whom it is available will have virtually pushbutton access to up-to-date information. The ultimate impact of the computer upon retail business lies in the automation of financial interchange. An integrated data-processing system can link customer with store and bank so as almost to eliminate the need for money or check writing. A person need only carry a bank identification card for insertion into a communication device between store and the computer of his banks; for cash transactions the computer could deduct the amount from the customer's account and credit it to the store's or flash an instantaneous credit rating to the store concerning installment purchases or credit transactions. Even utility and telephone bills could be paid by using one's home telephone.

The plans to build supersonic transports (SST) promise a most remarkable transportation advance for intensifying man's adjustment of space. An airplane carrying 350 passengers for 4000 miles at 1780 miles per hour would double the capacity and triple the speed of today's jets. A flight from

London to New York would require 2 hours 35 minutes, and from Tokyo to San Francisco 5 hours 40 minutes; Asia will then become as close in time to the United States as Europe is now. The SST is not just a larger, faster plane but one designed to cope with the physical forces to be met while flying faster than the speed of sound. As the most productive long-range vehicle in history, one SST can carry more passengers to and from Europe per year than six *Queen Mary's*, which is why the former "Queen of the Seas" was retired from service and is now used as a floating hotel-convention center at Long Beach, California. One objective, of course, in intensifying space adjustment is to increase the scarcest resource, skilled human productivity; another is to move valuable cargo in large volume from one end of the earth to the other.

Intensification through Regional Development

The Lower Mekong Basin project (Fig. 11.6), currently being developed in mainland Southeast Asia, is symbolic of all the efforts to modernize vast parts of the world through the simultaneous application of techniques for resource extraction, resource conversion, space adjustment, and space intensification in a coordinated manner. A high level of international technical, financial, and administrative collaboration is being achieved, and the social implications of the enterprise are far-reaching.

The vast program launched by the United Nations Economic Commission for Asia and the Far East (ECAFE) embodies the extensive development of the world's greatest international water-

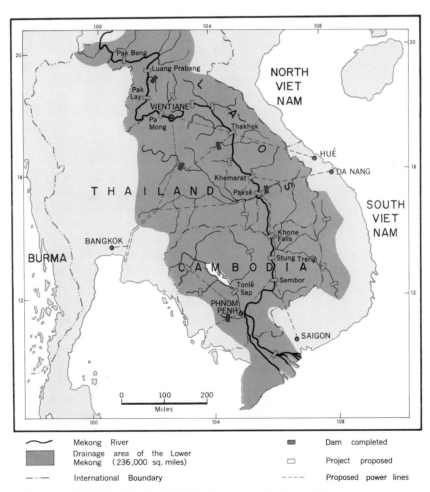

FIG. 11.6 THE LOWER MEKONG RIVER PROJECT. (Compare with Fig. 1.7B).

way. The initial project, under the direction of the Committee for Coordination of Investigations of the Lower Mekong Basin involves the almost complete harnessing of the river and its tributaries by means of gigantic engineering works. Four fifths of the drainage basin's area lies along the lower half of the Mekong River which passes through four countries: Laos, Thailand, Cambodia, and South Viet-Nam. The Lower Mekong Basin, in 1967, contained about 20 million people: about two million in Laos, mainly in towns along the river; about seven million in northeast Thailand, distributed between large towns and rural areas; some five million in Cambodia, whose capital Phnom Penh is the river's largest city; and about six million in the Mekong delta area of South Viet-Nam.

The lower Mekong River has a gentle but irregular gradient, but several rapids and falls render it nonnavigable above its delta. Altitudes above sea level are 15 feet at Phnom Penh, 200 miles from the sea, and 500 feet at Vientiane, 1050 miles from its mouth. The basic idea, for which preliminary plans were drawn in 1953, is to build a series of dams to (1) divide the river into steps, a series of connected, navigable lakes, each of which would generate a very large amount of hydroelectric power (installed capacity totaling five million kilowatts); (2) regulate and reduce the damage from wet-season floods; and (3) make available the irrigation of vast areas that now suffer annually from prolonged droughts. In 1956 a mission from the United States Bureau of Reclamation outlined the kinds of needed information: hydrology, map making, agriculture, climate, and others, all the surveys began in 1960.

In addition to the four Lower Mekong countries, 10 United Nations agencies, 20 donor countries, and numerous nongovernmental organizations are involved. Representatives of the four countries compose the Committee, a policy-making board of directors, which is served by an Advisory Group of engineering, economic, and educational experts and a General Manager who is the project's executive officer. The international scope and involvement is as immense as that of the river itself. The spectacular engineering achievements are expected to create new bases for social advancement of the regions affected. Local populations already are undergoing occupational training and being encouraged to diversify their diets and commercialize their products, for it is obvious that the massive

program for hydroelectric and irrigation storage development, flood control, and navigation improvement will have extensive repercussions. Rural areas will be protected against the calamities of seasonal drought and floods. Diet will be improved through regularization of supply and increase in yields of rice and fish, and diversification of crops. Excess production of food and agricultural raw materials can be exchanged for town-produced manufactured goods. Urban areas will benefit from new sources of foodstuffs, a plentiful supply of electric power, and vastly increased industrialization. Levels of living will be raised in the whole of the Lower Mekong. Further, there will be established the experience, the incentive, and the need for continued political, economic, and technical cooperation to operate and maintain the international system for water control, navigation, and electric power distribution.

A Summing Up

The space-intensification techniques include all those ways in which man utilizes space to its greatest advantage for himself. In part this has been achieved by the "feedback" process, in which the products of industrial technology are applied to intensify resource extraction, resource conversion, and space adjustment. But it also has meant the supplanting, in part, of wild and cultivated landscapes by an artificial or man-made landscape. The creation of urban concentrations has led the way to a new era of human densities on the earth; urban areas are demonstrative of how to support the most people in the least space. Cities, thus, are the most efficient areal technique invented by man for maximizing production and consumption. For example, on an area of about 200 acres located just north of Herald Square in New York City, about 150,000 workers are engaged in the women's clothing industry. The population supported by work in this small area exceeds the rural farm population in the entire state of Kansas.

The invention and innovation of a new technology rarely make all existing means of achieving a given end obsolete. Rather, a new technology makes it possible to do some things that previously could not be done at all. The choice of which technology to use in any situation in a free market depends on relative costs and profits, as the market allocates the gains and losses from the new technology's displacement of older technologies. The process of creative destruction is the critical function, and essential fact, of capitalism.

Human disasters in past time have generally been localized. The destructions of Crete and Carthage and Angkor were so severe that they never recovered, but, for mankind as a whole, the spread of civilization has been an almost continuous territorial expansion. Probably the total urban population of the world has never appreciably declined, except for rare periods of particular centuries. The awesome destruction during World War II did not diminish modern man's preference for city life; the damage was largely repaired in 20 years or less.

The evidence of the 20th century seems clear that man has expressed a preference for living in or in close contact with urban areas and their amenities for prolonging and enhancing life. The urbanization process and its industrial-technological by-products of improved shelter, food, health, transport are avidly followed and sought by most of the world's people. The urban way is an idea deemed true, useful, and valuable, and is in process of worldwide diffusion without much need of persuasion or compulsion. International agencies and sources of funds are speeding the process of change. Perhaps it always has been part of the human story that those with a clear vision of the evolutionary potential of a significant and exciting future are more likely to dedicate their lives to creative efforts to effect changes. The humanized earth has prevailed, and so will it continue to evolve.

SELECTED REFERENCES

Bibliography
Berry, B. J. L. and Allan Pred
    1961 *Central Place Studies: A Bibliography of Theories and Applications*. Philadelphia: Regional Science Research Institute. 153 pp.

About Cities as Concentrations
Kraeling, Carl H., and Robert M. Adams (eds.)
    1960 *City Invincible*. Chicago: University of Chicago Press. 446 pp.
Mumford, Lewis
    1961 *The City in History*. New York: Harcourt, Brace & World. 657 pp.
Weber, Max
    1958 *The City* (translated and edited by Don Martindale and Gertrud Neuwirth). Glencoe, Ill.: The Free Press. 242 pp. (Also available in paperback edition, 1966.)

About Evolution of the Industrial City
Adams, R. M.
    1966 *The Evolution of Urban Society*. Chicago: Aldine Publishing Co. 191 pp.
Handlin, Oscar, and John Burchard (eds.)
    1963 *The Historian and the City*. Cambridge, Mass.: The M.I.T. Press and Harvard University Press. 299 pp.
Polanyi, K., C. M. Arensberg, and H. W. Pearson
    1957 *Trade and Market in Early Empires*. Glencoe, Illinois: The Free Press. 382 pp.
Reissman, Leonard
    1964 *The Urban Process; Cities in Industrial Societies*. New York: Free Press of Glencoe. 255 pp.
Sjoberg, Gideon
    1960 *The Preindustrial City*. Glencoe, Ill.: The Free Press. 353 pp.
Taylor, Miller Lee, and Arthur R. Jones, Jr.
    1964 *Rural Life and Urbanized Society*. New York: Oxford University Press. 493 pp.

About the Rise of Urban America
Green, Constance M.
    1965 *The Rise of Urban America*. New York: Harper. 208 pp.

Kohn, Clyde F. (ed.)
  1961   *Urban Responses to Agricultural Change: a collection of papers.* Iowa City. 207 pp.
McKelvey, Blake
  1963   *The Urbanization of America, 1860–1915.* New Brunswick, N.J.: Rutgers University Press. 370 pp.
Smith, Wilson (ed.)
  1964   *Cities of our Past and Present, A Descriptive Reader.* New York: Wiley. 292 pp.
Strauss, Anselm L. (ed.)
  1968   *The American City: A Sourcebook of Urban Imagery.* Chicago: Aldine Publishing Co. 480 pp.
Tunnard, Christopher, and Henry Hope Reed
  1956   *American Skyline* (Mentor Book). New York: New American Library. 224 pp.
White, Morton, and Lucia White
  1962   *The Intellectual Versus the City.* Cambridge, Mass.: Harvard University Press and the M.I.T. Press. 270 pp.

About Urban Areas and Metropolitan Regions

Bollens, John C. and Henry J. Schmandt
  1965   *The Metropolis: Its People, Politics, and Economic Life.* New York: Harper & Row. 643 pp.
Dickinson, Robert E.
  1964   *City and Region; A Geographical Interpretation.* London: Routledge and K. Paul. 588 pp.
Hall, Peter
  1966   *The World Cities* (World University Library). New York: McGraw-Hill. 256 pp.
Hauser, Philip M., and Leo F. Schnore
  1965   *The Study of Urbanization.* New York: Wiley. 554 pp.
International Urban Research
  1959   *The World's Metropolitan Areas.* Berkeley: University of California Press. 115 pp.
Kiang, Ying-Cheng
  1964   *Urban Geography.* Charleston, Ill.: Privately Published. 265 pp.
Mayer, Harold M., and Clyde F. Kohn (eds.)
  1959   *Readings in Urban Geography.* Chicago: The University of Chicago Press. 625 pp.
Murphy, Raymond E.
  1966   *The American City, An Urban Geography.* New York: McGraw-Hill. 464 pp.

About Conurbations and Megalopolis

Chapin, Francis Stuart, Jr., and Shirley F. Weiss (eds.)
  1962   *Urban Growth Dynamics in a Regional Cluster of Cities.* New York: Wiley. 484 pp.
Gottman, Jean
  1961   *Megalopolis: The Urbanized Northeastern Seaboard of the United States.* New York: The Twentieth Century Fund. 810 pp.
Osborn, F. J., and A. Whittick
  1963   *The New Towns: Answer to Megalopolis.* New York: McGraw-Hill. 376 pp.
Tietze, Frederick J., and James E. McKeown (eds.)
  1964   *The Changing Metropolis.* Boston: Houghton Mifflin. 210 pp.
Von Eckardt, Wolf
  1964   *The Challenge of Megalopolis.* New York: Macmillan. 128 pp.

About Vertical Intensification of Space Use

Eckko, Garrett
  1964   *Urban Landscape Design.* New York: McGraw-Hill. 248 pp.
Spreiregen, Paul D.
  1965   *Urban Design: The Architecture of Towns and Cities.* New York: McGraw-Hill. 243 pp.

About Complexity of Internal Differentiation

Andrews, Richard B.
  1962 *Urban Growth and Development.* New York: Simmons-Boardman Publishing Corporation. 420 pp.

Fitch, Lyle C., et al.
  1964 *Urban Transportation and Public Policy.* San Francisco: Chandler Publishing Company. 279 pp.

Gist, Noel P., and Sylvia F. Fava
  1964 *Urban Society* (5th ed.). New York: Crowell. 623 pp.

Lang, Albert S., and Richard M. Soberman
  1964 *Urban Rail Transit: Its Economics and Technology.* Cambridge, Mass.: Massachusetts Institute of Technology Press. 139 pp.

Schnore, Leo F.
  1965 *The Urban Scene; Human Ecology and Demography.* New York: Free Press. 374 pp.

About Penalties of Human Concentration

Adrian, Charles R.
  1961 *Governing Urban America* (2nd ed.). New York: McGraw-Hill. 508 pp.

Berry, B. J. L.
  1963 *Commercial Structure and Commercial Blight.* Chicago: Department of Geography, University of Chicago, (Research Paper No. 85). 235 pp.

Berry, Brian J. L., and Jack Meltzer (eds.)
  1967 *Goals for Urban America.* Englewood Cliffs, N.J.: Prentice-Hall. 152 pp.

Doxiades, K. A.
  1966 *Urban Renewal and the Future of the American City.* Chicago: Public Administration Service. 174 pp.

Greer, Scott A.
  1966 *Urban Renewal and American Cities; The Dilemma of Democratic Intervention.* Indianapolis, Ind.: Bobbs-Merrill. 201 pp.

Jacobs, Jane
  1961 *The Death and Life of Great American Cities* (Vintage Book, V-241). New York: Vintage Books. 458 pp.

Meyer, John R. et al.
  1965 *The Urban Transportation Problem.* Cambridge, Mass.: Harvard University Press. 427 pp.

Mitchell, Robert B. (ed.)
  1964 *Urban Revival: Goals and Standards* (Annals of the American Academy of Political and Social Science, Vol. 352). Philadelphia: Academy of Political and Social Science. 234 pp.

Self, Peter
  1961 *Cities in Flood: The Problems of Urban Growth* (2nd ed.) London: Faber and Faber. 189 pp.

Smerk, George M.
  1965 *Urban Transportation; the Federal Role.* Bloomington, Ind.: Indiana University Press. 336 pp.

Vernon, Raymond
  1962 *The Myth and Reality of Our Urban Problems.* Cambridge, Mass.: Joint Center for Urban Studies, Massachusetts Institute of Technology and Harvard University. 84 pp.

Weaver, Robert C.
  1964 *The Urban Complex: Human Values in Urban Life.* Garden City, N.Y.: Doubleday. 297 pp.

Wilson, James Q. (ed.)
  1966 *Urban Renewal: The Record and the Controversy.* Cambridge, Mass.: Massachusetts Institute of Technology Press. 683 pp.

About Urbanization as a Worldwide Process

Ahmad, Qazi Shakil
  1965 *Indian Cities; Characteristics and Correlates* (Research Paper No. 102). Chicago: Department of Geography, University of Chicago. 184 pp.

Breese, Gerald W.
   1966   *Urbanization in Newly Developing Countries.* Englewood Cliffs, N.J.: Prentice-Hall. 151 pp.
Hauser, Philip M. (ed.)
   1961   *Urbanization in Latin America, Proceedings.* Paris: UNESCO. 331 pp.
Hoyt, Homer
   1962   *World Urbanization: Expanding Population in a Shrinking World* (Technical Bulletin 43). Washington, D.C.: Urban Land Institute. 50 pp.
Pitts, Forrest R. (ed.)
   1962   *Urban Systems and Economic Development.* Eugene, Ore.: University of Oregon, School of Business Administration. 126 pp.
Scientific American
   1965   *Cities.* New York: Alfred A. Knopf. 211 pp.
Sovani, N. V.
   1966   *Urbanization and Urban India.* New York: Asia Publishing House. 160 pp.
Turner, Roy (ed.)
   1962   *India's Urban Future.* Berkeley: University of California Press. 470 pp.
Unesco Regional Seminar on Urban-Rural Differences and Relationships in Southern Asia
   1964   *Urban-Rural Differences in Southern Asia.* Delhi, India: Unesco Research Centre on Social and Economic Development in Southern Asia. 147 pp.

PUBLIC BUILDINGS

GEORGE HOLTON, PHOTO RESEARCHERS

Angkor Wat, Cambodia

W. L. THOMAS, JR.

Buddhist Stupa, Thailand

JAPAN NATIONAL TOURIST ORGANIZATION

Hall of the Great Buddha, Nara, Japan

506

Old-Style Roman Catholic Church, Philippines

W. L. THOMAS, JR.

Taj Mahal, Agra, India

GEORGE HOLTON, PHOTO RESEARCHERS

507

*Roman Catholic Church,
Batalha, Portugal*

KATHERINE YOUNG, D.P.I.

HEILPERN PHOTOGRAPHY

508

Secondary School, Glastonbury, Connecticut, U.S.

Moscow University, U.S.S.R.

J. ALLEN CASH, RAPHO GUILLUMETTE

Parliament, Apia, Western Samoa

CHRISTA ARMSTRONG, RAPHO GUILLUMETTE

509

Statehouse, Annapolis, Maryland, U.S., 1774

M. E. WARREN, PHOTO RESEARCHERS

CONSULATE GENERAL OF FINLAND

510

Council of State, Helsinki, Finland

The Kremlin, Moscow, U.S.S.R.

LYNN PELHAM, RAPHO GUILLUMETTE

511

*United Nations
Building,
New York, U.S.*

HOWARD JOHNSON

An American Motel, United States

Hotel Row, Miami Beach, Florida, U.S.

512

LYNN PELHAM, RAPHO GUILLUMETTE

MEXICAN NATIONAL TOURIST COUNCIL

AMERICAN AIRLINES

A Bullring, Mexico

Candlestick Park, Baseball Stadium, San Francisco, U.S.

513

On the Beach at Coney Island, Brooklyn, U.S.

LITTON INDUSTRIES—AERO SERVICES DIVISION

A Vehicleless Mall, Ottawa, Canada

CANADIAN NATIONAL FILM BOARD

514

Urban Buildings of the Modern City, Plaza Colon, Mexico City

MARC AND EVELYNE BERNHEIM, RAPHO GUILLUMETTE

PART FIVE

The Human Prospect

The past two centuries have been witness to the fulfillment of human aspirations to a measure greater than the world has ever known. Men have fulfilled the potential to make the whole earth their home. A universal human habitat has been created. The earth has been humanized.

No other animal, save man, so dominates the earth and has the power through control of both inanimate energy and the organization of society to direct the earth's physical and biotic forces toward ends of its own choice. Whether he likes it or not or knows it or not, man is now the sole agent for the future of the whole evolutionary process on the earth. He is responsible not only for his own future but also the future of all the life-forms on the planet Earth.

Part Four of this book has set forth in considerable detail the many ways by which man, through the cumulative growth of culture, has learned to interpret and use the earth's materials and its space. The emphasis has been on the techniques acquired, and on how these have been applied in an ever-widening pattern until the whole earth has become caught up in a universal application of modern industrial-urban-high-speed-transport technology. In portraying the effects of human actions, the holistic view of all earth phenomena and processes has been retained, because all regions of the earth have relevancy for, and each has become interconnected with, all the others.

Man's role in changing the face of the earth has been part agent, part manager. Human phenomena and processes have always operated in particular places and, through time, have come to be both affected by and in turn modify the environments of those places. The changes that man has effected on the earth have been enormous. Man not only has removed thousands of square miles of forest communities, but he has also learned to create whole new forests of desired kinds. His appetite for mineral substances is gargantuan, but he has learned to appreciate the "limiting factor" of the valuable trace elements. Although he has tried almost everything harvestable from the sea, he has found the cultivation of fish in man-made ponds to be most productive. Water is his near-universal solvent, but so great are man's demands that fresh water is no longer either pure or free, and some quite humid regions barely have enough of it. In prehistoric time the most productive crops and animals were domesticated for use as food and fiber, but in recent centuries they not only have been transferred all round the world as favored life-forms but also have been so transformed through selective breeding as to be scarcely recognizable, compared to their sixteenth-century ancestors.

From the host of raw materials that man has discovered and learned to produce and use, a whole new world has been created by techniques for their transport and assembly. Conversion of raw materials involved techniques not only for their processing, but also for manufacturing a seemingly endless variety of items in all shapes, sizes, materials, and uses, many of which in turn are component items for further assembly into industrial products of considerable complexity (books, automobiles, jukeboxes, electronic computers). Yet man's conquest of matter has been more than material: the invention and diffusion of specific techniques (double-entry bookkeeping, cost accounting, legal codes, insurance, public ownership of corporate stocks) have gone hand in hand with general technological progress to give rise to the means and methods, the organizational "mix" of capital, labor, and management for production, distribution, and consumption of the contents of our modern cornucopia.

Man's further achievement has been the increased ease and speed by which things, people, and ideas can be conveyed round the world. Space has been adjusted by shortening the effective distance of travel and transport, by the evolution of trade in increasing volumes over increasing distances, by increasing the speed and accuracy of communication, and by evolving political and administrative organizations responsible for regional or worldwide jurisdiction of special processes or forces.

The true measure of man's organized complexity lies in the ways that he has learned to intensify the use of the space at his disposal. More and more is being produced: per plant, per animal, per acre, per man-hour. The traditional methods no longer suffice; man has learned to enhance quality as well as quantity. Cities, through the concentrations of men made possible by multilevel architecture, are the most efficient instrument yet devised by man for utilizing resources in most types of production, distribution, and consumption. They are also the centers of increased intellectual contacts which stimulate cross-fertilization of ideas, recognition of opportunities, and facilities for research; all these are conducive to increases in future productivity. Industrialization and urbanization have infinitely augmented the puny power of man the animal: tools by which man is transforming the surface of the earth are urban-produced.

Part Five of this book examines the effects of man's actions on man himself, his numbers and his prospects for continued longevity on the earth. All unforeseen, man's creation of culture has included a fundamental change in the balance of births and deaths which control man's numbers on earth. In the slow transition from primitive societies to the modern urban-industrial civilization, men applied death control before they learned to apply a simultaneous control to births. Ours is the age of the intense peopling of the earth, a wholly new phenomenon. Compared to most of human time on the earth, our present rate of growth is something like the speed of an express train compared to the pace of a tortoise.

The inherent quality of the earth's basic resources has not changed. The earth continues to intercept solar energy at the same rate. Neither has there been a change in the inherent nature of the human animal. Men had the same basic structure, arrangement of muscles, and brain ten thousand years ago as today. The change in human numbers has resulted from the changes in methods that men have learned to apply in their dealings with the earth's resources. Even more of a decisive factor for man's future longevity on the earth than the sheer press of numbers of men is the rise in per capita consumption of food, materials, and energy. People in remote corners of South America, Asia, and Africa are learning to use European-American derived means of production, transportation, and communication, and are adjusting their institutions and ways of life to Western patterns that perforce require an increase in their rates of consumption. The Western nation-states, in the cause of exporting their ways of life to other peoples, are engaged in a great competitive enterprise to raise the "levels of living" (read, "rates of consumption") for most of the rest of the world. Can everyone be as profligate as a modern American?

Because of culture, human populations are unique in the rapidity with which they have been able to change their environments and thus their requisites. There seems little doubt that the present era of rapid change is an unusually exciting period in which to be living on the earth. The character of its surface, the direction of its physical-biotic forces, the patterning of its regions, the intensity in organization of its political, economic, and social space all are unique. No earlier men experienced anything like our humanized earth, although, as culture bearers and as transmitters of culture to ensuing generations they played a role in shaping it.

But clearly the present pace of rapid technological and population change cannot long continue. What *are* the limits of the earth? What are the limits in numbers of men, in food supply, in kinds and volumes of materials, in the amounts of energy to be harnessed, in the skills that men can learn and apply, and in the ideas to be added to the cultural level already attained by man? It has been suggested that Science teels that the limits are still far off in the future, although just how far is somewhat arguable. To a population total that increases in the future at exponential rates, even Science cannot hold out an endless prospect. To a population that levels off at a controlled figure not more than two or three times that of the present total, Science can hold out the technological goal of reasonable sufficiency for all for a very considerable period.

And yet! There remain bothersome questions. Will continued technological improvement in material things suffice? Has biopsychological man improved in keeping with technological man? Will the limits of the earth, and its life pattern, lie within the earth, or will those limits lie within the cultural nature of man himself? Is the physical nature of the planet Earth to be the determinant (the resource of energy and materials), or is it the behavioral pattern of mankind that will be the determinant (social, economic, political, and psychological customs in practice)? There are those human beings who worriedly fear that tremendously able technologic mankind may at any moment, in a frenzy of brutish anger and hatred, not only extinguish his whole species but also destroy all life on the planet Earth, or even may destroy the planet as a finite unit in the universe. The latter is not yet conceivable, for the earth has withstood far greater stresses than man can apply, but the former is not totally inconceivable. It is not, however, the threat of total destruction of life-forms on the earth that is of real concern. The significant thing is whether man, having come to evolutionary dominance on an earth which he has remade, can live in relative peace with himself in all of his ethnic diversity, cultural variety, and biopsychological heterogeneity.

There is little doubt that biological mankind has diversified greatly, during the last 35,000 years of the reign of *Homo sapiens sapiens,* into a congeries of slightly dissimilar ethnic stocks as man spread to the far corners of the earth, there to work out his localized living systems and breed local strains of man. Biological convergence is a very recent phenomenon, in one sense, shown in such territories as the United States, Brazil, and Argentina. But biological convergence has far to go before mankind is socially and psychologically united. Will technological man be able to live with biopsychological man in the near future? Physical Science has expressed concern about Cultural Practice, but physical scientists are themselves subject to all the biopsychological vagaries of mankind in general. The historic record of competitive struggle for units of space on our earth, in which to elaborate particular human living systems, does not make the prospect for peaceful Utopia very immediate. The modern record of cultural strife within individual societies, such as within South Africa, India, and the United States does not improve the chances of the prospect. A sort of supreme question may not be that of the duration of continuance of the resources of the earth, but whether biosociopsychologic man can devise unified cultural systems whereby all mankind may share in the harvest of human material technology. Can mankind enjoy the humanized earth now created and technologically procedured, or must there continue an evolutionary kind of competitive struggle between varieties of man to some end no man may now envision?

Part Five views the immediate future of the humanized earth on the basis of the discernible present trends in human cultural evolution. All the past is prologue to the future human prospect!

CHAPTER *12*
The Population Spiral

Animals which exist in superabundance are those, unlike men, whose body size is small and whose reproductive cycles are short. Many fish and insects, for example, are clearly more numerous than men: codfish, shrimp, sardines, ants, grasshoppers, flies, and moths, among others, come immediately to mind. Among the mammals, however, astounding as it may seem, man at present is the most abundant single species. This does not mean, for instance, that there are more men than rats or mice or squirrels, because the total number of living rodents is much greater than the total number of living men. But all living men are of one species whereas the rodents number more than 300 different species.

The Numbers of Man and Animals

Among the primates, man is not only the most numerous single species, but also his present numbers exceed the sum total of numbers of all the other 500-plus living species of primates. This fact becomes all the more spectacular when the growth periods of the several primates are compared (Table 12.1). Man is not much different from the other anthropoid apes in the length of his gestation or prenatal period (the sequence of events from conception to birth). But after birth, man's growth pattern differs markedly; the child-bearing period (onset of puberty) is long delayed, the completion of general growth is even further extended. The anthropoids, not man, have the edge in reproductive potential. That is, chimpanzees can produce offspring which in turn produce offspring far more quickly than man, so that in a 45-year period, say,

potentially six times the numbers of chimpanzees as of men can be produced.

What is astounding, then, about the extreme abundance of human beings is not that it is a recent phenomenon, but that an abundance ever could have occurred at all. In his reproduction cycle, man is at an overwhelming disadvantage compared with most other life-forms. A bacterium, for example, can produce itself in a half hour or so, whereas a human baby takes nine months of gestation and then a long period of growing up through infancy, childhood, and adolescence. So much time is spent in reaching sexual maturity that the average human generation covers a span of about 25 years.

Man's specialization lies in the marked elongation of his fertile period (28 years in man compared to 16 in the chimpanzee), and in the long postponement of the onset of senility (man's total life span is now more than twice that of other primates). The increased opportunity for successful completion of full reproductive cycles by more individuals is a consequence of biologic adaptation to the acquisition of culture. There are *more than* $3\frac{1}{3}$ billion (3,333,333,333) people on the earth's surface. Considering that man is a land animal and that the earth's surface is 70 per cent water, the numbers of mankind can be described only in terms of abundance.

Man's Capacity to Reproduce

The number of children actually born to each couple is generally far less than the maximum number possible. The decisions to produce fewer children than the maximum possible are personal,

TABLE 12.1 AVERAGE DURATION OF GROWTH PERIODS IN DIFFERENT PRIMATES

Primate Species	Gestation (Weeks)	Beginning of Puberty (Years)	Eruption of Last Permanent Teeth (Years)	Completion of General Growth (Years)	Life Span (Years)
Lemur	18	?	?	3	14
Macaque	24	2	6.4	7	24
Gibbon	30	8.5	8.5	9	30
Orangutan	39	?	9.8	11	30
Chimpanzee	34	8.8	10.2	11	35
Gorilla	?	9	10.5	11	?
Man	38	13.7	20.5	20	75

but invariably culturally influenced. If these cultural impediments to productivity were cast aside, some very significant patterns of population increase would result.

For example, around the beginning of the nineteenth century English and American women were having seven or eight children, on the average. Families of 15 to 20 were not unknown. John Wesley was the 15th child in a family of 19 children, and Benjamin Franklin was the sixth son in a family of ten children! Today, there are many places in the world (such as among settled Arabs in Southwest Asia) where each woman has, on the average, about eight children. Under conditions in which women live through their full span of reproductive years and exercise their full reproductive capacities, they would bear on the average well over eight children. Since almost half of all infants are girls, each woman could contribute, on the average, four potential mothers to the next generation. If we assume there are four generations in a century, a wholly unimpeded exercise of human productive capacity could give a 256-fold increase in the span of 100 years:

One mother could produce

4 girl babies of second generation, who could produce

16 girl babies of third generation, who could produce

64 girl babies of fourth generation, who could produce

256 girl babies a century after their great-great-grandmother was born.

Continuation of the fertility pattern of Colonial America would have yielded an approximation of this trend. Obviously, the pattern has not prevailed, or else the population of the present United States (without any further influx of immigrants

since Independence) would have exceeded by a thousandfold the present total population of the world.

It is not difficult to see that a 256-fold increase in one century or a 16,384-fold increase over two centuries could give rise to insuperable problems. But these figures are cited only to indicate what is biologically possible, that the potential for population growth is explosive. Fortunately, no large population or nation has ever produced at maximum capacity. The actual number of live births (fertility) has always been far below the maximum reproductive capacity (fecundity).

What is, and has been, the actual situation of population increase? For our answer, we look first at the human fossil record and contemporary primitive societies to secure some indications of human living conditions prior to the development of food raising. Second, we shall look at the actual record of population growth over the world to the present time. Our concern, first, is to arrive at an understanding of why a difference exists in human reproduction between a biologically maximum capacity and a culturally inhibited productivity of lesser quantity, and second to determine the order of magnitude of this difference. If man is biologically capable of reproducing himself 256-fold in a century, but is not doing so, then at what rates has he increased?

Primitive Society and Its Vital Statistics

Most of the human time span on the earth was passed at a strictly food-gathering stage of culture, with local circumstances (shellfish, salmon runs, abundant large game) favorable for semisedentary food collectors, including hunters. It takes about two square miles of fertile territory, on the average, to support a human individual under a gathering and collecting economy. Since only about one third of the earth's land surface could ever have been used successfully (eliminating the bulk of the earth's land surface which is too dry, too high, or too cold), the maximum possible food-gathering population for the whole world would have totaled about 10 million. More likely, the mid-Paleolithic era population of gatherers and collectors scarcely exceeded half that number. Surely any population change over the several hundreds of millennia prior to the invention of food growing (marked by the establishment of sedentary farming life following man's domestication of plants and animals) was all but imperceptible. Local declines were offset by small increases elsewhere, but always without causal connections between regions isolated from one another.

The life cycle of early men and the length of an average generation were very short; only the rare individual survived to pass through a full reproductive cycle into old age. For example, among the 38 individuals identified from the fossil skeletal remains of Peking man (*Homo erectus*) from the Lower Cave at Choukoutien, 15 were children no more than 14 years of age. Among the seven adults whose age at death could be determined with some accuracy, three died before age 30, three between 40 and 50, and one between 50 and 60. Similar evidence comes from the Upper Cave at Choukoutien, and from study of the 187 human fossils found in Europe. Through fragmentary, the evidence clearly suggests that an advanced age was seldom reached. Human survival, from predators, diseases, and famines, was in such a delicate balance that the extremely high mortality could only have been offset by high fertility. Thus, for early man, birthrates and death rates were both high; but, since man did survive, births obviously held a narrow margin.

The difficulties in securing vital statistics for peoples living without cultivation are enormous. About the best that can be done is to observe the sizes of populations that can be supported by contemporary gatherers and collectors, determine the sizes of territories over which they range, and calculate their population densities, assuming that conditions in the past were somewhat similar. Australian Aborigines, for example, inhabited a continent that provided meager resources for the support of people having only very simple equipment and little property of any sort. Populations had to be dispersed in relatively small groups. The search for sustenance required long seasonal migrations during which aged or infirm persons sometimes had to be abandoned. The inhabitants of the whole island continent of Australia at the time of its discovery by Western man probably numbered between one quarter and one third of a million. The crude population density of Aboriginal Australia was thus of the order of magnitude of one person per ten square miles.

Man's cultural circumstances place many "roadblocks" in the way of maximizing births. Any number of taboos and customs surround sexual behavior and create a considerable gap between fecundity and fertility. Marriage customs can postpone the arrival of a woman's first child until long after puberty. Some cultural traits interfere with copulation or otherwise block the biological sex function, whereas others lead to abortions. A further ancient practice that served to keep population numbers in harmony with territorial resources was infanticide, which was widely practiced, as we know from accounts of ancient Greece, and from China and Japan.

The conclusion reached is that the growth of the population of the world prior to the invention of food production was so slow as to be all but imperceptible. Regional fluctuations, a gain in one area offsetting a decrease elsewhere, tended to cancel each other. For the world's population to reach a total just short of 10 million by about 9000 B.C., an overall growth in man's numbers of about two tenths of one per cent per century was all that was necessary.

Evolution of Population

Reconstruction, within reasonable limits of error, of the estimated population of the world from 10,000 or 9000 B.C. (end of the Paleolithic period in southwest Asia) to the present time, discloses that an enormous increase has occurred, especially in the past three centuries, not only in the numbers of the world's peoples, but also in the rate of growth of population (Table 12.2).

Most of the hundreds of millennia of man's time on earth were required to produce a total population of one billion persons (about A.D. 1850). A doubling of numbers, the production of a population of two billion persons, was reached only 75 years later (1925); only 37 years more were necessary for a population of three billion persons

TABLE 12.2 WORLD POPULATION GROWTH OVER THE PAST 12,000 YEARS

Time	World Population Total
10,000–9000 B.C.	Between 5 and 10 million
Time of Christ	Between 200 and 300 million
A.D. 1650	500 million
A.D. 1850	1,000 million (1 billion)
A.D. 1925	2,000 million (2 billion)
A.D. 1962	3,000 million (3 billion)

(1962). For all the long time span prior to the beginnings of cultivation of food, population growth among the world's gatherers and collectors could only have averaged about 0.02 per thousand per year, or a 2 per cent increase in a thousand years. By contrast, the rate of present world population growth approximates 20 per thousand per year. Hence, there has occurred a thousandfold increase in man's rate of growth in numbers during his habitation of the earth.

Of the total number of men that were ever born (Table 12.3) about 4 per cent are now living. Granted that there is a wide range of possible error in estimating prehistoric and early historic populations and that the numbers can never be known precisely, the conclusion is nevertheless clear: in his creation of a humanized earth, man has experienced a fantastic acceleration in his growth rate.

Thomas Robert Malthus and His Principle of Population

The person credited with drawing attention to the problems created by the trend toward a rapid increase in man's numbers, is the Reverend Thomas Robert Malthus. In A.D. 1798 there was published in London a small book, entitled *An Essay on the Principle of Population as it Affects the Future Improvement of Society.* For the second edition in 1803, longer and more carefully docu-

TABLE 12.3 TOTAL NUMBERS OF PEOPLE WHO HAVE LIVED

Time	Number of Births	Per Cent of Total of All Persons Ever Born
600,000 to 9000 B.C.	12 billion	16
9000 B.C. to A.D. 1650	42 billion	54
A.D. 1650 to 1962	23 billion	30

mented, Malthus discarded anonymity when setting forth the basic statement of his principles.

Unchecked, Malthus said, populations tend to grow in a geometric progression, 1, 2, 4, 8, 16, 32 . . . , doubling in successive generations about every 25 years. However, he reasoned, man's food supplies, so necessary for his continued existence, could not be increased in more than arithmetic progression: 1, 2, 3, 4, 5, 6, ... A doubling of food production over a 25-year period, by improved farming methods or by opening new lands to cultivation, carries no assurance that another doubling can occur in the next 25 years. During each period, the increase in food production could not be expected to be equal, Malthus contended, as greater energy and ingenuity are required to wrest more food from marginally less valuable land not previously in use. Hence, Malthus concluded, population growth inevitably outruns food supplies.

Malthus' *Principle of Population* stated:

1. Population is necessarily limited by the means of subsistence.
2. Population invariably increases where the means of subsistence increases, unless prevented by some very powerful and obvious checks.
3. These checks, and the checks which repress the superior power of population and keep its effects on a level with the means of subsistence, all are resoluble into moral restraint, vice, and misery."

Malthus' "moral restraint" included continence and delayed marriage; these were the preventive checks which he felt man could exert to curtail his own numbers and reap the rewards of better living conditions. But he was not hopeful that the mass of the population would exercise sufficient restraint, even under the threat of poverty; he foresaw that the positive checks on population growth were starvation, disease, and war.

Malthus was not so much wrong as he was premature. Although he recognized that migration and improved techniques of production would temporarily postpone the difficulties engendered by population increase, he could not have been expected to foresee the tremendous burst of productivity in the modern West during the nineteenth and twentieth centuries, which brought progressive release from the positive checks on population growth. Malthus also could not foresee that Europe during the same period would exercise a preventive check by drastically reducing its birthrates through the spread of birth-control practices. It was not poverty and disease in Europe but the improved living conditions and rising aspirations that motivated the trend toward birth regulation. Not necessity among the suffering poor induced restraint, but the exercise of human choice (combining foresight with prudence) among the middle and upper classes started the trend toward reduced fertility. And the modern trend, which resulted in a slowing of Europe's rate of increase, came late, only after several centuries during which Europeans and their descendants had increased faster than the rest of the world.

Increased Human Longevity

Very great differences in rates of growth of population have occurred among the different regions of the world. During the three centuries of the modern era (1650 to 1950) when the world's population underwent a fivefold increase (from about 500 million to about 2½ billion), it was Europe and especially the overseas areas to which Europeans migrated and settled that experienced the most rapid population growth (Table 12.4).

Many technologic, social, and economic changes that had their origin in Europe have combined to accelerate the rate of population growth, principally through a drastic drop in death rates which has resulted in an unprecedented increase in average longevity. For example, the average life expectancy of a Roman at the beginning of the Christian Era was no more than 30 years; for people in western Europe and North America by 1650 to 1700, about 33 years. As recently as 1880, death rates in Massachusetts allowed only about 40 years of life on the average to each infant; by 1900 longevity had increased to 48 years. Now, life expectancy at birth in western Europe and North America is just over 70 years (all insurance companies will "bet" you on this), a tremendous increase during the present century of more than 20 years of added life. Life expectancy in the Soviet Union and Japan is not far distant from 70 years. Perhaps no other achievement of modern civilization has been so glorified as having added so much to human happiness.

Three factors have contributed to the decline in death rates first evident in Europe and areas of European settlement:

1. The rise in levels of living owing to
   (a) technological advances, and
   (b) peace and tranquility as a result of the establishment of relatively powerful and stable governments.
2. The achievements in public health (environmental sanitation) and improved personal hygiene (e.g., purifying food and water, thus reducing parasitic and infectious diseases).
3. The growing contributions of modern medicine (e.g., recent progress in insecticides and chemotherapy).

What happened was an upset of the previous near equilibrium between high birthrates and equally high death rates which typified the previous millennia of human evolution. The European realization of the significance of the old Chinese invention of vaccination for smallpox was but the first of a number of dramatic discoveries that led to the deferment of death in infants and children. The increased application of new findings in biology and medicine, combined with improved agricultural production, better transportation, and the emergence of an industrial society, created a set of circumstances which drastically lowered death rates and thereby greatly increased the efficiency of human reproduction. Data from France provide an example of the effects of increasing longevity:

Era	Births	Alive at Age 1	Alive at Age 20	Alive at Age 60
Eighteenth century	1000	767	502	214
Present-day	1000	960	940	754

While mortality in western Europe was declining sharply toward the end of the eighteenth century and in the early part of the nineteenth century, fertility maintained its usual high levels. Only with a considerable time lag (of as much as a century or more) did birthrates begin to decline to their present levels between 15 to 20 births per 1000 persons per year.

Until 25 years ago most of the world's people

TABLE 12.4 POPULATION GROWTH BY CONTINENTS, A.D. 1650 TO 1950

Region	Population (in Millions)		
	A.D. 1650	A.D. 1950	Increase
Europe (including U.S.S.R.)	100	590	6 times
North America	1	168	168 times
Latin America	7	163	23 times
Oceania (including Australia)	2	13	6½ times
Asia	290	1450	5 times
Africa	100	200	2 times

had a life expectancy at birth no greater than did western Europeans during the Middle Ages. Only Japan, among nations of non-European stock, had appreciably increased longevity through decrease of its death rate. But now the situation has been dramatically changed. Death rates have been, and are being, drastically curtailed (e.g., Algeria, Mexico, Costa Rica, Malaysia, all have cut mortality rates by more than 50 per cent in 20 years), while birthrates continue high. The major force of change has been scientific and technological. For example, in late 1946 and early 1947 the public health services of Ceylon had the houses of the island sprayed with DDT. The death rate fell 40 per cent within a single year. As a direct result of ever more people living longer lives, population growth is now greater among non-Europeans than among those of European stock. Most of the rest of the world is entering its phase of "death control" that European peoples have already experienced.

Differing Patterns of Population Change

Thus, in forming a true picture of the world population situation, a further important consideration is that different areas are experiencing different rates of growth. A map of world population distribution is analogous to a snapshot or still picture taken of the surface of a cauldron of boiling soup, whereas in reality some elements are stationary or nearly so and others are in rapid motion. An empirical consideration of all the countries for which some kind of statistical information is available reveals five categories or phases of population changes: (1) high stationary, (2) early expanding, (3) late expanding, (4) low stationary, and (5) declining. Figure 12.1 portrays the worldwide patterns, by countries, of these five categories.

High Stationary Phase

Growth of population in regions of this category is nil, or only sporadic. Birthrates and death rates are both high, ranging between 40 and 50 per thousand each year. Agrarian populations live near or at subsistence levels, as tendencies toward population increase are offset by frequent and rarely controlled famines, epidemics, floods, and droughts. For most of human time, the entire world must have been in this phase, until, with improvements in levels of living, certain Western countries left the rest of the world behind.

Countries still in this high stationary category are Afghanistan, Ethiopia, Indonesia (outside of Java), Iran, Saudi Arabia, parts of South America, and most of Negro Africa (see Table 12.4). If and when modern health services and measures for combating famine by increased industrialization are introduced, these countries have the potential for tremendous population increases.

Early Expanding Phase

This category is marked by continuation of high birthrates but with a lowering or decline in previously high death rates. Birthrates of about 40 per thousand per year with death rates of 20 to 25 per thousand per year are typical. The differences between such figures provide large net increases of population. Countries experiencing this category of population change are predominantly agrarian, but have benefited from technological advances which have led to increased agricultural production, the beginning of industrialization, and the development of transport and communications systems. Public health services have begun to check disease and epidemics. A school system, although inadequate for all, has reduced illiteracy. A measure of peace is being experienced, as a relatively strong central government has curtailed insecurity and civil strife.

Countries now in this early expanding category are the former colonial territories of Asia, such as India, Pakistan, Burma, Ceylon, Malaysia, Viet-Nam, Java, and Korea. In addition, this category prevails in China, Turkey, Egypt, Madagascar, Mexico, Central America, most of highland South America, and Brazil. Modest rates of increase have meant huge additions in population to those countries, such as China, India, and Pakistan, where populations were massive before recent growth began.

Late Expanding Phase

Birthrates have declined in this category, but death rates have declined more rapidly, and a net population increase continues to be registered. Countries in this category typically have birthrates ranging from 30 to 35 per thousand per year and death rates of less than 20 per thousand. Relatively advanced agriculture and modern industry have brought urban patterns of living accompanied by modern sanitation and public health services. Countries in this late expanding category include the Soviet bloc (U.S.S.R., Poland, Rumania, Yugo-

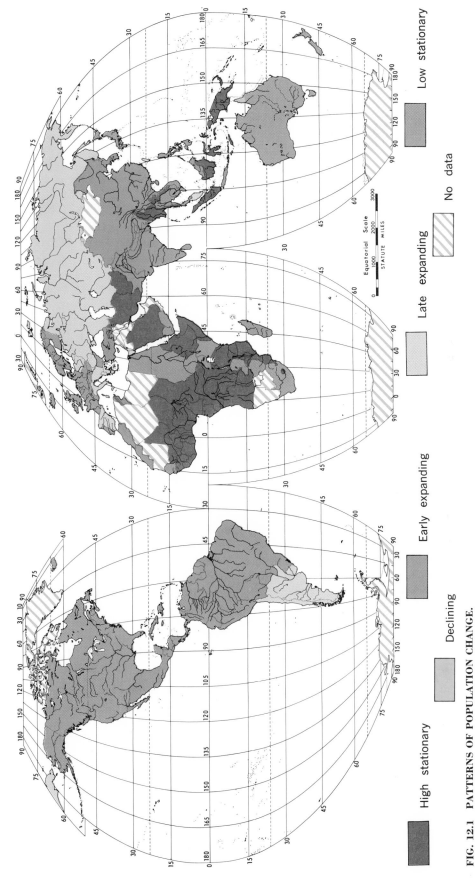

High stationary   Early expanding   Late expanding   Low stationary

Declining   No data

Equatorial Scale
0   1000   2000   3000
STATUTE MILES

FIG. 12.1 PATTERNS OF POPULATION CHANGE.

525

slavia), Italy, Spain, Puerto Rico, Argentina, Chile, Uruguay, Israel, and Taiwan. These are mostly countries which are experiencing conflicts between political or religious ideologies desirous of population expansion and the humanitarian or economic needs for population stability. The Soviet Union, for example, can exercise a choice between raising the level of living for its present population through increased production or diluting the present relatively modest level of living of its people by a further increase in population.

Low Stationary Phase

The low stationary category is marked by birthrates and death rates which are both low and roughly equal so that the population is kept relatively stationary. During the 1930s more than a dozen countries of western, northern, and central Europe (those with the highest standards and levels of living in the world) were in this phase, as well as the United States, Australia, and New Zealand. Significantly, only one country in the whole of Asia, Africa, or South America has ever attained the low stationary category. Japan, with a birthrate less than that of the United States, entered this phase in the mid-1950s. The country currently with the stablest population is East Germany.

Declining Phase

This category is marked by an actual decline in the total population of a country through an excess of deaths over births. It is not so much that the death rate is excessively high as that the birthrate is extremely low. The depopulation of certain islands, such as Tasmania, or the drastic reductions in populations of tropical Caribbean or Pacific islands (for example, the decimation of the Marianas from more than 50,000 people in 1521 to less than 1,800 by 1764) were negative reactions to the expansion of Europeans and their diseases. Only Hungary at the present time is in this declining phase category.

The foregoing five categories are represented in the mosaic (compare Fig. 12.1 with both end-paper maps) of total world population growth at the present time. Clearly, each country is experiencing its own phase of population change. Such change can also be viewed dynamically for particular countries. Great Britain, for example, was in the high stationary category before the advent of the agricultural and industrial revolutions. With ad-

vances in medicine, sanitation, and rising levels of living sustained by overseas emigration and colonialism, Great Britain moved successively through the early expanding and late expanding phases to the present low stationary category.

Each of the five categories of population change is gradational or transitional, one with another. A particular country or region may be a "borderline" case and in successive short periods alternate between one category or another; or a country, after many years in one category, may switch to another category as a result of an abrupt change in either its birth or death rate. Two examples will suffice to demonstrate such changes. France, for the ten years between 1936 and 1946, when its death rate exceeded the birthrate, was the outstanding example of a country in the declining phase category. After World War II, France became very population-conscious and experienced a relatively marked excess of births over deaths, to the extent that in recent years it has moved from the declining to the late expanding category. During the 1930s, the United States was in the low stationary phase, but since World War II it also has been in the late expanding category. The birthrate for 1965 was 19.4 per thousand, whereas the death rate was only 9.4 per thousand, creating an annual excess of births over deaths of almost two million. However, the United States trend is toward return to the low stationary category: Since 1954 the annual death rate has nearly stabilized, fluctuating upward only in those years marked by influenza epidemics, whereas the birthrate has been declining continuously since 1957. In 1965, for example, registered births totaled just under four million, the smallest number for any year since 1953 and the fourth consecutive annual decrease.

The Modern Prevalence of People and Their Distribution over the Earth

No one can ever know *exactly* how many people there are in the world. Births and deaths are recorded incompletely, or not at all; censuses are inaccurate or nonexistent for large areas of the world. The census results and estimates in current use are those collected from each country and evaluated by the Statistical Office and the Population Division of the United Nations. The United Nations estimate for midyear 1965 was that the world population totaled about 3285 million.

TABLE 12.5 POPULATION BY CONTINENTS, 1965

Area	Number	Per Cent
Asia	1,840,000,000	56
Europe (including U.S.S.R.)	674,000,000	20.5
Africa	302,000,000	9 +
North America	287,000,000	9 −
South America	164,000,000	5
Oceania (including Australia)	18,000,000	0.5
Total	3,285,000,000	100

Breaking this down by continents results in the distribution shown in Table 12.5.

The world's population is, and always has been, unevenly distributed over the earth's surface (see endpaper maps). Some areas are empty or nearly so, whereas other areas literally swarm with humanity. It is truly astounding that about two thirds of the people now present on the earth live on about 7 per cent of the land surface, whereas more than half the land surface supports only 5 per cent of the people. The four regions of greatest population concentration, eastern Asia, south Asia, western and central Europe, and the northeastern United States, are the positive results of man's historic adjustment to and development of world resources. And the eight great nearly empty areas, Greenland, Northern Canada and Alaska, Siberia, central Asia, Sahara, Amazon Basin, central and northern Australia, Antarctica, are the negative results of the same historic adjustment.

Asia contains two great areas of population concentration (see back endpaper)—eastern and southern; yet within each general area there are clearly observable variations of intensity. In eastern Asia, the zones of densest population are (1) the three southern islands of Japan; (2) the western zone of Korea extending north into the Manchurian lowlands; (3) within China, several regions that stand out—the North China plain south to include the Yangtze River lake basins and delta, the Szechwan basin, lower valley of the Si River, and the southeast coast; and (4) the offshore islands of Taiwan and Hainan. By contrast, Southeast Asia reveals only small clusters of dense population concentrations, the two largest being coastal North Viet-Nam and the island of Java. The great populations of India and Pakistan are prominent (1) from the Ganges River delta westward to the Indus River and (2) along both coasts of peninsular India. Southwestern Ceylon is also part of this high population cluster of south Asia.

The striking feature of Europe is the concentration of population that focuses upon the Low Countries at the southern end of the North Sea. The heavily populated coastal zone extends from the mouth of the Elbe River in Germany to the mouth of the Seine River in northern France. Two arms extend inland: one south up the Rhine River to Switzerland, down the Rhone River through southern France, thence to northern Italy; the other arm stretches east along the southern margin of the North European Plain into the Russian Ukraine. In addition, there are several separate clusters: in England and northern Ireland, around Barcelona along the east coast of Spain, around Oporto in northwest Portugal. However, north of 60° N. latitude (north of Stockholm, Sweden), Europe is nearly empty; another sparsely settled zone occurs in the depression north of the Caspian Sea. But, in general, there is not the sharp transition in Europe that there is in Asia between the heavily populated areas and the empty areas. The correlation between peoples and plains, so prominent in Asia, cannot be so clearly illustrated in Europe, where the hill zone from France to Poland contains a denser population than most of the plains of European Russia.

The population pattern of Africa is particularly striking. The densest zone is in the lower valley of the Nile River, a phenomenon similar to the dense zones of Asia and quite unlike anything else in Africa. The clusters are widely scattered: along the Atlas coast in the northwest, the southern Gold Coast and Nigeria, the eastern highlands between Lakes Tanganyika and Victoria, and around the coastal ports of South Africa.

The fourth world region of greatest population concentration is in eastern North America. The "triangle" between Boston, Chicago, and Washington, D.C., contains the densest population clusters, but the concentration of population is less clear-cut than in either Asia or Europe. A spotted or clustered pattern is even more noticeable than in Europe: whereas the eastern United States is somewhat uniform, dense population in the western half definitely is clustered, as in Southern California, the San Francisco Bay region, or around Puget Sound in the northwest. The empty lands are in the great north (Alaska and Canada), extending southward through the western mountains and deserts into northern Mexico.

In South America, the population clearly is arranged in clusters about the fringes of the continent, concentrated in the highlands, in the temperate south, or along the coastlines, with each cluster isolated by empty or nearly empty land. Clockwise from the eastern tip of Brazil are the clusters around the cities of Recife, Salvador, Rio de Janeiro, São Paulo and Santos, Montevideo and Buenos Aires (in this largest cluster, the former contains almost half the population of Uruguay, the latter over one quarter of Argentina's population), and in the north around Caracas and in the uplands of Colombia, with Bogotá as the principal center. Strikingly apparent are the huge empty interior between the coastal zone and the highlands and the sparsely inhabited zone south of the 40th parallel of latitude.

Australia is the most nearly empty of all the continents except Antarctica. There are five nuclear cities: Perth in the southwest, and Adelaide, Melbourne, Sydney, and Brisbane in the southeast, but no extensive "filled-up" areas anywhere. The contrast between the nearly empty expanses of Australia–New Guinea and densely settled Java to the north is as great as between Mongolia and north China, or between the highlands of Tibet and the Ganges plain of north India.

Not only is the greater part of the world's population concentrated in four major regions, but these, except for Java, are all located in the northern hemisphere. The densely populated regions are further located in the midlatitudes of the northern continents of Eurasia and North America. Only tropical south India and Southeast Asia are the major exceptions. These midlatitude regions are the sites of the historically most productive agricultural lands, with at least a 100-day growing season, a favorable precipitation-evaporation ratio (or supplemented by irrigation), and relatively extensive lands of low relief, suitable for cultivation.

But the four major world regions of greatest population densities are not alike. Peoples of the dominantly agrarian cultures extending from Egypt across south Asia to China are concentrated within the alluvial valleys of great rivers where irrigation agriculture has been most highly developed. The most populous zones of Europe and North America lie in areas where access to coal and iron in combination has encouraged the growth of modern manufacturing and of cities based on industry and transportation. The northwest Euro-

pean belt of dense settlement, in central England and reaching eastward from French Flanders through the Low Countries and the lower Rhine into Bohemia and Polish Galicia is an example. Petroleum and natural gas, in more recent decades, have served other industrial concentrations, as along the Gulf Coast of Louisiana and Texas or in Southern California.

The world's sparsely settled areas are of three main types: high-altitude and high-latitude, arid and semiarid, and tropical or equatorial. The sparsely settled parts of the world are dotted with small spots of denser settlement, depending almost entirely on local resources. Where water is available in arid regions, as on the alluvial piedmont of Sinkiang (westernmost China) or in exotic rivers such as the Amu Darya or the Nile, oases or strips of dense settlement are certain. Where commercially exploitable industrial minerals exist, particularly petroleum (Arabia or South Sumatra) or metals such as copper (northern Chile, or Arizona, Nevada, and Utah in the United States), isolated dense settlements in otherwise empty regions also occur.

Some general conclusions can be drawn from an examination of the map of world population distribution:

1. Men are to be found in numbers only where there is a supply of usable fresh water (cultures differ widely in the efficiencies of their technologies for securing water and rendering it usable).
2. Men are sparse in mountain uplands and subarctic lands with inadequate growing seasons.
3. Men in numbers in agrarian-based civilizations are a function of the amount of level land in combination with the amount of water available.
4. Men in numbers in industrial-based civilizations are a function of the amount and quality of industrially usable minerals, particularly coal and iron, available to an area (either locally mined or imported via world trade).

Variations in Population Densities: Rural versus Urban-Industrial Patterns

The earth has a little more than 57 million square miles of land surface. If the numbers of mankind were equally distributed, there would be about 58 people on each square mile. But this average density for the world as a whole is matched in only a few places (such as the United States' average). As we have just seen, the map of world population distribution is striking for the disparities revealed.

Java's 66 million people (1965 estimate) are contained in an area of 51,039 square miles (about equal to that of the state of New York), thus *averaging* over 1290 persons per square mile, or two per acre for the whole island. Java, the most populous island of Indonesia, is frequently cited as the most overcrowded place on earth, since the Javanese are essentially agrarian peasants who must depend directly on the produce of their farmlands for their livelihood. On the other hand, the megalopolis stretching from Boston to Washington, D.C., the most well-to-do sector of the northeastern United States, has a population density of more than 2000 per square mile. Crowding is not synonymous with poverty. What are the factors that determine whether a country, island, or region may be said to be "underpopulated" or "overcrowded," or whether its space is simply being used intensively and highly efficiently by its "population optimum"?

The ratio of total population to total area, the "crude" population density so far used for our comparisons, is not as effective a measure of the relationship of men to the land they occupy as is the ratio of total population to the area of land under cultivation (termed the "nutritional" density). A comparison of crude versus nutritional densities for ten selected countries of the world (Table 12.6) reveals their varied meanings.

According to crude densities (column 1), the five most densely settled countries among the ten are (in order): Japan, Great Britain, India, France, and China. But according to nutritional densities (column 2), the five most densely settled countries

TABLE 12.6   POPULATION DENSITIES AND RURAL-URBAN RATIOS FOR TEN SELECTED COUNTRIES

Country	Population Density per Square Mile of		Population Ratio (Per Cent)	
	Total Area	Cultivated Land	Rural	Urban
Argentina	21	188	38	62
Australia	3	96	35	65
Brazil	24	796	70	30
China	233	1682	87	13
France	254	581	52	48
Great Britain	624	1932	25	75
India	401	773	86	14
Japan	678	4104	46	54
Soviet Union	26	257	60	40
United States	55	267	30	70

among the ten are (in order): Japan, Great Britain, China, Brazil, and India. The rank order of the first two countries is not changed, but the disparity between them (4104 versus 1932 persons per square mile of cultivated land) is clearly greater. Japan's nutritional density is equal to 6.4 persons per acre; import of foodstuffs is an even greater necessity for Japan than for Great Britain. The change in position of China on the two lists, from fifth to third, recognizes that most of China's land area (Tibet, Sinkiang) is sparsely inhabited because it is too high, too dry, or too cold for cultivation; the nutritional density better reveals the pressures of the Chinese on their land. In crude population density (24 per square mile), Brazil is almost at the bottom of the list of ten countries; in nutritional density it is fourth, slightly surpassing India, again a recognition that the vast tropical rain forest and savanna areas of interior Brazil are nearly uninhabited and that almost all the population is densely concentrated on the eastern and southern coastal lowlands and near-coastal uplands.

Table 12.6 also shows that high nutritional population densities (over 500 per square mile of cultivated land) occur not only in countries that are predominantly rural, such as China, Brazil, or India, and not only in countries that are predominantly urban-industrial, such as Great Britain and Japan, but also in countries that are rather evenly balanced between rural and urban, such as France. But the highest nutritional densities of all appear to occur in predominantly urban-industrial countries, such as Japan and Great Britain.

The question then is raised: What are the highest nutritional densities that have been achieved by agrarian civilizations? Data from Java, East Pakistan, and Egypt disclose a remarkable similarity: an areawide average nutritional density of about 2000 persons per square mile of cultivated land, with local districts exceeding 4000 per square mile.

Java's cultivated land (irrigated rice fields, nonirrigated fields, gardens, fishponds, estates) totals 21,148,000 acres or 66 per cent of the island's land surface. Uncultivated estates, state forests, roads, water bodies, village sites, etc., total 11,512,000 acres or 34 per cent of the island's area. The nutritional density (1965) for the whole island is 1997 persons per square mile of cultivated land. The predominantly rural district of Adiwerno along the irrigated north coastal plain of central Java, from which two (and sometimes three) crops per year are harvested, reported a crude density of 4240 persons per square mile as long ago as the census of 1930.

Egypt affords an excellent illustration of population variability in adjustment to changed economic and social conditions within a particular physical setting. When Egypt was the granary of the Roman Empire, its population was about 8 million. At the time of Napoleon's conquest 18 centuries later, the population was only 2½ million. Today, the United Arab Republic contains over 29½ million. In every one of these periods, the valley and delta of the lower Nile has seemed overcrowded. The average nutritional density (a rural population in 1965 of 18.4 million on 6 million acres of cultivated land) for the U.A.R. is 1958. Completion of the High Dam project at Aswan and related land reclamation and irrigation projects will add two million acres of cultivated land; but meanwhile the rural population may have increased by seven million and all the additional output may barely maintain the present low level of living.

The greatest population clusters in all the world, however, are to be found in cities. Metropolitan areas in which more than a million people are grouped together are reasonably common (the 139 black dots in Fig. 11.4, pp. 484–485, and on each endpaper map). There are 45 containing more than two million each. The largest single cluster is the Tokyo-Yokohama metropolitan area with its 16 million people.

It is not surprising that Europe, among the four major world regions of greatest population density (East Asia, South Asia, Europe, and North America), contains the largest number (46) of metropolitan areas over one million. What is perhaps surprising is that East Asia has 28, the same number as North America. China, noted as one of the most rural countries in the world, has 17 such "million cities" and is second only to the United States, which has 25, among the world's countries in total number of metropolitan areas over one million people. The U.S.S.R. has ten, Germany nine, India eight, Great Britain and Japan seven each. No other country has more than four.

Cities contain the world's highest densities of population. The national average density of urban populations is remarkably the same, about 5500 persons per square mile, for such diverse countries as Japan, Germany, Great Britain, and the United States. But such a figure masks a wide range of variation among cities, or even within a single city. The world's largest cities, whether Asian, European, or American, attain densities about five times as high as the national urban average, that is, between 25,000 and 30,000 per square mile. Maximum densities for certain sections of great cities reach four to eight times even this figure. For example, in Chicago, two small census tracts reported over 100,000 per square mile: in the Tokyo-Yokohama metropolitan area, maximum densities are 240,000 per square mile (or 375 persons per acre of land, which is a ground space averaging a bit less than ten by twelve feet for each person!).

Mass Movement: Population Redistribution Through International Migration

There are only three ways to slow down the rate of growth of a population in a particular region: (1) by raising the death rate, (2) by lowering the birthrate, or (3) by increasing the rate of migration (shifting people from one population to another). It appears to be neither humane nor politic to raise the death rate, so this solution is rarely discussed (although inaction to relieve famines or to check epidemics has achieved the same end). The solution available and utilized so wholeheartedly by Europe following the discovery and opening of the New World was intercontinental migration. Over a period of more than 400 years many different types of migration took place, both conservative and innovating (see Chapter 5, p. 194). Socially impelled flight, freely chosen group movement, and mass settlement all tended toward the transfer of European agrarian forms to the New World.

During the period 1821–1932 (between the Napoleonic Wars and the Great Depression), there was relatively unrestricted, but reasonably well-recorded, mass movement. At least 59 million people, mostly Europeans, moved overseas during the period; of these, over 90 per cent settled either in North or South America. During the twentieth century, the largest volume of population transfers has been through forced migration negotiated and organized by national governments. After World War I, over a million Germans moved into Germany from Alsace-Lorraine and the areas ceded to Poland. In the exchange of populations between Greece and Turkey decreed by the 1923 Treaty of Lausanne, about 1,200,000 Greeks were moved out of Asia Minor and eastern Thrace, and about

600,000 Turks were moved from various Balkan countries, mostly from Greece. The German conduct of World War II resulted in vast movements of refugees and forced labor, and the collapse of Germany set in motion a gigantic series of redistributions. The separation of Pakistan and India in 1947 led to an exchange of population estimated in 1949 at seven million in each country.

The first phase of emigration from Asia to countries of America, Australia, and eastern Africa began as a result of the abolition of slavery in the British colonies in the 1830s. The demand for plantation labor was met by the recruitment of indentured laborers from India, and later from China, Japan, and the Philippines. Although this class of socially induced migration dominated Asian migration throughout the nineteenth century, it practically ceased after the 1920s.

The decline in intercontinental migration has been offset by an increase in interregional migrations within Asia. Immigrants have contributed greatly to the economic development of Malaysia (Chinese and Indians), Burma (Indians), Ceylon (Indians), Borneo (Chinese), and Manchuria (Chinese and, for a while, Japanese). International movements of migrants within Asia continued throughout the 1920s and 1930s, despite the near cessation of mass migration in the West. The chief countries of emigration have been China, India, Japan, and Korea. For all the emigration, principally to eastern Africa and Southeast Asia, the effects on the population of the country of origin have been negligible. For example, the urban areas of Japan between 1920 and 1940 increased by 17.5 million persons, ten times the number of emigrating Japanese civilians. As another example, about 30 million Indians are estimated to have settled abroad between 1834 and 1937, but, since 24 million eventually returned to India, the net outward balance was only six million over the span of more than a century.

Since 1945, with the gaining of political independence by former colonies, the new Asian nations have focused attention on internal migration and the achievement of economic development by labor of their own people rather than by that of immigrants. As a consequence, international migration in Asia has sharply declined.

The period immediately following World War II saw the revival of mass international migration in the West, including the transfer of some 1,200,000 refugees. Intercontinental migration during 1945–1952 may be summarized as follows:

Emigration from Europe	4,452,000
Immigration into Europe	1,150,000
Other intercontinental migration	710,000
Total	6,312,000

The chief countries of emigration and the main receiving countries during 1945–1952 were as indicated in Table 12.7. North and South America, it is to be noted, have continued to receive more than two thirds of the "new" intercontinental migrants.

But if intercontinental mass movement, despite the stimulus of World War II, amounted to the transfer of less than one million people per year during the eight-year period 1945–1952, then it is fair to conclude that only an extremely small percentage of mankind now is being affected by migration.

Migration has been a way of postponing the inevitable problem of population growth. Wherever man has migrated, sooner or later the density of population in the new territory rises to equal or exceed that of the home country. The migrations of the last centuries have changed certain local patterns of population densities and have resulted in racial and cultural mixing to an unprecedented degree. But migration has not truly solved the problem posed by man's increase in numbers. The migration process effects a redistribution of only a very small proportion of the world's people. The overall effects of immigration, in "smoothing out" or equalizing the great disparities in the world's population distribution, have been rendered insignificant by the natural increase in numbers of people in the already dense zones. Present population growth is of such dimensions that international migration, as a future means of re-

TABLE 12.7 MIGRATION FROM EUROPE, 1945 TO 1952

Emigration		Immigration	
Great Britain	1,107,000	United States	1,104,000 (27%)
Italy	741,000	Argentina, Brazil, and Venezuela	883,000 (21%)
Netherlands	318,000		
Spain	272,000	Canada	726,000 (17%)
Portugal	152,000	Australia	697,000 (17%)
		Israel	526,000 (13%)
		South Africa	125,000 (3%)
		New Zealand	75,000 (2%)

solving the grossly uneven distribution of the world's population, is wholly impracticable. For example, every year there are now 12 million more people in India than in the previous year. Where could they possibly go, even if all had the propensity, not to mention the financial subsidy, to migrate?

Most countries, today, are concerned about the growth of their own populations. Few are interested in adding to their problems by taking on any great quantity of foreigners. The present world situation is unlike the European past because there are no longer any nearly empty hemispheres awaiting development by modernizing Asians and because the blocking out of all the world's lands into independent nation-states has created barriers both to the movement of migrants and to the willingness of countries to receive immigrants.

Transport of Surplus Food: The Dilemma Compounded

Widespread poverty, hunger, and famine exist in the world. Malnutrition is a direct result of ever worsening low levels of living. The food supply, both in quantity and quality, of the world's people has not improved during the twentieth century. On the whole, per capita consumption has definitely decreased. Figure 12.2 represents the worldwide pattern of average per capita dietary standards for each country according to a fourfold classification: good diet, adequate diet, slightly deficient diet, grossly deficient diet.

An obvious solution to the problem of starvation, hunger, and malnutrition affecting most of the world is for surplus food from the favored areas to be transported to the areas of great need. What is the feasibility of such a proposal? Let us take a specific case, India, for example. To feed 10 per cent of its total population (about 48 million people) for one year would require the importation of about 10 million tons of grain. The bulk transport of this grain would require 1000 round trips between India and North America by large ships at least 500 feet in length, hence the dispatch of at least three such ships per day during the entire year. Who pays? And how? And would not the distribution of free or "cut-rate" food from the surplus areas to needy countries disrupt international economic systems as presently constituted? Obviously, the distribution of food surpluses is far from a simple matter.

In any case, currently existing surpluses in any country are at best minor factors in the world food problem. Their distribution is a temporary relief measure, not a permanent solution. If we assume that nutritional standards can be, or are being, slowly and steadily improved throughout the world, the consequence of such improvements will be reflected in a reduction of infant and childhood mortality and an increase in the life span. No longer, for example, would one in ten women in India die in childbirth or one in four Indian babies born die during their first year. Herein the dilemma is compounded: the net effect of nutritional improvements is to increase the potential rate of population growth.

Limits of Mankind: The Population Ahead

The present rate of increase in world population is estimated at 2 per cent per year. Two per cent may seem rather insignificant, yet it is truly an astounding growth, as may easily be demonstrated. From a base of three billion people (1962 world population), a growth rate of 2 per cent per year will produce in 650 years (A.D. 2612) a population density of one person for each square foot of land surface on the globe. In 1566 years (A.D. 3528), the mass of humanity would weigh as much as the planet Earth itself!

If the present era with its growth rate of 2 per cent a year is most abnormal, the conclusion is clear: the present growth rate cannot possibly persist for long into the future (Table 12.8, p. 534) without exhausting the earth's resources and living space. Some parts of mankind have already faced up to the problem of restricting their rates of growth in order to maintain a better balance between man's numbers and the fixed dimensions of the planet he calls home, but other parts have not.

Very great differences in rates of growth of population continue to occur among the different regions of the world. Latin America, Africa, and Asia, those areas that already contain seven of every ten of the world's people, now are increasing at faster rates than the rest of the world (Table 12.9, p. 534).

In the western hemisphere, a reshift in population relationships has recently taken place. Aboriginal Meso-America (principally Andean South America and highland Mexico-Guatemala) contained a larger population than North America before European conquest. Despite the widespread decimation of the North American Indian popula-

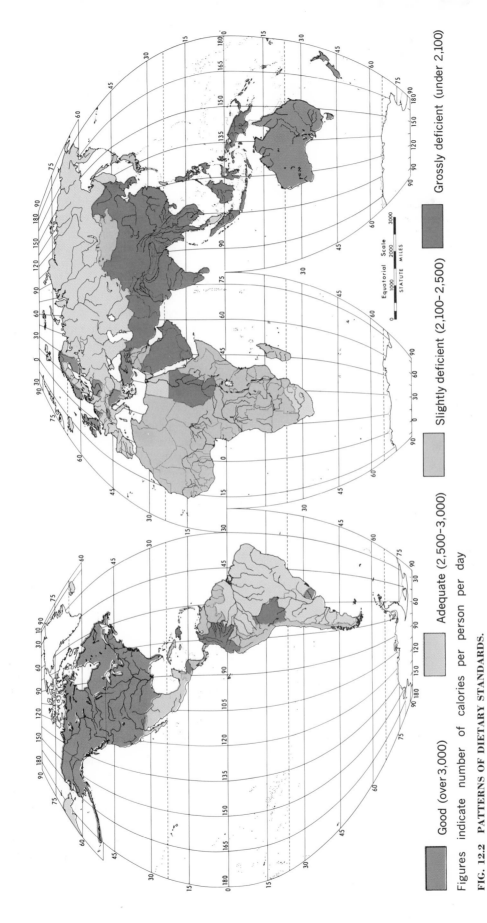

Good (over 3,000)　　Adequate (2,500–3,000)　　Slightly deficient (2,100–2,500)　　Grossly deficient (under 2,100)

Figures indicate number of calories per person per day

FIG. 12.2　PATTERNS OF DIETARY STANDARDS.

533

TABLE 12.8 PROJECTED WORLD POPULATION GROWTH (*at 2 Per Cent Annual Increase*)

Year	World Population Total	Number of Years to Add One Billion People
1962	3,000 million (3 billion)	
1977	4,000 million (4 billion)	15
1988	5,000 million (5 billion)	11
1997	6,000 million (6 billion)	9
2005	7,000 million (7 billion)	8
2012	8,000 million (8 billion)	7
2018	9,000 million (9 billion)	6
2023	10,000 million (10 billion)	5

Compare with Table 12.2.

tion, the earlier and more rapid economic development of Anglo-America coupled with heavier European immigration created a larger population than in Latin America. But since 1960 the number of persons in Latin America once again has exceeded the Anglo-American population. By the end of the twentieth century, Latin America's population will be almost twice that of Anglo-America; indeed, Latin America's absolute increase of people during the last four decades of the twentieth century will approach that of the whole world population in 1650.

Yet, all the differentials in growth of regional populations are but details (however startling!) compared to the overriding significance of what is happening in Asia. The projected increase in Asia's population during the remainder of this century is as great as the whole world population of 1958! The peoples of Europe, Anglo-America, and Australia–New Zealand are but dwindling minorities on the earth: from 36 per cent of the

TABLE 12.9 PROJECTED REGIONAL POPULATION GROWTH, 1962–2005

Region	Population (in Millions)			Percentage of Total World Population	
	A.D. 1962	A.D. 2005	Increase	A.D. 1962	A.D. 2005
Latin America	200	656	3+	6.6	9.3
Africa	250	666	2½	8.3	9.5
Asia	1700	4335	2½	56.6	61.7
Oceania (including Australia)	17	30	8/10	0.6	0.5
Europe (including U.S.S.R.)	640	1009	6/10	21.3	14.3
Anglo-America	200	333	6/10	6.6	4.7

world's people in 1900, they are now less than 30 per cent, and will constitute less than 20 per cent by the end of the century.

Population Problems: A Cultural Interpretation

In a very real sense, all problems of rapid population growth are of man's own creation. Each major upward step in man's numbers has followed some major discovery or invention: agriculture, the initiation of urban life and trade, the harnessing of inanimate power, or the establishment of public health services. In recent centuries, cultural evolution reached a state that enabled Europeans to precipitate a technological, industrial, scientific, and democratic revolution that made possible the application of scientific medicine and profoundly altered the long-established near equilibrium between man's birth and death rates all over the world. Many of the problems of modern living (urban congestion, suburban sprawl, longer-distance journeys to work or to recreation, automobile parking problems, higher costs of land, refuse disposal, and pollution abatement) are directly related to an increase in numbers of people competing for space, facilities, or services. In most other parts of the inhabited world the problems are more serious: hunger and shared poverty are spreading, lowering the existing levels of living and further reducing the chances for individual prosperity. The gulf in subsistence levels that exists today between peoples of the earth is widening. Life is better than ever for those in Western industrial countries, but the majority of the world's people still live close to the subsistence level and squalor reminiscent of medieval Europe. The odds are stacked against the developing countries of Africa, Asia, and Latin America, which are unable to add to their per capita wealth and productivity because rates of population growth are greater than rates of economic development. Funds expended for food consumption or housing construction are not available for capital investment to increase future productivity.

Man, however, is not only a culture builder but also a problem poser and problem solver. Perceiving the consequences of his actions, man has become increasingly aware of the implications of accelerating population growth. A greater degree of attention is being paid to reduction of birthrates, both by the United Nations and its specialized agencies and by a growing number of individual nations. The governments of India, Pakistan, Taiwan, Japan, and Korea sponsor active programs of birth control; Malaysia, Ceylon, Hong Kong, Barbados, and Puerto Rico have programs sanctioned by their governments; and Singapore, Tunisia, Turkey, and the United Arab Republic (Egypt) have formulated population policies. Their purpose is to ensure man's continuing control of his increasing numbers, so that means other than the Malthusian checks of vice, misery, famine, and war, can provide solutions to man's population problems.

Clearly, civilization has increased the average life span of men and has cut down the inroads of death by famines, pestilence, and war. Almost every one of the many human cultures is now faced with the fact that an unprecedented expansion of its numbers of people not only is possible or probable, but is in actual process. Is there no constant limit to population increase, no longer a foreseeable limit to the numbers of mankind that are capable of being produced? Is the true end of man merely to populate the earth with the maximum number of human beings that can be fitted into its finite space and kept alive simultaneously by the world's maximum food supply?

The question is not just one concerned with sufficient food and an adequate dietary standard for billions of additional hungry mouths, but rather one involving opportunities for education and employment and the development of social standards of living compatible with human dignity. There has been perhaps too great a tendency to seek a quantitative solution to human problems, whereas, in truth, the total answer can be given only in qualitative terms.

SELECTED REFERENCES

Ackerman, Edward A.
　　1959　"Population and Natural Resources," pp. 621–648 in P. M. Hauser and O. D. Duncan (eds.), *The Study of Population: An Inventory and Appraisal.* Chicago: University of Chicago Press. 864 pp.

Appleman, Philip
　　1965　*The Silent Explosion.* Boston: Beacon Press. 161 pp.

Barbour, K. M., and R. M. Prothero
　　1961　*Essays on African Population.* London: Routledge. 336 pp.

Bates, Marston
　　1955　*The Prevalence of People.* New York: Scribner's. 293 pp. (reprinted 1962 in the Scribner Library, paperback edition).

Bogue, Donald J.
　　1959　"Population Distribution," pp. 383–399 in P. M. Hauser and O. D. Duncan (eds.), *The Study of Population: An Inventory and Appraisal.* Chicago: University of Chicago Press. 864 pp.

Broek, Jan O. M.
　　1958　"The Man-Land Ratio," pp. 52–63 in Roy G. Francis (ed.), *The Population Ahead.* Minneapolis: University of Minnesota Press. 160 pp.

Cépède, Michel, et al.
　　1964　*Population and Food.* New York: Sheed and Ward. 461 pp.

Chandrasekhar, Sripati
　　1954　*Hungry People and Empty Lands.* London: George Allen & Unwin, Ltd. 306 pp.

Chen, Kuan-I
　　1960　*World Population Growth and Living Standards.* New York: Bookman Associates. 93 pp.

Cipola, Carlo
　　1962　*The Economic History of World Population.* Baltimore: Penguin Books. 126 pp. 126 pp.

Clarke, John I.
　　1965　*Population Geography.* Oxford: Pergamon Press. 164 pp.

Cragg, J. B. (ed.)
　　1955　*The Numbers of Man and Animals.* Edinburgh: Oliver and Boyd. 152 pp.

Darwin, Charles Galton
    1958   *The Problems of World Population* (The Rede Lecture). Cambridge, England: University Press. 40 pp.

Davis, Kingsley
    1967   "Population Policy: Will Current Programs Succeed?" *Science*, Vol. 158, No. 3802, pp. 730–739.

Durand, John D. (ed.)
    1967   *World Population* (The Annals of the American Academy of Political and Social Science, Vol. 369). Philadelphia: The Academy. 163 pp.

Francis, R. G. (ed.)
    1958   *The Population Ahead.* Minneapolis: University of Minnesota Press. 160 pp.

Freedman, Ronald (ed.)
    1964   *Population: The Vital Revolution.* Garden City, N.Y.: Anchor Books. 274 pp.

Geisert, Harold L.
    1962   *Population Growth and International Migration.* Washington, D. C.: Population Research Project, George Washington University. 57 pp.

Ginsburg, Norton
    1961   *Atlas of Economic Development.* Chicago: University of Chicago Press. 119 pp.

Hardin, Garrett (ed.)
    1966   *Population, Evolution, Birth Control: A Collage of Controversial Readings.* San Francisco: W. H. Freeman & Co. 341 pp.

Hauser, Philip M. (ed.)
    1958   *Population and World Politics.* Glencoe, Illinois: The Free Press. 297 pp.
    1964   "Man and More Men: The Population Prospects," *Bulletin of the Atomic Scientists*, June, pp. 4–8.
    1965   *World Population Problems.* New York: Foreign Policy Association. 46 pp.

Hauser, Philip M., and Otis Dudley Duncan (eds.)
    1959   *The Study of Population: An Inventory and Appraisal.* Chicago: The University of Chicago Press. 864 pp.

Hooson, David J. M.
    1960   "The Distribution of Population as the Essential Geographical Expression," *Canadian Geographer*, No. 17, pp. 10–20.

Hubbert, M. King
    1964   "Earth Scientists Look at Environmental Limits in Human Ecology," *News Report, National Academy of Sciences—National Research Council*, Vol. 14, July–August, pp. 58–60.

Huxley, Julian S.
    1963   *The Human Crisis.* Seattle, Wash.: University of Washington Press. 88 pp.

International Urban Research
    1959   *The World's Metropolitan Areas.* Berkeley and Los Angeles: University of California Press. 115 pp.

Landis, Paul H., and Paul K. Hatt
    1954   *Population Problems: A Cultural Interpretation* (2nd ed.). New York: American Book Company. 554 pp.

Lorimer, Frank, et al.
    1954   *Culture and Human Fertility, A Study of the Relation of Cultural Conditions to Fertility in Non-industrial and Transitional Societies.* Paris: UNESCO. 514 pp.

Mudd, Stuart (ed.)
    1964   *The Population Crisis and the Use of World Resources.* Bloomington, Ind.: Indiana University Press. 562 pp.

Ng, L. K. Y. and Stuart Mudd
    1966   *The Population Crisis: Implications and Plans for Action.* Bloomington, Ind.: Indiana University Press. 364 pp.

Petersen, William
    1964   *The Politics of Population.* Garden City, N.Y.: Doubleday. 350 pp.

Phelps, Harold A., and David Henderson
    1958   *Population in its Human Aspects.* New York: Appleton-Century-Crofts. 512 pp.

Royal Statistical Society
  1963 *Food Supplies and Population Growth (A Symposium)*. Edinburgh: Oliver and Boyd. 85 pp.
Shryock, H. S.
  1964 *Population Mobility in the United States*. Chicago: University of Chicago, Community and Family Study Center. 470 pp.
Sorre, Maximilien
  1955 *Les Migrations des Peuples: Essai Sur la Mobilite Geographique*. Paris: Flammarion. 265 pp.
Stamp, L. Dudley
  1960a "The Geographical Study of Population," pp. 26–36 in his *Applied Geography*. London: Penguin Books. 217 pp.
  1960b "The Interpretation of the Population and Land-Use Patterns," pp. 51–60 in his *Applied Geography*. London: Penguin Books. 217 pp.
Stycos, J. Mayone
  1964 "The Outlook for World Population," *Science*, Vol. 146, No. 3650, December 11, pp. 1435–1440.
Thomlinson, Ralph
  1965 *Population Problems* (5th ed.). New York: McGraw-Hill. 593 pp.
         Change. New York: Random House. 576 pp.
Thompson, Warren S., and David T. Lewis
  1965 *Population Problems* (5th ed.). New York: McGraw-Hill. 593 pp.
United Nations, Department of Economic and Social Affairs
  1958 *The Future Growth of World Population* (Population Studies, #28). New York: United Nations. 75 pp.
Watson, James Wreford
  1956 "Population Pressure and Marginal Lands," *Scottish Geographical Magazine*, Vol. 72, pp. 117–121.
Zelinsky, Wilbur
  1962 *A Bibliographic Guide to Population Geography* (Research Paper No. 80). Chicago: Department of Geography, University of Chicago. 257 pp.
  1966 *A Prologue to Population Geography*. Englewood Cliffs, N.J.: Prentice-Hall. 150 pp.

CHAPTER *13*

Man's Dominance of the Earth, and Its Consequences

This chapter assays a brief and simple summary of the comparative position of the earth in the second half of the twentieth century, by reviewing the several cultural aspects of its human occupance.

Benchmarks in Human Advancement

To gain a certain perspective, the human achievement should be measured against the comparative positions of other life-forms presently inhabiting the biotic earth; such a comparison makes clear that Man has done well in his struggle for mastery. Suppose that we begin by looking briefly at the earth through three nonhuman sets of eyes in figurative but simple comparative views. First, let us presume the reaction of an eagle as he soars above the earth in narrowing circles, speculating on the state of affairs. For eagles, the earth has deteriorated tremendously in the last few thousand years as man has suddenly grown so numerous and developed such curious habits and abilities. The cities, towns, villages, field systems, and grasslands that man has spread over much of the good parts of the earth are useless things. Most of our former good hunting grounds have been ruined, and the birds and the rodents have decreased rapidly; it is hard for us to find a living and it is unsafe to venture now into many sectors of the earth. The future looks grim, and all that we know to do is to retreat toward the remaining forest zones and hope that man will make a mess of things so that nature may reclaim her own before we eagles become extinct.

Next let us assume the reaction of a poodle as he commands his master to take him for his evening walk. Things appear in pretty fine shape, although there are many minor nuisances for dogs in the curious human systems of artifacts and in the more curious human habit systems. By our early liking for man and his curious ways we dogs succeeded in getting man to love, care for, and cater to us in wondrous fashion, even though some of the expressions of love are bothersome at times. We no longer have to hunt for a living, predators are few, and man now seldom eats dogs, so that our future seems assured. The dog population of the earth is greater than at any time in the past, and poodles currently rate very high in status, so that it is good to be a poodle. A curious feature is the great number of kinds of dogs that man has recently bred in many different parts of the earth, theoretically capitalizing on our native abilities as we express them in our avocational activities. Fortunately, dogs do not have to live by those supposed abilities, since man is now pleased to look after almost all kinds of dogs in a manner quite pleasing to most of us. He has even displayed great inventiveness and ingenuity on our behalf. The future of dogs looks almost as good as the future for cats, but, alas, we cannot have everything. We certainly hope that man does not get himself into trouble so great he cannot care for dogs.

Finally, let us assume the reaction of an elephant. The earth has changed tremendously since we were lords of the earth, from near the poles to the tropics. The earth has become very warm in several sudden bursts which found many of our kind unable to adapt to the changes. Unfortunately, during the period of change man became able to kill more and more elephants, and we have had a rather hard time adapting both to our environments and to the curious habits of man. The insatiable human demand for ivory has been hard on our population dynamics, and we seem to be a dying race. Man has been willing to use elephants now and then in a few parts of the world, but he has not been very skillful at it, and we have not found just the right means to get man to care for us as he does for dogs and cats. Perhaps our future looks best in a few forest preserves man is talking about. If he does not succeed in that effort it may be that our best other future prospect lies in the zoos man does seem to like around the world. We find the exhibition life rather dull and hardly worth our effort, but we may have to accept that, since the curious circus system seems to have little future and is not much of an alternative to hiding out in the few remaining tropical forests.

If we now come back to the human view of the earth, how does it seem? Well, it is a humanized Earth, operated by Man for the supposed good of all mankind, despite its inefficiencies, problems, and troubles. If we then think very quickly over what man has accomplished in his own behalf, the human prospect seems much better than that for eagles or elephants, if not quite so leisurely luxurious as for dogs and cats. The earliest hominoids outwitted their predators until evolutionary biological change set them upon a developmental sequence that led to *Homo sapiens*. While primordial man was learning extremely slowly, the physical earth went through changes that eventually made it a better place for mankind in general. By the time *Homo sapiens sapiens* had evolved, human action had implemented the forces of physical change in altering the earth's surface, and man had learned a great many basic lessons about using the environment to his own advantage. Man took off on an ascending spiral of learning, discovering, and inventing new ways to improve his competitive status on an Earth now more suitable to his own kind. Having spread over almost all the planet, man tested out the qualities of almost every kind of environmental complex. Some of the more rigorous ecological niches proved too difficult for human progress at the stage of slightly compounded human skills, but innately a few of the milder niches were sufficiently productive of elementary resources for the human population to grow in numbers. The human ability to communicate learning began to compound achievement,

rendering cumulative advantages over eagles, dogs, and elephants, as well as over the myriad of other life-forms. With greater numbers came more numerous discoveries and inventions, yielding further increases in man's numbers, which in turn led to further discoveries and inventions; shared cumulatively, the cultural spiral began and progressed.

Control over production of basic resources was achieved through plant and animal domestication, and was followed by technological control over mineral and wood resources for the improvement of utensils, tools, weapons, shelter, and clothing. Technological advancement on both land and sea gave man a new degree of mobility in both human movement and the movement of resources. Formulation of religious systems and social constructs gave man means of inspiring and organizing his growing numbers into effective working units which could tackle larger and more productive projects of improving upon the circumstances of nature. Unfortunately the same developments set man against man in the control over choice ecological niches and in the elaboration of biological territorialisms into militant regionalisms. Political organization culminated in the cultural construct of the state, which could enforce territorialisms more efficiently than before, to put a premium upon the organizing of ecological environments in several parts of the earth. The broad spread of Man over the Earth and the steady diffusion of techniques, customs, habits, and patterns of knowledge led to the elaboration of many different living systems in the innumerable local environments, but these very patterns led to steady advancement in the better environments to the end that there began to appear strong differentials in living systems between the most advanced and the slowest laggard groups. The rise of civilization, capitalizing upon all kinds of human abilities, furthered the divergence between the levels of living of mankind in different parts of the earth. But civilization brought to its participants ever greater strengths in remaking and improving upon the latent qualities of environments occupied. In the short-range view the centers of population, power, and human achievement shifted from one region to another in the Old World as diffusion carried human technologies to new groups in succeeding millennia. Such shifts culminated in the full exploration of the earth by one set of culture groups (Europeans), ending in the integration of the whole of the earth into one large operating region. In the long-range view the abilities of mankind became more widely spread to the peoples of the earth, and more variants in human living systems were compounded by further discoveries and inventions to the end that man finally comprehended the whole of his earth and was able to begin living from the whole rather than from restricted sectors only.

The increased mobility developed by man in his exploration of the earth has, more recently, been greatly compounded by the further development of transport technologies to the end that man now can go anywhere on the surface of the earth, and return home, within a short time interval. Such mobility has now been turned outward, with man now attempting the exploratory investigation of space-beyond-earth. Recent achievements in mobility have done more, however, than to make human movement willfully earthwide, for they have also made possible the movement of material things and ideas in ever-increasing volumes from any regional source to any other regional center desired. Man has about conquered the Earth in terms of life-form dominance and in terms of the ability to mobilize its resources where he will. A simple continuous review of the several clusters of photographs presented in this volume clearly gives a picture of diversity, but, equally, it also yields a realization of the progress and power in the hand of Man.

Man as an Agent of Physical Change

One of the basic elements in the human dominance of the earth is the ability of man to interfere with the natural processes of earth sculpture, erosion, deposition, drainage, the hydrologic cycle, and other processes of related significance. The very first little diversion ditch dug by man to bring potable water into a new channel closer to his home or onto fields where he then planted crops was not a very significant development, for it did not upset many natural processes. The ability to build a long string of flood control dams up the headwaters of a major river system (see Fig. 11.6, p. 499) so as to regulate the whole flow pattern of that river basin, seems at first glance both a notable accomplishment and a boon to mankind. The sheer leveling and filling of a hilly-to-swampy tract on the island of Singapore, on which to create a planned industrial district, is a measure of man's ability to remold his world to suit himself. The ability of the Dutch to tie together the whole string of Frisian Islands, by dikes that will enable the reclamation of a relatively large tract of coastal sea, seems a project quite worthy of an industrial society that needs more farmland—a project now in planning. The potential transfer of a significant volume of Yangtze River water, at a point in midwestern China, into the basin of the Huang Ho in order to make it available to the often parched North China Plain, is a notably worthy project, though it will require years to complete. These and many other possible illustrations demonstrate the calculated cultural ability of mankind to remake aspects of significant regions of the earth.

So far as we can determine the construction and reclamation projects that man thus far has been able to mount have been productive of more good than harm. Most great dams have been built in lightly occupied areas; the areas inundated by the reservoirs thus created have not been tremendously valuable. Most diking systems have restrained rivers or coastal seas without upsetting major basic natural processes. Rivers build up their beds, between dike systems, again to overflow sometime, whereupon the dikes must be raised higher. This has been the history for the Huang Ho, in North China, and it is proving the case in the Mississippi Basin. Is there a point at which man can disrupt the basic aspect of regional geomorphology? We only know that when man lives in a depositional plain he must continue to cope with depositional floods; diking systems are a means of coping, but once begun such diking must be maintained in perpetuity.

Man has learned to dig wells in dry regions from which to pump water for domestic and agricultural use. Often he has lowered the water table to the point at which the old technology no longer sufficed to produce water. Pumping technology has markedly progressed, and water can be drawn from depths of several hundred feet today. In the San Joaquin Valley of California deep wells now are taking out water that probably entered the rock systems high in the Sierra Nevada at a date early in the Pleistocene. What will the long-term effect be of such overuse in the drying out of rock strata at depth? The short-term answer, of course, is to bring in water from northern California and forget the matter of depleted rock strata. The introduction of large amounts of fresh water into the dry margins, whereby fresh water may percolate downward, is known to dissolve and loosen the cementing in heavy clays and clay shales, causing compaction and settling, and to lubricate particular planes, causing slippage, slumps, and landslides along bluff fronts and oversteepened slopes. The cut-and-fill patterns of reconstructing hilly areas for the development of residential communities is known to initiate fairly large-scale patterns of slippage and readjustment of local terrain as weight loads shift under lubrication by garden and lawn watering or by unusually heavy rains.

Man so far has not been able to upset drastically the "ecologic balance" of major morphological processes on the surface of the earth. Where he has cut off forests, he has put back farm landscapes filled with growing plants. His occasional severe cases of soil erosion are not so bad that care cannot restore the balance in soils in time, through land leveling, soil filling, and soil replenishment, or that migration cannot occur to areas still possessing cultivable soils. His major actions so far even seem puny when compared to the explosion that occurred when the volcanoes Krakatoa and Tambora in Indonesia blew up. Rainmaking so far has done nothing very significant to natural precipitation systems. Air conditioning uses considerable amounts of power but does nothing to alter the basic processes of weather that create climate in a region. The total energy involved in a single summer monsoon season for India, Pakistan, and Burma is more than man can yet marshal for the execution of a single project.

Thus it may seem that as able as man is at specific small projects he cannot yet create and concentrate sufficient energy to alter the basic geomorphic system of the earth's surface. And yet, perhaps we are overlooking little items that cumulatively become stresses on the system and cause major adjustments. What will be the long-run effect on basic physical processes of the removal of *all* the petroleum and natural gas that man can take out of the earth? In a very few shallow petroleum fields, such as that of Long Beach harbor, the effect is subsidence of the land surface sufficient to cause local disturbance to harbor installations. There can be a cumulative effect to the acts of man on the surface of the earth.

What we are suggesting is that relatively small individual actions, or sets of actions, in themselves do not constitute changes sufficient to bring prompt morphologic response of a major sort in specific cause-and-effect terms. However, the continued small actions of man are cumulative in many areas and in many respects. The responses may be neither immediate nor specific, they may not be measurable in the short term, and they may not even be in matters of physical morphology. Some of them may be in such indirect matters as the alteration of the biotic ecology of a region; these can be countered by further human actions of some sort when they become known and judged important. However, in the long run man must expect some kinds of environmental change to result from all his interference with, and disturbance of, purely natural processes affecting the surface of the earth. Whether these changes take the localized form of destructive landslides wiping out settlement patterns, the silting up of low-lying sectors, the future dike-topping flood, the induced regional earthquake, or the more generally distributed subtle change in environmental conditions is impossible to determine. May there come a time at which man's constant reconstruction and interference upsets some delicate balance in geomorphic ecology, or other environmental condition, to bring on a new and culturally induced set of changes of major importance crudely equivalent to an "Ice Age" or something similar? Perhaps for generations now living this is quite theoretical. Again, we are not trying to be alarmist, but we wish to point out that man's modern ability to modify his physical environment has reached proportions of possible long-term significance to the surface of the earth.

Through soils technology, water resources, oceanography, and climatic conditioning, the control of elements of the physical environment is coming within the technological capacity of man. The continuance of experiment, the devising of technology, and the application of power of specific kinds of physical problems and local environments can both correct past human mistakes and improve on conditions as nature developed them. In some regions the obvious problem elements are still too large for present technological capacity, but a significant factor in these circumstances is the continued inefficiency of human operation.

The Control of Biotic Environments

The human ability to alter the environment in ways significant to varied patterns of daily living is far greater than it ever was. Implicit in this ability is the power of correction of errors committed during an era when man understood neither the consequences of his own actions nor the power of his own collective impact. A prime example is the present plant cover of the earth. There are many plants whose continuance is a bother, there are many plants that could be immeasurably improved in their utility to man, and there are many that could be employed in landscape beautification that are not now so used. The present plant cover of the earth is ragged and ill-arranged, the consequence of natural process subjected to over a million years of human impact. There are barrens or poor grasslands where forests once stood, and where there could be forests again, both for beautification of the earth and for economic use. The commercial forester of today knows how to grow forests and grasslands of man's own arrangement, and within the very near future the reformation of the earth's plant cover will be well within the technological ability of man. The sacred groves, for the communing with nature, can be arranged as easily as can the tree farms for the production of peeler logs in the making of plywood—though it may take centuries to fill an order for giant redwoods. The cropping technology itself can be vastly improved in many parts of the world, to yield a range of agricultural crops in production patterns far more valuable than at present.

Overall the effect of man's redistribution of plants and animals is that the wilderness is in retreat. Man has so altered the earth's land surface, and much of its fresh water, that it is covered with communities of plants and animals enormously different from what they were a few centuries ago. The trend is toward man's management of the landscape, even of the wildscapes, to eliminate, to simplify, to standardize. The exploited lands of the earth have been decreased in richness and variety of species by extensive cultivation of a relatively few desired crops reinforced with massive seeding, spraying, and harvesting practices, by establishment of pastures of pure grass population, by planting stands of quick-growing conifers in forest plantations, and by the cleaning off of waste patches, as in the spraying of roadsides. For purposes other than agriculture man has deliberately shaped biological systems, determining their floristic composition and structure. Whole new forests have been moved or grown, as parks and roadside screens, to add visual variety and amenity to local regions. A golf course, for example, is an artificially constructed dune system, mostly grassy and stabilized, for a recreational purpose.

Man-induced environmental changes have not always been beneficial. Some human actions are already lowering the efficiency of land use for production of economically significant crop plants and decreasing the optimum conditions for all other organisms, including man himself. The causes for such deleterious modifications are readily apparent: the rising density and increasing mobility of men, the expansion of industrialization, and the increasing everyday use of technological products. Some of the problems have long been recognized: soil alkalinity, soil impoverishment, soil erosion, and endemic diseases. These age-old problems are far from being solved. But the present day has added others, those of changes in chemical compositions of soils, inland waters, and the atmosphere. "Pollution," "contamination," "nuisance," all are emotion-laden words expressing negative reactions by some men to the actions of others. However, the problems are real: (1) poisons in industrial effluents and mine seepage; (2) organic matter in sewage and industrial wastes from food processing and from paper and chemical manufacture; (3) suspended solids from treating organic residues and from mining, quarrying, farming, and construction; (4) heating of water in cooling processes, especially electricity generation; (5) nontoxic salts as waste products of industry, including petroleum drilling; (6) pesticides or toxic chemicals used in agriculture and horticulture; and (7) radioactive isotopes from industrial reactors, as nuclear power has begun to replace mineral fuels.

Man has effected drastic changes in the numbers of animals, as well as their distribution. The long-term trend has been to decrease the variety of animal forms through reduction in the numbers of most varieties, sometimes to the point of extinction. The expression "Dead as a dodo bird" is our recognition of a process that still continues: the dodo was sketched by a Dutchman in the seventeenth century, and so we have a record of a form that was last reported on the island of Mauritius in 1681. That giant flightless bird of New Zealand, the moa, was reported by Captain Cook on South Island, New Zealand, but was thereafter efficiently hunted and extirpated. Passenger pigeons, once described in flocks "that darkened the sun," are no more in North America. The lyrebird, the koala, and the platypus of Australia have needed stringent protection to save them from extinction. More recently, international treaties have been signed as agreements to protect the blue whale, the whooping crane, and many others. Why does extermination at the hands of men always seem to be inflicted upon the harmless?

The favoring and care of certain animal species by man for sport and spectacle is well established in horse and dog racing, in circuses, and in zoological gardens (colloquially known as "zoos"). The techniques of artificial insemination and the transplantation of ova have rationalized breeding methods and population controls of the domestic animals: cattle, pigs, sheep, horses, and chickens. The breeding of some other animal forms has become big business simply because the human demand for luxury products exceeds the supply that otherwise could be gathered from the wild. How else to explain the fur-farms of Peruvian chinchillas, Persian caracul sheep, silver foxes, and mink, of ostrich farms for plumes, of alligator and crocodile farms for leather, and of oyster beds for artificial pearls.

The displacement of animals has been widespread. First they lost their monopoly in the field of transport and then of traction in cultivation to faster and stronger machines. Then came a decline in the need for many animal products for food and clothing. The introduction of sugarcane and later the sugar beet in Europe reduced beekeeping to minor status, kept going as the supply of candlewax. Since the late nineteenth century, when petroleum production increased and gas-lighting came to be used in homes and streetlamps, bees have been kept more for pollination than for their products. Margarine and soap, produced from vegetable oils as a branch of the chemical industry, have been successful, cheaper substitutes for animal fats. Lightweight cellulose fibers produced from wood and cotton, and first called rayon, have all but replaced silk, produced from the silkworm, *Bombyx*. Nylon and other synthetic fibers produced from coal have proved more durable than silk and become far more popular. Artificial wool, produced from wood, has become a serious permanent competitor with sheep's wool, to the dismay of Australians. The modern demand for fertilizers in agriculture long ago exceeded the supply of animal manure; the phosphate and potassium mines and the nitrate chemical factories are the chief dispensers of fertilizers.

Man's numbers are greater than those of all the large domestic animals taken together. In the world, there are more swine than horses, more sheep than swine, more cattle than sheep. The

horse population has been in actual decline since 1920; the others are only slowly increasing in numbers, but not in pace with the increase in human population. Though the animals know it not, man today is the principal deciding factor whether animals shall live or die.

A Regional Example: Southern California

The theme of the modern dominance of man on the earth can best be demonstrated by a regional example. Whenever man comes in numbers into a region new to him, he promptly modifies the natural environment according to the cultural configuration he brings with him. An excellent case study of the rapid transformation of a region, in accordance with modern men's changing evaluations of what a land "is good for," as based on their technological and sociopolitical capabilities for effecting change, is afforded by Southern California (Table 13.1).

A huge area of the American Southwest was characterized in prehistoric time by a seed-gathering economy. What happened in Southern California was that men with an exceedingly simple way of life entered this area early and, despite great end-of-the-Pleistocene changes of climate and sea level with all the attendant ecological shifts, held on to their mode of existence. Here was an ideal environment for human existence, which provided enough easily collected plants, animals, and shellfish for foodstuffs. The record simply reads: vast time, great change in the natural environment, very little cultural change. Seeming to resist change, the California Indians remained collectors down to historic time. The dominant force was cultural, not physical-environmental.

Remarkably peaceful and stable, California Indians constituted the greatest concentration of Indian population in North America; about $7\frac{1}{2}$ per cent of all North American Indians are estimated to have lived in Southern California. These people effectively occupied the region for tens of thousands of years down to two centuries ago. The character of both the oak-park grassland and the chaparral was the result of periodic disturbance of the wild vegetation by Indian-set fires, presumably to improve hunting conditions of a future season. The conclusion one comes to is that Indians in the coastal zone–alluvial lowlands and grizzly bears in the mountains had, through evolution by natural selection, effectively established a remarkable equilibrium in competing for domi-

TABLE 13.1 SOCIAL AND TECHNICAL DEVELOPMENTS CONTRIBUTING TO THE TRANSFORMATION OF SOUTHERN CALIFORNIA
(*First to a Cultivated Land, Then to an Urban-Industrial Complex*)

"In the hands of an enterprising people, what a country this might be."
Richard Henry Dana, Jr., *Two Years before the Mast* (1840)

Year of Change	Social Factors	Plant and Animal Introduction	Technological Development	Southern California Population
To A.D. 1769	Indian tribes	Collectors of seeds and shellfish Wild plants of no commercial interest	No agriculture; no domestication	75,000? Indians
1542	European discovery (Cabrillo)			
1602	Coastal exploration (Vizcaino)			
1769	Spanish colonial settlement: First mission, presidio, and port at San Diego (Portola and Serra); 21 missions by 1820, 9 in Southern California	Orange, olive, grape, fig, wheat, vegetables, onion, potato, peppers, horse, longhorn cattle, sheep, goat, pig, mule, donkey	First irrigation; gravity flow; brush and earth dams; clay tile; mission gardens; patio, arches, adobe masonry and stucco; land survey by "metes and bounds"	
1774	Overland route from Sonora (Anza)			
1781	Pueblo of Los Angeles		Plaza as urban focus; gold placers in Cargo Muchacho	600 whites
1784	Private land grant system extended to Southern California (Nieto, Dominguez, Verdugo)			
1800				1200 whites
1803–1804	First American ships from New England engaged in sea-otter trade to Canton, China			
1815	Last of the Manila Galleons (Acapulco-Manila since 1565)			
1817	First school in Los Angeles			
1821	Mexican declaration of independence from Spain		Cattle ranchos (1820–1862); hides and tallow exported	3270 whites 48,000 Indians
1826	First American fur trappers (Jedidiah Smith) arrived overland			
1833–1834	Secularization of mission properties begun			
1841	First American settlers arrive overland to Los Angeles			
1842	Discovery of gold (Newhall)			
1847		English walnut		
1848	Gold Rush begins in north: Treaty of Peace with Mexico		Hydraulic engineering skills: flumes, aqueducts, pipes	
1850	Statehood; annexation to U.S.A.; 3 Southern California counties created: Santa Barbara, Los Angeles, San Diego; Trespass or "No Fence" Act; first Chinese in Los Angeles			Less than 8000 whites (*Continued*)

Table 13.1 (Continued)

Year of Change	Social Factors	Plant and Animal Introduction	Technological Development	Southern California Population
1851	First American settlement: El Monte; Private Land Title Claims Act		Lumbering (sawmill) in San Bernardino Mountains	
1852	Mormon settlement: San Bernardino	Alfalfa	San Bernardino Baseline & Meridian; Range & Township survey applied to Southern California lands outside Spanish-Mexican land grants	
1853	San Bernardino County formed			
1854		Prune		
1856		Almond; beekeeping		
1857–1858	First cooperative agricultural society (Anaheim, the German colony)		Commercial wine making; extensive surface irrigation	
1858	Los Angeles County Hospital established; Butterfield Overland Mail Company; Wilmington founded			
1859			Food preservation: tin containers	
1860	Bullfights banned in Los Angeles, baseball club formed		Food preservation: natural dehydration	25,000
1861			Transcontinental telegraph extended from San Francisco to Los Angeles	
1861–1862	Great flood			
1862	Smallpox epidemic; Homestead Act (U.S.); Morrill Act, land-grant colleges (U.S.)			
1862–1865	Drought: collapse of cattle grazing; switch to sheep pasturing; breakup of the ranchos			
1868	University of California (Berkeley); First banks in Southern California; Hayward & Co., Hellman, Temple & Co.		Metal-bladed windmills and first artesian water well (Wilmington)	
1869			Railroad: Los Angeles and San Pedro; Cerro Gordo Mine (lead), Inyo Mountains	
1870	Santa Ana founded; Riverside founded by Southern California Colony Association; beginning of irrigated commercial fruit		Food preservation: artificial dehydration	32,000
1872	"No fence" law; expansion of unfenced farmland marked completion of change from cattle and sheep grazing		Steam-powered pumps (L.A.)	
1873	Ventura County formed; Pasadena founded; L.A. Library Assoc.; L.A. High School	Navel orange	Cast-iron irrigation pipe; Panamint district (silver)	

(Continued)

Table 13.1 (*Continued*)

Year of Change	Social Factors	Plant and Animal Introduction	Technological Development	Southern California Population
1874	Pomona and San Fernando founded	Lemon (Lisbon)	Darwin mines (lead-silver-zinc)	
1875	First commercial oil well, in Pico canyon (near Newhall); Santa Monica founded	Cotton	Barbed wire for field enclosure Railroad: Southern Pacific	
1876			First oil refinery (Newhall)	
1877	Desert Land Law (U.S.)			
1880	Present State Constitution adopted; University of Southern California, first Protestant college	Valencia orange Lemon (Eureka)	Refrigerated railroad cars; diatomite quarried at Lompoc	65,000 (including 20,000 Chinese and 15,000 Indians, all California)
1882	Chinese Exclusion Act (prohibited immigration)		Railroad: California Southern; Concrete irrigation pipe; hydroelectric power (Etiwanda);	
1884	*Ramona* published (Southern California's first novel)		Bear Valley dam; water storage reservoir	
1885–1887	Railroad rate "wars"; heavy immigration from eastern and central U.S.; Boom of the Eighties: 100 towns platted, of which 38 remain today		Railroad: Atchison, Topeka & Santa Fe Electrically powered pumps First major oil field (Puente Hills)	
1886	Common law doctrine of riparian water rights upheld by Supreme court			
1887	Wright Act: first irrigation districts formed as cooperatives; collapse of "land boom" Orange Growers Protective Association of Southern California founded			
1888	Los Angeles Chamber of Commerce; commercial resurrection of mission tradition		Concrete irrigation dams	
1889	Tournament of Roses (Pasadena); beginning of recreation industry based on tourism; Orange County formed			
1890		Grapefruit (seedless)	Beet-sugar refinery at Chino; frost protection: oil-fired orchard heaters; food preservation: mechanical refrigeration	201,000
1892	San Gabriel Forest Reserve proclaimed (December 20)		Mt. Lowe Railway	
1893	Riverside County formed; also Southern California Fruit Exchange (marketing cooperative); San Bernardino Forest Reserve proclaimed (February 25)			

(*Continued*)

Table 13.1   (*Continued*)

Year of Change	Social Factors	Plant and Animal Introduction	Technological Development	Southern California Population
1894			Colton Plant, California Portland Cement Co.	
1896	Tideland oil wells drilled (Summerland)			
1900				304,000
1902	Reclamation Act (U.S.)			
1904			Yuma irrigation project and dam (opening of Imperial Valley)	
1905	Incorporation of Vernon, a planned industrial city	Melon (honeydew)		
1906	Mt. Wilson astronomical observatory	Avocado	Glenn Martin's first airplane	
1907	Imperial County formed		First utilization of natural gas	
1909	State Highways Act			
1910	San Pedro breakwater finished (man-made deep water harbor)		First aviation sporting meet (Dominguez Field)	752,000
1912		Date palm (Deglet Noor)		
1913	California Alien Land Act (Webb Act)		Motion pictures: beginning of entertainment industry	
			Owens River aqueduct completed (232-mile import of water to L.A.)	
1914	Panama Canal opened			
1915	Import of Mexican field laborers		Heavy-duty earth-moving machinery	
1917			Rotary well drilling; automobile assembly plant (Ford Motor Co.)	
1920	Los Angeles passes San Francisco in population size; consumption needs of increasingly large local market means import economy: meat, eggs, butter, cheese, feed grains Seven major oil fields discovered (1919–1925)		Highways: shipment by truck Rubber company plant	1,345,000
1922–1924	Boom of the "Twenties"			
1924	Federal Immigration Act: exclusion of Oriental labor; sharp drop in immigration from abroad			
1927	"County of Origin" water law			
1929	"Watershed Protection" act			
1930			Shipments by refrigerated truck	2,933,000
1934	Depression years		Seaways: Freon-refrigerated ships	
1935			Food preservation: quick freezing	
1936			Hoover Dam completed: electrical power imported to Southern California	

(*Continued*)

Table 13.1 *(Continued)*

Year of Change	Social Factors	Plant and Animal Introduction	Technological Development	Southern California Population
1939	More than one half of state population in Southern California			
1940			First Freeway (Arroyo Seco, 6 miles)	3,674,000
			All-American canal (Imperial Valley)	
1941			Colorado River Aqueduct completed (242 miles import of water to coast)	
1942–1945	World War II (Pacific orientation)			
1942			Kaiser Steel Plant (Fontana); military production program, especially aircraft and metal-products industries	
	Boom of the "Forties"—continuation and intensification of industrialization begun in 1920s; tremendous upsurge			
1947	in population (part of world's greatest peacetime migration), including large-scale Negro immigration		Interstate natural gas pipeline (from New Mexico and west Texas)	
1947–1953	Industrial growth greater than any other state			
1950	Two thirds of the people in cities; occupy 1 % of state area			5,653,000
1951			Import of crude oil from Saudi Arabia	
1957			Feather River project begun (first unit of California Water Plan, diverting water 750 miles from north of state to Mexican border)	
1960	Voters approve $1750 million bond issue for financing California Water Plan;			9,025,694
	Manufacturing now principal source of income			

Bibliography

Beattie, George W., and Helen P. Beattie, *Heritage of the Valley, San Bernardino's First Century*. Oakland, Calif.: Biobooks, 1951.

Cleland, Robert Glass, *Cattle on a Thousand Hills*. San Marino, California: Henry E. Huntington Library, 1951.

Dumke, Glenn S., *The Boom of the Eighties in Southern California*. San Marino, Calif.: Henry E. Huntington Library, 1944.

Gentilcore, R. Louis, "Ontario, California and the Agricultural Boom of the 1880's," *Agricultural History*, Vol. 34, No. 2, April, pp. 77–87, 1960.

McWilliams, Carey, *Southern California Country: An Island on the Land*. New York: Duell, Sloan, and Pearce, 1946.

Raup, Hallock F., "San Bernardino, California. Settlement and Growth of a Pass-Site City," *University of California Publications in Geography*, Vol. 8, pp. 1–64, 1940.

Raup, Hallock F., "Piedmont Agriculture in Southern California," *Yearbook of the Association of Pacific Coast Geographers*, Vol. 6, pp. 26–31, 1940.

Raup, Hallock F., "The German Colonization of Anaheim, California," *University of California Publications in Geography*, Vol. 6, pp. 123–146, 1932.

Raup, Hallock F., "Land Use and Water Supply Problems in Southern California; The Case of the Perris Valley," *Geographical Review*, Vol. 22, pp. 270–278, 1932.

Robinson, W. W., *Ranchos Become Cities*. Pasadena, Calif.; San Pasqual Press, 1939.

Thomas, William L., Jr. (ed.), *Man, Time, and Space in Southern California* (Supplement to *Annals* of the Association of American Geographers, Vol. 49, No. 3, Part 2), Washington, D.C., 1959.

nance of Southern California's space. Staying in their home territories, learning of resources and how to exploit them for food, each group (Indians and bears) substantially filled its area. The Southern California Indians were distinctly a part of nature, dependent for their livelihood on the acquisition of foodstuffs produced by natural biotic processes over which they exerted little control.

After Cabrillo's voyage of discovery in 1542, a period of 227 years elapsed before permanent Spanish settlement began, at San Diego presidio and mission. After 1769, bears could no longer compete with men on horseback possessing guns, and Southern California's future lay wholly as man directed. Spanish settlement and missionary zeal focused on the coastal zone and alluvial lowlands, where Indians were most numerous, and where overland transport and communication were easiest. As a result, a significant portion of the wild landscape of Southern California was subjected to drastic reinterpretation. But Spanish occupancy was never wholehearted or very successful. The best efforts of the military and missionaries failed to make the chain of 21 California missions self-supporting, and after 52 years, partly as a result of Mexican independence, the system fell apart.

Nevertheless, Southern California inherited an important Spanish legacy (see Table 13.1). Permanent European settlements began 200 years ago in a region whose natural environmental characteristics were remarkably similar to Mediterranean Spain. In a familiar setting, the Spanish readily introduced their technology, which made possible a productive agriculture based on domestic plants and animals and the use of gravity-flow irrigation, on Spanish schemes of settlement, their architectural styles, their place-names, systems of water rights, and systems of land tenure. The Spanish evaluation of the natural environment followed Judaeo-Christian thought, which distinguished man from nature as epitomized in the injunction of the Deity that man not only should be fruitful and multiply like the plants and animals, but that, in addition, he should:

"fill the earth and subdue it; and have dominion over the fish of the sea and over the birds of the air and over every living thing that moves upon the earth" (*Genesis*, I, 28).

These kinds of biblical commands are best understood and followed by a people of an agricultural and pastoral tradition, who could thus interpret a natural environment as being provided by God for man's use.

Spanish tenure was brief and insecure, but the transformation of Southern California to a cultivated land, once begun, continued at an increasingly rapid pace. New England "Yankees" discovered Southern California in 1803–1804, while poaching for sea otters, to begin a lucrative China trade, and only a few decades elapsed before Americans came to stay; in 1850 California became part of the Union. But most of the earliest settlers in Southern California came from the greatest distances: from Germany, France, Poland, Great Britain, and China. Only after the late 1870s was Southern California engulfed by a tidal wave of Americans.

The accompanying chart (see Table 13.1) shows the quickening pace of change:

1. The social factors (cooperative societies, laws, institutions, significant events) that marked the change first to a commercial agricultural export economy and thence to a society now industrial-based and consumer-oriented.
2. The later introductions of domesticated plants. Since the native plants of the natural environment provided no staple food products, and there were no domesticated crop plants, the creation of an agricultural economy was dependent on importation of many new species and varieties from all parts of the world.
3. The technological developments (such as transportation improvements, irrigation techniques, and other inventions and processes) that contributed first to the advance of agriculture and then to the rise of an urban-industrial complex.
4. The fantastic growth in total population, decade by decade, for the eight southern counties of California. Nearly ten times as many people are now in Southern California as were there in 1920.

The land called Southern California has been caught up in and vastly changed during the very abnormal period in world history of the last century and a half. It is a unique circumstance, combining abundance of capital, high quality of labor, complex technology, and an efficient social system with our particular evaluation of natural resources, that makes the present time so exceptional, far surpassing any previous occasion in human history. When the world's population reached about 500 million by 1700, one person in 7000 lived in Southern California. One in 350 persons in the world now lives there, probably one in 200 by century's end. Since 1963, California has been the most populous state in the United States; since 1938 the eight southern counties have contained more than half the state's population.

Present-day Southern California is man-made—a gigantic, magical improvisation. Virtually everything in the region has been imported: forage grasses, herbs, shrubs, trees, flowers, weeds, rats, birds, water, iron ore, gas, electrical energy—even its people. The movement of people to this region during and since World War II has been the largest migration in American history. Almost all have gone to the cities and suburbs, with the result that a distinctly artifical (man-made) urban-industrial landscape has been spread over the lowlands and adjoining hills. For example, more than one third of all buildings in Southern California have been constructed since 1945. And no region of such a size in America is dominated by one city to the extent that Los Angeles, with its 454 square miles, dominates Southern California. It is no wonder that other Americans scoff at the artificiality of Southern California, for there is nothing like it elsewhere in the United States. But the clincher is that many people seem to like this human creation, for the influx of population continues.

Man's evaluation of the natural environment of Southern California has been determined by the cultural configurations, including values and attitudes, of the peoples making the settlement. The Spanish worked in a familiar environmental framework and managed to construct a pattern that reproduced the Mediterranean cultural landscape of their homeland. Their applecart was upset by Indians who did poorly at forced labor because of many lacks: of education, of a sense of group cohesiveness, of resistance to disease; also, a government decision left the missions without support. Whereas the Spanish were really comfortable here, accepting the seasonal regime of winter moisture and summer drought, the Anglo-Saxons took a somewhat different approach. They adopted many of the Spanish ways but, where these did not suffice, they made over the natural environment to suit their purpose, such as importing water from Northern California and the Colorado River, natural gas from western Texas, and installing air conditioners. It does seem a bit ironic that the society that has made the greatest changes in the natural environment yet has had the least longevity in Southern California should now be the one most concerned about assuring its own future.

Questions: On the Futures of Human Technologies and Human Habits

If we grant that man has by now learned major and significant lessons in material cultural technology and that he is now quite able to manipulate many aspects of his earthly environment to his own ordering, questions arise concerning the future. What are the limits of material technology? Has material technology outreached social technology? What can man now do about his habituated non-material cultural systems that stand in the way of future material technological development of the earth as the home of man?

In egoistic pride, concerning human ability to manipulate the earth, some of us occasionally daydream about the future, and about what human life may be like when man has been able to put into practice all the material technological procedures he now has learned, and is still learning, in the research laboratory. Such dream constructs often imply that no man will need to perform heavy physical labor in order to live, that quiet green spaciousness will intermingle with and surround each living community, that each such community will be air-conditioned to a temperature-humidity regime most favorable to human biology, that recreational play and enjoyment of the finer things in life will be for all, and that man will live to be 150 years of age on the average. Other daydreams put things somewhat differently, such as that cities will be built at the bottom of the sea, or under mountain ranges with elevators to the tops, and so on. Do not laugh at this, as did the friends of Leonardo da Vinci when he talked of flying machines and as did the friends of John Wilkins when he talked of traveling to the moon! If man has learned the basic lessons in Science, the future development and extension of human manipulation of the earth may be even more revolutionary than that which man has accrued in the last four hundred years. But to what end, and for whom?

In the long evolutionary history of the planet Earth the competitive struggle brought to dominance in the biological world a species of life-form we call Man. Many species were eliminated during that history by their own evolutionary tangents. As a species of life-form, man proved more and more successful in the competitive struggle. He, alone, evolved naturally to the biologic form that could, by his own purposeful manipulative skills (culture and cultural technology), alter his competitive position among other life-forms, even using some of them to further his own advancement. Man finally has come to dominance. But dominance finds him with large numbers of his own species, spread over the earth in great variety of size and color, varying further in minor biological attributes, all possessed of the same general ability to look to the future of his own kind. Dominance finds man with almost infinite varieties of habituated living systems. It finds man still possessed of numerous instinctive animal urges and reactions, all inherited from his far past and not intrinsically altered by his formulation of social living systems. The material technology of man now almost conclusively demands that the earth be merged into one operative reservoir of resources for all mankind. The variety of human living systems need not be merged into one great system, but there is need for a kind of system by which mankind, as a whole, can utilize that reservoir so that all members of the species may live happily.

In the second half of the twentieth century man is nearing a crossroads, a crossroads of his own making, in the ultimate sense. His very success at inheriting the earth now impels the further question of how he shall use that earth. Now that man has come to dominate the earth, what will he do about mankind as the possessor of the earth? Either the numbers of mankind will increase further, accompanied by bitter struggle for territoriality and the possession of the resources of the earth, or man will decide on some patterns of cultural compromise, through which social technology may make life satisfactory for restricted numbers of mankind.

Fortunately, perhaps, man has not totally mastered the technological control of the earth. He cannot yet shut off a hurricane before it does damage; he cannot make it rain year after year in the deserts of the earth; he cannot yet live on the bottom of the sea; he cannot submerge a continent in a fit of anger. Man still is subject to certain of the physical systems that combine to make the earth what it is. Unfortunately, surely, man has not yet really mastered the social control of the earth, either. One societal system cannot prevent poverty and suffering in another system, although the technological means are available by which the second system can live a better life. The

operative physical systems of the earth, however, can be lived with until such time as man can alleviate the painful stresses from them. The habituated cultural systems pose more of a threat to the future of mankind today than do the physical systems. The technological means are available to alleviate these painful stresses, too, but a twentieth-century problem lies in how to put those means to use.

Patently, we two authors cannot set forth here the specifics of the necessary choices. As authors, we are part and parcel of the American societal living system, partial to that system, and bound by its cultural mores. Each of us has lived within other cultural systems, enjoying virtues and finding shortcomings in them, even as we find both in our own system. The kindred feeling for many aspects of the way of life in other societies impels us to the conviction that the good in human living is shared by all mankind, and that the search for a common, peaceful, and friendly solution is a worthy search for twentieth-century man.

Imbalances Amid Advancements: The Reorientation of World Technical Mores

At the present the earth contains great contrasts in levels of achievement. Neolithic crop-growing procedures are still in practice, and Neolithic simple-household industry in still the rule among some peoples. Since other societies employ highly technological and highly powered systems, the gap between the most advanced and the lagging remains very wide. In the twentieth century the earth shows a greater range of economic, technologic, political, and sociopsychologic development than has ever been present in any past era. This simply means that there is greater imbalance among the societies of men today than has ever been true in the past on an earth now belonging to and dominated by man. At the same time cultural convergence is in process, in that the whole earth is becoming integrated toward the pattern of one resource region, and economic exchange from one industrial region touches most consuming regions of the earth, through the integration of modern space-adjusting processes.

There are those, of course, who insist on the view that some varieties of the species *Homo sapiens sapiens* are biologically superior to other varieties, and that superior varieties deserve more than do inferior ones. Biologically, we hold this to be a primitive, misguided, erroneous concept, one that cannot be preserved in the cultural development of mankind as a series of societies possessing bodies of culture. On the other hand, there can be no question whatsoever that the cultural system in force in one society is superior in systematic constructs to the cultural system in force in another society, and that in some societies there is strong internal imbalance in the understanding of, and sharing of, the advanced elements of the cultural system.

Nevertheless, the ultimate concern of mankind, on the planet Earth, must be the utilization of the resources of the globe for the greatest advancement of all mankind. To that end all societies of mankind must eventually strive for the lessening of human labor, the lessening of environmental stresses, the lessening of intersocietal stresses, the greater use of technological knowledge and skills in the employment of energy, the more efficient production of basic and primary economic goods, the more equitable sharing in consumption of these goods, and the limitation of human numbers to a total commensurate with the effective capacity of the earth. This sort of aim is no less than the utopian search for universal peace, prosperity, and freedom in perpetuity on this planet. The aim is not the search for privilege. It clearly involves the assumption of responsibility by all societies of mankind, for the ultimate common good of the species. It is a natural evolutionary conclusion to the emergence of man as a species of life-form on the planet Earth. In the twentieth century it is still, unfortunately, somewhat utopian; but is it beyond ultimate reach?

In the twentieth century the varieties of advancement in the material aspects of human culture have become much greater than ever, but the cultural stresses are greater, too. Not only is resource technology becoming more efficient, but the technologies of sharing are also improving tremendously, through space-adjusting techniques, to permit diffusion of knowledge over the whole earth in a way never possible during the Neolithic. Although many are impatient at what seems slow progress of the so-called developing regions and the most underdeveloped portions of the earth, this is a short-term view. It derives chiefly from the heavy intersocietal cultural stresses that suddenly have taken shape in the articulate expression of unhappinesses over Neolithic and post-Neolithic cultural systems that today seem unsatisfactory. The strains produced by those stresses have been

militant revolution, pillage, and suffering. There is more of all this now because the population of the earth is larger than ever and very unequal in distribution; the possibilities of worldwide cultural change are greater than ever within an equal time period; there is greater imbalance in world culture than ever; and the members of a given society in a far country can now know better than ever what are the cultural systems of another far country. Revolutions are best mounted not by the poor and ignorant, but by those who know enough to know they want more.

The outlook is not totally clouded, however. The strong demands of societies, in the face of greater imbalance, can be met by collective human action in ways never possible in an earlier era. There is both challenge and opportunity for resident mankind of the late twentieth and early twenty-first centuries. The reorientation of world technical mores is a first-order priority that must take into account both the cultural systems and the environmental characteristics of the homelands of the congeries of human societies residing on the earth today. There is collective responsibility, for all mankind, in this reorientation of the human culture that has brought man to his position of dominance. The continued dominance of the earth by man depends on his success in repairing the imbalances in cultural systems and technical mores.

Demands for Resources, and the Future of Industrialization

All kinds of maps portraying production, distribution, and consumption clearly demonstrate that patterns of demand are high in a few parts of the earth and range down to negligible amounts in other sectors of the earth (Fig. 13.1). The United States is the largest single producer-consumer of power, raw materials, and productive agents, followed by Northwest Europe, the Soviet Union, Japan, India, Canada, Mediterranean Europe, China, Australia, Brazil, and South Africa. The United States is a high-ranking producer of nearly half the minerals and industrial agents important to current world industrialization. The Soviet Union is slightly ahead or not very far behind the United States in many of these items. This underscores, of course, the significant positions of the large countries, each of which possesses a complex geological structure and rich endowment of mineralization. A number of small countries have long

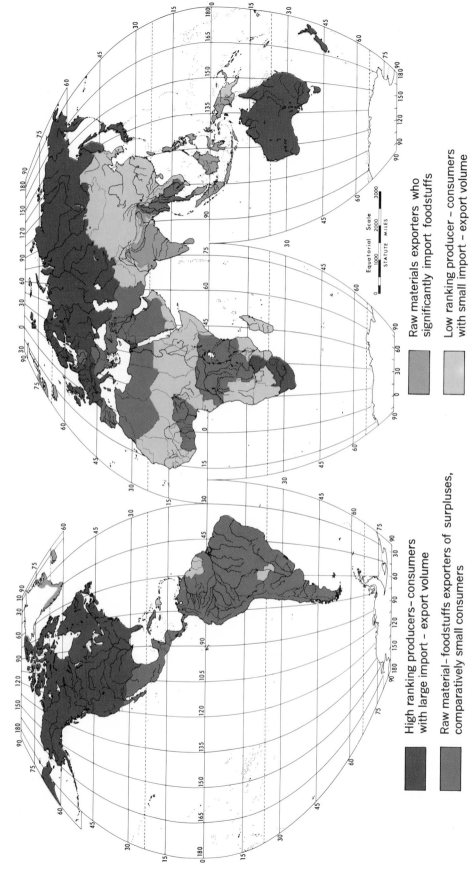

Raw materials exporters who
significantly import foodstuffs

Low ranking producer – consumers
with small import – export volume

High ranking producers–consumers
with large import – export volume

Raw material–foodstuffs exporters of surpluses,
comparatively small consumers

FIG. 13.1 COMPARATIVE PRODUCTION AND CONSUMPTION LEVELS.

554

been ranking producers of single mineral raw materials, or small raw-materials groups.

There is every expectancy, for the near future at least, that the aforenamed countries will continue, or intensify, their heavy demands for the same raw materials, as well as for some of the newer types of resources just beginning to come under technological control. The fractionation of the rest of the world into relatively small political states or economic unions means that tabulations of production, export, and import will always show a wide scattering and relatively smaller totals. At the same time, however, the demand patterns for many of the fuels, raw materials, and agents are bound to increase around the earth, for the very progress of industrialization dictates that this be so. For example, the Philippines has long appeared on exporter lists for a variety of materials and for wood products, and has appeared on importer lists for most of the range of manufactured commodities and for petroleum products. Now, government planning programs have been established for the broad-scale industrialization of the country, protective tariffs have been established and will increase, and investment control is functioning. A small iron and steel industry is in production-expansion, wood-products manufacture is steadily increasing in wide range, the manufacture of many of the simpler consumer commodities is expanding, and many kinds of processing now are carried on to turn out semifinished goods and industrial agents. Industrial maturity, however, is a good way off at present.

The Philippines is a relatively small country with a comparatively small demand for many kinds of industrial products. The export production of iron ore and the ferroalloys may also serve home industry, and copper and a number of other minerals are in adequate supply for a home industrial program. The export of some lines of manufactures will soon become normal, and the range will expand. However, until the Philippine industrial program has come fully of age there can only be an increasing demand for many raw materials and for industrial agents not yet produced. Geological surveys still incomplete may find resources not now known, particularly petroleum-natural gas, but the Philippines may never produce all of its resource requirements. Its power sources lie chiefly in hydroelectricity, but these cannot serve all industrial needs.

The potential industrialization of Jamaica, now coming into a ranking position as a bauxite miner and soon to be a significant processor of alumina, can only present a more extreme case for a long-continued wide range of demand. The example of Nigeria is not so extreme but is significant, nonetheless. Long an exporter of agricultural products, more recently also an exporter of particular minerals, and perhaps destined to produce significant amounts of petroleum, the raw material-agent demands of Nigerian industrialization will be very significant for considerable time.

The simple fact is, of course, that no political state has a full sufficiency of everything needed by modern industrialization. In part this is a matter of continuing incompleteness of geological survey, particularly in the newer minerals. Partly it is a matter that the domestic materials of any one country may present technological problems in mining-smelting-refining, and that it has been cheaper in the past to buy an easily refined mineral abroad. In good part it is that modern industrialization has such a tremendous range of demands for raw materials that only the far ends of the earth may fill them. Future development of industrialization can only increase this interdependence of all industrial societies upon the resources of the whole earth.

The world demand for all kinds of raw and finished materials is regionalized according to localized rates of population growth, progressive economic expansion, and the specific rates of industrialization. Regional rates of industrialization, in turn, will probably remain rather closely related to the harnessed sources of power available. The regional inequality in the distribution of the fossil fuel and hydroelectric sources of power will continue to be a factor in economic development so long as the transport of power over long distances remains costly or difficult, or until some of the currently unharnessed sources of power become practical. This means that the present distribution of power sources is a key to the regional development of the earth's industrial economy in the more immediate future, barring some now totally unexpected breakthrough in technology. The argument returns, therefore, toward a final generalization that the northern hemisphere sectors of Anglo-America, Northwestern Europe, the Soviet Union, and China will continue to develop and to lead in the dual patterns of demand for raw materials and in industrialization. The technological development of some of the new sources of power will find these same regions able to employ the new technologies also, to give a further reach to the time dimension. In the southern hemisphere only Australia, and Argentina-Chile (as a regional unit), currently show significant potential in development. The day of the large-scale pattern of tropical development is coming, but for the more immediate future the prospect is one of growing development as a region of plant raw-material production. It will take significant technological maturity to bring the tropics strongly into the industrial world.

Currently, industrialization is viewed as the means for lifting the levels of living in the developing countries and in those far countries still pursuing Neolithic and post-Neolithic living systems. Occasionally, one is provoked to consider the question of what happens next, when all the world has become maturely industrialized? But one form of partial answer lies in the further question of what shall constitute mature industrialization? Can it ever be reached by all the far countries of the earth at any one given time? May it not be that continued research into the laws of physical matter will continuously extend the limits of resource extraction and conversion to that society most perseveringly pressing the search? Industrial chemistry is approaching the point at which solar energy may convert a large variety of presently inert materials into desired products of a different nature and composition. The ultimate question of the final future of manufacturing, then, can be construed as a question of how long will the sun in our universe continue to pour effective amounts of solar energy onto the surface of the earth.

An almost certain conclusion of the inquiry into the future of industrial procedure yields the generalization that technological industrialization has limits sufficiently extended so that it is not resources, or industrial technology, that pose threats to the future of human existence. It is, rather, social, psychological, economic, and political limits that pose the threat to the continuance of industrial manufacture. If mankind cannot learn to control its own numbers, if mankind cannot devise a process of settling human differences other than by the wasteful expenditure of resources in war, if mankind cannot restrict criminal behavior toward its own kind, and if mankind cannot achieve egalitarian social practice toward all members of its own species, then industrial manfacturing has limits outside its own field.

This is not to say that all present systems of industrial manufacture shall continue unabated for all times. This never has been true in the past, and it is unlikely to be true in the future. The predictive ability of modern Science is not sufficiently highly developed for man to predict the form and nature of the chief manufactured product a thousand years hence, and no more can man predict the precise technology that will be involved or the shape of the factory in which it will be produced. So long as man is able to create power, so long will he be able to process materials into different forms.

The Long-Run Balance: Extraction, Production, and Consumption

There is no casual and easy way to express the facts of present total energy production balanced against total consumption in the course of a year for the earth as a whole. The accuracy of data on both counts and of assumptions in values to be set is not very high. How many calories of energy should suffice a person for a year for all consumption needs? What might he like to consume? The issue is not sheer physiologic support of the human body in a nonactive state, but total consumer requirements. There are obvious differences throughout the earth at present, and we can provide only crude and assumed approximations at any point (Fig. 13.2). There is a basis for assuming a long-term human need for just over 2000 calories per day per person for biologic existence, yielding a total annual per capita requirement of about 750,000 calories. The assumed 5,000,000 inhabitants of the mid-Paleolithic era would have consumed about 3,750,000,000,000 calories per year (more briefly expressed as 3.75×10^{12}). The material resources of the earth then must have provided a considerable surplus, although we cannot put a measure to the annual availability of directly consumable plant, animal, and marine resources. The present world total population need, for food alone, is a bit less than twice *per day* what the Paleolithic total was *per year*; the present annual food requirement is not far from 2.5×10^{15} calories. It is obvious that such an amount must be grown or manufactured, since gathering and collecting could never yield this total from the wild resources of the earth.

We can make no sound assumption regarding the nonfood energy requirement for mid-Paleolithic man, but there are population groups resident

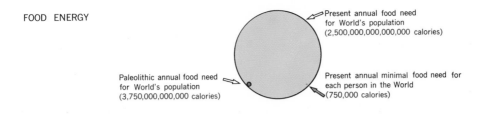

FOOD ENERGY

Present annual food need
for World's population
(2,500,000,000,000,000 calories)

Paleolithic annual food need
for World's population
(3,750,000,000,000 calories)

Present annual minimal food need for
each person in the World
(750,000 calories)

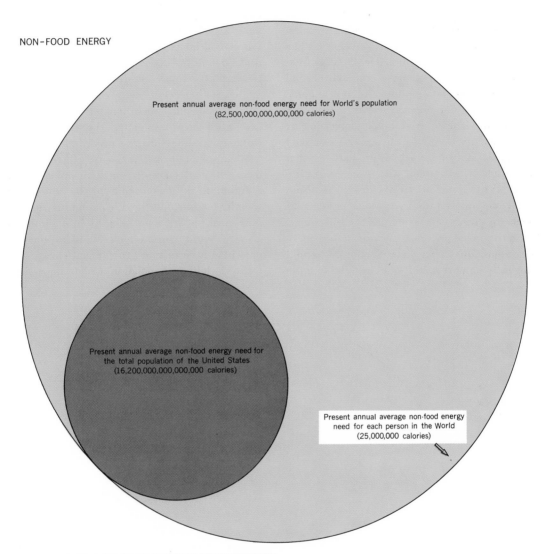

NON-FOOD ENERGY

Present annual average non-food energy need for World's population
(82,500,000,000,000,000 calories)

Present annual average non-food energy need for
the total population of the United States
(16,200,000,000,000,000 calories)

Present annual average non-food energy
need for each person in the World
(25,000,000 calories)

FIG. 13.2   COMPARISONS IN ENERGY CONSUMPTION.

on the earth today that probably require not much more nonfood energy than did Paleolithic man. Most of the earth's present population lives at levels far above the Paleolithic, however, and there are grounds for an assumed average annual consumption of energy per capita at about 2.5×10^7 (25,000,000) calories, yielding an annual world requirement of about 8.25×10^{16}. The wide dis-

crepancies in present world consumption levels range from about 8.25×10^5 to about 8.1×10^7 (that is, from 825,000 calories per person per year to about 81,000,000). The latter figure is near the average often employed to characterize per capita energy consumption per year in the United States during the late 1950s.

It is obvious that some of the earth's present

inhabitants require only a little energy beyond that contained in the food they consume, whereas other inhabitants consume or utilize nearly 100 times as much energy as needed for biologic continuance. The latter consumption is involved in what is customarily termed a high level of living. Such a level utilizes huge amounts of coal, hydroelectric power, petroleum, natural gas, wood products, and other energy sources to process the industrial commodities (the natural growth items themselves consuming energy) purchased, used, and "consumed." The American level of living, of course, includes food supplies that have a net energy cost well beyond the simple calorie consumption of food per capita. The steak eaten for dinner involves a relatively low level of efficiency in resource conversion by the bovine animal yielding the steak. An old and crude maxim in Chinese agriculture has been that a man could live on about what it cost to feed a cow, so why keep a cow? In American agriculture steaks come out at little more than 15 per cent efficiency in energy conversion, and the 160 pounds of meat consumed per capita per year in the United States approximates an energy total that could biologically support several more people were the

cattle source foods converted directly into human food.

Will it be possible for the United States to go on consuming so great a supply of the world's energy, to the exclusion of other sectors of the earth? Will it be possible for the rest of the earth's inhabitants to raise their energy consumption to a satisfactory rate without penalizing Americans? Will it be possible for all the earth's people to live at the same high level as present-day Americans? These are the ultimate questions to be faced in any discussion of the reserves, or the conservation, of the earth's natural resources. Assuming that the United States level of energy consumption is lifted only a reasonably small amount during the next two or three decades, and that the rest of the world makes outstanding progress toward modern industrial consumption patterns, what will the requirements then be? There are too many unknowns and assumptions in this question for the answer to be soundly realistic, but the calculation may be made for the sake of argument (Fig. 13.3). Assuming the average world consumption at about one-third present American rates, the annual energy needs for a 5 billion population could approximate

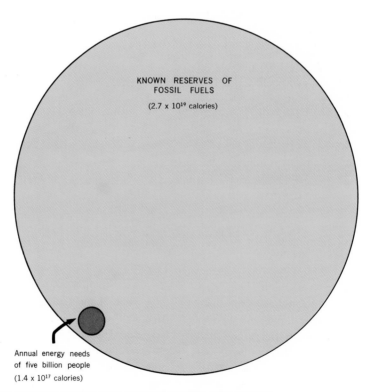

KNOWN RESERVES OF
FOSSIL FUELS

(2.7 x 10^{19} calories)

Annual energy needs
of five billion people
(1.4 x 10^{17} calories)

FIG. 13.3 FUTURE ENERGY NEEDS AND KNOWN POWER RESOURCES.

1.4×10^{17} calories. The known recoverable fossil fuels in the standard resource table approximates 2.7×10^{19} calories, yielding an expectable exhaustion date of about 200 years, give or take a little for now unexpected future finds and for recovery at somewhat less than currently estimated rates. But this obviously would mean power-conversion equipment that could substitute fuel sources, and it would mean a total world sharing of the fossil fuel resources, of which the United States has an overly large share in its coal and oil shale deposits. Any further increase in world consumption would shorten the period prior to exhaustion. Our calculation does not include water power, nor does it include the uranium group of power minerals, and it makes no allowance for the use of solar energy in direct applications. Neither does it involve the possible increase in efficiency of resource conversion, which could stretch out the use of known resources. Future improvement in energy production can be very marked. There already is considerable sharing of total energy consumption in the shipment of manufactured goods from one region to another, but the foregoing assumptions on energy sharing would involve a far greater application, probably in ways not now taking place.

The Control of Cultural Environments

Mankind is the despair of Science. When not perverted by man, Science is often held to be orderly, rather deterministic, always at least highly probabilistic, and highly objective. The consequence of a known set of procedures can be relied upon to produce a calculated result. Human performance, on the other hand, often seems subjective, susceptible to irregularity, and normally has been held to be sufficiently nonregular in reaction to that a known set of stimuli will produce varieties of responses. Certain types of human performance, of course, contain a high degree of probabilism, and one sector of contemporary geographic thought is concerned to demonstrate that a great deal of human activity is rather distinctly probabilistic in performance. One of the very features that brought man to the dominance of the earth, however, was his ability to think of a different response to given conditions. The hunch, the startled response, the calculated devious act, and the act of desperation are most often barely probabilistic. In the social tendencies of man there is a strong aggregative trend to do things alike, derived from his gregarious and social tendencies, but there also is the trend to individualism, which rejects the aggregative principle for the individual decision in an unpredictable direction.

Social scientists, therefore, have been wary of predicting the behavior of man in the possession of culture. The very differences between the Occident and the Orient have been held up as proof of the nonregularity of cultural performance. The variable outlook of the Latin, the Slav, the Bantu, and the Malay are adduced to the support of irregular variation in human behavior. The past patterns of change in societal culture, including the sheer diversifications of very primitive culture into innumerable systems of culture, had a very significant element of irregularity in them. Whether these past changes possessed an irregularity fully random, or less than random in the statistical sense, cannot be proven now. Within the last several centuries, as we have repeatedly suggested, there has been taking place a convergence of culture, a lessening of diversification, and a centering upon more significant common attributes. Since 1800 the rates of convergence have accelerated. The planned reorganization of Japanese industrial culture, for example, since the 1860s is a specific case. Within the last few decades the rates of convergence have increased still more rapidly, as the diffusion of industrialization and of its products, such as sewing machines and flashlights, has spread over the earth. In the trends of converging cultures there must be an increase in the probabilistic elements of cultural performance.

As the body of human culture has increased, individual cultures have increased internally in the elements that bind them together. The individual progressive body of culture, the cultural environment surrounding a single person or the whole society, has increased in depth, in range, in technology, in institutions, in artifacts, and in occupational specialization, but it has also increased in total strength. As we come toward the modern era it can be seen that ranking cultures have a strength and a context almost apart from the persons of the society possessing a given culture. American culture is what Americans make it, yet the very strength of American culture in the second half of the twentieth century imposes cultural mores on Americans toward patterns of collective decision to greater degree than ever was true in the past. It sometimes appears that evolving American culture controls Americans, as in the mechanistic trends toward greater automation, whether we like it or not.

Prior to about 1700 it could be said that group status counted for more than individual status; that is, a person was a member of a group within his society. The modern rise of the code of the rights of the individual would seem to be a trend toward sheer individualism within the society accepting the code. And yet there may be as great probabilistic performance among members of modern societies as among those of a far earlier day because of the institutionalized content and strength of the modern culture.

Among modernized contemporary societies there are numerous agencies that work toward the control of the cultural environment just as there were agencies in an earlier era. From first entrance into such groups as Cub or Brownie Scouts, the Sunday school class, or the regular day school kindergarten, on through the rest of his life the average American citizen is touched by agencies that work at controlling the American cultural environment. To the degree that such agencies are now widely spread elements of cultural control around the earth, such controls are effective in patterning cultural environments. These many personal agencies are augmented by impersonal agencies such as the five-year plan, the national economic plan, quasi-governmental programs for specific kinds of development, and the more formal governmental efforts at shaping, directing, and controlling the systems of culture.

Despite the trends toward cultural convergence exhibited in many ways, the individualism of societal cultures remains and will continue to remain. Many of the societal agencies working at control of the cultural environment aim directly at societal individualism, at those kinds of differences that distinguish one holistic society from another. The trends toward convergence are not yet trends toward world culture as a single mode. It might be added that the patterns of protest at cultural controls, within single cultures, seem to be taking probabilistic trends all over the earth. Although these protestors think of themselves as working toward individualisms, they are actually part of a pattern of convergence of world culture.

The Remaining Steps

Material technology and the integration of the earth into a single operating unit are sufficiently advanced for man to manage his own material welfare on the basis of known earth resources. It no longer is the lack of means of production, the absence of transport, or the ignorance of technological procedure that handicap the satisfactory level of living anywhere on the earth for the present population. Problems of satisfactory levels of living for our present population now lie in the inadequacies of the cultural systems of the earth, in the socio-psycho-econo-political structuring between and among the human culture groups that exist on the earth today. These inadequacies exist in the fields of both external and internal relations. Whereas Paleolithic man understood neither his physical world (and how to make it produce for him) nor the kinds of cultural systems that could make life comfortable, twentieth-century man has largely solved the primary problems of operating the physical environment to productive ends. However, twentieth-century man has not put into operation the kinds of cultural systems throughout the earth that would make life both comfortable and peaceful for all members of the human race. The steps remaining by which mankind can live satisfactorily in all parts of the earth lie entirely within the understanding of mankind, but there exists a basic human refusal to put into operation those cultural systems that could make worldwide life both satisfactory and peaceful.

We describe as Paleolithic any society that engages in a hunting-gathering-collecting economy, that is band-tribal in sociopolitical structure, that employs animistic ritualism by which to supplicate the gods of production of game and vegetable foods, that goes to war to protect its tribal territorial lands, that does not engage in economic procedures to accumulate wealth applicable to productive ends. What is it that forces such a group to continue its Paleolithic culture system during the twentieth century? It is *not* the limitations of the physical-biotic environment. Rather it is the historic drag within the minds of the members of the culture group that causes them to cling to the old ways in spite of the cultural patterns that may surround them, patterns that offer innumerable avenues of cultural change by which to bring themselves toward a balanced relationship with more advanced culture groups.

We describe as feudal, backward, underdeveloped, and poverty-ridden any society that concentrates the material wealth in the hands of a small class of multiprivileged aristocrats (be it great landed estates, the ownership of mines, or the ownership of other productive elements), that imposes a restrictive system of political management by which a few hold power, that maintains a social structure that strongly enforces stratification ranging from artistocrat-above-the-law to outcasts below having neither rights nor access to the law, that does not operate an educational system that extends the privileges of cultural improvement to all members of the society to the highest possible level, and that really has no plans or procedures by which to alleviate the poverty of its largest population component. It is indulging in Paleolithic thinking to place the blame for this compounded situation on the physical-biotic environment. The cure is available in world culture, the initiative is open to leadership of the society, and the means exist by which to lift the level of living; it is human failure that permits the continuance of the circumstances. The human failure lies in the selfish greed of human beings who continue the operation of the society in the traditional manner against collective need.

Science often holds that its rules transcend political, physiographic, and climatic boundaries, that the laws of physics or molecular biology are the same in the United States, in Patagonia, along the banks of the Congo River, or at the northern end of the Ural Mountains. The technologies of copper smelting can be operated anywhere on the earth, radio messages can be effectively relayed everywhere, and the planting of hybrid varieties of crop plants can be technologically systematized in all climatic zones except the severe microclimatic. Sociopsychologic and econo-political laws are equally applicable to all parts of the earth, among all societies. All members of the species *Homo sapiens sapiens* possess the capacities for learning, an equitable social system needs know no physiographic, climatic, or political boundary, and industrial technology can be applied in any society. It is patent that any cultural system can be put into operation in any part of the earth.

The biologic trait of exclusive territorialism may have been necessary in its elemental form to the first of the hominids, but is it any longer necessary for *Homo sapiens sapiens*? Is it beyond civilized man's capacity to devise cultural systems of territorialism for orderly living commensurate with the one-world technology operable in research in industrial chemistry? We saw, in the failure of the League of Nations, the unwillingness of mankind to integrate political management of the earth to a one-world cultural system. Do we see, in the United Nations, really revolutionary advancement commensurate with the need? In political management we see profound reluctance to take the needed steps; in many other aspects of United Nations programs and activities we do see systematic and progressive advancement of the highest order.

This is not the place in which to enlarge upon the world needs of mankind in general. We set down a simple list of the kinds of objectives that must form the remaining steps in cultural evolution necessary to the future satisfactory residence of *Homo sapiens sapiens* on the planet Earth. These are:

1. The open sharing of world natural resources.
2. The freeing of all human beings from restrictive social stratification prohibitive of individual development, and the establishment of systems of international law operative throughout the world permitting peaceful settlement of problems external to individual societal boundaries.
3. The worldwide development of educational systems of common bases providing minimal levels of individual advancement, and the establishment of systems of cultural "custom" operative on a worldwide basis for economic development.
4. The worldwide acceptance of population restriction to limits within world technological productive capacity.

The list is a minimal one, suggestive rather than inclusive, problem-minded rather than moralistic. Man has come a long way since the start of the Pleistocene, and his inventiveness has brought him to domination of the earth, but man's satisfactory continuance on the earth now depends on human initiative, tolerance, cooperation, and willful limitation, and on the devising of cultural systems commensurate with huge numbers of people as residents of the planet.

The chief direction of the foregoing comments was to external relations between human groups scattered over the earth. It is obvious, however, that within human cultural boundaries some of the same needs apply. No human society today provides potential satisfaction for all of its members within its own sets of rules, mores, and customs. The continuance of satisfactory life, within cultural groups, depends significantly on the working out of cultural procedures satisfactory to all members of the group. No longer may a dissident group emigrate to an empty land in which to indulge its own demands for new freedoms in new systems of culture.

We have repeatedly made the point that cultural advancement of human society has been by many small but cumulative steps taken in development of technological or institutional ways. We have also made the point that diffusion of new culture traits and trait complexes has gone around the earth eventually, to the end that many similar culture complexes have been adopted in most parts of the earth. We have made a third point that there has long been a contrast in the levels of living between the levels achieved by the leaders and those persisted in by the laggers. Although there are some who feel that the Industrial Revolution is just moving into full rates of achievement, may we momentarily assume that industrial and institutional technology has reached a degree of maturity constituting a "plateau"? The question then becomes: how long will it take for the established advanced culture complexes of the creative regions and societies to diffuse among all the regions and societies of the earth? Are all societies now ready to accept the new elements, to permit the levels of living throughout the earth to reach comparable planes of development? In other words, can we equate the Industrial Revolution, including all its subsidiary revolutions in agriculture, system of government, transportation, housing, music, and the like, with the Neolithic as an era of extremely rapid, worldwide advancement? May we equate the era of the seventeenth to twentieth centuries with the era that saw the crystallization of civilization in the Old World?

The twentieth century, particularly, is a period of extremely rapid cultural change throughout the earth. Diffusionary movements during the seventeenth to twentieth centuries have carried resource-extraction and resource-conversion procedures, space-adjustment and space-intensification procedures, consumer systems, living systems, governmental systems, and all kinds of ideas about societal operation to all parts of the earth. The Industrial Revolution is now available everywhere on earth. What will the congeries of human societies do about the issues of acceptance or refusal? How far will they go in any acceptance? We have noted that, in the twentieth century, there still are remnantal societies clinging to the systems of the Paleolithic. In the twenty-second century, will it be recorded that there still are societies that refuse to accept significant shares of the cultural revolution effected by the Industrial Revolution? Will such societies be few and remnantal or will they be both numerous and populous? Significant aspects of the future of man on the planet Earth depend on the completeness of acceptance of all elements of the Industrial Revolution, and upon the regional distribution of those acceptances over the globe. The regional differentiation of the Earth undoubtedly will present a variable pattern of advancement in the twenty-second century, just as it always has presented a variable pattern in the past. But where will the balance fall? Will there have been acceptance of material technology only, without change in cultural institutions? Will the integration of the earth's peoples into a peacefully working combine be significantly farther along? Will some balance in population control be sufficiently widely accepted that *Homo sapiens sapiens* will have achieved a balance among resources, technology, and consumption? Or will certain societies be threatening the overwhelming of the whole earth by their own kind, and the extermination of other peoples? The cultural revolution, properly managed by man, could ensure the cultural preservation of many ways of life. How far will it go?

The Irreversibility of Cultural Evolution

Occasionally the cartoonist, the science-fiction writer, or the prophet of doom projects man forward through time to the odd circumstance at which his culture has been reversed clear back to the level of the Paleolithic-Neolithic. This is an interesting speculation but one most unlikely to come to pass. It may not be beyond the power of Man, in a sudden fit of animal rage, to press some trigger on a technological system which could drastically reduce the numbers of mankind and poison the surface of the Earth and its atmosphere for an interval. The numbers of mankind who then continue to survive might well need their maximum skills in survival training, but those skills would not be at the same level as those by which Paleolithic and Neolithic man survived. The earth would then be a very different earth from that of Paleolithic man. Such survival would most certainly require all the compounded skills of the Industrial Revolution. Within a relatively short time span it becomes inconceivable that man could lose total touch with all elements of culture and technology devised since the Paleolithic. Even assuming that he lost many of them, mankind's new base and starting circumstances would be quite different from those that faced mankind at the start of the Neolithic.

The first men who made metal tools picked up pieces of pure copper ore or smelted simple carbonates or oxides obtained from the ground level. The earliest coal was available from surface exposures. Today, because the easiest available and purest substances have already been extracted and diffused through use, modern man has to probe ever more deeply with far more ingenuity for leaner ores at ever greater cost. It is more difficult and costly to drill an oil well 5 miles deep than to dig 50 feet for water. The complex processes of our industrial world can be continued for only so long as our tools and spare parts continue to be produced and our elaborate network of communication-transport-trade is maintained. Neolithic society could not begin again on our present-day world; too much has been disturbed, eradicated, and consumed. How could the simplest phases of an age of metals or of inanimate energy ever again come into being without easily available copper and iron and without easily available coal seams? It is conceivable that surviving remnants of our present population, in a postbomb world freed again from radioactive content, could live a curious kind of life scavenging off the artifacts of the prebomb era. However, it would be a new kind of living system, one not only lacking the characteristics of the old Neolithic but also lacking many elements of the present world order, and who knows what ecologic balance would obtain and what mutation change would have taken place in man? How long would it take such remnants, isolated in particular niches over the earth, to put together a reasonable system of world culture?

Man cannot turn back to a full-scale facsimile of the Neolithic world in which to elaborate a Neolithic operating program for any kind of activity possible in the future world. We may turn back to a lesson learned in earlier time, whose point we have perhaps recently neglected, but application of that old knowledge must be on terms commensurate with contemporary circumstances. It still is possible for a single family, or a small group of people, to go off into a wilderness and live a Neolithic life, but there are no longer sufficient wildernesses for the world's present population to do so. Similarly, Jeffersonian democracy, in the full sense, is simply not open by choice to the 200 million citizens of the United States. Our present environment is normal for us, and it includes such environmental components as clothing, housing, heating, modern technology, and modern medicine. The Paleolithic and Neolithic environments are now abnormal. We will not live in those environments, and since we are no longer fit to live in them, this may make us nostalgic but perhaps not unduly alarmed. We and our descendants are not able to dispense with the services of medicine (to maintain health) and technology (to maintain food supplies). The remedy for our dependence on technology is more, not less, technology.

The advances in public health and sanitation in most parts of the world, in the past half century, have lengthened the life of the human being remarkably, but they have also promoted the illusion that this is a one-way street and that man has totally conquered the whole of the biotic world. The truth is that no disease affecting man has yet been eliminated from the complex ecosystem in which he lives; the endemic repositories still retain all of the world's ailments, and if man becomes careless with his waste disposal procedures, the traffic could turn in the other direction. The biotic ecology of the surface of the earth is still an active system which, if thrown too badly out of balance in any one direction, reacts strongly in compensation in some counterdirection. Man so dominates all other life-forms on the earth that lions and tigers, for example, pose no real threat to man, but the world of insects, viruses, fungi, and the like is very much alive, very evolutionary, and capable of strong pressure on mankind as a whole. In an urbanizing and industrializing world, where the disposal problem becomes steadily more acute, disposal technologies are poorly developed and often given little thought. Our concern is not for the continued use of sewage on the vegetable gardens of China, Korea, and Japan, but for the disposal of the total variety of cultural wastes from such centers as New York, the Chicago industrial region, Southern California, greater Moscow, greater Tokyo, and greater Rio de Janeiro, from the whole of the northeastern manufacturing region of the United States, from the growing manufacturing region of central western India, and from other such regions.

Some new problems in biotic ecology have emerged out of industrialization, but most of the old problems remain with us in latent or merely quieted states. There was a year, not very long ago, when much of the world laughed at the smog problem of the Los Angeles Basin; today smog hangs over many of the world's cities in thickening layers which presage only trouble for mankind if its disposal technology is not revolutionized. There are those who are already worrying about the disposal of nuclear wastes from the coming power plants. These are symtomatic of the new cultural wastes problem not faced by the people of Egypt who went through the ten great plagues.

The ability of industrial chemistry has so far sufficed to maintain sanitary controls over water supplies in regions that both dump sewage and industrial wastes into rivers and then take their domestic water from the same rivers. Such heavily populated regions as the Rhine Basin, the lower Yangtze Basin, the lower Brahmaputra-Ganges Basin, and even the Mississippi Basin face a somewhat tenuous balance in control over water supply. But the margins need augmenting as both waste disposal and consumer demand for water from a larger population increase annually. Aside from the matter of quantity, the issue of quality raises questions for even the near future. It was remarked earlier that in humid regions, in particular, man has not been very careful of water.

The disregard for the equilibrium in biotic ecology has caused man many problems in the past, through either his elimination of a biological agent in an involved cycle or his disregard for the buildup of a regional situation that threw the biotic balance out of line. Although the uses of pesticides seem primarily to increase productivity in agriculture and to maintain control over vectors of disease, it is by no means certain what the long-term repercussions may be. Just as a Chinese campaign, in the late 1950s, to kill grain-eating sparrows probably did save some grain one year, it brought on increases in plant pests the next year which taxed the grain supply. The modern industrial era is a period of marked variation in human living systems, and one seriously threatening the balance of the biotic world. So far, man has shown little awareness of this threat to the implicit balance brought on by his cultural systems newly evolved during the modern revolutionary period. Mankind is still making progress in the obvious aspects of human disease, simple sanitation, and general public health, but some of the waste disposal systems are increasingly heightening the risks that present cultural controls may break down

at some point, to unleash a modern series of great plagues as the ecosystem's other elements move toward a new balance. These plagues could wreak havoc on a human world basically unexposed to many elements. We are not sounding any alarmist note, here, but simply pointing out that man does live within a large and complicated biotic ecosystem onto which his present cultural practices are throwing heavy stresses.

It sometimes is said that human technological achievement has reached the plane on which it may be possible for man to reverse at least some of the trends in human development. Population control does represent such a potential line of reversibility, but the cultural procedures by which such control may be made effective in themselves represent a further element in cultural evolution, and not a reversal. The success of population control, as a worldwide phenomenon, patently depends on advanced technologies, and it depends on the common participation of all societies on the face of the earth; such participation in a common program would represent cultural evolution of a significant order, since it has never yet been fully achieved in any other program. Equally, any other reversing trends will require unanimous consent and participation, furthering cultural evolution.

Man faces a unique set of circumstances in his present world, circumstances never before operative. There are three primary aspects to the present state of uniqueness: the total numbers of man, the levels of his culture, and the present face of the earth. None of these has ever obtained in its present pattern in any earlier time. To deal with the compounded problems they represent, no cultural system of the past is applicable. From lack of a cultural system mankind has moved to differing kinds of cultural systems; from maladjustments of his systems man has moved to new systems; from new successes he has created new circumstances that eventually produced new maladjustments; still newer systems have repaired the ills and brought still newer successes, creating still newer circumstances. It is crudely possible to see a certain kind of cyclic pattern in the succession of problems that cause search for solutions, in solutions that make possible new levels of achievement but also create maladjustments, in renewed searches for solutions and new breakthroughs. The Industrial Revolution has, in a sense, constituted a tremendous breakthrough, but it has in turn created a host of problems that require still newer solutions for the greatly expanded population that resulted from the breakthrough. The cultural solutions to twentieth-century problems must represent some new kinds of solutions never before deduced by man.

Responsibility for Achieving a Balance among Environment, Man, and Culture

Mankind, as a species controlling the earth in the twentieth century, is in a peculiar position. We have finally achieved a degree of technological mastery over our environment that enables us to do almost what we wish with the surface of our planet, so far as making it yield the kinds of things we know and like. Knowledge is power, and man has finally mastered many of the secrets of power. Power brings freedom for mankind, freedom from the drudgery of incessant human manual labor by which to carry on daily life. Power has brought predictability in production and has released man from the uncertainty of the bounty of Nature. But freedom brings issues of responsibility. Are the inventive, aggressive, and ambitious to hoard what they have, defying the rest of mankind? Or do they share their results and work out worldwide systems by which all mankind can live satisfactorily? Does mankind go on fighting itself for possession of the choice ecological environments, leaving to the irreversible trends of biologic and cultural evolution the whole future of mankind, wherever it may trend? Or does mankind use its accumulated cultural technology to stabilize certain elements of the progression in order that man may retain the leadership and control of the physical world that he now dominates. In the dire prediction of the prophet of doom there does lie the potential reality that unless mankind takes steps toward some controls mankind may face problems much too great for its cultural ability.

The peculiar position of mankind at present is that man knows what it is that man needs to do, but mankind cannot bring itself to take those steps. There are four culture complexes in which responsible evolutionary development in cultural systems must take place for a wholly humanized planet. Repeating in briefer listing the steps itemized on an earlier page, these four fields are: systems of worldwide sharing of raw materials and sources of power, systems of international civil adjudication of all common problems, systems of worldwide sharing of cultural technologies that will no longer permit any society to remain far below the level of general world technology, and systems of population control applicable to all societies.

To many people in all parts of the earth, including people in the United States, each of these steps is at present wholly unacceptable. Attitudes of nationalism, exclusivism, and the devil-take-the-hindmost are cultural patterns out of the past that remain strongly planted in human consciousness. Each was possible on an earth inhabited by relatively small numbers of people, an earth separated by time and distance into units that could be made to accord with some physical components making up the landforms, climatic regions, vegetative associations, soil zones, and water supply basins. Mankind went through a long series of eras during which biologic and cultural divergence took place to the end that mankind became a veritable congeries of differing societies practicing increasingly differing systems of culture. Most of human time on the earth fell within that broad trend of divergence: 1,999,500 years out of 2,000,000 years. Only for the last 500 years, in round terms, has mankind been on the other trend of convergence, and our heritage still is too clearly with us. It may take a while for mankind to come to terms with its own past and the problems of its future. Meanwhile the problems grow more urgent, and they must be solved in revolutionary steps, if man is to continue in the mastery of the Earth. Man now faces the responsibility of living up to the culture-creating creature he has become.

The sheer diversity of mankind is one of the major problems facing man today. In the twentieth century man must work at the procedures needed to bring his kind back toward the types of groupings that can live on the one earth which man has recognized the planet to be. The balance between one earth and the large number of "little worlds" is tenuous, almost constantly being broken by militant action of man against man, so that war seems more frequent than peace. Whether this issue is viewed as biological territorialism or as militant sociopolitical regionalism makes little difference.

The solution must be worked out to the end that man retains his control over the earth, even against himself, lest he threaten mankind by upsetting the whole systems of balances and by accumulating in too great numbers. The solution must include at least three kinds of values, in finding a lasting balance among physical-biotic environment, man, and culture. These are *self-realization* (or identity, or status) sufficient to the biological ego of individual men as members of a species, *stimulus* sufficient to keep the species from dying of boredom or committing too much crime against its own kind, and *security* in terms of biological support and a home territory for each member of the species. There is not much hope of the physical-biotic environment changing markedly within the required interval, nor is there much hope that man can by then drain off his surplus numbers to some other planet. Without culture there is little hope that man can attain any solution at all. The key element in the balance is Culture in the hands of Man. The inquiry into the nature of the ecosystem, the exploration of additional technologies, and the search for effective means of repairing errors of commission and omission against the environment, all in the hands of Science, are one segment in the achievement of that balance. The other segment must lie in the psycho-sociopolitical field. The sublimation of militant nationalism into cultural regionalism of a nonmilitant variety, the development of international institutional systems suitable to single-earth operation, and the development of social institutions encompassing all members of the species are the requisite elements on this front. The development of philosopho-psychologic cultural viewpoints amenable to the present technological skills of medicine, in the extension to worldwide practice of population control, becomes the most critical element in the whole question of balance.

The finding of cultural systems sufficient to the development of the environment-man-culture balance is not really an issue of the next ten years, although the problems become more pressing with every decade. The problems are those of the next century or two, for man has a short breathing space, still, in which to work out his solutions to them. The problems are sufficient to present opportunities for self-realization and stimulus in ample volume for all interested mankind. Security could be the result of success.

SELECTED REFERENCES

Addison, Herbert
    1955   *Land, Water, and Food.* London: Chapman & Hall. 248 pp.

Arensberg, Conrad M., and Arthur H. Niehoff
    1964   *Introducing Social Change.* Chicago: Aldine. 214 pp.

Baade, Fritz
    1962   *The Race to the Year 2000; Our Future: A Paradise or the Suicide of Mankind.* Garden City, N.Y.: Doubleday. 246 pp.

Boserup, Ester
    1965   *The Conditions of Agricultural Growth; The Economics of Agrarian Change Under Population Pressure.* London: George Allen & Unwin, and Chicago: Aldine. 124 pp.

Boyko, Hugo (ed.)
    1961   *Science and the Future of Mankind.* Bloomington, Ind.: Indiana University Press. 563 pp.

Brown, Harrison S.
    1954   *The Challenge of Man's Future; An Inquiry Concerning the Conditions of Man During the Years that Lie Ahead.* New York: Viking Press. 290 pp.

Burton, Ian
    1968   "The Quality of the Environment: A Review," *Geographical Review*, Vol. LVIII, pp. 472–481.

Carr, Donald E.
    1966   *Death of the Sweet Waters.* New York: Norton. 257 pp.

Ciriacy-Wantrup, S. V., and James J. Parsons (eds.)
    1967   *Natural Resources: Quality and Quantity.* Berkeley and Los Angeles: University of California Press. 217 pp.

Cottrell, Fred
    1955   *Energy and Society: The Relation Between Energy, Social Change, and Economic Development.* New York: McGraw-Hill. 330 pp.

Crombie, A. C. (ed.)

    1963   *Scientific Change: Historical Studies in the Intellectual, Social, and Technical Conditions for Scientific Discovery and Technical Invention, from Antiquity to the Present.* New York: Basic Books. 896 pp.

deSchweinitz, Karl, Jr.

    1964   *Industrialization and Democracy; Economic Necessities and Political Possibilities.* New York: Free Press of Glencoe—Macmillan. 309 pp.

Durand, John D. (ed.)

    1967   *World Population,* The Annals of the American Academy of Political and Social Science, Vol. 369, 163 pp.

Ewald, William R., Jr. (ed.)

    1967   *Environment for Man: The Next Fifty Years.* Bloomington, Ind.: Indiana University Press. 308 pp.

Finkle, Jason L., and Richard W. Gable

    1966   *Political Development and Social Change.* New York: Wiley. 599 pp.

Fisher, J. L., and N. Potter

    1964   *World Prospects for Natural Resources; Some Projections of Demand and Indicators of Supply to the Year 2000.* Baltimore: The Johns Hopkins Press, for Resources for the Future. 73 pp.

Foster, George M.

    1962   *Traditional Cultures and the Impact of Technology.* New York: Harper. 292 pp.

Gabor, Dennis

    1963   *Inventing the Future.* London: Secker and Warburg. 231 pp.

Garst, Jonathan

    1963   *No Need for Hunger.* New York: Random House. 182 pp.

Gordon, Theodore J.

    1965   *The Future.* New York: St Martin's Press. 184 pp.

Graubard, Stephen R. (ed.)

    1966   "Conditions of World Order," *Daedalus,* Vol. 95, No. 2, pp. 455–703, of the Proceedings of the American Academy of Arts and Sciences.

    1967   "The Year 2000—The Trajectory of an Idea," *Daedalus,* Vol. 96, No. 3, pp. 639–977, of the Proceedings of the American Academy of Arts and Sciences.

Hatt, Paul K.

    1952   *World Population and Future Resources.* New York: American Book Company. 262 pp.

Heilbroner, Robert L.

    1962   *The Making of Economic Society.* New York: Prentice-Hall. 242 pp.

Highsmith, R. M., Jr.

    1962   *Conservation in the United States.* Chicago: Rand-McNally. 322 pp.

How, R. C.

    1959   *The Conservation of Natural Resources.* London: Faber & Faber. 255 pp.

Jarrett, Henry (ed.)

    1966   *Environmental Quality in a Growing Economy.* Baltimore: The Johns Hopkins Press, for Resources for the Future. 173 pp.

Jennings, Burgess H., and John E. Murphy (eds.)

    1966   *Interactions of Man and His Environment.* New York: Plenum Press. 168 pp.

Kahn, Herman, and Anthony J. Wiener

    1967   *The Year 2000: A Framework for Speculation on the Next Thirty-Three Years.* New York: Macmillan. 431 pp.

Landsberg, H. H.

    1964   *Natural Resources for the U.S. Growth; A Look Ahead to the Year 2000.* Baltimore: The Johns Hopkins Press, for Resources for the Future. 260 pp.

Landsberg, Hans H., L. L. Fischman, and J. L. Fisher

    1963   *Resources in America's Future; Patterns of Requirements and Availabilities, 1960–2000.* Baltimore: The Johns Hopkins Press, for Resources for the Future. 1017 pp.

Langbein, W. B., and W. G. Hoyt

    1959   *Water Facts for the Nation's Future.* New York: Ronald Press. 288 pp.

Liebenstein, Harvey

    1957   *Economic Backwardness and Economic Growth: Studies in the Theory of Economic Growth.* New York: Wiley. 295 pp.

MacIver, Robert M.
    1964   *Power Transformed.* New York: Macmillan. 244 pp.

Mead, Margaret
    1964   *Continuities in Cultural Evolution.* New Haven, Conn.: Yale University Press,
          471 pp.

Meier, Richard L.
    1966   *Science and Economic Development: New Patterns of Living.* Cambridge,
          Mass.: M.I.T. Press. 2nd edition, 273 pp.

Mudd, Stewart (ed.)
    1964   *The Population Crisis and the Use of World Resources.* Bloomington, Ind.:
          Indiana University Press. 563 pp.

Nash, Roderick
    1967   *Wilderness and the American Mind.* New Haven, Conn.: Yale University Press.
          256 pp.

Platt, John R.
    1966   *The Step to Man.* New York: Wiley. 216 pp.

Rosovsky, Henry (ed.)
    1966   *Industrialization in Two Systems.* New York: Wiley. 289 pp.

Seidenberg, Roderick
    1961   *Anatomy of the Future.* Chapel Hill, N.C.: University of North Carolina Press.
          173 pp.

Shannon, Lyle W. (ed.)
    1957   *Underdeveloped Areas; A Book of Readings.* New York: Harper. 496 pp.

Stewart, Harris B., Jr.
    1963   *The Global Sea.* Princeton, N.J.: Van Nostrand. 126 pp.

Thomas, William L., Jr. (ed.)
    1959   *Man, Time, and Space in Southern California* (Supplement to *Annals* of the
          Association of American Geographers, Vol. 49, No. 3, Part 2). Washing-
          ton, D.C.: Association of American Geographers. 120 pp.

Tinberger, Jan, L. H. Klassen, and E. H. Mulder
    1956   *Observations on the Planned Provision of Nitrogen Fertilizer for the World.*
          Leiden: Stenfert Kroese, for the Netherlands Economic Institute. 45 pp.

Ward, Barbara
    1966   *Spaceship Earth.* New York: Columbia University Press. 152 pp.

Wolstenholme, Gordon (ed.)
    1963   *Man and His Future.* London: J. & A. Churchill. 410 pp.

Index

Numbers in italics refer to illustrative materials, as keyed by the parentheses following the numbers.

*Most animals are not individually indexed, but all domesticated animals are included by source of domestication in Table 4.2, p. 157. A few animals are individually indexed in connection with extended discussions.

Beachcombing, as fishing technique, 143–144
  Paleolithic origins of, 351
Beadle, G. W., 410
Beals, R. L., 175
Beating club, *140* (drawing)
Beattie, G. W., 549
Beattie, H. P., 549
Beaumont, Texas, 433
Beauty, role of, in human biological evolution, 278
Bedouin, Algerian women, *50* (photo)
Beehive, form of housing, *135* (drawing)
Belgian Congo, 444
Belgium, 94, 426, 437, 444, 487
  irregular fieldscape, *182* (photo)
Belshaw, C. S., 228, 457
Belt conveyor, *470* (photo)
Benchmarks, in human achievement, 539–541
Beneficiation, of iron ore, 349
Bengali, language, speakers of, 19
Bergen, 416
Bering Sea, 206
Bering Strait, 73
  as land bridge, *70* (map), *74* (table)
Berlin, 476, 477, 483
Berry, B. J. I., 378, 410, 437, 458, 501, 503
Beryllium, in modern use, 349
Bhargava, K. D., 228
Biologic divergence, of human species, 278–279
Biologic evolution, replacement by cultural processes, 110–112
Biotic ecology, evolutionary aspects of, 563–564
Birmingham, 485
Birth rate, changes in, 523–524
  current world, 15
Bishop, W. W., 112
Black Sea, 251, 253
Blow gun, use of, 139, *140* (drawing)
Boat peddlers, *414* (photo)
Boesch, H., 378, 458
Bogota, 484
Bogue, D. J., 535
Bohemia, 528
Boiling, of foods, early, 143
Bola, use of, 139, *140* (drawing)
Bolivia, 68, 439
Bollens, J. C., 502
Bombay, 456, 485
Bone tools, *96* (drawing)
Boomerang, use of, 139, *140* (drawing)
Borneo, 68, 74, 262, 339, 435, 531
Boserup, E., 410, 566
Boston, Massachusetts, 433, 484, 527, 529
Botswana, 36, 37
Boulding, K. E., 325
Bouquet, A. C., 325

Bow and arrow, *140* (drawing)
Boyko, H., 566
Boy Scouts, International, countries with, *29* (map)
Brace, C. L., 112
Brahmaputra River, 68, 564
Braidwood, R. J., 112, 176, 228
Brainerd, G. W., 228
Brasilia, 483
Brazil, 66, 109, 151, 155, 264, 278, 281, 343, 364, 394, 437, 444, 518, 524, 528, 529, 553
  coffee plantation, *185* (photo)
  egg boxing, *337* (photo)
Breese, G. W., 410, 502, 504
Brisbane, 528
Britain, 253
Broek, J. O. M., 535
Broiling, of foods, early, 143
Bronze manufacturing, in Thailand, 400
Brown, A. J., 410
Brown, G. N., 228, 325
Brown, H. S., 566
Brown, R. T., 458
Brunei, 25
Brush peddler, *414* (photo)
Brussels, 485
Buchanan, R. O., 378, 411
Bucharest, 485
Budapest, 485
Buddhism, as reform of God-King concept, 171
  renunciation of the physical world by, 409
Buddhist temple, *506* (photo)
Buenos Aires, 484
Buettner-Janusch, J., 112
Buffalo, New York, 433, 484
Buggy, *463* (photo)
Bull ring, Mexico, *513* (photo)
Burchard, J., 501
Bureaucracy, evolution of the, 171
Burkitt, M. C., 113, 176
Burkoe, R. W., 411
Burma, 68, 90, 217, 315, 442, 499, 524, 531
Burton, I., 566
Butzer, K. W., 81, 113

Cadiz, 278
Cairo, 211, 278, 485
Calais, 425, 457
Calcutta, 278, 477, 485
Caldwell, J. R., 228
California, 264, 350, 420, 445, 541, 551
  general store, *420* (photo)
Cambodia, 68, 283, 314, 500
  Angkor Wat, *505* (photo)
  bamboo pile house, *238* (photo)
Cambodian, writing forms, *315* (diagram)
Camel, introduction into Africa, 221

Cameroon, 282
Canada, 44, 45, 189, 224, 268, 278, 290, 291, 301, 366, 373, 392, 394, 405, 422, 436, 439, 440, 444, 445, 487, 489, 526, 527, 553
  core area, *480* (map)
  log cabin, *235* (photo)
  logger, *58* (photo)
  shopping center, *422* (photo)
  as trade region, 440–442, *441* (map)
  urban settlement, *124* (photo)
Canadian Shield, 493
Canals, as space-adjustment techniques, 456–457
Canary Islands, 282
Canberra, Australia, *122* (photo), 483
Cannibalism, by *Homo erectus,* 90
Canoe, *141* (drawing)
Cantilever, as engineering problem, *134* (drawing)
Canton, 278, 485
Cape Town, 15
Capital buildings, Finland, *510* (photo)
  Maryland, U. S., *509* (photo)
  Samoa, *509* (photo)
  U.S.S.R., *510* (photo)
  United Nations, *510* (photo)
Capitalism, as changing system, 390
  regional origin of, 390
Capitals, names of, of political states, *292–297* (table)
Caracas, 278, 484, 528
Carpathian Mountains, 253
Carr, D. E., 566
Carrying basket, use of, 139, *141* (drawing)
Cart, *163* (drawing)
Carthage, 500
Casablanca, 485
Caspian Sea, 75, 527
Casting, of metals, 166
Cast net, *144* (drawing)
Catholic church, Philippines, *506* (photo)
  Portugal, *507* (photo)
Cattle, brahmin breeds, 158
  taurus breeds, 158
Cattle station, Australia, *179* (photo)
Cavalry, Mongol use of, 223
Cave, housing, *237* (photo)
Caves, used as early housing, 133
Celebes, 66
Cenozoic, meaning of, 63
Central American Common Market, 439
Central Asia, 21, 71, 158, 159, 168, 201, 217, 223
Central Asian Corridor, 151
  as a cultural crossroads, 206
Central business district, growth of the, 480–481
Central China, 360
Central Europe, 286
Cépède, M., 535

*Varieties not individually indexed, but all common crop plants included by source of domestication in Table 4.1, pp. 150–151. Crop plants separately indexed only when some extended discussion occurs or when mapped in some other context.

Meyer, J. R., 503
Miami, 484
Miami Beach, 512
Michigan, 514
Microbiology, changes in productive, 496–497
Middle America, 150, 155, 156, 168, 172, 173, 360, 367
  as early center of civilization, 172, 173 (map)
Middle East, 139, 146, 158, 169, 171, 383, 402, 440
Midlatitudes, European settlement of, 266–268
Miehl, H. E., 378
Migration, animal, by land bridges, 73–74
  colonization as result of, 196
  definition of, 194
  as factor in diffusion, 194–195
  new patterns of, 127
  and the slave trade, 195
  types of, 195 (diagram)
Milan, 420, 476, 483, 485
Military defense, as instrument of political state, 171
  rise of systems of, 170–171
Mill, grain, 336 (photo), 142 (drawing)
Milton, J. P., 378
Milwaukee, 484
Mindanao, 222
Minerals, cycle of mining of, 167, 346–349
  intensification of extraction, 493–494
  mining and comparative technologies of, 345–351
  per capita use of, 351
  where mined, 347 (map)
Miniaturization, electronic, 498
Mining, cycle of, 167, 346–349
  diffusion of, 166 (map)
  distribution of, 347 (map)
  evolution of, 165–167
  growth of, in medieval Europe, 252
  intensification of, 493–494
Ministers of religion, function of, 131
Minneapolis, 484
Minnesota, 383, 389, 444
Minority, defined, 19
Mississippi Basin, 564
Mississippi River, 13, 69, 71, 431
Missouri River, 69
Mitchell, R. B., 503
Mixed economy, United States, as a, 391
Mobile, Alabama, 433
Mobile housing, tent, 231 (photo)
  trailer, 247 (photo)
  yurt, 232 (photo)
Mobility, as expressed in exploration and migration, 194–196
  of gatherer-collectors, 100–101

among pastoralists, 204–206
  of population after 7000 B.C., 206
  restrictions on earliest man, 87
Modesty, cultural concept of, 168
Mohenjo-Daro, 13, 213
Monaco, 25, 283, 375
Mongolia, 169, 217, 528
Mongols, evolution of military cavalry tactics among, 205
Monkeys, rise of, 77 (chart)
Monopoly, regional in crops and minerals, 361, 364
Montagu, M. F. A., 112, 114
Montevideo, 484, 528
Montpelier, 288
Montreal, 484
Morocco, 91, 94, 191
  retail market stands, 418 (photo)
Mortality rates, decline in, 523–524
Mortar and pestle, 142 (drawing)
Moscatti, S., 229
Moscow, 289, 476, 477, 485, 491, 510, 563
  urban area, 491 (map)
Mountain building, and climatic change, 68–69
  during Pleistocene, 66
  in shaping coastlines, 73
Mountain ranges, recent, 68–69
  relations to climatic change, 68–69
Mountains, as refuge zones, 136
Mount Blanc Tunnel, 457
Mt. Everest, 68
Mount Fuji, 16
Mountjoy, A. B., 378
Mousterian, tool types, 96 (drawing)
Mozambique, 36, 37
Mud and wattle, use of in housing, 135 (drawing)
Mudd, S., 412, 536, 568
Mukden, 485
Mulder, E. H., 568
Mumford, L., 486 (credited), 501
Munn, N. L., 114
Murdock, G. P., 229
Murphy, J. E., 567
Murphy, R. E., 502
Myers, C. A., 411
Myrdal, G., 378
Myres, J. L., 276
Mysticism, as factor in promoting religious system, 130

Nagato, 493
Nagoya, 485
Nakayama, I., 325
Nanking, 485
Naples, 476, 485
Nash, M., 229
Nash, R., 568
Nation, political organization of a, 290–291

Nationalism, declining role of, 321
  as European concept, 319
  rise of, 288–291
National sovereignty, passing of, concept of, 456
NATO, 25
  members of, 31 (map)
Natural gas, see Petroleum
Natural resources, comprehension of, 342
Navaho Indian, woman, 49 (photo)
Navigation, growth of knowledge of, in Europe, 259
Near East, 165, 166, 170, 171, 172, 206, 249
Needham, J., 176, 229
Nef, J. U., 379, 409 (credited), 412
Neighborhood, 10 (map)
  nature of the, 11
Neolithic, architecture of the, 133
  continuance of agricultural systems of the, 361
  contrasts in culture levels during the, 225
  defined as a time period, 152
  domestic housing of the, 133
  end of, defined, 165
  as era of production systems, 152
  forests as a problem during the, 341
  maturing of cultural processes during the, 206
  migrations resulting from increasing aridity, 205
  mining technology, 166–167
  origins of fishing technologies, 351
  as period of flowering of technology, 165
  rapid advance of culture of, 130
  textile technologies, 168
Nepal, 283
  Ghurka couple, 51 (photo)
Net, cast, 144 (drawing)
  draw, 144 (drawing)
Netherlands, 437, 440, 444, 487
  greenhouse farms, 189 (photo)
Netschert, B. C., 412
New Brunswick, 493
New Caledonia, 389, 444
Newcomen, Thomas, 383
New England, 155, 260, 264, 341, 353, 444, 550
New Guinea, 65, 68, 107, 262, 279, 286, 351, 361, 384, 385, 392, 394, 435, 528
  Chimbu tribesman, 48 (photo)
New Haven, 451
New nations, as of 1939, 322 (map)
  as of 1963, 323 (map)
New Orleans, 13, 15, 433, 484
Newsstand, sidewalk, Paris, 417 (photo)
New World, earliest appearance of man in the, 107–109
New World culture hearths, 217–219

in mineral extraction, 493–494
in resource extraction, 488–494
role of transport in, 425–426
summary notes on, 500–501
techniques of, 340, 475
Spain, 75, 91, 94, 222, 249, 302, 316, 318, 321, 426, 445, 525, 527, 550
cave housing, *237* (photo)
educational system of, 316–318
olive orchards, *186* (photo)
Spanish language, speakers of, 19
Spanish March, 255
Spears, fishing, *144* (drawing)
Spear thrower, use of, 139, *140* (drawing)
Specialization, in gathering-collecting, 97–101
Speciation, of angiosperms, 64–65
Species, defined, 63
as taxonomic grouping, 64
Speech, in evolution of language, 102–103
Spencer, J. E., 177
Spinning, 168
machines, *335* (photo)
shop for equipment, Iran, *415* (photo)
Splintering-off, as social grouping, 137
Spooler, thread, *334* (photo)
Spreiregen, P. D., 502
Srok Khmer, as native name for Cambodia, 314
Stacker, mechanical, *470* (photo)
Stamp, L. D., 537
Standard metropolitan statistical area, 481
Starr, C. G., 230, 276
State, concept of political, 170
genesis of the political, 207–208
god-King concept and the political, 171, 207
States, list of political, *292–297* (table)
new political, as of 1939, *322* (map)
as of 1963, *323* (map)
political, eastern hemisphere, *301* (map)
lacking access to the sea, *300* (table)
western hemisphere, *300* (map)
Steam engine, related to urbanism, 479
Steamship, early, *465* (photo)
Steel, scarcity of, in ancient world, 167
in 1850, 345
Steel industry, integrated mill, *338* (photo)
mechanization of, 497
Steward, J. H., 177, 412
Stewart, H. B., 568
Stockholm, 485, 527
Stone architecture, England, *240* (photo)
housing, *135* (drawing)
Peru, *234* (photo)

Stone tool technology, chopping, 87
chronology of, *99* (table)
early New World, 108
flaking, 96, 104, 106
grinding, 107
illustrations of, *88* (drawing), *96* (drawing), *105* (drawing)
Storage dam, for water, 354, 356
Storehouse, Neolithic origin of, 133
Straits of Dover, 457
Strasbourg, 485
Strauss, A. L., 502
String village, *136* (drawing)
Stupa, Buddhist, *506* (photo)
Stycos, J. M., 537
Suberman, R. M., 503
Subsistence groups, living system, 23–24
location, *22* (map)
Suburbs, as related to cities, 481–484
Succession, meaning of, as term, 423
Sudan, 133, 211, 220, 402, 444
village settlement, *119* (photo)
Suez Canal, as space-adjustment technique, 456–457
Sumatra, 15, 68, 74, 133, 278, 528
wood carving in domestic housing, 133
Sunda Islands, mammals, *79* (table)
Sunda Shelf, 73
Sunda Strait, as land bridge, *70* (map), *74* (table)
Sun dried brick, housing, *236* (photo)
Superior, Minnesota, 433
Supermarket, Mexico City, *421* (photo)
Supernatural phenomena, interpretation of, 130, 131
Surabaja, 485
Surinam, 439
house, *235* (photo)
Sutlej River, 68
Sverdlovsk, 485
Swaziland, 36, 37
Sweden, 255, 439, 444, 487, 527
housing, *246* (photo)
Switzerland, 66, 94, 302, 319, 426, 439, 527
educational system of, 319
Sydney, 483, 485, 528
Syria, 215, 288, 470
clay house, *232* (photo)
cotton picking, *331* (photo)
waterwheel, *420* (photo)
Szechwan Basin, 361, 526
crop assemblage of, 360

Tailoring, origin and diffusion of, 169
T'aipei, 485
Tai Ping Rebellion, 15
Taiwan, 444, 525, 527, 535
Taiyuan, 485
Taj Mahal, *507* (photo)
Tambora, 542
Tanker, *465* (photo)

Tanzania, 85, 94, 283
Taoism, renunciation of the physical world, 409
Tarim Basin, 68, 205
Tarim River, shift of, 15
Tashkent, 485
Tasmania, 65, 109, 525
demise of Tasmanian culture, 291
disappearance of Tasmanian ethnic stock, 278–279
Taton, R., 177, 230, 276
Tatooing, *49* (photo), as adornment, 168
Tax, S., 177
Tax assessor, origins of function of, 171
Taxonomic classification system, hierarchy in, 64
Taylor, M. L., 501
Technological civilization, as product of Northwest Europe, 281
Technology, in agriculture, *362* (map), *363* (map)
evolution of processing, 164–165
future demands on, 560–562
and future resources, 376–377
limits of, 516
maturing as civilization appeared, 174–175
in production of earth resources, *370* (map)
relationships to culture, 110–112, 321
reorientation of future, 551–553
spread of, 281–282
systems of manufacture, 384–385
Telephones, world distribution of, *450* (map)
Television stations, world distribution of, *452* (map)
Temperatures, during Pleistocene, 75–76
Temple, Angkor, *505* (photo)
institutionalizing of the, 170–171
Japan, *506* (photo)
Neolithic origin of the, 133
Thailand, *506* (photo)
Tenneco, Inc., areas of operations of, *387* (map), *388* (map)
organization of, *386* (chart)
Tent, as moveable housing, *134* (drawing)
pastoral, *231* (photo)
Terraces, Brazil, *185* (photo)
Indonesia, *180* (photo)
Japan, *181* (photo)
Territoriality, biologic, 131
and civilization, 172
competition for space as, 138, 175
early cultural growth of, 131–132
environmental change and, 132
in European political states, *255* (map), *256* (map)
expression of, in European conquests, 266

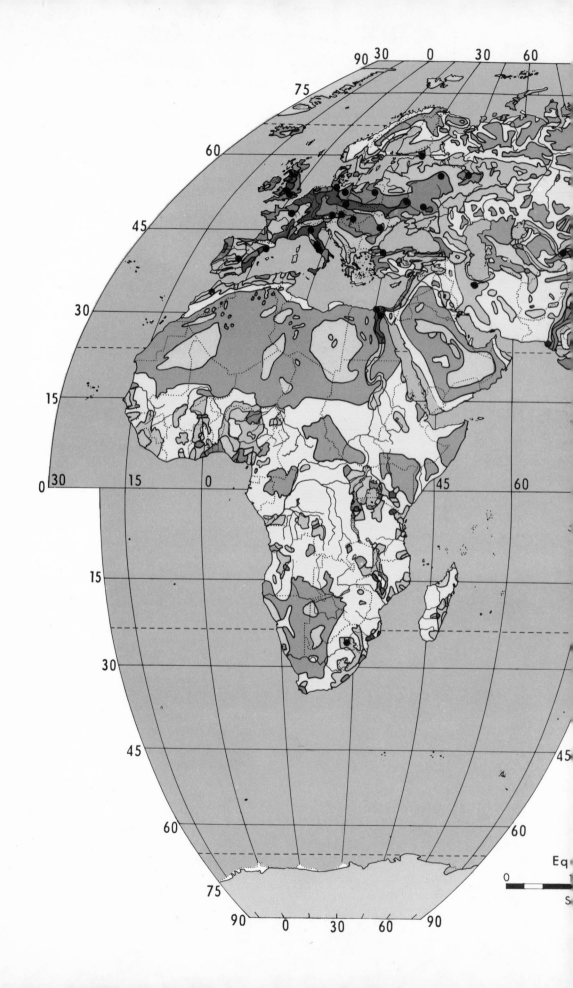